# Legal Issues of Services of General Interest

**Series editors**

Johan Willem van de Gronden
Markus Krajewski
Ulla Neergaard
Erika Szyszczak

More information about this series at http://www.springer.com/series/8900

Markus Krajewski
Editor

# Services of General Interest Beyond the Single Market

## External and International Law Dimensions

ASSER PRESS

Springer

*Editor*
Markus Krajewski
Fachbereich Rechtswissenschaft
FAU Erlangen-Nürnberg
Erlangen
Germany

Legal Issues of Services of General Interest
ISBN 978-94-6265-062-6 ISBN 978-94-6265-063-3 (eBook)
DOI 10.1007/978-94-6265-063-3

Library of Congress Control Number: 2015936621

Published by T.M.C. ASSER PRESS, The Hague, The Netherlands www.asserpress.nl
Produced and distributed for T.M.C. ASSER PRESS by Springer-Verlag Berlin Heidelberg



Printed on acid-free paper

Springer Science+Business Media B.V. Dordrecht is part of Springer Science+Business Media
(www.springer.com)

## Series Information

The aim of the series *Legal Issues of Services of General Interest* is to sketch the framework for services of general interest in the EU and to explore the issues raised by developments related to these services. The Series encompasses, inter alia, analyses of EU internal market, competition law, legislation (such as the Services Directive), international economic law and national (economic) law from a comparative perspective. Sector-specific approaches will also be covered (health, social services). In essence, the present Series addresses the emergence of a European Social Model and will therefore raise issues of fundamental and theoretical interest in Europe and the global economy.

*Series Editors*

Ulla Neergaard
Faculty of Law
University of Copenhagen
Studiestræde 6
1455 Copenhagen K
Denmark
e-mail: ulla.neergaard@jur.ku.dk

Johan Willem van de Gronden
Faculty of Law
Radboud University
Comeniuslaan 4
6525 HP Nijmegen
The Netherlands
e-mail: j.vandeGronden@jur.ru.nl

Erika Szyszczak
Sussex Law School
University of Sussex
Brighton, BN1 9SP
UK
e-mail: E.Szyszczak@sussex.ac.uk

Markus Krajewski
Fachbereich Rechtswissenschaft
Universität Erlangen-Nürnberg
Schillerstraße 1
91054 Erlangen
Germany
e-mail: markus.krajewski@fau.de

# Preface

After six volumes dealing with internal dimensions of the law of services of general interest, the present contribution of the series "Legal Issues of Services of General Interest" focuses on external and international law. It hopes to address new and pertinent questions and contribute to the ongoing debate about the future of services of general interest in the EU with fresh ideas and perspectives. Given the contentiousness of international trade and investment agreements as well as the EU's external policies, the issues discussed in this volume seem timely and relevant.

The chapters of this volume were developed on the basis of papers first presented at a workshop entitled "Beyond the Single Market" held on 18 and 19 September 2013 at the University of Erlangen-Nürnberg. The papers were redrafted in light of the conference proceedings and supplemented with two additional contributions. Our thanks go to the authors and other workshop participants who created a fruitful academic setting of the workshop and allowed in-depth discussions of the various matters. We are also grateful for the rich and stimulating written contributions which turned this collection into a comprehensive treatise on the external and international law dimensions of services of general interest in the EU.

We gratefully acknowledge the support of the German Research Foundation (Deutsche Forschungsgemeinschaft—DFG), the Alfred Vinzl-Stiftung and the Luise Prell-Stiftung for financially supporting the initial workshop. We are indebted to the Law School of the University of Erlangen-Nürnberg for hosting the conference. Special thanks are owed to Kathrin Schuster who was in charge of all organisational matters of the workshop as well as to Johanna Goldbach and Anja Nestler for assisting with the workshop organisation and for checking footnotes and citation styles in the final manuscripts. Without their help this could not have been done. The Language Service Centre of the University of Erlangen-Nürnberg helped us with final proofreading.

Finally, we are as ever thankful to Philip van Tongeren, Marjolijn Bastiaans and Antoinette Wessels at T.M.C. Asser Press for their tremendous help and support in producing this book.

Erlangen Markus Krajewski
February 2015

# Contents

# Contributors

**Amedeo Arena** Assistant Professor of European Union Law, University of Naples 'Federico II', Department of Law, Napoli, Italy; Visiting Researcher (STAR Fellow), University College London Faculty of Laws, London, UK;

**Olga Batura** Lecturer in European Law, European Humanities University and University of Bremen, Bremen, Germany

**Pierre Bauby** Researcher and Professor of Political Science, Paris 8 University, Science Po Paris, Centre National de la Fonction Publique Territoriale, Saint-Denis, France

**Francesco Costamagna** Associate Professor of European Union Law, University of Turin, Turin, Italy

**Panagiotis Delimatsis** Professor of European and International Trade Law and Director, Tilburg Law and Economics Center (TILEC), Tilburg University, Tilburg, The Netherlands

**Piet Eeckhout** Professor of European Union Law, University College London Faculty of Laws, London, UK

**Narine Ghazaryan** Lecturer in Law, Brunel University London, Uxbridge, UK

**David Hall** Director of the Public Services International Research Unit (PSIRU), University of Greenwich Business School, London, UK

**Meri Koivusalo** Senior Researcher, National Institute for Health and Welfare, Helsinki, Finland

**Markus Krajewski** Professor of Public and International Law, University of Erlangen-Nuremberg, Erlangen, Germany

**Britta Kynast** Doctoral Candidate, University of Erlangen-Nuremberg, Erlangen, Germany

**Johan van de Gronden** Professor of the Law of European Integration, Radboud University Nijmegen, Nijmegen, The Netherlands; Staatsraad at the Raad van State (judge at the Dutch Council of State), The Netherlands

**J. Anthony VanDuzer** Professor of Law, Common Law Section, Faculty of Law, University of Ottawa, Ottawa, Canada

**Wolfgang Weiß** Professor of European and Public International Law, German University of Administrative Sciences Speyer, Speyer, Germany; Honorary Research Fellow, Oxford Brookes University, Oxford, UK

# Chapter 1
# Introduction

**Markus Krajewski**

**Abstract** The chapters of this book address the external and international dimensions of the European legal framework for services of general interest which are often overlooked in the debates about public service in Europe. The questions raised in this context are analysed from three different angles: The chapters in Part I of the book approach the special nature of services of general interest from the perspective of the different dimensions of international economic law including international trade, procurement, investment and competition law. Part II then turns to the EU's external policy dimension and asks if and how the EU pursues its constitutional value of services of general interest in its general external policy as well as in its common commercial and neighbourhood policies. Finally, Part III turns to sector-specific analyses in the fields of telecommunications, energy, water supply and health services. The contributions within this part illustrate and deepen the general discussions of the first two parts of the book.

## Contents



---

M. Krajewski (✉)
University of Erlangen-Nuremberg, Erlangen, Germany
e-mail: markus.krajewski@fau.de



M. Krajewski (ed.), *Services of General Interest Beyond the Single Market*, Legal Issues of Services of General Interest,
DOI 10.1007/978-94-6265-063-3_1

## 1.1 Services of General Interest in EU International Law and External Policies

Services of general interest remain high on the political and legal agenda of the European Union. However, the debates about the impact of EU law on services of general interest usually focus on internal market law such as the free movement of services, competition law, state aid rules and the law of public procurement.[1] The external and international dimensions of the European legal framework for services of general interest are often overlooked, even though the EU is party to a number of international agreements which may influence providing, financing, commissioning and organising services of general interest. Most prominently these agreements include the World Trade Organization's General Agreement on Trade in Services (GATS),[2] but also recently negotiated bilateral free trade agreements such as the Comprehensive Trade and Economic Agreement (CETA) between the EU and Canada. As the EU is about to conclude its first agreements on investment protection, the impact of international investment law on public services is also becoming more relevant.[3]

The impact of trade and investment agreements, in particular the GATS, on public services has been subject to a general debate for more than a decade.[4] However, this debate seems largely de-linked from the general EU debate about services of general interest. This is especially noteworthy, since the general themes of both debates are comparable. The inherent tension between rules aimed at establishing and securing undistorted competition on markets and the logic of organising, financing and supplying services in the public interest can be shown with regards to the EU internal law as well as with regards to international economic law. Key questions relevant in both contexts are the scope and definition of services of general interest or public services, the legality of monopolies and other restrictions on competition or market access, procurement requirements, the preservation of regulatory autonomy and the discretion of national, regional and local authorities in regulating and providing services of general interest, and the general balance between open and competitive markets and public interest regulation.

The Treaty of Lisbon added two aspects which connect external and internal aspects of the law of services of general interest even further. First, it firmly established protecting and maintaining the special situation of services of general interest as a core constitutional value of EU law and further defined the contents of this value in Protocol No. 26 on services of general interest.[5] Second, it affirmed

---

[1]See the contributions in Van de Gronden et al. 2011; Szyszczak et al. 2011; Neergaard et al. 2013 and Szyszczak and van de Gronden 2013.

[2]See Chap. 2 in this volume.

[3]See Chap. 4 in this volume.

[4]Krajewski 2003; Adlung 2006; Arena 2011.

[5]Protocol (No. 26) on services of general interest, *OJ* 2008 C 115/308.

the value-driven nature of EU external policies. Article 21 para 1 TEU declares that the EU's "action on the international scene shall be guided by the principles which have inspired its own creation, development and enlargement (…)". This includes the principles of equality and solidarity. In its 2006 Trade Policy Paper "Global Europe" the European Commission concurred with this perspective when it stated: "As we pursue social justice and cohesion at home, we should also seek to promote our values, including social and environmental standards and cultural diversity, around the world."[6] Arguably, the general constitutional values of the EU are among the principles which Article 21 TEU refers to and encompass the special nature of services of general interest.[7]

As the EU is required to pursue its internal values which include the special situation of services of general interest in its external policies, the EU's common commercial policy including current trade negotiations in the field of services needs to be assessed in this light. This includes two dimensions: First, international agreements should not limit the EU's and Member States' abilities to organise and provide services of general interest. Second, agreements signed by the EU should not impede the ability of the EU's trading partners to provide and organise public services according to their own political interest and legal framework. The former aspect is increasingly accepted in the public and academic debate. The latter still needs to be developed further. For example, can it be reconciled with the values of services of general interest if the EU requests its trading partners to open their markets in key public services sectors such as water supply or postal services?

The EU Commission seemed to have acknowledged that the impact of trade agreements on services of general interest needs to be carefully monitored and managed in a "Reflections Paper on Services of General Interest in Bilateral FTAs" published in February 2011[8] and a paper entitled "Commission Proposal for the Modernisation of the Treatment of Public Services in EU Trade Agreements" of October 2011.[9] Even though these documents did not contain official trade policy statements, they showed that the relationship between public services and free trade agreements needed special attention. It is also noteworthy that the directives for the negotiation of the plurilateral Trade in Services

[6]European Commission, External Trade, Global Europe—Competing in the World, A Contribution to the EU's Growth and Jobs Strategy, available at http://trade.ec.europa.eu/doclib/docs/2006/october/tradoc_130376.pdf (last accessed on 30 January 2015), p. 5.

[7]See Chaps. 8 and 9 in this volume.

[8]European Commission, Reflections Paper on Services of General Interest in Bilateral FTAs (Applicable to both Positive and Negative Lists), TRADE.B.1/SJ D(2011), 28 February 2011, available at http://www.epsu.org/IMG/pdf/Reflections_Paper_on_SGIs_in_Bilateral_FTAs.pdf (last accessed 30 January 2015).

[9]European Commission, Commission Proposal for the Modernization of the Treatment of Public Services in EU Trade Agreements, TRADE.B.1/SC/am D(2011) 1146318, 26 October 2011, available at http://www.epsu.org/IMG/pdf/154b-11_EC_paper_on_public_services_pdf (last accessed 30 January 2015).

agreement (TiSA) and for the Transatlantic Trade and Investment Partnership (TTIP) between the EU and the US connect Protocol No. 26 and trade negotiations for the first time. They state: "The high quality of the EU's public utilities should be preserved in accordance with the TFEU and in particular Protocol No. 26 on Services of General Interest, and taking into account the EU's commitments in this area, including the GATS".[10] It can be argued, that these references to Protocol No. 26 in recent trade negotiations directives reflect the special value of services of general interest which the EU's negotiators of trade agreements should respect.

The contributions collected in this volume address the questions raised in this context from three different angles: The chapters in Part I of the book approach the special nature of services of general interest from the perspective of the different dimensions of international economic law including international trade, procurement, investment and competition law. Part II then turns to the EU's external policy dimension and asks if and how the EU pursues its constitutional value of services of general interest in its general external policy as well as in its common commercial and neighbourhood policies. Finally, Part III turns to sector-specific analyses in the fields of telecommunications, energy, water supply and health services. The contributions within this part illustrate and deepen the general discussions of the first two parts of the book.

## 1.2 Public Services in International Trade, Investment and Competition Law

International economic law consists of different regimes. As a consequence, the impact of international economic law on services of general interest (or public services) depends on the scope, contents and principal obligations of each regime. The chapters of the first part of the book therefore address public services in the context of the regimes of international economic law.

Chapter 2 addresses the impact of the GATS on public services. *Amedeo Arena* revisits the pertinent debates and shows inconsistencies between the requirements of public services regulation and key GATS provisions such as market access and national treatment. Based on this finding he analyses the layers of GATS exemptions for public services including Article I:3(b) and (c) GATS which exempts services supplied in the exercise of governmental authority from the scope of the GATS. Arena concludes that the GATS remains "agnostic" towards

[10]Council of the European Union, Directives for the negotiation on the Transatlantic Trade and Investment Partnership between the European Union and the United States of America, ST 11103/13, 17 June 2013, available at http://data.consilium.europa.eu/doc/document/ST-11103-2013-DCL-1/en/pdf (last accessed on 29 January 2015). See also Council of the European Union, Draft Directives for the negotiation of a plurilateral agreement on trade in services, 8 March 2013, on file with author.

public services. While the actual impact of the GATS on services of general interest may be limited, the ideological focus of the GATS could interfere with a global concept of public services. This finding resonates with some of the outcomes of the debates on services of general interest in the EU internal market order which also showed that the conceptual differences may be more fundamental than the actual conflicts.

The global procurement rules established in the framework of the World Trade Organisation are at the centre of Chap. 3 by *Wolfgang Weiß*. He addresses the revised plurilateral Government Procurement Agreement (GPA) of 2012 and its impact on services of general interest. In particular, the chapter analyses whether and to which extent the GPA disciplines limit the ability of public entities to provide services of general interest directly ("in-house") and through public private partnerships. It is shown that these questions which are at the core of the debates on services of general interest and procurement in EU law[11] are yet to be answered with regards to global procurement law. While concessions and public-private partnership arrangements are not covered by the GPA, it is unclear whether the term "government procurement" extends to "in house" procurement. However, it needs to be kept in mind that the GPA and procurement chapters in free trade agreements only apply to sectors which have been specifically opened to the procurement market by the respective party. So far, environmental services including sewage services are the only services of general interest which the EU submitted to global procurement rules.

Chapter 4 moves the focus from trade to investment law. *Francesco Costamagna* relates the general debate about the impact of international investment law on regulatory autonomy to the concrete questions of public services regulation. He points in particular to the privatisation of key services sectors and subsequent regulatory challenges which may lead to investment disputes. Given the broad wording of many provisions of investment agreements and the lack of specific provisions for public services this is hardly surprising. In fact, Costamagna notes that investment tribunals showed an agnostic approach towards the needs and specialities of regulating public services in the past. More recent state-investor dispute settlement practice however, seems to show a greater appreciation for public services regulation. In light of the agnosticism diagnosed by Arena in his chapter on GATS, it could be asked whether the trade regime can learn from the investment regime in this context.

Rules on trade, procurement and investment cannot only be found at the global level, but also in regional and bilateral free trade agreements. One of the best-known regional agreements is the North American Free Trade Agreement (NAFTA). *J. Anthony VanDuzer* assesses in Chap. 5 NAFTA's approach towards public services which can be used as an important comparison with the GATS approach and the approach of EU free trade agreements. One of the most important differences between NAFTA and GATS is that the former follows a

---

[11]See e.g. ECJ, Case C-26/03 *Stadt Halle* [2005] ECR I-1 and ECJ, Case C-458/03 *Parking Brixen* [2005] ECR I-8585.

"negative list-approach" towards services liberalisation while the latter adopts a "positive list-approach". VanDuzer shows how public services can be protected in the context of a negative list which is important for the EU, because recent EU trade agreements such as CETA and possibly TTIP also follow a negative list-approach. Another difference is that NAFTA does not rely on functional exemptions for certain types of activities, but on sector-specific lists with specific reservations. This seems to lead to greater legal certainty, but also entails a more fragmented approach than the GATS according to VanDuzer. Yet, in light of the limited scope of the GATS exemption for governmental authority and the importance of sectoral commitments (and the absence thereof) in the GATS the differences between GATS and NAFTA may be less significant from a practical perspective than in theory. Another key difference between NAFTA and GATS is that the latter also contains investor protection which extends to all public services. In fact, NAFTA investment arbitration practice was among the first to also contain cases relating to public services. Finally, NAFTA contains chapters on procurement, telecommunications and energy which also allow us to draw comparisons with the global approach towards these fields as discussed in the chapters by Weiß (3), Batura (12) and Delimatsis (13).

Chapters 6 and 7 address fields of law which have not yet been thoroughly codified on the basis of public international law treaties. The first relates to international competition law which is still a relatively new and emerging field of international economic law. Its rules can be found in a variety of legal sources, such as bilateral and regional trade agreements, specific competition law treaties and customary law. *Johan van de Gronden* assesses whether services of general interest which are a key concept in the context of EU competition law are also of relevance in international competition law. He distinguishes between a "market approach" and a "carve-out approach". While the former is the dominant thinking within internal EU competition law as exemplified in Article 106(2) TFEU and weighs the benefits of competition in public services, the latter exempts of public services from the scope of competition law. It can be said that this approach would be comparable to the function of the GATS carve-out for services supplied in the exercise of governmental authority. The market approach, however, can only be found in a few EU bilateral trade agreements. If future trade and investment agreements were to include robust rules on competition law including provisions on monopolies, relying on a market approach could be an option to safeguard public services without fully shielding them from competition law.

The last chapter of Part I, Chap. 7, looks at the global financial system and addresses services of general interest in relation to international and European austerity policies. *David Hall's* chapter takes a political economy perspective and is hence less concerned with legal questions of these programmes, but rather with the social and economic impact of structural adjustment programmes of international financial institutions such as the IMF and the EU on services of general interest. After placing the current austerity programmes in their historic context and addressing their general impact on public spending and economic growth, the chapter shows that austerity programmes had a particular devastating effect on public services. Hall links the current programmes also to their legal and constitutional framework which are—in the case of the EU—the rules on debt and deficit of the Maastricht Treaty and new instruments developed as a reaction to the financial crisis of 2008, namely the European Stabilisation Mechanism (ESM). It seems striking that these instruments and their counterparts at the global level "constitutionalise" a certain neoliberal economic paradigm without any room for balancing market rationales with the special requirements and logic of public services. This observation clearly calls for further research of the matter from a international and constitutional legal perspective.

## 1.3 External Policies of the European Union and Services of General Interest

Part II of the book turns specifically to the EU's external policies and asks how the special role and value of services of general interest can be protected and guaranteed within the framework of the EU's relations with other countries. Apart from a political interest in protecting services of general interest as part of its external policies, the EU might even legally be obliged to do so. The chapters by *Piet Eeckhout* (Chap. 8) and *Pierre Bauby* (Chap. 9) explore this perspective, while the chapters on the EU's trade and investment agreements (Chap. 10) and on the EU's Neighbourhood Policy (Chap. 11) concretise this general perspective on the basis of two specific fields of EU external relations.

Articles 3(5) and 21 TEU stipulate that EU foreign policy should be guided by the same principles which guided the internal development of the EU. *Piet Eeckhout* takes these provisions seriously and asks whether they provide a legally binding normative basis for EU external relations. He frames his analysis in the context of the wider concept of a Normative Power Europe and argues that the EU is obliged to be guided by the values underlying the protection of services of general interest in its external policies. This argument rests on the assumption that the protection of services of general interest is a value in the meaning of the provisions on external relations, an assumption which is based on the human rights element of services of general interest (Article 36 Charter of Fundamental Rights) and the solidarity aspects of these services (Article 3 TEU). As a consequence the EU must respect the principles of services of general interest in its common commercial policy. Eeckhout develops a broader constitutional framework for external policies of the EU but does not focus on what this could mean in concrete terms for services of general interest. Further research seems necessary, but the framework is clearly spelled out: The values which the EU is obliged to take into account when developing its trade and investment policies include the values mentioned in Article 14 TFEU ("the place occupied by services of general economic interest in the shared values of the Union") and spelled out in Protocol No. 26 on Services of General Interest.

In Chap. 9, *Pierre Bauby* reinforces this call by placing the development of the common commercial policy and of the EU approach towards services of general interest into their historic and political contexts. Like Eeckhout, Bauby is convinced that the protection of services of general interest is included in the values the EU is required to pursue in its external economic policies and negotiations. This requires a clear strategy which may—in Bauby's view—support the objectives, aims and values of the European Union in international trade negotiations.

*Markus Krajewski* analyses the EU's trade policy agenda concerning trade agreements vis-à-vis services of general interests in Chap. 11. It shows that this agenda recognises these services as special and developed a number of legal and institutional tools to mitigate a negative impact of trade agreements on the provision and organisation of services of general interest. These include excluding "public utilities" from certain market access obligations, limiting commitments in education, health and social services to publicly funded services and to generally exclude activities in the exercise of governmental power. The chapter develops a framework of assessing the effectiveness of these "public service exemptions" based on the substantive scope and the level of protection offered by each of these exemption clauses. However, the chapter also shows that without such exemption clauses trade agreements would clearly have a negative impact on public services.

The EU's influence on its neighbouring countries is often overlooked in debates about services of general interest in EU law and policy. *Narine Ghazaryan* therefore addresses in Chap. 11 the role of services of general interest in the European Neighbourhood Policy (ENP) vis-à-vis its Eastern and Southern Neighbours. She shows that the ENP is especially value-driven and that many instruments and agreements of the ENP aim to export the EU social model which includes services of general interest. Even though the term is explicitly mentioned for the first time only in 2013, it is clear that many elements of sectoral policies in the ENP context have been promoting the specific EU model of regulating services. For example the idea of universal service in telecommunications or general affordability and accessibility issues with regards to health and social services have been addressed through instruments of the ENP. In the recently negotiated trade agreements with the ENP partners the EU also incorporated competition rules which have an exemption for services of general economic interest similar to Article 106(2) TFEU. However, the actual impact of EU agreements or the ENP in general on public services models in the partner countries and which elements of these models can and should be preserved and further developed, is still unknown and hardly ever debated. Nevertheless it can be shown that the EU is trying to protect and promote services of general interest as an element of the European social model at the same time.

## 1.4 Sector-Specific Perspectives: Telecommunications, Energy, Water and Health Services

Finally, Part III contains four sectoral case studies which exemplify some of the current challenges. The rules on liberalising and regulating telecommunications (electronic communications) are of crucial importance in the EU's internal market and the WTO's services regime. In Chap. 12 *Olga Batura* analyses common elements and shows how the two regimes are different. She also considers which approach is better equipped to deal with the social and regulatory needs of the sector at the moment. Since the EU approach combines market efficiency with protecting social needs she considers this approach to be superior. Would it be possible to reach such an approach also at the global? Batura remains sceptical. She argues that the current global regime is split into a trade institutional approach based on the WTO legal framework and an approach attempting to reach common standards and regulations in the International Telecommunications Union (ITU). This shows that a key to the successful management of public services values and trade liberalisation is to realise that liberalisation presupposes regulation and that they go hence hand in hand with each other. Even though the current global trade system contains elements of telecommunications regulation Batura concludes that a framework linking liberalisation and social regulation for this sector is not to be expected at the international level in the near future.

*Panagiotis Delimatsis* (Chap. 13) chooses the energy sector to analyse the impact of services of general interest on the EU's external policies. Like the telecommunications sector, there is a rich and complex regulatory framework of the sector in the internal market, but no comparable system at the international level. In fact, the EU does not even seem to have a coherent external energy policy. After briefly recalling the current state of the energy sector in internal EU policies, Delimatsis addresses various instruments of energy regulation in trade and investment agreements. He shows that the global legal framework for trade and competition lacks a clear focus with regards to energy policies. Even the Energy Charter Treaty only employs traditional means of trade liberalisation and investment protection. In international trade agreements, energy-related activities are often carved out which may also explain why there is no global regulatory regime. The usual parallel development of internal market liberalisation and external trade commitments is lacking in the field of energy services. However, this picture may change according to Delimatsis as the EU will develop outward-looking strategies towards energy security and sustainability.

The impact of trade agreements on water provision is one the most controversial questions in the present context. *Britta Kynast* (Chap. 14) uses the case study of the provision and regulation of water supply through local entities in Germany to show the potential impact of trade agreements on water. She recalls the relevance of Article 4(2) TFEU which specifically requires the respect of local self-government and argues that this also applies to the negotiations and conclusion of free trade agreements. Hence, liberalising water services through a trade agreement could violate this requirement, because some of the key obligations of trade agreements such as national treatment or procurement regulations may negatively affect the possibilities of local governments to regulate and provide the supply of water. Kynast also recalls Protocol No. 26 which points to the essential role of—inter alia—local authorities in providing, commission and organising services of general interest "as closely as possible to the needs of the users". Kynast concludes that opening water supply services through international trade agreements would also violate the proportionality principle, because the negative results of liberalisation outweigh any positive effects.

A new and emerging field is the regulation of transnational health care provision. Chapter 15 by *Meri Koivusalo* begins with a short overview of the development of health policies in the framework of the European treaties addressing both the challenges posed by the free movement of patients and the approach adopted by the Treaty of Lisbon regarding EU competence in the field. She then points out that the special nature of health services is also recognised in the decision-making process of the common commercial policy (Article 207(4) TFEU). In light of recent health policy reforms in many EU countries which involved an increased reliance on commercial and contractual elements, Koivusalo develops her main argument which concerns policy space for health systems both in the negotiations of trade agreements and the actual agreements themselves. She warns that a new generation of comprehensive trade and investment agreements with high-income countries such as Canada or the US may have negative effects on the necessary policy space in particular with regards to cost-containment, equity and quality. In this context, she also recalls the problems associated with patient mobility within the EU. She concludes by questioning the benefits of the inclusion of health services in free trade agreements and consequently prefers a carve-out for the entire sector. Such a sectoral carve-out would go beyond the current EU practice which only excludes publicly-funded health services from the commitments of trade agreements, but not services which are entirely funded through private means.

## 1.5 Main Themes and Agenda for Future Research

The chapters in this volume indicate that many conflicts and debates concerning services of general interest which exist in the internal market can also be seen in the legal regimes outside the internal market. However, often the conflicts seem more relevant at a systematic and general level involving clashes between different rationales and regulatory objectives and less so at the technical and practical level. In fact, the chapters of this volume suggest that practical challenges to the organisation, financing and commissioning of services of general interest can still be expected more from internal EU law (competition, state aid, procurement and free movement) than from the EU's international obligations. However, it seems clear that the relative lack of concrete challenges and risks is due to the fact that many trade and investment agreements do not contain specific requirements in this regard. In addition, the chapters in this volume also show that the relationship between services of general interest and the logic of trade liberalisation is often managed on a mere technical level through specific exemption provisions.

Another important lesson to be drawn from the contributions in this book is the importance of the connection between regulation and the possibility to legislate and liberalisation requirements at the international level. Liberalisation of key public services sectors within the EU has been accompanied by establishing the necessary regulatory framework often specifically dedicated at the protection of social goals such as universal access. At the international level this connection is largely missing and it is not to be expected that a coherent regulatory and liberalisation regime will emerge anytime soon. This leads to the question how regulation and liberalisation can be reconciled in the future: Should the approach rely on incorporating regulatory principles in trade agreements or should sectoral liberalisation and regulation be addressed by sector-specific international organisations such as the ITU?

Maintaining policy space or national regulatory autonomy is also a theme which shapes both the internal and the external dimension of services of general interest. The compromise reached in the EU internal market includes the power of the Member States to define what services of general interest are and to institutionalise special regimes for the provision while EU law controls deviations from the general principles of competition and free movement. Such a compromise is also yet to be found at the international level. In fact, in most cases the definition of which activities constitute public services is generally not left to the parties themselves, but depends on the definition of key terms of an international agreement. In this context it should also be noted that both the international and the internal regime are challenged by the lack of a clear understanding of what services of general interest are. It is striking that the terminology used by the EU in its trade in services commitments ("public utilities") differs from the terminology derived from the TFEU and used internally ("services of general interest"), but that both terms are equally unclear.

These brief and preliminary observations of the main themes of the chapters of this volume suggest a two-fold research agenda for the future: First, the general and specific (potential) impact of international economic law and the EU's free trade agreements needs to be further studied and analysed, because these agreements may be binding on the EU and supersede secondary EU legislation. Second, the approaches and compromises found in the internal market can be used as a reference point in order to assess the effectiveness and appropriateness of approaches found in international trade and investment agreements or other international legal instruments. Future research along those lines may help implementing the normative basis of the EU's external policies and may also contribute to the development of international tools and instruments which seek to balance the policy goals of competition and market efficiency on the one side and the public interest in regulating services of general interest in a manner which make them accessible and affordable for all on the other side.

## References

Adlung R (2006) Public services and the GATS. J Int Econ Law 9(2):455–485

Arena A (2011) The GATS notion of public services as an instance of intergovernmental agnosticism: comparative insights from EU supranational dialectic. J World Trade 45(3):489–528

Krajewski M (2003) Public services and trade liberalization: mapping the legal framework. J Int Econ Law 6(2):341–367

Neergaard U, Szyszczak E, van de Gronden JW, Krajewski M (eds) (2013) Social services of general interest in the EU. T.M.C. Asser Press, The Hague
Szyszczak E, Davies J, Andenæs M, Bekkedal T (eds) (2011) Developments in services of general interest. T.M.C. Asser Press, The Hague
Szyszczak E, van de Gronden JW (2013) Financing services of general economic interest—reform and modernization. T.M.C. Asser Press, The Hague
Van de Gronden JW, Szyszczak E, Neergaard U, Krajewski M (eds) (2011) Health care and EU law. T.M.C. Asser Press, The Hague

# Part I
# Public Services in International Economic Law

# Chapter 2
# Revisiting the Impact of GATS on Public Services

**Amedeo Arena**

**Abstract** The impact of the WTO's General Agreement on Trade in Services (GATS) on public services is the subject of intense debates. This chapter analyses the potential effects of the main GATS disciplines, such as most-favoured-nation treatment, market access, national treatment and rules on domestic regulation, on the provision of public services at the national and local level. It also examines the instruments WTO members are afforded by the GATS to mitigate those effects by exempting what they regard as public service from the GATS disciplines. In addition, this chapter examines the GATS overall approach to the notion of public services and its impact on the conceptualisation of public services beyond national borders through regional economic integration.

## Contents



---

Assistant Professor of European Union Law, University of Naples 'Federico II' Department of Law; and Visiting Researcher (STAR Fellow), University College London, Faculty of Laws.

---

A. Arena (✉)
Department of Law, University of Naples 'Federico II', Naples, Italy
e-mail: a.arena@unina.it

 
M. Krajewski (ed.), *Services of General Interest Beyond the Single Market*, Legal Issues of Services of General Interest,
DOI 10.1007/978-94-6265-063-3_2

## 2.1 Introduction

The General Agreement on Trade in Services (GATS), the world's foremost agreement on services in terms of membership, constitutes an unavoidable reference in current and, possibly, future negotiations at the bilateral and plurilateral level. Just as Economic Integration Agreements (EIAs) take over ready-made clauses from the GATS or build upon their wording, they also share a more controversial legacy: the allegations of undermining the provision of public services in the countries concerned. The impact of the GATS on public services has been the subject of a lively academic discussion.[1] The purpose of this chapter is to assess, with the benefit of 20 years of hindsight, the impact that GATS has actually had on public services and the role it might play in regional service negotiations.

To this end, this chapter will first analyse the potential effects of GATS' cornerstone trade disciplines (i.e. Most-favoured-nation treatment, market access, national treatment, domestic regulation, etc.) on the provision of public services at the national and local level. Second, this chapter will examine the instruments WTO members are afforded by the GATS to mitigate those effects by exempting what they regard as public service providers from the above trade disciplines. Third, regard will be had to the GATS overall approach to the notion of public services and its impact on the conceptualisation of public services beyond national borders through regional economic integration.

Before delving into that analysis, a definitional note is in order. For the purpose of this chapter, the notion of 'public services' should be regarded as an inherently *domestic* pre-understanding (*Vorverständnis*).[2] To wit, 'public services' should be understood as comprising all activities functional to the pursuit of goals regarded as being in the general interest by a public authority *at the national or local level* and, for that reason, subject to rules different, in whole or in part, from those applying to other services and including elements compulsoriness (such as 'public service' or 'universal service' obligations).[3]

[1]For a comprehensive literature review, see Kulkarni 2009, pp. 247–248.

[2]See, generally, De Ruggiero 1984, pp. 596–597.

[3]See generally Marcou 2004, pp. 7–51; Marcou 2001, p. 386; Brancasi 2003, p. 30.

## 2.2 The Potential Impact of GATS Trade Disciplines on Public Services

The GATS seeks to pursue economic growth through 'progressive liberalization'. In essence, that agreement lays down a number of trade disciplines whose function is to constrain WTO members' ability to adopt measures affecting the provision of services through the four modes of supply described in Article I(2) GATS.

As noted by Krajewski, however, not all those constraints have the same impact on WTO member's ability to regulate, fund, and operate public services.[4] This section, therefore, will focus on GATS trade disciplines that are most likely to affect the provision of those services at the national and local level, viz. Most-Favored-Nation (MFN) treatment, market access, national treatment, domestic regulation, and a number of other horizontal and sectoral provisions. To that end, examples of public service regulation and support schemes that may be inconsistent with those disciplines will be provided.

Before turning to the specificities of each provision, it must be noted that, in general, GATS trade disciplines are 'import-related',[5] in that they seek to prevent WTO members from restricting supply of foreign services or by foreign suppliers, rather than from placing regulatory constraints on domestic services or service suppliers.[6] Accordingly, as it will be explained in greater detail in the following sections, certain regulatory schemes designed to ensure the availability of public services to domestic users lie outside the scope of the GATS trade disciplines altogether.

### *2.2.1 Most-Favoured-Nation Treatment*

According to Article II GATS, each WTO member must accord to services and service suppliers of any other Member treatment no less favorable than that it accords to like services and service suppliers of any other country.

The MFN clause does not interfere with public services so long as only *national* providers supply those services.[7] The picture changes substantially, however, if also *foreign* suppliers are involved in the provision of public services. The MFN stipulates that all like foreign services and like service providers should be on equal footing, thus precluding reciprocity-based arrangements between WTO members.

---

[4]See Krajewski 2003, p. 359.

[5]But see *China—Certain measures affecting electronic payment services*, Report of the Panel, WT/DS413/R, para 7.618 ("Nothing in the GATS suggests that the supply of a service through commercial presence in the territory of a Member does not extend to the "export" of services from that Member's territory to a recipient in the territory of another Member or to a foreign recipient located in the "exporting" Member's territory").

[6]Krajewski 2003, p. 347.

[7]Adlung 2006, p. 467; Krajewski 2003, p. 359.

Some examples may elucidate that proposition. If WTO member A and WTO member B enable their healthcare professionals to practice in one another's territory (mode 4), the MFN clause requires those WTO members to extend that treatment also to practitioners from every other WTO member. Likewise, if WTO member A reimburses expenses incurred by its nationals for medical treatments undergone in the territory of WTO member B (mode 2) on the basis of reciprocity, it must also cover the costs of medical care received by its nationals in other WTO members. Moreover, the MFN clause prohibits discrimination between suppliers of telecommunication or audiovisual services from different WTO members having a commercial presence in the same WTO member as regards access to the radio spectrum and to network infrastructure.

The MFN principle may also interfere with the regulation of public services provided across the border (mode 1), such as the international postal service.[8] When mail is sent from one country to another, the receiving postal administration charges the sending postal administration for access to its delivery network (the so-called 'terminal dues'). The MFN clause precludes WTO members to apply different terminal dues based on the incoming mail's country of origin.[9]

The liberalization potential of the MFN principle is, however, subject to constraints. First, it only applies to 'like' services and 'like' service providers. Moreover, since the MFN principle is aimed at measures affecting the 'import' of services, each WTO member remains at liberty to treat incoming service recipients from different WTO members in a different manner. Thus, WTO member A may grant preferential access to hospital facilities located in its territory to patients that are nationals of WTO member B, with which a reciprocity arrangement is in place, relative to citizens of other WTO members, which are not bound by an equivalent agreement. Moreover, outbound movements of domestic suppliers are not subject to the MFN clause. Therefore, a WTO member may provide financial assistance only to domestic educators wishing to teach at academic institutions located in WTO members that have tighter cultural or economic links with the former WTO member.

### *2.2.2 Market Access*

Article XVI requires WTO members to refrain from applying six types of measures that may hinder market access: quantitative restrictions (on the number of service suppliers, on the value of service transactions or assets, on the number of

[8]See WTO, Background Paper by the Universal Postal Union, Informal Note from the Secretariat, JOB(02)/17, 4 March 2002.

[9]See Perrazzelli and Vergano 2000, pp. 744–746; Luff 2002, pp. 77–78; T.M.C. Asser Instituut, The Study of the Relationship between the Constitution, Rules, and Practice of the Universal Postal Union, the WTO Rules (in particular the GATS), and the European Community Law, Final Report, prepared for the European Commission. http://ec.europa.eu/internal_market/post/doc/activities/tmc-asser-final-report-300604_en.pdf. 30 June 2004, p. 79. Accessed 20 October 2014.

operations or quantity of output, and on the number of natural persons supplying a service) as well as limitations on forms of legal entity, and on the participation of foreign capital.

The obligations flowing from Article XVI may interfere with regulatory arrangements commonly adopted by national and local governments in the field of public services, notably special and exclusive rights. WTO members may entrust the provision of public services to a limited number of providers to achieve cost efficiency (e.g., in the case of natural monopolies or natural oligopolies) or to allocate scarce resources (such as the broadcasting spectrum). Moreover, exclusive rights may enable public service providers to operate in conditions of economic equilibrium by offsetting profitable activities (e.g. courier services) against unprofitable ones (e.g. the universal postal service). By the same token, in concession contracts, the concessionaire's exclusive right to exploit the works or services constitutes its consideration for the provision of those works or services in addition or as an alternative to payment. Yet, those schemes may fall within the mischief of Article XVI:2(a), insofar as they limit the number of service providers, thus hindering market access.[10]

Article XVI may also preclude public ownership requirements, as well as restrictions on foreign investment in the share capital of public service providers. Economic theory has shown that under conditions of contract incompleteness public ownership may prove more efficient than regulation of private firms.[11] Several WTO members have thus discontinued the privatization trend of their utilities or even reversed it, through remunicipalisation of certain essential services. Some WTO members have also imposed foreign equity ceilings in the field of audio-visual, education and postal services.[12] However, those measures may be inconsistent with Article XVI:2(f), which outlaws restrictions on foreign capital and investment.

Moreover, the GATS provision on market access may bar WTO members from regulating the legal form of public service providers.[13] In several countries, for instance, higher education institutions may only be constituted as non-profit organizations.[14]

---

[10]Choudhury 2012, p. 78; Krajewski 2003, p. 360.

[11]See Laffont and Tirole 1993, p. 644.

[12]WTO Council for Trade in Services, Education Services, Background Note by the Secretariat, S/C/W/313, 1 April 2010, para 78; WTO Council for Trade in Services, Audiovisual Services, Background Note by the Secretariat, S/C/W/310, 12 January 2010, para 67; WTO Council for Trade in Services, Postal and Courier Services, Background Note by the Secretariat, S/C/W/319, 11 August 2010, para 77.

[13]A. Ostrovsky, E. Türk and R. Speed, GATS and Water: Retaining Policy Space to Serve the Poor. Center for International Environmental Law 3–4. http://www.ciel.org/Publications/GATS_5 Sep03.pdf. 5 September 2003, pp. 3–4. Accessed 20 October 2014.

[14]APEC, Measures Affecting Cross-Border Exchange and Investment in Higher Education in the APEC Region. http://aplicaciones2.colombiaaprende.edu.co/mesas_dialogo/documentos/mesa8 0/21113MeasuresAffectingCrossBorderexchangeanfinvestmentinHEintheAPECregion.pdf. May 2009. Accessed 20 October 2014.

Other WTO members have placed restrictions on the type of legal entity through which audio-visual services can be provided.[15] In many jurisdictions, likewise, only natural persons can only provide notary services.[16]

### 2.2.3 National Treatment

Article XVII GATS requires WTO members to accord to services and service suppliers of any other Member, in respect of all measures affecting the supply of services, treatment no less favorable than that it accords to its own like services and service suppliers.

Several measures employed by national and local governments in respect of public services may come into conflict with that provision. The most relevant example is state aids accorded to public service providers. Those subsidies can either be addressed to the supplier (e.g. university funding based on the number of enrolled students) or to the recipient (e.g. tax deductibility of medical treatments) of the service.

As to the former, while Article XVII GATS requires that foreign service suppliers established in a WTO member (modes 3 and 4) be granted the same financial incentives as their domestic counterparts,[17] WTO members are under no obligation to extend subsidies to suppliers located in the territory of other members,[18] whose services are either consumed abroad (mode 2) or provided on a cross-border basis (mode 1). This means that while a domestic university and a foreign university established in the same WTO member are entitled to receive the same funding per enrolled student,[19] no funding is due to universities established abroad for tuition provided to students from the above WTO member.[20]

In contrast, recipient-based subsidies should be extended also to services provided to domestic consumers by foreign suppliers either abroad (mode 2) or on a cross-border basis (mode 1).[21] Accordingly, patients of a WTO member should be entitled to deduct medical treatments received in another WTO member at the

[15]WTO Council for Trade in Services, Audiovisual Services, Background Note by the Secretariat, S/C/W/310, 12 January 2010, para 67.

[16]WTO Council for Trade in Services, Legal Services, Background Note by the Secretariat, S/C/W/318, 14 June 2010, para 58.

[17]Choudhury 2012, p. 77 (noting that, as a result of the obligation to extend subsidies on a national treatment basis, states may be unable to use subsidies altogether).

[18]WTO Trade in Services, Guidelines for the Scheduling of Specific Commitments under the General Agreement on Trade in Services (GATS), S/L/92, 28 March 2001, para 16.

[19]Cf. Krajewski 2003.

[20]Adlung 2007, p. 245. (noting that it would be "unreasonable to expect the authorities of an importing country to assess the competitive conditions in committed sectors across all other Members that may have trade interests—and then try to level the 'playfield' *vis-à-vis* each of these Members").

[21]Ibid., p. 246.

same conditions governing deductibility of medical care received domestically. Likewise, if a WTO member grants scholarships to unemployed citizens to attend on-line vocational training courses, also courses provided by foreign suppliers should be eligible for that subsidy.

As in the case of the MFN clause, also the national treatment obligation mainly catches import-related measures. Accordingly, WTO members may accord domestic consumers preferential access to public services provided by domestic suppliers. Reduced transport fares for nationals living in certain parts of a country, therefore, need not be extended to tourists from other WTO members. Likewise, WTO members can set higher tuition fees for foreign students relative to domestic students attending the same courses.[22] Cases like *China—Electronic Payment Services,* however, suggest the 'export' of services by foreign suppliers having a commercial presence in a host WTO member is also subject to the national treatment obligation. If domestic universities in WTO member A receive a subsidy based on the number of enrolled students, also foreign universities established in that WTO member must be eligible for funding, even if they only accept foreign students.

### 2.2.4 Domestic Regulation

Article VI GATS concerns measures of general application and administrative measures affecting trade in services. Article VI:1 requires that those measures be 'administered in a reasonable, objective and impartial manner'. Article VI:4 provides for that the Council for Trade in Services is to develop disciplines aimed to ensure that qualification requirements and procedures, technical standards, and licensing requirements be: (a) 'based on objective and transparent criteria' (e.g. the competence and the ability to supply the service); (b) 'not more burdensome than necessary to ensure the quality of the service'; (c) as far as licensing procedures are concerned, 'not in themselves a restriction on the supply of the service'. Although to date those disciplines have only been adopted in the accounting sector,[23] pursuant to Article VI:5 GATS Members are required, in all sectors where they have undertaken specific commitments, not to apply their licensing and qualification requirements and technical standards in a manner inconsistent with the three criteria laid down in Article VI:4 GATS, that nullifies or impairs the

[22]WTO Council for Trade in Services, Education Services, Background Note by the Secretariat, S/C/W/313, 1 April 2010, para 76.

[23]See WTO Working Party on Professional Services, Report of the Working Party on Professional Services to the Council for Trade in Services, S/WPPS/3, 4 December 1998 and WTO Trade in Services, Decision on disciplines relating to the Accountancy Sector, S/L/63, 15 December 1998. The accounting disciplines essentially lay down a standstill obligation: '3. Commencing immediately and continuing until the formal integration of these disciplines into the GATS, Members shall, to the fullest extent consistent with their existing legislation, not take measures which would be inconsistent with these disciplines.'

scheduling member's commitments, and that could not reasonably have been expected of that Member at the time the specific commitments in those sectors were made.

Many public service and universal service obligations imposed by WTO members in the form of, notably, licensing requirements may fall short of the above necessity test, focusing exclusively on the 'quality of the service'.[24] Indeed, virtually all public service and universal service obligations can be regarded as 'burdensome' and most of them pursue general interest goals (e.g. affordability, continuity, equal treatment, universal access) other than service quality. For instance, ferries that are required to guarantee service to an island every day of the year may not provide a service as comfortable as that provided by commercial companies that only operate at the peak of the tourist season. A licensing requirement for commercial hospitals to reserve a certain number of beds to customers to be treated on a *pro bono* basis can hardly be described as necessary to ensure the 'quality of the service'.[25] It is noteworthy that in the only area where GATS disciplines on domestic regulation were adopted, i.e. accountancy services,[26] the necessity test based on the 'quality of the service' has been replaced by a more openly defined criterion, viz. the fulfilment of a 'legitimate objective'.[27]

Some authors, however, have taken the view that the impact of Article VI:5 GATS on WTO members' ability to impose universal service and public service obligations is, in fact, very limited.[28] Indeed, a WTO member challenging a regulatory measure by another member on the basis of Article VI:5 GATS must also prove that it amounts to a 'nullification or impairment' of the scheduling member's commitments and that it could not have reasonably been expected when those commitments were made. In essence, Article VI:5 boils down to a 'standstill-clause', which only applies to regulatory measures introduced after the adoption of a member's specific commitments and not foreseen or anticipated in those commitments.[29] Even the amendment of existing regulatory measures would escape the ban under Article VI:5, unless it can be regarded as a substantial departure from the original content of those measures.

---

[24]See, generally, Trachtman 2003, pp. 57, 68. For a summary of the arguments in favor and against the necessity test laid down in Article VI:4(b) GATS, see Krajewski 2008a, pp. 186–187.

[25]Assuming that such requirement is framed as a licensing requirement, it is submitted that it might still be justified as a measure necessary to protect human health under Article XIV(b).

[26]WTO Working Party on Professional Services, Report of the Working Party on Professional Services to the Council for Trade in Services, S/WPPS/3, 4 December 1998 and WTO Trade in Services, Decision on disciplines relating to the accountancy sector, S/L/63, 15 December 1998.

[27]Adlung 2006, pp. 481–482.

[28]See ibid., p. 481. (observing that the provisional application of Article VI:4 GATS 'lacks teeth').

[29]Krajewski 2008a, p. 194.

### 2.2.5 Other GATS Obligations

A number of other GATS obligations may also have an impact on the regulation of public services by WTO members. The rules on statutory monopolies[30] and exclusive service suppliers[31] laid down in Article VIII GATS are a case in point, insofar as WTO Members often bestow special or exclusive rights upon their public service providers. Article VIII:1 GATS requires every WTO Member to ensure that its monopoly suppliers do not act inconsistently with the MFN treatment and, if applicable, with specific commitments (national treatment, market access and additional commitments). The goal of that provision is not only to prohibit trade-restrictive conduct on the part of monopoly suppliers as such, but also to prevent WTO members from 'privatising protection', i.e. circumventing their obligations and commitments under the GATS by acting through their exclusive suppliers.[32] Thus, just like the MFN principle precludes a WTO member from applying different terminal dues to mail originating in different countries, Article VIII:1 GATS requires that member to ensure that its monopoly postal service provider does not accord priority to the delivery of letters from one WTO member over letters from other WTO members.[33]

Article VIII:2 GATS requires WTO members to ensure that their monopoly suppliers do not abuse of their position outside the scope of their monopoly rights in markets where they compete with other firms. Therefore, if a WTO member has entrusted the operation of postal services to a public monopolist but has undertaken liberalization commitments in courier services, the postal monopolist cannot leverage its market position to foreclose competition on the liberalized segment. The scope of the notion of 'abuse of monopoly position' is, however, still unclear. For instance, it is still open to debate whether Article VIII:2 GATS requires monopoly suppliers to grant access to facilities they control that are essential to operate in another sector,[34] such as the rail network in the case of rail transport services.

[30]The provisions under Article VIII do not seem to apply to natural monopolies (unless they are backed by legal monopoly rights), as apparent from the definition of a 'monopoly supplier' under Article XXVIII(h) (referring to any public or private person which 'in the relevant market … is authorized or established formally or in effect by that Member as the sole supplier of that service'). See Adlung 2006, p. 473; Bigdeli and Rechsteiner 2008, p. 216.

[31]See Article VIII:5 GATS ('The provisions of this Article shall also apply to cases of exclusive service suppliers, where a Member, formally or in effect, (a) authorizes or establishes a small number of service suppliers and (b) substantially prevents competition among those suppliers in its territory').

[32]*Cf. Japan—Measures Affecting Consumer Photographic Film and Paper (United States v Japan)*, Report of the Panel, WT/DS44/R, adopted 22 April 1998 (highlighting the 'risk that WTO obligations could be evaded through a Member's delegation of quasi-governmental authority to private bodies').

[33]Bigdeli and Rechsteiner 2008, p. 211.

[34]See the discussion in ibid., p. 216.

An access obligation, instead, is clearly laid down in Section 5(a) of the Annex on Telecommunications, which requires WTO members to ensure that any service supplier of any other member is accorded 'access to and use' of public telecommunication transport networks and services on 'reasonable' and 'non-discriminatory' terms and conditions for the supply of a service included in that member's schedule of commitment. Thus, if a WTO member has undertaken commitments in the banking service sector—which requires access to telecommunications services to be provided effectively on a cross-border basis—foreign providers of banking services of must be granted access to the telecommunication network of that WTO member.[35] As clarified by the panel in *Mexico—Telecoms,* the same also holds true if a WTO member has undertaken commitments in the basic telecommunications service sector.[36]

A number of WTO members took on additional commitments in the field of basic telecommunications services under the so-called Reference Paper: as per Section 2(2) thereof, those members must ensure that their major suppliers enable interconnection under non-discriminatory terms, in a timely fashion at cost-oriented rates, and upon request, at points in addition to the network termination points offered to the majority of users; Section 3 of the Reference Paper further requires scheduling WTO members to prevent their major suppliers from engaging in certain anti-competitive practices, such as cross-subsidisation, using information obtained from competitors with anti-competitive results and refusal to grant technical information about essential facilities to other suppliers. In an extremely controversial passage of the *Mexico—Telecoms* report, the panel ruled that also a governmental measure requiring horizontal price-fixing between providers of telecom services must be regarded as an anti-competitive practice prohibited by the Reference paper.[37]

## 2.3 GATS Public Service Exemptions

The GATS offers WTO members several solutions to preserve their power to regulate, support, and operate public services. Indeed, just like other EIAs, the GATS includes several 'public service exemption clauses' (or 'public service exemptions'), i.e. provisions that can be relied upon to take certain activities considered to be in the general interest outside the scope of the agreement's trade disciplines.

As far as the notion of 'public service exemptions' is concerned, two caveats are in order. First, the expression 'public service' only indicates one of the *potential* uses of those clauses, regardless of their *intended* use by the drafters or

---

[35]See Burri Nenova 2007, p. 843.

[36]See *Mexico—Measures Affecting Telecommunications Services (Mexico-Telecoms),* Report of the Panel, T/DS204/R, paras 7.273–7.288.

[37]See *Mexico—Measures Affecting Telecommunications Services (Mexico-Telecoms),* Report of the Panel, T/DS204/R, para 7.234.

their *typical* use by the parties, institutions or dispute settlement bodies. Second, the word 'exemption' is employed in its broadest sense of an EIA provision that causes another EIA provision to become inapplicable. That notion, therefore, should be understood as including derogations, exceptions, exclusions, immunities, and carve-outs of all sorts.

Just as with trade disciplines, not all public service exemptions carry the same weight. Their ability to effectively protect public services from the trade disciplines laid down in an EIA is a function of, at least, four variables: (i) the exemption's *subjective scope*, i.e. the EIA parties to which the exemption applies; (ii) the exemption's *objective scope* (or 'exempted sectors'), i.e. the services or activities covered by the exemption; (iii) the exemption's *affected rules*, i.e. the EIA trade disciplines which, by virtue of the exemption, become inapplicable; and (iv) the exemption's *conditionality*, i.e. the requirements or criteria that must be met in order to trigger the exemption clause.

The subjective scope of EIA exemption clauses usually includes all EIA parties, in accordance with the principle of reciprocity.[38] This, however, is not always the case. For instance, parties can make reservations to an EIA to exclude its application to certain activities or sectors. Alternatively, EIA provisions may be framed in a way so that they only apply (or do not apply) to matters included in each party's list, as exemplified by the six annexes to the NAFTA. In these cases, EIAs can be said to include 'individual' public service exemption clauses, insofar as they only affect the applicability of EIA provisions to one of its parties.

From the perspective of their objective scope, public service exemptions can be classified into 'horizontal' and 'sectoral', depending on whether they cover all or some of the services that would otherwise be caught by the affected EIA provision(s). EIA drafters can employ different drafting techniques to define the objective scope of an exemption clause. One is referring to the exempted sectors by recourse to *generalklauseln* (i.e. generic expressions to be clarified at the stage of implementation or dispute resolution, such as 'governmental authority') or criteria (e.g. features common to all exempted sectors, such as being provided 'on a non-commercial basis'). Another is the so-called 'list-approach', consisting in an express enumeration of the exempted sectors (negative-list approach) or, conversely, of the sectors subject to the agreement (positive-list approach).

Having regard to the affected rules, public service exemptions can be divided into 'total' and 'partial': total exemptions determine the non-applicability of all trade disciplines set out in the relevant EIA; partial exemptions, instead, preclude the application of one or more specific EIA provisions, but are without prejudice to other provisions of the relevant EIA.

Public service exemptions, moreover, can be 'conditional' or 'unconditional' depending on whether their applicability is contingent on the fulfilment of one or more given requirements. Generally, conditionality serves the purpose of limiting the scope of permissible public intervention in the exempted sectors. This is the

---

[38]See, generally, Parisi and Ghei 2003, p. 93.

case, for instance, of public service exemptions subject to a proportionality test, whereby public intervention is allowed so long as it does not exceed what is necessary to achieve the relevant public interest goal.

The GATS contains a number of provisions that may be relied upon to exempt public services from its trade disciplines. Regard will be had, first, to the 'individual' public service exemptions laid down in the GATS, then to exemptions applying to all WTO members, either across all sectors or only in specific sectors.

### *2.3.1 Individual Exemptions*

The structure of the GATS affords each WTO member considerable discretion to tailor to its needs the application of the agreement's trade disciplines. This remarkable flexibility, which has been aptly nicknamed the '*à la carte*' application of the GATS,[39] is achieved by allowing WTO members to adjust the scope of GATS trade disciplines in three different ways.

First, each WTO Member can define the *sectoral coverage* of GATS obligations. Every WTO member can exempt any service sector from the MFN treatment by listing that sector in its list of Article II exemptions (negative-list approach). Specularly, market access, national treatment, and additional commitments only apply to sectors included in each Member's schedule of specific commitments (positive-list approach). Moreover, other GATS provisions known as 'conditional obligations', notably those concerning domestic regulation, only apply to sectors where specific commitments are undertaken. While WTO members usually refer to the sectors and subsectors listed in the WTO Secretariat's Services Sectoral Classification List (SSCL) for the purpose of drafting their schedules of commitments and MFN exemptions, they can further fine-tune the scope of GATS obligations by employing custom-made sub-sectoral classification or definitions.

Second, for each service sector, WTO Members can determine the *modal coverage* of their specific commitments. Thus, a WTO member may undertake a market access commitment on the cross-border provision of a service but no commitments on the consumption abroad of the same service. Likewise, WTO members may undertake commitments affecting also the provision of a service through commercial presence or the presence of natural persons.

Third, for each sector and mode of supply, WTO members can determine their *level of commitment*, which can range from no commitment ('unbound') to full commitment ('none'). In between those extremes, WTO members can schedule partial commitments, that is to say commitments subject to horizontal or sectoral limitations.

The following sections will show how WTO members have employed those three layers of flexibility to remove several activities that are customarily regarded as public services from the scope of GATS trade disciplines.

---

[39]See, generally, VanGrasstek and Sauvé 2006, p. 837.

#### 2.3.1.1 Sectoral Scope

A survey of WTO members' schedules of specific commitments via the I-TIP portal[40] shows that some activities traditionally regarded as public services, such as human health services and social services, attracted a lower number of commitments (respectively 26 and 18 commitments) than services that are usually provided on a commercial basis, such as hotel and restaurant services (139 commitments) and professional services (102 commitments). Moreover, within each sector, segments that are generally regarded as unprofitable attracted fewer commitments than commercially viable segments, as in the case, respectively, of postal services (13 commitments) and courier services (60 commitments).

WTO members instead appeared less reluctant to assume MFN obligations in public service sectors. Education and postal services, for instance, attracted as little as one MFN exemption each.[41] Moreover, in spite of a potential inconsistency between the Universal Postal Union Convention provisions on terminal dues and Article II GATS, no WTO member has scheduled MFN exemptions regarding terminal dues. This seems to confirm that the MFN clause is—or at least is perceived as—less intrusive than other GATS obligations *vis-à-vis* the regulation and financing of public services.

WTO members have also extensively relied on custom-made service subcategories. In the field of education services, for instance, several members have circumscribed their commitments either by source of funding (e.g. 'privately funded education services') or by programme of study (e.g. 'secondary education services [...] excluding compulsory education'). Likewise, in the postal and courier services sector, 7 out of the 13 members that have undertaken commitments have restricted them to specific postal products (e.g. 'parcels', 'items above 500 grams', 'letters up to 350 grams', etc.).

#### 2.3.1.2 Modal Scope

WTO members have also taken advantage of their prerogative to differentiate between modes of supply to protect what they possibly regard as the most vulnerable segments of certain public services from the application of GATS trade disciplines.

In the education sector, for instance, countries have appeared more ready to liberalize cross-border provision (e.g. distance learning) and consumption abroad (i.e. study abroad by their nationals) than the provision of those services through commercial presence (e.g. establishment in their territory of foreign academic

[40] http://i-tip.wto.org/services/.

[41] WTO Council for Trade in Services, Postal and Courier Services, Background Note by the Secretariat, S/C/W/319, 11 August 2010, para 17; WTO Council for Trade in Services, Education Services, Background Note by the Secretariat, S/C/W/313, 1 April 2010, para 69.

institutions, satellite campuses or joint ventures with domestic institutions) or the presence of foreign educators.[42]

In the health sector, instead, WTO members were more inclined to liberalize consumption abroad (i.e. domestic patient mobility to foreign healthcare providers) and commercial presence (the establishment of foreign health institutions in their territory),[43] than cross-border provision (e.g. telemedicine, distance processing of laboratory samples etc.), partly due to doubts as to the technical feasibility of that mode of provision.[44] Moreover, most countries have chosen not to accept commitments concerning the provision in their territory of health service by foreign natural persons.[45]

#### 2.3.1.3 Level of Commitment

Also the levels of commitment by WTO members among the various service sectors seem to suggest certain patterns. Several WTO members, notably developing countries, have made full commitments on cross-border, consumption abroad and provision through commercial presence of health services, possibly with a view to attracting foreign healthcare providers as well as their skills and expertise.[46] Most WTO members, instead, have only assumed partial commitments with regard to the provision of health services by foreign professionals.[47] While some members have merely extended their horizontal limitations to health services,[48] other members have scheduled sector-specific entries, e.g. adding nationality and residency requirements.[49]

Horizontal limitations by some WTO members sometimes contain direct references to public services or related legal notions. The EU, Montenegro and, with some minor differences, Russia have qualified their market access commitments under mode 3 in all sectors by specifying that 'services considered as public utilities at a national or local level may be subject to public monopolies or to exclusive rights granted to private operators'. Similarly, Canada stipulated that the 'supply of a service, or its subsidization, within the public sector is not in breach' of its national treatment commitments. The Dominican Republic, moreover, stated that

---

[42]Choudhury 2012, p. 210.

[43]Ibid., p. 270.

[44]WTO Council for Trade in Services, Health and Social Services, Background Note by the Secretariat, S/C/W/50, 18 September 1998, paras 52–53.

[45]Choudhury 2012, p. 271.

[46]WTO Council for Trade in Services, Health and Social Services, Background Note by the Secretariat, S/C/W/50, 18 September 1998, para 51.

[47]Ibid., para 57.

[48]Horizontal limitations are qualifications to a WTO member's commitments in all service sectors. Horizontal limitations must not be confused with Horizontal exemptions, which for the purpose of this chapter are defined as exemptions applicable to all WTO members.

[49]WTO Council for Trade in Services (fn. 49), para 57.

registration of foreign investment is 'totally prohibited in public services, such as drinking water, sewage and postal services'.

Sector-specific limitations can be employed to provide an additional layer of protection to certain public service arrangements. In the field of education, for instance, Japan specified that only non-profit foreign institutions may provide education services in its territory; Sierra Leone stipulated that foreign educators must hold certain academic qualifications and obtain prior approval from the Ministry of Education; China made access to its territory by foreign teachers and lecturers conditional upon receiving an invitation by or securing employment at a Chinese education institution. Telecommunication services have also attracted a varied pattern of sector-specific limitations, such as exclusive rights, economic needs tests, restrictions on the type of legal entity, restrictions on foreign equity, routing and commercial presence requirements, etc.[50]

## 2.3.2 *Horizontal Exemptions*

Apart from the individual exemption clauses resulting from the '*à la carte*' application of the GATS liberalization provisions, that agreement contains a number of public service exemptions that can be regarded as 'horizontal', in that they apply to all WTO Members. In this section, regard will be had to horizontal public service exemptions, both of an unconditional nature (i.e. the exemption for services supplied in the exercise of governmental authority and that for government procurement) and subject to conditionality (i.e. the general and security exceptions).

### 2.3.2.1 Services Supplied in the Exercise of Governmental Authority

The exemption clause for 'services supplied in the exercise of governmental authority' (hereafter: 'governmental services') set out in Article I:3(b) GATS is horizontal, total, and unconditional.[51] As most WTO Members' governments are directly or indirectly involved in the provision, financing, or organization of public services, Article I:3(b) GATS might appear as the GATS public service clause *par excellence*. The myriad exemption clauses in FTAs mirroring the language of Article I:3(b) GATS further add to the relevance of that provision. The objective scope of Article I:3(b) GATS, however, has given rise to considerable controversy.[52] Article I:3(c) GATS defines

[50] WTO Council for Trade in Services, Telecommunication Services, Background Note by the Secretariat, S/C/W/299, 10 June 2009, para 24.

[51] Article I:3 GATS ('For the purposes of this Agreement … (b) 'services' includes any service in any sector except services supplied in the exercise of governmental authority; (c) 'a service supplied in the exercise of governmental authority' means any service which is supplied neither on a commercial basis, nor in competition with one or more service suppliers.').

[52] See Howse and Türk 2002, pp. 1, 3 (noting that the exact scope of the Article I:3(b) GATS is 'far from clear').

'services supplied in the exercise of governmental authority' as 'any service which is supplied neither on a commercial basis, nor in competition with one or more service suppliers'.

The wording 'on a commercial basis', according to some legal commentators, should be interpreted as meaning 'with a view to making a profit'. That construction is supported by the definition of 'commercial presence' in Article XXVIII:(d) GATS, which refers to 'business or professional establishment', i.e. activities that are usually set up to make a profit.[53] The supplier's profit intention can be inferred from several elements, such as recourse to marketing and advertising.[54] Other authors,[55] however, argued that businesses and professional establishments under Article XXVIII:(d) GATS also include juridical persons, which are defined in letter l) of the same article as 'any legal entity duly constituted or otherwise organized under applicable law, *whether for profit or otherwise*' [emphasis added]. Moreover, as highlighted by the *Canada—Renewable Energy* panel, 'loss-making sales can be, and often are, a part of ordinary commercial activity'.[56] Thus, the meaning of the expression 'on a commercial basis' cannot be restricted to 'profit-seeking', but should also include non profit-seeking activities, whenever they are provided for remuneration.[57] Yet, according to that approach, public hospitals and even courts and tribunals would not be eligible for exemption, insofar as patients and plaintiffs are often required to pay charges or fees, sometimes of a symbolic amount, aimed at preventing excessive demand or at cost reduction. Other commentators, therefore, opined that the notion of 'commercial basis' implies some measure of strategic economic behaviour on the part of the service provider, i.e. taking into account the preferences of potential users and the availability of potential substitutes.[58] But making the 'commercial' nature of an activity dependant upon how well it is run does not.

The expression 'in competition with one or more service suppliers', in turn, evokes a typical antitrust law question: how should the relevant market for the services concerned be defined? Some authors, establishing a parallel with the notion of

[53]See Krajewski 2003, pp. 341, 351; Leroux 2006, pp. 345, 349 (noting that this interpretation is also supported by the definition of 'commercial presence' in Para D.2. of the Understanding on Commitments in Financial Services).

[54]Marchetti and Mavroidis 2004, pp. 511, 531.

[55]Adlung 2006, pp. 455, 463.

[56]*Canada—Certain Measures Affecting The Renewable Energy Generation Sector* and *Canada—Measures Relating To The Feed-In Tariff Program*, Report of the Panel, WT/DS412/R and WT/DS426/R, 19 December 2012, 7.151 (discussing the notion of 'commercial resale' for the purpose of Article III:8(a) of the GATT 1994).

[57]But see Krajewski 2008b, pp. 199–200 (arguing that the definition of juridical persons in Article XXVIII:1 GATS refers to the service supplier, whereas Article I:3(c) GATS focuses on the service itself).

[58]Adlung 2006, p. 463; Zacharias 2008a, pp. 64–65.

'like products' within the meaning of Article III:1 GATT, contended that regard must be had to all substitutable services,[59] as well as, possibly, potential competition.[60] Therefore, courts could be regarded as competing with arbitral tribunals in the market for legal services. Moreover, the question has been raised whether competition from other modes of supply should also be taken into account. According to this reading,[61] even national healthcare monopolists would not qualify for exemption, for so long as patients can travel to other WTO Members, foreign healthcare providers may be regarded as competitors.[62]

Other commentators thus suggested that the meaning of 'in competition' should be restricted to a notion of 'one-way competition'.[63] According to that approach, which relies on the definition of competition provided by the panel in *Mexico-Telecoms*,[64] a service is supplied 'in competition' only if the provider concerned acts competitively, 'striving for custom' against other suppliers.[65] Therefore, the governmental services exemption would cover cases where a supplier, such as a public school or hospital provides a service pursuant to a public service or universal service obligation, rather than because it seeks to increase its revenues by attracting more consumers. Under that perspective, the presence of competing suppliers, such as private schools or hospitals operating in the same relevant market, would be irrelevant.[66] The practical application of that criterion, nonetheless, appears problematic: how much 'loving neglect' is required on the part of a service provider to be regarded as *not* acting 'in competition'? National regulatory schemes often offers incentives to public service providers to increase the quality and quantity of their output, yet even so can those providers be regarded as 'striving for custom'? Paradoxically, according to the 'one-way competition' approach, the best candidates for exemption would be the least efficiently managed public services—an outcome which is clearly at odds with GATS welfare enhancement goals. Besides, it is perhaps no coincidence that market definition for the purpose of antitrust law in virtually

---

[59]See *Japan—Taxes on Alcoholic Beverages*, Report of the Appellate Body, WT/DS8-11/AB/R, paras 6.22 and 6.28.

[60]Van de Gronden 2013, p. 127.

[61]See Leroux 2006, pp. 345, 384.

[62]See Adlung 2006, pp. 454–465.

[63]See VanDuzer 2004, p. 388.

[64]*Mexico—Measures Affecting Telecommunications Services* (*'Mexico-Telecoms'*), Report of the Panel, T/DS204/R, para 7.250.

[65]*Mexico—Measures Affecting Telecommunications Services* (*'Mexico-Telecoms'*), Report of the Panel, T/DS204/R, para 7.230 (citing the *The Shorter Oxford English Dictionary*, 3rd edition, (Clarendon Press, 1990), Vol. II, p. 382: 'The word "competition", in its relevant economic sense, is in turn defined as "rivalry in the market, striving for custom between those who have the same commodities to dispose of"').

[66]VanDuzer 2004, p. 412.

all jurisdictions focuses on demand-side substitutability (and, in some cases, on supply-side substitutability), rather than on a firm's competitive intent.[67]

Another source of uncertainty is whether the two criteria under Article I:3(c) GATS define the notion of governmental services inclusively. If they do, as suggested by the verb 'means',[68] then all services provided on a commercial basis or in competition with other suppliers may be subject to the GATS, whatever their nature.[69] That could be the case of notaries, insofar as they compete with each other for clients and, in several jurisdictions, provide their services for a fee.[70] Other authors, instead, have taken the view that the wording 'governmental authority' has an autonomous meaning and that it contributes to define the scope of the governmental services exemption along with to the two criteria under Article I:3(c) GATS.[71] According to this view, services provided on a non-commercial basis and in a non-competitive environment are still subject to the GATS if they are supplied by private companies having no governmental involvement, such as certain religious institutions.[72]

In an earlier contribution on the GATS notion of public services,[73] it has been submitted that the wording 'governmental authority' should be understood as antithetical to the expressions 'on a commercial basis' and 'in competition'. Accordingly, governmental services should comprise those activities that are so inherently connected to the notion of 'governmental authority' as to be ontologically incompatible with those of 'commerce' and 'competition'.[74] It has also been

---

[67]See, e.g., European Commission notice on the definition of relevant market for the purposes of Community competition law, *OJ* 1997 C 372, para 13; U.S. Department of Justice and the Federal Trade Commission, Horizontal Merger Guidelines (19 August 2010, available at: http://ftc.gov/os/2010/08/100819hmg.pdf) p. 7; UK Competition Commission and the Office of Fair Trading, Merger Assessment Guidelines, (OFT1254, September 2010, available at: http://www.oft.gov.uk/shared_oft/mergers/642749/OFT1254.pdf), Section 5.2. See also International Competition Network, Draft Report on Merger Guidelines and Market Definition, (available at: http://www.internationalcompetitionnetwork.org/uploads/library/doc562.pdf) para 1.17 ("In virtually all of the Guidelines, the process of defining the product market begins with … demand side substitutability").

[68]See Leroux 2006, pp. 345, 348 (arguing that the use of the verb 'includes' rather than the verb 'means' would have opened a different interpretative scenario).

[69]See Krajewski 2003, pp. 347–349.

[70]See also WTO Council for Trade in Services, Legal Services, Background Note by the Secretariat, S/C/W/43, 6 July 1998 (noting that while in some countries notarial services may be regarded as provided in the exercise of governmental authority, notaries often supply their services on a commercial basis and should thus be covered by the GATS).

[71]See, e.g. *United States—Continued Dumping and Subsidy Offset Act of 2000,* Report of the Appellate Body, WT/DS217/AB/R, WT/DS234/AB/R, para 271 (holding that the 'internationally recognized interpretive principle of effectiveness should guide the interpretation of the WTO Agreement, and, under this principle, provisions of the WTO Agreement should not be interpreted in such a manner that whole clauses or paragraphs of a treaty would be reduced to redundancy or inutility').

[72]Krajewski 2003, p. 353; Zacharias 2008a, p. 61.

[73]Arena 2011, p. 502 et seq.

[74]Cf. Leroux 2006, pp. 345, 352 (stating that the exercise of governmental authority 'has little to do with commerce') and p. 362 (arguing that the notion of competition 'is generally absent in the case of the exercise of governmental authority').

argued that such a 'connection' should be of a functional, rather than an institutional, nature, on the model of Article 5 of the International Law Commission ('ILC') Articles on Responsibility of States for Internationally Wrongful Acts,[75] which holds States accountable for wrongful acts by entities that exercise 'elements of governmental authority', viz. that are entrusted with 'certain public or regulatory functions' and act in that capacity.[76] The choice of a functional approach is supported by the wording of Article I:3(b)–(c) GATS, which refers to '*services* supplied in the exercise of governmental authority' rather than to 'service *suppliers*', and by Article 5(c)(i)–(ii) of the Annex on Financial Services, which defines 'public entity' (for the purposes inter alia of the sector-specific governmental service exemption clauses under Article 1(b)(i) and (iii) thereof) focusing on the functions rather than on the public or private character of the entity concerned.[77]

Still, even according to that interpretation, the scope of the governmental service clause would be extremely narrow, and would only cover *acta jure imperii* and the so-called '*fonctions régaliennes*',[78] i.e. activities inherent to core sovereignty functions exercised by WTO members such as regulation, supervision and enforcement.[79] As a consequence, the vast majority of public services would still lie outside the scope of the governmental services exemption,[80] thus making that exemption clause of limited practical relevance.

[75]International Law Commission, Articles on State Responsibility, annexed to UN General Assembly Resolution no. 56/83, UN Doc. A/CN.4/L.602/Rev.1 (2001) (recalled by resolutions no. 59/35 and 62/61). Those Articles were previously published (along with a detailed commentary by the ILC) as International Law Commission, 'Draft articles on Responsibility of States for Internationally Wrongful Acts, with commentaries', Yearbook of the International Law Commission, 2001/2, Part Two, 42.

[76]See Commentary to Article 5 of the Draft Articles, para 5.

[77]Article 5(c)(i)–(ii) of the Annex on Financial Services ('"Public entity" means … an entity owned or controlled by a Member, that is principally engaged in carrying out governmental functions or activities for governmental purposes, not including an entity principally engaged in supplying financial services on commercial terms; or … a private entity, performing functions normally performed by a central bank or monetary authority, when exercising those functions.').

[78]'Fonctions régaliennes' include those 'regal' functions that belong ontologically to the State, such as lawmaking, judicial adjudication, national security, monetary policy, and diplomacy. See, generally, Hauriou 1929, p. 116; Pontier 2003, p. 194.

[79]See *Canada–Measures Affecting the Importation of Milk and the Exportation of Dairy Products*, Report of the Appellate Body, WT/DS103/AB/R, WT/DS113/AB/R, para 97 ("The essence of 'government' is … that it enjoys the effective power to 'regulate', 'control' or 'supervise' individuals, or otherwise 'restrain' their conduct, through the exercise of lawful authority. This meaning is derived, in part, from the functions performed by a government and, in part, from the government having the powers and authority to perform those functions").

[80]See Krajewski 2003, pp. 341, 350.

#### 2.3.2.2 Government Procurement

Pursuant to Article XIII GATS, 'laws, regulations or requirements governing the procurement by governmental agencies of services purchased for governmental purposes and not with a view to commercial resale or with a view to use in the supply of services for commercial sale' are exempt from MFN, national treatment and market access obligations.

This horizontal, partial, and unconditional exemption is relevant to the topic of public services because it may cover purchases made by firms entrusted with the operation of those services. A public hospital, therefore, can chose to contract out laboratory testing only to national providers or to providers from a specified foreign country.[81]

The material scope of the exemption is delimited by four criteria, which are not defined by the GATS and thus have given rise to a number of uncertainties. The notion of 'procurement' consists in the acquisition of services for consideration by any contractual means,[82] including management contracts (i.e. entrusting a private company with specific tasks, such as billing, meter reading etc.) and, possibly, Build-Operate-Transfer contracts (i.e. requiring a private company to build a public facility, such as a bridge or a motorway, to operate it for a specified time, and ultimately revert it to the government).[83] 'Governmental agencies', in turn, include central and local governmental entities[84] and, according to the unadopted GATT panel report in *United States—Procurement of a Sonar Mapping System,* also private entities in the presence of certain linking factors such as payment by the government, government possession etc.[85] To be eligible for exemption, moreover, services must be procured 'for governmental purposes' and 'not with a view to commercial resale or with a view to use in the supply of services for commercial sale'. In this respect, one commentator suggested that procurement of maintenance services by a company supplying water would be subject to the GATS if that company charges its users for water supply.[86] Another commentator, instead, took the view that the main aim of that provision is preventing WTO members from relying on procurement 'as a pretext to by and resell particular [...] services with a view to affording them a competitive edge over alternative suppliers'.[87]

Moreover, it is not clear whether measures concerning procurement by entities supplying governmental services within the meaning of Article I:3(b)–(c) GATS

---

[81]See Kulkarni 2009, pp. 245–283, 252.

[82]Arrowsmith 2003, p. 100.

[83]Zacharias 2008b, pp. 279–280.

[84]WTO 1995, Analytical Index: Guide to GATT Law and Practice, p. 191.

[85]*United States—Procurement of a Sonar Mapping System*, Report of the Panel, GPR.DS1/R, (unadopted), paras 4.5–4.13.

[86]Zacharias 2008b, p. 281.

[87]Adlung 2006, p. 466 (footnote 28).

are always covered by the exemption under Article XIII GATS.[88] While the two negative requirements dealing with 'commercial resale' under the last-mentioned provision seem to reflect the 'commercial basis' criterion under Article I:3(c) GATS, it still has to be seen to what extent 'governmental purposes' and 'governmental agencies' are akin to 'governmental authority' under that Article. The expression 'governmental agencies', in particular, seems to imply an institutional approach, focusing on subjective features such as the public ownership or control of the service provider concerned or, alternatively, to its subjection to public law.[89] But the question is still open.

#### 2.3.2.3 General and Security Exceptions

Articles XIV and XIV bis GATS can be regarded as total and conditional exemptions in that they allow WTO Members to adopt national measures at variance with any GATS obligation so long as those measures meet the conditions laid down in those provisions.[90] In view of the similarity of the language used in Article XIV GATS and Article XX GATT on the one hand, and in Article XIV bis GATS and Article XXI GATT on the other, a wealth of Appellate Body and panel reports can be taken to elucidate those conditions.[91] This section, therefore, will only attempt to illustrate how Articles XIV and XIV bis GATS can be employed to exempt national public service arrangements from the GATS in sectors where liberalization commitments have been undertaken.

Article XIV GATS may come into play in the field of public healthcare reimbursement schemes and universal service obligations. Arguably, Members that have undertaken commitments in the healthcare sector can still justify similar regulatory schemes on the basis of Article XIV(b) GATS, allowing measures 'necessary to protect human, animal or plant life or health'.[92] Indeed, WTO case law suggests that WTO members have a broad margin of discretion in defining what

---

[88]See, generally, Adlung 2006, p. 474.

[89]See Musseli and Zarrilli 2005, p. 571 (arguing that the procurement of energy services by a national oil company is subject to GATS obligations).

[90]In the case of Article XIV GATS, requirements are laid down both in the *chapeau* and in paras (a)–(e) of that Article; in that of Article XIV bis GATS, instead, regard must be had only to its paragraphs.

[91]See *United States—Measures Affecting the Cross-Border Supply of Gambling and Betting Services*, Report of the Appellate Body, WT/DS285/AB/R, para 291 (holding that previous decisions under Article XX GATT are relevant for the interpretation of Article XIV GATS owing to the similarity of the language used in those provisions).

[92]Cf. WTO Council for Trade in Services, Health and Social Services, Background Note by the Secretariat, S/C/W/50, 18 September 1998, para 7 (posing the question whether Article XIV might 'provide legal cover' for policy intervention in the health services sector by to deal with the migration of qualified personnel abroad).

constitutes health and what is their desired level of protection.[93] However, the necessity requirement under that provision, as well as the additional requirements under the *chapeau,* should ensure that public service arrangements are designed and implemented—to paraphrase the Appellate Body in *US-Shrimp*—so as to strike a fair balance between intervention 'rights' and liberalization 'duties'.[94]

Article XIV bis GATS, in turn, could provide protection in the field of national security in addition to that granted by Article I:3(b)–(c) GATS. Indeed, even thought the suggested interpretation of the exemption under Article I:3(b)–(c) GATS would cover core sovereignty functions such as national defence, the functional application of that carve-out would leave out ancillary services, such as the operation of military recreational facilities. WTO Members seeking to regulate those activities could nonetheless rely on Article XIVbis(b)(i) GATS, enabling Members to 'take any action [they] consider necessary' to protect their 'essential security interests' relating inter alia to the supply of services for the 'provisioning of military establishments'. Once again, the necessity requirement laid down in that provision should prevent abuse.

## *2.3.3 Sectoral Exemptions*

Sectoral exemptions apply to certain service sectors, such as maritime transport, air transport, and telecommunications, which are traditionally regarded as public services in several jurisdictions. The rules affected by those exemptions are remarkably different: while the air transport services exemption precludes the application to those services of all GATS provisions, the exemption for maritime transport only takes those services outside the scope of the MFN provisions. The telecommunications exemptions, instead, only affect the application of the sector-specific obligations laid down in the Annex on Telecommunications and in the Reference Papers. Moreover, while the two telecommunications exemptions are subject to necessity tests, the exemptions for air transport services and maritime services are unconditional.

### 2.3.3.1 Air Transport Services

The exemption set out in Article 2 of the Annex on Air Transport Services (ATS Annex) is sector-specific, total, and unconditional. It applies to measures affecting 'air traffic rights' and 'services directly related to the exercise of traffic rights'. The relationship between that exemption and public services is self-evident, as air transport is an important network industry, which in many countries is regarded as a public service and is subject to heavy government regulation, public ownership, and

[93] See *European communities—Measures affecting Asbestos and Asbestos-containing products*, Report of the Appellate Body, WTO/DS135/AB/R, para 168. See also Cottier et al. 2008, p. 313 et seq.

[94] Cf. *United States—Import Prohibition of Certain Shrimp and Shrimp Products*, Report of the Appellate Body, WT/DS58/AB/R, para 156.

widespread governmental subsidization.[95] Moreover, international aviation is subject to a dense network of bilateral treaties, based on the doctrine of airspace sovereignty, the right to restrict cabotage (i.e. transport between domestic destinations) to national airlines, and the exchange of air traffic rights on the basis of reciprocity.

Unlike the exemption for governmental services, the exemption for air transport services does not cover the whole sector, but only certain types of intervention in that sector, i.e. air traffic rights, which are defined in para 6(d) of the ATS Annex. Paragraph 3 of the ATS Annex further restricts the scope of the exemption by setting out three categories of services that are subject to the GATS: (i) 'aircraft repair and maintenance services'; (ii) the 'selling and marketing of air transport services'; and (iii) 'computer reservation system' services. The exemption laid down in the ATS Annex, instead, also covers 'services directly related to the exercise of air traffic rights', an expression that is not defined by the ATS Annex and whose boundaries are not entirely clear. While it is clear that the exemption does cover the so-called 'hard rights' (e.g. traffic and route rights, the designation of rights, capacity controls and pricing), there is no consensus as to whether it also applies to the so-called 'soft rights' (e.g. currency exchanges, ground and baggage handling, catering, marketing, and airport usage). According to one view, those services cannot be regarded as 'directly related' to air traffic rights and thus fall within the scope of the GATS. Others have argued that para 3 of the ATS Annex sets out an exhaustive list of air transport services that are covered by the GATS, so all other services should be regarded as eligible for exemption.

The ATS Annex provides yet another layer of protection by stating that the GATS is without prejudice to pre-existing bilateral and multilateral agreements. The GATS therefore only takes precedence over agreements that came into effect after 1 January 1995, subject to the broad exemption laid down in the ATS Annex. This seems to confirm that not only the drafters of the GATS were unwilling to replace the complex network of bilateral agreements in place in the field of air transport with a single multilateral agreement,[96] but also that they wanted to afford WTO members a broad margin of discretion to continue regulating international aviation as they most saw fit.

#### 2.3.3.2 Maritime Transport

Maritime transport is operated as a public service in several WTO Members due inter alia to the strategic role of ports as essential facilities. The Annex on Negotiations on Maritime Transport Services (the NMTS Annex) provides for a sector-specific, partial, and unconditional public service exemption.

The material scope of the exemption includes 'international shipping', 'auxiliary services' and 'access to and use of port facilities', but the NMTS Annex does not define any of those expressions. International shipping, in essence, consists in

[95]For an overview, see Köbele 2008, pp. 600–607.

[96]Lehner 1995, pp. 436, 446.

the transportation of cargo on board a vessel from one country to another.[97] Auxiliary services include cargo storage and handling, warehousing, container station and depot services.[98] Port services and facilities, in turn, include pilotage, towing and tug assistance, provisioning, fuelling, garbage collection, port captain services, navigation aids, emergency repairs, anchorage, berthing etc.[99]

Turning to the rules affected by the exemption clause under scrutiny, regard must be had, first and foremost, to the MFN clause, whose application to the maritime transport sector is suspended until the conclusion of the trade negotiations. In other words, as long as the trade talks are on-going, WTO members can maintain measures that are at variance with the MFN treatment principle without listing an exemption under Article II GATS, as they would be required to for other service sectors. WTO members that have scheduled specific commitments in the area of maritime transport must apply those commitments on an MFN basis, but may improve, modify, or withdraw those commitments before the conclusion of the negotiations without offering compensation, as Article XXI GATS requires for the modification of schedules.

Those provisions are hardly related to the public service aspects of maritime transport, but rather reflect the on-going lack of consensus in trade negotiations: suspending the MFN regime was perceived as a lesser evil relative to WTO members listing a multitude of Article II exemptions, which would have further hindered the trade talks.[100] For the same reason, in spite of the increased flexibility afforded by the NMTS Annex, few WTO members undertook commitments in the maritime transport sector.[101]

#### 2.3.3.3 Telecommunications

Among the remaining GATS public service exemptions, regard must be had, in particular, to Section 5(e)(i) of the Annex on Telecommunications and Section 3 of the Reference Paper.

According to the former, the 'access to and use' obligation under Section 5(a) of the Annex on Telecommunications may be subject to conditions 'necessary … to safeguard the *public service responsibilities* of suppliers of public telecommunications transport networks and services, in particular their *ability to make their networks or services available to the public generally*' (emphasis added). The rationale underlying that provision is that telecommunications networks and services are subject to capacity

---

[97]C. Fink, A. Mattoo and I.C. Neagu IC, Trade in international Maritime Services: How Much Does Policy Matter? World Bank Policy Research Working Paper No. 2522. http://siteresources.worldbank.org/EXTEXPCOMNET/Resources/2463593-1213975515123/03_Fink.pdf. January 2001, p. 6. Accessed 27 February 2015.

[98]Parameswaran 2008, p. 674.

[99]Ibid.

[100]Parameswaran 2008, pp. 668–669.

[101]WTO Council for Trade in Services, Maritime Transport Services, Background Note by the Secretariat, S/C/W/315, 7 June 2010, para 139.

constraints: the duty to provide access to and use of those networks and services to foreign service providers must, in some circumstances, yield to responsibilities such as ensuring universal access, the interoperability of public telecommunications services, or compliance with international standards for global compatibility.[102] The Annex on Telecommunications, therefore, attempts to strike a fair balance 'between the needs of users for fair terms of access and the needs of the regulators and public telecommunications operators to maintain a system that works and that meets public service objectives'.[103]

As per Section 3 of the Reference Paper, each Member has 'the right to define the kind of universal service obligation it wishes to maintain' in the telecommunications sector. Those obligations are not regarded as per se anti-competitive, provided that they are, first and foremost, 'administered in a transparent, non-discriminatory, and competitively neutral manner'. In essence, universal service obligations must be made publicly available, must not penalize certain operators *vis-à-vis* others and must not distort competition between different suppliers.[104] Since universal service obligations are also 'measures of general application affecting trade in [telecommunications] services', they must 'be administered in a reasonable, objective and impartial manner' pursuant to Article VI(1) GATS.[105] To be eligible for exemption, moreover, universal service obligations must not be 'more burdensome than necessary for the kind of universal service defined by the Member'. The wording of that provision reminds of that of Article VI:4(b) GATS, but unlike that provision, which only recognizes the 'quality of the service' as a legitimate goal, Section 3 of the Reference Paper allows for a broader range of general interest objectives to be factored in.[106]

## 2.4 GATS 'Agnostic' Approach to the Notion of Public Services

Sections 2.2 and 2.3 above analysed the potential impact of GATS trade disciplines on public services and the discretion that GATS public service exemptions afford WTO members to exclude those services from the scope of liberalization. The focus of the present section is, instead, conceptual, in that it seeks to examine the GATS approach to the *notion* of public services.

As public services have for a long time been provided and regulated at the national or local level, a number of different domestic legal notions have been

[102]Section 7(a) Annex on Telecommunications.

[103]WTO, Explanation of the Annex on telecommunications, available at: http://www.wto.org/english/tratop_e/serv_e/telecom_e/telecom_annex_expl_e.htm.

[104]Gao 2008, p. 742.

[105]Ibid., p. 743.

[106]See Arena 2011, pp. 514–515.

developed. Transnational economic integration, however, and notably positive integration through the harmonisation of national regulatory schemes relating to public services has, in certain cases, brought about the development of novel public service concepts and categories. The most striking example, in that respect, is the EU notion of 'services of general interest', which, although not originally envisaged in the Treaty of Rome, emerged over time through the practice of the European Commission, the jurisprudence of the European Court of Justice, and the writings of legal commentators.[107]

Is there a GATS notion of public services? Is that agreement conducive to the development of a global notion of public services? In order to answer those questions, regard must be had to whether the GATS does or does not recognise the specificity of those services and of the goals they pursue.

### *2.4.1 The GATS Indifference to Public Service Goals*

As a rule, GATS trade disciplines apply to all 'measures affecting trade in services' regardless of the nature of the service and aim of the measure. As outlined in Sect. 2.3, several GATS provisions allow WTO members to exempt what they regard as public services from those obligations, but asserting the public service nature of those activities is hardly ever a requirement for exemption.

The GATS '*à la carte*' application provides a clear illustration of GATS agnosticism *vis-à-vis* public services: WTO members, indeed, are under no obligation to state the goal they pursue in scheduling an Article II exemption or in refusing to undertake commitments in a given sector. Ensuring universal access to a given services or sheltering domestic suppliers from foreign competition are equally acceptable aims: the GATS, simply, asks no questions.

The agnosticism characterizing the GATS approach to public services is further highlighted by the privilege vested in WTO Members to employ their own classification systems in their schedules of specific commitments.[108] The EU schedule, for instance, stipulates that 'services considered public utilities at a national or local

[107]See, e.g., Nistor 2011, p. 228 et seq.; Karayigit 2009, p. 575; Neergaard 2009, pp. 17–50.

[108]WTO, Services Sectoral Classification List, Note by the Secretariat, MTN.GNS/W/120, 10 July 1991. As WTO Members are not required to adopt the SSCL as a basis for scheduling their commitments, any two Members may refer to the same sector employing different expressions. But see *United States—Measures Affecting the Cross-Border Supply of Gambling and Betting Services*, Report of the Appellate Body, WT/DS285/AB/R (The Appellate Body upheld the panel's finding that the US schedule must be interpreted as including gambling and betting services based on WTO nomenclature, reflecting that erroneous scheduling can limit the policy space of Members. The Appellate Body also found that the measure did not meet the requirements of the public moral defence, since it did not place this ban on domestic operators, leading to an unjustifiable and arbitrary discrimination.).

level may be subject to public monopolies or to exclusive rights granted to private operators',[109] thus setting out a *renvoi* to an inherently protean legal category.

Moreover, as noted above, according to some commentators the public service nature of 'services supplied in the exercise of governmental authority' does not come into play for the purpose of the exemption set out in Article I:3(b) GATS: what really matters is that the non-commercial basis and non-competition criteria set out in letter (c) are met. The same holds true for the exemption laid down in the ATS Annex: although air transport services are regarded as public services in several jurisdictions, the exemption applies regardless of the aims pursued by WTO members in the management of air traffic rights or directly related services. Likewise, international shipping, auxiliary services and access to and use of port facilities are temporarily exempted from the substantive and procedural provisions relating to MFN regardless of the policy objectives WTO members may seek to pursue with regard to those services.

In sum, the GATS simply does not recognise the specificity of public services and does not seem to take their goals into any account: as a matter of fact, what have been so far referred to as 'public service' exemptions can be employed to pursue a broad range of different objectives, even of a protectionist nature (as in the case of economic needs tests).[110]

That general trend, however, is not without exceptions. Articles XIV and XIV bis GATS can be invoked to justify measures pursuing a number of specific aims, which do not explicitly include (but might impliedly encompass) public service goals. Article XIII only applies to measures governing procurement of services purchased 'for governmental purposes'. Likewise, Section 5(e)(i) of the Annex on Telecommunications and Section 3 of the Reference Paper expressly recognise, respectively, 'public services responsibilities' and 'universal service obligations' as worthy of protection. Most importantly, those provisions set out substantive requirements (and, in the case of Section 3 of the Reference Paper, also procedural safeguards) to ensure that such measures are effectively applied to pursue general interest goals. However, while those provisions can be regarded as a deviation from the GATS agnostic trend, they are of limited relevance: in Articles XIV and XIV bis GATS enable WTO members to pursue broader public policy goals; Article XIII can, at best, cover the procurement of public services rather than their provision by WTO members or their suppliers, Section 5(e)(i) of the Annex on Telecommunications and Section 3 of the Reference Paper have a rather narrow objective scope—and, in the case of the Reference Paper, also a limited subjective scope.

---

[109]GATS, European Communities and their Member States Schedule of Specific Commitments, GATS/SC/31, 15 April 1994, p. 2.

[110]See Marchetti and Mavroidis 2004, pp. 519–520 (arguing that the economic needs tests can be employed 'to serve a purpose other than restricting access on a non-discriminatory basis, i.e., to restrict access in a discretionary manner').

### 2.4.2 The Indeterminability of the GATS Concept of Public Services

The autonomy WTO members enjoy under the GATS in drafting their schedules of commitments is not conducive to a spontaneous convergence towards a common notion of public services. Rather, as shown by the language of several schedules, WTO members have taken advantage of that autonomy to reassert their own legal notions and classifications relating to public services.

Although most schedules are based on the SSCL rather than custom-made service subcategories, no GATS notion of public services can be inferred from the sectoral distribution of WTO members' commitments. While it has been observed that activities traditionally regarded as public services at the domestic and local level have attracted, by and large, fewer commitments than other services, it would be erroneous to assume that all sectors with few commitments are related to activities provided in the general interest. For instance, real estate services, which are commonly regarded as a commercial activity, attracted fewer commitments (31) than typical public services, such as primary education (40) and hospital services (52). As stated above, WTO members must not disclose the policy objectives they pursue when drawing up their schedules, so the reasons for not undertaking commitments in a given service sector can be imponderable.

The WTO Secretariat, in turn, has so far been unable to promote convergence around a common GATS notion of public services. Although the Secretariat has referred to the governmental services exemption in a number of background notes,[111] it has no authority to provide a binding interpretation of GATS provisions or of the legal notions employed in WTO Members' schedules.

By the same token, a general GATS notion of public services cannot be gleaned from the other public service exemptions laid down in the agreement. The material scope of the governmental services exemption is still unclear and it has not been the subject of dispute settlement. In that respect, the Chairman of the Group of Negotiations on Services, in a statement of December 1993, added that 'it is assumed that participants would refrain from taking issues arising in this area to dispute settlement but would try to settle them through bilateral consultations'.[112] Equally ambiguous are the expressions employed in Article XIII GATS to frame the boundaries of the government procurement exemption. In any case, as noted above, that exemption would only cover the procurement of public services by WTO members, not their provision.

Turning to conditional exemptions, it has been suggested that the security exception under Article XIV bis GATS could protect public service regulatory

[111]But see Leroux 2006, p. 357 (arguing that the WTO Secretariat's background notes 'raise more questions than answers' as to the scope of the exemption for governmental services).

[112]Multilateral Trade Negotiations the Uruguay Round, Group of Negotiations on Services, Informal GNS Meeting—10 December 1993, Chairman's Statement, MTN.GNS/49, 11 December 1993.

schemes in the area of national security, in particular in the case of ancillary services. However, it still has to be seen whether that provision can be put to that use. It has also been argued that the general exceptions under Article XIV could be relied upon to safeguard universal service obligations in sectors characterized by a strong general interest ethos, such as healthcare, but again that hypothesis has not yet been validated by any panel or Appellate Body report. Besides, as noted in the previous section, not all measures pursuing the general interest objectives listed in Article XIV can be regarded as relating to public services: a notion of public services inferred from Article XIV GATS would thus be excessively broad.[113]

The remaining public service exemptions provide no further guidance in the quest for a GATS notion of public services. The exemption for Maritime Transport, as discussed above, merely reflects the difficulty to reach consensus in that area through trade negotiations. The exemption set out in the ATS Annex, instead, has wide-ranging effects and a sufficiently clear-cut coverage, but is entirely agnostic as to the aims pursued by WTO Members in managing air traffic rights.

Section 5(e)(i) of the Annex on Telecommunications and Section 3 of the Reference Paper actually seem to constitute expressions of a GATS notion of public services, albeit limited to the field of telecommunications. Indeed, as discussed in the previous section, both provisions recognise the general interest goals that underlie the imposition of certain performance requirements on telecoms operators (i.e. public service and universal service obligations) and accordingly grant those services a special legal status by exempting them from the regulatory provisions set out, respectively, in the Annex on Telecommunications and in the Reference Paper. Nonetheless, due to the limited attention WTO dispute resolution organs have so far devoted to Section 5(e)(i) of the Annex on Telecommunications and Section 3 of the Reference Paper[114] and to their narrow scope of application, those provisions can hardly constitute a template for the development of a general GATS notion of public services.

### 2.4.3 The GATS Impact on the Emergence of a Global Notion of Public Services in Non-WTO Contexts

According to Article V GATS, WTO members are entitled to conclude EIAs providing for the preferential liberalization of trade in services provided that those agreements comply with a number of requirements. First, EIAs must have a

[113]For instance, imposing qualification requirements as a prerequisite for the access to the medical profession can be regarded as a measure necessary to protect human health within the meaning of Article XIV(b) GATS. It does not follow, however, that all medical doctors can be regarded as providers of a public service.

[114]But see, *Mexico—Measures Affecting Telecommunications Services ('Mexico-Telecoms')*, Report of the Panel, T/DS204/R, para 7.327 (holding that rates charged for the access to and use of public telecommunications transport networks are not 'conditions' within the meaning of Section 5(e) of the Annex on Telecommunications).

substantial sectoral coverage. Second, EIAs must eliminate substantially all discrimination between or among the parties through proscription of existing discriminatory measures or prohibition or new or more discriminatory measures. Third, EIAs must facilitate trade between their parties and must not raise the overall level of barriers to trade in services *vis-à-vis* third parties.

The 'substantial coverage' requirement may have an impact on the development of regional notions of public services. With reference to the equivalent provision set out in Article XXIV GATT 1994, the Appellate Body in *Turkey—Textiles* ruled that, while that expression 'is not the same as *all* the trade', it is 'something considerably more than merely *some* of the trade'.[115] Accordingly, while an EIA exempting some public services, such as primary education or public healthcare, appears in line with the 'substantial coverage' requirement,[116] doubts arise whether an EIA setting out an across-the-board exemption for public services would still comply with the above requirement.

Moreover, while EIA provisions are not required to comply with the MFN obligation enshrined in Article II GATS—because it is in the very nature of EIAs to accord preferential treatment to select trading partners—it is doubtful whether EIAs can also depart from other GATS trade disciplines that are relevant to the regulation and funding of public services, such as the ones on transparency and domestic regulation.[117] That EIAs must comply with the principle of national treatment, instead, is expressly stipulated in Article V:1(b), which requires those agreements to provide for 'the absence or elimination of substantially all discrimination' in the sectors they cover.

The impact of the requirements set out in Article V GATS on the actual content of bilateral and plurilateral EIAs must not be overestimated. As a matter of fact, deviations from Article V requirements and GATS-minus commitments abound.[118] With particular reference to public services, some EIAs embody detailed provisions relating to subsidies, government procurement, domestic regulation and some relatively broad public service exemptions.[119] Accordingly, some commentators have rejected the 'hierarchical' or 'top-down' relationship between EIAs and the GATS that Article V GATS purports to establish.[120]

---

[115]*Turkey—Textiles*, Report of the Appellate Body, WT/DS34/AB/R, para 48 (italics in the original).

[116]See Cottier and Molinuevo 2008, p. 132.

[117]See WTO Committee on Regional Trade Agreements Twenty-Seconds Session, Note on the meetings of 29–30 April and 3 May 1999, WT/REG/M/22, 4 June 1999, paras 17 and 18; WTO Committee on Regional Trade Agreements, Synopsis of 'Systemic' Issues Related to Regional Trade Agreements, Note by the Secretariat, WT/REG/W/37, 2 March 2000, para 33.

[118]See Adlung and Miroudot 2012.

[119]See Krajewski 2006; M. Krajewski, Public services in bilateral free trade agreements of the EU. http://www.epsu.org/IMG/pdf/PublicServicesFTAs_FinalVersion.pdf. Accessed 20 October 2014.

[120]See Fabbricotti 2010.

Still, even if Article V GATS does not constitute a peremptory constraint for bilateral and plurilateral negotiations on trade in services, the language of GATS provisions undoubtedly represents a 'focal point' around which trade negotiations tend to converge. Indeed, GATS-like public services exemptions abound in EIAs.[121] The governmental services exemption laid down in Article I:1(b)–(c) GATS appears in several EIAs, including the most elaborate and detailed ones. Considering that the language of that exemption still remains unclear, WTO members could have drafted and employed clearer public service exemption clauses for their EIAs. The circumstance that, in most cases, they have failed to do so suggests that GATS agnosticism *vis-à-vis* public services can, at least to some extent, hinder the emergence of a global notion of public services through regional economic integration.

## 2.5 Conclusions

The purpose of this chapter was to assess the impact of the GATS on public services. To that end, regard has been paid, in Sect. 2.2, to the potential incidence on those services of GATS trade disciplines, i.e. MFN treatment, market access, national treatment, domestic regulation, and a number of other provisions. That assessment yielded disparate results. The MFN obligation was found not to be relevant to the provision of public services so long as they are supplied by national providers, but to preclude arrangements between WTO members based on the principle of reciprocity, such as access to the radio spectrum or reimbursement of medical treatment received in select foreign countries. Instead, it has been observed that market access commitments may impede the granting of special and exclusive rights, a common form of entry regulation employed in the provision of public services, as well as other relevant requirements such as those on public ownership, legal form and foreign investment. Possible inconsistencies have also been detected between the GATS principle of national treatment and the funding of domestic public service providers. If a WTO member undertakes national treatment commitments in a given service sector, it is not required to grant its supplier-addressed subsidies also to providers of like services established in other WTO members, but must extend its recipient-based subsidies to like services provided to domestic consumers by foreign suppliers either abroad (mode 2) or on a cross-border basis (mode 1). Also the provisional application of domestic regulation requirements was found to be potentially incompatible with public service and universal service obligations, insofar as the necessity test based on the 'quality of the service' laid down in Article VI:4(b) GATS may be unable to accommodate the broader policy goals (e.g. affordability, continuity, equal treatment, universal access) pursued by public service and universal service obligations. The rules on statutory monopolies and exclusive service providers as well as the sector-specific provisions set out

[121]For a survey and an in-depth analysis of GATS-like public service exemptions, see Krajewski 2011, p. 17 et seq.

in the Annex on Telecommunications and in the Reference Paper were also found to have implications on the regulation and operation of public services.

Against the background of such a potentially far-reaching impact on public services, Sect. 2.3 sought to examine the discretion the GATS grants WTO members to exempt what they regard as public services from the above trade disciplines. In particular, it has been observed that WTO members enjoy a remarkable discretion in adding 'individual' public service exemptions to the agreement. A survey of WTO members' GATS schedules revealed that activities that have traditionally been regarded as public services attracted fewer commitments in terms of sectoral and modal scope, as well as lower levels of commitment. The exemption for 'services supplied in the exercise of governmental authority', instead, was found to have a minor impact, due to its narrow material scope. Account was taken to the autonomy afforded to WTO members by Article XIII GATS in the procurement of public services. Regard was also had to how general and security exceptions could be employed to cover regulatory measures concerning the operation of public services. Other sector-specific public service exemptions were surveyed, such as the ones for air transport services and maritime services and the ones laid down in the Annex on Telecommunications and in the Reference Paper. The overall conclusion of that assessment is that, in spite of the potentially far-reaching effects of GATS trade disciplines on public services, WTO members are afforded ample opportunities to tailor those effects to their needs.

Section 2.4 examined the GATS approach to the notion of public services, an approach that was described as inherently 'agnostic'. Most GATS provisions were found not to recognise the specificity of those services or of the goals they pursue. As a consequence, the provisions WTO members can rely on to exempt what they regard as public services from liberalization can actually be employed to exclude other services or to pursue other policy goals, including protectionist ones. Therefore, a GATS notion of public services could not be established. It could neither be gleaned from a survey of WTO members' schedules nor from the interpretation of GATS public service exemptions. Moreover, regard was had to the impact of GATS on the emergence of a global notion of public services through bilateral and plurilateral economic integration agreements (EIAs). While the hierarchical relationship envisaged by Article V GATS between that agreement and EIAs hardly reflects the reality of international practice, it was submitted that GATS agnosticism *vis-à-vis* public services may nonetheless constitute a 'focal point' around which bilateral and plurilateral negotiations tend to converge, thus hindering the emergence of a global notion of public services.

In conclusion, while the GATS may have a very limited *practical* impact on the provision, regulation, and funding of public services at the national and local level, the agnostic model embodied by that agreement might interfere with the conceptualisation of public services beyond national borders. To paraphrase Victor Hugo, '*On résiste à l'invasion des armées; on ne résiste pas à l'invasion des idées*.'[122]

[122] Hugo 1877.

## References

Adlung R (2006) Public services and the GATS. J Int Econ Law 9(2):455–485
Adlung R (2007) Negotiations on safeguards and subsidies in services: a never-ending story? J Int Econ Law 10(2):235–265
Adlung R, Miroudot S (2012) Poison in the wine? Tracing GATS-minus commitments in regional trade agreements. J World Trade 46(5):1045–1082
Arena A (2011) The GATS notion of public services as an instance of intergovernmental agnosticism: comparative insights from the EU's supranational dialectic. J World Trade 45(3):489–528
Arrowsmith S (2003) Government procurement in the WTO. Kluwer Law International, The Hague
Bigdeli S, Rechsteiner S (2008) Article VIII GATS. In: Wolfrum R, Stoll P-T, Feinäugle C (eds) WTO—trade in services, vol 6. Martinus Nijhoff Publishers, Leiden, pp 205–220
Burri Nenova M (2007) The law of the World Trade Organization and the communications law of the European Community: on a path of harmony or discord? J World Trade 41(4):833–878
Brancasi A (2003), Il servizio pubblico di trasporto terrestre e la liberalizzazione dei servizi pubblici a carattere imprenditoriale. In: Brancasi A (ed) Liberalizzazione del trasporto terrestre e servizi pubblici economici. Il Mulino, Bologna, pp 11–38
Choudhury B (2012) Public services and international trade liberalization. CUP, Cambridge
Cottier T, Molinuevo M (2008) Article V GATS. In: Wolfrum R, Stoll P-T, Feinäugle C (eds) WTO—trade in Services, vol 6. Martinus Nijhoff Publishers, Leiden, pp 125–151
Cottier T, Pagagiotis D, Diebold NF (2008) Article XIV GATS. In: Wolfrum R, Stoll P-T, Feinäugle C (eds) WTO—trade in services, vol 6. Martinus Nijhoff Publishers, Leiden, pp 287–328
De Ruggiero L (1984) Sul concetto di precomprensione. Politica del diritto 15:577–598
Fabbricotti A (2010) The WTO and RTAs: a 'bottom-up' interpretation of RTAs' autonomy over WTO law. In: Kolsky LM, Frankel S (eds) International economic law and national autonomy. CUP, Cambridge, pp 116–140
Gao H (2008) Telecommunications services: reference paper. In: Wolfrum R, Stoll P-T, Feinäugle C (eds) WTO—trade in services, vol 6. Martinus Nijhoff Publishers, Leiden, pp 718–747
Hauriou M (1929) Précis de droit constitutionnel. Sirey, Paris
Hugo V (1877) Histoire d'un Crime. J. Hetzel, Paris
Howse R, Türk E (2002) The WTO negotiations on services: the regulatory state up for grabs. Canada Watch 9(1–2):3–6
Karayigit MT (2009) The notion of services of general economic interest revisited. Eur Public Law 15(4):575–595
Köbele M (2008) Annex on air transport services. In: Wolfrum R, Stoll P-T, Feinäugle C (eds) WTO—trade in services, vol 6. Martinus Nijhoff Publishers, Leiden, pp 598–617
Krajewski M (2003) Public services and trade liberalization: mapping the legal framework. J Int Econ Law 6(2):341–367
Krajewski M (2006) Services liberalization in regional trade agreements: lessons for GATS 'unfinished business'? In: Bartels L, Ortin F (eds) Regional trade agreements and the WTO legal system. Oxford University Press, Oxford, pp 175–200
Krajewski M (2008a) Article VI GATS. In: Wolfrum R, Stoll P-T, Feinäugle C (eds) WTO—trade in services, vol 6. Martinus Nijhoff Publishers, Leiden, pp 165–196
Krajewski M (2008b) Protecting a shared value of the union in a globalized world: services of general economic interest and external trade. In: Van de Gronden J (ed) EU and WTO law on services: limits to the realization of general interest policies within the services markets. Kluwer Law International, The Hague, pp 173–213
Krajewski M (2011) Public services in bilateral free trade agreements of the EU. Available at SSRN: http://ssrn.com/abstract=1964288

Kulkarni P (2009) Impact of the GATS on basic social services redux. J World Trade 43(2):245–283

Laffont JJ, Tirole J (1993) A theory of incentives in procurement and regulation. MIT Press, Cambridge

Lehner RD (1995) Protectionism, prestige and national security: the alliance against multilateral trade in international air transport. Duke Law J 45(2):436–478

Leroux EH (2006) What is a "Service Supplied in the Exercise of Governmental Authority" under Article I:3(b) and (c) of the general agreement on trade in services? J World Trade 40(3):345–385

Luff D (2002) International regulation of postal services: UPU vs. WTO rules. In: Geradin D (ed) The liberalization of postal services in the European Union, 34 European monographs. Kluwer Law International, The Hague, pp 39–88

Marchetti JA, Mavroidis PC (2004) What are the main challenges for the GATS framework? Don't talk about revolution. Eur Bus Organ Law Rev 5(3):511–562

Marcou G (2001) De l'idée de service public au service d'intérêt general. In: Marcou G, Moderne F (eds) L'idée de service public dans le droit des Etats de l'Union Européenne. L'Harmattan, Paris, pp 365–412

Marcou G (2004) Il servizio pubblico di fronte al diritto comunitario. Il Filangieri 1:7–51

Musseli I, Zarrilli S (2005) Oil and gas services: market liberalization and the ongoing GATS negotiations. J Int Econ Law 8(2):551–581

Neergaard U (2009) Services of general economic interest: the nature of the beast. In: Krajewski M, Neergaard U, van de Gronden J (eds) The changing legal framework for services of general interest in Europe: between competition and solidarity. T.M.C. Asser Press, The Hague, pp 17–50

Nistor L (2011) Public services and the European Union. Springer, Heidelberg

Parameswaran B (2008) Annex on negotiations on maritime transport services. In: Wolfrum R, Stoll P-T, Feinäugle C (eds) WTO—trade in services, vol 6. Martinus Nijhoff Publishers, Leiden, pp 667–682

Parisi F, Ghei N (2003) The role of reciprocity in international law. Cornell Int Law J 36(1):93–123

Perrazzelli A, Vergano P (2000) Terminal dues under the UPU convention and the GATS: an overview of the rules and of their compatibility. Fordham Int Law J 23:736–751

Pontier J-M (2003) La notion de compétences régaliennes dans la problématique de la répartition des compétences entre les collectivités publiques. Revue du Droit Public et de la Science Politique en France et à l'Etranger 119:193–237

Trachtman JP (2003) Lessons for the GATS from existing WTO rules on domestic regulation. In: Mattoo A, Sauvé P (eds) Domestic regulation & services trade liberalization. The World Bank, Washington, D.C

Van de Gronden J (2013) Transnational competition law and public services. Eur Yearb Int Econ Law 4:109–146

VanDuzer JA (2004) Health, education and social services in Canada: the impact of the GATS. In: Curtis JM, Ciuriak D (eds) Trade policy research. International Trade Canada, Ottawa, pp 287–518

VanGrasstek C, Sauvé P (2006) The consistency of WTO rules: can the single undertaking be squared with variable geometry? J Int Econ Law 9:837–864

World Trade Organization (1995) Analytical index: guide to GATT law and practice, 6th edn. World Trade Organization, Geneva

Zacharias D (2008a) Article I GATS. In: Wolfrum R, Stoll P-T, Feinäugle C (eds) WTO—trade in services, vol 6. Martinus Nijhoff Publishers, Leiden, pp 31–69

Zacharias D (2008b) Article XIII GATS. In: Wolfrum R, Stoll P-T, Feinäugle C (eds) WTO—trade in services, vol 6. Martinus Nijhoff Publishers, Leiden, pp 272–286

# Chapter 3
# WTO Procurement Rules: In Particular the Government Procurement Agreement (GPA) and Services of General Interest

**Wolfgang Weiß**

**Abstract** The global procurement rules have been revised in 2012. This chapter therefore addresses the impact of the new Government Procurement Agreement (GPA) on services of general interest. A detailed analysis of the GPA's scope is given which delineates it from the purview of the GATT and the GATS as these agreements also address the issue of public procurement and provide useful guidance in the understanding of the new definition of covered procurement used in the new GPA 2012. Subsequently, the substantive and personal scope of the GPA rules is discussed in order to determine the relevance of GPA obligations to the provision of public services. The last section proceeds by considering the notion of government procurement in order to establish whether specific regimes used in the procurement of public services, such as concession contracts and in-house procurement, are covered by GPA rules.

## Contents



W. Weiß (✉)
European and Public International Law, German University of Administrative Sciences Speyer, Speyer, Germany
e-mail: weiss@uni-speyer.de

W. Weiß
Oxford Brookes University, Oxford, UK
e-mail: wweiss@brookes.ac.uk



M. Krajewski (ed.), *Services of General Interest Beyond the Single Market*, Legal Issues of Services of General Interest,
DOI 10.1007/978-94-6265-063-3_3

## 3.1 Introduction

The provision of services, in particular the provision of services in the general interest, i.e. public services, may be subject to WTO procurement rules as governments may decide either to procure these services or to procure goods or services for use in the public production or supply of these services. Hence, the economic transactions and operations used in the provision of such services may be determined by WTO procurement rules. This presupposes, of course, that WTO procurement rules are applicable to these transactions.

Besides rules dealing with public procurement in the multilateral GATT and GATS, WTO procurement rules are mainly collected in the plurilateral Government Procurement Agreement (GPA) which is included in Annex 4 to the WTO agreement. As a plurilateral agreement, the GPA is not binding for all WTO members but only for those who have specifically accepted it (Article II:4 WTO Agreement). The GPA rules were subject to a protracted revision process based on Article XXIV:7 GPA which began in 1996/7, and after gaining momentum in 2002 finally ended in 2012 with the adoption of a new, revised text and newly negotiated annexes.[1] The text of the GPA 2012 actually corresponds, by and large, to a provisional text agreed upon at the end of 2006.[2] The revision process strived for an improved text updating the GPA with regard to electronic procurement methods, eliminating remaining discriminatory practices (such as offsets and buy national rules which are in place under the GPA 1994[3]), and expanding the GPA's coverage, and was finally intended to make the disciplines of the GPA clearer and easier to implement so that protectionism in public procurement could effectively be reduced.[4]

[1]See WTO Committee on Government Procurement, Adoption of the results of the negotiations under Article XXIV:7 of the Agreement on Government Procurement, GPA/113, 2 April 2012.

[2]See WTO Committee on Government Procurement, Revision of the Agreement on Government Procurement of 8 December 2006, prepared by the Secretariat, GPA/W/297, 11 December 2006.

[3]Offsets are banned under the GPA 2012, see Article IV:6.

[4]See also Arrowsmith 2002, p. 761.

The new GPA 2012 which recently entered into force in April 2014 involves a new definition of covered procurement according to which procurement in the sense of the GPA covers procurement for governmental purposes which does not include procurement with a view to commercial sale or resale, or for use in the production or supply of goods or services for commercial sale or resale (see Article II:2 (a) GPA 2012). The understanding of the definition is pivotal to the scope of the new GPA 2012 and in particular to the question as to whether the procurement of services of general interest will be covered by the GPA 2012, as services of general interest (such as energy, water supply, the provision of public transport and of travel infrastructure)—even though their provision is widely seen as part of government responsibility—are usually sold by public entities to consumers (generally with the exception of infrastructure and basic education). Hence, one could consider that these genuine public services are not government services in the sense of the GPA coverage but commercial services, as the state may act like an ordinary private market-oriented service supplier in this respect. Hence, the procurement of most services of general interest will not be covered by GPA 2012 disciplines. Such an understanding would imply a considerable shift from the GPA 1994, as the latter does not contain an equivalent definition of covered procurement, meaning that the procurement of public services is subject to GPA disciplines in any case.

Furthermore, it is usually local authorities or enterprises run by public authorities on the sub-central level which provide for public services. Local authorities and state enterprises, however, may not be bound by GPA disciplines because local authorities and state enterprises are subject to the procurement disciplines only insofar as the GPA parties list them in Annex 2 or 3 to the GPA (see Article I fn. 1 GPA 1994 and Article II:4 lit. (b) GPA 2012).

Hence, the new GPA 2012 gives occasion for an analysis of the relevance of WTO government procurement rules for the provision of services of general interest.

This chapter will proceed as follows: after a brief look at the notion of services of general interest, in particular in view of its specific use in EU law (Sect. 3.2), and a likewise brief introduction to the GPA (Sect. 3.3), a detailed analysis of the GPA's scope will be given which delineates it from the purview of the GATT and the GATS as these agreements also address the issue of public procurement and provide useful guidance in the understanding of the new definition of covered procurement used in the new GPA 2012 (Sect. 3.4). Subsequently, the substantive and personal scope of the GPA rules will be discussed in order to determine the relevance of GPA obligations to the provision of public services (Sect. 3.5). The last section proceeds by considering the notion of government procurement in order to establish whether specific regimes used in the procurement of public services, such as concession contracts and in-house procurement, are covered by GPA rules (Sect. 3.6). A summary will conclude (Sect. 3.7).

## 3.2 The Notion of Services of General Interest in WTO Law and in EU Law

In contrast to EU law, the term "services of general interest" does not exist in WTO law. In EU law, services of general (economic) interest are subject to fierce debate about the role of member states and their remaining leeway in unilaterally determining the conditions under which such public services are performed. Hence, in EU law the concept of services of general (economic) interest plays an important role in assessing how intensive EU common market law may impact on the domestic provision of such types of services and what role the specific exception to the application of EU competition rules contained in Article 106 para 2 TFEU plays. The European concept of services of general interest captures a specific category of public services. A comparable notion of services of general interest does not exist in WTO law. Neither the GATS nor the GPA use this term.[5] Comparably to EU law, however, WTO agreements exclude specific services from their scope of application, meaning that there are also specific types of services which are treated differently from others in WTO law. According to Article I:3 GATS, GATS disciplines do not apply to services supplied in the exercise of governmental authority, i.e. services supplied neither on a commercial basis nor in competition with one or more service suppliers.[6]

The two concepts of services of general interest or services of general economic interest in EU law, on the one hand, and of governmental services in WTO law, on the other, are not necessarily co-extensive, all the more since the term "governmental" used in Article I:3 (b) GATS or Article II:2 GPA 2012 may not have exactly the same meaning. These conceptual discrepancies between EU and WTO law give rise to the problem of determining whether and, if so, how far WTO procurement disciplines apply to the specific type of services encompassed by the European notion of "services of general interest".

EU law differentiates between the general category of services of general interest and the sub-category of services of general economic interest.[7] Services of general interest are services whose provision is important for everyone as these services meet the basic needs of any human being, such as water, energy, infrastructure, and telecommunications. Hence, their provision is in the general interest. Services of general economic interest are a sub-group of these services; they

[5]Adlung 2006, p. 456.

[6]A specific exclusion from the GATS is provided for in para 1 lit. (b) and (c) of the Annex on Financial Services concerning "activities forming part of a statutory system of social security or public retirement plans" as long as they are not conducted in competition of a public entity or a financial service supplier. Lack of competition is the decisive criterion here; Marchetti and Mavroidis 2004, p. 534.

[7]See for example Protocol (No 26) on services of general interest, *OJ* 2010 C 83/308.

comprise those services of general interest which are supplied in an economic way. They are supplied commercially on a market like any other economic activity.[8]

Due to the reliance of any human being on services of general (economic) interest, these services cannot be left to uncontrolled market forces, as market forces may not guarantee their availability in good quality to everyone, everywhere they are needed and at affordable prices. In addition, these services are special due to the need for network infrastructure. The provision of at least some of these services requires costly infrastructure which may lead to natural monopolies as there will be—for various reasons—only one network available for the provision of these services (water, energy supply, transport infrastructure; technological development has changed this in the telecommunications sector). Hence, these services cannot be compared to other commercial products as the market entrance barrier is very high. The specific character of services of general interest is perceived in a domestic way in most states since they have specific concepts of public involvement or public responsibility in these sectors, the expression of which is usually the existence of sector-specific rules and regulations laying down public service obligations. In the EU, services of general interest are perceived as important for social coherence (Article 174 TFEU) and hence enjoy a specific status as a shared value (Article 14 TFEU; see also Article 1 Protocol No 26), and to some extent receive unique treatment with regard to economic rules on the internal market.[9]

National concepts determining the unique status of services provided in the general interest vary, as does the concrete allocation of services to this specific category. Hence, it is unsurprising that WTO rules do not enshrine a specific concept of services of general interest. Consequently, one cannot discuss the relevance of WTO procurement rules to a specific concept of services which is particular to the European Union. Nevertheless, one can assess the significance of WTO procurement rules for the autonomy of WTO members to decide the institutional setting for the provision of services which are in the general interest and therefore must be available to all citizens in a reliable and affordable fashion. Moreover, the European differentiation between services of general interest and services of general economic interest is irrelevant here, all the more given that the differentiation is not beyond doubt even in the EU context.

## 3.3 A Brief Introduction to the GPA

The GPA provides for specific obligations for the public procurement of its parties. Since public procurement for governmental purposes is excluded from the general disciplines on trade in goods and services enshrined in the GATT and the GATS (for more detail see Sect. 3.4), there was a need for a specific agreement laying down rules to combat protectionism in the public procurement of WTO members. The GPA

[8]Compare the definition by the European Commission given in its Communication: A Quality Framework for Services of General Interest in Europe, COM(2011) 900 final, 20 December 2011, p. 3.

[9]For an overview of developments under EU law cf. Krajewski et al. 2009.

1994 is therefore based on similar basic disciplines as the whole of WTO law, in particular the ban on any discrimination (see Article III GPA 1994 and Articles IV:1, 2 GPA 2012), so that the GPA parties are obliged to immediately and unconditionally accord treatment to the goods, services or suppliers of any other party that is no less favourable than the treatment accorded to domestic goods, services or suppliers.

The personal and substantive coverage of the GPA disciplines, however, is restricted in different ways, in particular by the agreement's positive list approach. Under the positive list approach, only those public entities which have been listed explicitly in the parties' annexes are subject to GPA disciplines. In addition, this applies only to those goods and services listed in these annexes, and whose value equals or exceeds the relevant thresholds which are non-uniformly set by the parties in their annexes. As a consequence, the extent to which the GPA disciplines apply to each GPA party and its public procurement varies.

Beyond the core discipline of non-discrimination, the GPA contains rules that counteract unnecessary obstacles to international trade due to technical specifications (Article VI GPA 1994; Article X:1–6 GPA 2012) and that foster the transparency of procurement rules (Article XIX GPA 1994; Article VI GPA 2012), and provide for concrete procedural requirements in the tendering procedures (Articles VII, IX ff. GPA 1994), for rules on qualifications (Article VIII GPA 1994, Article IX GPA 2012), the awarding of contracts, and finally domestic review (Article XX GPA 1994; Article XVIII GPA 2012).

## 3.4 Delineation of Scope: GPA Versus GATT and GATS

### *3.4.1 (Some) Consonance in Exceptions*

The provision of services by public entities may be covered by the disciplines of the GATS and of the GATT agreement. Both the GATS and the GATT agreement, however, specify that their central disciplines on market access and non-discrimination do not apply to the procurement of goods or services for governmental purposes by governmental agencies; see Article III:8 lit. (a) GATT[10] and Article

[10]Even though Article III:8 GATT explicitly only excludes national treatment, and not most-favoured nation treatment, the reference in Article I GATT to Article III:2 and 4 GATT also leads to the exclusion of Article I obligation, as confirmed by practice, see *European Communities—Measures Affecting Trade in Commercial Vessels*, Report of the Panel, WT/DS301/R, paras 7.85–90; Arrowsmith 2003, pp. 61–63; Dischendorfer 2000, pp. 15–17; Jackson 1997, p. 225. *Contra* Reich 1997, p. 142 et seq. Another argument reads that MFN obligation does not cover procurement as procurement is not mentioned there, see Trepte 2005, p. 1126. See also Article XVII:2 GATT according to which the obligation of state trading enterprises to respect the non-discrimination obligation (which includes the MFN obligation of Article I GATT, see *Korea—Measures Affecting Imports of Fresh, Chilled and Frozen Beef*, Report of the Panel, WT/DS161/R, WT/DS169/R, para 753) does not apply to imports of products for immediate or ultimate consumption in governmental use. In this respect, only the requirement of a fair and equitable treatment of the trade of other WTO members exists which does, however, not impose any specific obligation; see Dischendorfer 2000, p. 17.

XIII:1 GATS.[11] Hence, government procurement is exempt from the main market access and non-discrimination obligations of the GATS and from the non-discrimination requirement under the GATT. The rationale behind this appears rather clear: since core GATT and GATS disciplines do not apply, WTO members need not open their domestic procurement activities to international competition (and there are good reasons for this, such as protection of domestic industries, or pursuit of non-economic, social policies that favour small and medium sized undertakings or undertakings from rural, poor areas[12]; the most important historic reason for exclusion of public procurement from international disciplines was analysed by Evenett and Hoekman who showed the prevalence of the Keynesian idea at that time that an increase in government expenses contributes to a greater increase in national wealth the smaller the share of goods produced abroad[13]). WTO members can thus still discriminate against companies from other WTO members in their public procurement of goods or services. Foreign companies' entrance to the domestic procurement market is subject to reciprocity by virtue of the GPA disciplines if the WTO member is bound by this plurilateral agreement. As the GATS and GATT disciplines step back by virtue of their exceptions, they make way for the GPA obligations.

Article III:8 (a) GATT and Article XIII:1 GATS do however contain a commercial sale/resale counter-exception: governmental procurement is covered by the above-mentioned GATT and GATS disciplines if procurement is done "with a view to commercial resale or with a view to use in the supply of services for commercial sale" (see Article XIII:1 GATS; similarly Article III:8 lit. (a) GATT and Article XVII:2 GATT[14]). In other words, in the case of commercial activities, GATT and GATS disciplines fully apply to public procurement. GPA rules may then not apply. As already mentioned, the new GPA 2012 explicitly gives a definition of covered procurement, according to which the GPA 2012 rules do not cover such commercial government procurement. The explicit definition in Article II:2 lit. (a) (ii) GPA 2012, according to which procurement with a view to commercial sale or for use in the production or supply of goods or services for commercial sale is not covered governmental procurement, almost repeats verbatim the wording of the counter-exception in Article III:8 (a) GATT and Article XIII:1 GATS, with one notable difference: both Article III:8 (a) GATT and Article XIII:1 GATS only refer to "governmental agencies" which—in reverse conclusion—excludes public enterprises. Public enterprises are not covered by the term "governmental agencies" as there is a specific rule on state trading enterprises: Article XVII

[11]Instead, Article XIII:2 GATS provides for multilateral negotiations on services procurement which take place in the multilateral Working Party on GATS Rules (WPGR), established by the Services Trade Council in 1995.

[12]See Zacharias 2008, para 1 et seq.

[13]Mavroidis 2012, p. 799.

[14]"and not otherwise for resale or use in the production of goods for sale".

GATT.[15] Article XVII GATT regulates the relevance of GATT rules for public enterprises, and in para 2 exempts government procurement by state enterprises from the non-discrimination disciplines. Hence, while governmental agencies are exempted from core GATT rules by Article III:8 lit. (a) GATT, public enterprises are exempted by Article XVII:2 GATT. Thus, Article XVII:2 GATT complements the exceptions from non-discrimination for government procurement in Article III:8 lit. (a) GATT.[16] Governmental agencies and state enterprises are hence allowed to procure for government purposes in a discriminatory manner. In accordance with this scope of exemptions, the GPA covers governmental agencies in Annex 1 and 2 and state trading enterprises in Annex 3. Hence, the scope of application of the GPA disciplines mirrors the scope of exclusion of government procurement from core GATT disciplines.

The situation is slightly different, however, under the GATS. The limitation of the exclusion from core GATS principles in Article XIII:1 GATS to governmental agencies is not complemented by a GATS provision similar to Article XVII:2 GATT on state trading enterprises. Article VIII GATS only addresses monopolies and exclusive service suppliers, meaning that other public undertakings are not covered by GATS disciplines, such as public undertakings operating in a competitive environment.[17] If public undertakings not covered by Article VIII GATS do not come under the scope of the GPA either (for example, due to the commercial nature of their activities), their business conduct is subject to neither GPA disciplines nor GATS rules.[18]

Apart from this small difference, the consequence of this verbatim consonance between the exceptions from the GATT/GATS, on the one hand, and the scope of the GPA 2012, on the other, allegedly is that the scope of the GPA and the scope of the GATT and GATS exemptions are the same.[19] As a consequence, their coverage, in essence, is mutually exclusive. If public entities act like a commercial entity, their purchases of goods and services in the conduct of their commercial activities of selling goods and services on the marketplace are not subject to the specific GPA provisions, but have to respect the relevant obligations under the GATS and the GATT.

---

[15] *Canada—Certain Measures Affecting the Renewable Energy Generation Sector, Canada—Measures Relating to the Feed-In Tariff Program*, Report of the Appellate Body, WT/DS412/AB/R, WT/DS426/AB/R, para 5.61, according to which the term "governmental agency" "refers to those entities acting for or on behalf of government in the public realm within the competences that have been conferred on them to discharge governmental functions. "This further confirms our understanding that a governmental agency is an entity acting for or on behalf of government and performing governmental functions within the competences conferred to it".

[16] Dischendorfer 2000, p. 17.

[17] Mattoo 1998, p. 51.

[18] The telecommunication rules, however, go beyond Article VIII GATS; see Mattoo 1998, p. 55 et seq.

[19] Reich 2009, p. 1006.

The practical effect of such distinction in the coverage of the GPA, the GATS and the GATT is that WTO law also differentiates between different types of services: (at least) under the GPA 2012, the GPA rules are intended to apply only to the public procurement of goods and services for governmental purposes and not for public commercial purposes such as state trading. State commercial activities are subject to multilateral GATT/GATS disciplines and not subject to plurilateral GPA 2012 rules. In contrast, the purchase of the specific type of government services is subject to plurilateral GPA disciplines only, which presupposes that the state has acceded to the plurilateral GPA. Otherwise, specific governmental services would not be subject to core WTO disciplines at all. As a result, the delineation of genuine governmental purposes from commercial purposes becomes highly relevant and will be looked at in more detail below in Sect. 3.4.3. However, before turning to this issue, one has to explore whether this distinction has the same relevance under the present GPA 1994 as under the future GPA 2012.

### *3.4.2 Differences in Coverage Between GPA 1994 and GPA 2012 with Regard to Commercial Purchases*

The mutual exclusivity of the scopes of the GPA, on the one hand, and of the GATS and the GATT, on the other, may not apply to the same extent to the current, still relevant GPA 1994 since the definitional elements for the notion of government procurement in Article II:2 lit. (a) (ii) GPA 2012 ("not procured with a view to commercial sale ... or for use in the production or supply of goods or services for commercial sale") are not present in the GPA 1994. Some authors, however, allege that it is implied that the GPA 1994 also did not cover commercial purchases but only procurement for governmental purposes, as the scope of the Article III:8 GATT exemption was the very *raison d´etre* of the GPA.[20] They also refer to the fact that GPA parties already under the GPA 1994 had included such a definition in their annexes.[21] Indeed, under the GPA 1994, some parties made specific restrictions in their annexes which exclude procurement for commercial sale from GPA coverage. For example, Korea excludes products and services purchased with a view to resale or to use in the production of goods or provision of services for sale. Japan excludes the purchase of goods and services for resale or for use in the production of goods for sale; with regard to entities under Annex 3, Japan excludes contracts for purposes of daily profit-making activities which are exposed to competitive forces in markets. The EU drafted its restriction to the coverage of entities in Annex 3 in different terms, as it excludes purchases for resale only when the entity does not enjoy special or exclusive rights and other entities

[20]Reich 2009, p. 1006. *Contra* Wang 2007, pp. 895, 905; Wang 2009, p. 682.

[21]See Reich 2009, p. 1006.

are free to sell or hire it under the same conditions as the procuring entity.[22] The most extensive specific definition was used by Canada, according to which "[p]rocurement in terms of Canadian coverage is defined as contractual transactions to acquire property or services for the direct benefit or use of the government. … It does not include non-contractual agreements or any form of government assistance including but not limited to co-operative agreements, grants, loans, equity infusions, guarantees, fiscal incentives and government provisions of goods and services, given to individuals, firms, private institutions, and sub-central governments. It does not include procurements made with a view to commercial resale or made by one entity or enterprise from another entity or enterprise of Canada".[23]

One has to consider, however, that even though several GPA parties had already included restrictions to their GPA coverage in their annexes to the GPA 1994 which use similar elements as are now contained in the definition of covered procurement in Article II:2 GPA 2012, it was not done by all. Hence, one cannot state that the explicit limitation to the notion of covered procurement present in Article II:2 GPA 2012 by excluding commercial procurement only mirrors an understanding already prevalent under the GPA 1994. On the contrary, extending exceptions from the GPA 1994 coverage (which exclude commercial procurement) present only in some parties' annexes to all GPA parties under the GPA 2012, and hence standardizing the scope of application of GPA disciplines to all GPA parties, could in the end even be criticized for reducing GPA coverage.[24] Furthermore, even though the GPA 2012 excludes these types of commercial activities from its coverage, some GPA parties still maintain their traditional definitions and exclusions to the GPA 1994 coverage in their annexes under the GPA 2012; see for example Annex 3 to the European Union, which not only excludes procurement in activities which are exposed to competitive forces in the market but also procurement "for purposes of re-sale or hire to third parties, provided that the procuring entity enjoys no special or exclusive right to sell or hire the subject of such contracts and other entities are free to sell or hire it under the same conditions as the procuring entity",[25] or the General Note by Canada in its future Annex 7, according to which procurement is contractual acquisition of goods or services for the direct benefit or use of the government.[26] This recurrence might be ascribed to the interpretive uncertainties caused by the broad formulations used in Article II:2 GPA 2012 (a lack of a clear and workable definition of covered procurement in the GPA 2012

[22]See Wang 2009, p. 682 with fn. 62 for references.

[23]See Canada's General Notes on its annexes. This extract is quoted from Wang 2007, p. 894, fn. 23.

[24]Reich 2009, p. 1006.

[25]See the notes on Annex 3 of the European Union, Committee on Government Procurement, Adoption of the results of the negotiations under Article XXIV:7 of the Agreement on Government Procurement, GPA/113, 2 April 2012, p. 188.

[26]Note 4, Annex 7 to Canada's Appendix I to the GPA 2012, GPA/113 (above note 1), p. 62.

has also been bemoaned[27]), so that for the sake of clarity the GPA parties still continue with their traditional derogations and exclusions under the GPA 2012, despite the danger of being repetitive as the traditional exclusions might now exclude goods and services from GPA coverage which will be excluded anyway by the definition of covered procurement in Article II:2 GPA 2012. The interpretive uncertainties of the new definitional elements given in Article II:2 GPA 2012 will be analysed in more detail below in Sect. 3.4.3.

The analysis here has shown that the coverage of the GPA 1994 appears not to be exactly the same, and not as uniform, as will be the coverage under the GPA 2012 concerning procurement for commercial purposes. Procurement for commercial purposes does NOT appear to be excluded a priori from the coverage of the GPA 1994. This is important for public services in the general interest: they are not excluded from the GPA 1994 coverage from the outset even if they are (re)sold by the public entity to the consumer. The exclusion of purchases of commercial services or goods appears relevant in order to meet a different challenge: to define the GPA coverage *vis-à-vis* state trading enterprises and countries with a huge number of state-owned commercial activities.[28]

As a further consequence, the mutual exclusivity between the scopes of the GATT and GATS agreements, on the one hand, and the GPA, on the other, which has been observed above may not necessarily apply to the same extent for all GPA parties under the GPA 1994.

### 3.4.3 *Covered Procurement: Governmental Versus Commercial Purposes*

#### 3.4.3.1 Preliminary

As has already become clear, the application of the GPA 2012 depends on two qualifiers to the notion of "covered procurement": firstly, the requirement of "governmental purposes" and, secondly, the requirement of "not procured with a view to commercial sale or resale, or for use in the production or supply of goods or services for commercial sale or resale" (Article II:2 (a) (ii) GPA 2012). The meaning of these prerequisites for the procurement of goods and services covered by the GPA 2012 is subject to contestation and debate[29] and is decisive in particular for the GPA coverage regarding services of general interest, as they are usually sold by public entities to the consumer, meaning that they could be perceived as being for commercial sale.

The interpretation of these qualifiers is also important for the reason that under the GPA 2012 the GPA parties still have the freedom to exclude the procurement of

[27]Wang et al. 2011, p. 271.

[28]See Anderson and Osei-Lah 2011a, p. 84.

[29]See, for example, Wang 2007, pp. 905–910.

certain services from the GPA's coverage; this is explicitly provided for in Article II:2 lit. (e) GPA 2012 (which allows parties' annexes to exclude services from GPA coverage) and is the corollary of the positive list approach. The parties, however, may no longer have the freedom to expand their GPA coverage to services to which the GPA explicitly does not apply. Such an implication could be concluded *e contrario* from Article II:3 GPA 2012 which grants the parties the freedom to exclude services actually covered by GPA coverage but does not grant the leeway to expand GPA coverage ("except where provided otherwise in a party's annexes..., this Agreement does not apply to"). This appears to be different in the GPA 1994 as the GPA 1994 coverage does not depend on any unified definition of covered procurement (as there is none) but solely on the coverage as defined in the parties' positive lists and the individual descriptions and derogations contained therein; under the GPA 1994 parties could more or less include their own definition of covered procurement in their annexes.[30] Hence, parties enjoyed the freedom to extend the coverage to rather commercial services which, under the GPA 2012, would be excluded by virtue of the insurmountable definition in Article II:2 (a) (ii) GPA 2012. A consequence of this deliberation is that whereas under the GPA 1994 the determination of GPA coverage by the parties in their annexes was binding, constitutive and hence decisive, the coverage of the GPA 2012 is now fixed by the definitions in Article II GPA, and the descriptions and derogations in the parties' annexes may only impact on the interpretation of these definitions, in accordance with the rules of treaty interpretation set out in the Vienna Convention. In this respect, the descriptions and derogations in the annexes are no longer constitutive as the purview of the GPA 2012 is determined by the treaty definitions. The annexes continue to have constitutive force insofar as the positive list approach applies.

#### 3.4.3.2 Interpreting the Definitional Elements to Determine the GPA 2012 Scope

Now we turn to the interpretation of the above-mentioned qualifiers in Article II:2 GPA 2012.

**Wording**

Firstly, one might doubt whether the requirement of *governmental purposes* has its own stand-alone meaning, or whether its significance is exhausted in being the confirmation of the second qualifier and the antonym to procurement with a view to commercial sale/resale.[31] If so, then there was actually only one qualifier as the

---

[30]See Wang 2007, pp. 894, 898.

[31]An interpretive issue not further addressed here is the question of what kinds of procured goods/services are "for use in the production or supply", and what is meant by "use". Does this only encompass commodities and other starting material which is directly used for production, or also manufacturing equipment or energy used/consumed during the production process? Does it also cover the purchase of computers used for management and not for mere production purposes?

decisive issue was then to determine whether a procurement has been made for governmental purposes or not. The second phrase ("not procured with a view to commercial sale…") then merely determined when the procurement was not made for governmental purposes. The development of the texts speaks for the latter approach as the term governmental purposes has already been used in Article III:8 lit. (a) GATT and Article XIII:1 GATS. Hence, the phrase "for governmental purposes" was inserted into Article II:2 GPA 2012 in order to conform to the wording of Article III:8a GATT and Article XIII:1 GATS.[32] The wording in the latter rules allows for the conclusion that the requirement of "not with a view to commercial resale …" appears to be the explanation of governmental purposes due to the use of the conjunction "and" instead of "or". One may, however, as did the Appellate Body recently with regard to Article III:8 lit. (a) GATT,[33] conclude that the conjunction "and" points exactly to the opposite, i.e. that the two requirements of "governmental purposes" and "not with a view for commercial sale …" are different and cumulative. This deliberation, however, cannot be applied to the formulation used in Article II:2 GPA 2012 due to the different wording: the term "governmental purposes" is not linked to the other phase by an "and". Instead, the text of Article II:2 GPA 2012 allows for an understanding that the second phrase is an explanation of the term "procurement for governmental purposes".

Furthermore, Article XVII:2 GATT does not use the term "governmental purposes" but the phrase "immediate or ultimate consumption in governmental use" instead. Hence, this could be taken as an indication that the notion of governmental purposes used in the other rules refers to immediate use for governmental purposes, instead of use for the production or supply of products for sale. To draw such a conclusion (that governmental purposes are only present if the procurement refers to goods or services immediately used for the fulfilment of government tasks, i.e. for the government's own consumption, excluding any subsequent offer of services to consumers/citizens) would lead to a very narrow conception of the exception provided in Article III:8 lit. (a) GATT and in Article XIII:1 GATS and also of—consequently—the coverage of the GPA.

**Context**

The interpretation of the notion of "governmental purposes … not with a view to commercial sale/resale" must furthermore consider the ***context*** in which Article XIII:1 GATS is placed: Article I:3 GATS a priori excludes from the GATS' scope of application services supplied in the exercise of governmental authority which are defined as services neither supplied on a commercial basis nor in competition with other service suppliers. Hence, if Article I:3 lit. (b) GATS was conceived broadly, so as to exclude governmental services from the scope of the GATS, what scope would remain for the exclusion from GATS core principles brought about by Article XIII

---

[32] Wang 2007, p. 910.

[33] *Canada—Certain Measures Affecting the Renewable Energy Generation Sector, Canada—Measures Relating to the Feed-In Tariff Program*, Report of the Appellate Body, WT/DS412/AB/R, WT/DS426/AB/R, para 5.69.

GATS? The very existence of the exception provided in Article XIII GATS points to the fact that the concepts of governmental services used in Article I:3 GATS and of governmental procurement services used in Article XIII GATS are not identical. Instead, the general exclusion of governmental services in Article I:3 GATS must be interpreted much more narrowly than the specific exclusion for procurement for governmental purposes provided for in Article XIII:1 GATS. Thus, non-commercial, non-competitive services in the sense of Article I:3 GATS must be a different, and much narrower concept than non-commercial government services in the sense of Article XIII:1 GATS. From reading Article I:3 GATS and Article XIII:1 GATS it follows that commercial services and relevant purchases are covered by the GATS, irrespective of whether public or private entities supply them. Furthermore, there must be a type of commercial, non-governmental service to which the general exclusion of Article I:3 GATS does not apply, but with regard to whose purchase Article XIII:1 GATS excludes the application of core GATS principles as these services are assessed as serving non-commercial, governmental purposes under that rule.

These deliberations are confirmed by recognized interpretive practice as the definition of governmental services in Article I:3 GATS is perceived very narrowly[34] since the concepts of commercial basis and competitiveness are conceived rather broadly: in this respect, "commercial" refers to the existence of economically viable transactions; competitiveness draws on the existence of at least one other supplier.[35] Part of these broadly conceived commercial services, however, must be assessed as nevertheless working for governmental purposes and not for commercial resale in the sense of Article XIII:1 GATS, otherwise its exception from core GATS principles would become futile. Hence, the term "commercial" used in Article I:3 lit. (c) GATS and in Article XIII:1 GATS (and in Article III:8 lit. (a) GATT) has to have different meanings; the meaning of "commercial" in Article XIII:1 GATS must be narrower than that in Article I:3 lit. (c) GATS, and vice versa that of governmental purposes broader than in Article I:3 lit. (c). *This is a clear indication that governmental purposes in the sense of Article II:2 GPA 2012 should not be conceived to be confined to the ultimate government consumption*, as deliberated above in Sect. 3.1. Instead, government purposes can still be present, and the GPA disciplines apply, if the government procures services or goods for direct resale or for use in the production of goods and services for resale to consumers/citizens in the context of public services such as utilities, for Article II:2 GPA 2012 does not exclude any resale but only commercial resale. (Accordingly, with regard to Article III:8 lit. (a) GATT, the Appellate Body also recently concluded that this rule covers both situations, i.e. when procured goods are consumed by the government and when procured goods are used by the government in the provision of services to recipients in discharge of public functions.[36])

[34]See Krajewski 2003, p. 73.

[35]Krajewski 2011, p. 459.

[36]*Canada—Certain Measures Affecting the Renewable Energy Generation Sector, Canada—Measures Relating to the Feed-In Tariff Program*, Report of the Appellate Body, WT/DS412/AB/R, WT/DS426/AB/R, paras 5.68, 5.74.

A further argument against a broad notion of "commercial" in Article II:2 GPA 2012 is that a broad notion might exclude all procurement for resale by public enterprises—which clearly would contradict the whole purpose of GPA coverage of public enterprises in Annex 3.[37]

**Conclusions**

Public procurement in the context of the supply of services of general interest which are resold to citizens is hence NOT a priori, from the outset, excluded from the procurement covered by the GPA. The notion of "commercial" in Article II:2 lit. (a) (ii) GPA 2012 has to be interpreted—in accordance with the notion of commercial in Article XIII:1 GATS or Article III:8 lit. (a) GATT—rather narrowly, so that a sale or resale under any market environment is not sufficient to exclude the procurement from GPA coverage.

#### 3.4.3.3 Distinguishing Genuine Government Procurement from Commercial Activities

The question remains: what are the decisive criteria for the differentiation between genuine government procurement and commercial purchase? The basic distinction between procurement subject to the GPA 2012, on the one hand, and public purchase covered by multilateral core GATT and GATS disciplines, on the other, could be summarized as lying in the **differentiation** between the purchase of goods and services **for commercial, entrepreneurial objectives** (either in the context of state trading directly by government, public authorities or their agencies or indirectly by way of state trading enterprises) and purchase for the **fulfilment of genuine government tasks**. Hence, one could consider intentions to be relevant. However, it might not be acceptable to assess the intentions of the state as being the decisive criterion. Intentions are subjective, may change easily, and may differ in different member states. There is considerable difference among WTO members in their conception of appropriate government activity and hence among the domestic definition of government agencies and governmental purposes.[38] In addition, the Appellate Body recently showed with regard to the wording of Article IIII:8 lit. (a) GATT, on the basis of comparison with the Spanish and French versions, that the phrase "governmental purposes" does not refer to the intentions of government, but to the issue of whether a product is needed for government purposes in discharge of government functions.[39] This reasoning applies also to Article II:2 GPA 2012 as there too the French and Spanish versions read "pour les besoins des pouvoirs publics" and "la contratación realizada a efectos

---

[37]Wang 2007, pp. 906–907.

[38]Jackson 1997, p. 225.

[39]*Canada—Certain Measures Affecting the Renewable Energy Generation Sector, Canada—Measures Relating to the Feed-In Tariff Program*, Report of the Appellate Body, WT/DS412/AB/R, WT/DS426/AB/R, para 5.67.

gubernamentales" respectively. Accordingly, one should base the application of GPA rules on objective reasons and circumstances of government functions. Consequently, criteria for a commercial purchase might be whether the state behaves like a private service supplier on the market, in particular whether the state is seeking profit, or whether there is competition with other private service suppliers. GATT practice with regard to Article III:8 (a) GATT, however, shows that the mere fact that there was a governmental monopoly in itself was not sufficient to exclude its trade activities from the non-discrimination requirement of Article III GATT. If a governmental monopoly was a domestic sales monopoly of products on the market to the consumer, its activity was assessed as being of commercial character (as in such circumstance these products were procured with a view to commercial resale, they would not have to be assessed as being for genuine governmental purposes), meaning that the counter-exception from the exemption in Article III:8 GATT applied, with the consequence that the national treatment obligation of Article III GATT had to be respected.[40] In these cases, the question of whether the state monopoly makes profit was not addressed, meaning that such a requirement was not decisive. Recently, the Appellate Body, however, opined—with regard to Article III:8 (a) GATT—that commercial sale might on a regular basis imply profit orientation, but the Appellate Body also admitted that there was need for assessment of the entire transaction and of the seller's long-term strategy.[41]

The term "commercial" thus carries wider connotations than simply seeking profit[42] or the presence of a further competitor. It appears sufficient in itself that the public service provision was organized like the provision of services on competitive markets. Hence, procurement for government purpose refers to conditions and circumstances for service provision which do not take place in a competitive manner. The notion of commercial provision of services in the sense of Article II:2 GPA 2012 refers to institutional settings under which services can be performed under a workable competitive environment with no restrictions to market access and no involvement of governmental authority for establishing markets. The coverage of services by the GPA 2012 does not depend on the type of services or their properties and characteristics, but on the circumstances of their supply and the way in which their supply is organized by the state. Therefore, the assessment depends on whether a service is supplied by the state to its citizens for free, merely financed by tax revenues, or whether a service is offered to citizens or consumers in exchange for a quid pro quo as if there were a competitive market.

[40]See WTO 1995, Analytical Index: Guide to GATT Law and Practice, pp. 122–123.

[41]*Canada—Certain Measures Affecting the Renewable Energy Generation Sector, Canada—Measures Relating to the Feed-In Tariff Program*, Report of the Appellate Body, WT/DS412/AB/R, WT/DS426/AB/R, para 5.71. The Appellate Body did not need to make a conclusive statement about the notion of the term "with a view to commercial resale"; see ibid. para 5.84 et seq.

[42]Adlung 2006, p. 466, fn. 28.

This can be exemplified with regard to public health services: if health services are offered to the citizens in the framework of a national health service which is a tax-financed genuine government service, then the procurement of such services is covered by the GPA rules.[43] If the public health service is offered to the citizen in exchange for payment in a competitive context where the public supplier acts like a private undertaking, the public service has to be assessed as a commercial activity and hence is not covered by GPA rules, at least not under the GPA 2012. In many countries, however, public health services may not be supplied in either of these two ways, but in the context of a social security scheme where the quid pro quo is not paid by the patient but by a health insurance system which is either run or overseen by the state and which is subject to specific public regulations which decouple the service provision from the individual contribution. In such cases, the procurement of services or goods used by public health suppliers for the supply of health services does not operate in a competitive framework.[44] As a consequence, these services are then not to be seen as procured for commercial purposes in the sense of Article II:2 lit. (a) (ii) GPA 2012 but for governmental purposes, meaning that the GPA disciplines apply. The Appellate Body recently gave a comparable example of a procurement for governmental purposes: a public hospital purchases pharmaceuticals and provides them to patients.[45]

## 3.5 Public Procurement of Services: The Substantive and Personal Coverage of Procurement Rules

### *3.5.1 Substantive Ambit: Essentially All Goods and Some Services*

As mentioned above, the GPA does not apply to all types of services but only to certain specific procurement acts (so-called "covered procurement") which are listed in the parties' annexes to the GPA. Besides the parameters of *value* of procurement (only contracts beyond a certain value threshold), of *identity of the*

[43]Such tax financed national health services are excluded a priori from the scope of GATS disciplines by virtue of Article I:3 lit. (c) GATS; see Krajewski 2011, p. 459.

[44]Likewise, the CJEU will then assess the activities of social insurance systems as not being of commercial character so that EU competition rules will not be applied; cf. CJEU, Case C-244/94 *Fédération francaise des sociétés d'assurance a.o.* v. *Ministère de l'Agriculture et de la Pêche* [1995] ECR I-4013, para 17; CJEU, Joined Cases C-264/01, C-306/01, C-354/01 and C-355/01 *AOK Bundesverband a.o.* v. *Ichthyol-Gesellschaft Cordes, Hermani & Co. a.o.* [2004] ECR I-2493, paras 52–54.

[45]*Canada—Certain Measures Affecting the Renewable Energy Generation Sector, Canada—Measures Relating to the Feed-In Tariff Program*, Report of the Appellate Body, WT/DS412/AB/R, WT/DS426/AB/R, para 5.68, fn. 514.

*procuring entity* (central government institutions; some sub-central government entities and also some other entities[46]; only those listed by each party in its annexes 2 and 3), and of *origin* of the goods or services (the GPA of course merely applies between GPA parties), the GPA only covers certain types of *goods or services*. The GPA 1994 applies to all goods, apart from those explicitly excluded by a party (so-called negative list approach). With regard to services, the GPA 1994 runs a positive list approach so that it applies only to those services explicitly listed by each party in its annexes. The negative list approach for goods and the positive list approach for services prevalent under the GPA 1994 (see Article I and fn. 1) will be altered with the GPA 2012 (Article II:4) and even goods will then only be covered if listed in Annex 4. In practice, however, this change from a negative to positive list approach also for goods will not impede the increased coverage of the GPA 2012, including with regard to goods through deletion or reduction of existing derogations and additions of goods in the non-sensitive defence sector.[47] Future GPA 2012 Annexes 4 of the parties briefly state that the GPA covers all goods procured by the entities included in Annexes 1 through 3, unless otherwise specified. Hence, the coverage of goods by the GPA 2012 remains extensive.

With regard to services, generally speaking, the GPA disciplines cover public procurement of construction services and certain other services, as set out in the annex of each party. Once the GPA 2012 enters into force, the coverage of the GPA will be expanded (the WTO website mentions a "significant extension of the coverage of the Agreement"[48]) by lowering thresholds and adding new entities and sectors to the parties' commitments. This also concerns the procurement of services as additional services coverage has been added by almost all parties (for examples see below Sect. 3.5.3).

Even though GPA parties are subject to the requirement of non-discrimination (see Article III GPA 1994 and Article V GPA 2012), the GPA 1994 and the GPA 2012 allow for extensive derogations from these principles.[49] GPA parties can limit their commitments with regard to GPA coverage, for example by restricting non-discriminatory treatment to certain GPA parties which offer the same or at least equivalent concessions regarding the access to their domestic procurement markets as they do themselves in order to enforce reciprocity. GPA parties do so by introducing exceptions and deviations from the general GPA coverage in their General Notes to their Appendix I or by notes in their Annexes 1–3. This of course

[46]This is a residual category titled "all other entities whose procurement is covered by this Agreement"; see Article I:1, fn. 1 GPA 1994 and Article II:4 lit. (c) GPA 2012. This formula reflects the difficulty negotiators to have with common definition of entities such as public enterprises or public utilities; Dischendorfer 2000, p. 22.

[47]Williams 2013, p. NA 94.

[48]WTO, The re-negotiation of the Agreement on Government Procurement (GPA), available at: http://www.wto.org/english/tratop_e/gproc_e/negotiations_e.htm.

[49]With regard to the GPA 1994; see De e Silva 2008, pp. 64, 74.

increases discriminatory effects.[50] The GPA does not restrict the parties' discretion to make various types of party-specific derogations which then also depart from the MFN obligation.[51] In effect, the MFN treatment requirement between GPA parties has been abrogated.[52] The legality of this practice under the GPA 1994 has been confirmed by an explicit clause to this effect in Article II:2 lit. (e) GPA 2012 which allows for exclusions from GPA coverage in a party's annexes. Hence, the original aim for the GPA revision of eliminating exceptions and derogations aiming for reciprocity[53] has not been met.

### *3.5.2 Personal Scope: Entities Covered*

The GPA 1994 and, in future, the GPA 2012 cover sub-central authorities and other entities if listed in Annexes 2 and 3 of the GPA parties' Appendix I. Annex 3 is designed to typically cover state enterprises or entities performing public utility functions such as energy or water supply, public transport services and infrastructures (airports, ports).[54] This does not, however, mean that any party subdues such public services to GPA disciplines.

The positive list approach applicable for the annexes has a considerable disadvantage: entities not affirmatively listed in the annexes are not covered by GPA disciplines. A panel explicitly held that entities not listed in annexes are only covered by the GPA in exceptional circumstances of which the panel named two: "(i) where the entity in question is essentially a part of, i.e. legally unified with a listed entity; (ii) where the entity in question is procuring on behalf of a listed entity."[55] This means that the GPA will only cover non-listed entities if they are either a branch or a procuring agent of a listed entity.[56] The reluctance to expand GPA coverage to entities not explicitly provided in the parties' annexes reflects the efforts not to undermine the negotiations.[57] As a consequence, the positive list approach engenders the opportunity that, with regard to public enterprises, for example, a

[50]See, for example, Note 6 on Annex 3 to the GPA 2012 Appendix I of the European Union according to which certain services are not covered by the GPA "until such time, the EU has accepted that the parties concerned provide satisfactory reciprocal access to EU goods, suppliers, services and service providers to their own procurement markets", GPA/113 (above note 1), p. 190.

[51]Wang 2007, p. 893.

[52]Trepte and De Graaf 1994, p. CS 71.

[53]Dischendorfer 2000, p. 33.

[54]Wang 2007, p. 895.

[55]*Korea—Measures Affecting Government Procurement*, Report of the Panel, WT/DS163/R, para 7.59.

[56]Wang 2009, p. 681.

[57]Trepte 2005, p. 1139, fn. 77.

state can easily circumvent GPA disciplines by establishing a new entity not mentioned in annex 3 so that its procurement is not subject to GPA rules.

The situation is different only if a GPA party determines the entities listed in Annex 3 in a more general way through generic approaches to entity coverage, for example by referring to all companies whose procurement is covered by domestic procurement law.[58] Yet even then an alteration of domestic procurement law instantly impacts on the coverage of the GPA. Additionally, in other states a reference to domestic procurement law would be hollow, as domestic procurement rules may not cover state enterprises.[59] Most GPA parties still indicate the covered entities in an exhaustive way so that those not mentioned are not covered.

As is the case with the GPA 1994, the list of entities given in Annexes 2 and 3 to the GPA 2012 is not free from overlap. Whereas some GPA parties list public enterprises in Annex 3, other GPA parties indicate some types of public enterprises in Annex 2. The list on Germany given in Annex 2 to the European Union's Appendix I to the GPA 2012, for example, also indicates legal persons governed by private law, including utilities enterprises run by local authorities, as sub-central entities in Annex 2. The GPA 2012 disciplines will hence apply in Germany to "[n]on-industrial and non-commercial establishments subject to State control and operating in the general interest, including … municipal utilities" in the health sector (hospitals, health resort establishments, medical research institutes, testing and carcase-disposal establishments), in the area of culture (public theatres, orchestras, museums, libraries, archives, zoological and botanical gardens), in the social welfare, sports, safety, education, science and other sectors, always indicating the entities covered in more detail.[60]

The new GPA 2012 will considerably expand the GPA coverage with regard to both the personal and the substantive scope. GPA parties revised their concessions and thus ameliorate market access to their procurement markets by adding more than 200 new contracting entities at the central and sub-central levels, increasing goods and services, including construction services coverage, and reducing the pertinent thresholds.[61]

### *3.5.3 GPA Coverage According to the Annexes with Regard to Public Services, in Particular Utilities*

The GPA coverage of public services under the GPA 1994 is determined by the various individual concessions and derogations, and sometimes also specific definitions made by the GPA parties in their annexes. This reflects the rather strict reciprocity

---

[58]See Annex 3 of the Republic of Armenia, GPA/113 (above note 1), p. 43.

[59]As is the case with China, currently a non-member of the GPA which is negotiating its accession to the GPA, Wang 2009, p. 680.

[60]GPA/113 (above note 1), p. 152.

[61]Williams 2013, p. NA 94.

approach described above adopted by GPA parties with regard to GPA coverage. The different domestic status of utility companies, for example, contributes to the differing scope of application of the GPA 1994 to services of general interest.[62]

Usually, the utility sector is covered by the GPA disciplines on the basis of reciprocity. Under the present GPA 1994 all parties except Canada and the USA offered access to utilities procurement to different extents and subject to various derogations.[63] Canada and the USA will still exclude public utilities under the GPA 2012.[64]

In concrete terms this means, for example, that EU undertakings have access to procurement regarding ports and airports in Japan, Korea, Hong Kong, Israel, Switzerland, and, of course, the EEA countries, regarding urban transport in Hong Kong, Switzerland and the EEA, and for electrical utilities in Korea, Israel, Switzerland and the EEA. Accordingly, undertakings from these countries enjoy access to public procurement in the EU.[65]

With the entry into force of the new GPA 2012, the parties' commitments with regard to services of general interest increases as GPA coverage will be extended in this respect. For example, this means for the telecommunications sector that—whereas under the GPA 1994 telecommunications had not been included[66]—almost all parties will cover telecommunications services in their revised annexes,[67] apart from the USA and Canada which will only cover enhanced or value-added telecommunication services.[68]

## 3.6 The Notion of "Government Procurement"

Procurement refers to acquisition, by any contractual means, of goods, services or a combination thereof,[69] see Article I:2 GPA 1994 and Article II:2 (b) GPA 2012. Article II:3 (b) GPA 2012 furthermore provides that non-contractual agreements are only covered by the GPA if explicitly provided in a GPA party's annexes. Under the GPA 1994, due to the lack of a pre-set definition of covered procurement, what government procurement precisely means is subject to debate. Therefore, as already

[62]Trepte and De Graaf 1994, p. CS 71.

[63]Williams 2010, p. NA 41.

[64]See Note 3 lit. (b) on Annex 5 to Canada's Appendix I to the GPA 2012, GPA/113 (above note 1), 2 April 2012, p. 60 and Annex 5 to the USA's Appendix I to the GPA 2012, GPA/113 (above note 1), p. 431.

[65]See Trepte and De Graaf 1994, p. CS 72.

[66]See Trepte and De Graaf 1994, p. CS 71.

[67]Anderson 2012, p. 85.

[68]See Note 2 on Annex 5 of Canada's Appendix I to the GPA 2012, GPA/113 (above note 1), p. 60, and Annex 5 to the USA's Appendix I to the GPA 2012, GPA/113 (above note 1), p. 431.

[69]See also WTO Working Group on Transparency in Government Procurement, Work of the working group on the matters related to the items I-V of the list of the issues raised and points made, Note by the Secretariat, WT/WGTGP/W/32, 23 May 2002, para 13.

mentioned, certain parties included their own definition of procurement in their annexes. In reaction to this, the new GPA 2012 gives an authentic definition of government procurement in Articles II:2 and 3 GPA 2012, which has been analysed in detail above. Despite this rather elaborate definition of the notion of government procurement in the GPA 2012, some of the old discussions about the reach of the GPA to specific procurement activities still have not been clarified. This relates in particular to specific procurement arrangements such as concession contracts (see Sect. 3.6.1) and the issue of in-house procurement (see Sect. 3.6.2).

### *3.6.1 Procurement, Concession Contracts and PPP*

The first issue relates to the question as to whether the notion of government procurement also covers **concession contracts**, since such agreements between public and private entities are contracts as well. However, a concession does not involve the acquisition of a good or service of a private entity by a public entity, as under concessions a (usually private) entity provides a service to the users who have to pay in exchange for its use, meaning that the remuneration for the service comes from them.[70] The concessionaire is not usually paid by the state; it may even be asked to pay a fee to the authorities in exchange for the temporary right of exploitation. Hence, there is no public purchase situation in this context. The supplier is granted the exclusive and temporary right by a public entity to provide the (remunerated) service in the common good which is first defined by the responsible central, sub-central, or even local authorities. They are responsible for the existence of such services or facilities.

Nevertheless, concessions are also an expression of arrangements based on mutuality: the state has the job done by private entities, and in exchange the concessionaire is given the right to charge the users. Such contractual arrangements are similar to procurement activities, but at the same time they are different due to their long-term nature, their complex remuneration mechanism and their use of private finances.[71] Due to the lack of a classic purchase context, concession contracts are not seen as covered by the GPA rules, even though, basically, the rationale of procurement rules may be convenient to them as well. The state does not purchase goods or services but the fulfilment of governmental tasks, in exchange for specific rights instead of financial remuneration. In the EU's internal market law, concession contracts are also not subject to procurement rules as the relevant directives explicitly exclude concession contracts from their purview.[72]

---

[70]Arrowsmith 2002, p. 784.

[71]Arrowsmith 2002, p. 785.

[72]See Articles 17 and 18 of Directive 2004/18/EC of the European Parliament and of the Council of 31 March 2004 on the coordination of procedures for the award of public work contracts, public supply contracts and public service contracts, *OJ* 2004 L 134/114 and of Directive 2004/17/EC of the European Parliament and of the Council of 31 March 2004 coordinating the procurement procedures of entities operating in the water, energy, transport and postal services sectors, *OJ* 2004 L134/1.

Comparable to concession contracts but slightly different are so-called **build-operate-transfer (BOT) arrangements** under which a contractor finances, builds and operates an infrastructure facility for a limited period of time, at the end of which the government is given the facility, usually free of charge. In Korea's future Annex 6 on Construction Services under the GPA 2012, BOT contracts are defined as "any contractual arrangement the primary purpose of which is to provide for the construction or rehabilitation of physical infrastructures, plants, buildings, facilities, or other government-owned works and under which, as consideration for a supplier's execution of a contractual arrangement, a procuring entity grants to the supplier, for a specified period of time, temporary ownership or a right to control and operate, and demand payment for the use of such works for the duration of the contract." State and private undertakings thus enter into a contract whereby the undertaking is obliged to build and maintain, for example, a motorway or port in exchange for the right to collect tolls, or a hospital in exchange for the right to operate it. Such contracts contain elements of public procurement as they provide for construction of a good for the government (which will ultimately be transferred to it), like in a purchase context, but also elements from concession regimes due to the temporary right to exploitation. Hence, BOT arrangements are perceived as complementing the usual method of public procurement. BOT contracts come particularly close to procurement contracts with regard to construction services (which are covered) if the right to operate a facility or to provide a service stands not at the centre of contractual arrangements (as it only serves as means of making the investment finance itself) but where the contract is primarily aimed at public acquisition of an infrastructure. Hence, in such a situation, BOT contracts could be assessed as government procurement covered by the GPA as the means of financing public infrastructure, either directly or indirectly by novel ways, should not determine the coverage of the GPA.[73]

The assignment of concession contracts and BOT contracts to the scope of the GPA is subject to controversy (unless country specific definitions of covered procurement in the parties' annexes settle this issue[74]). Whereas the USA favour their coverage by procurement rules, the EU opposes it,[75] in accordance with intra-EU rules which exclude concession contracts from the procurement regime.

Under the GPA 2012, the definition of procurement in Article II:2 GPA also pleads against their inclusion under GPA coverage as, in particular, the exclusive right to charge fees granted to the concessionaire documents their commercial background.[76] The conclusion, however, may be different where BOT contracts are an innovative means of infrastructure procurement by public entities, as construction services are covered by the GPA and defined in broad terms in Article I (c)

[73]Zacharias 2008, para 16; see also Reich 2009, p. 1007.

[74]Anderson and Arrowsmith 2011, p. 51.

[75]Arrowsmith 2002, p. 785.

[76]Compare Adlung 2006, pp. 466–467, with regard to Article I:3 GATS.

GPA 2012 as the "realization by whatever means of civil or building works", which may also refer to innovative ways in which public authorities realize their construction plans.[77] Arguing on the basis of this broad definition of construction services, however, is built on shaky ground as even under the GPA 1994 this wording can be found in the common definition of construction services in Annex 5 of most GPA parties' Appendix I (such as the EU, Chinese Taipei)[78] and many of them still maintain that such innovative arrangements are not covered by their GPA obligations.[79]

The conclusion that concession contracts and BOT arrangements are not usually covered by the definition of government procurement is finally confirmed by domestic practice as many countries adopt specific legislation for concession contracts.[80] UNCITRAL Model rules on procurement also do not cover concession contracts; instead, separate model rules for this type of arrangements were drafted.[81]

In conclusion, the text of the GPA 2012 did not bring about any more clarity in the issue of GPA coverage of concession contracts and BOT contracts than the GPA 1994,[82] apart from allowing new arguments to be drawn in the debate over the definition of covered procurement in Article II:2 GPA 2012.

Innovative developments will result from some parties' revised annexes as the GPA 2012 will expand the GPA coverage to works concessions and BOT contracts because three parties will enter into concessions for the first time, i.e. the EU,[83] Korea[84] and Japan.[85] Hence, here the issue of country specific coverage due to the parties' formulations in the annexes may arise again. As explained above

[77]Reich 2009, p. 1001.

[78]Cf. Trepte 2005, p. 1139; Anderson and Osei-Lah 2011b, p. 156.

[79]See again Reich 2009, p. 1007, fn. 85.

[80]Anderson and Arrowsmith 2011, p. 50; Arrowsmith 2002, p. 784.

[81]See United Nations Commission on International Trade Law (UNCITRAL), Model Legislative Provisions on Privately Financed Infrastructure Projects (2003), available at: http://www.uncitral.org/pdf/english/texts/procurem/pfip/model/03-90621_Ebook.pdf. For an analysis see S. Son, Legal Analysis on Public-Private Partnerships regarding Model PPP Rules. http://www.uncitral.org/pdf/english/colloquia/public-private-partnerships-2013/20120704_Report_on_PPP_legal_IssuesSon_Seungwoover.11.pdf. June 2012. Accessed 12 December 2013.

[82]Reich 2009, p. 1007; see also Anderson and Arrowsmith 2011, p. 49.

[83]See Annex 6 of the EU's Appendix I to the GPA 2012, GPA/113 (above note 1), p. 250: "Works concessions contracts, when awarded by Annex 1 and 2 entities, are included under the national treatment regime for the construction service providers of Iceland, Liechtenstein, the Netherlands on behalf of Aruba and Switzerland … and for construction service providers of Korea." The relevant thresholds are SDR 5 million or SDR15 million.

[84]See Korea's Annex 6, according to which construction services contracts include BOT contracts. The annex gives a definition of BOT contracts. The threshold is SDR 5 million or SDR 15 million. See GPA/113 (above note 1), p. 319.

[85]The Note on Japan's Annex 6 provides that procurement with regard to a construction project based on the Act on Promotion of Private Finance Initiative 2011 is covered, GPA/113 (above note 1), p. 306.

(Sect. 3.4.3), under the GPA 2012 it is subject to doubt whether parties can unilaterally—by virtue of their formulations or definitions in the annexes—expand the coverage of GPA rules beyond the confines of the definition of covered procurement spelled out in Article II:2 GPA 2012. Such confines to GPA coverage with regard to concession contracts and BOT arrangements, however, cannot be clearly derived from Article II:2 GPA 2012, as shown above. Hence, it is indeed advisable and preferable to have the issue of coverage of concession contracts and BOT contracts resolved in the parties' annexes rather than through dispute settlement.[86]

### *3.6.2 Coverage of In-house Procurement*

The second contested issue regarding the definition of "covered procurement" concerns government acquisition of products from other public entities which can have different forms, such as purchase from or via collective purchasing agencies, or purchase from other public entities or even subsidiaries of the procuring entity.[87] Under the GPA 1994, as well as under the GPA 2012, some parties explicitly exclude procurement between covered entities from the GPA coverage. Canada, as already quoted, has the widest formulation and excludes procurement made by one covered entity from another entity or enterprise of Canada which reflects the conception of the state of Canada to be treated as one legal person.[88] This formulation, although slightly redrafted, will not change in essence in the GPA 2012.[89] Other parties exempt procurement from undertakings or entities which are affiliated with or dependent on the procuring entity.[90] The significance of this coverage issue will arise again when more countries with a large state sector like China join the GPA.[91]

Again, the treatment of such "intra-public sector procurement"[92] is far from clear if the issue is not decided in the annexes of the GPA parties as neither the texts of the GPA 1994 nor of the GPA 2012 rule on this. As regards the EU, the GPA 1994 concessions in the EU's annexes did not address the issue of in-house procurement at all and hence did not include derogations in this respect (except some reference to exceptions in domestic Finish and Swedish law[93]), which gives rise to the problem that the scope of the GPA obligations of the EU might be broader than

---

[86] Anderson and Arrowsmith 2011, pp. 51–52.

[87] Anderson and Arrowsmith 2011, p. 52; Arrowsmith 2002, p. 785.

[88] Wang et al. 2011, pp. 273–274.

[89] See General Note 4, Annex 7, GPA/113 (above note 1), p. 62.

[90] Cf. Wang 2009, p. 683.

[91] Arrowsmith 2002, p. 785.

[92] Wang 2007, p. 910.

[93] See also Wang et al. 2011, p. 274.

the purview of domestic EU procurement rules as the relevant CJEU case law[94] provides for exceptions for in-house procurement.[95] Hence, whereas domestic EU procurement rules do not apply to specific types of in-house procurement, the EU's obligations under the GPA 1994 are broader in scope. The situation will alter, however, with the entry into force of the GPA 2012 as the new notes to Annex 3 to the EU's commitments excludes procurement to an affiliated undertaking or procurement by a joint venture, in accordance with intra-EU procurement law.[96]

One starting point for assessing GPA coverage for intra public arrangements in case of lack of derogations in the annexes may be the notion of covered entities. Covered procurement is the procurement made by a procuring entity, see Article II:2 in conjunction with Article I (o) GPA 2012. Hence, any procurement made by them is covered by GPA disciplines. On the other hand, the internal organisation of a covered entity is up to each party. Thus, it should not make any difference, in terms of GPA coverage, whether a covered entity provides a service internally by an internal division or whether, after reorganisation, it purchases the same service from the same division which has then become legally separated but is still a wholly owned subsidiary. The same deliberation must apply if several local authorities set up a joint venture which provides services for them. Such transactions then have to be regarded as purely internal administrative arrangements to which GPA rules do not apply.[97] Hence, intra-public procurement should not be regarded as government procurement for the purposes of the GPA if the providing entity is controlled by the procuring entity (even if jointly with other procuring entities[98]), in contrast to procurement activities from legally separate and economically independent entities.[99] Objections could be made to the latter understanding as the establishment of legally separate, non-affiliated entities may as well be seen as an expression of the national organisation autonomy regarding the domestic administrative regime, in conformity with Canada's understanding as reflected in Canada's annex, according to which the state has to be assessed as one indivisible legal person. As already mentioned, other GPA parties have a much narrower approach in excluding intra-public arrangements from the GPA coverage. This divergence in national conceptions is caused by the positive list approach. Hence, it is hardly unavoidable that coverage varies from party to party as it mirrors the different approaches and understandings present among GPA parties, given the lack of clear treaty language and the lack of a principled approach in the GPA for defining its coverage.

---

[94]For an analysis see Wang et al. 2011, pp. 256–263.

[95]Wang et al. 2011, p. 277.

[96]See Notes 4 and 5 on Annex 3 of the EU's Appendix I to the GPA 2012, GPA/113 (above note 1), pp. 188–189.

[97]Wang 2007, p. 910.

[98]See also the explicit exclusion from the GPA coverage of cooperative agreements in Article II:3 lit. (b) GPA 2012.

[99]Arrowsmith 2002, p. 785.

## 3.7 Summary and Assessment: The Autonomy of the GPA Parties in Providing Services of General Interest

Both the GPA 1994 and the GPA 2012 apply to the procurement of services in the general interest. The explicit exclusion of service provision for commercial purposes enshrined in the GPA 2012's definition of government procurement hardly confines the scope of application of GPA rules to services of general interest due to its imprecise notion. It is therefore again the parties who by their annexes to the GPA determine the coverage of GPA rules. The analysis shows that procurement law leaves considerable discretion to the GPA parties in the organization of the provision of services for the common good. Their flexibility in formulating their annexes has been confirmed by Article II:2 (e) GPA 2012, as has been their freedom to base commitments on reciprocity, despite the MFN principle.

Innovative means of service provision through concession contracts and BOT arrangements are only covered if explicitly provided for in the parties' individual annexes. Determining GPA coverage has been left to the parties in this respect. Intra-public procurement arrangements are not usually covered due to respect for the organisational autonomy and the sovereignty of the nation states with regard to their administrative entities. Hence, the ability of public entities to provide services of general interest directly or through public private partnerships is hardly limited. These results, however, are subject to change if the Appellate Body adopts a different interpretation of the relevant GPA rules. This does not appear probable given the imprecise terms in the definition of covered procurement in Article II:2 GPA 2012 and the lack of common rules and general principles regarding GPA coverage.[100]

## References

Adlung R (2006) Public services and the GATS. J Int Econ Law 9(2):455–485

Anderson R (2012) The conclusion of the renegotiation of the World Trade Organization Agreement on Government Procurement: what it means for the agreement and for the world economy. Public Procure Law Rev 21:83–94

Anderson R, Arrowsmith S (2011) The WTO Regime on Government Procurement: past, present and future. In: Arrowsmith S, Anderson R (eds) The WTO Regime on Government Procurement: challenge and reform. CUP, Cambridge, pp 3–58

Anderson R, Osei-Lah K (2011a) Forging a more global procurement market: issues concerning accessions to the Agreement on Government Procurement. In: Arrowsmith S, Anderson R (eds) The WTO Regime on Government Procurement: challenge and reform. CUP, Cambridge, pp 61–91

Anderson R, Osei-Lah K (2011b) The coverage negotiations under the Agreement on Government Procurement: context, mandate, process and prospects. In: Arrowsmith S, Anderson R (eds) The WTO Regime on Government Procurement: challenge and reform. CUP, Cambridge, pp 149–174

[100] See Wang et al. 2011, p. 279.

Arrowsmith S (2002) Reviewing the GPA: the role and development of the Plurilateral Agreement after Doha. J Int Econ Law 5:761–790

Arrowsmith S (2003) Government Procurement in the WTO. CUP, Cambridge

Lima De, Silva VG (2008) The revision of the WTO Agreement on Government Procurement: to what extent might it contribute to the expansion of current membership. Public Procure Law Rev 17:61–98

Dischendorfer M (2000) The existence and development of multilateral rules on government procurement under the framework of the WTO. Public Procure Law Rev 9:1–38

Jackson J (1997) The World Trading System: the law and policy of international economic relations. MIT Press, Massachusetts

Krajewski M (2003) National regulation and trade liberalization in services. Kluwer Law International, The Hague

Krajewski M (2011) Patient mobility beyond Calais: health services under WTO law. In: van de Gronden JW et al (eds) Health care and EU law. T.M.C. Asser Press, The Hague, pp 453–480

Krajewski M, Neergaard U, van de Gronden JW (2009) The changing legal framework for services of general interest in Europe between competition and solidarity. T.M.C. Asser Press, The Hague

Marchetti JA, Mavroidis P (2004) What are the main challenges for the GATS framework? Don't talk about revolution. Eur Bus Organ Law Rev 5:511–562

Mattoo A (1998) Dealing with monopolies and state enterprises: WTO rules for goods and services. In: Cottier T, Mavroidis PC (eds) State trading in the twenty-first century. University of Michigan Press, Michigan, pp 37–70

Mavroidis P (2012) Trade in goods, 2nd edn. OUP, Oxford

Reich A (1997) The new GATT Agreement on Government Procurement. J World Trade 31(2):125–151

Reich A (2009) The new text of the Agreement on Government Procurement: an analysis and assessment. J Int Econ Law 12:989–1022

Trepte P (2005) The Agreement on Government Procurement. In: Macrory PFJ, Appleton AE, Plummer MG (eds) The World Trade Organization: legal, economic and political analysis. Springer, New York, pp 1123–1163

Trepte P, De Graaf G (1994) The revised GATT procurement agreement. Public Procure Law Rev 3:CS 70–73

Wang P (2007) Coverage of the WTO's Agreement on Government Procurement: challenges of integrating China and other Countries with a large state sector into the global trading system. J Int Econ Law 10:887–920

Wang P (2009) China's accession to the WTO Government Procurement Agreement—challenges and the way forward. J Int Econ Law 12:663–706

Wang P, Cavallo Perin R, Casalini D (2011) Addressing purchasing arrangements between public sector entities: what can the WTO learn from the EU´s experience? In: Arrowsmith S, Anderson R (eds) The WTO Regime on Government Procurement: challenge and reform. CUP, Cambridge, pp 252–281

Williams R (2010) Access to utilities procurement markets of non-EU countries. Public Procure Law Rev 19:NA 39-NA 44

Williams R (2013) European Commission proposals in relation to third country access to EU procurement markets. Public Procure Law Rev 22:NA 91-NA 94

World Trade Organization (1995) Analytical index: guide to GATT law and practice, 6th edn. Geneva

Zacharias D (2008) Art. XIII GATS. In: Wolfrum R, Stoll P-T, Feinäugle C (eds) WTO–Trade in Services, vol 6. Martinus Nijhoff Publishers, Leiden, pp 272–286

# Chapter 4
# Regulating Public Services and International Investment Law

**Francesco Costamagna**

**Abstract** International investment law is increasingly becoming an important reference field of international economic law. The chapter examines if, and the extent to which, investment arbitral tribunals sought to meet the need to respect host State's capacity to regulate in the public interest. Preliminarily, the chapter deals with the notion of regulation in the public service sector, by exploring its categorization as a right and as a duty of States. Subsequently, it assesses whether the regulation of public services is a matter falling within international investment law's scope of application and whether all regulatory measures used to govern public services' provision may fall under international arbitral tribunals' scrutiny. It then analyses the controversial distinction between lawful regulation and regulatory expropriation under international investment law. To this purpose, the chapter takes into consideration the different approaches adopted by arbitral tribunals, in order to evaluate their capacity to meaningfully contribute to find a balance between investors' and States' competing interests with regard to public services. Lastly, the analysis turns to the increasingly important role played by the fair and equitable treatment standard in arbitral practice, also with regard to public services' cases. In particular, this part of the chapter looks at the difficulties in finding an equilibrium between stability and regulatory change in the public services' sector, by examining the impact of the legitimate expectations doctrine upon host States' regulatory autonomy.

## Contents



F. Costamagna (✉)
Associate Professor of European Union Law, University of Turin, Turin, Italy
e-mail: francesco.costamagna@unito.it



M. Krajewski (ed.), *Services of General Interest Beyond the Single Market*, Legal Issues of Services of General Interest,
DOI 10.1007/978-94-6265-063-3_4

## 4.1 Introduction

The international regime for the protection of foreign investments has gained unprecedented visibility over the last decade, thanks to the growth in the number of international investment agreements and, more importantly, the boom of investor-State arbitration. This evolution has raised concerns because of its impact on States' regulatory autonomy. Indeed, the reach of these disputes goes well beyond mere commercial matters, touching upon key aspects of host States' socio-economic order.

The regulation of public services[1] represents one of the main examples in this regard. Over the last few years there has been a growing number of cases concerning measures taken by host States to regulate foreign investments in this sector. This evolution has been aided and abetted by liberalization and privatization policies that, starting from the late-'70s, have spread all over the world. The process opened up new spaces for the participation of private actors in a sector that had been traditionally dominated by State-owned or State-controlled entities. However, the relationship between the private party and the public authority has often

[1]The term has not a uniform definition under international law. This paper will use it as indicating all those activities that States subject to specific obligations in order to meet objectives of general interest. The term will mostly, albeit not exclusively, cover services provided through network industries, such as electricity, gas and water. On the definition of the notion of "public service" see below Sect. 4.2.

proven difficult, because of both technical and socio-political reasons, often ending up in front an international arbitral panel.

The analysis of these cases shows the potentially deep impact that international investment law may have on States' regulatory autonomy with regard to public services. Much depends on the approach taken by international arbitrators to define international agreements' vaguely worded provisions and, in particular, to their capacity and willingness to pay due regard to the fact that these activities are not ordinary business operations, as they are functional to the pursuit of fundamental social objectives. Therefore, in assessing whether national regulatory interventions comply with international protection standards, there is the need to respect host State's capacity to regulate in the public interest.

This chapter examines if, and the extent to which, arbitral tribunals sought to meet this need, by focusing on some key aspects. Preliminarily, the paper deals with the notion of regulation in the public service sector, by exploring its categorization as a right and as a duty of States. Subsequently, it assesses whether the regulation of public services is a matter falling within international investment law's scope of application and whether all regulatory measures used to govern public services' provision may fall under international arbitral tribunals' scrutiny. The following paragraph analyses the controversial distinction between lawful regulation and regulatory expropriation under international investment law. To this purpose, it takes into consideration the different approaches adopted by arbitral tribunals, in order to evaluate their capacity to meaningfully contribute to find a balance between investors' and States' competing interests with regard to public services. Lastly, the analysis turns to the increasingly important role played by the fair and equitable treatment standard in arbitral practice, also with regard to public services' cases. In particular, this part of the chapter looks at the difficulties in finding an equilibrium between stability and regulatory change in the public services' sector, by examining the impact of the legitimate expectations doctrine upon host States' regulatory autonomy.

## 4.2 Public Services' Regulation as State's Right (or as a Duty?)

The role of the State in the provision of public services has markedly changed over the last decades, mainly because of the impact of liberalization and privatization policies that have been variously adopted and implemented by several countries around the world. Some of the functions traditionally exercised by States' authorities have been progressively transferred to private or mixed actors. However, public authorities are still expected to intervene in order to ensure that public services are organized and provided in a way that preserves their specific function. Indeed, these services cannot be fully equated to other economic activities, as they are vital to fulfil peoples' daily needs, to enhance social cohesion and to foster economic growth. For all these reasons, today ensuring (universal) access to high-quality public services is to be regarded as one of the key aims of the State.

Especially in those cases where public services have been liberalized or privatized, regulation represents the main instrument at the disposal of public authorities to achieve this aim. Before proceeding with the analysis, it is worth observing that the notion of 'regulation' has an uncertain legal meaning, at least under international law. This chapter will use the term in a broad sense, encompassing all the measures taken by public authorities in order to "influenc[e], control[...] and guid[e] economic or other private activities with impact on others",[2] with the aim of achieving specific socio-economic policy objectives.[3] It must be highlighted that the term 'public authorities' is meant to cover not just central authorities, but also independent agencies or bodies, as well as local authorities, which, as it will be seen later on, play a major role in the regulation of public services.

A distinction is often made between economic and social regulation, depending on the objectives it pursues.[4] Economic regulation mainly aims at correcting market failures[5] that, according to the neo-classical economic theory, may lead to an inefficient allocation of resources if not properly regulated. Some of these failures[6] are particularly relevant with regard to public services, as it is the case of natural monopolies. Indeed, the supply of public services often require the existence of expensive network infrastructure that cannot be duplicated so to allow the entry of new competitors. Therefore, there is the need to avoid that the provider could exploit its monopolistic power, by, for instance, charging excessive fees to end-users.

Regulation performs functions that go beyond the correction of market failures, as it may address distortions that occur even in cases where the market works properly. Indeed, economic efficiency does not ensure a fair distribution of costs and benefits and, consequently, there is the need for the State to intervene in order to ensure that public services might contribute to the achievement of fundamental social objectives.[7] This may occur through the imposition of public service obligations upon the provider or the providers. These obligations, which may take different forms and which may have different scopes, are generally geared toward ensuring affordability, geographical coverage and quality of public services' supply.[8]

---

[2]Krajewski 2003a, p. 4.

[3]The *Glossary of Industrial Organisation Economics and Competition Law*, compiled by R.S. Khemani and D.M. Shapiro, commissioned by the Directorate for Financial, Fiscal and Enterprise Affairs, OECD, 1993 defines regulation as the "imposition of rules by government, backed by the use of penalties that are intended specifically to modify the economic behaviour of individuals and firms in the private sector". An equally broad definition is used by Mitnick 1980, 1. The A. defines regulation as "[...] the intentional restriction of a subject's choice of activity by an entity not directly party or involved in that activity".

[4]This distinction is not to be taken too rigidly, as regulatory measures normally pursue different types of objectives simultaneously. See Krajewski 2003a, p. 18.

[5]Baldwin and Cave 1999, Chap. 2. Conversely, according to the private interest theories of regulation, regulatory functions are not meant to serve the public interest, as they are captured by powerful private groups. See Stigler 1971, pp. 122–126.

[6]Baldwin and Cave 1999, p. 9.

[7]Palast et al. 2003.

[8]Houben 2008, pp. 7–27.

Public services are by no mean the only economic sector where States exercise their regulatory functions. However, in this context regulation plays a role that is far more important than in other economic sectors, having a 'constitutive' value. Indeed the exercise of regulatory functions by public authorities, through the imposition of specific obligations on the supply of the service, is key to identify the existence of a 'public service' and to distinguish it, also with regard to its legal status, from other economic activities. This approach goes beyond the traditional 'subjective' understanding of the notion, which derives from the French doctrine of *service public* and tends to consider public services only those directly provided by State's entities.[9] The objective definition of public services has gained increasing recognition in recent times, as it better reflects the evolution of the role of the State in the provision of public services. For instance, this approach has been constantly employed by the European Union to define the notion of services of general economic interest, which is used in the attempt to avoid the ambiguities of 'public services'.[10] For instance, in 2003 the European Commission explained that the concept, which can be found in Article 106.2 TFEU, refers to "services of an economic nature which the Member States or the Community subject to specific public service obligations by virtue of a general interest criterion".[11]

As observed by Lowe with regard to regulation in general, the exercise of regulatory functions is "an essential element of the permanent sovereignty of each State over its economy"[12] and it has, thus, to be considered as a sovereign right. The existence of such a right has been recalled by the GATS, whose Preamble reiterates the need to respect "the right of members to regulate, and to introduce new regulation, on the supply of services within their territories in order to meet national policy objectives".[13]

This is even truer with regard to public services, as their provision represents one of State's core sovereign functions and, ultimately, its very *raison d'être*. The role of public services as constitutive elements of the State had already been emphasised in the early XIX century, by the so-called School of Bordeaux. In particular Leon Duguit, the founder of the School, criticized the assimilation of the

[9]See Hauriou 1927; Jèze 1926, pp. 171–172.

[10]But these efforts seems to be to no avail, as the notion of services of general economic interest, as well as its relationship with other related concepts, such as that of services of general interest, is still uncertain and it has generated much confusion. See generally Neergaard 2009, pp. 17–50.

[11]European Commission, *Green Paper on Services of General Interest*, COM(2003) 270 final, 21 May 2003, para 17.

[12]Lowe 2002, pp. 450–451.

[13]The recognition of this right sought to respond to the concerns that the adoption of GATS could jeopardise States' capacity to regulate services and, in particular, public services. The WTO website also features a section devoted to "Misunderstanding and scare stories: The right to regulate" (http://www.wto.org/english/tratop_e/serv_e/gats_factfiction11_e.htm). On the relationship between trade and public services see Arena 2011, pp. 489–528; Krajewski 2003b, pp. 341–367; Adlung 2006, pp. 455–485.

State to the concept of *puissance public*,[14] instead conceiving it as a "cooperation de services publics organisés et controlés par des gouvernants".[15] This approach still retains its value, as public services keep on being "a key element of the modern social and welfare state"[16] and a building block of its legitimacy.

The adoption of a less State-centric vision has opened up new perspectives on the regulation of public services, which has been conceived, albeit only tentatively, as a duty of the State and not just as a sovereign right.[17] This evolution has mainly taken place with regard to human rights, and, in particular, social and economic rights. It is worth observing, due to its relevance for this inquiry, that the debate mostly centred on States' responsibilities in those cases where the supply of essential services has been entrusted with private operators.[18] There is now consensus on the fact that the choice to outsource public services' provision to private actors does not relieve the State from the realization of rights and, hence, from making use of all the regulatory tools at their disposal to this end. For instance, in 2007 the UN High Commissioner for Human Rights, after having recalled that international human rights law is neutral with respect to the economic model for the provision of services, confirmed that "Governments and public officials remain primary responsible for ensuring progress toward the realization of rights" and, consequently, they "must take measures to ensure that limited resources, public as well as private, are used in the most effective manner to promote the realization of rights, giving particular attention to improving the situation of those most in need".[19] This argument has been reiterated and further specified with particular regard to the right to water and sanitation. The Human Rights Council, in a Resolution adopted in 2010, reaffirmed that "the delegation of the delivery of safe drinking water and/or sanitation services to a third party does not exempt the State from its human rights obligations" and called upon States to adopt a detailed series of measures to fulfil their duties. Inter alia, States are urged to develop appropriate tools and mechanisms "to achieve progressively the full realization of human rights obligations related to safe drinking water and sanitation, including in

---

[14]See Hariou 1901, pp. 26–27.

[15]Duguit 1925, p. 55.

[16]M. Krajewski, Investment Law and Public Services http://papers.ssrn.com/sol3/papers.cfm?abstract_id=2038514. 1 April 1 2012. Accessed 20 November 2014.

[17]See High Commissioner for Human Rights, *Economic, Social and Cultural Rights. Handbook for National Human Rights Institutions*, United Nations: New York—Geneva (2005), 18 where it says that "[t]he obligation to fulfil economic, social and cultural rights [...] can entail issues such as [...] the provision of basic public services and infrastructures".

[18]Graham 2005, pp. 33–56.

[19]UN Economic and Social Council, Report of the United Nations High Commissioner for Human Rights (focusing on the concept of progressive realization of economic, social and cultural rights), E/2007/82, 25 June 2007, paras 34–36.

currently unserved and underserved areas" and "to adopt and implement effective regulatory frameworks for all service providers in line with the human rights obligations of States".[20]

## 4.3 The Regulation of Public Services and the Scope of Application of International Investment Law

### *4.3.1 Public Services and the Substantive Scope of International Investment Agreements*

The assessment of the impact of international investment law upon States' capacity to regulate public services needs, first of all, to determine whether these activities fall within international investment agreements' substantive scope of application. The answer to this question must be a resounding "yes", barring few exceptional cases.

On the one side, international agreements tends to define their substantive scope of application quite loosely, by incorporating open-ended asset-based definitions of what can be considered as an "investment".[21] Arbitral tribunals have contributed to consolidate and even amplify this tendency, by interpreting this notion in an over-extensive manner. On the other side, investment agreements, unlike trade agreements, rarely contains so-called "public services exemptions clauses", i.e. "provisions [...] which exempt public services or aspects of their provision, financing and regulation from all or some disciplines of [the] agreements".[22]

However, the situation is progressively changing, also in response to the stance adopted by arbitral tribunals. In a limited (but growing) number of cases, States have introduced in their investment agreements exemption clauses, aimed at safeguarding or restoring their regulatory capacity also with regard to public services. One of the earliest examples in this regard is NAFTA. Indeed, in this context Canada, Mexico and the US all reserved, with regard to both cross-border services and investment, to adopt and maintain "any measure" with regard to the provision of services "established or maintained for a public purpose" such as, inter alia, social security and insurance, social welfare, public education, health and child

[20]UN General Assembly, Resolution adopted by the Human Rights Council. Human Rights and Access to Safe Drinking Water and Sanitation, A/HRC/RES/15/9, 6 October 2010.

[21]UNCTAD, Scope and Definition, Series on Issues in International Investment Agreements II. UN Publication, 2011, pp. 7–12. New York, Geneva.

[22]M. Krajewski, Public Services in Bilateral Free Trade Agreements of the EU http://www.epsu.org/IMG/pdf/PublicServicesFTAs_FinalVersion.pdf, p. 7. Accessed 20 November 2014. See also Arena 2011, pp. 495–496.

care.[23] The very same provision can be found in a number of FTA concluded by the US with countries such as Australia[24] and Colombia.[25]

In the Korus FTA[26] this very broad exemption clause applies to investments "to supply a service in the exercise of governmental authority". The provision reproduces the wording of Article I:3(b) GATS, without, however, making any reference to the clarification contained in letter (c) of the same provision. Therefore, it is not clear whether this clause is meant to allow the concerned States to adopt any measure with regard to "any service which is supplied neither on a commercial basis, nor in competition with one or more service suppliers". If this is the case, the effect of the clause would be fairly limited, at least with regard the preservation of State's capacity to exercise its regulatory functions in the public services sector. Despite some uncertainties concerning the definition of the requirements set by the provisions,[27] it has been convincingly demonstrated that public services sit mostly outside the scope of the clause.[28] This is even more the case in the context at hand, as the existence of an investment, which presupposes the presence of subject acting for profit, make it difficult, if not impossible, to argue that the service is not supplied on a commercial basis. On the other side, it could be argued that the absence of the clarification contained in Article I:3(c) GATS paves the way for a broader interpretation of the clause, so to allow national authorities to adopt any measure also with regard to activities that, albeit supplied on a commercial basis or in competition with other suppliers, represent an exercise of governmental authority. However, the adoption of this reading is potentially problematic, due to the uncertainty on what can be considered as an exercise of governmental authority in the absence of any meaningful guidance in the text of the agreement.

### 4.3.2 Public Services' Regulatory Measures and International Arbitral Tribunals Jurisdiction: The Case of ICSID

Public services' regulatory frameworks often have a multi-tiered structure, as the conditions for their supply are set in different legal instruments, such as constitutional norms, legislative acts, administrative regulations and contractual agreements stipulated between the competent authority and the provider. Doubts have

---

[23] *North American Free Trade Agreement between the Government of Canada, the Government of the United Mexican States and the Government of the United States of America*, 12 December 1992, Annex II.

[24] *Australia—United States Free Trade Agreement*, 18 May 2004, Annex II.

[25] *Colombia—United States Free Trade Agreement*, 22 November 2006, Annex II.

[26] *Republic of Korea—United States Free Trade Agreement*, 30 June 2007, Annex II.

[27] On the different interpretation of the words "on a commercial basis" see Arena 2011, p. 502.

[28] Krajewski 2003b, p. 350.

arisen as to whether arbitral tribunals can exercise their scrutiny over all these regulatory measures, in order to assess their compatibility with norms and standards contained in international investment agreements. These doubts mainly concerned those measures having a general character, i.e. aiming at implementing general policy choices and not just directed toward a specific investment.

The issue has been raised and discussed in most of the so-called Argentine cases,[29] concerning the measures adopted by Argentina in response to the dramatic economic crisis that hit the country at the end of the '90s and that led to a substantial modification of the regulatory framework governing private investments in public services.[30] Indeed, Argentina challenged the competence of ICSID tribunals to hear these cases by contending that a controversy concerning the application of measures having a general nature cannot be said to be "a dispute arising directly out of an investment", as required by Article 25 ICSID Convention.[31] The Respondent State read the word "directly" as meaning "specifically" and, thus, restricting the competence of arbitral tribunals to those measures that, according to the *Methanex* decision,[32] have "a legally significant connection" with the investment or the investor. Conversely, admitting the possibility to deal with measures having a wider focus would allow an international adjudicatory body to put under scrutiny "the wisdom of general economic measures taken by the government".

Arbitral tribunals have constantly rejected Argentina's interpretation of Article 25 ICSID Convention and, consequently, the possibility to exclude regulatory measures having a general character from the scope of application of international investment law. Their reasoning rested on the distinction between, on the one side, the measures and, on the other, their effects on the investment. In the *CMS* case, for instance, the Tribunal conceded that it "does not have jurisdiction over measures of general economic policy adopted by the Republic of Argentina and cannot pass judgement on whether they are right or wrong", but, at the same time, it forcefully claimed to have "jurisdiction to examine whether [...] measures of general economic policy having a direct bearing on such investment have been adopted in violation of legally binding commitments made to the investor in

[29]See generally Burke-White 2010, pp. 407–432.

[30]In the second half of the '90s the growth of public debt drove the country into recession that caused massive protests and social rests, as most of Argentina's households were no longer able to cope with everyday life expenses. In order to guarantee the access to basic public services, the Government first forced private investors to accept a temporary tariffs' freezing. Subsequently, in January 2002, it adopted the *Ley de Emergencia*, which terminated tariffs' automatic adjustment mechanism, based on the US Producer Price Index (PPI), as well as the peso-to-dollar 1-to-1 peg.

[31]Schreuer 1996, pp. 318–492.

[32]*Methanex Corp. v. United States of America*, UNCITRAL Case, Award on Jurisdiction and Admissibility of 7 August 2002, para 139. This notwithstanding the fact that Article 1101 NAFTA only speaks of measures "relating to" investments or investors of another party.

treaties, legislation or contracts".[33] This distinction aimed at ensuring a proper balance between the conflicting interests at stake. Indeed, as observed in *AES*, while a State has "a right to adopt its economic policies; [...] this does not mean that the foreign under a system of guarantees and protection could be deprived of their respective rights".[34]

However, while theoretically clear, the distinction between the measure and its effects might be more difficult to draw in practice. Admittedly, the recourse to other criteria, such as the nature of the measure, could be equally problematic, giving the possibility to national authorities to easily evade international obligations by resorting to measures having a general character. At the same time, this approach ends up widening the jurisdiction of international arbitral tribunals, allowing them to exercise their scrutiny virtually over any type of regulatory measure, irrespective of its nature and status. In this sense, there is little doubt that this regime "obliging States to arbitrate dispute arising from sovereign acts, [it] establish[es] [...] a mechanism to control the exercise of public authority",[35] imposing potentially far-reaching constraints to their regulatory autonomy.

## 4.4 Legitimate Regulation or Regulatory Expropriation? Looking for an Elusive Answer in the Context of Public Services

### *4.4.1 Regulatory Expropriation: An Overview*

The exercise of regulatory functions by the host State may have adverse economic effects on investments. This is very much evident with regard to public services where the profitability of the activity carried out by the investor is heavily dependent on the regulatory choices adopted by competent authorities with regard, for instance, the obligations that must be fulfilled in supplying of the service or the mechanism for the calculation of tariffs.

---

[33] *CMS Gas Transmission Company v. The Republic of Argentina*, ICSID Case No. ARB/01/8, Decision on Objections to Jurisdiction of 7 July 2003, para 33. See also *Total S.A. v. The Argentine Republic*, ICSID Case No. ARB/04/1, Decision on Objections to Jurisdiction of 25 August 2006, para 59; *Suez, Sociedad General de Aguas de Barcelona S.A. and Vivendi International S.S. v. The Argentine Republic*, ICSID Case No. ARB/03/19 and *AWG Group Ltd. v. The Argentine Republic*, UNCITRAL Case, Decision on Jurisdiction of 3 August 2006, paras 27–31; *Telefonica S.A. v. The Argentine Republic*, ICSID Case No. ARB/03/20, Decision of the Tribunal on Objections to Jurisdiction of 25 May 2006; paras 62–67; *Gas Natural SDG S.A. v. The Argentine Republic*, ICSID Case No. ARB/03/10, Decision on Preliminary Questions on Jurisdiction of 17 July 2005, paras 37–39.

[34] *AES Corp. v. The Argentine Republic*, ICSID Case No. ARB/02/17, Decision on Jurisdiction of 26 April 2005, para 57.

[35] Van Harten and Loughlin 2006, p. 146.

In certain cases, the impact of regulation may be as severe as to amount to an expropriatory act, which is usually identified as 'regulatory expropriation'. Investment treaties do not contain any explicit reference to this notion. In the *Suez* case it has been defined as follows: "[i]n case of an indirect expropriation, sometimes referred to as a 'regulatory taking', host States invoke their legislative and regulatory powers to enact measures that reduce the benefits that investors derive from their investments but without actually changing or cancelling investors' legal title to their assets or diminishing their control over them".[36] The relationship between regulatory expropriation and indirect expropriation[37] is still uncertain, despite having being extensively discussed in literature[38] and case-law. However, clarifying and differentiating between these and other related concepts is essentially a terminological problem, having little relevance from a legal perspective. Indeed, any expropriation—be it direct, indirect, regulatory, de facto, creeping or consequential—to be lawful under international law must fulfil the same conditions, i.e. it must be in the public interest, non-discriminatory, in accordance with due process of law and accompanied by the payment of a prompt, adequate and effective compensation.[39] The assimilation, which is explicitly provided for by many international investment agreements,[40] had already been sanctioned by the Permanent Court of Arbitration,[41] the Permanent Court of International Justice,[42] the Iran-US Claims Tribunal[43] and it has been subsequently confirmed by several arbitral tribunals.

---

[36] *Suez, Sociedad General de Aguas de Barcelona S.A. and Vivendi International S.S. v. The Argentine Republic,* ICSID Case No. ARB/03/19 and *AWG Group Ltd. v. The Argentine Republic,* UNCITRAL Case, Decision on Liability of 30 July 2010, para 132.

[37] One of the best-know definitions of indirect expropriation is that elaborated by the Iran-US Claims Tribunal in the *Starrett Housing* decision, where it has been observed that "[...] it is recognized in international law that measures taken by a State can interfere with property rights to such an extent that these rights are rendered so useless that they must deemed to have been expropriated, even though the State does not purport to have expropriated them and the legal title to the property formally remains with original owner" (*Starret Housing Corp. v. Government of the Islamic Republic of Iran*, Award No. ITL 32-24-1 of 19 December 1983, Iran-US CTR, 4, 154).

[38] See generally, Newcombe 2005, pp. 1–57; Coe and Rubins 2005, pp. 597–667.

[39] See Sacerdoti 1997, p. 381; Higgins 1983, p. 324; Christie 1962, pp. 310–311.

[40] For an overview of these references in some international investment agreements, see UNCTAD, Expropriation. A Sequel, Series on Issues in International Investment Agreements II. UN Publication, 2012, pp. 8–12. New York, Geneva.

[41] *Norwegian Shipowners Claims*, 13 October 1922, UNRIAA, I, 1922, 334.

[42] *Case concerning certain German interests in Polish Upper Silesia (The Merits)*, 25 May 1925, PCIJ, Ser. A, 7, 1926; *Interpretation of Judgements Nos. 7 and 8 (The Chorzów Factory)*, 16 December 1927, PCIJ, Ser. A, 13, 1927; *The Oscar Chinn Case*, 12 December 1934, PCIJ, Ser. A, 63, 1934.

[43] *Starrett Housing*, above n 37, para 154. The Iran-US Claims Tribunal's contribution to the development of the legal notion of indirect expropriation has been substantial, also from a quantitative perspective as this issue has been dealt with in more than 60 cases. See Brower and Brueschke 1998.

### 4.4.2 The Distinction Between Regulation and Expropriation from a Quantitative Perspective: The Sole-Effect Doctrine

In the case of regulatory expropriation, the main issue is not the respect of the conditions seen above, but rather the distinction between instances of legitimate regulation and cases of compensable expropriation.[44] This distinction remains fairly obscure,[45] as demonstrated by the divergent solutions adopted, in public services' cases, by different arbitral tribunals dealing with same factual scenario. In the *AWG/Suez* case, the arbitral tribunal admitted that is unclear "when governmental action that interferes with broadly-defined property rights…crosses the line from valid regulation to a compensable taking, and it is fair to say that no one has come up with a fully satisfactory means of drawing this line".[46]

The approach traditionally adopted by arbitral tribunals has a distinct quantitative nature, focusing primarily, and almost exclusively, on the effects of the regulatory measure upon the investment and the investor. As observed in several decisions, "[e]xpropriation tends to involve the deprivation of ownership rights, regulation a lesser interference".[47] The elements taken into consideration to determine the impact of the regulatory measure on the investment are both legal and economic. As for the first dimension, in a decision concerning gas distribution,[48] the arbitral Tribunal clarified that expropriation may result, inter alia,[49] "from depriving the investor of the control on the investment, managing the day-to-day operations of the company, arresting and detaining company officials or employees, supervising the work of officials, interfering in administration, impeding the distribution of dividends, interfering in the appointment of officials or managers, or depriving the company of its property or control in whole or in part".[50] As for the second dimension, the main item taken into consideration is the impact on the investment's economic viability and profitability. In a number of cases, even concerning public services, arbitral tribunals have seemingly given priority to the first dimension over the second one. In *CMS*, for instance, the tribunal opined that "[t]he essential question is therefore whether the enjoyment of property has been

---

[44]See Lowe 2002, pp. 457–460.

[45]Reinisch 2008, p. 432.

[46]*AWG/Suez,* above n 36, para 132.

[47]*S.D. Mayers Inc. v. Government of Canada*, UNCITRAL, Partial Award of 13 November 2000, para 282.

[48]*Sempra Energy International v. The Argentine Republic*, ICSID Case No. ARB/02/16, Award of 28 September 2007, para 284.

[49]The same paragraph pointed out that "[t]he list of measures could be expanded significantly".

[50]See also *PSEG Global Inc., The North American Coal Corp., and Konya Ilgin Elektrik Üritim ve Ticaret Limited Sirketi v. Republic of Turkey*, ICSID Case No. ARB/02/25, Award of 19 January 2007, para 278.

effectively neutralized".[51] Correspondingly, in *LG&E* the arbitral panel concluded that no expropriation had occurred, since the measures, despite having an "impact on Claimants' investment, especially regarding the earnings that the Claimants expected", did not "deprive the investors of the right to enjoy their investment".[52] Conversely, in other cases the economic items played a more prominent role. In a case concerning the privatization of water and sanitation services in the Argentina's Province of Tucmán, the arbitral tribunal found that the regulatory measures had to be considered as an act of expropriation, as they deprived Claimants "of the economic use and enjoyment of their investment, the benefits of which (i.e. the right to be paid for services provided) had been effectively neutralised and rendered useless".[53]

This line of reasoning, aptly dubbed as the "sole-effects doctrine",[54] gives little, if any, relevance the regulatory intent or purpose. In most public services cases, Respondent States sought to justify their measures by recalling their fundamental social functions, such as ensuring universal access to essential services. However, arbitral tribunals have constantly adopted an agnostic approach,[55] remaining indifferent to these considerations. While incidentally recognizing that a "State has the right to adopt measures having a social or general welfare purpose",[56] in fact they stuck to the idea that "State's intent, or its subjective motives are at most a secondary consideration", as "the effect of the measure on the investor, not the State's intent, is the critical factor".[57]

Such a rigidly objective approach reflects the perception of State's regulation more as a risk than as the exercise of a fundamental sovereign function. This perception is particularly acute with regard to public services, due to the high incidence that this form of risk, commonly known as 'regulatory risk', has in this context. This is due to the high political sensitivity of the objectives pursued though the provision of these services, as well as to the fact that they mostly require extensive network infrastructures entailing high levels of fixed capital and long payback periods.[58]

---

[51] *CMS Gas Transmission Company v. The Republic of Argentina*, ICSID Case No. ARB/01/8, Final Award of 12 May 2005, para 262.

[52] *LG&E Energy Corp., LG&E Capital Corp. And LG&E International Inc. v. The Argentine Republic*, ICSID Case No. ARB/02/1, Decision on Liability of 3 October 2006, para 199.

[53] *Compañia de Aguas del Aconquijia S.A. and Vivendi Universal S.A. v. The Argentine Republic*, ICSID Case No. ARB/97/3, Award of 20 August 2007, para 7.5.34.

[54] Dolzer 2003, p. 78.

[55] Arena 2011, pp. 515–516. The author uses the concept to describe GATS approach toward public services.

[56] *LG&E*, above n 52, para 195.

[57] *Vivendi II*, above n 53, para 7.5.20. The same approach has been consistently adopted also by the Iran-US Claims Tribunal: see, for instance, *Tippets, Abbett, McCarthy, Stratton v. TAMS-AFFA Consulting Engineers of Iran*, Award No. 141-7-2 of 29 June 1984, Iran-US CTR, 21, para 115.

[58] See Wälde and Dow 2000, pp. 1–61; Sacerdoti 1999.

The sole-effect doctrine, if taken in absolute terms, raises issues of compatibility with the idea of a right to regulate. Indeed, corollary of this idea is the principle according to which a lawful exercise of State's regulatory authority cannot amount to expropriation even if it affects foreign investments considerably.[59] As duly observed in *Azurix*, "[i]n the exercise of their public policy function, governments take all sort of measures that may affect the economic value of investments without such measures giving rise to a need to compensate".[60] Conversely, when applying the sole-effect doctrine international arbitrators may well end up imposing upon host States a duty to compensate even for measures adopted in the exercise of public policy functions, by looking only to the material consequences of the action.

The impact of the doctrine has been partially softened by looking at the degree and intensity of the interference. Indeed, as expounded in several cases, "[t]he impact must be substantial in order that compensation may be claimed for the expropriation".[61] In order to be 'substantial' the interference must be "more than adverse effect", requiring that "the investor no longer be in control of its business operation, or that the value of the business has been virtually annihilated".[62] Such a severe reading of the 'substantial impact' criterion represents a constant feature of arbitral decisions concerning public services,[63] contributing much to the limited number of cases in which States' regulatory measures have been considered as an expropriatory act.[64]

### *4.4.3 Beyond the Quantitative Perspective: Police-Power Exception and Proportionality Analysis*

The solution seen above solution fails to address the main lacuna of the sole-effect doctrine, as it does not allow for adequate consideration of the reasons that justify States' regulatory intervention. To fill it, some authors[65] proposed to rely on the

[59] Reisman and Sloane 2004, p. 129; Brownlie 2003, p. 509.

[60] *Azurix v. Argentine Republic*, ICSID Case No. ARB/01/12, Award of 14 July 2006, para 310.

[61] *LG&E*, above n 52, para 191.

[62] *Sempra*, above n 48, paras 284–285.

[63] *Vivendi II*, above n 53, para 7.5.11; *Enron Corporation and Ponderosa Assets, L.P. v. Argentine Republic*, ICSID Case No. ARB/01/3, Award of 22 May 2007, 245; *CMS*, above n 51, para 262. In this regard Coe and Rubins 2005, p. 621 observe that "the sense often conveyed is that interference must approach total impairment".

[64] This leniency would represent a counterbalance to the far stricter interpretative stance adopted with regard to the fair and equitable treatment. In this manner, arbitral tribunals would seek to "comfort loosing respondents—"giving them something"—by declaring that there was no expropriation". See Paulsson 2006, p. 7.

[65] See Christie 1962, p. 388; White 1961, p. 145.

police power doctrine in order to identify a cluster of measures that, due to their nature and objectives, are in any case exempted from compensation. This doctrine has been originally elaborated by the US Supreme Court in its takings jurisprudence[66] and, subsequently, it has progressively made its way in some international normative instruments and judicial decisions. The exception is explicitly recognized in the US Third Restatement, which speaks about "[...] actions of the kind that is commonly accepted as within the police powers of States".[67] Other instruments, while not expressly using the concept, follow the same path as they try to identify those measures that cannot be considered as an act of expropriation. For instance, the Article 11(a)(iii) MIGA Convention[68] excludes from the notion of expropriation "non-discriminatory measures of general application which governments take for the purpose of regulating economic activity in their territories". Likewise, Annex B of the 2012 US Model BIT establishes that "[e]xcept in rare circumstances, non-discriminatory regulatory actions by a Party that are designed and applied to protect legitimate public welfare objectives, such as public health, safety, and the environment, do not constitute indirect expropriations".

The police power doctrine remains a controversial tool for the identification of non-compensable regulatory measures. Indeed, there is not an internationally-accepted definition of this notion, which has been often stretched as an accordion. According to a narrower understanding, the exception only "allows the State to protect essential public interests from certain types of harms".[69] Conversely, other scholars see it as covering not only 'traditional' non-economic interests, such as health, safety, social welfare or the environment, but also competition, consumer protection, securities and land planning.[70] This situation of uncertainty is particularly acute with regard to public services, being it a context in which States pursue a disparate set of socio-economic objectives through several different instruments. Therefore, the scope of the exception should be wide enough to include all the different measures that may be functional to achieve these objectives and flexible enough to accommodate 'future' measures to be necessarily adopted in a context that is subject to a continuous process of change and adaptation. The risk is that this process might end up diluting too much the normative value of the exception, making it impossible to identify its boundaries.

Furthermore—and, to some extent, more importantly—the transposition of this doctrine in the international legal order poses problems of compatibility with the customary principle according to which the fact that a measure has been adopted

---

[66]See recently Karkkainen 2006.

[67]American Law Institute 1987, para 712(1).

[68]*Convention Establishing the Multilateral Investment Guarantee Agency*, 12 April 1988.

[69]Newcombe 2005, p. 26.

[70]H. Mann, The Final Decision on Methanex v. United States: Some New Wine in Some New Bottles. International Institute for Sustainable Development http://www.iisd.org/pdf/2005/commentary_methanex.pdf. August 2005. Accessed 20 November 2014; Freeman 2003, p. 208. See also Clough 2005, p. 563.

for a public purpose does not exclude compensation.[71] This point has been raised in the *Azurix* case, which concerned the privatization of water and sewage services in the Province of Buenos Aires. The arbitral tribunal, after having found the police power criterion contradictory and uncertain, proposed to move beyond it and take into account additional elements.[72] Among the others, it proposed to look at the proportionality of the relationship between the regulatory measure, as well as its impact upon the investment, and the aim to be achieved. In so doing, the tribunal referred to the jurisprudence of the European Court of Human Rights[73] and to the *Tecmed* case,[74] which, at that time, was the only arbitral decision that had applied, or at least made a passing reference to, the proportionality test. Subsequently, this approach has progressively made its way in the international arbitral practice,[75] albeit at a pace that is far less impressive than the attention that this evolution has gained in the literature.[76]

Far from representing "a magical formula, susceptible of mechanical application",[77] proportionality analysis is a judicial technique that may contribute at "managing disputes between rights involving an alleged conflict between two rights claims, or between a rights provision and a legitimate state or public interest".[78] The analysis can, thus, represent a tool that can help to draw a line between legitimate regulation and compensable expropriation,[79] going beyond the rigidities that affect the effect doctrine/police powers exception dichotomy. Indeed, rather than pitting quantitative against qualitative considerations, the proportionality test brings both these sets of factors within the same analytical framework, allowing for a case-by-case balancing exercise.[80] This may lead to exempt from compensation regulatory measures having a negative effect on foreign investments, when the burden is justified in the light of the objective pursued. At the same time, it avoids

[71]Schreuer 2005a, p. 28.

[72]*Azurix*, above n 60, paras 310–311. See Costamagna 2006.

[73]Cross-regime comparison has been often advocated as a way to increase the capacity of international arbitral tribunals to deal with non-economic values and, implicitly, enhance their legitimacy. However, this approach has been criticized, highlighting that boundary crossing is not always desiderable and that, in any case, international arbitrators engaging in it should pay greater attention to the context. In this sense see J.E. Alvarez, Beware: Boundary Crossing. http://www.law.yale.edu/documents/pdf/sela/Bewareboundarycrossings_nofootnotes_%282%29.pdf. 19 March 2013. Accessed 20 November 2014.

[74]*Técnicas Medioambientales Tecmed, S.A. v. United Mexican States*, ICSID Case No. ARB(AF)/00/2, Award of 29 May 2003, paras 121–122.

[75]See Henckels 2012, pp. 234–237.

[76]See, *ex multis*, Schill 2012, pp. 87–119; Leonhardsen 2012, pp. 95–136, Stone Sweet 2010, pp. 47–76; Kingsbury and Schill 2010, pp. 75–104.

[77]Paulsson 2006, p. 2.

[78]Stone Sweet and Matthews 2008, p. 83. See also Wälde and Kolo 2001, pp. 827–835.

[79]Contra Burke-White and von Staden 2010, p. 287.

[80]Henckels 2012, p. 239; Kingsbury and Schill 2010, p. 79.

creating a loophole that states might exploit by simply claiming that their measures pursue a legitimate objective.

It has been rightly pointed out that "proportionality analysis is only half of the story",[81] as the result will mostly depend on the standard of review adopted by tribunals in distinguishing between a regulatory measure and an act of expropriation. Proportionality analysis is a flexible tool, whose impact varies according to the intensity of review, i.e. to the degree of scrutiny applied by arbitral tribunals in evaluating regulatory measures compatibility with international investment rules. This can go from complete deference to the arguments put forward by a State in order to justify its regulatory measure to de novo review of the adopted measures by the adjudicatory body.[82] Given the structure of international investment arbitration, it is far from surprising that arbitral tribunals are yet to develop a coherent standard of review[83] reflecting the eminently public nature of disputes that touch upon key aspects of States' socio-economic constitution.[84] In some cases, they have adopted a very permissive standard: the *LG&E* tribunal stated that measures having a social or general welfare purpose must be "accepted without any imposition of liability, except in cases where the State's action is obviously disproportionate to the need being addressed".[85] Conversely, in other cases, they went as far to second-guess the necessity of the measures adopted by the respondent State.

It can be safely argued that arbitral tribunals should opt for an adequately deferential approach "in their assessment of matters that are more appropriately in the province of national decision-makers".[86] The need for a high degree of deference rests upon various considerations, such as national authorities' greater democratic legitimacy and proximity to the polity or their superior expertise and competence in dealing with complex matters. Furthermore, deference is also considered as a proxy of the separation of powers principle, contributing to a correct allocation of power between primary decision-makers and their adjudicators.[87]

The adoption of a lenient standard of review is all the more necessary with regard to public services. Indeed, "the provision and regulation of public services is intrinsically linked to democratic autonomy"[88] and it is, thus, a field in which national decision-makers should enjoy broad discretionary power.

---

[81]Henckels 2012, p. 238.

[82]Kavanagh 2008, p. 186.

[83]Henckels 2012, p. 240.

[84]Burke-White and von Staden 2010, pp. 287–295.

[85]*LG&E*, above n 52, para 195.

[86]Henckels 2012, p. 255.

[87]S. Schill, Deference in Investment Treaty Arbitration: Re-Conceptualizing the Standard of Review through Comparative Public Law. http://ssrn.com/abstract=2095334. 28 June 2012, p. 27. Accessed 20 November 2014.

[88]Krajewski, above n 16, p. 3.

Furthermore, regulating public services is one of States' core sovereign functions, which is essential for the well-being of their population and for the enjoyment of fundamental human rights. Therefore, arbitral tribunals should adjust the intensity of review in order to fully respect national authorities' regulatory autonomy in this context.

## 4.5 Regulatory Change and Stability of the Regulatory Framework in the Context of Public Services: The Role of the Fair and Equitable Treatment Standard

### *4.5.1 Fair and Equitable Treatment, Stability and Investors' Legitimate Expectations*

The fair and equitable treatment (FET) standard has acquired an increasingly important role in the debate on the balance between hosts States' regulatory flexibility and foreign investors' need for regulatory stability under international investment law, progressively taking the precedence over the discipline of expropriation. The standard has long been "a sleeping beauty"[89] in the international regime for the protection of foreign investors, as arbitral tribunals 'discovered' it only in the 2000s. However, in few years it has become the most frequently invoked standard in investment disputes[90] or, as pretentiously stated in *AWG/Suez*, "the *Grundnorm* or basic norm of international investment law".[91]

There are two main reasons for its success. First, the standard is politically less burdensome, as "it provides a more supple way of providing a remedy appropriate to the particular situation as compared to the more drastic determination and remedy inherent in the concept of regulatory expropriation".[92] Second, the intrinsic vagueness[93] of an "amorphous concept"[94] enabled international arbitrators to progressively broaden the scope of application of the standard to foreign investors' advantage. This contributed to make the clause a sort of "catch all provision which may embrace a very broad number of governmental

[89]Schreuer 2007, p. 92.

[90]Dolzer 2005, p. 87.

[91]*AWG/Suez*, above n 36, para 188.

[92]*International Thunderbird Gaming v. The United Mexican States*, UNCITRAL (NAFTA), Arbitral Award of 26 January 2006, Separate Opinion of Prof. T. Wälde. See also *Sempra*, above n 48, para 301.

[93]S. Schill, Fair and Equitable Treatment under Investment Treaties as an Embodiment of the Rule of Law. Global Administrative Law Series, IILJ Working Paper 2006/6, p. 5.

[94]Choudhury 2005, p. 297.

acts",[95] having a potentially considerable impact on the freedom of a government to regulate its economy.[96]

One of the elements included in the FET standard is host States' obligation to respect and protect foreign investors' legitimate expectations with respect to the investment they have made. Quite surprisingly, there is still a considerable amount of uncertainty as to the justification for the inclusion of this element in the standard.[97] Some arbitral tribunals referred to the good faith principle as the element requiring "the Contracting Parties to provide to international investments treatment that does not affect the basic expectations that were taken into account by the foreign investor to make the investment".[98] Other relied on a purposive reading of the notion of fair and equitable treatment, as the preamble of some BITs recognizes "that the fair and equitable treatment is desirable in order to maintain a stable framework for investments".[99] In many cases, arbitral tribunals have not even tried to offer a convincing justification, as they simply pointed to the existence of "an overwhelming jurisdictional trend" going in that direction.[100]

This notwithstanding, this aspect has rapidly gained a prominent role in the definition of FET, becoming one of its major component[101] and even "the dominant element of that standard".[102] Furthermore, the use of legitimate expectations in this context is "highly relevant to the need for reconciling the competing interests of legal predictability and regulatory flexibility".[103] Indeed, as aptly observed in a recent UNCTAD report on FET, "[t]he concept of legitimate expectations is

---

[95]Dolzer 2005, p. 88.

[96]Lowe 2002, p. 455. See also Haynes 2013, pp. 114–146.

[97]See Potestà 2013, pp. 90–93. See also *Suez, Sociedad General de Aguas de Barcelona S.A. and Vivendi International S.S. v. The Argentine Republic,* ICSID Case No. ARB/03/19 and *AWG Group Ltd. v. The Argentine Republic,* UNCITRAL Case, Decision on Liability of 30 July 2010, Dissenting Opinion of Arbitrator Pedro Nikken, para 3, arguing against the possibility of including this item in the FET.

[98]*Tecmed*, above n 74, para 154. See also *Sempra*, above n 48, para 299. *Contra* Gazzini 2009, p. 117.

[99]*Treaty between United States of America and the Argentine Republic Concerning the Reciprocal Encouragement and Protection of Investment*, 14 November 1991.

[100]*El Paso Energy International Company v. The Argentine Republic*, ICSID Case No. ARB/03/15, Award of 31 October 2011, para 355. See also *AWG/Suez*, above n 36, para 222. In this case, the Tribunal simply observed that "[i]n an effort to develop an operational method for determining the existence or non-existence of fair and equitable treatment, arbitral tribunals have increasingly taken into account the legitimate expectations that a host country has created in the investor and the extent to which conduct by the host government subsequent to the investment has frustrated those expectations".

[101]*EDF v. Romania*, ICSID Case No. ARB/05/13, Award of 8 October 2009, para 216.

[102]*Saluka v. Czech Republic*, UNCITRAL, Partial Award of 17 March 2006, para 301.

[103]Hirsch 2011, p. 786.

connected to the phenomenon of 'change'"[104] and, in particular, to the possibility for national authorities to exercise their regulatory power in a way that modifies, even substantially, the legal environment in which the investment was decided and made.

### *4.5.2 Making Investors' Expectations Prevail Over States' Regulatory Autonomy in the Context of Public Services: The Early Argentine Cases*

Striking a balance between the protection of investors' legitimate expectations and the respect of host States' regulatory autonomy is a key concern in the context of public services. As seen above, regulatory changes may sensibly affect the economic profitability of projects that normally presuppose the existence of large network infrastructures and, consequently, entail high levels of sunk costs and payback periods, while assets cannot be moved elsewhere. These investments are particularly exposed to the so-called obsolescing bargain phenomenon,[105] which may occur after the bulk of the investment has been made and the host government, mostly for political reasons, seeks to force a revision of the terms of the agreement with the investor by resorting to its sovereign powers. This is what happened in the *Vivendi II* case, where the newly elected authorities of the Province of Tucumán did all what in their power to undermine the privatization of water and sewage services. To this purpose, they mounted what the arbitral tribunal defined "an illegitimate campaign against the concession",[106] by using their regulatory powers to put pressure on the concessionaire.

On the other hand, there is the need to ensure an adequate regulatory space to national authorities, so that they may continuously exercise their sovereign function by adapting the regulatory framework to ever-changing needs and challenges. The case of Argentina represented an extreme example in this regard, as arbitral tribunals have been called upon to evaluate the legitimacy of far-reaching regulatory changes that had been taken in response to a crisis that was excluding large sectors of the population from having access to basic services.

The need to find a balance between these competing interests has been recognized in all cases concerning public services. All arbitral decisions acknowledge that the duty to ensure stability and predictability of the regulatory framework does not entail the immutability of the legal order. Or, as said in *CMS*, "[i]t is not a question whether the legal framework might need to be frozen as it can always evolve and be adapted to changing circumstances, but neither is it a question of whether

[104]UNCTAD, Fair and Equitable Treatment. A Sequel. Series on Issues in International Investment Agreements II. UN Publication, 2012, p. 63. New York, Geneva.

[105]See Vernon 1967, pp. 81–89. See more recently, Woodhouse 2006, pp. 121–219.

[106]*Vivendi II*, above n 53, para 7.4.19.

the framework can be dispensed with altogether when specific commitments to the contrary have been made".[107] This dictum has progressively acquired an iconic status, being constantly recalled in all subsequent decisions dealing with the matter. However, in many cases it turned out to be an empty formula, or, as purposely observed in *El Paso* with regard to *CMS*, "a general statement of principle with no legal consequences on the settlement of the case".[108]

Although quite harsh in its tone, this remark reflects the criticisms levelled against an early line of decisions that adopted a markedly pro-investor stance, paying little attention to host State's capacity to adapt the legal framework governing the provision of public services to a deteriorating economic situation. All these cases concerned the measures taken by Argentina to deal with the dramatic economic crisis that hit the country at the end of the'90s and that led to a substantial modification of the legal framework devised in the early-'90s to support public utilities' privatization programme. Prospective investors were encouraged to participate by offering them extremely favourable conditions, such as tariffs calculated in U.S. dollars, automatic and periodic adjustments to the tariffs based on the US Producer Price Index (PPI) and a clear legal framework that could not be unilaterally modified. In the aftermath of the crisis, the Argentine government intervened by first forcing private investors to negotiate a temporary tariffs' freezing[109] and, then, with the Emergency Law in 2002,[110] establishing that tariffs and prices for public services were to be calculated in pesos, abolishing all clauses calling for tariff adjustments in U.S. dollars or other foreign currencies, eliminating all indexing mechanisms and directing the executive branch to renegotiate all public service contracts.

Private investors challenged these measures in front of different international arbitral tribunals, by arguing, inter alia, that they violated the FET standard, as they frustrated the expectations created by the guarantees on which private investors relied when deciding to invest in Argentina's public service sector. Early arbitral decisions, such as *CMS*, *LG&E*, *Sempra* and *Enron*, were swift to side with claimants, as they adopted a far-reaching understanding of host States' duty to ensure the stability of the environment in which foreign investment operate.

In *CMS*, the arbitral tribunal held that Argentina's measures resulted in a breach of the FET standard as they "in fact entirely transform and alter the legal and business environment under which the investment was decided and made".[111] This conclusion rests on a purposive reading of the notion of FET, as the tribunal noted that the Preamble of the applicable BIT recognize the close link between this standard and the maintenance of "a stable framework for investments and

[107]*CMS*, above n 51, para 277. See also Schreuer 2005b, p. 374.

[108]*El Paso*, above n 100, para 371.

[109]Doak Bishop and Aguirre Luzi 2005, p. 432.

[110]Law No 25.561 of 6 January 2002.

[111]*CMS*, above n 51, para 275.

maximum effective use of resources". Therefore, "there can be no doubt" that ensuring the stability of the legal and business framework is "an essential element" of the standard.[112] Subsequent decisions adopted the same line of reasoning, as they considered it "an emerging standard of fair and equitable treatment in international law".[113] The *LG&E* decision stands for the same proposition, while further adding that "the fair and equitable standard consists of the host State's consistent and transparent behaviour, free of ambiguity that involves the obligation to grant and maintain a stable and predictable legal framework necessary to fulfil the justified expectations of the foreign investor".[114] Likewise, in *Enron*, the tribunal found "an objective breach" of FET, since "the guarantees of the tariff regime that had seduced so many foreign investors were dismantled" and "the stable legal framework that induced the investment is no longer in place".[115]

The focus of these decisions was firmly on investors' position and on their expectations, while paying little consideration to the position of the host State and its right to regulate.[116] Such a bias clearly emerges from 'incomplete' reference to the Preamble of the BIT made by the *CMS* and *LG&E* decisions. In both cases, tribunals only retained the first prong of the provision, being it functional to demonstrate that stability is a constitutive element of FET, while dropping the second one, which would have called for greater consideration of State's capacity to guarantee to its population maximum effective use of its resources. This one-sided sided approach appears to be ill suited to define the content of a standard "entailing reasonableness and proportionality".[117]

### *4.5.3 Looking for a Better Definition of the Legitimacy of Expectations: Is There a Need for Specific Commitments?*

Subsequent decisions tried to distance themselves from this over-expansive reading of the FET standard, by tentatively working out a more balanced definition of

---

[112]Ibid., para 274.

[113]*LG&E*, above n 52, para 125.

[114]Ibid., para 131. This conclusion echoes the very demanding, and much criticized, standard developed in *Tecmed* (para 154). Douglas observed that "[t]he Tecmed 'standard' is not a standard at all; it is rather a description of perfect public regulation in a perfect world, to which all States should aspire but very few (if any) will ever attain". See Douglas 2006, p. 28.

[115]*Enron*, above n 63, paras 266–268.

[116]This approach seems to reflect what Crema convincingly described as the international investment regime's cultural bias against domestic regulation. Indeed in this framework "excessive domestic regulation, discriminatory or not, unfair or not, is in any case problematic: it is a local, particularistic obstacle to the bigger game of reallocating resources in a better way for the good of a greater number of persons". See Crema 2014, pp. 60–61.

[117]*El Paso*, above n 100, para 373.

the concept of legitimate expectations and of the related duty to ensure the stability of the regulatory framework. To this purpose, arbitral tribunals sought to identify a number of qualifying requirements to determine whether an expectation may be said 'legitimate' and, thus, subject to protection under the FET standard. One of the most delicate issues in this regard is the definition of the sources from which legitimate expectations may arise.

The question is whether private investors can claim to have enforceable expectations by simply relying on legislative or regulatory instruments having a general character or whether they have to show the existence of more specific promises by the host State.[118] The answer is key to strike a balance between regulatory stability and change, as it determines the scope of host State' duty to maintain 'a stable legal environment'. Indeed, if investors can claim to have *legitimate* expectations by simply relying on the general legislative and regulatory framework in force when they made the investment, any modification of such a framework may entail a violation of FET. This would transform the standard in a sort of general stabilization clause,[119] fettering States' capacity to regulate their economy and going "beyond what the investor could legitimately expect".[120]

It is worth observing that, by adopting this approach, international arbitral tribunals end up ensuring private investors a higher level of protection than national judges. Indeed, the latter have traditionally been extremely cautious in this regard, as "only exceptionally has the concept of legitimate expectations been the basis of redress when legislative action by a State was at stake".[121] As observed by Steele with regard to the English legal system, "it seems likely that protecting an expectation in a 'change of policy' scenario will have more wideranging implications for decisions-maker's freedom of action".[122] This proposition finds support in the case law of the Court of Justice of the European Union, which has constantly held that "traders cannot have a legitimate expectation that an existing situation which is capable of being altered by the Community institutions in the exercise of their discretionary power will be maintained".[123]

Conversely, early public services' arbitral decisions took a different path. In *LG&E*, for instance, the tribunal established that Argentina acted unfairly and

[118]See generally Potestà 2013, pp. 100–117; Hirsch 2011, pp. 787–797.

[119]See recently Bertoli and Crespi Reghizzi 2014, p. 36.

[120]Schreuer 2005b, p. 374. *Contra* Boute 2011, pp. 523–526.

[121]*Total S.A. v. The Argentine Republic*, ICSID Case No. ARB/04/01, Decision on Liability of 27 December 2010, para 129.

[122]Steele 2005, p. 303.

[123]CJEU, Case C-245/81, *Edeka Zentrale AG v Germany* [1982], ECR 2745, para 27; CJEU, Case C-52/81, *Offene Handelsgesellschaft in Firma Werner Faust v Commission*, [1982], ECR 3745, para 27; CJEU, Joined Cases 424-425/85, *Cooeperative Melkproducentenbedrijven Noord-Nederland BA (Frico) and Others v Voedselvoorzienings In—en Verkoopbureau* [1987], ECR 2755, para 33. See generally Craig 2006, pp. 635–639; Tridimas 2006, pp. 273–280.

inequitably by frustrating Claimant's reliance upon "certain key guarantees in the Gas Law and implementing regulation".[124] Likewise, in *Enron*, the arbitral tribunal found that the dismantling of the tariff regime amounted to a violation of the FET standard, as "it was in reliance upon the conditions established by the Respondent in the regulatory framework for the gas sector that Enron embarked on its investment in TGS. Given the scope of Argentina's privatization process, its international marketing, and the statutory enshrinement of the tariff regime, Enron had reasonable grounds to rely on such conditions".[125] Despite some passing reference to the need for "specific commitments",[126] these dicta convey the idea that guarantees included in domestic legislative and regulatory acts of general application may be sufficient to create legitimate expectations.[127] According to this line of cases, the decisive element to assess the legitimacy of the expectations is not the origin or the nature of the guarantees, but the fact that investors relied upon them when deciding to invest.

Subsequent arbitral decisions tried to work out a less investor-centred and more principled approach to the issue. In *Continental Casualty*, a case concerning Argentina's insurance market, the tribunal tried to shed more light on the link between the source of the expectation and its legitimacy. To this purpose, it distinguished between different types of expectations, by pointing out that general legislative statements engender only reduced expectations, while "unilateral modification of contractual undertakings by government [...] deserve clearly more scrutiny".[128] The key element to establish the legitimacy or, *rectius*, the legal strength of the expectation is the specificity of the undertaking relied upon by the investor. The *El Paso* decision tried to further clarify the point, by arguing that a commitment is to be considered 'specific' when it is directly made to the investor, "for example in a contract or in a letter of intent, or even through a specific promise in a person-to-person business meeting" and "its precise object was to give a real guarantee of stability to the investor".[129]

This approach has gradually made its way also in decisions concerning public services. The *Total* decision represents a good case in point, concerning an investor that had no contractual relationship with the host country, as it invested after the original privatization process by acquiring and indirect share in the Argentinian gas transportation company (Transportadora de Gas del Norte) from another investor in 2001. To determine whether Argentina's modification of the tariff regime violated Total's legitimate expectations, the arbitral tribunal started by making clear that signing a BIT cannot be a taken a sign of States' will to

[124] *LG&E*, above n 52, para 133.

[125] *Enron*, above n 63, para 265.

[126] *CMS*, above n 51, para 277.

[127] Potestà 2013, p. 112. *Contra* Hirsch 2011, pp. 789–790.

[128] *Continental Casualty Company v. The Argentine Republic*, ICSID Case No. ARB/03/9, Award of 5 September 2008, para 261.

[129] Ibid., paras 376–377 (emphasis in the original).

"relinquish their regulatory powers [or] limit their responsibility to amend their legislation". Therefore, "in the absence of some 'promise' by the host State or a specific provision in the treaty itself, the legal regime in force in the host country at the time of making the investment is not automatically subject to a "guarantee" of stability". According to the tribunal, expectations are "undoubtedly legitimate" when based upon contracts, concessions or stabilization clauses "on which the investor is [...] entitled to rely as a matter of law".[130] The same holds true with other types of representations, albeit less formal, provided that they are sufficiently clear and specific.[131]

However, the tribunal also acknowledges that problems may arise with regard to certain specific sectors, such as "operation of utilities under a licence", where expectations "rooted in regulation of a normative and administrative nature that is not specifically addressed to the relevant investor" may be legitimate, due to the "inherently prospective nature of the regulation at issue aimed at providing a defined framework for future operations".[132] In fact, unilateral modifications to the guarantees contained therein cannot be considered irrelevant when assessing whether the host State acted equitably and fairly. Only, as duly warned by the *Total* tribunal, there is the need for greater caution, as these expectations are inherently weaker that those originating from more specific undertakings. This element is, thus, to be taken into account when weighting investors' expectations and host State's regulatory interest in order to determine whether there has been a breach of the FET standard.

### 4.5.4 Balancing Investors' Expectations and States' Regulatory Purpose

Early public services cases excluded that the reasons behind host States' regulatory intervention could be an element to be taken into account when assessing whether the frustration of investors' expectations amounts to a violation of the FET. Once again, in these cases arbitral tribunal adopted an agnostic approach,[133] showing a "deplorable lack of sensitivity with regards to regulatory issues".[134] Indeed, they focused exclusively on the effects of regulatory changes on investors' position, while disregarding host State' legitimate interest to adopt such measures. For instance, the *Enron* and *Sempra* decisions curtly observed that "[e]ven assuming that the Respondent was guided by the best of intentions, what the Tribunal

[130]*Total*, above n 121, para 117.

[131]Ibid., para 121.

[132]Ibid., para 122.

[133]Arena 2011, pp. 515–516.

[134]Krajewski 2012, p. 366.

has no reason to doubt, there has here been an objective breach of the fair and equitable treatment due under the Treaty".[135]

Even a cursory comparative analysis demonstrates that his approach is at odd with the line of reasoning traditionally followed in domestic and other supranational jurisdictions. Weighting individual expectations with the public interest pursued through the challenged measures represents a constant feature of the EU Court of Justice case law on this matter. This is well exemplified by *Dieckmann & Hansen*,[136] a judgement of the then Court of First Instance concerning an importation ban of fishery product from Kazakhstan, in view of the systemic deficiencies with the general regime of health supervision. A German company, which had concluded a contract to import caviar from that country, brought an annulment action against this decision, arguing that the act violated its legitimate expectations by not including transitional provisions in the decision to remove a country from the list of third countries from which the import of fishery products is authorised. The Court dismissed this claim, as it held that the choice was then taken to protect consumers' health, which is an overriding public interest within the meaning of the case law.[137] This is a way to recognise that the legitimate expectations doctrine is not absolute as it "must give way where [its] application becomes incompatible with the free and proper exercise of an authority's powers on the due performance of its duties in the public interest".[138]

More recent arbitral awards have progressively abandoned the agnostic approach, by emphasising the need to balance investors' expectations against the regulatory goals of the host country. Interestingly enough, the *Total* decision motivated the adoption of this approach by referring to the fact that "TGN's gas transportation is not an ordinary business operation but it is qualified as a 'national public service'".[139] Consequently, the assessment of whether the modification of the regulatory framework constitutes a breach of investor's legitimate expectations and, thus, a violation of the FET standard must take into account "the purposes, nature and objectives of the measures challenged", so to determine that they are "reasonable and proportionate".[140] In the same vein, the *AWG/Suez* tribunal, ruling on a case concerning "one of the world's largest water distribution and waste water treatment privatizations in a great city" such as Buenos Aires, held that to interpret

[135] *Sempra*, above n 48, para 304; *Enron*, above n 63, para 268. The only exception in this regard is the *LG&E* decision, which recognized the economic hardship and "certain political and social realities that may have influenced the Government's response to the growing economic difficulties", but considered that Argentina "went too far" (para 139).

[136] CFI, Case T-155/99, *Dieckmann & Hansen* [2001], ECR II-3143; See Craig 2006, pp. 639–641.

[137] Ibid., para 81.

[138] Wade and Forsyth 2000, p. 242.

[139] *Total*, above n 121, para 160.

[140] Ibid., para 162.

the FET standard it "must balance the legitimate and reasonable expectations of the Claimants with Argentina's right to regulate the provision of a vital public service".[141]

The recourse to a balancing test as a tool to reconcile investors' expectations and States' right to adapt the regulatory framework to changing need and circumstances may allow a more flexible and comprehensive evaluation of all the interests at stake. However, as already noticed with regard to regulatory expropriation, the balancing test is just part of the story. Indeed the decisive factor is the level of scrutiny that arbitral tribunals apply in carrying out this balancing exercise. In particular, the key question is determining where the standard of review will stand on the sliding scale that goes from complete deference to de novo reconsideration of the choices made by national authorities.[142]

The analysis of the arbitral case-law on public services does not show the existence of a coherent pattern in this regard. In some cases, such as *Total*, the arbitral tribunal afforded a high degree of deference to the national decision makers, by applying a loose reasonability test to evaluate the legitimacy of the contested measures. Accordingly the tribunal found that the measures adopted by Argentina to respond to the crisis. i.e. the de-dollarization of tariffs and the abolition of mechanisms for automatic adjustment, were neither unfair not inequitable, as they reflected "a legitimate exercise of the host State's governmental power".[143] Conversely, in the *AWG/Suez* case the tribunal resorted to a strict necessity test, as it found that Argentina's could have "employed more flexible means" to achieve the stated ends. It even went as far as to put forward some alternative measures that Argentina could have taken instead than altering the legal framework and the concession. In particular, the tribunal opined that to protect the poor from increased tariffs, national authorities "might have allowed tariff increases for other consumers while applying a social tariff or a subsidy to the poor". In so doing, it intruded into matters that lie at the heart of States' regulatory space, entailing delicate political choices over the allocation of scarce resources.

A comparative analysis of domestic and supranational legal systems protecting legitimate expectations may provide useful guidance to work out a more principled approach for the development of a correct and coherent standard of review in this context. It is worth noting that national and supranational courts tend to use different types of balancing tests, which may go from the manifest unreasonableness test to a proper "weighting [of] the requirements of fairness against an

[141]*AWG/Suez*, above n 36, para 236. See Tanzi 2013, pp. 592–596. See also Tanzi 2014, pp. 318–335.

[142]See above para 4.4.3.

[143]*Total*, above n 121, para 164. This conclusion is opposite to the one reached in *CMS*, despite the fact that these two cases concerned the very same measures and the very same situation, as both Total and CMS we shareholders of TGN.

overriding interest",[144] according to a variety of factors. Among the others, two of these factors are worth to be briefly taken into consideration, because of their potential relevance with regard to future investment disputes concerning public services.

The first element is the origin of the expectations. National and supranational courts tend to adopt a more deferential approach when general measures are at stake. As for the English legal system, in the *Begbie* case the Court of Appeal pointed out that "[t]he more the decision challenges in what may inelegantly be called the macro-political field, the less intrusive will be the court's supervision. More than this: [...] changes of policy [...] may more readily be accepted as taking precedence over the interests of groups which enjoyed expectations generated by an earlier policy".[145] A similar attitude can also be found in the EU legal order.[146] Schømberg noted that the EU Court of Justice "will be more reluctant to interfere with general changes of policy embodied in the shift from one regulatory scheme to another".[147] In these circumstances the Court tends to make the expectation prevail only when there is a significant imbalance between the interests of those involved and the policy considerations behind the regulatory change.[148]

The other element that is potentially relevant in this regard is the importance of the public interest at stake. For instance, the European Court of Human Rights grants a wider margin of appreciation to national authorities when the State is performing one of its core sovereign functions, such as the protection of the environment and fiscal policy. In *Gorraiz Lizarraga* acknowledged that "[u]rban and regional planning policies are, *par excellence*, spheres in which the State intervene, particularly through control of property in the general or public interest" and thus its "margin of appreciation is greater than when exclusively civil rights are at stake".[149] A similar stance has also been adopted by the EU Court of Justice. In the above-mentioned *Dieckmann & Hansen* judgement, the Court took the view that it had to afford a wide margin of discretion to the Commission in this case, due to the importance of the public interest at stake, which was ensuring a high level of protection of human health.[150]

---

[144] *R. v. North and East Devon Authority ex p. Coughlan*, 1999, LGR703, para 57. Clayton 2003, pp. 98–102 which highlights that the categorization may result over simplistic in the light of a much more complex reality. See also Craig 2006, p. 650 which observes that "[t]he ECJ and the CFI have been rather reluctant to assign a discrete legal label to this exercise. It has therefore been left to commentators to divine the legal test for the courts' reasoning".

[145] *R. v. Secretary of State for Education and Employment, ex p. Begbie*, 2000, 1 WLR 1115, para 82.

[146] See Quinot 2004, p. 72, which notes that "the ECJ is generally as deferential to administrative discretion, especially in matters regarding policy, as its English counterparts".

[147] Schømberg 2001, p. 150.

[148] See Craig 2006, pp. 649–652.

[149] *Gorraiz Lizarraga et al. v. Spain*, Judgment of 27 April 2004, Ap. No. 62543/00 (emphasis added).

[150] *Dieckmann & Hansen*, above n 136, paras 47–56.

If these criteria were to be employed in international investment disputes concerning the provision of public services, they would lead to the adoption of a deferential approach by arbitral tribunals. This holds especially true in those cases, as in *Total*, where expectations are rooted in general legislative or regulatory instruments not directly addressed to the investor. The existence of more specific undertakings, especially if in the form of a contract concluded between the host State and the investor, would seemingly militate for the adoption of a more intrusive standard of review. However, other factors would still suggest a softer approach. Among the others already seen above, international arbitrators should pay due consideration to the fact that is one of State' core sovereign functions, as it is key to pursuit of fundamental social objectives.

## 4.6 Conclusion

The international regime for the protection of foreign investments has the potential to fetter host States' autonomy in regulating public services.[151] In this sector, regulation represents the main tool for public authorities to pursue fundamental social objectives by ensuring to their population access to high-quality services. Indeed, over the last decades many States have privatized or liberalized the provision of public services, by progressively transferring to private actors some of the functions traditionally performed by public entities. However, the choice to move along this path does not deprive States of their right to regulate the organization and the supply of public services, nor it relieves them from their duty to guarantee the continuous realization of the rights that depend on the provision of these services.

In exercising these functions, States resort to a variety of regulatory tools, which are often contained in different legal instruments, such as constitutional norms, legislative acts, administrative regulations and contractual agreements stipulated with the private provider. Foreign operators investing in this sector may challenge in front of an international arbitral tribunal any regulatory measure taken by the host State if it violates rules or standards contained in an international investment agreement. In several public services cases, host States sought to exclude from arbitral tribunals' jurisdiction those measures having a general character, arguing that this would amount to put under scrutiny the wisdom of measures of general economic policy taken by competent domestic authorities. Arbitral tribunals have constantly rejected the plea, taking the view that their jurisdiction extends over any measure having a direct bearing on an investment, no matter its legal form.

The impact of international investment law on States' regulatory autonomy in the field of public services depends on the definition of vaguely worded provisions and, in particular, on arbitral tribunals' willingness to pay due regard to the

[151] *Contra*, although not with regard to the public services sector, see De Luca 2014, pp. 151–152.

specific social value of these activities. Early arbitral decisions adopted an agnostic approach, by showing a deplorable lack of sensitivity in this regard. This was the case with regard to the discipline of expropriation, as arbitral tribunals tended to focus exclusively on the quantitative impact of host States' regulatory measures upon the investment's legal viability and economic profitability. The approach, aptly dubbed as the "sole effect doctrine", excludes that State's regulatory intent can play any role in distinguishing between legitimate regulation and regulatory expropriation.

A similar approach has also been adopted with regard to the FET standard, as arbitral tribunals sought to progressively broaden its scope. In particular, they have taken the view that one of the FET's main components is hosts States' duty to ensure the stability of the investment's regulatory framework, by avoiding any modification that may frustrate investor's legitimate expectations. If taken to rigidly, this duty may fetter host States' capacity to adapt the legislative environment to ever changing needs and challenges. Despite acknowledging the need to guarantee an adequate regulatory space to national authorities, especially in a sector such as public services, some early decisions adopted an over-broad reading of the duty to protect investor's expectations, paying little attention to States' regulatory purposes.

More recent decisions have shown a bit more sensitivity towards these concerns. Both with regard to the definition of regulatory expropriation and the protection of legitimate expectations under the FET, arbitral tribunals have started to rely upon balancing techniques to accommodate host States' and investors' competing interests. Far from being a panacea, these tools could help international arbitrators to pay greater regard to hosts States' regulatory purposes when assessing whether their measures violated foreign investors' rights. In some cases, arbitral tribunals motivated the shift toward a more balanced approach by making reference to the fact that the activity was not an ordinary commercial one, but a public service.

There is still the need to elaborate a more principled and coherent approach for the determination of the standard of review to be adopted by arbitral tribunals when applying these balancing techniques. As for public services, the analysis has shown the existence of various elements that call for the adoption of a deferential approach in weighting regulatory measures against their impact upon investor's rights. Above all, international arbitrators should pay due consideration to the fact that regulating public services is a core sovereign function which is essential for the well-being of the population and which touches upon key aspects of States' democratic autonomy and legitimacy.

## References

Adlung R (2006) Public services and the GATS. J Int Econ Law 9(2):455–485

American Law Institute (1987) Restatement (third) of the foreign relations law of the United States. American Law Institute Publishers, Saint Paul

Arena A (2011) The GATS notion of public services as an instance of intergovernmental agnosticism: comparative insights from the EU's supranational dialectic. J World Trade 45(3):489–528
Baldwin R, Cave M (1999) Understanding regulation—theory, strategy and practice. OUP, Oxford
Bertoli P, Crespi Reghizzi Z (2014) Regulatory measures, standards of treatment and the law applicable to investment disputes. In: Treves T, Seatzu F, Trevisanut S (eds) Foreign investment, international law and common concerns. Routledge, London, pp 26–49
Boute A (2011) Challenging the re-regulation of liberalized electricity prices under investment arbitration. Energy Law J 32(2):497–539
Brower CH, Brueschke JD (1998) The Iran-United States Claims Tribunal. Martinus Nijhoff, The Hague
Brownlie I (2003) Principles of public international law, 6th edn. OUP, Oxford
Burke-White WW (2010) The argentine financial crisis: state liability under BITs and the legitimacy of the ICSID system. In: Waibel M (ed) The backlash against investment arbitration: perceptions and reality. Kluwer Law International, The Hague, pp 407–432
Burke-White WW, von Staden A (2010) Private litigation in a public sphere: the standard of review in investor-state arbitrations. Yale J Int Law 35(2):283–346
Coe J Jr, Rubins N (2005) Regulatory expropriation and the Tecmed case: context and contributions. In: Weiler T (ed) International investment law and arbitration: leading cases from ICSID, NAFTA, bilateral treaties and customary international law. Cameron May, London, pp 597–667
Choudhury B (2005) Evolution or devolution? Defining fair and equitable treatment in international investment law. J World Invest Trade 6(2):297–320
Christie GC (1962) What constitutes a taking under international law? Br Yearb Int Law 38:310–311
Clayton R (2003) Legitimate expectations, policy and the principle of consistency. Camb Law J 62(1):93–105
Clough D (2005) Regulatory expropriation and competition under NAFTA. J World Invest Trade 6(4):553–584
Costamagna F (2006) Legitimate regulation vs regulatory expropriation in public infrastructure investments after Azurix. Transnatl Dispute Management 4(2)
Craig P (2006) EU administrative law. OUP, Oxford
Crema L (2014) Investors' rights and well-being. Remarks on the interpretation of investment treaties in light of other rights. In: Treves T, Seatzu F, Trevisanut S (eds) Foreign investment, international law and common concerns. Routledge, London, pp 50–70
De Luca A (2014) Non trade values protection and investment protection in EU investment policy. In: Treves T, Seatzu F, Trevisanut S (eds) Foreign investment, international law and common concerns. Routledge, London, pp 137–153
Doak Bishop R, Aguirre Luzi R (2005) Investment claims: first lessons from Argentina. In: Weiler T (ed) International investment law and arbitration: leading cases from the ICSID, NAFTA, bilateral treaties and customary international law. Cameron May, London, pp 425–469
Dolzer R (2003) Indirect expropriation: new developments? NYU Environ Law J 11(1):64–93
Dolzer R (2005) Fair and equitable treatment: a key standard in investment treaties. Int Lawyer 39(1):87–106
Douglas Z (2006) Nothing if not critical for investment treaty arbitration. Arbitr Int 22(1):27–51
Duguit L (1925) Traité de droit constitutionel. Vol 5, Les libertés publiques, 2nd edn. Ancienne Librairie Fontemoing, Paris
Freeman EM (2003) Regulatory expropriation under NAFTA chapter 11: some lessons from the European Court of Human Rights. Columbia J Transnatl Law 42:177–215
Gazzini T (2009) General principles of law in the field of foreign investment. J World Invest Trade 10(1):103–119
Graham C (2005) Human rights and the privatization of public utilities and essential services. In: De Feyter K, Gómez Isa F (eds) Privatization and human rights in the age of globalization. Intersentia, Antwerp, pp 33–56

Haynes J (2013) The evolving nature of the fair and equitable (FET) standard: challenging its increasing pervasiveness in light of developing countries' concerns: the case for regulatory rebalancing. J World Invest Trade 14(1):114–146
Hauriou M (1927) Précis de droit administratif et de droit public, 11th edn. Sirey, Paris
Henckels C (2012) Indirect expropriation and the right to regulate: revisiting proportionality analysis and the standard of review in investor-state arbitration. J Int Econ Law 15(1):223–255
Higgins R (1983) The taking of property by the state: recent developments in international law. Recueil des Courses—Hague Acad Int Law 176:259–391
Hirsch M (2011) Between fair and equitable treatment and stabilization clause: stable legal environment and regulatory change in international investment law. J World Invest Trade 12(6):783–806
Houben I (2008) Public services obligations: moral counterbalance of technical liberalization legislation. Eur Rev Private Law 16(1):7–27
Jèze G (1926) Le service public. Revista de Drept Public, pp 167–179
Karkkainen BC (2006) The Police power revised: phantom incorporation and the roots of takings "muddle". Minn Law Rev 90:826–913
Kavanagh A (2008) Deference or defiance? The limits of the judicial role in constitutional adjudication. In: Huscroft G (ed) Expounding the constitution: essays in constitutional theory. OUP, Oxford, pp 184–216
Kingsbury B, Schill S (2010) Public law concepts to balance investor's rights with state regulatory actions in the public interest—the concept of proportionality. In: Schill S (ed) International investment law and comparative public law. OUP, Oxford, pp 75–104
Krajewski M (2003a) National regulation and trade liberalization in services—the legal impact of the general agreement on trade in services (GATS) on national regulatory autonomy. Kluwer Law International, The Hague
Krajewski M (2003b) Public services and trade liberalization: mapping the legal framework. J Int Econ Law 6(2):341–367
Krajewski M (2012) The impact of international investment agreements on energy regulation. Eur Yearb Int Econ Law 3:343–369
Leonhardsen E (2012) Looking for legitimacy: exploring proportionality analysis in investment treaty arbitration. J Int Dispute Settl 3(1):95–136
Lowe V (2002) Regulation or expropriation? Curr Legal Prob 55:447–466
Mitnick BM (1980) The political economy of regulation. Columbia University Press, New York
Neergaard U (2009) Services of general economic interest: the nature of the beast. In: Krajewski M, Neergaard U, van de Gronden J (eds) The changing legal framework for services of general interest in Europe. TMC Asser Press, The Hague, pp 17–50
Newcombe A (2005) The boundaries of regulatory expropriation in international law. ICSID Rev Foreign Invest Law J 20(1):1–57
Palast G, Oppenheimer J, MacGregor T (2003) Democracy and regulation: how the public can govern essential services. Pluto Press, London-Sterling
Paulsson J (2006) Indirect expropriation: is the right to regulate at risk? Transnatl Dispute Manage 3(2):8–9
Potestà M (2013) Legitimate expectations in investment treaty law: understanding the roots and the limits of a controversial concept. ICSID Rev Foreign Invest Law J 28(1):88–122
Quinot G (2004) Substantive legitimate expectations in South African and European administrative law. Ger Law J 5(1):65–85
Reinisch A (2008) Expropriation. In: Muchlinski P, Ortino F, Schreuer C (eds) The Oxford handbook of international investment law. OUP, Oxford, pp 407–458
Reisman RW, Sloane RD (2004) Indirect expropriation and its valuation in the BIT generation. Br Yearb Int Law 74:115–150
Sacerdoti G (1997) Bilateral treaties and multilateral instruments on investment protection. Recueil des Courses Hague Acad Int Law 269:251–460

Sacerdoti G (1999) The source and evolution of international legal protection for infrastructure investments confronting political and regulatory risk. CEPMLP On-Line J 5(3):7
Schill S (2012) Cross-regime harmonization through proportionality analysis; the case of international investment law, the law of state immunity and human rights. ICSID Rev Foreign Invest Law J 27(1):87–119
Schømberg S (2001) Legitimate expectations in administrative law. OUP, Oxford
Schreuer C (1996) Commentary on the ICSID convention. Article 25. ICSID Rev Foreign Invest Law J 11(2):318–492
Schreuer C (2005a) The concept of expropriation under the ECT and other investments protection treaties. Transnatl Dispute Manage 2(5)
Schreuer C (2005b) Fair and equitable treatment in arbitral practice. J World Invest Trade 6(3):357–386
Schreuer C (2007) Fair and equitable treatment in investment treaty law. In: Ortino F, Liberti L, Sheppard A, Warner H (eds) Investment treaty law, current issues II. British Institute on International and Comparative Law, London, pp 92–96
Steele I (2005) Substantive legitimate expectations: striking the rights balance. Law Q Rev 121:300–328
Stigler G (1971) The theory of economic regulation. Bell J Econ Manage Sci 2(1):3–21
Stone Sweet A (2010) Investor-state arbitration: proportionality's new frontier. Law Ethics Hum Rights 4(1):47–76
Stone Sweet A, Matthews J (2008) Proportionality balancing and global constitutionalism. Columbia J Transnatl Law 47:72–164
Tanzi A (2013) Recent trends in international investment arbitration and the protection of human rights in the public services sector. In: Boschiero N, Scovazzi T, Pitea C, Ragni C (eds) International courts and the development of international law. Essays in Honour of Tullio Treves, TMC Asser Press, The Hague, pp 587–598
Tanzi A (2014) Public interest concerns in international investment arbitration in the water services sector. Problems and prospects for an integrated approach. In: Treves T, Seatzu F, Trevisanut S (eds) Foreign investment, international law and common concerns. Routledge, London, pp 318–335
Tridimas T (2006) General principles of EU law, 2nd edn. OUP, Oxford
Van Harten G, Loughlin M (2006) Investment treaty arbitration as a species of global administrative law. Eur J Int Law 17(1):121–150
Vernon R (1967) Long-run trends in concession contracts. Proc Am Soc Int Law 61:81–89
Wade W, Forsyth C (2000) Administrative law, 8th edn. OUP, Oxford
Wälde T, Dow S (2000) Treaties and regulatory risk in infrastructure investment. J World Trade 34(2):1–61
Wälde T, Kolo A (2001) Environmental regulation, investment protection and 'regulatory taking' in international law. Int Comp Law Q 50:827–835
White G (1961) Nationalization of foreign property. Praeger, London
Woodhouse EJ (2006) The obsolescing bargain redux? Foreign investment in the electric power sector in developing countries. New York J Int Law Policy 38:121–219

# Chapter 5
# NAFTA's Approach to Protecting Public Services: Fragmentary, Asymmetrical, Rigid and Limited

**J. Anthony VanDuzer**

**Abstract** The chapter surveys NAFTA's approach to protecting public services with a view to drawing some conclusions regarding its costs and benefits. The chapter first discusses the scope of NAFTA's application to public services, focussing on the obligations relating to trade in services and investment and the relevant reservations taken by each NAFTA party state. This is followed by an examination of how the specific NAFTA obligations relating to financial services, telecommunications services, energy, government procurement, and competition as well as the treaty's exceptions provisions address public services. Finally a synthesis is provided of NAFTA's approach to public services with a view to identifying its costs and benefits in relation to the approach in GATS and EU trade agreements.

## Contents



J.A. VanDuzer (✉)
University of Ottawa, Ottawa, Canada
e-mail: Anthony.VanDuzer@uOttawa.ca



M. Krajewski (ed.), *Services of General Interest Beyond the Single Market*, Legal Issues of Services of General Interest,
DOI 10.1007/978-94-6265-063-3_5

## 5.1 Introduction

Public services are treated differently under the North American Free Trade Agreement (NAFTA) compared to the WTO General Agreement on Trade in Services (GATS) and European Union (EU) trade treaties.[1] The approach in NAFTA, which is followed in many bilateral and regional agreements worldwide,[2] has three main distinctive characteristics.

First, NAFTA is a negative list agreement—meaning that all of the obligations in the treaty, including those related to services and investment, apply to all state actions except to the extent specifically carved out through reservations or exceptions. By contrast, GATS and EU trade treaties are positive list agreements under which some services obligations only apply to a sector or activity if and to the extent that a state lists it in an national schedule of commitments to the treaty.[3] A positive list approach makes it easier in practice for state parties to limit the scope of their obligations to areas they choose and avoid unanticipated consequences of their obligations, including in relation to public services.

Second, NAFTA contains no general exception from all treaty obligations for any category of public service. There is no exception for services delivered in the exercise of governmental authority as is found in the GATS and many EU trade treaties, nor is there any unifying concept of public services in the treaty. Instead, there are a variety of limited exceptions and country-specific reservations that exclude the application of certain treaty obligations to some categories of public services and to specific kinds of measures that may be related to public services, like subsidies. Reservations vary by country.

Third, NAFTA contains comprehensive obligations relating to investment, which are not found in the GATS or EU trade treaties. These obligations are similar to those found in the bilateral investment treaties of EU member states.[4] NAFTA provides specific protections to the investments of foreign investors, including those in public services where such investment is permitted. Only some of these obligations are subject to exceptions and reservations. As in most bilateral investment treaties, if a country fails to comply with a NAFTA investment obligation, an investor that suffers a loss as a result may seek compensation in binding arbitration.

---

[1] Krajewski 2011a. See e.g. European Community–CARIFORUM Economic Partnership Agreement (2008).

[2] Houde et al. 2007.

[3] Although the final text of the Comprehensive Economic and Trade Agreement between Canada and the EU has not been agreed to, it is reported that it will be the first EU negative list agreement: Council of the European Union, EU Canada Comprehensive Economic and Trade Agreement—landing zones, Note by the Commission, DS 1744/12, 6 November 2012. Apparently, the Parliament has said that this should not be considered a precedent for future agreements, see Krajewski 2011a, p. 9.

[4] Of course, this may change for treaties concluded after the Treaty on the Functioning of the European Union [TFEU] came into force on December 2009. The Comprehensive Trade and Investment Agreement between Canada and the EU may be the first EU treaty with comprehensive investment obligations.

Canada and the United States have essentially followed the NAFTA approach in most subsequent trade treaties.[5] In part, this may be because there has been little political or academic discussion in either country regarding the application of NAFTA to public services generally.[6] There have been significant concerns vocally and consistently expressed by labour organizations and progressive NGOs regarding the risk to particular public services, especially health care, which NAFTA (and other trade obligations) represent.[7] But the Canadian government's consistent response to these concerns has been to flatly deny that the delivery of health, education, social services and other public services is threatened by Canada's existing commitments under the NAFTA.[8] Perhaps as a result of the government's position, there has been limited policy discussion in government or academia about alternative ways to address public services in trade agreements. Even less attention has been paid to these issues in the United States.

Undoubtedly, one other reason for the lack of discussion of trade and public services as a distinct subject of enquiry has been the absence in Canada and the United States of a domestic policy-making framework that uses a concept of public services as starting point for developing general principles that qualify the application of market-based legal disciplines to public services. There is no equivalent to the provisions of the Treaty on the Functioning of the European Union[9] or the European Charter[10] dealing with services of general interest in Canada or the United States.[11] There are no North American institutions comparable to the EU Commission, the Parliament or the Social Protection Committee[12] that deal with these issues. The Biennial Reports on social services of general interest[13] and the

[5]Canada and, to a lesser extent, the US has followed the same approach in its investment treaties.

[6]There has been some academic writing on NAFTA and health care. E.g. Epps and Flood 2002; VanDuzer 2004.

[7]E.g. Grieshaber-Otto and Sanger 2002, pp. 46–84. More recently similar concerns have been expressed regarding possible obligations under a Comprehensive Economic and Trade Agreement between Canada and the EU: see Sinclair 2010.

[8]This commitment was expressed repeatedly by former trade Minister Pierre Pettigrew (e.g. Canada 2000).

[9]TFEU, Articles 14, 106, and Protocol No. 26 on Services of General Interest.

[10]Charter of Fundamental Rights of the European Union, Article 36.

[11]Arguments have been made regarding entitlements to certain public services under Canada's Charter of Rights, e.g. Jackman and Porter 2008. Some public service issues have been addressed in Canadian intergovernmental agreements: Agreement on Internal Trade—Consolidated Version, available at http://www.ait-aci.ca/en/ait/ait_en.pdf, accessed 14 January 2014, and the New West Partnership Agreement entered into by the provinces of British Columbia, Alberta and Saskatchewan, see Compendium of the New West Partnership Agreements available at http://www.gov.sk.ca/nwp, accessed 14 Jan 2014. Under these agreements, most obligations do not apply to government regulation taken for a legitimate purpose. Each agreement goes on to list what legitimate purposes are.

[12]The Social Protection Committee was created in accordance with Article 160 of the TFEU, through Decisions of the European Council in 2000 and 2004. The Committee facilitates cooperation between Member States and the European Commission on social inclusion, health care and long-term care, including pensions.

[13]E.g. European Commission, Commission Staff Working Document, 3rd Biennial Report on Social Services of General Interest, SWD(2013) 40 final, 20 February 2013, p. 40.

forums on such services sponsored by the Presidency of the Council of the European Union have no North American equivalents.

Another reason for the limited attention to public services in North America may be that, despite the concerns noted above, there has been no state-to-state dispute between NAFTA countries in which one party claimed that some public service measure was inconsistent with the agreement. Claims have been made by private investors under NAFTA's investor-state arbitration procedures related to various public services, including waste disposal, water distribution, postal services, and health services. But few of these cases have been successful. As well, the issues in these cases have typically related to the manner in which the state has acted in dealing with the investor, such as whether it met acceptable standards for administrative process or acted in an arbitrary or discriminatory way, rather than the public service character of the measure.[14] While the public nature of the services at issue has played a role in the analysis by the tribunal in at least one case, a distinct approach to public services has not developed.[15]

In this chapter, I will survey NAFTA's approach to protecting public services with a view to drawing some conclusions regarding its costs and benefits. Section 5.2 discusses the scope of NAFTA's application to public services, focussing on the obligations relating to trade in services and investment and the relevant reservations taken by each NAFTA party state. This is followed by an examination of how the specific NAFTA obligations relating to financial services, telecommunications services, energy, government procurement, and competition as well as the treaty's exceptions provisions address public services. Section 5.3 provides a synthesis of NAFTA's approach to public services with a view to identifying its costs and benefits in relation to the approach in GATS and EU trade agreements.

## 5.2 Survey of NAFTA

### *5.2.1 Introduction*

As noted above, NAFTA does not have a general exclusion for any category of public service. There is no equivalent to GATS exception for services "supplied in the exercise of governmental authority" meaning services "supplied neither on a commercial basis, nor in competition with one or more service suppliers."[16]

[14]Concerns about how investor-state tribunals were interpreting the balance between investor-protection and state's right to regulate caused Canada and the US to adopt an interpretation of indirect expropriation that better protected the right to regulate in subsequent US and Canadian trade and investment agreements. Krajewski notes that many investor-state cases have dealt with public services, especially public water services, but the issues have been characterized as human rights issues rather than public services issues, see Krajewski 2012.

[15]*United Parcel Service of America Inc. v. Government of Canada,* UNCITRAL Arbitration, Award on the Merits, 24 May 2007, discussed below.

[16]GATS, Articles I.3(b) and (c).

Instead, various provisions of the treaty limit its application to different aspects of public services. As a negative list agreement, the starting point is that treaty obligations apply to all services, including public services, except to the extent specifically excluded. NAFTA's approach to protecting public services from the application of the market-based disciplines in the treaty has three features: (i) exceptions and country-specific reservations that exempt identified services activities and measures from certain services and investment obligations, (ii) specific chapters on financial services, telecommunications, energy and government procurement that address, among other things, the distinctive public service characteristics of these services and (iii) limited disciplines on state monopolies and state enterprises that recognize their public service responsibilities. In short, the NAFTA approach is not based on an over-arching conception of what defines a public service. For the most part, it provides limited protection to whole areas of public services policy-making, like public health services, and to specific public services measures, but no protection at all for other areas typically considered to be public services like water distribution.

This somewhat fragmentary approach is not surprising given that the overall goal of NAFTA is to promote trade and investment within North America. Public services are not a signficant focus of the treaty. The preamble to the agreement expresses the parties' resolution to "...preserve their flexibility to safeguard the public welfare,..." but only as one of fifteen matters addressed. This aspect of the preamble has not been referred to in cases decided under NAFTA's dispute settlement mechanisms. The preamble makes clear that the principal purpose of the agreement is to "create an expanded and secure market for the goods and services produced in [the party states'] territories." The priority accorded to trade and investment in the preamble is confirmed in a separate objectives provision, which states that the objectives of the agreement are to "eliminate barriers to trade in, and facilitate the cross-border movement of, goods and services" and to "increase substantially investment opportunities".[17] Nowhere in the objectives provision is public welfare mentioned.

The features of NAFTA that address or are likely to affect public services are described in turn below, beginning with the rules most likely to be relevant to public services: NAFTA obligations relating to trade in services and investment.

## *5.2.2 Services and Investment Rules*

### 5.2.2.1 Introduction

Both NAFTA's Chapter 11 on investment and Chapter 12 on services contain an interpretive direction regarding the application of its provisions to some public services. As well they include exceptions and reservations that exclude certain public services and particular existing public services measures from some investment obligations and most services obligations.

[17]NAFTA, Article 102. This approach to interpretation was adopted in *In the Matter of Cross-Border Trucking Services*, USA-Mex-98-2008-01, Final Report of the Panel, 6 February 2001.

#### 5.2.2.2 Scope of Application

**Services**

Chapter 12 applies to measures relating to cross-border trade in services, including public services. Cross-border trade in services is defined to mean the provision of a service

- from the territory of a NAFTA party state (a *Party*) into the territory of another Party (such as medical advice given over the telephone by an American doctor in the United States to a Canadian patient in Canada);
- in the territory of a Party by a person of that Party to a person of another Party (such as an American doctor providing medical treatment to a Canadian who has travelled to the United States); and
- by a national of a Party in the territory of another Party (such as a Mexican doctor providing medical treatment while temporarily in Canada).[18]

These three modes of services supply correspond to GATS mode 1 (cross-border supply), mode 2 (consumption abroad) and mode 4 (presence of natural persons). Unlike the GATS, Chapter 12 does not cover measures related to GATS mode 3, the provision of a service in the territory of a Party through a commercial presence, such as a US business operating a private school in Canada. As discussed under 'Investment' below, Chapter 11 creates extensive and distinctive rules relating to the protection of NAFTA investors and their investments in other NAFTA states that apply to services supplied through a commercial presence, as well as a wide range of other forms of investment.

As well, the services chapter does not apply to government procurement or financial services, each of which is the subject of a separate chapter in NAFTA,[19] or to "subsidies or grants provided by a Party or state enterprise, including government-supported loans, guarantees and insurance."[20] This broad exclusion for state financial support, which is similar to provisions found in EU trade agreements,[21] provides substantial flexibility for the NAFTA countries to provide financial support for public services. As discussed below, the investment chapter provides a more limited exception for procurement, subsidies and grants.

---

[18]NAFTA, Articles 1201(1) and 1213(2). NAFTA also has a separate chapter setting out commitments regarding the temporary entry of business persons (Chapter 16).

[19]NAFTA Chapters 10 and 14 respectively.

[20]NAFTA, Article 1201(2).

[21]Krajewski 2011b, p. 14. There are no obligations in GATS that are tailored to subsidies. Subsidies disciplines were left for future negotiations (GATS, Article XV). Nevertheless, general GATS obligations apply, including national treatment for services listed in national schedules of commitments. For this reason, many countries have included provisions in their schedules preserving their ability to subsidize in a discriminatory way. E.g. European Communities and their Member States, Schedule of Specific Commitments (the European Communities are not bound in relation to subsidies in the public sector), and Canada, Schedule of Specific Commitments (Canada is not bound to grant national treatment in relation to "[t]he supply of a service, or its subsidization, within the public sector" or "[s]ubsidies related to research and development").

**Investment**

Chapter 11 obligations apply in relation to an "investor," which is defined to mean:

- a NAFTA Party state;
- a state enterprise of a NAFTA Party state;
- a natural person who is a national of a NAFTA Party state; and
- an enterprise constituted or organized under the laws of a NAFTA Party state and a branch located in the territory of a NAFTA Party state and carrying out business activities there.[22]

In order to be eligible for protection under the treaty, an investor, as defined, must "seek…to make, be making or [have] made an investment." By including investors who "seek" to make or are in the process of "making" an investment, the definition of investor extends the protections of the agreement to investors even before any investment has actually been made. As discussed below, this intention to provide pre-establishment rights is expressly confirmed by the language in the non-discrimination obligations in Chapter 11, national treatment and MFN, the obligations most likely to be relevant to investors before their investment is in place. In this way, the investment provisions address market access for investors, as well the treatment of investors after they have entered the market. This is a distinctive feature of NAFTA as well as other Canadian and US investment treaties, compared to investment treaties of EU Member states.

The definition of investment in NAFTA is extremely broad. It includes virtually any kind of economic interest, such as ownership interests in enterprises, debt and equity securities issued by an enterprise, all forms of real and personal property including intellectual property, interests that entitle the owner to share in income or profits or that arise out of commitments of capital or other resources and certain contracts and loans. Concessions by states to private parties, such as those that might be given for the distribution of water or gas, are expressly included.[23] The definition goes far beyond investments representing control of an enterprise to include much less significant interests, such as portfolio investment. As well, an "enterprise" is defined to include government-owned entities and not-for-profit entities.[24]

[22]NAFTA, Article 1139. "[E]nterprise" is defined broadly to mean "any entity constituted or organized under applicable law, whether or not for profit, and whether privately-owned or governmentally-owned, including any corporation, trust, partnership, sole proprietorship, joint venture or association" (NAFTA, Article 201).

[23]NAFTA, Article 1139.

[24]The investment chapter provides that if the investor is an enterprise constituted or organized under the laws of a NAFTA Party state but is owned or controlled by persons who are investors of a state or states not party to NAFTA and the enterprise has no substantial business activities in the territory of the NAFTA Party state under whose law it is constituted or organized, the NAFTA Party state complained against may deny that investor the benefits of the agreement, including access to investor-state dispute settlement (NAFTA, Article 1113). In order to deny benefits to such an investor, notification to the NAFTA Party state under whose laws the enterprise is constituted or organized is required in accordance with Article 1803. The NAFTA Party state notified may request consultations under Article 2006. A NAFTA Party state may also deny access in certain other circumstances. The services chapter has a provision (NAFTA, Article 1211(2)) that is identical to Article 1113.

Consequently interests in not-for-profit and public or publicly-controlled entities engaged in public service delivery are investments for the purposes of NAFTA.

Eligible investors of a NAFTA Party may seek compensation through binding arbitration in relation to measures of another NAFTA Party that do not conform to the obligations of that state under Chapter 11.[25] An investor-state case dealing with public services is discussed below. With respect to claims that a NAFTA Party has not fulfilled its obligations under other provisions of NAFTA, including those relating to services, there is no such private right to relief. Such claims may only be addressed through state-to-state dispute settlement under NAFTA Chapter 20. While investor-state arbitration is common in the investment treaties of member states, it is unknown in WTO agreements and EU trade treaties.

#### 5.2.2.3 Interpretive Direction

Pursuant to NAFTA Articles 1101(4) and 1201(3), nothing in the investment or services chapters respectively shall be construed to

> prevent a Party from providing a service or performing a function such as law enforcement, correctional services, income security or insurance, social security or insurance, social welfare, public education, public training, health, and child care in a manner *not inconsistent with this Chapter*. [emphasis added]

These provisions have never been interpreted in NAFTA dispute settlement proceedings. Nevertheless, since they relate only to a Party state performing services in a manner "not inconsistent with this Chapter," they are not exceptions from the substantive services and investment obligations discussed below. Indeed, if this direction were interpreted as an exception it would make some of the exceptions and reservations related to public services in NAFTA redundant.[26] For example, the list of services used in these provisions is identical to that in Annex II reservations taken by all three NAFTA countries. Consequently, there is no basis to interpret these provisions as exceptions.[27] Nevertheless, these provisions are part of the context for interpreting the substantive obligations in each chapter. Any interpreter of an obligation should seek an interpretation that would permit a Party to provide services of the kinds indicated. This list of services benefiting from this interpretation is expressed not to be exhaustive, but there is no general language indicating what other kinds of services should be included. Accordingly, the character of what fits within this provision is likely to be determined by reference to the items on the list.

---

[25]The investor-state dispute settlement process is described in VanDuzer 2002, pp. 51–71. This right to seek compensation is also available in relation to certain provisions of Chapters 14 and 15.

[26]Such an interpretation would be contrary to the effectiveness principle of treaty interpretation. Lennard 2002, p. 17; Maki 2000.

[27]A similarly worded provision describing states right to act to protect the environment (Article 1114(1)) has been interpreted as an interpretive direction only (Kinnear et al. 2008).

#### 5.2.2.4 Services and Investment Obligations Subject to Canadian Reservations

Some of the obligations in Chapters 11 and 12 are subject to reservations. In this section, these obligations are described. Other obligations that cannot be reserved against are discussed later in the chapter.

With respect to cross-border trade in services, Chapter 12 obliges each NAFTA Party to provide the better of national treatment and most favoured nation (*MFN*) treatment to services providers from another NAFTA Party.[28] So, for example, Canada is obliged to treat US water services suppliers no less favourably than it treats, in like circumstances, Canadian water services providers *and* no less favourably than water service providers from any other country.[29] Chapter 12 also provides that no NAFTA Party can impose requirements for a local presence in its national market as a condition of allowing NAFTA services suppliers to operate in the market.[30]

With respect to services delivered through an investment, Chapter 11 imposes similar rules. Canada, the US and Mexico must each provide the better of national treatment and MFN treatment in relation to investors of the other NAFTA Parties and their investments.[31] In the investment chapter, the obligations are expressed to apply with respect to the "establishment, acquisition, expansion, management, conduct, operation, and sale or other disposition of investments."[32] Because the scope of the national treatment and MFN obligations extends to the "establishment, acquisition, [and] expansion" of an investment, they benefit investors' investments prior to the moment that their investments enter the national market of a NAFTA Party. As noted, such pre-establishment rights are not commonly found in investment treaties entered into by European countries but are characteristic of those entered into by the US and Canada.[33] Because of these pre-establishment rights, the carve-outs from these obligations in the Annex I and Annex II

---

28 NAFTA, Article 1204.

29 NAFTA, Articles 1202 and 1203.

30 NAFTA, Article 1205.

31 NAFTA, Articles 1102, 1103, and 1104. Chapter 11 clarifies that the national treatment obligation means that requirements of a NAFTA Party that its nationals hold a minimum level of equity in a NAFTA investor are prohibited and NAFTA investors cannot be required to sell their investments simply because of their nationality (NAFTA, Article 1102(4)).

32 In the case of measures of a state or province, the national treatment obligation is modified. States and provinces are only obliged to grant treatment no less favourable than the most favourable treatment accorded, in like circumstances, to investors and investments of the Party of which it forms a part (NAFTA, Article 1102(3)).

33 See US Model Bilateral Investment Treaty, Articles 3 and 4 and Canadian Model Foreign Investment Promotion and Protection Agreement, Articles 3 and 4. Also investors eligible for protection are defined to include persons seeking to make an investment (Canadian Model Foreign Investment Promotion and Protection Agreement, Article 1; US Model Bilateral Investment Treaty, Article 1). Pre-establishment rights are also found in some Japanese and Australian investment treaties.

reservations for each country described below are essential for public services schemes that permit only local private suppliers, including not-for-profit organizations, such as local not-for-profit private hospitals to provide services.

Chapter 11 prohibits a NAFTA Party state from imposing specified requirements (referred to as *performance requirements*) in connection with the "establishment, acquisition, expansion, management, conduct or operation" of an investment of a NAFTA investor, such as requirements

- to source inputs locally or meet domestic content requirements,
- to meet export performance targets or restrict imports, or
- to transfer technology to a person in its territory.[34]

Again, because the scope of this performance requirement obligation extends to the "establishment, acquisition, [and] expansion" of an investment, these obligations apply to new investments prior to the moment that they enter the national market of a NAFTA party.[35] For example, none of the listed performance requirements could be imposed by the United States as a condition allowing a Mexican investor into the country. The performance requirement obligation does not prohibit the kinds of requirements typically imposed on public service providers, such as those related to public access, quality or affordability. They do prohibit requirements for an investor to be an exclusive supplier of goods or services to a specific region.[36] Such a requirement might be imposed in relation to a public service like a requirement to provide passenger rail transportation services in a part of the country. NAFTA Party states may not condition the receipt by an investor of an advantage, such as a subsidy, on a subset of these performance requirements. These prohibited performance requirements include domestic sourcing or content requirements but not exclusive regional supply.[37]

As well, under Article 1107, NAFTA prohibits the imposition by a Party of nationality requirements for senior managers of enterprises formed under its laws that are investments of investors from other NAFTA countries. This obligation does not apply to nationality requirements regarding a majority of members of the board of directors of an enterprise, so long as these requirements do not affect control of the enterprise.

All these investment obligations in Chapter 11 are subject to some exceptions. The national treatment, MFN and prohibition on nationality requirement obligations do not apply to government procurement or to "subsidies or grants provided by a Party or state enterprise, including government-supported loans, guarantees and insurance."[38] In this way, NAFTA permits financial support for public services

[34]These obligations go beyond the requirements of the WTO Agreement on Trade-related Investment Measures, (1994).

[35]Again, this obligation may be subject to reservations as discussed below.

[36]NAFTA, Article 1106(1)(g).

[37]NAFTA, Article 1106.

[38]NAFTA, Article 1108(7).

that discriminates in favour of local suppliers of such services.[39] The performance requirement prohibition is subject to some more narrowly targeted exceptions.[40] The application of country-specific reservations to the services and investment obligations described in this section that apply to public services are discussed in the next section.

## *5.2.3 NAFTA's Annex I and Annex II Reservations*

### 5.2.3.1 Introduction

NAFTA permits Parties to take reservations against NAFTA services and investment disciplines relating to national treatment and MFN as well as—in the case of cross-border services—the prohibition on local presence requirements and—in the case of investments—the prohibitions on certain performance requirements and nationality requirements for senior managers. Annex I reservations apply only to existing non-conforming measures of the NAFTA Parties, while Annex II reservations apply to existing and future measures in discrete areas of policy-making identified in each reservation, including certain public services. The annexes are the most important limit on the application of the disciplines in NAFTA to public services.

### 5.2.3.2 Annex I Reservations

Annex I to NAFTA contains a national schedule for each NAFTA Party in which it lists specific non-conforming measures that are to be excluded from the obligations in the treaty identified in the reservation. No Party may add new non-conforming measures to this list and an amendment to a measure is only protected against the application of the treaty "to the extent that the amendment does not decrease the conformity of the measure, as it existed immediately before the amendment."[41] Also, once a measure subject to the reservation is liberalized, in the sense that some non-conforming aspect of it is removed, the obligations apply to the measure as amended. As a result, if a Party state changes a listed measure to, for example, remove a preference in favour of domestic businesses, then the reservation continues to apply to the amended measure. However, the Party state cannot subsequently reinstate the preference or change the measure in any other

[39] An example would be discrimination against foreign education services suppliers.

[40] NAFTA, Article 1108(8). These exceptions provide that certain of the prohibitions do not apply to government procurement, requirements to qualify for export promotion programs, foreign aid programs or preferential tariffs or quotas.

[41] NAFTA, Articles 1206(1)(c) and 1108(1)(c). For financial services, reservations are permitted under Articles 1409(1) and (4).

way that makes it less consistent with the Party's obligations under the treaty. This so-called "ratchet" effect means that when a state liberalizes a measure listed in its Schedule to Annex I, it becomes bound to the new level of openness provided by the liberalized measure.[42]

All three NAFTA states have listed certain federal-level measures in their schedule to Annex I, few of which implicate public services. One example related to public services is a reservation in relation to the privatization of state assets taken by Canada from the national treatment obligation, the prohibition on certain performance requirements and nationality requirements for senior managers.[43] Under this reservation, if Canada sold off assets employed in the delivery of a public service, like publicly-owned hospitals that provide medical care to military veterans, it could favour a Canadian purchaser over a purchaser from the US or Mexico.

At the time NAFTA was signed, the Parties intended that each of their states and provinces would prepare a list of measures to be included in their schedule to Annex I. In a subsequent exchange of letters, the three NAFTA Parties agreed that all non-conforming provincial and state measures in existence prior to the date NAFTA came into force, 1 January 1994, would benefit from this reservation.[44] All existing non-conforming local government measures were also excluded in the treaty.[45]

In summary, Annex I reservations provide protection for any listed federal measure as well as public services regimes in the NAFTA Parties that are within provincial, state nor local jurisdiction and were in place on 1 January 1994. This would include, for example, most health, education and social services in Canada and the United States. In practice, however, the effective scope of these reservations will likely diminish over time as federal, provincial and state programs evolve.[46] As noted by Krajewski and others, public services are inherently dynamic.[47] In many North American jurisdictions, this dynamism is reflected in new government measures reducing the scope of public funding and direct state provision of services in favour of private provision or public/private partnerships.[48] The result of such liberalizing measures is the diminution of protection from NAFTA obligations under Annex I reservations.

[42]Krajewski 2011a; and VanDuzer et al. 2013, p. 241.

[43]It is not clear why this is not an Annex II reservation, since it applies to an area of activity rather than a specific measure.

[44]Exchange of Letters between Canada, the U.S. and Mexico (29 March 1996), cited in de Mestral 1998.

[45]NAFTA, Articles 1206(1)(a)(iii) and 1108(a)(iii).

[46]Johnson 2002.

[47]Krajewski 2011b, p. 41. This is also noted by the European Commission in European Commission, A Quality Framework for Services of General Economic Interest in Europe, COM(2011) 900 final, 20 December 2011.

[48]Though they take many forms, most public/private partnerships provide a service through a partnership with one or more private parties and a government entity. Typically, the private party undertakes some financial or operational risk related to the provision of the service.

Whether an Annex I reservation applies or not, NAFTA Parties cannot introduce new measures in relation to public services that discriminate against services providers from other Parties or are otherwise inconsistent with applicable NAFTA obligations. To do that an Annex II reservation must be available, as discussed below.

#### 5.2.3.3 Annex II Reservation for Social Services

Annex II reservations apply to federal, state, provincial and local government[49] measures in areas identified by each NAFTA country in its schedule to Annex II of NAFTA. Within the areas identified in their reservations, governments may introduce new measures that are more restrictive than the regime that existed at the time NAFTA entered into force notwithstanding that such measures do not conform to the obligations reserved against. All three NAFTA parties took identical Annex II reservations relating to certain public services (the *Social Services Reservation*). Each country

> …reserves the right to adopt or maintain any measure with respect to the provision of public law enforcement and correctional services, and the following services to the extent that they are social services established or maintained for a public purpose: income security or insurance, social security or insurance, social welfare, public education, public training, health, and child care.[50]

Canada's schedule provides that its Annex II reservation for these social services only applies to the national treatment and MFN obligations, the prohibition on requirements for a local presence to be able to provide a service and nationality requirements for senior management in Chapters 11 and 12.[51] Canada's reservation does not extend to the performance requirements prohibition in Chapter 11. One result of Canada's reservation is that the market access guaranteed by the national treatment and MFN obligations need not be provided in the areas identified in the Social Services Reservation. The Annex II reservations of Mexico and the United States also apply to national treatment but not to the MFN obligation or the performance requirements prohibition. Mexico's reservation extends to the prohibition on nationality requirements for senior managers.

This Social Services Reservation has not been addressed in state-to-state or investor-state dispute settlement but Canadian and American officials have suggested divergent interpretations. Canadian government representatives have said

[49] Though NAFTA Annex II is not clear as to whether it applies to measures by governments below the national level, it appears to be understood as applicable to such measures: Johnson 1994, p. 309.

[50] NAFTA, Canada's Schedule to Annex II, Sector: Social Services.

[51] Canada's Annex I and II reservations regarding national treatment and most favoured nation treatment are deemed to apply to the financial services obligations in Articles 1405 and 1406 (NAFTA, Article 1409(4)). Additional reservations are permitted under Article 1409.

that the broad wording of the Social Services Reservation was adopted intentionally to permit the provision to be interpreted flexibly and, significantly, that it is largely up to each Party to decide whether it views a particular service as falling within the reservation or not.[52] By contrast, in a 1995 communication to states, the US Trade Representative (USTR) suggested the following interpretation of the reservation.

> The reservation…is intended to cover services which are similar to those provided by a government, such as childcare or drug treatment programs. If those services are supplied by a private firm, on a profit or a not-for-profit basis, Chapter Eleven [investment] and Twelve [services] apply.

Elsewhere in the same document the USTR expressed the view that Chapters 11 and 12 apply once "[a] state allows private providers to offer similar services on a commercial basis."[53] Such after-the-fact unilateral statements regarding the meaning of a treaty are not likely to affect its interpretation should the matter come before a dispute settlement panel.[54] Statements regarding the subjective interpretation of a Party will not be relied on to replace a textual analysis.[55] Nevertheless, both cannot be right and the existence of such a large disparity in understanding suggests a real prospect for disputes arising between Canada and the United States regarding the scope of the Social Services Reservation. None have arisen so far, however.

Some support may be offered for both interpretations. The NAFTA preamble and objectives might be relied on to argue for a narrow interpretation of the Social Services Reservation. Consistent with the approach adopted in Cross-Border Trucking, one of only three (3) state-to-state panel decisions under NAFTA, the reservation may be viewed as being in the nature of an exception to the overall

---

[52]Letter from John Weekes dated 31 January 1995 to the provinces and Letter from Douglas Waddell dated 22 September 1995 to the provinces, quoted in Schwartz 1997. Professor Schwartz also cites some criticism of this interpretation from the government of Ontario.

[53]USTR 1995. In effect, the USTR's interpretation appears to be close to the governmental services exception defined in GATS, Article 1.3.

[54]This is consistent with the approach in *In the Matter of Cross-Border Trucking Services*, USA-Mex-98-2008-01, Final Report of the Panel, 6 February 2001, where the Panel refused to consider the subjective intent of the United States in relation to its moratorium on Mexican trucking operations in the US (at para 214). In limited circumstances, statements by WTO Members regarding the meaning of certain provisions have been held by dispute settlement panels to be relevant for interpreting a Member's obligations. In *United States—Sects. 301-310 of the Trade Act of 1974*, Report of the Panel, WT/DS152/R, statements made in a panel proceeding by persons with authority to bind the state and intending to bind the state were held to be relevant.

[55]There is no NAFTA case on this precise issue. In *European Communities—Customs Classification of Certain Computer Equipment,* Report of the Appellate Body, WT/DS62/AB/R, WT/DS67/AB/R, WT/DS68/AB/R, the WTO Appellate Body refused to adopt an interpretation of "automatic data processing equipment" that the UK had relied on in its negotiations with the US, even in the face of US argument that the meaning adopted in negotiations had informed its expectations. The Appellate Body ruled that the interests of all Members in being able to rely on the text of an agreement meant that interpretation had to be grounded in the text alone. See Maki 2000, pp. 354–356, Lennard 2002, pp. 72–73.

trade and investment liberalization objectives of the agreement,[56] and so should be interpreted narrowly. Such an approach would be consistent with the American position. However, giving effect to the very narrow US position that any private provision takes a service outside the Annex II reservation would virtually exclude the application of the Annex II exemption to many public services. For example, most doctors' and hospital services in Canada are delivered by private parties that are fully funded by the state. Under the US approach, these would be fully subject to the obligations of NAFTA. The US approach would limit services excluded by the Social Services Reservation to those delivered by the state, in a manner similar to the GATS exclusion for services in the exercise of governmental authority, but the Social Services Reservation would be narrower in scope because it only applies to services in the discrete areas identified in the reservation.

On the other hand, it is possible to argue for a broader interpretation. The phrase "social service established or maintained for a public purpose" has a broad ordinary meaning.[57] Neither social service nor public purpose is defined in the agreement. "Social service" is defined broadly in the *Oxford English Dictionary* as "a service supplied for the benefit of the community, esp., one provided by the state, as education, health care, housing, etc."[58] This definition suggests that social services typically are services provided directly by the state but may include private supply. For privately delivered services, such as private schools, it would seem necessary to demonstrate that a particular measure was related to services with respect to which a state had undertaken some responsibility to ensure that they were being delivered for the benefit of the community. This might include a consideration of the nature and extent of state involvement in the delivery of the service, including the degree of public funding and the role played by the state in ensuring that the services were provided by private parties in a manner that achieves a public benefit. The interpretive direction in Chapters 11 and 12 discussed above provides no support for a broad interpretation of the reservation that

[56]This view is consistent with how the WTO Members have agreed to interpret the exclusion for services in the exercise of governmental authority (see Krajewski 2011a, p. 29, citing WTO Council for Trade in Services, Report of the Meeting Held on 14 October 1998, Note by the Secretariat, S/C/M/30, 12 November 1998, para 22(b)). Such an approach, however, is not consistent with WTO case law holding that there is no distinctive approach to interpreting exception provisions like GATT Article XX. In *European Communities—Measures Concerning Meat and Meat Products (Hormones)*, Report of the Appellate Body, WT/DS26/AB/R, WT/DS48/AB/R, para 104, the Appellate Body said that "merely, characterizing a treaty provision as an 'exception' does not by itself justify a 'stricter' or 'narrower' interpretation of that provision that would not be warranted...by applying the normal rule of treaty interpretation." See generally, Newcombe 2011, p. 361.

[57]This is also the conclusion of Schwartz 1997.

[58]*Oxford English Dictionary* 2009: "A public purpose has for its objective the promotion of the public health, safety, morals, general welfare, security, prosperity, and contentment of all the inhabitants or residents within a given political division, as, for example, a state, the sovereign powers of which are exercised to promote such public purpose or public business." http://www.oed.com. Accessed 14 January 2014.

would allow private supply of public services, since it is restricted to services provided directly by the state.

A broader approach does not, however, require adopting the Canadian position that, in effect, the content of the social service reservation may be defined by each Party. In the absence of clear language to this effect, what falls within the Social Services Reservation cannot be whatever a state asserts is a measure related to "social services established or maintained for a public purpose." The attributes of the funding, delivery and regulation of the service, among other things, would have to be examined. Regardless of the meaning of the public purpose limitation, it will not always be obvious what falls into some of the categories of services identified in Annex II. For example, what are considered health services provided for a public purpose will vary over time with a state and from one state to the next.

In short, while a narrow interpretation can be supported to some extent, there is also support for a broader view. Given the untested nature of the Social Services Reservation, there is residual uncertainty regarding how it will be applied. Reliable conclusions about the extent to which NAFTA commitments apply to the listed public services are difficult. Some such uncertainty is the inevitable consequence of applying a short, broadly worded treaty provision to services subject to a range of complex regulation like public services. What is clear is that the Social Service Reservation represents a different approach to dealing with public services than is found in the GATS or EU trade treaties, as discussed below. It provides an exhaustive list of specific areas that are protected, to a limited extent, from the obligations in the treaty. Many services considered public services in most countries, such as water services, are not listed. By contrast, as discussed below, GATS and EU trade treaties exclude public services based on their functional and operational characteristics and provide scope for states to decide for themselves what constitutes a public service in some cases.

#### 5.2.3.4 Other Annex II Reservations Related to Public Services

Several other Annex II reservations in NAFTA relate to particular public services or aspects of public services.[59] Canada, the United States and Mexico have each taken a reservation against the national treatment obligation and the prohibition on local presence requirements in relation to "any measure according rights or preferences to socially or economically disadvantaged minorities,…". Canada has also taken a reservation against these obligations as well as MFN and the performance requirements prohibition permitting it to deny to foreign investors and service providers any right or preference that it gives to aboriginal peoples. These would include a wide range of social assistance and other sorts of preferences for the benefit of the identified groups.

[59]The Appendix to this chapter summarizes the Parties' reservations under Annex II.

All three countries have listed telecommunications networks and telecommunications services in their schedules to Annex II, though the forms of these reservations vary.[60] The United States reservation applies only to national treatment, MFN treatment and the prohibition on local presence requirements. Canadian and Mexican reservations extend to the prohibition on nationality requirements for senior managers as well as these obligations. Other reservations common to the three countries relate to air and marine transport and cabotage.

In addition, Mexico has taken a reservation against the national treatment and MFN obligations and the prohibition on local presence requirements in relation to any measure that it adopts or maintains related to postal services as well as "telegraph services, radiotelegraphy services, satellite communications services…, and railroad services." Mexico has also taken reservations for measures related to broadcasting and energy services.[61]

## *5.2.4 Services and Investment Rules not Subject to National Reservations*

### 5.2.4.1 Introduction

A variety of NAFTA services and investment obligations are not subject to Annex I or Annex II reservations or the exception for subsidies and government procurement described above. These include rules regarding the licensing and certification of services suppliers in Chapter 12, as well as, more significantly, the prohibition on the expropriation of investments of NAFTA investors without compensation and the requirement to provide fair and equitable treatment to investments of such investors in Chapter 11. Any measure of a Party that is contrary to these latter obligations is a breach of the treaty and may be the subject of a claim by an investor of another Party that suffers loss as a result. An investor-state arbitration tribunal may award financial compensation to such an investor. These kinds of provisions do not appear in any EU agreement, though they are typical of the more than 1200 bilateral investment treaties negotiated by individual member states.[62] While it is generally recognized that the application of these standards must take into account the need for the state to be able to regulate and otherwise act in the public interest, there is substantial disagreement regarding what government actions are insulated from investors' claims.[63]

---

[60]This reservation does not apply to providers of enhanced or value-added services whose underlying telecommunications transmission facilities are leased from providers of public telecommunications transport networks.

[61]Mexico reserves to itself the provision of services and investment in electricity "supplied as a public service" (NAFTA, Annex 602.3(1)(c)).

[62]VanDuzer et al. 2013, p. 408.

[63]VanDuzer et al. 2013, pp. 410–415.

#### 5.2.4.2 Licencing and Certification Requirements

Chapter 12 seeks to ensure that measures related to licensing and certification of services suppliers do not operate as unnecessary barriers to trade and obliges each Party to "endeavor" to ensure that each such measure

- is based on objective and transparent criteria, such as competence and the ability to provide a service;
- is not more burdensome than necessary to ensure the quality of the service; and
- does not constitute a disguised restriction on the cross-border provision of a service.[64]

These rather general requirements follow language used in the GATS, though specific WTO disciplines based on these requirements are still being negotiated.[65] As has been noted by others, these standards are hard to apply in the context of public services like health and education services where a variety of goals other than quality of the service, narrowly conceived, are fundamental determinants of public policy. It is not clear, for example, to what extent a measure that imposes a universal service obligation on a supplier of hospital services as a condition of permitting the supplier to offer such services would be considered to relate to the quality of the service. Even if the measure was found to relate to quality, it is not clear to what extent a new universal service obligation would be considered no more burdensome than necessary to ensure the quality of the service. Alternative ways of ensuring the availability of hospital services to the population, such as some form of program providing financial incentives to suppliers, are certainly conceivable.[66]

As formulated in NAFTA, these obligations relating to licencing and certification are best endeavours undertakings only. Rather than a guarantee that the Parties' domestic regulation will meet these standards, these provisions require states simply to make a good faith effort to comply. As well, these kinds of provisions only become relevant when foreign supply of the service is allowed by a Party. As discussed in the next section, NAFTA Parties are not obliged generally to allow foreign supply.

#### 5.2.4.3 Market Access

NAFTA Parties have no obligation in NAFTA's services chapter to provide market access to services suppliers from other NAFTA Party states. Existing quantitative limitations on market access for cross-border trade in services, such as non-discriminatory limits on the number of service suppliers, may be maintained, subject to some specific

[64]NAFTA, Article 1210(1).

[65]GATS, Article VI. There is also an annex to the services chapter that obliges that NAFTA parties to encourage professional bodies in each country to develop mutually acceptable licensing standards for professionals (Annex 1210.5).

[66]Luff 2003, pp. 204–6; Krajewski 2011b; Adlung 2003, p. 455.

liberalization commitments undertaken, and while the Parties must negotiate with a view to removing existing restrictions, NAFTA allows Parties to adopt new market access restrictions.[67] By contrast, under GATS, market access obligations apply to sectors listed in a member's schedule of commitments subject to any limitation written into the schedule.[68] Consequently, NAFTA gives Canada, the US and Mexico significant flexibility to exclude foreign services suppliers through non-discriminatory market access limitations like quotas.

#### 5.2.4.4 Investment Obligations

In terms of their impact on the delivery and regulation of public services, the investment obligations in Chapter 11 that are not subject to reservations are likely to be more significant than the services commitments in Chapter 12. The next section discusses the most significant of the Chapter 11 obligations: the obligation to provide fair and equitable treatment to foreign investments and the obligation not to expropriate foreign investments without certain requirements being met including the payment of compensation.

**Fair and Equitable Treatment (FET)**

Article 1105(1) provides that investments of NAFTA investors must be given at least "treatment in accordance with international law, including fair and equitable treatment and full protection and security"[69] Arbitral tribunals have adopted inconsistent and, in some awards, quite broad interpretations of this standard. While it is far beyond the scope of this paper to try to define this inherently open-ended standard, a number of commentators have expressed concerns that the FET standard as it has been applied creates a significant risk that it will be used to constrain a state's sovereignty and its ability to regulate in the public interest.[70] A particular concern is that this obligation has been interpreted to protect an investor's legitimate expectations, based on the legal regime of the host country at the time the investment was made. Strong protection of investor's expectations in this regard would make it difficult for states to change their regimes. In particular, returning to public provision of a privatized service or the imposition of substantially more intrusive regulation of a service to ensure that it meets public goals could be prohibited in some circumstances on the basis that such a change was considered

---

[67]NAFTA, Articles 1207, 1208. Federal level restrictions must be listed by each party in its Schedule to Annex V of NAFTA. Local government restrictions do not have to be notified (Article 1207(3)). Market access for investors is guaranteed through the pre-establishment operation of the national treatment and MFN obligations, subject to the exceptions and reservations in NAFTA, including the Annex I and Annex II reservations described above.

[68]GATS, Article XVI.

[69]NAFTA, Article 1105.

[70]Kläger 2011, p. 241; Mayeda 2007, p. 273. For a synthesis of the standard see UNCTAD 2012b, pp. 62–63.

contrary to the investor's legitimate expectations when it made the investment.[71] A country that experiments with private supply or increased private supply of a public service might be constrained if it decided to return to public provision. In 2001, the NAFTA Parties adopted a binding interpretation of this obligation with a view to narrowing its application. They stated that the obligation imposes only the customary international law standard for the treatment of aliens. Despite this statement, significant uncertainty remains regarding what the standard requires.[72]

**Prohibition on Expropriation without Compensation**

As well, a NAFTA Party must not, directly or indirectly, nationalize or expropriate investments of investors of other Parties, or take a measure tantamount to nationalization or expropriation, except upon complying with certain requirements. The state action must be

- for a public purpose,
- on a non-discriminatory basis,
- in accordance with due process of law and Article 1105(1)(the FET obligation), and
- on payment of compensation equivalent to the fair market value of the investment immediately before the expropriation took place.

Compensation must be paid without delay in a form that is fully realizable.[73]

Like most investment treaties, NAFTA applies to both direct and indirect expropriation. Direct expropriation refers to a situation in which a state takes title to the property of a foreign investor or otherwise transfers the benefit of the foreign investor's investment to itself, typically through an outright seizure. What constitutes indirect expropriation is much more difficult to define and, potentially, much more problematic for public services provision. Indirect expropriation refers to state action that deprives the foreign investor of the ability to make use of its property in some substantial way, but ownership remains with the investor. An indirect expropriation can occur even if the host state does not benefit from the limitation

[71]This approach has been more common in investor-state arbitration awards interpreting similar obligations in other investment treaties. E.g. *Tecnicas Medioambientales Tecmed S.A. v. United Mexican States*, ICSID Case No. ARB(AF)/00/2, Award, 29 May 2003, para 154; *CME Czech Republic B.V. v. Czech Republic*, UNCITRAL Arbitration, Final Award, 14 March 2003, para 601; *Occidental Exploration and Production Company v. Republic of Ecuador*, LCIA Case No. UN 3467, Final Award, 1 July 2004, para 190.

[72]Free Trade Commission 2001. Where the Free Trade Commission established under NAFTA has interpreted a provision of NAFTA, the interpretation is binding on arbitral tribunals (NAFTA, Article 1131). There has been some controversy about the legitimacy of this interpretation: see VanDuzer 2002.

[73]NAFTA, Articles 1110(1), (2) and (3). Certain other obligations are also imposed in Chapter 11, which are not subject to reservations. NAFTA Article 1109 requires each NAFTA Party to permit all financial transfers, like profits, fees, dividends and loan repayments relating to an investment freely and without delay. Exceptions permit Parties to prevent transfers where they are applying their laws in areas like bankruptcy, such as to prevent preferences to be given to investors to the prejudice of other creditors.

on the foreign investor's ability to use its property. It can also occur through a series of acts, sometimes referred to as "creeping expropriation". Defining an indirect expropriation requires specifying the degree of diminished control necessary to qualify as an expropriation. It is impossible, however, to cite a single rule applicable in all circumstances that precisely identifies the degree of control that must be lost for an expropriation to have occurred.

Some NAFTA investor-state tribunals have considered that diminished control or deprivation of the benefits of property alone is sufficient to constitute an indirect expropriation applying what is called the "sole effects doctrine". For these tribunals, the host state's motivation for the measure is irrelevant.[74] Other tribunals have rejected this approach. Instead, deprivation is treated as a necessary but not sufficient condition for a finding of indirect expropriation. The character of the measure, including, in particular, whether it is a regulatory act for a public purpose needs to be considered.[75] Under this approach, non-discriminatory regulation for a public purpose undertaken in good faith would not be considered an indirect expropriation. Traditionally, this has been referred to as the "police power" of states. Thus, while most regulatory measures will not result in a deprivation substantial enough to be considered an expropriation in any case, even if a measure did reach this threshold, it would not be an expropriation if it is within the police powers. Such an approach could insulate most state measures related to public services from successful compensation claims by investors in investor-state arbitration.

To address uncertainty regarding the application of this provision, Canada and the US have adopted a more specific expression of the nature of these obligations in treaties subsequent to NAFTA. In particular, because of the existence of a broad police powers carve-out from expropriation is not universally acknowledged,[76] Canada and the US have adopted a detailed statement as to what constitutes an indirect expropriation requiring compensation to describe what should be considered regulatory measures that do not constitute an expropriation.[77] In the US model bilateral investment treaty, for example, whether or not an indirect expropriation has occurred is to be determined using several criteria:

- An indirect expropriation must have an effect equivalent to a direct expropriation, even though there is no formal transfer of title or an outright seizure;
- The determination of whether an indirect expropriation has occurred requires a case-by-case analysis, including a consideration of the character and economic impact of the government action and the extent to which the action "interferes with distinct, reasonable investment-backed expectations";

[74]E.g. *Fireman's Fund Insurance Company v. United Mexican States*, ICSID Case No. ARB(AF)/02/1, Award, 17 July 2006, para 176(f).

[75]E.g. *Chemtura Corporation v. Government of Canada*, UNCITRAL Arbitration, Award, 2 August 2010.

[76]E.g. Hoffman 2008, p. 165.

[77]UNCTAD identifies the adoption of such an approach as a "clear trend" (UNCTAD 2012a, p. 86).

- The fact that a measure or series of measures of a party state has an adverse effect on the economic value of an investment does not by itself establish that an indirect expropriation has occurred; and
- "Except in rare circumstances, non-discriminatory regulatory measures that are designed and applied to protect legitimate public welfare objectives, such as public health, safety, and the environment, do not constitute indirect expropriations".[78]

This kind of specification provides a relatively clear direction to interpreters of the treaty regarding whether a public service measure should be found to be an indirect expropriation. To the extent that this standard is applied there would appear to be substantial scope for states to take action in relation to public services. There is residual uncertainty, however regarding some elements of this specification. For example, what are the "rare circumstances" in which public welfare regulation will trigger a compensation obligation and what are public welfare objectives beyond those specifically enumerated?[79] Would measures revoking an investor's licence to provide water services on the basis that the service was poor or unpopular fall into this category? Nevertheless, even though this attempted clarification leaves significant residual uncertainty, it does represent an improvement over NAFTA's terse and vague formulation of the expropriation standard.[80]

### 5.2.5 *Investor-State Cases Related to Public Services*

The application of NAFTA Chapter 11's broad and uncertain standards of investor protection to public services has encouraged investors to make a number of investor-state claims in relation to public services measures of the NAFTA Parties, including waste disposal,[81] water distribution,[82] postal services,[83] and health

---

[78]US Model Bilateral Investment Treaty (2012), Annex B.

[79]For an example of the chilling effect that investment protections can have in this regard, see Sinclair 2014, fn 32.

[80]There is also a debate over whether the formulations adopted are different from what customary international law would require in any case (VanDuzer et al. 2013, pp. 253–255).

[81]*Robert Azinian, Kenneth Davitian, & Ellen Baca v. United Mexican States*, ICSID Case No. ARB(AF)/97/2, Award, 1 November 1999 (waste collection and disposal); *Metalclad v. United Mexican States*, ICSID Case No. ARB(AF)/97/1, Award, 30 August 2000 (toxic waste disposal facility); *Waste Management, Inc. v. United Mexican States*, ICSID Case No. ARB (AF)/00/3, Award, 30 April 2004 (waste collection and disposal); *S. D. Myers Inc. v. Government of Canada*, UNCITRAL Arbitration, Partial Award, 13 November 2000 (toxic waste remediation).

[82]*Bayview Irrigation District* et al. *v. The United Mexican States*, ICSID Case No. ARB(AF)/05/1, Award, 19 June 2007 (water distribution).

[83]*United Parcel Service of America Inc. v. Government of Canada,* UNCITRAL Arbitration, Award on the Merits, 24 May 2007 (postal services).

services[84] as well as government procurement.[85] Few, however, have been successful. Most of these cases have addressed a claim that an investor with concessions to perform some public service, like water distribution, was treated unfairly or arbitrarily or denied justice by the state in the way it terminated the concession. Only one has directly addressed the distinctive nature of public services in applying NAFTA's substantive standards of protection.

That case involved an American courier company, UPS, that competed for courier business with Canada Post, the entity of the Canadian federal government that provides basic mail delivery. Canada provided certain benefits to Canada Post, including a subsidy for Canada Post's delivery of Canadian magazines and periodicals. Canada did not provide these benefits to UPS or any other private courier. UPS claimed, among other things, that Canada's denial of these benefits to UPS was inconsistent with NAFTA's national treatment obligation.[86] The arbitration tribunal decided that there was no breach, however, because UPS and Canada Post were not "in like circumstances" as required under NAFTA Article 1102 and so Canada was entitled to treat Canada Post more favourably. In particular, for the purposes of the subsidies, UPS and Canada Post were not in like circumstances because (i) Canada Post has a universal service obligation under its governing legislation and (ii) under its statutory mandate Canada Post must fulfill a variety of "significant public policy functions,..., which are not governed solely by commercial considerations".[87] The tribunal found, for example, that through the subsidies and benefits Canada sought to ensure the widest possible distribution of Canadian magazines and other periodicals to individual Canadian consumers at affordable and uniform prices with the goal of promoting Canadian culture. Only Canada Post, with its universal service obligation and vast distribution network, was able to ensure that Canada achieved this goal.[88] Also, the volume carried by Canada

[84]E.g. *Melvin J. Howard, Centurion Health Corporation & Howard Family Trust v. Government of Canada*, PCA Case No. 2009-21, Order for the Termination of the Proceedings and Award on Costs, 2 August 2010 (health services).

[85]E.g. *ADF Group Inc. v. United States of America*, ICSID Case No. ARB(AF)/00/1, Final Award, 9 January 2003 (government procurement), *Mondev International Ltd v. United States of America*, ICSID Case No. ARB(AF)/99/2, Award, 11 October 2002 (government procurement).

[86]*United Parcel Service of America Inc. v. Government of Canada*, UNCITRAL Arbitration, Award on the Merits, 24 May 2007. The main benefit was to subsidize the distribution of Canadian magazines and other periodicals by Canada Post (paras 137–181). Other alleged benefits consisted of preferential treatment by Canada's national customs agency, including the provisions of certain services for free. The alleged benefits are listed in para 80. The tribunal found that any preference related to mail service as opposed to courier service was not relevant. The tribunal also found that fee-based services provided by one branch of government to another constituted government procurement and so was exempt from the NAFTA investment obligations.

[87]*United Parcel Service of America Inc. v. Government of Canada*, UNCITRAL Arbitration, Award on the Merits, 24 May 2007, para 142. The tribunal discussed the mandate of Canada Post under the Canada Post Corporation Act, Revised Statutes of Canada 1985, c C-10.

[88]*United Parcel Service of America Inc. v. Government of Canada*, UNCITRAL Arbitration, Award on the Merits, 24 May 2007, para 175.

Post resulted in substantial efficiencies in the delivery of Canadian magazines and periodicals. Canadian and US private courier companies, including UPS, might compete for some of the business of distributing Canadian magazines and periodicals but they do not and could not serve all addresses in Canada. US private courier companies, including UPS, were in like circumstances with Canadian courier companies, but they were treated identically so the national treatment obligation was complied with. Only Canada Post received the subsidy and other benefits.

This case provides the only example of a NAFTA investment tribunal recognizing the unique characteristics of a public service provider as a consideration relevant to its decision. It remains to be seen whether this approach will be followed in subsequent cases.

## *5.2.6 NAFTA Chapters Dealing with Particular Aspects of Public Services Provision*

### 5.2.6.1 Introduction

In addition to general framework rules for services and investment, NAFTA has chapters dealing with particular services that address aspects of public service provision: financial services, telecommunications, and energy. As well, NAFTA has separate chapters on government procurement and government monopolies that may have an effect on public services. Finally, NAFTA contains general exceptions that help define the scope for states to act in relation to public services. All these are discussed in the next sections.

### 5.2.6.2 Financial Services

Chapter 14 and not Chapters 11 or 12 apply to investment in and the cross-border supply of financial services.[89] The pattern of basic obligations in the investment and services chapters is followed in Chapter 14, but with certain modifications that tailor the provisions to the specific characteristics of financial services and address some of the public service dimensions of such services, including the protection of depositors.[90] The need to ensure cost-effective access to basic financial services, which has been characterized as a public service issue in Europe, is not addressed.[91]

---

[89]NAFTA, Articles 1101(3) and 1201(2)(a). "[F]inancial service" is defined as a "service of a financial nature, including insurance." NAFTA, Article 1416.

[90]GATS Annex on Financial Services; and European Communities–CARIFORUM Economic Partnership Agreement (2008), Title 2, Chapter 5, Section 5.

[91]European Commission, A Quality Framework for Services of General Economic Interest in Europe, COM(2011) 900 final, 20 December 2011.

In terms of its scope of application, Chapter 14 applies to measures of a Party relating to financial institutions[92] of another Party,[93] investors of another Party in financial institutions in the territory of the Party, and their investments in such institutions as well as cross-border trade in financial services,[94] which is defined to mean provision of a financial service through GATS modes 1, 2 or 4.[95] Most significantly for public services, the scope of Chapter 14 is limited by Article 1401(3), which provides as follows:

> Nothing in this chapter shall be construed to prevent a Party, including its public entities, from *exclusively* conducting or providing in its territory:
>
> (a) activities or services forming part of a public retirement plan or statutory system of social security; or
> (b) activities or services for the account or with the guarantee or using the financial resources of the Party, including its public entities.[96] [emphasis added]

This limitation carves out direct and exclusive state provision of services relating to retirement and social security programs, as well as other financial services to which the chapter would otherwise apply that are delivered exclusively on behalf of the state through public and private entities that the state fully funds or with respect to which it guarantees the payment of some identified return. An example of private supply might be below market rate government loans to students for their post-secondary education where the loans are administered by private banks but repayment is guaranteed by the state. The reference to "exclusively" in the NAFTA provision means that Chapter 14 does apply to services of these kinds where private parties are permitted to supply them alongside the state.

For the purposes of GATS, the Annex on Financial Services defines the kinds of services described in Article 1401(3) as "services in the exercise of governmental authority" so that they are excluded from the agreement. The absence of competition by private parties as a condition of the availability of the exception is more explicitly addressed in GATS Annex on Financial Services.

Most of the obligations in Chapter 14 are commitments by each Party in relation to financial services providers and investors in financial institutions from other NAFTA Parties regarding their access to the market of the Party and the security of their position in that market. While these provisions go beyond that commitments of WTO Members expressed in the Understanding on Commitments in Financial Services, they have limited implications for public services.

---

[92]Financial institution is defined in terms of the scheme of financial services regulation in each Party, rather than a discrete list of activities. It means "a financial intermediary or other enterprise that is authorized to do business and regulated or supervised as a financial institution under the law of the Party in whose territory it is located." NAFTA, Article 1416.

[93]A financial institution of another Party is one that is controlled by persons of the other Party and is located in the territory of that other Party (NAFTA, Article 1416).

[94]NAFTA, Article 1401(1).

[95]NAFTA, Article 1416.

[96]*See also* NAFTA, Article 1410(3).

Each Party must give national treatment to investors in financial institutions and their investments with certain caveats.[97] Like the national treatment obligation in Chapter 11, the Chapter 14 obligation extends expressly to the "establishment, acquisition, [or] expansion" of such investments in financial institutions meaning that the obligations extend to the pre-establishment period and provide a guarantee of market access. National treatment must also be provided to cross-border financial service providers of another Party.[98] However, national treatment need only be provided in relation to any particular service provided across the border, if the Party permits the service to be provided in that way. A Party is free to refuse to allow services to be provided cross-border. A Party might choose to do so due to the difficulty in regulating foreign service providers that have no presence in the territory to ensure that they comply with public service obligations imposed by the state, or because the state provides the service directly.

Chapter 14 imposes an MFN obligation in relation to investors in financial institutions and their investments, with certain caveats, and to cross-border services suppliers.[99] The MFN obligation is attenuated in that a Party may recognize prudential measures[100] of a particular Party (or a non-Party) without triggering an MFN obligation to recognize the prudential measures of the other Party or Parties. The recognizing Party must, however, "provide adequate opportunity to another Party to demonstrate that circumstances exist in which there are or would be equivalent regulation, oversight, implementation of regulation, and, if appropriate, procedures concerning the sharing of information between the Parties."[101]

Article 1408 prohibits nationality requirements for senior managers of financial services providers, reproducing the general prohibition on such requirements in Chapter 11.[102] As well, the Parties committed to allowing financial institutions of another Party to transfer data into and out of their territory for the purposes of data processing in the ordinary course of business.[103]

Chapter 14 incorporates by reference certain provisions from Chapter 11, including the obligation not to expropriate investments of other NAFTA Parties except in accordance with certain requirements, including compensation.[104]

---

[97] NAFTA, Articles 1405(1), (2) and (4).

[98] NAFTA, Article 1405(3).

[99] NAFTA, Article 1406(1).

[100] As discussed in more detail below, prudential measures include those designed to protect depositors and others dealing with financial institutions.

[101] NAFTA, Articles 1406(2), and (3).

[102] NAFTA, Article 1407(1). The Parties agreed that they would permit financial institutions of another Party to provide any new financial services that develop on the same basis as domestic institutions.

[103] NAFTA, Article 1407(1).

[104] NAFTA, Article 1401(2) incorporates by reference Articles 1109 (transfer of funds), 1110 (expropriation), 1111 (special formalities and information requirements), 1113 (denial of benefits), and 1114 (environmental measures). The denial of benefits provision is also carried over from Chapter 12 (Article 1211).

The investor-state arbitration scheme under Chapter 11 is incorporated to protect investments in financial services but only from violations of the obligations that are incorporated by reference from Chapter 11.[105]

Significantly, the same Annex I and Annex II reservations as were discussed above in relation to Chapters 11 and 12, including the Social Services Reservation, apply to the national treatment and MFN obligations in Chapter 14.[106] Without these reservations, provincial health care funding plans in Canada that operate as a kind of insurance might be caught by Chapter 14.[107]

Most important for public services, NAFTA includes a fairly broad prudential exception that is very similar to the carve-out for such measures in the GATS Annex on Financial Services. It ensures that NAFTA obligations do not apply to limit the ability of Parties to protect public interests implicated by financial services provision, including the interests of investors in financial institutions, bank depositors, and insurance policy holders as well as the public interest in the overall health of individual financial institutions and the financial system generally. The activities of central banking authorities in pursuit of monetary and related credit policies or exchange rate policies are also excluded from obligations in the chapter.[108]

The prudential exception applies not only to the obligations in Chapter 14 but also those in Chapters 11, 12 and 13 (telecommunications), Chapter 15 (competition) and Chapter 16 (the temporary entry of business persons). Where an investor makes a claim against a Party, and the Party invokes this exception, the issue is referred to a Committee established under Chapter 14 which makes a binding decision on whether the exception applies.[109]

Article 1411 imposes certain obligations regarding the transparency of measures relating to financial services and applications to be permitted to provide financial services. There is no obligation, however, on a Party to furnish confidential information or information regarding the financial affairs of individual customers.[110]

To summarize, Chapter 14 has a number of features relevant to public services. NAFTA contains a version of the governmental authority exclusion for public retirement and social security plans as well as other financial services supplied exclusively by public or private entities on behalf of the state with the

[105]NAFTA, Articles 1414 and 1415. Article 1401(2) incorporates by reference the dispute settlement provisions (Articles 1115–1138) of Chapter 11 into Chapter 14.

[106]NAFTA, Article 1409(4). Reservations in Schedules to Annexes III and IV are also incorporated.

[107]See VanDuzer 2004. Categories of non-conforming measures that are listed by each Party in their schedule to Annex VII are also excluded, though none of these relate to public services. Existing local government measures are also excluded.

[108]See Malloy 2004, p. 231.

[109]NAFTA, Article 1412 (Financial Services Committee), Article 1415 (procedure for dealing with claim that prudential exception applies).

[110]NAFTA, Article 1411(5).

financial resources or guarantee of the state. It also exempts prudential measures and central bank activities. NAFTA Annex I and Annex II reservations discussed above in relation to Chapters 11 and 12, including the Social Services Reservation, apply to the national treatment and MFN obligations in Chapter 14. Finally, Chapter 14 recognizes that Parties cannot be obliged to disclose confidential information or information regarding the financial affairs of individual customers.

#### 5.2.6.3 Telecommunications

NAFTA Chapter 13 deals with telecommunications. The main purpose of Chapter 13 is to establish some additional specific obligations that relate to the distinctive characteristics of this sector, including its public service dimension. One commentator has called the chapter a "code of regulatory conduct".[111] It does not commit the NAFTA countries to allowing foreign businesses to deliver basic telecommunications services, but, like the GATS Annex on Telecommunications Services, obliges them to guarantee access to these services and the telecommunications networks that deliver them on a reasonable and non-discriminatory basis. The chapter also establishes some requirements for licencing regimes for enhanced or value-added telecommunications services[112] and the operation of state monopolies. In dealing with inter-connection and anti-competitive practices, NAFTA Chapter 13 follows the GATS Annex on Telecommunications and the Reference Paper on Telecommunications,[113] though Chapter 13 is more detailed and specific.

Telecommunications services are fully subject to the obligations in Chapters 11 and 12, except to the extent that any obligation in Chapter 13 is inconsistent with these chapters, in which case, the Chapter 13 obligation prevails.[114] As noted, the impact of Chapters 11 and 12 is circumscribed by the Annex II reservations filed by each NAFTA Party relating to telecommunications networks and services.

In terms of scope, Chapter 13 provides rules governing

- access to and use of public telecommunications networks or public telecommunications services (meaning services, like telephone services, that involve only the transmission of information supplied by a customer between points that is not changed in form or content end-to-end);

---

[111] Johnson 2002, p. 328.

[112] NAFTA, Article 1310.

[113] Telecommunications Services 1996. GATS Annex on Telecommunications only commits members to providing access to public telecommunications networks and services.

[114] NAFTA, Article 1307. One implication of this is that the reservations in Chapters 11 and 12 do not prevail over any obligation in Chapter 13 (Johnson 2002, p. 327).

- licensing the provision of enhanced or value-added telecommunications services (meaning telecommunications services other than public telecommunications services as described, such as services that act on the form, content or other aspects of the customer's information,[115] like email or remote alarm services); and
- standards for attaching equipment to public telecommunications networks.[116]

Chapter 13 does not, however, grant any right to investors or services suppliers to establish, acquire or build a telecommunications network or provide public telecommunications services.[117]

Article 1302(1) establishes the basic rule that each Party must ensure that persons from other NAFTA countries have access to any public telecommunications network or service operated within its territory or across its borders on reasonable and non-discriminatory terms. Pricing of public telecommunications services has to reflect the costs directly related to providing the service.[118] NAFTA countries are expressly permitted to take steps to ensure the privacy of subscribers or the confidentiality of messages and impose conditions that are "necessary … to safeguard the public service responsibilities" of telecommunications networks or services providers, including their ability to make their networks or services available to the public.[119] No other conditions on access to or use of networks or services may be imposed. The explicit requirement for cost-based pricing would seem to prohibit charging higher prices to subsidize universal service or other public service obligations of providers of networks or services, except to the extent that they are based on the costs of meeting such obligations.[120] Mexico was found to have failed to ensure that cost-justified rates were charged by its public telecommunications network contrary to GATS in *Mexico-Measures Affecting Telecommunications Services*. The same result would likely have followed in a challenge under NAFTA. Cross-subsidization, however, is expressly permitted. For example, a telephone company may subsidize the cost of local service from revenues from long distance services.

NAFTA 1303 deals with the conditions upon which enhanced or value-added telecommunications services may be provided. Some of these commitments are of limited relevance to public services regulation. For example, registration and other procedures must be transparent and non-discriminatory, and any information required to be filed must be limited to that required to demonstrate the applicant's

[115]NAFTA, Article 1310.

[116]NAFTA, Article 1301(1). Chapter 13 does not deal with the distribution of television or radio programs except to require that persons operating broadcast stations and cable systems be given access to public telecommunications networks (NAFTA, Article 1301(2)).

[117]NAFTA, Article 1301(3)(b).

[118]NAFTA, Article 1302(3). Cross-subsidization between public services is permitted.

[119]NAFTA, Articles 1302(5) and (6).

[120]*Mexico—Measures Affecting Telecommunications Services,* Report of the Panel, WT/DS204/R.

solvency or compliance with technical standards. Of greater significance, NAFTA countries cannot impose on providers of enhanced or value-added services the kinds of requirements that are often imposed on public services providers, such as obligations to

(a) provide [services] generally to the public;
(b) cost-justify its rates;
(c) file a tariff; [[121]]
(d) interconnect its networks with any particular customer or network;
(e) conform with any particular standard or technical regulation for interconnection other than for interconnection to a public telecommunications transport network.

Certain requirements are also imposed in relation to standards imposed by the operators of such telecommunications networks for the attachment of equipment to networks.[122] One of the permitted categories of standards-related measures is to ensure users' safety and access to the network.

Where a NAFTA country maintains or designates a monopoly to provide certain telecommunications services and the monopoly competes with private firms in providing enhanced or value-added telecommunications, it must ensure that the monopoly does not engage in anti-competitive conduct when doing so.[123]

Finally, Chapter 13 does not permit reservations to be taken. By virtue of the reservations taken by each country in the investment and services chapters, however, the national treatment and MFN obligations as well as some other obligations in those chapters do not apply to telecommunications networks or the provision of public telecommunications services.[124] Consequently, discriminatory restrictions on investment in and cross-border supply of telecommunications services that would otherwise be contrary to Chapters 11 and 12 may be maintained. Chapter 13 prevails over Chapters 11 and 12, so the Annex II reservations cannot derogate from the obligations in Chapter 13. Since Chapter 13 does not address discrimination, except for the obligation of public monoplies described above, the likelihood of such derogation would appear to be small.

In summary, Chapter 13 provides certain guarantees of access to public telecommunications networks and services but allows conditions to be imposed on suppliers of public telecommunications networks and services to ensure that public service objectives are achieved. Parties can also impose other standards to achieve other public interest goals, such as the protection of public safety. With respect to the important area of enhanced or value-added services, however, public services obligations, like universal service obligations and rate specification are prohibited.

[121] A tariff, meaning rates to be charged, may be required if the provider is a monopoly or the tariff is needed to remedy an anticompetitive action (NAFTA, Article 1303(3)).

[122] NAFTA, Article 1304.

[123] NAFTA, Article 1305.

[124] Johnson 1994, p. 330. The wording of these reservations is not identical.

#### 5.2.6.4 Energy

Special rules regarding the supply of energy are not commonly found in trade or investment treaties. NAFTA has no rules that specifically address the provision of energy in the territory of a Party. Chapter 6, however, creates some special rules dealing with "energy and basic petrochemical goods".[125] NAFTA's provisions are mainly concerned with protecting energy security within North America by limiting the ability of NAFTA Parties to constrain exports to each other. Critics have expressed concerns that these obligations could be invoked to prevent a country from limiting exports to respond to a domestic shortage with the goal of ensuring adequate access to energy for its domestic population.[126] There is no evidence that this has occurred in practice, however.

For the most part, Chapter 6 incorporates the basic limitations on the ability of Parties to restrict imports and exports of energy and petrochemical goods to which each of the Parties is subject under the GATT.[127] The chapter expresses the Parties' understanding that GATT prohibits minimum and maximum export prices in most circumstances.[128] The Parties also agree that they shall not impose discriminatory export taxes. These are taxes that apply to exports to a Party but not to goods sold for domestic consumption or that do not apply to exports to other countries.[129]

Chapter 6 also imposes three further limitations on the ability of NAFTA Parties to restrict exports of energy and petrochemical goods. In general, export restrictions are prohibited, except where there are domestic shortages or a Party imposes similar restrictions related to domestic energy supply. These limitations apply even in circumstances where export restrictions would be permitted under the GATT.[130]

---

[125] These goods are defined with reference to specific classes of goods in the Harmonized System (NAFTA, Article 602). Consistent with the Mexican Constitution, Mexico reserves to itself the right to carry on most activities in the energy sector, including exploring for, exploiting, refining, processing and trade in petrochemical products and the supply of electricity as a public service. Private investment is not permitted and the services obligations in Chapter 12 only apply to the extent that the government grants a private party a right to perform services related to energy (NAFTA, Annex 602.3).

[126] E.g. Laxer and Dillon 2008. The critics' views are discussed Johnson 1994, pp. 206–210.

[127] NAFTA, Article 602. This provision excludes the application of the Parties' protocols of provisional application. One implication of this is that, for NAFTA purposes, the provision in Mexico's protocol that permitted Mexico to rely on the exception in GATT Article XX(g) based on "social and development needs" does not apply (see Johnson 1994, p. 204).

[128] NAFTA, Article 603(2). There is some uncertainty regarding whether the GATT requires this (Johnson 1994, pp. 204–205).

[129] NAFTA, Article 604.

[130] I.e. the exceptions in GATT Articles XI:2(a), XX(g), (i), or (j). NAFTA, Article 607 also imposes limitations on the Parties' ability to rely on the national security exception in GATT XXI. These limitations do not apply to Mexico or to Canada and the United States in relation to Mexico.

A Party cannot impose a restriction in relation to the export of an energy or petrochemical product to another Party unless the following conditions are met.

(a) The restriction does not reduce the proportion of the total export shipments… to that other Party relative to the total supply of that good of the Party maintaining the restriction as compared to the proportion prevailing for the most recent 36 month period…
(b) The Party does not impose a higher price for exports of an energy or basic petrochemical good to that other Party than the price charged for such good when consumed domestically, by means of any measure such as licenses, fees, taxation and minimum price requirements.
(c) The restriction does not require the disruption of normal channels of supply to that other Party or normal proportions among specific energy or basic petrochemical goods supplied to that other Party, such as, for example, between crude oil and refined products and among different categories of crude oil and of refined products.

These limitations only apply as between Canada and the US. Mexico is not subject to them and neither Canada nor the United States has to comply with these rules in relation to Mexico.[131] Apart from the basic GATT rules dealing with import and export restrictions, the Mexican energy sector is exempt from the obligations in the treaty. The obligations in the treaty of Canada and the United States dealing with goods, services and investment, as well as those in the energy chapter, all apply to the energy sector.

The rules in Chapter 6 are only likely to be relevant in the circumstances where there has been a decline in production or for some other reason supply within a NAFTA country has been reduced. In these circumstances, the main obligation on Canada and the US is not to restrict or otherwise limit exports to the other country except in proportion to reductions in domestic distribution. As noted, in Canada, this proportionality restriction has been a significant concern though there is no evidence that problems have arisen in practice to date. In light of new sources of resources coming into production in all three NAFTA countries, problems of this kind seem unlikely.

#### 5.2.6.5 Government Procurement

NAFTA Chapter 10 provides a set of rules to govern procurement by NAFTA country governments of goods and services. Like the World Trade Organization's Agreement on Government Procurement,[132] Chapter 10 imposes an obligation on specified government bodies of a Party not to discriminate against suppliers from the other Parties in making some procurement decisions, sets standards for

---

[131]Energy production and distribution in Mexico is reserved to the Mexican state. This is expressly provided for in Article 27 of the Mexican Constitution, see also Articles 25 and 28.

[132]WTO Agreement on Government Procurement (1994).

procurement bidding procedures and requires each Party to put in place a process to challenge procurement decisions. Similar kinds of commitments are found in EU trade agreements.[133]

In terms of scope, Chapter 10 applies to purchases of goods and services as well as leases and rentals by national governments and some national government enterprises that exceed specified financial thresholds. Provincial and state procurement is not caught by Chapter 10.[134] Of relevance to public services, procurement does not include:

> (a) non-contractual agreements or any form of government assistance, including cooperative agreements, grants, loans, equity infusions, guarantees, fiscal incentives, and government provision of goods and services to persons or state, provincial and regional governments;…

The basic financial threshold for the application of the Chapter 10 rules to procurements of goods or services by governments is US$50 000 but for procurement of construction services is US$6.6 million. For government enterprises, the threshold for procurement of goods or services is US$250 000 and US$8 million for construction services. Chapter 10 obligations do not apply to purchases of arms or other national security procurements.[135]

With respect to procurement measures covered by Chapter 10, the NAFTA countries commit not to treat goods of another Party, suppliers of such goods or service suppliers of another Party less favourably than the most favourable treatment they provide to their own goods and suppliers or the goods and suppliers of another Party. The provision goes on to specify that this means that local suppliers cannot be discriminated against because (i) they are affiliated with foreign firms of another Party or foreigners of another Party hold ownership interests in them or (ii) the goods or services they offer are goods or services of another Party. This would preclude discrimination in favour of local private suppliers of public services.

Significantly, all three countries have taken a variety of reservations for procurement of services related to research and development, transport services, public utilities services (including telecommunications, water and energy services). Canada also excluded health and social services.[136] Consequently, there is substantial flexibility for NAFTA governments to use procurement in these sectors to achieve economic development and social objectives, such as the promotion of

---

[133]E.g. European Communities–CARIFORUM Economic Partnership Agreement (2008), Title IV, Chapter 3.

[134]These obligations have been expanded in accordance with the Canada-US Agreement on Government Procurement of 2010, which resulted in some reciprocal provincial and state commitments under the WTO Agreement on Government Procurement.

[135]NAFTA, Article 1001(1)(c). As between Canada and the US, the lower threshold agreed to in the Canada-United States Free Trade Agreement (1989) applies to procurements of goods by some entities: US$25,000 (Annex 1001.2c). These categories were expressed with reference to a classification system established in NAFTA.

[136]NAFTA, Chapter 10, Schedule B.

local employment and research and development activity, notwithstanding the procurement rules. Discrimination in favour of local suppliers in these areas is permitted for any reason. In some cases, governments might want to discriminate in connection with public services to ensure that services are appropriate for local conditions.

The general exceptions in NAFTA do not apply to Chapter 10.[137] Chapter 10, however, has its own exceptions similar to those in GATT Article XX. Nothing in Chapter 10 prevents any Party from adopting measures:

(a) necessary to protect public morals, order or safety;
(b) necessary to protect human, animal or plant life or health;
(c) necessary to protect intellectual property; or
(d) relating to goods or services of handicapped persons, of philanthropic institutions or of prison labor.

Like the general exceptions in GATT Article XX, the exceptions are only available in relation to measures that "are not applied in a manner that would constitute a means of arbitrary or unjustifiable discrimination between Parties where the same conditions prevail or a disguised restriction on trade between the Parties".[138] Some public services measures might benefit from this exception, though it is hard to imagine that discriminatory procurement practices could ever be necessary to achieve the identified objectives. Alternatives are likely to be available in most circumstances.

The procurement rules of NAFTA limit the ability of NAFTA countries to discriminate against suppliers from other NAFTA countries but are subject to some significant limitations as applied to public services. Government assistance is generally not considered procurement. As well, procurement in relation to a list of public services, including telecommunications, energy and water services, are not subject to the procurement rules. Discrimination in favour of local suppliers is permitted in these areas. As well, actions otherwise inconsistent with the procurement rules that can be justified as necessary to protect health and the other interests identified in the general exceptions in Chapter 10 are permitted.

#### 5.2.6.6 Competition Rules

The provisions of NAFTA Chapter 15 dealing with monopolies and state enterprises have some relevance to public services, since these kinds of entities are often the mechanism for the delivery of such services. NAFTA Chapter 15 obliges the Parties to have in place competition law rules addressing anti-competitive conduct and to cooperate on enforcement.[139] Nevertheless, existing monopolies,

[137]The exceptions are discussed below. GATS contains identical exceptions (Article XXIII).

[138]NAFTA, Article 1018(2). A national security exception is also provided (NAFTA, Article 1018(1)).

[139]NAFTA, Article 1501.

including those delivering public services, may be maintained and new ones designated,[140] though certain requirements are imposed to minimize the consequences of monopoly conduct on the businesses of other Parties. These obligations are broadly similar to those regarding monopolies in GATS.[141] States must ensure that their monopolies operate in accordance with commercial considerations except where monopolies are acting to comply with their mandate. Regardless of their mandate, however, a monopoly must not be permitted to act in a discriminatory way in the market in which it has a monopoly or in a way that is anticompetitive to the extent that it also operates in a non-monopolized market.

Monopoly is defined in NAFTA as

> An entity, including, a consortium or government agency, that in any relevant market in the territory of a Party, is designated as the sole provider of or purchaser of a good or a service…

Article 1502(1) provides that a NAFTA Party may designate a monopoly, so long as the Party gives prior notice to the other Parties and the Party must "endeavour" to impose conditions on the operation of the monopoly that will minimize or eliminate the nullification or impairment of certain NAFTA provisions.[142] This is not an obligation to guarantee that nullification or impairment does not occur.

NAFTA Article 1502(1) applies only to newly designated monopolies. As a result, it has no application to monopolies in public services that pre-date NAFTA, such as existing Canadian provincial health care plans that are the sole funders of basic medical services. It would be relevant, however, with respect to any expansion of existing monopolies. For example, if the categories of health services funded exclusively by the state were expanded beyond those that were delivered on this basis on 1 January 1994 when NAFTA came into force, such a policy shift might be characterized as designating a monopoly in these services to the extent

[140] Designation includes the expansion of existing monopolies, such as a public monopoly health care provider being authorized to provide new categories of health services exclusively (NAFTA, Article 1505).

[141] GATS, Article VIII provides that each WTO member will ensure that any monopoly service supplier acts consistently with the MFN obligation in GATS and the member's specific commitments. Where a monopoly competes outside the monopoly in a sector in which the member has made specific commitments, the member shall ensure that the monopoly does not abuse its monopoly position in a manner inconsistent with its commitments. Notification is required for any new monopoly. Where a member authorizes a small group of exclusive service suppliers and substantially prevents competition among them, the same obligations apply. If a member makes a market access and national treatment commitment by listing a sector, subsequent designation of a monopoly supplier would require a member to withdraw the concession and negotiate compensation under GATS.

[142] NAFTA, Article 1502(2). Article 1502(2) refers to the benefits listed in Annex 2004. The Annex does not list the obligations under Chapters 11 (investment) or 14 (financial services). Any impact on rights protected under these chapters does not have to be taken into account under this provision. The effect on rights protected under Chapter 12 (trade in services) would have to be considered. The investment and financial services obligations would still apply however.

that it precluded private insurance companies from selling insurance to cover those services.[143]

NAFTA Article 1502(3) imposes certain other requirements to be observed by monopolies designated by a Party that are operated either by private firms or the federal government. Each Party must ensure that such a monopoly

(a) acts in a manner not inconsistent with the Party's obligations where it exercises any regulatory, administrative or other government power delegated to it…;
(b) *except to comply with any terms of its designation that are not inconsistent with sub-paragraph (c) or (d), acts solely in accordance with commercial considerations* in its purchase or sale of the monopoly good or service in the relevant market, including with regard to price, quality, availability, marketability, transportation and other terms and conditions of purchase or sale;
(c) provides non-discriminatory treatment[[144]] to investments of investors, to goods and to service providers of another Party in its purchase or sale of the monopoly good or service in the relevant market; and
(d) does not use its monopoly position to engage, either directly or indirectly, including through its dealings with its parent, its subsidiary or other enterprise with common ownership, in anticompetitive practices in a non-monopolized market in its territory that adversely affect an investment of an investor of another Party, including through the discriminatory provision of the monopoly good or service, cross-subsidization or predatory conduct.[145] [emphasis added]

Chapter 15 also deals with state enterprises. Unlike the monopolies subject to Article 1503(2), state enterprises include those set up by the sub-national governments of states and provinces.[146] In contrast to the obligation in Article 1502(3)

[143]Even if such a characterization were accepted, however, Canada would not have to worry about this obligation in relation to US or Mexican insurance companies based on the obligations in Chapter 14 (financial services) because the benefits of Chapter 14 are not among those protected against nullification and impairment under Article 1502(1) as a result of not being listed in Annex 2004. Nevertheless, the obligations in Chapter 14, including the prohibition on expropriation without compensation incorporated by reference from Chapter 11, would still apply.

[144]Non-discriminatory means the better or national or MFN treatment (NAFTA, Article 1515).

[145]This last obligation is broadly similar to GATS, Article VIII. Where a Member authorises a monopoly service supplier to operate, such as a single provider of telecommunications services, and the services supplier competes in the supply of a service that is outside the scope of its monopoly rights and in a sector listed in the Member's schedule, the member must ensure that the monopoly supplier does not abuse its monopoly position (GATS, Article VIII). Abuse would include, for example, subsidising its activities in the competitive market with its monopoly profits. Members are also obliged to ensure that monopoly service suppliers do not undermine access commitments undertaken in national schedules of commitments (GATS, Article VIII.1).

[146]State specific definitions of state enterprises are set out in NAFTA Annex 1505. The obligation on monopolies in Article 1502(3)(a) and state enterprises in Article 1503 can be the subject of an investor-state claim if they are breached in a way that breaches an investor-protection obligations in Chapter 11. NAFTA, Articles 1116(1)(b), 1117(1)(b). This basis for an investor-state claim is excluded for Mexico in Annex 1120.1.

for monopolies to comply with all of a Party's NAFTA obligations, state enterprises exercising delegated regulatory, administrative or other governmental authority are only required not to act in a manner inconsistent with Chapter 11 (investment) and Chapter 14 (financial services). Parties must also ensure that state enterprises give the better of national or MFN treatment when selling goods or services to investments of investors of another NAFTA country in the Party's territory.[147]

In summary, while monopolies and state enterprises, including providers of public services, can continue to operate and new ones can be designated by NAFTA states, some restrictions apply. Parties must try to avoid nullification and impairment of certain obligations when they designate a new federal level or private monopoly. This obligation does not extend to the obligations in Chapter 11 (investment) or Chapter 14 (financial services). That does not mean, however, that these obligations do not apply to all state measures related to monopolies. Nothing in Chapter 15 excludes the obligations in Chapters 11 or 14. The obligation not to expropriate without compensation, for example, in these chapters continues to apply and may discourage the establishment of new monopolies in public services or the expansion of existing monopolies.[148] As well, where a federal or private monopoly has been designated, Chapter 15 expressly provides that Parties are obliged to ensure that it complies with all obligations in NAFTA, including Chapters 11 and 14. State enterprises, which includes sub-federal level enterprises, must be required to comply with Chapters 11 and 14 only. Of the other obligations relating to monopolies, the requirement to ensure that federal and private monopolies act "solely in accordance with commercial considerations" could interfere with public service obligations of these monopolies. This obligation does not apply, however, to any public service obligation provided for in the terms of the designation of a monopoly. This protection is restricted in two ways. Actions of a monopoly in its monopoly market that are discriminatory and actions outside its monopoly market that are anti-competitive are not protected even if the actions would promote the monopoly's mandate. These provisions would not apply, however, to common, non-discriminatory public service obligations, such as universal service obligations.

#### 5.2.6.7 General Exceptions

Chapter 21 of NAFTA provides some general exceptions that apply to the Parties' obligations. One general exception permits measures that a Party considers necessary for the protection of its national security interests.[149] There is also a general

[147]NAFTA, Article 1503.

[148]Johnson 1994, p. 409.

[149]NAFTA, Article 2102.

exception for measures taken in response to a balance of payments emergency.[150] Taxation measures are generally excluded with some limitations.[151] A taxation measure may be found to be an expropriation contrary to Chapter 11, unless the appropriate authorities in the host state and the investor's state agree that it is not an expropriation.[152] Chapter 21 also incorporates the GATT Article XX exceptions relating to, among other things, measures necessary for the protection of public morals, human, animal or plant health and the conservation of exhaustible natural resources, but only for measures related to trade in goods.[153]

NAFTA does not contain the general exceptions from the services obligations that are found in GATS and many EU trade agreements.[154] There is one exception of some relevance to public services. The services rules in Chapter 12 and the rules on telecommunications in Chapter 13 are subject to the following exception for measures related to compliance with laws, including those relating to health, safety and consumer protection:

> Provided that such measures are not applied in a manner that would constitute a means of arbitrary or unjustifiable discrimination between countries where the same conditions prevail or a disguised restriction on trade between the Parties, nothing in: …
>
> (c) Chapter Twelve (Cross-Border Trade in Services), and
> (d) Chapter Thirteen (Telecommunications),
>
> shall be construed to prevent the adoption or enforcement by any Party of measures necessary to secure compliance with laws or regulations that are not inconsistent with the provisions of this Agreement, including those relating to health and safety and consumer protection.

The structure of this exception means that its application is subject to several significant limitations. First, a measure must be necessary, not for the protection of any public interest directly, but to secure compliance with laws that are not themselves inconsistent with the agreement. In cases interpreting similar WTO obligations, necessary has been interpreted as meaning that there must not be an alternative measure reasonably available to the state to achieve the defined objective that is less restrictive of trade.[155] Second, the measure must "not [be] applied in a manner that

[150]NAFTA, Article 1501.

[151]NAFTA, Article 2103(4). National treatment and MFN in Chapter 11 relating to investments apply to certain taxation measures and the national treatment obligations in Chapters 12 and 14 apply to income and capital gains tax as well as some other taxes.

[152]NAFTA, Article 2103(6).

[153]NAFTA, Article 2101.

[154]Under GATS, measures are excluded if they are necessary "to protect public morals or to maintain public order" or "to protect human, animal or plant life or health." As well, GATS provides an exception for the enforcement of laws relating to privacy. As an example of an EU agreement, see the European Communities–CARIFORUM Economic Partnership Agreement (2008), Articles 184 and 221.

[155]E.g. *European Communities—Measures Affecting Asbestos and Products Containing Asbestos*, Report of the Appellate Body, WT/DS135/AB/R.

would constitute a means of arbitrary or unjustifiable discrimination between countries where the same conditions prevail or a disguised restriction on trade between the Parties." This architecture follows GATT Article XX and GATS Article XIV. Finally and most importantly, this exception does not apply to obligations under Chapter 11 (investment) or 14 (financial services). In short, where necessary for the enforcement of regulatory standards that are consistent with NAFTA, a Party could treat foreign services suppliers (apart from financial services suppliers and investors) differently. This exception simply recognizes that it may be more difficult to take enforcement action against foreign suppliers that are outside the territory of the enforcing party. It provides little protection for public service measures.

## 5.3 Analysis of NAFTA Rules Applicable to Public Services

### *5.3.1 Introduction*

The survey of NAFTA provisions in this chapter discloses some distinctive features of the approach taken in the NAFTA to protecting public services from treaty disciplines as compared to the approach in the GATS and EU trade agreements. In this section, these differences in approach are discussed in detail and some of the relative costs and benefits identified.

### *5.3.2 Approaches to the Protection of Public Services in GATS and EU Trade Agreements*

The conceptual starting point for NAFTA, as a negative list agreement, is that all provisions of the agreement apply to all activities of a party state, including subnational governments.[156] In contrast, key provisions of GATS and EU trade agreements only apply to sectors and activities that are positively listed by each party.

GATS and EU trade agreements also limit their scope of application to public services by an exclusion for services in the exercise of governmental authority.[157]

[156]NAFTA, Article 105. Each Party commits to "take all necessary measures" to give effect to the provisions of the agreement, "including their observance, except as otherwise provided, by state and provincial governments." The international law rules of state responsibility regarding treaty obligations that relate to matters within the jurisdiction of subordinate state actors are clear: a state is internationally responsible for their actions that are not in compliance with the state's international obligations. A state cannot invoke any internal constitutional rules that allocate jurisdiction to subordinate levels of government as an excuse for non-compliance: Vienna Convention on the Law of Treaties (1980), Article 27; International Law Commission 2001, Article 3.

[157]E.g. European Communities–CARIFORUM Economic Partnership Agreement (2008), Article 129.

NAFTA contains no such exclusion, relying largely on sector specific reservations and exceptions. The governmental authority exclusion is defined typically to encompass only services that are delivered not on a commercial basis and not in competition with one or more services suppliers. There has been much debate about the scope and utility of the governmental authority exclusion[158] but, as yet, no authoritative interpretation.[159] One leading commentator concludes that there is an emerging consensus that the protection provided by the governmental authority exclusion is narrow, including only core services delivered directly by the state.[160] Services that typically are considered public services, like health and education, but that are delivered on a fee-paid basis or by private institutions may be outside the protection of the exclusion.

In GATS and EU trade agreements, in addition to the exclusion for services supplied in the exercise of governmental authority, the EU typically includes in its schedule of commitments an exclusion for a broader category of public services: public utilities. In practice, this exclusion is limited in three ways: it applies (i) only to the market access and national treatment obligations, (ii) only in relation to one mode of service delivery, commercial presence, and (iii) only to one kind of public service delivery: public monopolies and exclusive rights granted to private operators. For example, the EU's national schedule of commitments to the GATS contains the following horizontal limitation (i.e. one applying to all listed sectors) in relation to the supply of a service through a commercial presence.

> In all EC Member States services considered as public utilities at a national or local level may be subject to public monopolies or to exclusive rights granted to private operators.*[161]

This limitation is accompanied by the following note.

> *1) Explanatory Note: Public utilities exist in sectors such as related scientific and technical consulting services, R&D services on social sciences and humanities, technical testing and analysis services, environmental services, health services, transport services and services auxiliary to all modes of transport. Exclusive rights on such services are often granted to private operators, for instance operators with concessions from public authorities, subject to specific service obligations. Given that public utilities often also exist at the sub-central level, detailed and exhaustive sector-specific scheduling is not practical.[162]

This limitation provides examples of what might be considered a public utility but not an exclusive list. In effect, it is up to the relevant authority in each member state to determine what is a public utility. The ability of local authorities to make these determinations on an ongoing basis provides significant flexibility with

[158]E.g. Leroux 2006, p. 345; Krajewski 2003, p. 341; Luff 2003; Adlung 2003; VanDuzer 2005, p. 303.

[159]The similarly worded exemption in Article 51 Treaty on the Functioning of the European Union has been interpreted by the European Court of Justice.

[160]Krajewski 2011a, p. 23.

[161]European Communities and their Member States, Schedule of Specific Commitments (1994).

[162]European Communities and their Member States, Schedule of Specific Commitments (1994).

respect to the areas which benefit from the limitation. The scope of permitted policy-making in relation to public utilities, however, is constrained. Public monopolies may be set up and exclusive private service suppliers designated with specific public service obligations, but no other form of public service delivery is carved out. As well, in relation to such monopolies or exclusive services suppliers the obligations in the GATS, other than market access and national treatment, would continue to apply. As well, GATS obligations for listed sectors, including national treatment and market access, would apply to any particular listed public service that is not provided through a commercial presence. These obligations, however, are subject to any other limitations written into the EU schedule. In its other positive list agreements, the EU typically also includes limitations that cut back the commitments it undertakes in specific sectors.[163]

### *5.3.3 Possible Costs and Benefits of NAFTA's Approach to the Protection of Public Services*

In contrast to the functional approach adopted in the governmental services exception and the targeted flexibility offered by the horizontal limitation for public utilities in GATS and EU trade treaties, the general approach in NAFTA is to carve out specific public services areas and measures. For example, the Social Services Reservation in the NAFTA Parties' Schedules to Annex II specifically excludes all present and future measures related to a finite list of identified areas: "public law enforcement and correctional services, and … to the extent that they are social services established or maintained for a public purpose: income security or insurance, social security or insurance, social welfare, public education, public training, health, and child care."

As discussed above, the meaning of "public purpose" in the abstract is somewhat uncertain. The use of a specific list of policy areas does provide a higher degree of certainty and predictability regarding the areas of public services that fall within it, compared to functional definitions like services in the exercise of governmental authority, the content of which is inherently contestable, or public utilities the content of which is largely up to member states. The same observation may be made regarding the other Annex II reservations that relate to specific policy areas implicating public service considerations.[164] The Annex I reservations for existing measures have precisely defined content and, as a result, are even more certain, though certainty is somewhat compromised with respect to existing

[163]Krajewski 2011a, p. 30.

[164]As noted, the main categories of Annex II reservations that implicate public services are set out in the Appendix to this chapter.

state and provincial measures which are protected by Annex I but, contrary to the Parties' original intention, were never listed.[165]

The procurement, financial services and telecommunications chapters also provide important area-specific rules relevant to public services. Annexes to Chapter 10 on procurement list areas of policy-making and regulation identified by each NAFTA country to which the procurement obligations do not apply. Chapter 14 on financial services exempts identified categories of prudential measures and the telecommunications chapter preserves the right of states to impose public service responsibilities on suppliers of public telecommunications networks and services.

Despite being relatively certain and specific, the NAFTA approach has inherent limits. Because it relies on discrete lists of areas and measures, it is fragmentary. Some generally recognized public services, such as water services, are not on any list in NAFTA, other than the list of exceptions from the government procurement obligations. Lists are not the same for all three countries and vary depending on the obligation. The government procurement lists of sectors reserved by each Party, for example, are more extensive than the Annex II lists.

NAFTA's approach is also rigid. What constitutes a public service is both dynamic and context specific. Policies on what services should be delivered as public services are inherently subject to experimentation and change over time.[166] Fixed lists, like the list in the Social Services Reservation, are poorly adapted to accommodate inevitable changes in the categories and nature of public services. NAFTA Annex II reservations and other NAFTA provisions with implications for public services can only be changed by an amendment to the treaty, which has never occurred and is unlikely in the future. As well, the dynamic nature of public services means that the standstill protection for particular measures under Annex I based on the form they took on 1 January 1994 is likely to diminish over time. In particular, the operation of the ratchet will mean that experiments involving liberalization will be locked in as part of the liberalizing Party's obligations. By contrast, the functional approach in the governmental services exclusion means that states can bring public services within the exclusion by adopting a policy of providing the service directly.[167] The horizontal limitation for public utilities is even more flexible since its application is up to EU member states.

Exclusions for subsidies and procurement from the services and investment obligations and the exclusion of government assistance from the procurement rules mitigate the rigidity of NAFTA's list-based approach. Carving out

[165] Annex I and Annex II reservations are not symmetrical.

[166] Krajewski 2011a, p. 28.

[167] If a state were to begin supplying a service directly that was the subject of specific commitment in its national schedule of commitments certain other GATS obligations might apply. If the state became the exclusive supplier, for example, GATS Article VIII.4 would require the state to give notice to the Council for Trade in Services. In such a case, at the request of any Member, the state would be required to enter into negotiations to agree on a compensating adjustment of its trade concessions. Any such adjustment would have to be extended on a most favoured nation basis to all WTO Members (GATS, Article XXI).

particular policy instruments that are not tied to any particular sector or activity gives flexibility to states to use these instruments to support public services in all areas, even those not protected specifically by exceptions or reservations. As discussed above, EU trade agreements also carve out these kinds of policy measures.

A final concern regarding the NAFTA approach is that it carves out public services activities largely without regard to the way in which services are delivered or the nature of the challenge that particular obligations represent for public services. For example, activities listed in the Social Services Reservation are excluded in their entirety from some NAFTA obligations even if all of the suppliers are private businesses that compete with each other, subject to the uncertain requirement that they are social services for a public purpose. The areas carved-out from the government procurement obligations, as well as other Annex II reservations and the Annex I reservations, do not contain this qualification. Areas of services supply identified in these provisions are fully excluded. By contrast, in EU trade agreements, the governmental services exclusion and the public utilities limitation do not fully exclude whole areas of services supply. As noted above, the governmental authority exclusion is likely limited to public services offered directly and exclusively by the state. The EU's horizontal limitation for public utilities is even more limited. It only permits the continuation and designation of monopolies and exclusive rights holders for one mode of supply (commercial presence) and only protects them from the market access and national treatment obligations. While EU member states can decide if public utilities are to be state or private monopolies or exclusive rights holders, if private competition is allowed, this provision would not apply to permit member states to discriminate against foreign suppliers in favour of local suppliers contrary to the national treatment obligation or to restrict market access.[168] The absence of these functional limitations in NAFTA means that the protection from the treaty obligations in areas listed in reservations is broader that under GATS and EU trade treaties. Most public services areas that are not listed, however, enjoy no protection at all.

The survey of NAFTA provisions does disclose a slightly more nuanced and functional approach to public services in some areas. In the financial services chapter, direct public provision of services relating to public funding and operation of retirement and social security programs, or other services that are delivered by the state through public or private entities that the government fully funds or with respect to which it guarantees the payment of some identified return are not subject to the obligations in the financial services chapter. But the exclusion is only available if the public or private entities are the exclusive providers of the service. If competition is permitted, then the exclusion does not apply and private parties

---

[168]European Commission, Commission Proposal for the Modernization of the Treatment of Public Services in EU Trade Agreements, TRADE.B.1/SC/am D(2011) 1146318, 26 October 2011.

benefit from the protections against discrimination in the treaty. This is similar in approach to GATs and European trade treaties.[169]

The NAFTA provisions on competition also reflect a more nuanced approach that limits the scope of obligations to the extent that they interfere with the mandate of state maintained monopolies. Monopolies and state enterprises can continue to operate and NAFTA countries can designate new ones but the measures relating to them are subject to the obligations in the investment chapter, including investor-state dispute settlement. A federal or private monopoly must operate solely in accordance with commercial considerations in relation to its purchases or sales of its monopoly good or service, "except to comply with any terms of its designation", meaning the terms on which it was set up. Thus a public service mandate for a monopoly would be a basis to deviate from commercial considerations. Even if doing so would assist a monopoly to comply with its "terms of its designation," however, a monopoly cannot behave in a discriminatory way in its monopoly market or engage in anti-competitive conduct outside its monopoly market. While the recognition of the essential role to be played by the public service mandate of a state monopoly does protect the ability of state monopolies to fulfill their mandates, these limitations restrict the scope of that protection.

Competition disciplines in some EU trade agreements also protect public service mandates of state monopolies but more comprehensively. The ability of states to designate monopolies and other enterprises with special or exclusive rights is commonly preserved in EU trade treaties. Competition disciplines still apply to these monopolies and enterprises but not to the extent that they would "obstruct the performance, in law or in fact, of the particular tasks assigned to them."[170] This would seem to go beyond NAFTA in permitting anti-competitive conduct by a monopoly if such conduct would promote the achievement of a monopoly's mandate.

Finally, public services are fully subject to the obligations protecting investors that may not be reserved against in NAFTA Chapter 11. These include the obligation to provide fair and equitable treatment and not to expropriate unless

[169]The comparable provision in the EC-CARIFORUM EPA expressly denies the exclusion when a party's domestic law permits those activities to be carried out by financial service suppliers in competition with public entities or private institutions. See also European Union-Korea Free Trade Agreement (2011), Article 7.44; European Communities–CARIFORUM Economic Partnership Agreement (2008), Article 108. Decision No. 2/2001 of the EU-Mexico Joint Council of 27 February 2001 implementing Articles 6, 9, 12(2)(b) and 50 of the Economic Partnership, Political Coordination and Cooperation Agreement, *OJ* 2001 L 70/7, Article 26. The same approach is taken in the Canada-Europe Comprehensive Economic and Trade Agreement (CETA), consolidated text of 26 September 2014, available at http://trade.ec.europa.eu/doclib/docs/2014/september/tradoc_152806.pdf.

[170]E.g. European Communities–CARIFORUM Economic Partnership Agreement (2008), Article 129, European Union-Korea Free Trade Agreement (2011), Article 11.4, cited in Krajewski 2011a, p. 21. Special rights mean that the state has limited competition to the enterprises with special rights or confers advantages on the enterprises with special rights that affect the ability of other enterprises to compete.

certain conditions are met, including the payment of compensation. While the UPS case provides an example of an investment tribunal recognizing the unique characteristics of a public service provider, concerns remain regarding the broad scope of NAFTA's investment obligations and their ability to constrain the public service policy choices of NAFTA countries. NAFTA has not be updated to adopt some of the limitations on its investment obligations that that Canada and the US now routinely incorporate in their trade and investment treaties, such as a specification of when an indirect expropriation occurs. These kinds of provisions are not found in GATS or EU trade treaties, though they are likely appear in some form in future EU treaties now that competence for investment has been shifted to the EU level.[171]

## 5.4 Summary and Conclusions

NAFTA's main approach to protecting public services is to exclude specific identified areas of public service provision and certain public service measures from the application of most NAFTA treaty obligations. With a couple of exceptions, NAFTA does not treat public services in a functional way that focuses on their distinct characteristics, including whether they are delivered by or on behalf of the state, nor does the treaty seek to circumscribe exclusions to what is necessary to ensure that the public interest mandate of public services may be discharged. Instead, exclusions in NAFTA are defined by reference to discrete lists of policy areas and existing measures that are protected from particular NAFTA obligations as well as a few sector specific provisions that preserve some flexibility for states to provide or regulate public services in ways that might otherwise be contrary to the disciplines of the agreement in relation to these sectors. In general, the scope of these provisions is more certain than the broadly worded functional exclusions in GATS and some European trade agreements, though the NAFTA provisions have never been challenged or interpreted and remain subject to some residual uncertainty. The result is protection that is somewhat more predictable, but possibly over-inclusive for public service areas listed in reservations. Most areas of public service provision not listed in reservations, however, are not protected at all. Some public service activities, like waste removal services, are subject to all of the obligations in the treaty. Other public services, like postal services, have been protected by reservations by one country only. The result is that protection for public services is both fragmentary and asymmetrical.

Reliance on discrete lists of services also means that NAFTA's approach is rigid compared to the GATS and EU trade agreement provisions. The NAFTA approach

[171] Krajewski 2011b.

cannot easily accommodate changes in national policies regarding what are considered public services. This rigidity is mitigated through exclusions from the application of some NAFTA provisions of a few policy tools, like subsidies, that can be used to support the delivery of public services outside of listed sectors.

Protection of public services under NAFTA is also limited, though the impact of the limits remains hazy. Some obligations, notably the Parties' obligations not to expropriate investments of investors of other Parties without compensation and to provide fair and equitable treatment, continue to apply to all public services. The extent to which these provisions actually limit the policy choices of NAFTA Parties in relation to public services is uncertain and contested

The survey of NAFTA provisions does disclose a slightly more nuanced approach to public services in the financial services chapter where protection is limited to delivery of services on behalf of the state by public or private entities exclusively entitled to do so with the financial support of the state. As well, the provisions on competition recognize and provide some protection for the public services mandate of state maintained monopolies from the disciplines in the competition chapter. Generally, however, the NAFTA approach to public services is fragmented, asymmetrical, rigid and limited.

In contrast to NAFTA, the approach adopted in the GATS and EU trade agreements typically involves adopting an open-ended and functional characterization of public services that permits the content to vary over time and in different contexts and that focuses more precisely on protecting the aspects of public services that make them different and in need of special treatment. This sort of approach would address some of the problems with the NAFTA approach, though at the cost of diminished predictability and likely does not provide protection for public services that is as broad as NAFTA for the public services listed in NAFTA reservations. While it is far beyond the scope of this paper to conclude that the current EU approach or the new approach to public services proposed recently by the Commission[172] should be followed in Canada and the US, the foregoing analysis suggests that more serious attention needs to be paid to the application of trade and investment rules to public services in North America. In this context, EU practice provides one example of an attempt to do so.

---

[172]European Commission, Commission Proposal for the Modernization of the Treatment of Public Services in EU Trade Agreements, TRADE.B.1/SC/am D(2011) 1146318, 26 October 2011. The Commission proposed that in its future trade agreements, the EU would reserve "the right to adopt or maintain any measure that is not inconsistent with its obligations under Article XVI of the General Agreement on Trade in Services with respect to limiting the number of suppliers through the designation of a monopoly or by conferring exclusive rights to private operators, for services of general economic interest which are subject to specific public service obligations imposed by public authorities on the provider of the service in order to meet certain public interest objectives".

## Appendix: NAFTA Annex II Reservations Relevant to Public Services

| Country | Sector | Obligations reserved against |
|---|---|---|
| Canada | Aboriginal peoples | National Treatment (Articles 1102, 1202) |
| | | Most-Favored-Nation Treatment (Articles 1103, 1203) |
| | | Local Presence (Article 1205) |
| | | Performance Requirements (Article 1106) |
| | | Senior Management and Boards of Directors (Article 1107) |
| | Air Transport | National Treatment (Article 1102) |
| | | Most-Favored-Nation Treatment (Article 1103) |
| | | Senior Management and Boards of Directors (Article 1107) |
| Mexico | Postal services | Most-Favored-Nation Treatment (Article 1203) |
| | | Local Presence (Article 1205) |
| | Energy services | Most-Favored-Nation Treatment (Article 1203) |
| | | Local Presence (Article 1205) |
| | Rail transport | Most-Favored-Nation Treatment (Article 1203) |
| | | Local Presence (Article 1205) |
| | Air traffic, navigation and related telecommunications | National Treatment (Articles 1102, 1202) |
| | | Most-Favored-Nation Treatment (Articles 1103, 1203) |
| | | Local Presence (Article 1205) |

| Country | Sector | Obligations reserved against |
|---|---|---|
| All three countries (note the specific terms of these reservations vary by country) | Public law enforcement and correctional services, and the following services to the extent they are social services established or maintained for a public purpose: income security or insurance, social security or insurance, social welfare, public education, public training, health, and child care. | National Treatment (Articles 1102, 1202) |
| | | Local Presence (Article 1205) |
| | | Senior Management and Boards of Directors (Article 1107) |
| | | (Canada and US only) |
| | | Most-Favored-Nation Treatment (Article 1203) (Canada only) |
| | Marine transport | National Treatment (Articles 1102, 1202) |
| | | Most-Favored-Nation Treatment (Articles 1103, 1203) |
| | | Local Presence (Article 1205) |
| | | Performance Requirements (Article 1106) Canada only |
| | | Senior Management and Boards of Directors (Article 1107) (Canada and US only) |
| | Socially or economically disadvantaged minorities | National Treatment (Articles 1102, 1202) |
| | | Local Presence (Article 1205) |
| | | Performance Requirements (Article 1106) Canada only |
| | | Senior Management and Boards of Directors (Article 1107) (Canada and US only) |
| | Telecommunications networks and services | National Treatment (Articles 1102, 1202) |
| | | Most-Favored-Nation Treatment (Articles 1103, 1203) |
| | | Local presence requirements (Article 1205) |
| | | Senior Management and Boards of Directors (Article 1107) (Canada and Mexico only) |

## References


Adlung R (2003) Public services and the GATS. J Int Econ Law 9:455–485

Canada (2000) Standing Committee on Foreign Affairs and International Trade, Evidence, 36th Parliament 2nd Session meeting no. 57 at 1540 (P S Pettigrew). http://www.parl.gc.ca/InfoComDoc/36/2/FAIT/Meetings/Evidence/faitev57-e.htm. Accessed 30 Nov 2014

de Mestral A (1998) The North American Free Trade Agreement: a comparative analysis. Recueil des Cours 275:219–416

Epps T, Flood C (2002) Have we traded away the opportunity for innovative health care reform? The implications of the NAFTA for medicare. McGill Law J 47:747–790

Free Trade Commission (2001) Notes of interpretation of certain NAFTA provisions, issued 13 July 2001. http://www.international.gc.ca/trade-agreements-accords-commerciaux/topics-domaines/disp-diff/NAFTA-Interpr.aspx?lang=eng. Accessed 30 Nov 2014

Grieshaber-Otto J, Sanger M (2002) Perilous lessons: the impact of the WTO Services Agreement (GATS) on Canada's public education system. Canadian Centre for Policy Alternatives, Ottawa

Hoffman A (2008) Indirect expropriation. In: Reinisch A (ed) Standards of investment protection. OUP, Oxford, pp 151–170

Houde M-F, Kolse-Patil A, Miroudot S (2007) The interaction between investment and services chapters in selected regional trade agreements. OECD Trade Policy Papers, no. 55. OECD Publishing

International Law Commission (2001) Draft articles on state responsibility for internationally wrongful acts. Report of the ILC on the work of its fifty-third session, UN GAOR, 56th Sess, supp no 10, p 43, UN Doc A/56/10

Jackman M, Porter P (2008) Socio-economic rights under the Canadian Charter. In: Langford M (ed) Socio-economic rights jurisprudence: emerging trends in comparative international law. CUP, Cambridge, pp 209–229

Johnson JR (1994) The North American Free Trade Agreement: a comprehensive guide. Canada Law Book, Aurora

Johnson JR (2002) How will international trade agreements affect Canadian health care? Discussion paper no. 22 for commission on the future of health care in Canada

Kinnear M, Bjorklund A, Hannaford J (2008) Investment disputes under NAFTA: an annotated guide to NAFTA Chapter 11. Kluwer Law International, Alphen aan den Rijn

Kläger R (2011) Fair and equitable treatment and sustainable development. In: Cordonier Segger M-C, Gehring M, Newcombe A (eds) Sustainable development in world investment law. Wolters Kluwer, Alphen aan den Rijn, pp 241–259

Krajewski M (2003) Public services and trade liberalization: mapping the legal framework. J Int Econ Law 6:341–367

Krajewski M (2011a) Universal service provisions in international agreements of the EU: From derogation to obligation? In: Szyszczak et al (eds) Developments in services of general interest. TMC Asser Press, The Hague, pp 231–252

Krajewski M (2011b) Public services in bilateral free trade agreements of the EU. http://papers.ssrn.com/sol3/papers.cfm?abstract_id=1964288. Accessed 14 Jan 2014

Krajewski M (2012) Investment law and public services. http://papers.ssrn.com/sol3/cf_dev/AbsByAuth.cfm?per_id=1056790. Accessed 14 Jan 2014

Laxer G, Dillon J (2008) Over a barrel: exiting NAFTA's proportionality clause. Parkland Institute and Canadian Centre for Policy Alternatives, Ottawa

Lennard M (2002) Navigating by the stars: interpreting the WTO agreements. J Int Econ Law 5:17–89

Leroux E (2006) What is a 'Service Supplied in the Exercise of Governmental Authority' under Article I:3(b) and (c) of the general agreement on trade in services? J World Trade 40:345–385

Luff D (2003) Regulation of health services and international trade law. In: Matoo A, Sauvé P (eds) Domestic regulation and services trade liberalization. World Bank and OUP, Washington, pp 191–220

Maki P (2000) Interpreting GATT using the Vienna convention on the law of treaties: a method to increase the legitimacy of the DSU system. Minnesota J Global Trade 9:343–360

Malloy M (2004) Financial services regulation after NAFTA. In: Kennedy K (ed) The first decade of NAFTA: the future of free trade in North America. Transnational Publishers, New York, pp 231–251

Mayeda G (2007) Playing fair: the meaning of fair and equitable treatment in Bilateral Investment Treaties (BITs). J World Trade 41:273–291

Newcombe A (2011) General exceptions in international investment agreements. In: Cordonier Segger M-C, Gehring M, Newcombe A (eds) Sustainable development in world investment law. Wolters Kluwer, Alphen aan den Rijn, pp 351–371

Schwartz B (1997) NAFTA reservations in the areas of health care. Health Law J 5:99–117

Sinclair S (2010) Negotiating from weakness: Canada-EU trade treaty threatens Canadian purchasing policies and public services. Canadian Centre for Policy Alternatives, Ottawa http://www.policyalternatives.ca/publications/reports/negotiating-%E2%80%89weakness. Accessed 27 Feb 2015

Sinclair S (2014 forthcoming) Trade agreements, the new constitutionalism and public services. In: Gill S, Cutler C (eds) New constitutionalism and world order. CUP, Cambridge

Telecommunications Services (1996) Negotiating group on basic telecommunications, reference paper. http://www.wto.org/english/tratop_e/serv_e/telecom_e/tel23_e.htm. Accessed 14 Jan 2014

UNCTAD (2012a) Expropriation: a sequel, UNCTAD series on issues in international investment agreements II. UN Publication, New York, Geneva

UNCTAD (2012b) A review of fair and equitable treatment: a sequel, UNCTAD series on issues in international investment Agreements II. UN Publication, New York, Geneva

United States Model Bilateral Investment Treaty (2012) http://www.state.gov/documents/organization/188371.pdf. Accessed 27 Feb 2015

United States Trade Representative (1995) Draft U.S.T.R. Guidelines for U.S. States: NAFTA services reservations: guidelines for NAFTA non-conforming state measures in inside NAFTA, vol 2, pp 18–20

VanDuzer J (2002) NAFTA Chapter 11 to date: the progress of a work in progress. In: Dawson L (ed) Whose rights? The NAFTA Chapter 11 Debate. Centre for Trade Policy and Law, Ottawa, pp 47–97

VanDuzer J (2004) NAFTA's impact on health care: a serious issue, a non-issue or something in between. In: Kennedy K (ed) The first decade of NAFTA: the future of free trade in North America. Transnational Publishers, New York, pp 183–229

VanDuzer J (2005) Health, education and social services in Canada: the impact of the GATS. Trade Policy Res 2004:303–505

VanDuzer J, Simons P, Mayeda G (2013) Integrating sustainable development into international investment agreements: a guide for developing countries. Commonwealth Secretariat, London

# Chapter 6
# Emerging Principles of International Competition Law: Do Public Services Matter?

**Johan van de Gronden**

**Abstract** Over the years provisions on competition law have found their way into international trade agreements. Some of these provisions concern the supply of public services. This chapter explores how the various systems of international competition law deal with public services. Do principles for public services emerge in the various international systems of competition law? It will be argued that two approaches to public services have been developed: the 'carve-out approach' and the 'market approach'. The first approach focuses on the question whether the special nature of a public service is such as to justify a carve-out from the competition rules. The second approach takes the applicability of the competition rules as point of departure, but also weighs the benefits of competition and the advantages of public services. It balances competition concerns with public service considerations.

## Contents



Professor of the Law of European Integration, Radboud University Nijmegen and Staatsraad at the Raad van State (judge at the Dutch Council of State).

J. van de Gronden (✉)
Radboud University Nijmegen, Nijmegen, The Netherlands
e-mail: J.vandeGronden@jur.ru.nl



M. Krajewski (ed.), *Services of General Interest Beyond the Single Market*, Legal Issues of Services of General Interest,
DOI 10.1007/978-94-6265-063-3_6

## 6.1 Introduction

In modern society, competition law is regarded as an important instrument for organising the economy. The functioning of free markets should be protected by competition rules. As a result, not only systems of competition law have been adopted by countries all over the world,[1] but also many international trade agreements contain rules governing the competition process. In many treaties, opening-up national markets and privatisation go hand in hand with the introduction of competition rules. A very well-known example is, of course, contained in Articles 101–109 of the Treaty on the Functioning of the EU (hereafter: TFEU). In the European integration process competition law plays a key role. From the EU experience it is not only apparent that banning anti-competitive practices is an important condition for prospering trade, but it also shows that due consideration should be paid to public services. In EU law, these services are framed as Services of General (Economic) Interest (SG(E)I). Many judgments deal with the application of the competition rules to these services. Additionally, EU harmonisation measures that oblige the Member States to open up markets in public utilities also lay down provisions on Services of General Economic Interest (SGEI).[2] The main aim of the great value assigned to this concept is to ensure access for all to essential services.[3] Accordingly, in EU law SGEI are regarded as a tool to strike a fair balance between competition and solidarity. It is apparent from developments of the last 10 years that in EU law an overall concept has emerged, i.e., Services of General Interest, which concept includes essential services of both economic and non-economic nature.[4] The European Commission has defined this concept as services that

[1]For example, in 2008 competition laws entered into force in China. On this, see Wei 2011, p. 807 et seq.

[2]See e.g. Article 3(3) of Directive 2009/72/EC of the European Parliament and of the Council of 13 July 2009 concerning common rules for the internal market in electricity and repealing Directive 2003/54/EC, *OJ* 2009 L 211/55 and Directive 2002/22/EC of the European Parliament and of the Council of 7 March 2002 on universal service and users' rights relating to electronic communication networks and services, *OJ* 2002 L 108/51 (amended by Directive 2009/136/EC, *OJ* 2009 L 337/11).

[3]See e.g. European Commission, A Quality Framework for Services of General Economic Interest in Europe, COM(2011) 900 final, 20 December 2011, p. 5.

[4]See, for example, the Protocol on Services of General Interest (connexed to the Treaty of Lisbon), *OJ* 2007 C 306/158 and European Commission, A Quality Framework for Services of General Economic Interest in Europe, COM(2011) 900 final, 20 December 2011, p. 3.

the public authorities of the Member States classify as being of general interest and, therefore, subject to specific public service obligations.[5]

It could be argued that the emergence of the concept of SGEI should be explained against the background of EU and national policies of privatisation and deregulation (introducing market forces in various sectors).[6] In EU competition law, a tool has been developed in order to balance competition and non-competition values. Therefore, the question arises whether in other systems of competition law attention is also paid to services that are similar to SG(E)I, or, as they are usually called in many jurisdictions other than the EU, public services.[7] In this chapter, the definition of public services is taken from the European Commission (EU experience): services that public authorities of a country classify as being of general interest and therefore subject to specific obligations. In my view, a very important rationale of these special obligations is to ensure access for all.

In sum, this chapter aims at examining whether public services matter in international competition law. In this contribution, international competition law is defined as a set of rules introduced by an international agreement such as the TFEU. In addition to this, it should be noted that the USA is the cradle of competition law and, as a result, US anti-trust law has been an important source of inspiration for many other systems.[8] Therefore, my definition of international competition law includes US anti-trust law. In other words, this area of law will serve as source of inspiration for exploring the role of public services in competition law. Furthermore, it should be borne in mind that the Agreement establishing the World Trade Organisation (WTO) provides an overarching framework for the liberalisation of trade. It may be expected that countries concluding trade agreements will derive concepts and principles from the WTO rules. Although the WTO system does not contain any competition rules, the analysis of this system is capable of enhancing the understanding of the role of public services. It should be noted that in some WTO cases, competition concerns were raised,[9] as is apparent inter alia from the *Mexico—Measures Affecting Telecommunications Services* case,[10] where the Dispute Settlement Body found that Mexico had failed to take action against anti-competitive practices of a major telecommunications provider.[11] In WTO law, arguments based on the need to protect competition do play

[5]See European Commission, Commission Staff Working Document, Guide to the application of the European Union rules on state aid, public procurement and the internal market to services of general economic interest, and in particular to social services of general interest, SWD(2013) 53 final/2, 29 April 2013, p. 21 and European Commission, A Quality Framework for Services of General Economic Interest in Europe, COM(2011) 900 final, 20 December 2011, p. 3.

[6]See Prosser 2005, pp. 1–16.

[7]See previous note.

[8]See Gerber 2010, p. 121 et seq.

[9]See Abbott and Singham 2013, pp. 29–32.

[10]See *Mexico—Measures Affecting Telecommunications Services,* Report of the Panel, WT/DS204/R.

[11]See Abbott and Singham 2013, pp. 30 and 31.

a role. To my mind, the consequence of this is that, in so far as this area of law contains principles for competition, it should be part of the definition of international competition law.

All in all, in this chapter it will be explored to what extent traces of public services are discernible in international competition law. Do principles for public services emerge in the various international systems of competition law?

In order to address this question, first the traditional role that public services play in international trade agreements will be highlighted. Then, two solutions for taking public services into account developed in international competition law will be discussed. This chapter ends with some conclusions. In this regard it should be noted that the analysis does not include the treaties on the Transatlantic Trade and Investment Partnership (US-EU) and on the Comprehensive Economic and Trade Agreement (Canada-EU), as these treaties were not concluded yet at the moment of the writing of this chapter.

## 6.2 The Traditional Role of Public Services: Restrictive Monopolies

Traditionally, competition law prohibits restrictive agreements and abuse of a dominant position. At the end of the 19th century the USA adopted the Sherman Act, which took these two bans as point of departure. The first section of the Sherman Act precludes firms from concluding contracts that lead to restraints. The second section of this act forbids firms from being engaged in monopolization or from attempting to monopolize. These 'dual bans' have made their appearances in EU competition law too. Article 101 TFEU forbids agreements having the object or effect of restricting competition, whereas Article 102 TFEU prohibits dominant companies from abusing their position. It should be noted, however, that the Treaty on the Functioning of the EU has extended the set of competition rules, to provisions that also deal with the role of the State. Article 107 TFEU prohibits the EU Member State from granting State aid to undertakings. Furthermore, Article 106 TFEU contains provisions on exclusive and special rights and on top of that also on SGEI. It is interesting to note that according to the second section of this provision the need to provide SGEI is a reason for justifying restrictions of competition.

It is striking that the WTO Treaties do not contain any provisions of competition law. But, in regional trade agreements many provisions on competition appear.[12] The regional treaties have fostered the emergence of a widespread conglomerate of international competition law considerably.[13] Many of them are modelled on the EU experience. For example, the West African Economic and Monetary Union (WAEMU) is based on the 'Traite de l'Union Economique et Monétaire Ouest Africaine' (TUEMOA),[14] which contains provisions that on the

[12]See Papadopoulos 2010, p. 259 et seq.

[13]See in this respect Hilpold 2013, pp. 84–86.

[14]This treaty is available at http://www.uemoa.int/Documents/TraitReviseUEMOA.pdf.

one hand ban restrictive practices of companies and State aid[15] and on the other hand deal with public services.[16]

Another interesting example is the Treaty establishing the Caribbean Community including the CARICOM Single Market and Economy (hereafter: the CARICOM Treaty).[17] This treaty contains provisions similar to those of the TFEU, in so far as the antitrust rules (cartel prohibition and dominance) are concerned.[18] But the CARICOM Treaty has no rules on public services.

It goes without saying that the international agreements that the EU has concluded with its partners are also based on the competition provisions of the TFEU. For example, the Euro-Mediterranean Agreement establishing an Association between the European Community and its Member States, on the one hand, and the People's Democratic Republic of Algeria, on the other[19] (hereafter: Euro-Mediterranean Agreement with Algeria) prohibits cartels and abusive behaviour of dominant companies in the same way as the TFEU does.[20] Article 43 of the Euro-Mediterranean Agreement with Algeria contains provisions on exclusive and special rights and on SGEI similar to Article 106 TFEU. Remarkably, Article 42 obliges the parties concerned to progressively adjust any State monopolies in order to guarantee that discrimination in the marketing of goods is abolished. In other words, State monopolies are regarded as serious obstacles to free trade in this agreement.

A significant example is the EU-South Korea Treaty.[21] Not only cartels and abusive practices (of dominant enterprises) are banned, but also concentrations that significantly impede effective competition.[22] Moreover, it is stipulated that it is not permitted for the parties to the agreement to adopt, with respect to companies having exclusive or special rights, measures that are contrary to the principles of competition and trade liberalisation; furthermore these parties should ensure that enterprises vested with such rights are subject to competition law.[23] It is, however, acknowledged that the Treaty does not prevent the parties from establishing or maintaining a State monopoly, provided that the principle of non-discrimination is observed.[24]

---

15 See Article 88 TUEMOA.

16 See Article 89 TUEMOA and Règlement 02/2002/CM/UEMOA relatif aux pratiques anticoncurrentielles à l'intérieur de l'UEMOA (available at http://www.uemoa.int/Pages/Actes/NewPages/reglement_2_2002_CM_UEMOA.aspx).

17 This treaty can be found at http://www.caricom.org/jsp/community/revised_treaty-text.pdf.

18 See Article 177 of the CARICOM Treaty.

19 Council Decision of 18 July 2005 on the conclusion of the Euro-Mediterranean Agreement establishing an Association between the European Community and its Member States, of the one part, and the People's Democratic Republic of Algeria, of the other part, *OJ* 2005 L 265/1.

20 See Article 41 of the Euro-Mediterranean Agreement with Algeria.

21 Free Trade Agreement between the European Union and its Member States, of the one part, and the Republic of Korea, of the other part, *OJ* 2011 L 127/6.

22 See Article 11.1(3) of the EU South Korea Treaty.

23 See Article 11.4 of the EU South Korea Treaty.

24 See Article 11.5 of the EU South Korea Treaty.

Other regional trade agreements have competition provisions that are different from the EU model. The NAFTA, for instance, has only a modest set of competition rules, as the aim of this treaty is not to transfer the trading block concerned into an advanced form of integration.[25] This treaty confines itself to stipulating that the NAFTA members must enforce their national competition laws. Remarkably, the NAFTA treaty does lay down concrete provisions on monopolies, which are mainly concerned with preventing these monopolies from leading to competition restrictions.

Another example is the Treaty that China has concluded with ASEAN.[26] This treaty only states that particular business practices may restrain competition and that, therefore, the parties to the treaty, if needed, should enter into consultation with each other with a view to eliminate the competition distortions concerned.[27] However, in the same vein as the NAFTA, it also explicitly provides that action should be taken, if monopolies are operated "…in a manner inconsistent with…" the commitments of the Treaty.[28]

What can be derived from the foregoing? Two categories of systems of international competition law can be distinguished. Many international trade agreements lay down substantive rules on competition. In line with the classic approach adopted in US anti-trust law agreements restraining competition and anti-competitive behaviour of firms having market power are forbidden. In other words, US anti-trust law has set an important example for many systems of international competition law. However, some systems of international competition law do not contain such substantive rules. These systems are limited to acknowledging that the parties to the agreement concerned should have in place a set of competition rules. In fact, such systems solely refer to the domestic rules and contain, accordingly, a 'light competition law regime'. It is remarkable that the US itself is party to an international agreement based on such a regime. In my view, the explanation for this could lie in the ambition regarding trade liberalisation. If this ambition is high, the parties concerned are more inclined to include substantive competition rules in an agreement, than they would be prepared to do if the ambition for opening-up markets is moderate.

It is striking that many systems of international competition law contain rules and principles that are of interest for the position of public services. In US anti-trust law rules that regulate these services in a comprehensive way are

---

[25]Nsour 2010, p. 200.

[26]Agreement on Trade in Services of the Framework Agreement on Comprehensive Economic Cooperation between the People's Republic of China and the Association of Southeast Asian Nations. This Treaty is available at http://www.asean.org/news/item/agreement-on-trade-in-services-of-the-framework-agreement-on-comprehensive-economic-co-operation-between-the-association-of-southeast-asian-nations-and-the-people-s-republic-of-china-2.

[27]See Article 8 of the Treaty mentioned in the previous note.

[28]See Article 7 of the Treaty concerned.

absent. Why have various systems of international competition law, which are all somehow rooted in the US experience with anti-trust law, come up with provisions related to public services? In my view, this can be explained by the following reasons. Traditionally, public services are provided through monopolies and similar rights in many countries, like the delivery of mail, the supply of electricity, health services and education. The provision of public services was shielded from market forces. When concluding trade agreements these monopoly-type rights are questioned and negotiations may be aimed at abolishing these rights. [29]

In this regard, it should be noted that for example in the EC-Chile Agreement, the EU has made commitments in order to open up some modes of supply of particular postal services and even of some educational services, i.e., the provision of services by privately funded universities.[30] Then again, other public services, referred to as 'public utilities', remain subject to monopolies and are precluded by the EU from the trade in services with Chile.[31] Also health and social services are not subject to commitments that allow for market access from operators from Chile.[32]

In the same vein, the EU-South Korea Agreement contains commitments of trade liberalisation related to, for example, some medical professional services[33] telecommunication and postal services,[34] rail transport services[35] and some energy services.[36] Even educational services and health care and social services are part of the commitments made; however, these commitments are limited to privately funded education services[37] (which mirrors the commitments of the EC-Chile Agreement). Furthermore, some restrictions on the opening-up of the markets for educational services and for health care and social services are set out in the EU-South Korea Agreement.[38] Moreover, the liberalisation of services does not include audio-visual services, in so far as establishment (the supply of these services on a permanent basis) is concerned.[39] As with the EC-Chile Agreement,

---

[29]Article 106(1) TFEU, for example, forbids Member States to take measures with regard to companies having a special position on the market contrary the competition rules. A similar provision is found in many trade agreements the EU is party to. Also in other trade blocks such as those of the WAEMU countries or the parties to the NAFTA, monopoly and similar rights are placed under critical scrutiny.

[30]See Krajewski 2008, p. 211.

[31]See Krajewski 2008, pp. 209 and 210.

[32]See Krajewski 2008, p. 212.

[33]See Annex 7-A-1 (cat. 1.A.j) and Annex 7-A-2 (cat. 6.h, j and k) of the EU South Korea Agreement.

[34]See Annex 7-A-1 (cat. 2) and Annex 7-A-2 (cat. 7) of the EU-South Korea Agreement.

[35]See Annex 7-A-1 (cat. 11.C) an Annex 7-A-2 (cat. 16.C) of the EU-South Korea Agreement.

[36]See Annex 7-A-1 (cat. 14) of the EU-South Korea Agreement.

[37]See Annex 7-A-1 (cat. 5 and 8) and Annex 7-A-2 (cat. 10 and 13) of the EU-South Korea Agreement.

[38]See previous note.

[39]See Article 7.10 of the EU-South Korea Agreement.

trade concerning public utilities has not been liberalised by the EU-South Korea Agreement.[40] Interestingly, the EU South Korea Agreement also provides that the parties should ensure competition in postal and courier services and the provision of these services should not be reserved to a monopoly.[41] This agreement has also introduced provisions aiming to foster competition in telecommunications.[42] Nevertheless, it is permitted for the parties to impose obligations upon telecommunication operators in order to guarantee the provision of universal services.[43]

One could argue that in trade agreements public services meet with a hostile approach, as the national regulation governing these services constitutes obstacles for free trade. In other words, national measures adopted in order to pursue public interests, such as access for all, are framed as restrictions to free trade. It goes without saying that this does not mean that the aim of countries negotiating trade agreements is abolishing these types of national regulation. On the contrary, much pressure will be on the negotiators to preserve the proper functioning of a wide range of public services. The point is that public services are perceived as a problematic category of services that complicates the liberalisation process of trade. As a result, countries are forced to examine with great care whether national measures protecting and guaranteeing the provision of public services cause unnecessary distortions of competition or trade.

Strikingly, in many national jurisdictions it is acknowledged that public services play a significant role on the market and their role is to mitigate the harsh effects of competition law. In contrast, in trade agreements the concept of public service is regarded as a problem that needs to be resolved. Therefore, the question arises how the trade agreements have dealt with this problem. Which models have been developed in order to accommodate considerations of public services in the application of international competition law? In my view, in general two categories of approach can be identified in this respect.[44] The first group focuses on the question whether the special nature of a public service is such as to justify a carve-out from the competition rules. This category is referred to as the 'carve-out approach' in this chapter. The second group takes the applicability of the competition rules as point of departure but also weighs the benefits of competition and the advantages of public services. This category is referred to as the 'market approach'. Below both categories will be discussed.

In this regard, it should be noted, as was pointed out above, that some treaties do not introduce a 'brand new' set of rules of international competition law but confine themselves to referring to domestic competition rules that are in place in the countries party to these treaties. It goes without saying that the impact that such a system could have on the provision of public services depends largely on the drafting

---

[40]See Annex 7-A-2 of the EU-South Korea Agreement.

[41]See Article 7.26 of the EU-South Korea Agreement.

[42]See Articles 7.27–7.33 of the EU-South Korea Agreement.

[43]See Article 7.34 of the EU-South Korea Agreement.

[44]See also Van de Gronden 2013a, p. 143.

of the domestic competition rules. Accordingly, it is clear from the outset that the 'stand alone-effect' of the competition provisions of a treaty that only refers to domestic systems is very limited. Nevertheless, some attention will be paid to these treaties, as lessons can be learned from how the treaties try to strike a balance between the general trade rules and concerns related to public services.

## 6.3 The Place of Public Services in International Competition Law: The 'Carve-Out Approach'

The approaches developed in several systems of international economic law in order to pay due consideration to the special role of public services boil down to excluding these services from the scope of the competition and trade rules. The first step to be taken is to examine whether public services are caught by a particular set of rules. If not, the public authorities of a particular State remain free to regulate these services. In contrast, if the competition and trade rules kick in, the public services concerned are subject to the economic rules at issue. Accordingly, the providers of the services involved must observe prohibitions such as the ban on concluding restrictive agreements and the ban on the abuse of a dominant position. The same is, of course, true for the provisions dealing with exclusive rights, special rights and State aid. On top of that, it should be pointed out that the applicability of trade rules laid down in an international agreement could entail the obligation for a country to open up (partly) the market for the public service concerned. In sum, in the 'carve-out approach' the special features of a particular public service justify that a safe harbour is created: the providers of these services are not bound by the competition rules and, furthermore, the national State measures governing these providers are not caught by the trade rules laid down in the international agreement concerned.

In international competition law several tests have been developed, when it comes to deciding on the applicability of the competition and trade rules. In essence, two main categories of tests can be distinguished.[45] The first one takes the institutional design of the national legal framework of a particular service as point of departure. The second one focuses on the question whether a specific set of national laws and rules allows for competition or commercial activities.

### *6.3.1 Institutional Design Test*

A very important example of the 'institutional design test' can be found in US anti-trust law. In this jurisdiction, no special rules are in place for public services. However, a specific doctrine, which is of great interest for the position of

[45] See previous note.

these services, has been developed: the State action doctrine.[46] According to this doctrine, the US antitrust rules do not apply if a State of the US takes a measure leading to displacing competition by creating a particular regulatory regime.[47] It goes without saying that public services are immune from US anti-trust law, if these services are governed by such a regime. For the State action doctrine to be applicable two conditions must be met.[48] In the first place, the restraint under review must be a practice that is clearly articulated and affirmatively expressed as State policy. In the second place, the policy at hand must be actively supervised by the State itself. The first condition requires that the anti-competitive effect is foreseeable,[49] whereas the second condition is concerned with adequate supervision of a State organ having the power of both disapproving and evaluating/regulating the conduct concerned.[50] It is clear that anti-trust immunity only kicks in, if specific institutional conditions are fulfilled. At the end of the day, it is not of importance whether the proper provision of a particular public service is at stake. What matters, however, is whether the State exercises control over the practices concerned.

It is interesting to note that traces of the test of the US State action doctrine is discernible in EU competition law. In EU competition law, the question arose as to whether undertakings could escape anti-trust liability by arguing that national laws forced them to engage in anti-competitive behaviour. In Ladbroke the Court of Justice of the EU (CJEU) held that firms only escape from this liability, if the relevant national laws did not leave any room for manoeuvre. [51] In other words, the institutional design of a particular framework can justify the non-applicability of the Treaty provisions on competition. The provision of public services may benefit from the 'Ladbroke approach', but concerns related to the specific nature of such services do not play any role in finding anti-trust liability. In my view, the approach adopted by the CJEU in Ladbroke is modelled on the US experience, as this approach has much in common with the US State action doctrine.

Accordingly, companies providing public services will be immune from European competition law, if EU Member States oblige them to conclude restrictive agreements or to abuse their dominant position. The problem is, however, that in such circumstances the EU Member States themselves will likely be found liable under the European competition rules. The CJEU has derived the

---

[46]Supreme Court of the United States, *Parker v. Brown*, 317 U.S. 341, 63 S.Ct. 307 (1943).

[47]See Hovenkamp 2005, p. 332.

[48]See Supreme Court of the United States, *California Retail Liquor Dealers Ass'n v. Midcal Aluminum Co.*, 445 U.S. 97, 100 S.Ct. 937 (1980).

[49]See e.g. Trujillo 2006, pp. 367–372.

[50]See Areeda and Hovenkamp 2006, p. 73.

[51]CJEU, Joined Cases C-359/95 and C-379/95 *Commission of the European Communities and French Republic v. Ladbroke Racing Ltd.* [1997] ECR I-6265. See also CFI, Case T-387/94 *Asia Motor France SA a.o. v. Commission of the European Communities* [1996] ECR II-961.

so-called ‘useful effect doctrine’[52] from Article 4(3) TEU and the Treaty provisions on competition. According to Article 4(3) TEU these States must refrain from taking measures that could jeopardise compliance with obligations of EU law. It is settled case law of the CJEU that, therefore, EU Member States are precluded from requiring or encouraging the adoption of restrictive agreements, decisions or concerted practices or from reinforcing their effects.[53] Moreover, these States are not permitted to delegate their powers to intervene on the market to private economic operators.[54] Consequently, whereas national regulatory measures could pre-empt antitrust issues from arising for private enterprises, these measures could lead, nevertheless, to competition law liability for the Member State concerned. Unlike in US antitrust law, regulatory State measures do not enjoy a ‘completely safe harbour’.

In this respect, it should be noted that State supervision is an important argument for finding the non-applicability of the competition rules. As already was pointed out, in US anti-trust law one of the requirements for the State action doctrine is that the State concerned has foreseen the anti-competitive effect. In my view, this requirement requires the State to exercise ex-ante supervision. In other words, ex ante supervisory State mechanisms justify that the provision of the public services concerned is not subject to the competition rules.

### *6.3.2 Test Based on the Room for Competition/Commercial Activities*

In some systems of international competition law, arguments related to the role of competition or commerciality play an important role. Approaches are developed that focus on how much room for competition or commercial activity is allowed within a particular legal framework for the provision of public services. The main difference with the test of the institutional design is that in these approaches formal considerations are not taken into account; rather they embark from substantive benchmarks, as they examine whether the State has introduced genuine elements of competition so as to justify the application of the rules of the ‘market game’.

In my view, it is important to examine WTO law in this regard. As already stated, this area of law does not contain any provisions of competition law. Nevertheless, considerations related to competition play a role in WTO law, more in particular in the General Agreement on Trade in Services (GATS), which imposes obligations related to free trade in services on the WTO

---

[52]See e.g. Vedder 2003, pp. 5 and 237–246.

[53]See e.g. CJEU, Case 267/86 *Van Eycke v. ASPA NV* [1988] ECR 4769.

[54]See previous note.

members. It is apparent from the drafting of this agreement that the absence of competition could constitute a reason for not applying the rules obliging the opening up of markets to particular services. This has to do with the concept of 'services supplied in the exercise of governmental authority'. This concept plays a significant role for matters of applicability, as Article I:3(b) GATS states that 'services supplied in the exercise of governmental authority' are not caught by this treaty. Article I:3(c) GATS defines this concept as any service that is supplied neither on a commercial basis, nor in competition with one or more service providers. In other words, in establishing the applicability of the GATS, WTO law takes the room for competition or commercial activities as point of departure. In legal doctrine, the interpretation of what is meant by competition or commercial activity has given rise to much debate. Controversy has arisen as to whether the reference made to competition means that potential competition would already trigger the applicability of the GATS rules[55] or whether a particular degree of actual competition is necessary.[56] In any event, it is clear from the outset that it should be scrutinised whether the national legislature of a WTO member has allowed for market forces to play some role in the provision of public services. If so, the public service at hand falls within the scope of the GATS. Under this approach, it is, in fact, in the hands of the national legislature whether the supply of these services should be made subject to the trade rules. It could be argued that the GATS provisions obliging the liberalisation of the trade in services are the 'rules of the market game', which should only apply, in so far as the national legal framework concerned allows for a substantial level of competition.

The approach developed in WTO law is mirrored by a line in the CJEU's case law on the EU competition rules. This case law concerns the issue as to whether the Treaty provisions on competition apply to social security schemes. In my view, these schemes ensure the provision of a significant form of public services, that is, the services that play an essential role in the social welfare State. EU competition law applies, in so far as the operators concerned qualify as undertakings, which means that they must be engaged in economic activities[57] (defined as the offering of goods or services on the market).[58] When it comes to social security schemes, it must, accordingly, be examined whether the bodies managing these schemes perform economic activities. In deciding this matter, the CJEU took the way the social security schemes at hand were drafted as point of departure. As with the GATS concept of 'services supplied in the exercise of governmental authority', the point in case was how much room for competition was left, as is apparent from a

[55]Cf. Krajewski 2009a, p. 201.

[56]See e.g. Adlung 2006, p. 465; VanDuzer 2004, p. 396.

[57]See CJEU, Case C-41/90 *Höfner and Elser v. Macrotron GmbH* [1991] ECR I-1979.

[58]See CJEU, Case 118/85 *Commission of the European Communities v. Italian Republic* [1987] ECR 2599.

huge body of case law.[59] From these judgments it could be derived that the CJEU focuses on the principle of solidarity. If a particular scheme is predominantly based on solidarity (because, for example, the social benefits are fixed in national law and the entitlements do not depend on the rate of the contributions due), the competition rules do not apply.[60] If the schemes concerned are based on a mix of competition and solidarity, the competition rules do kick in.[61] Since the handing down of the judgments of Kattner Stahlbau[62] and AG2R,[63] however, this approach has been changed: bodies managing schemes predominately based on solidarity only escape from EU competition law, provided that they are subject to substantial State control. In other words, the involvement of the State should justify the non-applicability of the competition rules. The AG2R judgment is illustrative of the change of approach of the CJEU. In this case the CJEU found that the scheme concerned was predominately based on solidarity but concluded, nevertheless, that the body managing this scheme might be an undertaking for the purposes of EU competition law. The reason for this was that it could not be excluded that the State control with regard to this scheme was limited, as considerable room for manoeuvre was left to the market parties.[64] It was for the referring court to examine whether this was the case.[65] If so, this national court had to conclude that the Treaty provisions on competition applied to the social security scheme at issue.

[59]See, e.g. CJEU, Joined Cases C-264/01, C-306/01, C-354/01 and C-355/01 *AOK Bundesverband a.o.* v. *Ichthyol-Gesellschaft Cordes, Hermani & Co. a.o.* [2004] ECR I-2493; CJEU, Case C-67/96 *Albany International BV v. Stichting Bedrijfspensioenfonds Textielindustrie* [1999] ECR I-5751; CJEU, Joined Cases C-115/97, C-116/97 and C-117/97 *Brentjens' Handelsonderneming BV v. Stichting Bedrijfspensioenfonds voor de Handel in Bouwmaterialen* [1999] ECR I-6025; CJEU, Case C-219/97 *Maatschappij Drijvende Bokken BV v. Stichting Pensioenfonds voor de Vervoer- en Havenbedrijven* [1999] ECR I-6121; CJEU, Case C-244/94 *Fédération Française des Sociétés d'Assurance a.o. v. Ministère de l'Agriculture et de la Pêche* [1995] ECR I-4013; CJEU, Joined Cases C-159/91; C-160/91 *Poucet v. Assurances Générales de France and Caisse Mutuelle Régionale du Languedoc-Roussillon* [1993] ECR I-637 and CJEU, Case C-205/03 *Federación Española de Empresas de Tecnología Sanitaria (FENIN) v. Commission of the European Communities* [2006] ECR I-6295.

[60]See, for instance, CJEU, Joined Cases C-264/01, C-306/01, C-354/01 and C-355/01 *AOK Bundesverband a.o.* v. *Ichthyol-Gesellschaft Cordes, Hermani & Co. a.o.* [2004] ECR I-2493.

[61]See, for example, CJEU, Case C-67/96 *Albany International BV v. Stichting Bedrijfspensioenfonds Textielindustrie* [1999] ECR I-5751; CJEU, Joined Cases C-115/97, C-116/97 and C-117/97 *Brentjens' Handelsonderneming BV v. Stichting Bedrijfspensioenfonds voor de Handel in Bouwmaterialen* [1999] ECR I-6025 and CJEU, Case C-219/97 *Maatschappij Drijvende Bokken BV v. Stichting Pensioenfonds voor de Vervoer- en Havenbedrijven* [1999] ECR I-6121.

[62]CJEU, Case C-350/07 *Kattner Stahlbau GmbH v. Maschinenbau- und Metall-*Berufsgenossenschaft [2009] ECR I-1513.

[63]CJEU, Case C-437/09 *AG2R Prévoyance v. Beaudout Père et Fils SARL* [2011] ECR I-973.

[64]See also Neergaard 2013, p. 228.

[65]The issues of AG2R were raised in a preliminary procedure, where, pursuant to Article 267 TFEU, a domestic court of a Member State poses questions regarding, for example, the interpretation of EU law to the CJEU.

From this line of reasoning it can be inferred that the CJEU now carries out a two-prong test, which takes both the role of the principle of solidarity and the level of State control as point of departure. In fact, the CJEU has merged the elements of the test based on the room for competition with the institutional design test, as not only substantive elements but also institutional issues play a role in its reasoning. As a result, the threshold to escape from EU competition law in social security cases has been raised.

In this regard, it should be noted that if a social security service falls within the scope of EU competition law, an exception could be invoked. As already mentioned above, Article 106(2) TFEU provides that the need to provide a Service of General Economic interest (which is the EU term for public service) is capable of justifying restrictive practices. In Sect. 6.4, this Treaty provision will be discussed in more detail.

In sum, it has to be noted that, as in WTO law, the will of the national legislature is taken into account in cases concerning the applicability of the EU competition rules to social security schemes. It is in the hands of the national legislature to determine whether these rules should kick in. Apparently, the Treaty provisions on competition are regarded as the rules of the market game: they apply in so far as the set-up of the social security scheme concerned justifies that market-oriented rules, such as EU competition law, have to be applied.

### *6.3.3 Evaluation*

Various approaches have been discussed in this section. Although the details of these approaches may differ, they do have one important feature in common. Eventually, they draw on the will of the legislature of the State concerned, for the key question whether a framework for public services is introduced that justifies the application of the competition (and trade) rules. Some approaches address this question from a formal angle and others from a substantive angle. But this does not have any bearing on the finding that the national legislature is capable of shielding public services from the impact of competition law. The national legislature could set aside the competition (and trade) rules by basing the provision of public services on (substantial) State control (formal angle) and by not allowing for competition or commercial activities (substantive angle). In fact, it is, therefore, in the hands of the national legislature whether the competition (and trade) rules should be complied with in matters concerning public services.

To my mind, this comes down to paying due consideration to democratic legitimacy. It may be assumed that the will of the legislature is a genuine expression of the point of view (of the majority of) the national parliament. Democratic legitimation is, apparently, also a value that should be taken into account when deciding on the applicability of the competition (and the trade) rules.

## 6.4 The Place of Public Services in International Competition Law: The 'Market Approach'

In the previous section the 'carve-out approach', which has been developed in several systems of international competition law, was discussed. However, another solution for the accommodation of considerations related to public service is also discernible. Mainly in EU competition law, such a solution has been created. It should be pointed out that, apart from its case law dealing with the 'Ladbroke doctrine' and with social security schemes, the CJEU has handed down judgments that depart from a different point of view, when it comes to public services. The line of reasoning of this other case law does not focus on the intent of the national legislature; rather it emphasises the potential role that market forces could play and, at the same time, it balances competition concerns with public services considerations. As regards public services that are not social security services, the CJEU has dealt with the concept of undertaking in a way different from it did in the cases discussed above. Below this case law will be analysed. In this regard, it should be noted that in US anti-trust law an approach based on balancing competition concerns with public services considerations is absent. On the one hand the Rule of Reason, as developed in US anti-trust law, allows for assessing the pro and anti-competitive effects of a contract.[66] But the US-style Rule of Reason does not leave room for making a trade-off between competition restraints and social welfare gains and other non-competition values,[67] as is apparent from, for example, policy guidelines developed by the US authorities for the application of the anti-trust rules in health care matters.[68] As a result, considerations based on the specific features of public services do not play a significant role in US anti-trust law cases.

### *6.4.1 The Market Approach in EU Competition Law*

When it comes to the question as to whether the providers of these public services (other than the management of social security schemes) are undertakings, the CJEU starts by examining whether the provision of such a public service amounts

[66]See e.g. Nagy 2013, p. 101 et seq.

[67]See Elhauge and Geradin 2011, pp. 180–208. Cf. also Nagy 2013, pp. 123–127.

[68]See the Statements of Antitrust Enforcement Policy in Health Care, issued by the U.S. Department of Justice and the Federal Trade Commission, August 1996, available at http://www.ftc.gov/bc/healthcare/industryguide/policy/hlth3s.pdf. The following statements (taken from p. 70 of these guidelines) are illustrative for the approach adopted in this respect: "The Agencies emphasize that it is not their intent to treat such networks either more strictly or more leniently than joint ventures in other industries, or to favour any particular pro-competitive organization or structure of health care delivery over other forms that consumers may desire. Rather, their goal is to ensure a competitive marketplace in which consumers will have the benefit of high quality, cost-effective health care and a wide range of choices, including new provider-controlled networks that expand consumer choice and increase competition."

to an economic activity. It is striking that in cases other than those involving social security systems the CJEU has consistently held that public services are of an economic nature, unless they concern the exercise of State prerogatives. An interesting case in this regard is Eurocontrol,[69] since the facts of this case unfolded in an international setting. At issue was the question whether air traffic control, which was based on treaties concluded between various countries, amounted to economic activities for the purpose of EU competition law. The CJEU stressed that Eurocontrol provided air space control and was "...vested with rights and powers of coercion which derogate from ordinary law...".[70] The finding was, therefore, that this task belonged to the public domain and therefore constituted State prerogatives. Accordingly, the European competition rules did not apply. In the same vein, the CJEU decided that the police task of an Italian private cooperation, which entailed verifying compliance with public environmental laws, amounted to the exercise of a State prerogative and, therefore, was not of an economic nature. In my view, the CJEU has examined in these cases whether only the State is capable of providing a particular public service. If so, competition law does not apply; if not, competition law kicks in. This conclusion is confirmed by the CJEU's judgment in *Compass-Datenbank*.[71] Here, the CJEU had to decide on the task of a public authority of storing data that firms are obliged to report to a company register on the basis of statutory obligations. The authority managing this register was obliged to make this data available to the public on behalf of the government at rates fixed in national legislation. The CJEU ruled that this task was not of an economic nature. In my view, an important argument for this finding was that the collection of the data at issue and their provision at request to the public were based on a statutory obligation.[72] It is clear from the outset that only the State has the authority to impose such obligations upon enterprises; market operators do not have this competence. Consequently, the public service concerned can only be provided by the State.

In my view, by stressing that the competition rules do only not cover public services belonging to the public domain, the CJEU, in fact, accepts that these rules apply, as long as the services concerned can be provided on the market. In other words, if, from a theoretical point of view, it is possible to subject the supply of a particular service to market forces, competition law kicks in under this approach. Accordingly, what matters for establishing the applicability of the competition rules is whether the services under review have a 'market dimension'. In sharp contrast with the case law on social security schemes (discussed in the previous section), the national design of the public service organisation does not matter.

[69]CJEU, Case C-364/92 *SAT Fluggesellschaft mbH v. Eurocontrol* [1994] ECR I-43.

[70]See para 24 of CJEU, Case C-364/92 *SAT Fluggesellschaft mbH v. Eurocontrol* [1994] ECR I-43.

[71]CJEU, Case C-138/11 *Compass-Datenbank GmbH v. Republik Österreich* [2012] ECR I-449.

[72]See para 40 of CJEU, Case C-138/11 *Compass-Datenbank GmbH v. Republik Österreich* [2012] ECR I-449.

Even in cases where the national legislature has created an extensive legal framework that leaves virtually no room for competition, the EU anti-trust rules could be applicable, if, theoretically, it is not excluded that market operators provide the public services at issue. The benchmark to apply is, therefore, not whether a national legislature of a Member State has put in place a market-oriented model; rather the test revolves around the 'abstract' point of view as to whether it is possible to make the supply of particular public services subject to competition, irrespective of whether such a role for the market is envisaged by the State concerned. In other words, -apart from social security services- in EU law public services are only immune from the competition rules, if they cannot be performed in a market-based environment.[73]

Strikingly, EU competition law is capable of covering more public services than its equivalent system in the US, as the latter system only takes the institutional design of the public services as point of departure for establishing the applicability of the anti-trust rules. Above, it was put forward that the competition rules of many international trade agreements are modelled on Articles 101 and 102 TFEU. Consequently, it may be assumed that these competition rules should be interpreted in the light of the EU competition rules, which should, in fact, lead to the finding that these international competition rules also apply to a wide range of public services. Potentially, the approach developed by the CJEU to public services (other than social security activities) is capable of having a far-reaching impact, as it could prompt the application of the competition rules to these services. However, in legal doctrine, it is pointed out that the competition rules of many international agreements concluded between the EU and its partners are hardly enforced in practice.[74] This observation considerably mitigates the high expectations that the impact of the competition rules of trade agreements could have on public services.

In sum, in many cases the potential market dimension of public services will trigger the applicability of the EU competition rules. As a result, services such as public housing, health care services, transport services and social services fall within the ambit of Articles 101 and 102 TFEU.

This does not mean, however, that the public services falling within the scope of competition law are fully subjected to these treaty provisions. It is important to note, as already mentioned, that the EU experience with public services (SGEI) is based on balancing competition concerns with values that are typical for public services. As already pointed out, Article 106(2) TFEU lays down a 'public service specific' exception. Accordingly, the market approach leads to a balancing act: the advantages and disadvantages of applying the competition rules in a specific case must be weighed. Market and other values, such as those of a social nature, should be identified and on a case by case basis it should be decided which value should

[73]Van de Gronden 2004, p. 85.

[74]See in this regard Geradin and Petit 2004, p. 78. Cf. in this regard also Papadopoulos 2010, p. 184 and Tschaeni and Engammare 2013, pp. 63–67.

take precedence. In some circumstances competition restraints are permitted and in other circumstances they are not. In my view, the market approach is acceptable on the condition that a particular competition law system allows for balancing the positive and negative effects of subjecting the provision of public services to market forces, as EU law does. To put it differently, such a competition law system should contain exceptions to prohibitions not to be engaged in anti-competitive behaviour. The point is that a smart market approach lays down exceptions that allows for balancing the benefits and disadvantages of applying the competition rules to public services in a specific case.

According to Article 106(2) TFEU, restrictive practices and measures are permitted, provided that these practices and measures are necessary with a view to the adequate provision of Services of General Economic Interest (SGEI). As already mentioned, the TFEU prefers the term SGEI to that of public services. In any event, it is important to note that in Article 106(2) TFEU cases to a certain extent some value is assigned to the role of the national legislature: it is settled case law of the CJEU that for Article 106(2) TFEU to be applicable, a State body has to entrust a SGEI mission to a particular enterprise.[75] It could be argued that the State body entrusting such a mission to an operator derives its authority from the national legislature and, as a result, democratic legitimatization is one of the underpinning principles in the EU doctrine regarding Article 106(2) TFEU. Furthermore, apart from the requirement of entrustment, Article 106(2) TFEU can only be invoked if the principle of proportionality is met: the restrictive practice or measure should be necessary in order to guarantee the adequate supply of SGEI. In landmark decisions such as Corbeau,[76] the CJEU has allowed the EU Member States some flexibility in this respect.[77] The test to be applied does not come down to examining whether the SGEI concerned can be provided by less restrictive means.[78] Rather, the CJEU verifies whether a particular SGEI operator can only perform the task entrusted under economically acceptable circumstances by restricting competition. In my view, this test entails addressing the problems of cherry picking. A SGEI operator entrusted with the task of guaranteeing access for all is usually confronted with commercially oriented enterprises, which carry out the most profitable activities leaving the less profitable activities to this SGEI operator. In order to solve this problem, the CJEU has accepted that an EU Member Sate may enable a SGEI operator to cross-subsidise its less profitable activities with the revenues from profitable activities by, for example, giving this operator an exclusive or special right.

---

[75]See, for example, CJEU, Case C-475/99 *Firma Ambulanz Glöckner v. Landkreis Südwestpfalz* [2001] ECR I-8089.

[76]CJEU, Case C-320/91 *Corbeau* [1993] ECR I-2533.

[77]Cf. Buendia Sierra 1999, pp. 319 and 320; Schweitzer 2011, pp. 38–41.

[78]This stands in sharp contrast with the CJEU's case law on free movement. In this areas of law, the CJEU has held that an exception can only be relied upon, if a specific objective of general interest cannot be realized by less restrictive means than the measure under review. See e.g. para 37 of CJEU, Case C-55/94 *Gebhard v. Consiglio dell'Ordine degli Avvocati e Procuratori di Milano* [1995] I-4165.

For instance, in Ambulanz Glöckner[79] the exclusive rights of an ambulance organisation were designed in such a way as to enable public ambulance organisations to leverage their market power from the reserved market (which was the market for emergency patient transport) to the market open for competition (which was the market for non-emergency patient transport). The CJEU held that this restrictive measure was justifiable on the basis of Article 106(2) TFEU, as public ambulances needed the revenues from the market for non-emergency transport in order to finance the emergency transport of ill people, especially, in remote areas. In this regard it should be noted that competition restrictions could be caused by both the EU Member States (when setting up a scheme for the proper provision of SGEI) and by the SGEI enterprises (when carrying out the tasks entrusted to them). Therefore, the CJEU has accepted that both the EU Member States and SGEI enterprises are entitled to invoke Article 106(2) TFEU.[80]

To wind up, market failure is for the CJEU an important reason for applying Article 106(2) TFEU.[81] To date, in relation to SGEI/public services, the CJEU has acknowledged only one market failure, that is, cherry picking. It should be awaited whether the CJEU will accept that also other types of market failures could be regarded as reasons for justifying restrictive measures.

### *6.4.2 The Market Approach in International Trade Agreements*

Some other systems of international competition law have modelled provisions on public services on Article 106(2) TFEU and, accordingly, have introduced a market approach to these services based on competition concerns and public service values. Unsurprisingly, trade agreements that the EU has concluded with other countries refer to this provision of the TFEU. Article 43 of the Euro-Mediterranean Agreement with Algeria[82] and Article 36 of the Euro-Mediterranean Agreement with Egypt[83] recognise that the need to provide SGEI could justify restrictive practices. Similarly, the EC-Chile Agreement

---

[79]CJEU, Case C-475/99 *Firma Ambulanz Glöckner v. Landkreis Südwestpfalz* [2001] ECR I-8089.

[80]See, for example, CJEU, Case C-203/96 *Chemische Afvalstoffen Dusseldorp BV a.o. v. Minister van Volkshuisvesting, Ruimtelijke Ordening en Milieubeheer* [1998] ECR I-4075 and CJEU, Case C-437/09 *AG2R Prévoyance v. Beaudout Père et Fils SARL* [2011] ECR I-973 (already mentioned). See furthermore Jones and Sufrin 2014, p. 634.

[81]See Sauter 2008, pp. 179 and 180 and Van de Gronden 2006, pp. 133–135.

[82]Council Decision of 18 July 2005 on the conclusion of the Euro-Mediterranean Agreement establishing an Association between the European Community and its Member States, of the one part, and the People's Democratic Republic of Algeria, of the other part, *OJ* 2005 L 265/1.

[83]Euro-Mediterranean Agreement establishing an Association between the European Communities and their Member States, on the one part, and the Arab Republic of Egypt, on the other part, *OJ* 2004 L 304/39.

acknowledges that the need to assign particular tasks to enterprises having exclusive or special rights is capable of justifying restraints of competition.[84] Moreover, this agreement contains SGEI-type of provisions[85] for special sectors: it is permitted for the parties to the Treaty to impose universal service obligations on operators in telecommunications.[86] Also the EU South Korea Treaty provides that enterprises having exclusive and special rights are not subject to the competition rules, in so far as the application of these rules would obstruct the performance of the special tasks assigned to them.[87] This international agreement recognises too that in special sectors (postal and courier services as well telecommunications) the provision of universal services has to be guaranteed.[88] Furthermore, the Agreement establishing an Association between the European Union and its Members, on the one hand, and Central America on the other[89] (EU Central America Association Agreement) provides that particular tasks assigned to public enterprises and enterprises having exclusive or special rights are capable of justifying anti-competitive restraints.[90] This agreement also contains a provision on universal services in telecommunications.[91]

But it should be noted that even international trade agreements to which the EU is not a party include provisions that resemble Article 106(2) TFEU. In this respect, the TUEMOA is of interest. Under this treaty a special law, which is Regulation 02/2002,[92] was adopted. Pursuant to Article 6.2 of this regulation enterprises entrusted with the operation of a SGEI mission could put forward that compliance with the competition rules of the TUEMOA would obstruct the performance of the task assigned to them. Nevertheless, one striking procedural difference with the EU approach should be outlined: the enterprise intending to invoke the SGEI exception is obliged to apply for prior authorisation from a commission, which is vested with the task of implementing the TUEMOA. Even in the NAFTA, which has only a limited set of competition rules, concerns of public service are accommodated. It should, although, be pointed out that this treaty deals in an indirect way with these concerns. Article 1502 NAFTA provides that its Members are entitled to have in place monopolies and monopoly specific competition rules. Nevertheless, the Contracting Parties must ensure the fairness of the competition

[84]See Article 179(2) of the EC-Chile Agreement.

[85]See Van de Gronden 2013a, p. 140.

[86]See Article 115 of the EC-Chile Agreement.

[87]See Article 11.4(1) of the EU South Korea Treaty.

[88]See Articles 7.26, 7.27 (2 sub h) and 7.34 of the EU South Korea Treaty.

[89]Agreement establishing an Association between the European Union and its Member States, on the one hand, and Central America on the other, *OJ* 2012 L 346/3.

[90]See Article 280(2) of the EU Central America Association Agreement.

[91]See Article 191 of the EU Central America Association Agreement.

[92]Règlement 02/2002/CM/UEMOA relatif aux pratiques anticoncurrentielles à l'intérieur de l'UEMOA, available at http://www.uemoa.int/Pages/Actes/NewPages/reglement_2_2002_CM_UEMOA.aspx.

process, by, for example, banning anti-competitive practices in a non-monopolised market carried out by privately owned monopolies.[93] Furthermore, pursuant to Article 1503 NAFTA it is permitted for its Members to maintain or establish State enterprises. Accordingly, the States party to the NAFTA are able to guarantee the provision of public services through monopolies and State enterprises.

The question arises as to whether the provisions of international trade agreements modelled on the EU experience with SGEI should be interpreted in the light of Article 106(2) TFEU. This seems to make sense for agreements to which the EU is a party, but also other agreements could learn lessons from the EU experience with SGEI. Nevertheless, countries in other parts of the world could have traditions and views related to public services that are very different from those of the EU. These differences could justify diverging interpretations of public service-oriented provisions. To date, no experience with SGEI-type of obligations laid down in international trade agreements (other than the TFEU) is available to my knowledge

In sum, traces of the market approach to public services are not only discernible in EU law but also in other systems of international competition law. In sharp contrast with the EU experience, however, the rules and principles of this approach are virtually not worked out in concrete judgments in these other systems of international competition law.

### 6.4.3 The Market Approach and the EU State Aid Rules

The EU experience with public services has shown that mechanisms for financing these services play an important role in many countries. Providing SGEI (in EU terminology) can be very cost-intensive and it comes, therefore, not as a surprise that EU Member States have financed the provisions of these services. In EU law this could give rise to State aid issues, as Article 107 TFEU, in principle, precludes Member States from giving such aid to undertakings. In order to address these issues, the CJEU has developed an approach to SGEI and State aid. In Altmark[94] the CJEU has held that a national mechanism adopted in order to finance SGEI does not constitute State aid if the following conditions are satisfied: (1) the undertaking concerned is charged with the execution of a Public Service Obligation,[95] (2) the parameters of the amount of the compensation are calculated in an objective and transparent way (3) the compensation does not go beyond what is

[93]See Article 1502(3) NAFTA.

[94]CJEU, Case C-280/00 *Altmark Trans GmbH and Regierungspräsidium Magdeburg v. Nahverkehrsgesellschaft Altmark GmbH, and Oberbundesanwalt beim Bundesverwaltungsgericht* [2003] ECR I-7747.

[95]It is apparent from paras 161–162 of CFI, Case T-289/03 *British United Provident Association Ltd a.o. v. Commission of the European Communities* [2008] ECR II-81, that Public Service Obligations and Services of General Economic Interest are identical concepts.

necessary, and (4) the amount of the compensation is determined on the basis of the expenses of a well-run undertaking (if the contract concerned has not been granted in accordance with a public procurement procedure). Furthermore, it should be noted that Article 106(2) TFEU could be invoked, if a particular national State aid measure does not meet all Altmark conditions.

On the one hand, the *Altmark* ruling and subsequent CJEU judgments on State aid and SGEI have given some room for manoeuvre to the EU Member States, when it comes to financing public services. On the other hand, by setting out specific conditions for SGEI aid, the EU institutions have developed a powerful tool for influencing the supply of public services in the Member States.[96] That is exactly what happened the last years, as the Commission has adopted the so-called Altmark package.[97] In this package,[98] the Commission has obliged the EU Member States to adopt cost-effective policies when financing SGEI.[99] If they fail to do so, the risk exists that these policies will not be compatible with EU State aid law. Furthermore, the governance of the national SGEI organisation should satisfy particular conditions, such as compliance with the transparency principle, in order to meet the criteria set out by the Commission in the Altmark package.[100] Moreover, Member States should define clearly the contours of a particular SGEI mission and limit the aid given to the operator of this mission, and prevent the operator concerned from spending the public money on other activities. Accordingly, by clarifying all kind of questions, which at first sight may concern technicalities but on second thought involve fundamental matters, the EU institutions increasingly influence the way public services are supplied by the Member States.

The foregoing shows that in EU law a huge body of case law on policy interventions is available as regards the financing of SGEI. It is interesting to note that traces of issues that are in place in EU State aid law are discernible in other systems of international competition law. Also the NAFTA experience shows the importance of State aid in public service matters. The International Centre for Settlement of Investment Disputes, which has the authority to handle cases arising under the NAFTA, was called upon to settle a dispute on subsidizing the delivery

---

[96]See Szyszczak 2013, pp. 7–11.

[97]See the Communication from the European Commission on the application of the European Union State aid rules to compensation granted for the provision of services of general economic interest, *OJ* 2012 C 8/4; the Commission Decision of 20 December 2011 on the application of Article 106(2) of the Treaty on the Functioning of the European Union to State aid in the form of public service compensation granted to certain undertakings entrusted with the operation of services of general economic interest, *OJ* 2012 L 7/3; the Communication from the European Commission on a European Union framework for State aid in the form of public service compensation, *OJ* 2012 C 8/15 and Commission Regulation (EU) No 360/2012 of 25 April 2012 on the application of Articles 107 and 108 of the Treaty on the Functioning of the European Union to *de minimis* aid granted to undertakings providing services of general economic interest, *OJ* 2012 L 114/8.

[98]On this package, see e.g. Szyszczak and Van de Gronden 2013.

[99]See Kavanagh 2013, pp. 158 and 159.

[100]See Van de Gronden 2013b, pp. 282 and 283.

of post.[101] This case was brought to this body by the US based enterprise, UPS. The point was that the Canadian government allowed Canada Post to use its privileges resulting from its letter mail monopoly (subsidies) in order to cross-subsidize its services of express delivery. The International Centre contended that these practices were not contrary to NAFTA law, as the financing of the services concerned was justified on the basis of the so called 'cultural industries exceptions'. [102] This dispute settlement body emphasised the importance of the universal services obligations that were in place.[103] Interestingly, when rejecting UPS' claim that this company should get the same treatment as Canada Post, the International Centre referred to the obligation imposed on Canada Post to ensure the widest-possible distribution "…to individual Canadian consumers at affordable and uniform prices throughout the country…" and "… to deliver to every address in Canada (in fulfilment of Canada's universal service obligation)…".[104] This obligation justifies the finding that UPS and Canada Post are not in the same circumstances. Consequently, not only in EU law, but also in other systems of international competition law it is acknowledged that the need to ensure access for all to particular public services could constitute a reason for allowing national mechanisms to finance the provision of these services.

### *6.4.4 Some Observations on SG(E)I in EU Law*

In EU law important developments regarding public services have taken place and, accordingly, their position is reinforced. As a result the importance of the market approach to these services has increased.

Of eminent importance is the entering into force of the Treaty of Lisbon and, more in particular, the changes concerning SG(E)I brought upon by this treaty.[105] Article 14 TFEU now contains a legal basis for EU action for SGEI. The Protocol on Services of General Interest (SGI),[106] annexed to the Treaty of Lisbon, comes up with an overarching EU approach to SGI (being non-economic SGI and SGEI). To conclude, Article 36 of the EU Charter of Fundamental Rights, which was

---

[101] *United Parcel Service of America Inc. v. Government of Canada,* NAFTA/UNCITRAL Arbitration, Award on the Merits, 24 May 2007.

[102] Nsour 2010, p. 151.

[103] See *United Parcel Service of America Inc. v. Government of Canada,* NAFTA/UNCITRAL Arbitration, Award on the Merits, 24 May 2007, paras 139 and further.

[104] See *United Parcel Service of America Inc. v. Government of Canada,* NAFTA/UNCITRAL Arbitration, Award on the Merits, 24 May 2007, para 175.

[105] On this, see Van de Gronden and Rusu 2012, p. 413 et seq.

[106] Protocols to be annexed to the Treaty on European Union, to the Treaty on the Functioning of the European Union and, where applicable, to the Treaty establishing the European Atomic Energy Community, *OJ* 2007 C 306/148.

declared legally binding by the Treaty of Lisbon,[107] States that access to SGEI is a fundamental right. In other words, by setting out principles and requirements for SG(E)I on the European level the Treaty framers have paved the way for more EU action regarding public services in the near future.

### 6.4.5 Evaluation

In sum, under EU law Member States have to balance the benefits resulting from competition and the need to ensure access to public services for all. By introducing the test of economically acceptable circumstances, the CJEU has allowed the Member States to address market failures. Furthermore, as the market failure acknowledged by the CJEU is related to the problem of cherry picking, at the heart of the SGEI approach is ensuring access for vulnerable groups of citizens to essential services and, as a result, solidarity plays a key role in this regard.[108] Therefore, it does not make sense for EU Member States to deny that competition law is relevant for their public services organisation. Rather, they should shape this organisation in such a way as to strike a good balance between competition and the need to give access for all to public services/SG(E)I.

Furthermore, also in other systems of international competition law traces of the market approach to public services are discernible. Partly, provisions of these systems dealing with public services are modelled on the EU experience. One could argue that the EU has exported its SGEI oriented rules to other parts of the world. Partly, provisions of international systems of competition law govern the provision of public services in an indirect way. An important issue is, however, the implementation of the public service-specific competition rules. Whereas in EU law many judgments of the European courts, decisions of the European Commission and even EU legislation related to SGEI are available, in other systems of international competition law such experience is virtually absent. (The case brought upon by UPS against Canada under the NAFTA is a rare exception.)

## 6.5 Conclusions

In international competition law two approaches to public services have been developed: in this chapter they are labelled the 'carve-out approach' and the 'market approach'. On the one hand significant differences exist between both approaches, but on the other, there is a striking resemblance: under both approaches a considerable number of public services are caught by the competition

[107] See Article 6(1) Treaty establishing the EU.

[108] See Krajewski 2009b, pp. 504 and 505.

rules. The reason for applying these rules to these services is related to the goal of removing obstacles to free trade. In this regard, an important problem should be mentioned: apart from the EU and US anti-trust rules, the international competition rules contained in trade agreements are virtually not enforced.[109]

The 'market approach', which assigns great value to balancing competition and public concerns, has mainly been developed in EU competition law. This is not surprising, as balancing these two concerns requires the existence of strong administrative and judicial mechanisms. In the EU such mechanisms are in place, since the European Commission enforces the competition rules, whereas the decisions taken by this institution are subject to review by the General Court and the Court of Justice of the EU. These bodies have developed an extensive body of case law, which is capable of giving guidance on how to balance competition concerns with public service considerations. If other jurisdictions consider developing a market approach comparable to the EU experience, these jurisdictions should set up a strong administrative and judicial system for enforcing the competition rules as well. This raises the question whether various parties to trade agreements are prepared and have the courage to take measures in order to improve the effectiveness of the competition rules they have agreed upon.

Probably, the fear exists that better enforcement of the competition rules could have adverse effects on the proper functioning of many domestic public services. This fear could be addressed by combining the 'carve-out approach' with the 'market approach'[110]: as long as a particular essential service should be protected from market forces in the view of a State, it can be agreed that international competition rules do not apply to this service. As soon as the providers of the public services concerned are ready for facing competition, the exemption can be withdrawn. It should be noted that the providers of these services would not be exposed to unbridled competition, if a public service-specific exception based on balancing the competition and public concerns is to be put in place as well. This means, in my view, that, in line with the EU experience, administrative and judicial bodies should also be established in order to apply this exception. Such bodies are able to give guidance on how to balance competition and public services concerns. Probably, the bodies responsible for applying the competition rules to public services in various international jurisdictions could exchange best practices as to how to take into account the special features of public services. Lessons could be learned from the judgments handed down and decisions taken in the various systems of international competition law. To conclude, if the parties to international trade agreements introduce mechanisms that both improve the efficiency of enforcement and accommodate concerns related to competition and public services, they will contribute to the development of a smart international competition law system that is capable of increasing competitiveness and paying due consideration to social values at the same time.

---

[109]See in this respect the UNCTAD 2005, p. 31 and Nsour 2010, p. 153.

[110]See Van de Gronden 2013a, p. 146.

## References


Abbott AF, Singham S (2013) Competition policy and international trade distortions. In: Herrmann C, Krajewski M, Terhechte JP (eds) European yearbook of international economic law. Springer, Heidelberg, pp 23–38

Adlung R (2006) Public services and the GATS. J Int Econ Law 9(2):455–485

Areeda PE, Hovenkamp H (2006) Antitrust law, an analysis of antitrust principles and their application, vol IA, 3rd edn. Aspen Publishers, New York

Buendia Sierra JL (1999) Exclusive rights and state monopolies under EC law. Article 86 (former Article 90) of the EC Treaty. Oxford University Press, Oxford

Elhauge E, Geradin D (2011) Global competition law and economics. Hart Publishing, Oxford

Geradin D, Petit N (2004) Competition policy in the southern Mediterranean countries. Rev Netw Econ 3(1):65–82

Gerber D (2010) Global competition: law, markets and globalization. Oxford University Press, Oxford

Hilpold P (2013) Regulating international competition issues by regional trade agreements: a stepping stone towards a plurilateral trade agreement? In: Herrmann C, Krajewski M, Terhechte JP (eds) European yearbook of international economic law. Springer, Heidelberg, pp 71–86

Hovenkamp H (2005) Antitrust, 4th edn. Thomson/West, St. Paul

Jones A, Sufrin B (2014) EU competition law. Text, cases and materials, 5th edn. Oxford University Press, Oxford

Kavanagh J (2013) Financing services of general economic interest: the European Commission's economic test. In: Szyszczak E, van de Gronden JW (eds) Financing services of general economic interest. Reform and modernization. T.M.C. Asser Press, The Hague, pp 149–160

Krajewski M (2008) Of modes and sectors. External relations, internal debates, and the special case of (trade in) services. In: Cremona M (ed) Developments in EU external relations law. Oxford University Press, Oxford, pp 172–215

Krajewski M (2009a) Protecting a shared value of the Union in a globalized world: services of general economic interest and external trade. In: van de Gronden JW (ed) EU and WTO law on services. Limits to the realisation of general interest policies within the services markets? Kluwer Law International, Alphen aan de Rijn, pp 187–213

Krajewski M (2009b) Conclusion. In: Krajewski M, Neergaard U, van de Gronden JW (eds) The changing legal framework for services of general interest for Europe. Between competition and solidarity. T.M.C. Asser Press, The Hague, pp 499–506

Nagy CI (2013) EU and US competition law: divided in unity? The rule on restrictive agreements and vertical intra-brand restraints. Ashgate, Farnham

Neergaard U (2013) The concept of SSGI and the asymmetries between free movement and competition law. In: Neergaard U et al (eds) Social services of general interest in the EU. T.M.C. Asser Press, The Hague, pp 205–244

Nsour MFA (2010) Rethinking the world trade order. Towards a better legal understanding of the role of regionalism in the multilateral trade regime. Sidestone Press, Leiden

Papadopoulos AS (2010) The international dimension of EU competition law and policy. Cambridge University Press, Cambridge

Prosser T (2005) The limits of competition law. Markets and public services. Oxford University Press, Oxford

Sauter W (2008) Services of general economic interest and universal service in EU law. Eur Law Rev 33(2):167–193

Schweitzer H (2011) Services of general economic interest: European law's impact on the role of markets and of member states. In: Cremona M (ed) Market integration and public services in the European Union. Oxford University Press, Oxford, pp 11–62

Szyszczak E (2013) Introduction. In: Szyszczak E, van de Gronden JW (eds) Financing services of general economic interest. Reform and modernization. T.M.C. Asser Press, The Hague, pp 1–34
Szyszczak E, van de Gronden JW (eds) (2013) Financing services of general economic interest. Reform and modernization. T.M.C. Asser Press, The Hague
Trujillo E (2006) State action antitrust exemption collides with deregulation: rehabilitating the foreseeability doctrine. Fordham J Corp Fin Law 11(2):349–411
Tschaeni H, Engammare V (2013) The Relationship between trade and competition and free trade agreements: developments since the 1990s and challenges. In: Herrmann C, Krajewski M, Terhechte JP (eds) European yearbook of international economic law. Springer, Heidelberg, pp 39–70
UNCTAD (2005) Report, competition provisions in regional trade agreements: how to assure development gains. UN Publication, New York
Van de Gronden JW (2004) Purchasing care: economic activity or service of general (economic) interest? Eur Compet Law Rev 25(2):87–94
Van de Gronden JW (2006) The internal market, the state and private initiative. A legal assessment of national mixed public-private arrangements in the light of European law. Legal Issues Econ Integr 33(2):105–137
Van de Gronden JW, Rusu CS (2012) Services of general (economic) interest post-Lisbon. In: Trybus M, Rubini L (eds) The Treaty of Lisbon and the future of European law and policy. Edward Elgar Publishing, Cheltenham, pp 413–435
Van de Gronden JW (2013a) Transnational competition law and public services. In: Herrmann C, Krajewski M, Terhechte JP (eds) European yearbook of international economic law. Springer, Heidelberg, pp 109–146
Van de Gronden JW (2013b) Conclusion. In: Szyszczak E, van de Gronden JW (eds) Financing services of general economic interest. Reform and modernization. T.M.C. Asser Press, The Hague, pp 273–284
VanDuzer JA (2004) Health, education and social services in Canada: the impact of the GATS. In: Curtis JM, Ciuriak D (eds) Trade policy research 2004. Minister of Public Works and Government Services, Ottawa, pp 287–518
Vedder HHB (2003) Competition law and environmental protection in Europe; towards sustainability? Europa Law Publishing, Groningen
Wei D (2011) China's anti-monopoly law and its merger enforcement: convergence and flexibility. J Int Econ Law 14(4):807–844

# Chapter 7
# Services of General Interest Under Regimes of Fiscal Austerity

**David Hall**

**Abstract** This chapter discusses the political economy of the austerity programmes currently being applied throughout Europe and in many other countries worldwide. It examines the economic context of austerity, including its relations to the global financial crisis of 2008 and support for banks, its impact on economic growth, and links to long-term concerns of the IMF and the EU over public spending. Furthermore, the chapter looks at the roles of the IMF and EU, including the legal and economic bases of their interventions, the policy objectives being pursued, and the relationship between both bodies and national laws and political processes. It concludes that tensions between these institutional mechanisms and democratic processes are likely to continue and grow, in the absence of significant economic growth.

## Contents



D. Hall (✉)
Public Services International Research Unit (PSIRU), University of Greenwich Business School, London, UK
e-mail: d.j.hall@gre.ac.uk



M. Krajewski (ed.), *Services of General Interest Beyond the Single Market*, Legal Issues of Services of General Interest,
DOI 10.1007/978-94-6265-063-3_7

## 7.1 Introduction

This chapter attempts to shed some light on the political economy of the austerity programmes currently being applied throughout Europe and in many other countries worldwide. Firstly, it examines the economic context of austerity, including its relations to the global financial crisis of 2008 and support for banks, its impact on economic growth, and links to long-term concerns of the IMF and the EU over public spending. Secondly, it looks at the roles of the IMF and EU, including the legal and economic bases of their interventions, the policy objectives being pursued, and the relationship between both bodies and national laws and political processes. It concludes that tensions between these institutional mechanisms and democratic processes are likely to continue and grow, in the absence of significant economic growth.

## 7.2 Austerity: Origins and Impact

### *7.2.1 Crisis and Deficits*

The austerity policies are not simple economic consequences of the recession. And the crisis which led to the recession was not, in any sense at all, created by government spending policies. The world recession rather stemmed from the financial bubbles generated through a crisis of private finance, most notoriously the 'sub-prime' mortgages of the USA, and various forms of securitisation: a crisis of private, not public, finance.

It was rather the recession which led to government deficits rising everywhere in 2009, partly as an entirely healthy operation of the 'automatic stabilisers' whereby governments soak up part of the impact of recessions through a fall in taxes and a rise in spending on benefits, partly as a result of a globally coordinated deliberate expansion of public borrowing in most countries in 2009, which successfully injected a significant boost to the world economy, and partly through the massive debts adopted by various governments to rescue banks which would otherwise have collapsed. Economic recession was contained, through a sharp rise in public deficits and public spending. Public spending as a % of GDP rose significantly everywhere, restoring its long-term upward trend, reaching over 50 % of GDP across Europe as a whole.

### *7.2.2 Varieties of Austerity*

The concept of austerity implies a collective sacrifice of current consumption for some public or common good, in the context of limited economic resources which require planned prioritisation. In post-war Europe, it was applied to programmes where household consumption and income was restricted, often with some form of rationing to equalise the impact, to enable national economic reconstruction to take place, including the establishment of full employment. Public spending, public ownership and employment, by contrast, grew substantially, including public healthcare and pensions which were expanded as key elements of national reconstruction and building a better world. The impact was cushioned by the availability of Marshall aid from the USA, without conditionalities.[1] Large amounts of public debt were written off, thus freeing resources for other priorities. This included the cancellation of nearly all of the huge public debt of Germany, which had reached 675 % of GDP.[2]

In the European austerity policies of the 21st century, there are at least two great differences. Firstly, the public objective is very different, and less clear. It is not the reconstruction of productive capacity, full employment, or the development of the shared benefit of the welfare state, but rather the goal of fiscal soundness, formalised in targets for government debt and deficit, and the ability to borrow, and repay, in international financial markets. While it is asserted that these goals will lead to better economic growth and employment levels, these are not the key indicators of success—they are rather treated as externalities. Secondly, the austerity is focussed primarily on public spending, rather than consumer spending (reinforced by the objective focussing on the management of public, rather than private, debt.)

### *7.2.3 Unequal Austerity*

Most of the reduction in budget deficits has been made by cuts in spending rather than increases in taxes—in the UK for example the ratio has been about 85:15. The measures have included cuts in subsidies, cuts in pay and pensions of public employees, reduced eligibility for benefits and pensions, and cuts in healthcare

---

[1]Eichengreen 2007.

[2]R. Kuttner, Debtors' Prison: The Politics of Austerity Versus Possibility. Knopf, New York. http://knopfdoubleday.com/book/219148/debtors-prison/. Accessed 15 December 2014.

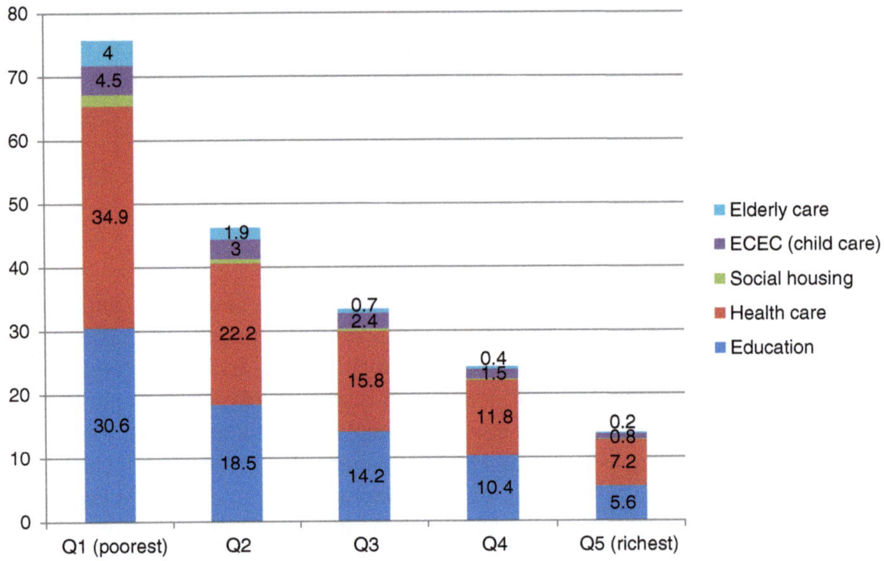


**Chart 7.1** Value of public services relative to disposable income, 27 OECD countries, *Source* calculated from Verbist et al. 2012, p. 35, http://dx.doi.org/10.1787/5k9h363c5szq-en

expenditure,[3] and the effects have been felt in terms of loss of income, loss of employment, insecurity, morbidity and mortality: "austerity is not only self-defeating but fatal".[4] While the programmes have been welcomed by banks and financial institutions, small businesses have been less enthusiastic, and they have been met with a wave of general strikes on an unprecedented scale, and by social movements of unemployed youth.[5]

Under austerity programmes, the poor are harder hit by cuts in public services as well as by cuts in benefits or subsidies. This is because the benefits of public services are very evenly distributed between households divided into five income bands, or quintiles, so each quintile receives roughly equal benefit from the services, in absolute terms. In relative terms, it means that the poor lose a greater proportion of their combined welfare from money income and public services from cuts in public services (Chart 7.1).[6]

[3]I. Ortiz and M. Cummins, The Age of Austerity: A Review of Public Expenditures and Adjustment Measures in 181 Countries. http://policydialogue.org/files/publications/Age_of_Austerity_Ortiz_and_Cummins.pdf. March 2013. Accessed 15 December 2014.

[4]Stuckler and Basu, How Austerity kills. New York Times, 12 May 2013.

[5]Cavero and Poinasamy 2013.

[6]Verbist et al. 2012.

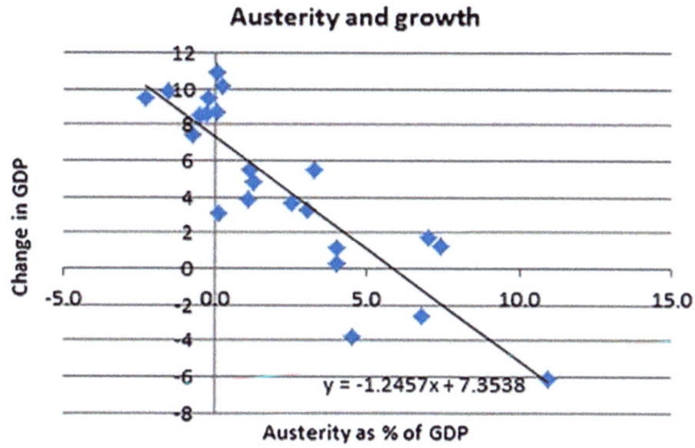


**Chart 7.2** Austerity and growth 2009–2011 (Krugman), *Source* http://krugman.blogs.nytimes.com/2012/04/24/austerity-and-growth-again-wonkish/

# 7.3 Austerity Without Growth

## *7.3.1 Actual Experience: Austerity Is Linked to Fall in GDP*

The supporters of austerity argue that it will restore confidence of markets and investors, and so result in stronger growth in the economy as a whole, as a result of which all groups will be better off. The sacrifices are thus worthwhile for everybody in the end. If this was true, then the case for austerity would be stronger, as there would be some benefits available to all groups, to compensate for the losses suffered as a result of the austerity measures themselves. But the empirical evidence, both from the current policies, and from previous experience, is that this is not happening. Moreover, there is much evidence dating from before the European crisis that austerity policies do not lead to growth.

As far as current policies are concerned, the simple evidence in Chart 7.2—from a Nobel prize—winning economist-show the opposite: the greater the austerity, measured in terms of reducing government deficit, the greater the fall in GDP. There is a strong correlation, but the reverse of what is promised. In addition to imposing austerity, the policies also impose lower growth.

## *7.3.2 Previous Evidence on Austerity and Growth*

Moreover, this is not surprising, least of all for the IMF, which has published some of the strongest evidence that policies of austerity and liberalisation do not lead to growth in GDP. Three reports are especially relevant.

The first is a research paper published in August 2012, with the extremely misleading title of "Successful Austerity in the United States, Europe and Japan".[7]

[7]IMF, Successful Austerity in the United States, Europe and Japan, IMF WP12/190. http://www.imf.org/external/pubs/ft/wp/2012/wp12190.pdf. Accessed 15 December 2014.

Its main results, however, did not identify any successes, but rather confirmed that, on the basis of past evidence, fiscal consolidation—that is, reducing government deficits—is extremely likely to damage growth, especially in recession. It concluded that: "withdrawing fiscal stimuli too quickly in economies where output is already contracting can prolong their recessions without generating the expected fiscal saving. This is particularly true if the consolidation is centred around cuts to public expenditure… and if the size of the consolidation is large." It also found that any 'confidence effects' "do not seem to have ever been strong enough to make the consolidations expansionary", so the supposed trade-off of restoring market confidence never compensates for the damage. As an analysis by Ronald Janssen concluded, this paper: "is simply devastating for traditional and mainstream recommendations on fiscal policy and austerity." [8]

The second report concerned the forecasts attached to austerity measures, which systematically claim that after the initial impact, there will be a positive effect on growth. In the October 2012 World Economic Outlook, the IMF reported that all such forecasts of economic growth following austerity have been systematically overstated by a large margin.[9] This finding applied to the forecasts of all the international institutions—the IMF, European Commission, and OECD—and one leading private forecaster, the Economist Intelligence Unit. It also confirms that the overstatements are not explicable by exceptional cases of high debt levels, or trade imbalances, or even the activities of financial markets. The WEO says bluntly that the relationship between forecasts and actual outcomes is "large, negative, and significant". The WEO attributes this to over-optimistic multipliers, that is, the ratio between austerity measures and subsequent change in GDP.

Moreover, the IMF had already known, for some years, that its growth forecasts for austerity packages were systematically over-optimistic. A detailed examination of fiscal adjustment in 133 IMF-supported programmes in 70 countries carried out by the IMF's own Independent Evaluation Office (IEO) in 2003 noted:

> There is a tendency to adopt fiscal targets based on overoptimistic assumptions about the pace of economic recovery leading inevitably to fiscal underperformance and frequent revisions of targets. The optimism about growth recovery in the short term is itself often the consequence of overoptimistic assumptions about the pace of revival of private investment when a more realistic assessment in certain circumstances could have justified the adoption of a more relaxed fiscal stance on contra-cyclical grounds.[10]

They were reminded of these results in a more recent analysis by UNCTAD of the failure of growth to materialise as promised after earlier IMF programmes in developing and transition economies. It found that in nearly all cases, the outturns in terms of GDP growth were worse than the IMF forecasts, and points up a more fundamental weakness underlying these forecasting failure—that the IMF is

[8]http://www.social-europe.eu/2012/10/blame-it-on-the-multiplier/.

[9]IMF, World Economic Outlook, October 2012. http://www.imf.org/external/pubs/ft/weo/2012/02/pdf/text.pdf. Accessed 15 December 2014.

[10]IMF, Fiscal Adjustment in IMF-Supported Programs. www.ieo-imf.org/ieo/files/completedevaluations/09092003main.pdf. Accessed 15 December 2014.

working on a set of false assumptions about how economies work: "Misjudging the effects of fiscal tightening seems to be the rule rather than the exception in IMF-backed programmes…. In country after country where fiscal tightening was expected to both reduce the budget deficit and boost investment and economic growth, the opposite happened. … This record of failed IMF-sponsored adjustment programmes suggests that they are based on a fundamental macroeconomic misconception."[11]

Although the IMF have effectively admitted that their forecasts were flawed, the reaction of the European Commission in 2012 was to attempt a tortuous theoretical defence of the possibility of austerity policies being compatible with growth in GDP, in its annual report on public finances.[12] The report does not address the empirical evidence, but instead dismisses the idea that austerity does not generate economic growth as "counter-intuitive".[13]

### *7.3.3 The Negative Effects of 'Good' Governance*

Apart from the cuts in government deficits, the IMF programmes, and the EU economic policies, also require changes in economic governance and regulation, so that business is less constrained by regulation of all kinds, including labour conditions and regulation of the financial sector. The World Bank publishes indices of good economic governance, based on business opinions.

The third of the relevant IMF papers, published in 2011, studied whether countries which scored better on 'good governance', as defined by the World Bank indicators of economic governance, had weathered the global economic crisis better.[14]

The results, however, show that the favoured policies are not just useless, but positively damaging: "….This variable is negative and highly significant …the countries with the best ratings in terms of public sector regulatory framework, as well as those countries with the most far reaching financial deregulation, were hit the hardest economically."

Nor is the IMF alone in reaching these results. An earlier paper, published by the OECD and co-authored by an ECB economist, also found that: "the indicators

[11]UNCTAD, Trade and Development Report: Post-crisis policy challenges in the world economy, UN Publication, New York, Geneva, 2011, p. 65.

[12]European Commission, Report on Public Finances in EMU 2012, European economy series 4/2012 http://ec.europa.eu/economy_finance/publications/european_economy/2012/pdf/ee-2012-4.pdf. Accessed 15 December 2014.

[13]EC 2012, p. 160.

[14]IMF, The Economic Crisis: Did Financial Supervision Matter? Masciandaro D, Vega Pansini R, Quinty M, IMF WP 11/261. http://www.imf.org/external/pubs/ft/wp/2011/wp11261.pdf. Accessed 15 December 2014.

of the quality of public sector regulations—which proxy the "market friendliness" of the economy—are negatively correlated with economic growth".[15]

## 7.4 Explaining Austerity: Bond Markets and Public Spending

If austerity policies cannot be expected to restore growth, it is necessary to look for other factors to explain why it has taken place, and why it has led to changes in EU law to enshrine the observation of austerity rules in future. Two key factors can be identified: the role of financial money markets, and the long-established concern of the IMF and the European Commission to limit the growth in public spending.

### *7.4.1 Bond Markets and Austerity*

In Eurozone countries, the austerity programmes were driven by financial markets speculation against those countries perceived to be potential risks for creditors. The close links between the financial markets and austerity programmes can be seen in Chart 7.3, which support the "strong perception that countries that introduced austerity programs in the Eurozone were somehow forced to do so by the financial markets". There is an almost perfect correlation between the interest demanded by the markets for debt of different countries, and the degree of austerity they adopted.[16]

These market pressures emerged because, from 2008, other Eurozone countries refused to confirm a continuation of the implied solidarity, which had previously resulted in more or less identical interest rates (spreads) on government bonds throughout the Eurozone. The consequent rescue packages by the Troika were then the vehicle for the application of austerity policies, followed by the restoration of Eurozone solidarity in 2012, when the ECB committed itself to unlimited support of the government bond markets. The spreads then dropped dramatically, despite a rise in the ratio of government debt to GDP in all countries.[17]

---

[15]IMF, The Economic Crisis: Did Financial Supervision Matter? Masciandaro D, Vega Pansini R, Quinty M, IMF WP 11/261. http://www.imf.org/external/pubs/ft/wp/2011/wp11261.pdf. Accessed 15 December 2014; D. Giannone, M. Lenza and L. Reichlin, Market freedom and the global recession OECD. http://www.oecd.org/economy/productivityandlongtermgrowth/46418753.pdf. Accessed 15 December 2014.

[16]P. De Grauwe and Y. Ji, Panic-driven austerity in the Eurozone and its implications. http://www.voxeu.org/article/panic-driven-austerity-eurozone-and-its-implications. 21 February 2013. Accessed 15 December 2014.

[17]P. De Grauwe and Y. Ji, Panic-driven austerity in the Eurozone and its implications. http://www.voxeu.org/article/panic-driven-austerity-eurozone-and-its-implications. 21 February 2013. Accessed 15 December 2014.

**Chart 7.3** Austerity measures and financial market borrowing 'spreads' in 2011, *Source* P. De Grauwe and Y. Ji, Panic-driven austerity in the Eurozone and its implications. http://www.voxeu.org/article/panic-driven-austerity-eurozone-and-its-implications. 21 February 2013. Accessed 15 December 2014

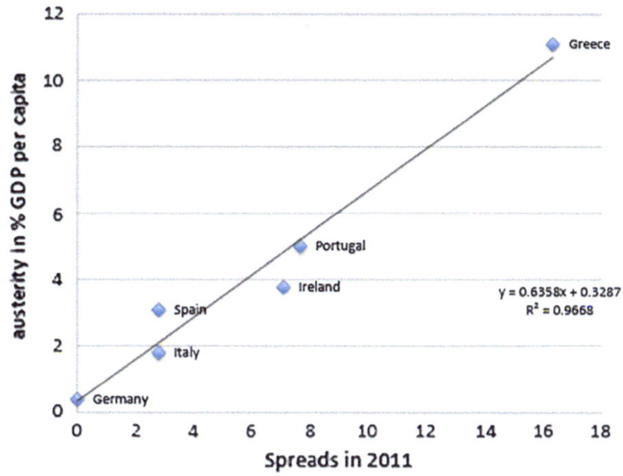


The prioritisation of bond-holders has long historical antecedents in Southern Europe and Mediterranean countries. Between the 1870s and 1920s, the governments of Britain, France and Germany installed committees to take over the management of public revenues in a number of countries (including Greece, Portugal, the Ottoman empire, Egypt and Morocco). These committees ensured that the first priority was given to paying interest to the banks of the northern countries who had invested in bonds of the southern governments. The Troika packages are the modern equivalent.

### *7.4.2 The Problem of Public Spending*

One core element of neoliberalism has been a commitment to reducing the role of the state, and the level of public spending has been a central aspect of this. In OECD countries as a whole, it had risen from around 13 % of GDP in the early 20th century to about 45 % by the mid-1990s, while in Europe it had risen to over 50 % (see Chart 7.4). National governments had mostly succeeded in slowing or reversing this growth, but the crisis and the reflationary policies of 2009 saw the levels leap up again, to over 50 %. If the expansionary policies had continued, the level of public spending would have also continued growing.

But well before the crisis, since the 1990s, the IMF, OECD, EU and national governments had been arguing that major cuts in public spending were needed, because of the 'demographic time-bomb' of ageing populations, requiring higher spending on healthcare and pensions. The European Commission's first report on the subject, in 1999, identified the problem simply as: "Ageing is consequently expected to result in substantial increases in age-related public expenditures", and also identified these services as 'culprits' in the post-war growth in public spending: "over the last 35 years, increases in these expenditures have been the main

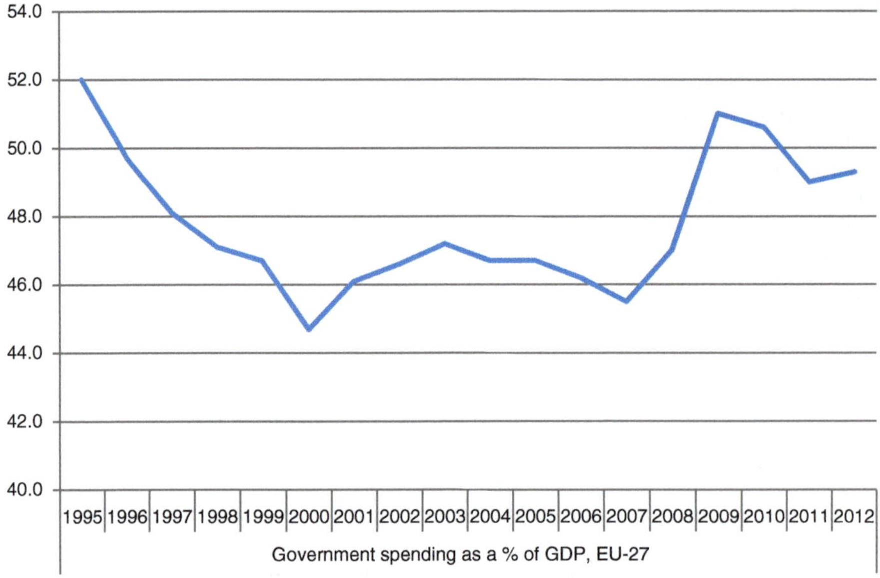


**Chart 7.4** Government spending as % of GDP, EU-27, 1995–2012, *Source* Eurostat Government revenue, expenditure and main aggregates [gov_a_main] http://epp.eurostat.ec.europa.eu/portal/page/portal/government_finance_statistics/data/main_tables

culprits in explaining the inexorable rise in the share of government expenditure in GDP". It then emphasised the large reversal needed, and its lack of confidence in elected governments to deliver it:

> It is important to stress the scale of the task facing governments in relation to controlling health and pension expenditure over the next 50 years.... Furthermore, and equally worrying, if past experience is anything to go by, Governments are going to have difficulty even keeping their pension and health care budgets to the, already rather large, percentage points increases which will emanate from purely demographic factors.[18]

The demographic time bomb was also used by the IMF to justify the abandonment of the Keynesian stimulus policies of 2009 in favour of long-term, global austerity policies. It projected that healthcare spending alone could rise by the equivalent of 3.5 % of GDP by 2030, and pensions spending by 1 % of GDP, and proposed a general austerity strategy, with the sole objective of containing future growth of public spending (see Chart 7.5).[19]

[18] K. McMorrow and W. Roeger, The economic consequences of ageing populations. (European Economy) Economic Papers 138, November 1999. http://ec.europa.eu/economy_finance/publications/publication11151_en.pdf, p. 16. Accessed 15 December 2014.

[19] IMF, From Stimulus to Consolidation: Revenue and Expenditure Policies in Advanced and Emerging Economies, 30 April 2010. www.imf.org/external/np/pp/eng/2010/043010a.pdf. Accessed 15 December 2014.

**Chart 7.5** IMF and the fear of future public spending, *Source* IMF, From stimulus to consolidation: Revenue and expenditure policies in advanced and emerging economies, 30 April 2010. www.imf.org/external/np/pp/eng/2010/043010a.pdf. Accessed 15 December 2014

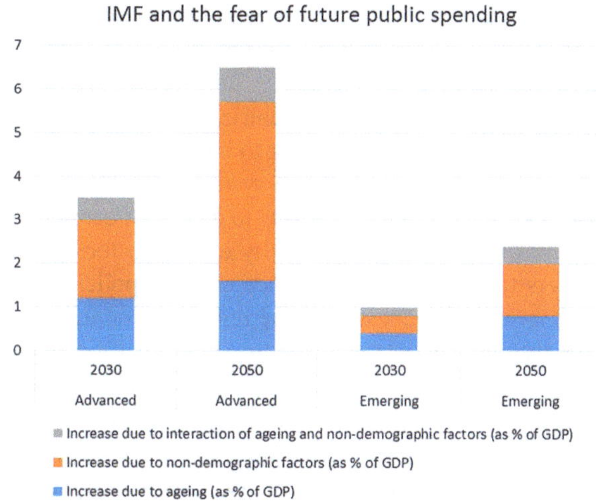


Thus by 2009 many governments had already adopted policies of reducing pension entitlements and pension levels, both in general and for public employees in particular, despite strong attempts at resistance. People now have to work longer, retire later, and receive lower pensions.

Public spending on public healthcare in Europe has also now started falling, from 9.2 % of GDP in 2009 and 9.0 % in 2010 for the first time in many years: exactly what the international institutions had been wanting to happen. Ireland and Greece recorded some of the biggest cuts.[20]

## 7.5 IMF

The power of the IMF to influence the economic policies of governments has existed long before the recession and the crises in European countries. This power derives not from any legal obligation on countries to follow particular policies, but from the economic significance of its surveillance and lending powers. It brings it into conflict with national law, and reflects a global role that is not only economic but, increasingly, geopolitical.

### *7.5.1 Informal Power and Conflicts of Interest*

The original remit of the IMF was drawn up in the context of the Bretton Woods exchange rate mechanism, and under article IV member states undertook "to collaborate with the Fund to promote exchange stability, to maintain orderly exchange

[20]OECD/EU 2012.

arrangements with other members, and to avoid competitive exchange alterations". The IMF was authorised to make loans to countries to assist in stabilising the value of currencies, and to help countries in balance of payments difficulties. There were also possible sanctions against countries which failed to maintain their proper exchange rates, including losing the right to borrow from the IMF, or loss of membership.

As the fixed exchange rate system came to an end in the 1970s, the IMF's remit was re-defined to provide loans to deal with economic crises, including those caused by the surge in oil prices, or by excessive foreign debts. The IMF was given new powers to monitor and influence national policies using "dialogue, persuasion, candour, even-handedness and due regard to country circumstances", as well as to provide technical assistance to central banks and finance ministries. The IMF also began to specify policies as conditions for loans, and in its advice to governments, with a standard set of measures including reductions in public spending, especially in the public sector wages bill, increased charges for public services, de-regulation and privatisation—the central features of the 'Washington consensus' and neoliberal economic policies. With the political approval of its most powerful members for these policies, the conditionalities attached to IMF loans became a key way of promoting and extending these policies world-wide, and a key part of globalisation.[21]

The IMF has been able to have such impact not because countries have any legal obligation to adopt a certain set of policies. Unlike membership of the EU, which requires countries to adopt a wide range of specific laws and policies on economic, environmental and other issues, there is no such obligation on members of the IMF. Nor is there a contractual obligation on borrowers which is legally enforced by the IMF—formally, the conditionalities are contained in a government statement of policies it proposes to follow.[22] The impact of the IMF rather stems from its unique ability to exercise economic power and influence over selected countries, as a result of its surveillance and lending powers.

The surveillance role gives the IMF a globally unique role as constant and universal economic policy adviser to all countries at all times, through the programme of annual visits and reports on national economies. Without the context of an IMF loan, these may function to encourage and reinforce existing policies: to take an improbable example, an IMF staff mission to Libya in 2010 congratulated the Gaddafi regime in Libya for a programme to make 340,000 public employees redundant, recommended that the process "should be accelerated", and added that "The mission would like to thank the authorities for their excellent cooperation and hospitality."[23] These visits are supplemented by regular reports on the world

[21]Thorstensen et al. 2013.

[22]J. Klein, The Battle for Rule of Law in Thailand, The Constitutional Court of Thailand, The Provisions and the Working of the Court, pp. 34–90. http://www.cdi.anu.edu.au/CDIwebsite_1998-2004/thailand/thailand_downloads/ThaiUpdate_Klien_ConCourt%20Apr03.pdf. Accessed 15 December 2014.

[23]Preliminary Conclusions of the Mission to Libya, 28 October 2010, http://www.imf.org/external/np/ms/2010/102810.htm; 'Egypt's Orderly transition? International Aid and the Rush to Structural Adjustment' *Jadaliyya*, 29 May 2011; Bond 2011.

economy, global financial issues, and a plethora of research and other papers on economic policy. At national level, this has repeated impact on the acceptable range of government policies: a bad report from the IMF surveillance makes it more difficult for a country to borrow the money it needs. At international level, the effect is magnified by constant media coverage, academic discussion, and attention from financial markets, which continuously reinforces the dominance of the orthodox economic ideology of the Washington consensus.

IMF loans create a more direct economic bargaining mechanism, in which the loan conditionalities enable the IMF to induce countries to adopt its preferred policies. This power is based on the potential sanction of postponing or withholding the loans—if the correct policies are not adopted, the loans may be withheld, and the money markets will be much less willing to lend money to the government. So the relationship is not simply a partnership cooperating to a single end. It is also an exchange relationship, in which the IMF receives its desired policies in exchange for a loan—even if those policies are not desired by the government or large sections of the population of those countries.

As shown in the previous section, these economic policies are not a technocratic and uncontroversial package, but rather a set of highly contentious policies. The role of conditionalities is thus to ward off the danger that democratic processes will not lead to the result desired by the IMF, because of a conflict of interests: "between the IMF as lender and the country as borrower, …between the country and other foreign lenders, or between sharply conflicting interests within a country."[24] The core of this conflict is between the interests of citizens as expressed through democracy and the interests of financial entities expressed through the market:

> The politics of public debt may be conceived in terms of a distributional conflict between creditors and citizens. Both have claims on public funds in the form of contractual-commercial and political-social rights, respectively. In a democracy, citizens have the possibility of electing a government responsive to them but "irresponsible" from the viewpoint of financial markets…. creditors will seek guarantees that … their claims will always be given priority over those of citizens.[25]

The impact of the IMF should thus be understood as the exercise of informal power, engaged in repeated conflicts with the framework of national law and democratic activity, as summarised by Ulrich Beck:

> This de-territorialised economic power requires neither political implementation nor political legitimacy. In establishing itself, it even bypasses the institutions of the developed democracies, including parliaments and courts. This meta power is neither legal nor legitimate; it is 'translegal'.[26]

---

[24] S. Drazen A, Conditionality and Ownership in IMF Lending: A Political Economy Approach, IMF Staff Papers, 2002. http://econweb.umd.edu/~drazen/ConditionalityIMFStaff.pdf. Accessed 15 December 2014.

[25] W. Streeck, The Politics of Public Debt, MPIfG Discussion Paper 13/7, 2013. Max-Planck-Institut für Gesellschaftsforschung, Köln. http://www.mpifg.de/pu/mpifg_dp/dp13-7.pdf. Accessed 15 December 2014.

[26] Beck 2005.

### 7.5.2 *IMF and National Constitutions*

The IMF has repeatedly encountered public and political resistance to its programmes. One form of this resistance has been through national court cases seeking rulings that measures required by the IMF are unconstitutional. As shown in Table 7.1, the constitutional courts of Latvia, Romania, Hungary and Portugal have ruled various elements of their countries' packages unconstitutional, mostly in relation to cuts in pensions entitlement, cuts in public sector pay, or cuts in healthcare provision. This form of resistance has also been encountered in previous IMF packages, including in Colombia in the early 2000s and Hungary in the 1990s.

This has become a matter of concern to the financial markets, who see the constitutions as undesirable obstacles to the economic policies desired by countries' creditors. The bankers JP Morgan issued a remarkable note on the crisis in June 2013 which discussed the progress of European countries on deleveraging, economic restructuring, and political reform. Under the heading of 'political reform', it warned that:

> there are deep seated political problems in the periphery, which, in our view, need to change if EMU is going to function properly in the long run. The political systems in the periphery were established in the aftermath of dictatorship, and were defined by that experience. Constitutions tend to show a strong socialist influence, reflecting the political strength that left wing parties gained after the defeat of fascism...... There is a growing recognition of the extent of this problem, both in the core and in the periphery. Change is beginning to take place.[27]

### 7.5.3 *Geopolitics and the Pattern of Loans*

Europe is now especially important to the IMF because many countries in other world regions have effectively rejected the possibility of an IMF loan as an instrument of policy. No country in South America, except for Colombia, currently has an IMF loan, in most cases because governments have taken policy decisions to pay off loans as fast as possible and avoid any future IMF loan, following their experiences with structural adjustment loans in the 1990s and 2000s. In Asia, many countries took similar decisions, explicitly or in practice, following their experiences with IMF loans after the Asian currency crisis of 1998, including Indonesia, Philippines and Thailand (see Table 7.2).

[27] J.P. Morgan, The Euro Area Adjustment: About Halfway There. https://11740092596917189242.googlegroups.com/attach/243626285e18f68b/JPM-the-euro-area-adjustment--about-halfway-there.pdf?part=7&vt=ANaJVrG2WGC_YZQfaQXY7PeR28q3XCWQFXiOlyP7FtL81IFFYTx9nRhv8FLQAMwGy9B4_Nq5ZCR738qsPF1-LI6OccRFEfijGnIQpBHSSNJv1SHRZ_0paUI; see also http://blogs.euobserver.com/phillips/2013/06/07/jp-morgan-to-eurozone-periphery-get-rid-of-your-pinko-anti-fascist-constitutions/. Accessed 15 December 2014.

**Table 7.1** National constitutional court decisions against IMF/Troika austerity

| Date | Country | Issues | |
|---|---|---|---|
| 1995 | Hungary | Benefits, labour law, | The court rejected a number of elements of a cuts package demanded by the IMF in 1995, e.g. on benefits and sick leave. The IMF demands were partly reduced, some cuts were made elsewhere, and privatisation was accelerated[a] |
| 2000–2004 | Colombia | Pensions, public sector pay, healthcare, | The constitutional court of Colombia heard a series of cases against the IMF structural adjustment programmes between 1999–2004, and ruled policies were unconstitutional in 39 cases: "The Court affirmed that the need to control the fiscal deficit is not a valid argument to maintain situations that can violate constitutional rights" |
| 21/12/2009 | Latvia | Pensions | The Court found the law [which decreased the amount received by current pensioners by 10 % and that by future pensioners who were currently employed by 70 %] unconstitutional and in violation of an individual's right to a pension because Parliament had not considered other less restrictive alternatives, had not provided an adequate transition period before the law came into effect and there was no plan for future compensation: even if the conditions had been externally imposed, those conditions "cannot replace the rights established by the Constitution" |
| 24/06/2010 | Romania | Pensions | The Romanian constitutional court provoked enormous upheaval by overturning a proposed 15 % cut in pensions government's plan to cut pensions by 15 % in 2010 in order to reduce public spending was "unconstitutional" |
| 10/2010 | Hungary | Public sector pay | The constitutional court struck down several laws as unconstitutional, including a 98 % tax on public sector severence pay packages worth more than €7,275. The government then passed a constitutional amendment by two thirds parliamentary vote, which allows the Constitutional Court the power to annul laws affecting the budget, the implementation of the budget, central taxes, contribution payments and duties **only** if they violate the right to life and dignity, the right to protect personal data, the freedom of thought, conscience and religion, and rights connected to Hungarian citizenship. The Constitutional Court can still declare laws outside of this unconstitutional, but cannot annul them |

(continued)

**Table 7.1** (continued)

| Date | Country | Issues | |
|---|---|---|---|
| 04/04/2013 | Portugal | Pensions, public sector pay | The constitutional court rejected cuts in state pensions and public sector pay equivalent to about 7 % of annual income as well as cuts in sickness and unemployment benefits. the measures deemed unconstitutional represented between €900 m and €1.3 bn in government revenue and savings, about 20 % of the €5 bn the government planned to gain from austerity measures this year |
| 28/08/2013 | Portugal | Public sector employment | Court has ruled that legislation enabling the government to fire public sector workers who cannot be retrained is illegal, the provision flouted Portugal's "job safety guarantee" |

*Sources Rodriguez 2005, D.* O'Donovan D, A Twilight of Sovereignty: Eastern Europe's Constitutional Courts, the IMF and Government Austerity Programmes, Human Rights in Ireland. http://humanrights.ie/constitution-of-ireland/a-twilight-of-sovereignty-eastern-europes-constitutional-courts-the-imf-and-government-austerity-programmes/. 25 November 2010. Accessed 15 December 2014, J. Klein, The Battle for Rule of Law in Thailand, The Constitutional Court of Thailand, The Provisions and the Working of the Court, pp. 34–90. http://www.cdi.anu.edu.au/CDIwebsite_1998-2004/thailand/thailand_downloads/ThaiUpdate_Klien_ConCourt%20Apr03.pdf. Accessed 15 December 2014

[a]Scheppele 2006

**Table 7.2** Countries which accelerated final repayment of IMF loans. *Source* IMF Annual Report 2007; Soren Ambrose "The decline (& fall?) of the IMF" 02 April 2007 http://www.focusweb.org/index2.php?option=com_content&do_pdf=1&id=1172

| Country | Date of final repayment to IMF |
|---|---|
| Argentina | 2005 |
| Brazil | 2005 |
| Bulgaria | 2007–2008 |
| Ecuador | 2007–2008 |
| Indonesia | 2008 |
| Philippines | 2006 |
| Serbia | 2007 |
| Thailand | 2003 |
| Turkey | 2013 |
| Uruguay | 2007–2008 |
| Venezuela | 1999 |

This had such an impact that the IMF was preparing to make 10 % of its staff redundant, when the global financial crisis arrived to give the IMF a new role in dealing with the consequences. However, Asian and Latin American countries have continued to distance themselves from the possibility of fresh interventions by the IMF. A Latin American initiative to create a 'Bank of the South' was

**Chart 7.6** IMF lending at a glance (March 2014), *Source* IMF lending at a glance (http://www.imf.org/external/np/exr/map/lending/index.htm)

followed by the east Asian countries developing an alternative regional system of support through the Chiang Mai Initiative Multilateralisation (CMIM), and now the BRICS countries have also agreed to create a New Development Bank.[28]

As a result, IMF loans are now heavily concentrated in Europe, Africa, and central America and Caribbean—with Europe representing by far the greatest amount by value. Chart 7.6 of IMF loans shows this pattern very clearly, and also shows how other loans are also clustered in regions of strategic geopolitical importance—eastern Europe, the Middle East, central Asia and the Indian Ocean.

The persistent attempts to offer loans to north African countries following the Arab spring, with only vague attempts at explaining why the loans are necessary (and the new loan to Ukraine in 2014) may also be best explained by their geo-political significance. In 2010 the IMF endorsed the policies of the Mubarak regime in Egypt as "Five years of reforms and prudent macroeconomic policies"; but since the 2011 uprising, the IMF has repeatedly offered Egypt a loan, which has been initially accepted by the interim military governments, and by the short-lived Morsi government, but then deferred as a result of widespread popular opposition. A somewhat different dynamic was at play in Russia in the 1990s, where

[28]S. Nissan, Guest Post: Brics without Mortar, Financial Times. http://blogs.ft.com/beyond-brics/2013/09/05/guest-post-brics-without-water/. Accessed 15 December 2014; Bretton Woods Project, The Future of Global Economic Governance and the IMF: Challenges and Opportunities for Europe, Emerging Economies and Developing Countries. http://www.brettonwoodsproject.org/wp-content/uploads/2014/03/Future-of-global-economic-governance-and-the-IMF.pdf. March 2014. Accessed 15 December 2014.

the IMF, unusually, was effectively indifferent to the apparent misappropriation of the money for the use of individuals: the core objective of supporting new free-market policies was more important to the IMF.

## 7.6 EU

The EU has revised the treaty and introduced new laws, directives and agreements which seek to strengthen the role of the EU in monitoring and directing the fiscal and economic policies of member states. These changes build on existing constraints on public services and fiscal policies, by providing the EU with new powers of fiscal supervision and surveillance, specifically designed to limit the possibility of policy changes arriving from national democratic activity.

### *7.6.1 Public Services and Trade: Liberalisation and Privatisation*

The subordination of public services (also known as services of general interest, SGI) to the requirements of policies of trade liberalisation and fiscal orthodoxy has developed over many decades in the EU. The early political framework for the development of the EU allowed for economic liberalisation to be central to the European level, while public services were for the most part left to national competences, a compromise which allowed support from a wide range of political positions on left and right.[29]

The provision of public services in Europe have been subject to more and more encroachment by treaty clauses and directives concerning trade, competition and the creation of the internal market. These include:

- Procurement law, intended to promote transparent competition for public contracts, has been used to restrict the ability of public authorities to use corporatized entities without tendering
- State aid rules, originally intended to prevent member states subsidising manufacturing companies to give them an unfair competitive advantage against competitors in other countries, came to be increasingly applied to restrict the financing of public service organisations in sectors where private providers wanted to expand their activities;
- Internal market rules extended to sectors previously part of the public sector in many countries, such as electricity, telecoms, rail, and post, requiring the end of public monopolies and the opening of markets in these sectors, and more general liberalisation of the services sector

[29] Bugaric 2013.

This process, which involved a series of directives and rulings by the Commission and judgments by the ECJ, has been politically contentious and vigorously contested, for example the long battle over the Services Directive in the mid-2000s. These conflicts continue: a recent example is the Concessions Directive, which facilitates the use of concessions and other PPPs, where the Commission felt obliged to exclude the water sector as a result of a Europe wide campaign. This process is driven by the primacy of trade policy in the EU, which has developed an "asymetric policy regime, with strong exclusive Commission competences in the field of competition and shared fragile EU competences in the realm of social policies", as part of a system based on insider consensus which resists conflict over the fundamental policies themselves, at the expense of undermining the political legitimacy of the EU itself.[30]

This subordination of public services to market liberalisation was not inevitable. In response to the recession, for example, the Commission applied a temporary framework enabling it to authorise state aid for the financial sector worth €592 billion in capital support measures and €906 billion in guarantees, a combined total worth 12.3 % of the GDP of the whole of Europe[31]—the decision to enable such support for banks, but not for public services, was a political choice, not a legal inevitability. Within the long-term framework of the treaty itself, it would be possible to give a blanket exemption for public services from all elements of the treaty, as has been done for arms and weapons (including biological, chemical and nuclear weapons) ever since the original Treaty of Rome in 1958, and continues in the latest version of the treaty: "The provisions of this Treaty shall not preclude the application of the following rules: .....(b) Any Member State may take such measures as it considers necessary for the protection of the essential interests of its security which are connected with the production of or trade in arms, munitions and war material". An order of the Commission lists the firearms, artillery, bombs, rockets, tanks, ships, aircraft, electronic and other equipment covered by this exemption, including "toxic, biological or chemical agents and radioactive agents adapted for destructive use in war against persons, animals or crops".[32]

### 7.6.2 *Maastricht Rules on Debt and Deficit*

A more fundamental problem for all forms of public spending arose from the construction of the EMU and the Euro, which created the first legal powers for the EU to intervene in the fiscal policies of member states, and thus decisions on financing public services. This was based on the premise that a common currency, and even a common economic union, required all member states to accept standardised

---

[30]Crespy 2013, 2014.

[31]EU, State Aid Scoreboard 2013, Aid in the context of the financial and economic crisis. http://ec.europa.eu/competition/state_aid/scoreboard/financial_economic_crisis_aid_en.html. Accessed 15 December 2014.

[32]Article 346 TFEU.

constraints on government annual deficits, set at a maximum of 3 % of GDP, and on accumulated government debt, set at a maximum of 60 % of GDP. These figures were not mathematically deduced from universally accepted economic laws and truths—indeed, the relationship between public deficit, debt, and economic growth continues to be a hotly contested issue—but simply the result of political negotiation as part of the Maastricht treaty revisions in 1993: "the rule is quite arbitrary…the only reason why 60 % seems to have been chosen at Maastricht was that at that time this was the average debt-GDP ratio in the EU".[33]

The Commission was given the power to apply fines on member states which breached these limits, but despite their legal status under the treaty, it was unable to apply these sanctions effectively against its largest member states—France, Germany, Italy and the UK—when they breached the limits in the early 2000s. This led to reforms which allowed the Commission to calculate 'medium-term objectives' for countries, but without additional sanctions.[34]

The fiscal rules, and the EU's inability to enforce them, have also led the EU to encourage PPPs—which are counted as private finance—as a way of allowing member states to finance borrowing which would otherwise exceed the limits, in order to improve the chances of fiscal rules appearing to be observed. As a result, while the EU is adamant that it will not issue Euro bonds as a risk-sharing tool to support *government* borrowing by member states, it is planning to issue 'Europe 2020 Project Bonds', which can then be used by member states to provide low-cost finance for PPPs. The impact of PPPs on public services is also multiply negative—they are more expensive than public borrowing, less efficient than public services, and have resulted in a high and damaging failure rate, for example in public transport PPPs in London.[35]

### *7.6.3 The Crisis and New Powers for the EU*

The financial and economic crisis of 2008 led to much greater economic policy intervention by the EU. The initial response to the crisis required the EU to play a key role in enabling the response of member states through providing support for the financial sector and, initially, stimulating economic demand. Subsequently, the use of conditionalities through the EU-IMF-ECB 'Troika' packages provided the first occasion when the EU could impose specific policy requirements on member states

[33] De Grauwe 2012, p. 138.

[34] R. Thillaye, L. Kouba and A. Sachs, Reforming EU Economic Governance: Is "more" any better? http://www.foreurope.eu/fileadmin/documents/pdf/Workingpapers/WWWforEurope_WPS_no057_MS84.pdf. March 2014. Accessed 15 December 2014.

[35] Spiegel, The coming EU summit clash: Merkel vows 'no euro bonds as long as I live. http://www.spiegel.de/international/europe/chancellor-merkel-vows-no-euro-bonds-as-long-as-she-lives-a-841163.html. 27 June 2012. Accessed 15 December 2014; EIB, The Europe 2020 Project Bond Initiative—Innovative infrastructure financing. http://www.eib.europa.eu/products/project-bonds/index.htm. Accessed 15 December 2014.

in relation to non-fiscal issues, albeit in conjunction with the IMF. The support packages for member states in crisis also led to demands from some member states for much stricter EU controls as a condition of assuring such support for the future.

Since the crisis, the EU has developed a series of new mechanisms, which effectively strengthen its power and influence over the economic and fiscal policies of member states. It has increased the scope of its economic surveillance, through the European semester, the Fiscal Compact, which requires countries to be constitutionally or at least statutorily bound to a balanced budget, and the European Stabilisation Mechanism (ESM) providing financial support for countries in crisis.

The 'European Semester' is a cycle of monitoring and coordination of the economic policies of member states, based on the annual submission of draft budgets and macroeconomic plans by governments. This semester was reinforced by further legislation known as the 'Six-pack' and Two-pack'. The fiscal rules are defined by reference to medium-term objectives for budget deficits (MTOs) for each member state, which are set following detailed formulae, and which member states are obliged to follow. The formulae for MTOs refer not only to targets for deficit and debt, but also to targets for expenditure levels as a % of GDP, calculated by reference to EU reports on the cost of age-related public expenditure. Public spending must not rise faster than medium-term potential GDP growth, unless it is matched by adequate revenues. There are new stricter sanctions, with more automatic procedures, for breaching the deficit and debt targets, and a clause making it harder for the member states to override the application of these sanctions.[36]

There is also a new Macroeconomic Imbalances Procedure (MIP), which allows the Commission to issue 'alerts', and preventive and corrective recommendations to member states. Member states who repeatedly fail to take action required can be fined 0.1 % of GDP per year. The procedure uses a 'scorecard' for macro-economic policies concerning trade deficits, investment, labour costs, exchange rates, private and public sector debt, and house prices. The March 2014 report from the Commission under the MIP illustrates the scope of these powers. It identifies fourteen countries as having imbalances (including Germany): Italy, Slovenia and Croatia have been singled out as having 'excessive imbalances'. The report also shows ten countries with excessive fiscal deficits under the SGP, of which France and Slovakia have received special warnings of the risk of non-compliance with the target deficit. The Commission can also use the new 'Excessive Imbalance Procedure', under which countries have to submit corrective action plans: if they fail to do so, then ultimately the countries can be fined up to 0.1 % of GDP.[37]

The new Treaty on Stability, Coordination and Governance (TSCG, also known as the Fiscal Pact), signed by all member states (now including the Czech republic) except

[36]EU, The EU's economic governance explained MEMO/13/979 12/11/2013. http://europa.eu/rapid/press-release_MEMO-13-979_en.htm. Accessed 15 December 2014; Regulation (EU) No 1175/2011; A, Kocharov, Another Legal Monster? An EUI debate on the fiscal compact treaty, EUI Working Papers LAW 2012/09.

[37]European Commission, Commission concludes in-depth reviews to identify macroeconomic imbalances and assesses progress in fiscal consolidation, Press Release, IP/14/216, 5 March 2014.

the UK, reinforces these fiscal rules by requiring Member States to enshrine balanced budget rules in national binding law, preferably of constitutional nature. The obligation applies not only to the balanced budget principle but also to the specific rules for calculating this and 'automatic' correction of policies. The treaty (Article 3) specifies:

- "the budgetary position of the general government of the Contracting parties shall be balanced or in surplus"
- This is defined as a balance which is equal to "country-specific medium-term objective", but the in any case the structural deficit should not exceed 0.5 % of the GDP.
- The parties commit to "rapid convergence towards their respective medium-term objective", with the time-frame defined by the Commission, and progress will be evaluated using an assessment "including an analysis of expenditure"
- In case they deviate from their path to achieving their MTO, countries must have "a correction mechanism" which "shall be triggered automatically"
- All of these rules must be incorporated in national legislation "through provisions of binding force and permanent character, preferably constitutional, or otherwise guaranteed to be fully respected and adhered to throughout the national budgetary processes". Countries must also create at national level their correction mechanism, in line with "common principles to be proposed by the European Commission, concerning in particular the nature, size and time-frame of the corrective action to be undertaken, also in the case of exceptional circumstances, and the role and independence of the institutions responsible at national level for monitoring compliance with the rules" enforceable by the ECJ.[38]

Finally, the European Stability Mechanism (ESM) was established in 2012 by a new treaty amongst the 17 member states of the Eurozone to safeguard the stability of the Euro area by creating a fund "to mobilise funding and provide stability support under strict conditionality". The conditionalities will be determined following an examination by the EU-ECB-IMF Troika. Governments have to sign agreement to the conditionalities, and also have to be signatories to the Fiscal Compact (Table 7.3).[39]

These new powers work by constraining the decisions which can be taken by future elected governments, especially on economic policy. They are intended to work this way: when the Fiscal Compact was agreed, Angela Merkel was reported as saying: "The debt brakes will be binding and valid forever. Never will you be able to change them through a parliamentary majority."[40] They also include a political bias: a government which prioritised maintaining a higher economic

---

[38]EU, Treaty on stability, coordination and governance. http://european-council.europa.eu/media/639235/st00tscg26_en12.pdf. Accessed 15 December 2014; EU, Specifications on the implementation of the Stability and Growth Pact, 3 September 2012. http://ec.europa.eu/economy_finance/economic_governance/sgp/pdf/coc/code_of_conduct_en.pdf. Accessed 15 December 2014.

[39]EU, Treaty establishing the European Stability Mechanism (ESM) 2012. http://www.european-council.europa.eu/media/582311/05-tesm2.en12.pdf. Accessed 15 December 2014.

[40]Guardian, Germany to set the terms for saving the euro 31 January 2012. http://www.theguardian.com/business/2012/jan/30/eu-summit-eurozone-treaty-deal. Accessed 15 December 2014.

**Table 7.3** EU surveillance and correction of macroeconomic and fiscal imbalances (March 2014)

| | Macroeconomic imbalances | | Fiscal deficit |
|---|---|---|---|
| | Finding | Follow-up | Finding |
| BE | Imbalance | Recommendations to be adopted under the European semester, including on MIP-related issues | Excessive deficit, deadline for correction: 2013 |
| BG | Imbalance | Recommendations to be adopted under the European semester, including on MIP-related issues | Not yet at MTO |
| DE | Imbalance | Recommendations to be adopted under the European Semester, including on MIP-related issues | Overachieving MTO |
| DK | No imbalance | Recommendations to be adopted under the European semester | Excessive deficit, deadline for correction: 2013 |
| IE | Imbalance | Recommendations to be adopted under the European semester, including on MIP-related issues. Specific monitoring: post-programme surveillance | Excessive deficit, deadline for correction: 2015 |
| ES | Imbalance | Recommendations to be adopted under the European semester, including on MIP-related issues. Specific monitoring: post-programme surveillance | Excessive deficit, deadline for correction: 2016 |
| FR | Imbalance | Recommendations to be adopted under the European semester, including on MIP-related issues. Specific monitoring to be put in motion | Excessive deficit, deadline for correction: 2015 |
| HR | Excessive imbalance | Recommendations to be adopted under the European semester, including on MIP-related issues. Decision to be taken in June on subsequent steps under the MIP. Specific monitoring to be put in motion | Excessive deficit, deadline for correction: 2016 |

(continued)

**Table 7.3** (continued)

| | Macroeconomic imbalances | | Fiscal deficit |
|---|---|---|---|
| | Finding | Follow-up | Finding |
| IT | Excessive imbalance | Recommendations to be adopted under the European semester, including on MIP-related issues. Decision to be taken in June on subsequent steps under the MIP. Specific monitoring to be put in motion | Not yet at MTO |
| LU | No imbalance | Recommendations to be adopted under the European semester | Overachieving MTO |
| HU | Imbalance | Recommendations to be adopted under the European semester, including on MIP-related issues | Not yet at MTO |
| MT | No imbalance | Recommendations to be adopted under the European semester | Excessive deficit, deadline for correction: 2014 |
| NL | Imbalance | Recommendations to be adopted under the European semester, including on MIP-related issues | Excessive deficit, deadline for correction: 2014 |
| SI | Excessive imbalance | Recommendations to be adopted under the European semester, including on MIP-related issues. Decision to be taken in June on subsequent steps under the MIP. Specific monitoring to be put in motion | Excessive deficit, deadline for correction: 2015 |
| SE | Imbalance | Recommendations to be adopted under the European semester, including on MIP-related issues | Overachieving MTO |
| FI | Imbalance | Recommendations to be adopted under the European semester, including on MIP-related issues | Not yet at MTO |
| UK | Imbalance | Recommendations to be adopted under the European semester, including on MIP-related issues | Excessive deficit, deadline for correction: 2014–2015 |

*Source* European Commission, Results of in-depth reviews under Regulation (EU) No 1176/2011 on the prevention and correction of macroeconomic imbalances, COM(2014) 150 final, 5 March 2014

stimulus through government borrowing—like the USA government, for example—would risk sanctions from the EU and its own constitutional court. The fiscal compact thus: "outlaws Keynesianism and its counter-cyclical economic policies and constitutionalizes austerity and balanced budgets as new fundamental principles of the EU constitutional order."[41] The EU is acting more like an international financial institution than a federal government.

It is worth noting that the new powers of the EU are far greater than those of the USA federal government, which has no powers either to rescue or sanction states with fiscal crises, or monitor and direct economic policies in general. There is no legal requirement for states to adopt balanced budget rules, but since the mid-19th century, most states have adopted a balanced budget rule, as a matter of fiscal prudence, partly to make it easier to access financial markets to borrow money. In 35 states this is enshrined in the constitution, in varying terminology, in 14 cases there are statutory or de facto requirements for a balanced budget: only one state, Vermont, has no such constraint.[42] In both Europe and the USA, the balanced budget rules mean that the states prevent themselves from countering economic downturns by borrowing money to finance economic stimulus—in effect, Keynesian economic policies are illegal. In the USA, the federal government can still borrow and create money to finance reflationary Keynesian policies in times of recession, but the EU itself has no comparable ability, and so the entire Eurozone is left unable to do so.[43]

A comparison between the new EU powers and those of the IMF is also illuminating. Firstly, the EU now has detailed macroeconomic surveillance powers, similar to those of the IMF, through the semester, reinforced by the MIP, using set criteria. This may not enhance the status of the EU in the way that it has the IMF, however, because the EU is already facing widespread difficulties in many countries for excessive interference in the affairs of member states, and the semester/MIP may reinforce these problems.

Secondly, the EU has embedded a strict set of neoliberal economic rules in the Fiscal Compact and the MIP mechanism, which gives these rules more legal and institutional authority than the informal status of the IMF's rules. However, the IMF retains flexibility to modify the rules in different times and places, whereas the EU rules are set in legislation in remarkable detail: the Fiscal Compact provides a very detailed and technical "golden rule," which defines in strict mathematical terms the yearly structural deficit permitted in every member state and specifies conditions for disrespecting the rule, as well as automatic mechanisms to ensure compliance.[44] Thirdly, the EU institutions now have the financial carrot of the ESM to use, as well as the sticks of the penalties and sanctions under the SGP. But unlike the IMF, the EU cannot threaten to walk away from a member state; and also unlike the IMF, the EU is directly affected by, and may be weakened by, public and political resistance from within countries.

---

[41]Bugaric 2013.

[42]Fabbrini 2013.

[43]Fabbrini 2013; Benczes 2013.

[44]Fabbrini 2013.

## 7.7 Conclusion

Austerity was not an automatic consequence of the crisis, but an exercise in political economy. It reversed the Keynesian policies which were remarkably successful in stemming the impact of the crisis in 2009, and it provides support for the banks who are the principal creditors of countries in crisis. This is appreciated by the banks—although they were rescued by enormous public debt under the brief Keynesian period—as it was in the crises of the late 19th century. The banks, the IMF and now the EU appear to share a belief that democratic processes and constitutions are left-wing threats to the stable continuation of neoliberal economic policies. This is probably true, as long as this set of economic policies does not deliver economic growth enjoyed by all in terms of employment and prosperity. The tensions between democratic politics at national level, and neo-liberal economic policies driven by international institutions, are likely to continue for the foreseeable future.

## Annex: The EU Semester

### The European Semester—Coordination Throughout the Year

*Glossary*: *AGS* Annual Growth Survey, *AMR* Alert Mechanism Report, *CSR* Country-specific recommendations, *EDP* Excess Deficit Procedure, *IDR* In-depth Review

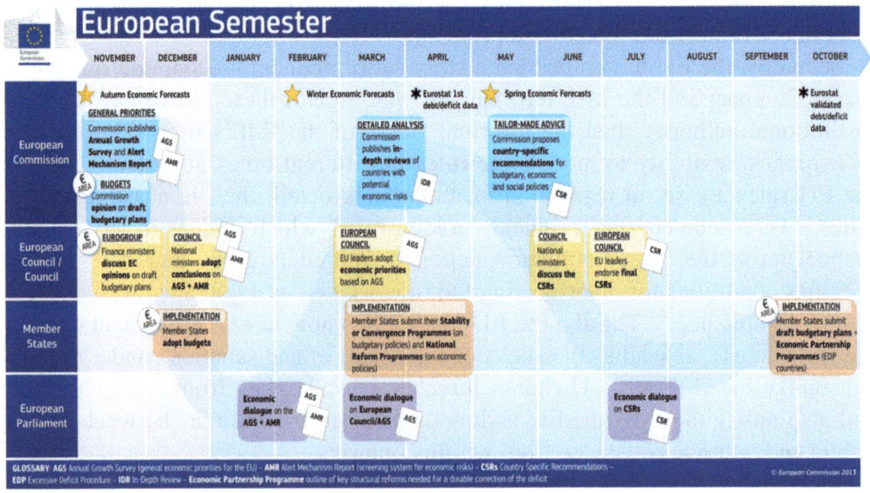


*Source* http://ec.europa.eu/economy_finance/economic_governance/the_european_semester/index_en.htm

## References

Beck U (2005) Power in the global age. Polity Press, Cambridge

Benczes I (2013) Fiscal rules and national ownership: a critical evaluation of past and current fiscal rules in the EU. In: Jensen J, Miszlivetz F (eds) Global challenges—European answers the rise of globality in Europe. Savaria University Press, Szombathely, pp 79–100

Bond P (2011) Neoliberal threats to North Africa. Rev Afr Polit Econ 38(129):481–495

Bugaric B (2013) Europe against the Left? On Legal Limits to Progressive Politics, LSE LEQS Paper No. 61/2013

Cavero T, Poinasamy K (2013) A cautionary tale: the true cost of austerity and inequality in Europe, Oxfam GB policy & practice. http://policy-practice.oxfam.org.uk/publications/a-cautionary-tale-the-true-cost-of-austerity-and-inequality-in-europe-301384. Accessed 15 Dec 2014

Crespy A (2013) Deliberative democracy and the legitimacy of the European Union: a reappraisal of conflict. Polit Stud 62(Supp. 1):81–98

Crespy A (2014) The vanishing promise of a more social Europe: public services before and after the eurocrisis, prepared for the conference of the Council for European Studies, Washington DC

De Grauwe P (2012) Economics of monetary union, 9th edn. Oxford University Press, Oxford

Eichengreen B (2007) Europe's post-war recovery. Cambridge University Press, Cambridge

Fabbrini F (2013) The fiscal compact, the "Golden Rule", and the paradox of European federalism. Boston Coll Int Comp Law Rev 36(1):1–38

Scheppele K (2006) Democracy by judiciary. In: Czarnota A, Krygier M, Sadurski W (eds) Rethinking the rule of law after communism. Central European University Press, Budapest, pp 25–60

Thorstensen V, Ramos D, Muller C (2013) The "Missing Link" between the WTO and the IMF. J Int Econ Law 16(2):353–381

Verbist G, Förster M, Vaalavuo M (2012) The impact of publicly provided services on the distribution of resources: review of new results and methods, OECD social, employment and migration working papers No. 130, 2012. OECD Publishing

# Part II
# External Policies of the European Union

# Chapter 8
# A Normative Basis for EU External Relations? Protecting Internal Values Beyond the Single Market

**Piet Eeckhout**

**Abstract** This chapter analyses the EU's obligation to uphold and promote its values and interests in its external polies, in particular as regards some of the values generally underpinning the EU's internal market, and the rules and principles concerning services of general interest in particular. The first part of the chapter offers a mapping exercise of the relevant Treaty provisions—seeking to establish connections and ways of reading them so that they may "inform" each other. The second part puts them in the context of the debate about Normative Power Europe (NPE)—a much used, but not undisputed international relations concept coined to express the nature of the EU's external policies and projection. The third inquires further into the "normative" nature and effect of the EU's constitutional values and objectives. It will be argued that the Treaty normative basis for the EU's external relations is meaningful and is to be taken seriously.

## Contents



## 8.1 Introduction

Over the last decade or so, the EU's external policies—now officially and rather inelegantly called "external action"—have grown in ambition, scope and stature. The trajectory is neither unproblematic nor linear. It is clear that some external

P. Eeckhout (✉)
Professor of European Union Law, University College London Faculty of Laws, London, UK
e-mail: p.eeckhout@ucl.ac.uk



M. Krajewski (ed.), *Services of General Interest Beyond the Single Market*, Legal Issues of Services of General Interest,
DOI 10.1007/978-94-6265-063-3_8

policies work better than others, and that the EU's constitutional ambition, as expressed in the Treaties, is difficult to realize. The overall tendency is clear, though. The EU—which when it comes to external policies is best understood as a conglomerate of the EU institutions and the Member States—seeks to become an ever more significant global actor,[1] not just in the economic field but across *and beyond* the range of its internal competences and policies. Indeed, the fledgling Common Foreign and Security Policy (CFSP) cannot be equated to the external projection of an internal policy; nor is that the case for the EU's external human rights policy.

The Lisbon Treaty was a scarcely veiled attempt to further constitutionalize the founding Treaties. As regards external action, that Treaty clearly constitutes the apex of the EU's constitutional and policy ambition—utopian at best, in the eyes of most.[2] It is worth recalling here the mere Treaty summary, in Article 3(5) TEU, of what the EU hopes to achieve in the wider world (the full version is in Article 21 TEU):

> In its relations with the wider world, the Union shall uphold and promote its values and interests and contribute to the protection of its citizens. It shall contribute to peace, security, the sustainable development of the Earth, solidarity and mutual respect among peoples, free and fair trade, eradication of poverty and the protection of human rights, in particular the rights of the child, as well as to the strict observance and the development of international law, including respect for the principles of the United Nations Charter.

It is easy to denigrate such utopian ambition. Yet this is a fundamental Treaty provision, and it is cast in mandatory terms: the EU *shall* uphold and promote its values and interests. This chapter seeks to inquire into the meaning of this Treaty obligation, in particular as regards some of the values generally underpinning the EU's internal market, and the rules and principles concerning services of general interest in particular. It is structured in three parts. Section 8.2 offers a mapping exercise of the relevant Treaty provisions—seeking to establish connections and ways of reading them so that they may "inform" each other. Section 8.3 puts them in the context of the debate about Normative Power Europe (NPE)—a much used, but not undisputed international relations concept coined to express the nature of the EU's external policies and projection.[3] Section 8.4 inquires further into the "normative" nature and effect of the EU's constitutional values and objectives. I will argue that the Treaty normative basis for the EU's external relations is meaningful and is to be taken seriously.

## 8.2 Mapping the Treaties

Reference was made above to Article 3(5) TEU, which sets out the EU's objectives "in its relations with the wider world". The EU must, first of all, uphold and promote its values. This of course raises the question as to what those values are,

[1] De Burca 2013, pp. 39, 43.

[2] Or perhaps EUtopian, cf Nicolaïdis and Howse 2002, p. 767.

[3] See the seminal article by Manners 2002, p. 235.

and how to define them. Article 2 TEU attempts to sum them up: they are "respect for human dignity, freedom, democracy, equality, the rule of law and respect for human rights, including the rights of persons belonging to minorities". There is no immediate connection here to the values underpinning the internal market, or to services of general interest. There is, however, a mediated one. The EU Charter of Fundamental Rights (EU Charter) contains a series of rights and principles grouped together in a title on "Solidarity" (Title IV), mostly concerned with social rights, but including Article 36 on "Access to services of general economic interest":

> The Union recognises and respects access to services of general economic interest as provided for in national laws and practices, in accordance with the Treaties, in order to promote the social and territorial cohesion of the Union.

This provision is not of course formulated as a human or fundamental right, and the Charter, as is well known, operates a cumbersome distinction between "rights" and "principles".[4] That however cannot mean that Article 36 is not part of the values referred to in Article 2 TEU. The Charter unifies civil and political rights, on the one hand, and social and economic rights on the other.[5] Its identity is singular: a Charter of Fundamental Rights of the European Union. The distinction between rights and principles is relevant to determining the effects of specific Charter provisions; but it is next to unarguable that, for the purpose of understanding the concept of respect for human rights as a Treaty-determined value of the EU, not all Charter provisions are to be included. It may further be noted that the Charter Title on Solidarity also refers to social security and social assistance (including housing assistance); to a right of access to health care; and to a high level of consumer protection.[6] The right to education in Article 14 Charter is also worth mentioning.

There are further links between the Treaty provisions on values and objectives, and the promotion of services of general interest. The Charter puts such services under the heading of "solidarity", and Article 2 TEU describes how the EU's "values are common to the Member States in a society in which… solidarity" (amongst others) prevails. Clearly, the principle of solidarity underpins the EU's concept of what Article 3 TEU describes as "a highly competitive social market economy", and justifies and explains the specific place occupied by services of general interest. The principle of solidarity is further expressly referred to as an objective of the EU's external action, in particular in Article 21(1) TEU, which includes it among "the principles which have inspired its own creation, development and enlargement, and which it seeks to advance in the wider world" and which need to guide the EU's action on the international scene.

[4]Article 52(5) EU Charter. See, for an excellent attempt to make sense of that distinction, the Opinion of AG P Cruz Villalón of 18 July 2013 in CJEU, Case C-176/12 *Association de Médiation Sociale* [2013] EU:C:2013:491, paras 43–80.

[5]Cf Anderson and Murphy 2012, pp. 155, 160.

[6]See Articles 34, 35 and 38 EU Charter.

There is further Treaty confirmation that services of general economic interest form part of the EU's values: Article 14 TFEU expressly confirms this by speaking of "the place occupied by services of general economic interest in the shared values of the Union as well as their role in promoting social and territorial cohesion". Protocol No 26 further elucidates what these shared values entail.

As a last section of this mapping exercise one may point towards the Treaty provisions on the common commercial policy. Both Articles 205 and 207(1) TFEU confirm that the common commercial policy must be conducted in the context of the principles and objectives of the EU's external action. Article 207 TFEU fully extends this policy to trade in services,[7] and it is of course in the context of international negotiations on such trade that the EU may seek to carve out a special position for services of general interest—both in the EU and elsewhere. This is not a consideration devoid of political and practical relevance in light of the sensitivity of international attempts at liberalizing trade in services in sectors such as water, energy and the like. Another type of sensitivity has found expression in the decision-making provisions of Article 207: by derogation from the standard qualified majority voting, unanimity governs negotiations in the field of trade in cultural and audiovisual services, where they "risk prejudicing the Union's cultural and linguistic diversity"; and in the field of trade in social, education and health services, where they "risk seriously disturbing the national organisation of such services and prejudicing the responsibility of Member States to deliver them".

It may be useful to sum up the main findings of this mapping exercise:

- in its external action the EU is subject to an obligation to uphold and promote its own values;
- those values include respect for human rights in a society in which solidarity prevails;
- the EU Charter lists access to services of general economic interest as a fundamental right, under the heading of solidarity;
- the principle of solidarity must be promoted as one of the express goals of EU external action;
- the EU's internal market is described as a highly competitive social market economy and services of general economic interest are part of it, occupying a place in the shared values of the EU;
- EU exclusive competence extends to international trade in services, but the decision-making provisions recognize that the liberalization of certain services is sensitive; and the common commercial policy must respect the principles and objectives of EU external action.

Taken together, these Treaty provisions confirm that services of general interest are part of the EU's values system. Precisely what that means, in substantive terms, is beyond the scope of this paper, as it would require an analysis of its own. It is clear though that, in its external action, the EU must take services of general

[7]See e.g. Krajewski 2012, pp. 292, 300.

interest into account. That Treaty command can be seen as a requirement for the EU's external dealings (for example when negotiating the liberalization of trade in services) not unduly to interfere with how services of general interest are organized within the EU Member States. But it could also be seen as a duty to respect and protect such services elsewhere, in third countries.

Further reflection is of course needed on the normative "thickness" of the Treaty command for the EU to respect and promote its values in its external action. What does this normativity entail? Can it be operationalized, or is it no more than a form of constitutionalized wishful thinking? A small detour via international relations theory may assist in this reflection.

## 8.3 Normative Power Europe?

Many legal scholars are generally critical of the attempt to constitutionalize the EU's values and objectives. As Larik reports, the manifold codified objectives of the EU have been described as a "Christmas tree" (in particular by the British delegation to the Convention on the Future of Europe), or a "hodgepodge" (von Bogdandy); or, specifically in relation to external objectives, as "redolent of motherhood and apple pie" (Dashwood and others), or a wish list for a better world (Drescher).[8] Even if he does not at length address the EU's external objectives, de Witte also complains that there is too much constitutional law in the EU's foreign relations.[9]

These scholars either regard the constitutionalization of values and objectives as rather meaningless, because of their vagueness and level of abstraction[10]; or as hopelessly idealistic for the cold world of foreign relations, thereby placing themselves in the realist camp of international relations commentators. De Witte's critique is of a different character: he worries about the level of entrenchment which the law of EU external relations suffers through the process of constitutionalization.

On the other hand, Larik argues that the EU's tendency to provide for a constitutional casting of the EU's external objectives is by no means unique, in that there is a general trend towards what he calls a "dynamic internationalization" in constitutional law.[11] Many States' constitutions, both in Europe and beyond,[12] are said to follow the same trend.

It is however remarkable that the general scepticism among lawyers is not shared by an important strand in international relations scholarship on the EU.

---

[8]Larik 2013, pp. 7, 18.

[9]De Witte 2008, p. 3.

[10]See also Leino 2008, pp. 259, 265.

[11]J. Larik, Shaping the international order as a Union objective and the dynamic internationalization of constitutional law. CLEER Working Papers 2011/5, pp. 1–41, at pp. 9 ff.

[12]Larik 2013, pp. 12–14.

Ian Manners' article on Normative Power Europe (NPE) is clearly seminal, and was shortlisted by the *Journal of Common Market Studies* as one of the 5 best papers of the 2002–2011 decade.[13] The article was published in the first half of 2002, at a time when the Convention on the Future of Europe was only beginning to meet, and had not even started to debate how to constitutionalize the EU's external action. And yet much of what Manners said about NPE is reflected in the provisions of the Constitutional Treaty and of the Lisbon Treaty.

It is not the purpose of this paper to offer a full analysis of the concept of NPE, and the debate pertaining to it among international relations scholars. I should merely like to note the remarkable convergence between this concept and the process of constitutionalization of the EU's values and objectives, in the sphere of its external action. This convergence can be illustrated with a brief *aperçu* of some of Manners's observations, analyses and concepts, as set out in his seminal article. His main aim was to move away from the dichotomy between military and civilian power, as it had been applied to the EU's external policies. He claimed that "by refocusing away from debate over either civilian or military power, it is possible to think of the ideational impact of the EU's international identity/role as representing normative power".[14] He argued that one of the problems with the notions of civilian and military power was "their unhealthy concentration on how much like a state the EU looks" and considered that they "need to be augmented with a focus on normative power of an ideational nature characterized by common principles and a willingness to disregard Westphalian conventions".[15] The EU's normative difference was argued to come from its historical context, hybrid polity and political-legal constitution.[16] Its constitutional norms were said to represent crucial constitutive factors determining its international identity, and the three above factors "accelerated a commitment to placing universal norms and principles at the centre of its relations with its Member States… and the world…." Manners argued that "we cannot overlook the extent to which the EU is normatively different to other polities with its commitment to individual rights and principles in accordance with the ECHR and the UN".[17] He rejected the assumption that normative power requires a willingness to use force in an instrumental way, instead contending that "the central component of normative power Europe is that it exists as being different to pre-existing political forms, and that this particular difference pre-disposes it to act in a normative way".[18]

Again, all of this was written prior to the drafting of the Constitutional Treaty and the Treaty of Lisbon. However, Manners's analysis was not confined to defining the concept of normative power in the rather abstract sense above. He digged

---

[13]Manners 2002, p. 235. On the nomination, see the journal's website at http://onlinelibrary.wiley.com/journal/10.1111/%28ISSN%291468-5965.

[14]Ibid at p. 238.

[15]Ibid at p. 239.

[16]Ibid at p. 240.

[17]Ibid at p. 241.

[18]Ibid at p. 242.

deeper into the EU's normative foundations, identifying five "core" norms within the *acquis communautaire* and the *acquis politique*. Those norms, he argued, were (1) the centrality of peace; (2) the idea of liberty; (3) democracy; (4) the rule of law; and (5) respect for human rights and fundamental freedoms. He further suggested four "minor" norms, but admitted that they were much more contested. Those norms were (1) social solidarity, (2) anti-discrimination, (3) sustainable development and (4) good governance.[19]

The convergence between this normative basis and the current TEU provisions setting out the EU's values and objectives is striking. Of course, Manners did not pick these core and minor norms out of thin air; except for the centrality of peace, the core norms were all referred to in Article 6 TEU, post Nice. However, the Lisbon Treaty has clearly built on the NPE concept, and its provisions are arguably closer to Manners's concept and normative basis analysis than previous Treaty versions. The point is not to show that the Treaty drafters embraced the NPE concept—though to some extent there may have been some influence.[20] Nor is it to argue that NPE is undisputed,[21] or that Manners' seminal article has exhausted the reflection on NPE. However, what the NPE literature does show is that the constitutionalization of the EU's values and objectives corresponds to conceptions widely held in international relations scholarship about the specificity of the EU's international identity. From this perspective, the Treaty catalogue of values and objectives cannot so easily be discarded as unrealistic, idealist, unspecified and vague; or as simply comparable to national constitutions, or constituting excessive constitutionalization. It is worth quoting one of Manners's final paragraphs[22]:

> The concept of normative power is an attempt to suggest that not only is the EU constructed on a normative basis, but importantly that this predisposes it to act in a normative way in world politics. It is built on the crucial, and usually overlooked observation that the most important factor shaping the international role of the EU is not what it does or what it says, but what it is. Thus my presentation of the EU as a normative power has an ontological quality to it—that the EU can be *conceptualized* as a changer of norms in the international system; a positivist quantity to it—that the EU *acts* to change norms in the international system; and a normative quality to it—that the EU *should* act to extend its norms into the international system.

Further literature on NPE has shown, however, that the concept of normative power is not straightforward—at least not for international relations scholars. The debate is in large measure about the meaning of "normative".[23] One question is the extent to which "normative" stands for universal norms and principles. Aggestam, for example, sees tension in EU foreign policy discourse between universalist

---

[19]Ibid at pp. 242–243.

[20]Cf Forsberg 2011, pp. 1183, 1186, where he refers to the adoption of NPE in policy papers and public diplomacy.

[21]For an overview of the criticism, see ibid at pp. 1187–1189.

[22]Manners 2002, p. 252.

[23]Forsberg 2011.

aspirations and attempts to shape the world in Europe's image.[24] She prefers focusing on the extent to which the EU is an ethical power, because that puts greater emphasis on questions of agency.[25] According to De Zutter, there is no need for a normative power to advocate and diffuse universal norms; normative power is an identity attributed to a political entity that diffuses its own norms in the international system.[26] However, such a conception of normative power would extend it to other international actors (States)—an express aim of De Zutter's analysis—and thereby dilute the idea that the EU is different. Manners, by contrast, continues to focus on universal norms and on the extent to which the EU "acts in a normative (i.e. ethically good) way".[27] De Wekker and Niemann argue that the emphasis placed on law is an indicator of normative power: "A true normative power would bind not only others but also itself to collective rules".[28] Again, however, it could be said that there are many other international actors which aim to exercise such normative power.

It is in this reflection on normative power that legal doctrine and scholarship may be able to assist, as notions of normativity are at the heart of law and legal systems. Put simply, the normativity of NPE could be regarded to be constitutionally normative, in the legal sense: the EU is required to act externally in accordance with its own constitutionally determined normative basis, i.e. its values and objectives. In Manners's terms, that idea would not answer the positive question—whether the EU *acts* as a normative power. But it is highly relevant to the ontological and normative questions—whether the EU *is* a normative power, and whether it ought to act as one. Furthermore, legal doctrine and scholarship may also assist in further defining the concept of "normative" in NPE, and in identifying the relevant norms as well as reflecting about their universal or universalizable character. It would for example be useful to start building bridges between the NPE literature and the literature on constitutionalism, European and international.

Much of this is beyond the scope of the present paper. Section 8.4 offers some initial ideas about the normative character of the EU's values and objectives.

## 8.4 The Nature and Effect of the EU's Values and Objectives as Norms for External Action

From a legal perspective, the analysis of the nature and effect of the EU's values and objectives naturally starts with some inquiry into their enforceability. The focus of that inquiry immediately turns on the EU Court of Justice (CJEU): to

[24]Aggestam 2008, p. 7.

[25]Ibid, p. 3.

[26]De Zutter 2010, p. 1107.

[27]Manners 2008, p. 45.

[28]T. De Wekker and A. Niemann, EU relations with Moldova: normative power Europe in action? European Foreign Policy Unit Working Paper No 2009/3, p. 13.

what extent is it possible to enforce, judicially, respect for the EU's fundamental norms in its external action. This immediate focus on the CJEU is a near Pavlovian reflex for EU legal scholars, and ought to be questioned, or at least contextualized.

To begin with, it is not obvious that litigation before the EU's own court would constitute a meaningful form of enforceability of the EU's values and objectives. In particular as regards external action, it could be argued that genuine enforcement ought to be located at the international judicial level, because of the stronger guarantees of independence offered by an "external" judiciary. However, there are few avenues at present for such external judicial control, though that may change once the EU joins the European Convention on Human Rights (ECHR).

There may be further concerns as to the relevance of internal, CJEU judicial control. There may well be a gap between the concept of enforceability, and its practical relevance. It may be easy to show that, in principle, respect for the EU's values and objectives is judicially enforceable; but whether such enforceability makes an empirically demonstrable contribution to such respect is another matter. Questions may also arise as to the "thickness" of enforceability, and the potential for tension between the different values and objectives. Is not their general character such that their enforceability may not be very meaningful for hard decisions and the daily practice of external action.

But even with those questions and doubts in mind, the inquiry into judicial enforceability before the CJEU continues to be useful, for a number of reasons. One of those is that the strong rule-of-law dimension of the EU is not just a lofty ideal which the Treaties uphold, but is a reality in day-to-day policy-making. Disagreements between the institutions, or between the Member States and the institutions, or between private parties and the institutions or Member States, quickly assume a strong legal dimension, and are easily judicialized. In the sphere of EU external relations law, many such disputes have a significant constitutional dimension: they may concern the division of competences between the EU and its Member States[29]; matters of legal basis determining the respective powers of the institutions[30]; the constraints imposed by the duty of cooperation between the EU institutions and the Member States[31]; or the protection of fundamental rights in the context of counter-terrorism policies.[32] The phenomenon of which de Witte complains—that there is too much constitutional EU external relations law[33]—is to some degree a function of this strong rule-of-law dimension, and therefore unavoidable. That is not to say that all of the case law excels in terms of constitutional quality and rigour. The critique that some of the judgments may be too

[29]For a recent example, see CJEU, Case C-414/11 *Daiichi Sankyo* [2013] ECLI:EU:C:2013:520, regarding the scope of the extension of the common commercial policy to intellectual property.

[30]See eg CJEU, Case C-130/10 *EP v Council* [2012] EU:C:2012:472, regarding the EP's involvement in counter-terrorist asset freezing measures.

[31]See eg CJEU, Case C-246/07 *Commission v Sweden* (*PFOS*) [2010] ECR I-3317.

[32]See eg CJEU, Joined Cases C-584/10 P, C-593/10 P and C-595/10 P *Commission, UK and Council v Kadi* (*Kadi II*) [2013] EU:C:2013:518.

[33]De Witte 2008.

complicated may well be justified. But the blame of judicialization, also of EU external policies, cannot be laid at the door of the CJEU: it is a function of the detailed and prolific Treaties which the Member States have drafted; of the wide scope of EU external action, in particular of a normative kind (it is no accident that so-called smart sanctions constitute the core of the CFSP); and of the EU's strong rule-of-law dimension. It may be added that the actual judgments of the CJEU are but the tip of the iceberg. Beneath the surface there is a panoply of legal opinions and advocacy nourished by the principles developed in the case law. In this basic sense, of extensive judicialization, there is a strong normative dimension to EU external action.

There is not much case law yet on the EU's values and objectives, in relation to external action—particularly in their Lisbon version, which for case law purposes is still quite young. Even so, there are some episodes and instances which clearly exemplify the potential for such case law to develop, and to determine the meaning of those values and objectives, and of the obligation to respect and promote them. Three of those episodes/instances are summarily recounted below. Two of them concern the requirement to respect fundamental rights; the third concerns the mandate to respect international law.

The first episode revolves around the EU's external human rights policy, more specifically the policy to include human-rights clauses in bilateral agreements which the EU concludes with third countries.[34] Those clauses were initially a response to difficulties which the (then) EC had with suspending development aid to ACP countries with regimes which grossly violated human rights, and with suspending the cooperation agreement with Yugoslavia at the time of conflict between the Yugoslav republics. In the latter case, there was litigation before the Court of Justice: a German wine importer, Racke, challenged the suspension of the agreement in response to the actions of the then Serbian regime and the attendant re-introduction of customs duties. The Court found in favour of the Council, which had suspended the agreement invoking the rather precarious *rebus sic stantibus* doctrine of customary international treaty law.[35] Despite this successful defence the institutions acknowledged that there was a legal need to provide for the possible suspension of free trade, cooperation and association agreements in cases of systemic violations of human rights. This need strongly contributed to what became a core component of the EU's external human rights policy: the requirement to include so-called "essential elements" clauses in bilateral agreements requiring the parties to respect fundamental rights. It is a policy which stands to this day, and which is not always convenient: witness the foundering of negotiations with Australia because of that country's refusal to accept such a clause.[36] It is further clear that the policy is not just a response to the legal difficulties which the *Racke* case revealed—the institutions deserve more than just defensive credit, and

[34]See e.g. Hoffmeister 1998; Arts 2000; Fierro 2003; Bartels 2005.

[35]CJEU, Case C-162/96 *Racke v Hauptzollamt Mainz* [1998] ECR I-3655.

[36]Fierro 2003, pp. 287–302.

the European Parliament in particular has always been a strong advocate for a meaningful external human rights policy. But it is equally obvious that the case law has assisted in crystallising the issues and has made a meaningful contribution.

The second episode is well known, and has given rise to an enormous amount of debate: the *Kadi* saga, which concerns the EU implementation of UN counter-terrorism policies and the requirement for the EU institutions to respect the fundamental rights of those suspected of supporting terrorism. The saga has now come to an end with the de-listing of Mr Kadi, a Saudi businessman, by the UN Security Council, and with the double victory he scored in the CJEU.[37] It is again an episode confirming the importance of the protection of fundamental rights in the EU's external action. Even in the face of a binding UN Security Council Resolution, the EU institutions must ensure that the listed person's rights of defence, of effective judicial protection, and to property are respected. It does not matter that the listed person is not a national of one of the Member States, and resides outside the EU: as a person subject to EU law by virtue of the freezing of his EU assets, Mr Kadi could claim the full protection of his EU law fundamental rights.

This dimension of the *Kadi* litigation, which has received very little commentary, is particularly noteworthy for the NPE debate. The protection of a person's human rights does not stop at the EU border; nor is it reserved to EU citizens. This approach, which is in consonance with the ECHR, builds a strong link between the EU Charter of Fundamental Rights and EU external action. It is highly relevant to EU policies on economic and financial sanctions, which are not confined to counter-terrorism, and which are currently under constant and intense judicial scrutiny in Luxembourg. But the link may be equally relevant to the EU's treaty-making practice, as the debate leading to the European Parliament's rejection of the Anti-Counterfeiting Trade Agreement (ACTA) has shown.[38] It is worth noting that the Commission tried to defuse that debate by requesting an Opinion from the CJEU, pursuant to Article 218(11) TFEU, on the compatibility of ACTA with the EU system of fundamental rights protection.[39] The request was later withdrawn, in the face of the Parliament's firm rejection, but nevertheless showed the potential for litigation on respect for human rights when the EU negotiates a trade agreement.

It is true that the *Kadi* episode also exposes the potential for tension between the requirement to uphold the protection of fundamental rights and the objective of ensuring "the strict observance and the development of international law, including respect for the principles of the United Nations Charter" (Article 3(5) TEU). Clearly, the EU's values and objectives will not always coexist as harmoniously as one would like. However, there is a reading of the *Kadi* saga which leaves room for some level of harmony. The protection and promotion of human rights is a UN objective, as much as it

---

[37]CJEU, Joined Cases C-402/05 P and C-415/05 P *Kadi and Al Barakaat* (*Kadi I*) [2008] EU:C:2008:461; for an overview of some of the relevant literature on this judgment see Poli and Tzanou 2009, p. 533; *Kadi II* (n 32 above).

[38]See Matthews and Zikovská 2013, p. 626.

[39]Request for an opinion submitted by the European Commission pursuant to Article 218(11) TFEU (Opinion 1/12) of 27 April 2013, *OJ* 2013 C 123, p. 14.

is an EU objective. The judgment in *Kadi I* led to a remarkable improvement in the UN's review system for counterterrorism listings, through the creation of the office of the Ombudsperson. This is NPE at work. The EU judicial challenge to the UN Security Council's practices focused attention on improving them, and led to a much stronger normative focus. It may further be noted that in its latest judgment the Court of Justice claims that judicial review of counterterrorism listings "is indispensable to ensure a fair balance between the maintenance of international peace and security and the protection of the fundamental rights and freedoms of the person concerned…, those being shared values of the UN and the European Union".[40] The Court thus strongly contributes to an international projection of the EU as a value-oriented actor, and advocates a similar conception for, and an allegiance to the UN.

The third instance concerns one of the first judicial applications of the new provision in Article 3(5) TEU—also relevant to the *Kadi* litigation—requiring the EU to promote the strict observance and the development of international law. In the litigation concerning the extension of the EU's emissions trading legislation to air transport (which, incidentally, can be seen as a tool to promote sustainable development, another objective of external action), the Court of Justice referred to Article 3(5) TEU in relation to the capacity of US airlines to rely on customary international law.[41] The airlines' challenge was unsuccessful, and the judgment was not the first in which the Court applied customary international law.[42] Those qualifications notwithstanding, it is definitely not excluded that the Court may display a greater willingness to hear international law arguments and become stricter in upholding the international rule of law, including against the EU's own institutions. The indicia are limited at this point in time, though, and what is stated here constitutes more a personal prediction than an established tendency.

These episodes/instances are exemplary rather than determinative. Some tentative conclusions can be drawn from them, but a more structured analysis of the normative dimension of the EU's values and objectives requires further reflection. It is nevertheless clear that the examples given are in line with the NPE concept. They show the legal significance of these values and objectives, often at the detriment of effective, purely interest-based external policies. It would be more straightforward to negotiate bilateral agreements if there was no need to include an essential elements clause. The EU's counter-terrorism and other sanctions policies would be easier to implement if the EU institutions could simply hide behind the Security Council. And the EU's legislative agenda is not inviting the constraint of international law.

The episodes narrated here also exemplify the scope for judicial enforcement of the EU's values and objectives, as well as indicating ways in which the case law of the CJEU may contribute to NPE by, for example, requiring respect for fundamental rights and for international law, and by instituting normative dialogue with other actors such as the UN Security Council.

---

[40] *Kadi II* (n 32 above), para 131.

[41] CJEU, Case C-366/10 *Air Transport Association of America* [2011] ECR I-13755.

[42] See also CJEU, Case C-162/96 *Racke v Hauptzollamt Mainz* [1998] ECR I-3655.

## 8.5 Some Concluding Remarks

The argument that the EU is primarily a normative power predates the strong constitutionalization of the EU's values and objectives through the Lisbon Treaty. Nevertheless, that constitutionalization invites a further reflection about the normativity of these values and objectives. The NPE literature is a useful backdrop for this reflection, which ought to be conducted also by legal scholars, who should take those values and objectives more seriously than has so far been the case. This paper has attempted to offer a first start, by focusing on normativity from a perspective of judicial enforceability. The preliminary conclusion is that the EU's values and objectives are meaningful to judicial discourse, and have some degree of enforceability.

This paper has not focused much on services of general economic interest, in contrast with the remainder of this volume. It is clear though that the EU's conception of such services is embedded in its value system, as confirmed by the Treaties and by the Charter. This means that the protection and, conceivably, the exportation of that conception need to be taken on board in the EU's external action. The identification of social solidarity as a norm which NPE embraces, confirms that finding.

That raises further questions about the nature of the norms which the EU ought to promote and diffuse in its external action. Is the recognition and protection of services of general economic interest a universal norm, or is it rather a typical, internal EU norm, which the EU seeks to export? That question can also be raised with respect to other norms which form part of the EU's fundamental values system. But it is not clear whether the NPE concept requires absolute universality, as distinguishable from a concept of fundamental norms, and a fundamentally normative approach, focusing on Europe's conception of the good life; norms lending themselves to universal application without constituting the emanation of a new form of imperialism.

## References

Aggestam L (2008) Introduction: ethical power Europe? Int Aff 84(1):1–11

Anderson D, Murphy C (2012) The Charter of Fundamental Rights. In: Biondi A, Eeckhout P, Ripley S (eds) EU law after Lisbon. OUP, Oxford, pp 155–179

Arts K (2000) Integrating human rights into development cooperation: the case of the Lomé Convention. Kluwer Law International, The Hague

Bartels L (2005) Human rights conditionality in the EU's international agreements. OUP, Oxford

De Burca G (2013) EU external relations: the governance mode of foreign policy. In: Van Vooren B, Blockmans S, Wouters J (eds) The EU's role in global governance—the legal dimension. OUP, Oxford, pp 39–58

De Witte B (2008) Too much constitutional law in the European union's foreign relations? In: Cremona M, De Witte B (eds) EU foreign relations law—constitutional fundamentals. Hart Publishing, Oxford, pp 3–15

De Zutter E (2010) Normative power spotting: an ontological and methodological appraisal. J Eur Public Policy 17(8):1106–1127

Fierro E (2003) The EU's approach to human rights conditionality in practice. Martinus Nijhoff Publishers, Leiden

Forsberg T (2011) Normative power Europe, once again: a conceptual analysis of an ideal type. J Common Mark Stud 49:1183–1204

Hoffmeister F (1998) Menschenrechts- und Demokratieklauseln in den vertraglichen Außenbeziehungen der Europäischen Gemeinschaft. Springer, Berlin

Krajewski M (2012) The reform of the common commercial policy. In: Biondi A, Eeckhout P, Ripley S (eds) EU law after Lisbon. OUP, Oxford, pp 292–311

Larik J (2013) Entrenching global governance: the EU's constitutional objectives caught between a sanguine world view and a daunting reality. In: Van Vooren B, Blockmans S, Wouters J (eds) The EU's role in global governance—the legal dimension. OUP, Oxford, pp 7–22

Leino P (2008) The journey towards all that is good and beautiful: human rights and common values as guiding principles of EU foreign relations law. In: Cremona M, De Witte B (eds) EU foreign relations law—constitutional fundamentals. Hart Publishing, Oxford, pp 259–289

Manners I (2002) Normative power Europe: a contradiction in terms? J Common Mark Stud 40(2):235–258

Manners I (2008) The normative ethics of the European Union. Int Aff 84(1):45–60

Matthews D, Zikovská P (2013) The rise and fall of the anti-counterfeiting trade agreement (ACTA): lessons for the European Union. Int Rev Intellect Property Competition Law 44(6):626–655

Nicolaïdis K, Howse R (2002) 'This is my EUtopia …': narrative as power. J Common Mark Stud 40(4):767–792

Poli S, Tzanou M (2009) The *Kadi* rulings: a survey of the literature. Yearb Eur Law 28(1):533–558

# Chapter 9
# Ambivalence of the European Strategy in External Relations on Trade Agreements

**Pierre Bauby**

**Abstract** This chapter claims that the values mentioned in Article 14 TFEU and spelled out in Protocol No. 26 on Services of General Interest must be respected when negotiating EU trade and investment agreements. The chapter discusses the development of the common commercial policy and of the EU approach towards services of general interest in their historic and political contexts. It is argued that the protection of services of general interest in the external economic policies requires a clear strategy which support the objectives, aims and values of the EU in international trade negotiations.

## Contents



## 9.1 Introduction

Since the Treaty of Rome of 1957, international trade negotiations have been subject to the exclusive competence of the European Union (formerly the European Community). The strategy of European integration, which was developed after the initial success of the European Coal and Steel Community and the failure of the European Defence Community, aimed to progressively build an "internal market" based on the free movement of goods, persons, services, and capital, thereby eliminating barriers to trade between the founding Member States. During the first

P. Bauby (✉)
Centre National de La Fonction Publique Territoriale, Paris 8 University, Science Po Paris, Paris, France
e-mail: bauby.pierre@orange.fr



M. Krajewski (ed.), *Services of General Interest Beyond the Single Market*, Legal Issues of Services of General Interest,
DOI 10.1007/978-94-6265-063-3_9

stage of European integration, the implementation of this strategy focused on trade in goods and therefore the progressive elimination of national customs duties. Beyond the creation of common European legislation to regulate barriers to trade within the Community—the Community competition law—it involved the definition of a common policy on trade with the rest of the world with, in particular, the establishment of a unified "common customs tariff",[1] of "customs duties", "to contribute, by means of a common commercial policy, to the progressive abolition of restrictions on international trade".[2]

Progressively, the development of international trade—i.e. globalisation—led to the opening of international negotiations and to the setting up of international organisations (GATT which became WTO in 1995), following an approach that became dominant which considers protectionism a factor of conflict and war, and free trade as a tool for development and progress.

The exclusive competence of the EU has led to the definition of common principles and procedures to ensure that the "Community interest" corresponds to the specific interests of each Member State.

Article 19 of the Treaty of Rome of 1957 states that "duties in the common customs tariff shall be at the level of the arithmetical average of the duties applied in the four customs territories comprised in the Community" and is accompanied by Annex I which lists industrial and agricultural products in categories which are subject either to the maximum duties of the common customs tariffs or, for some products, to negotiations between Member States.

Beyond the common customs tariff, the Treaty of Rome has defined a common "commercial policy" and its general approach: "By establishing a customs union between themselves Member States aim to contribute, in the common interest, to the harmonious development of world trade, the progressive abolition of restrictions on international trade and the lowering of customs barriers."[3] The Treaty of Rome conferred to the Commission the competence to conduct "tariff negotiations with third countries in respect of the common customs tariff (…) in consultation with a special committee appointed by the Council to assist the Commission in this task and within the framework of such directives as the Council may issue to it". For their part, "Member States shall aim at securing as high a level of uniformity as possible between themselves as regards their liberalisation lists in relation to third countries or groups of third countries. To this end, the Commission shall make all appropriate recommendations to Member States."[4] Furthermore, the Treaty states that it is for "the Commission to ensure the

[1]"… the activities of the Community shall include (…) (b) the establishment of a common customs tariff and of a common commercial policy towards third countries", Article 3 of the Treaty of Rome of 1957. The establishment of a common customs tariff is the subject of Articles 18–29 while the commercial policy of Articles 110–116 of the Treaty.

[2]Preamble of the Treaty of Rome of 1957.

[3]Article 110.

[4]Article 111 ff.

maintenance of all appropriate relations with the organs of the United Nations, of its specialised agencies and of the General Agreement on Tariffs and Trade".[5]

Without summarising all of the modifications to the Treaty of Rome that have intervened in the field of commercial policy during the last half-century, we shall examine here the new approaches detailed in the treaties currently in force which are contained in the Lisbon Treaty (the Treaty on European Union—TEU—and the Treaty on the Functioning of the European Union—TFEU).

Article 3 TEU, which establishes the objectives of the European Union, reveals a new approach: "In its relations with the wider world, *the Union shall uphold and promote its values and interests* and contribute to the protection of its citizens. It shall contribute to peace, security, the sustainable development of the Earth, solidarity and mutual respect among peoples, free and fair trade, eradication of poverty and the protection of human rights, in particular the rights of the child, as well as to the strict observance and the development of international law, including respect for the principles of the United Nations Charter" (my emphasis). It is not only about the "progressive abolition of restrictions on international trade"[6] but also aims to "promote its values and interests".

Article 3 TFEU includes the "common commercial policy" among the exclusive competences of the EU. Within the chapter "The Customs Union", Article 31 TFEU declares that "Common Customs Tariff duties shall be fixed by the Council on a proposal from the Commission" and Article 32 states that "the Commission shall be guided by: (a) the need to promote trade between Member States and third countries".

The common commercial policy is subject to Title II of Part Five of TFEU—The Union's External Action. Article 206 provides its objectives: "the Union shall contribute, in the common interest, to the harmonious development of world trade, the progressive abolition of restrictions on international trade and on foreign direct investment, and the lowering of customs and other barriers". Article 207 defines the conduct of negotiations:

> 3. The Commission shall make recommendations to the Council, which shall authorise it to open the necessary negotiations. The Council and the Commission shall be responsible for *ensuring that the agreements negotiated are compatible with internal Union policies and rules*. The Commission shall conduct these negotiations in consultation with a special committee appointed by the Council to assist the Commission in this task and within the framework of such directives as the Council may issue to it. The Commission shall report regularly to the special committee and to the European Parliament on the progress

[5]Article 229.

[6]Similar wording is used in Article 21 TEU—General Provisions on the Union's external action: "The Union shall define and pursue common policies and actions, and shall work for a high degree of cooperation in all fields of international relations, in order to: (…) e) encourage the integration of all countries into the world economy, including through the progressive abolition of restrictions on international trade" and in the Preamble of the TFEU: "desiring to contribute, by means of a common commercial policy, to the progressive abolition of restrictions on international trade".

> of negotiations. 4. For the negotiation and conclusion of the agreements referred to in para 3, the Council shall act by a qualified majority. For the negotiation and conclusion of *agreements in the fields of trade in services and the commercial aspects of intellectual property, as well as foreign direct investment, the Council shall act unanimously where such agreements include provisions for which unanimity is required for the adoption of internal rules*. The Council shall also act unanimously for the negotiation and conclusion of agreements: (a) in the field of *trade in cultural and audiovisual services, where these agreements risk prejudicing the Union's cultural and linguistic diversity*; (b) in the field of *trade in social, education and health services, where these agreements risk seriously disturbing the national organisation of such services and prejudicing the responsibility of Member States to deliver them* (emphasis added).

This Title contains key elements which outline the exclusive competence of European institutions and the role of European Commission. The international trade agreements must be "compatible with internal Union policies and rules"; this emphasises the primacy of these internal rules. Certain areas are subject to the qualified majority of the Council, while others are subject to unanimity, meaning they may be vetoed by a Member State. Meanwhile, the role of the European Parliament has become more important.

## 9.2 What European Strategies?

The primary law provides safeguards but it does not define the EU's strategic approach to international commercial negotiations. This is not a subject of the treaties, which define what Member States wish to do together and how they intend to do it. Neither the treaties of the European Community nor those of the EU define the specific details of the EU's approach, which rests on compromises, a convergence of the interests of each Member State and a common interest.

On the one hand, the strategic choices of the European Union during international trade negotiations rely on ambivalence between the role of the liberalisation of trade, the elimination of obstacles of all kinds, and therefore on confidence in the liberalisation of market forces. On the other hand, the objective is not only to "defend" the values and the European social model but also to enrich international exchanges with principles that can have a universal dimension.

At the same time, we see another vision, based on a rejection of any form of international trade negotiations and of any possible agreement, because of the domination of liberal content from international organisations such as WTO and because of the policies of the main economic stakeholders—businesses as well as states. Thus, the strategy is to put forward European specificities to exclude the maximum possible number of areas from international regulations and to systematically put forward the European exception.

Therefore, we see a recurrence of the issues of the 1990s when the European institutions searched for ways to Europeanise public services or services of general interest. At that time, public services—referred to as services of general interest in EU language—which had been defined and organised within the framework of national legislation became the subject of a process of European integration which was based on the elimination of barriers to trade. Three strategic approaches were then developed[7]:

- for some, it would be sufficient for these services to be made subject to the common law of competition and to the "invisible hand" of the market to improve their quality and lower their prices all around Europe;
- for others, liberalisation could only lead to new economic, social, territorial, generational, and financial polarisations, and the elimination of national and local monopolies also required recognition of public services' missions and obligations at European level to allow universal access to essential services and to develop European solidarities;
- for some, taking into account the liberal economic foundations of the European construct, this objective would not be compatible with the process of Europeanisation; it was therefore necessary to defend the national modes of organisation and regulation to exclude public services from Europeanisation or to hide behind a conception of subsidiarity meaning the respect of national specificities.

This third approach was predominant among a large number of economic and social stakeholders in many European countries for many years and the process of Europeanisation took time. However, the European construct could not go as far as to leave out the main communication, energy and transport services needed for the free movement of goods, services, persons and capital. Nevertheless, instead of searching for a positive balance between demonopolisation and the definition of Community public services objectives, in the 1990s and at the beginning of the following decade, an unbalanced approach based on the introduction of competition was developed. It appeared in the name of the required European integration which was presented as an unavoidable constraint to which national and local traditions had to conform.

Simultaneously, a process of rebalance allowing the emergence of a European conception has since been developed step by step, under the initiative of many stakeholders, and in particular of the European Parliament. The Treaty of Lisbon has consolidated this conception that can be summarised in ten acquis:

1. Member States (national, regional, local authorities) have the general competence in "providing, commissioning and organizing" SGI, as well as financing Services of General Economic Interest (SGEI).
2. European institutions have the same competence for European services that are necessary to accomplish EU objectives.
3. With regard to non-economic services of general interest (NESGI), the rules of competition and internal market do not apply; NESGI are only subject to the fundamental principles of the EU (transparency, non-discrimination, equal treatment, proportionality).

[7]See Pierre Bauby, L'européanisation des services publics. Presses SciencePo Paris, 2011.

4. As for services of general economic interest, public authorities must clearly define their "particular task" (principle of transparency).
5. On that basis, they may define appropriate means for the proper accomplishment of the "particular task" (principle of proportionality), including, if it is necessary and proportionate, aid and subsidies, exclusive or special rights.
6. Member states have free choice of management mode: internal, in-house, delegated, etc.
7. These definitions should clearly establish the objectives of "a high level of quality, safety and affordability, equal treatment and the promotion of universal access and of user rights".
8. Rules of competition and internal market apply only if they do not obstruct the performance, in law or in fact, of their particular tasks.
9. Member states have free choice of ownership of enterprises (principle of "neutrality").
10. In all cases, abuses may appear because of an "evident error" that the Commission may present under the control of the European Court of Justice.

However, these acquis remain precarious and many significant tensions continue to exist between internal market and competition approaches, public service or universal service obligations, the implementation of the subsidiarity principle and the promotion of economic, social and territorial cohesion.

A potential risk is the transposition of this European process on the level of international trade negotiations, which could lead to the same effects: today the liberalisation of exchanges, investments and trade at global level appears unavoidable within the framework of the process of globalisation; this would force Europeans to question our social model, our health and education systems, our culture, our services of general interest and the European rules on which they rest, and to open all of these sectors and public services, along with their missions and obligations, their definition and financing, to global competition.

A series of economic, political or institutional stakeholders promote this orientation which leads to the uniformity of all acquis stemming from the history of the European continent and social movements that have marked it. When we consider the difficulties of the majority of the Member States of the EU and of the European Parliament in imposing the exclusion of audiovisual services—on the basis of the "cultural exception"—from the mandate of negotiation of the European Commission for the Transatlantic Trade and Investment Partnership (TTIP), the importance of this approach in Europe is clear.

Faced with such a prospect, many stakeholders are organising themselves to propose a series of exceptions ranging from the area of public services to culture, education or health, and their exclusion from international trade negotiations, either at the level of the WTO or at the level of regional or inter-state negotiations.

A significant example of this strategy is to be found in the declaration adopted on 5 September 2013 by a large number of alternative or environmental organisations[8]: "To address the climate emergency we need to not only stop the expansion of the WTO and FTAs". The WTO, the World Bank and the International Monetary Fund aim at "promoting neoliberalism and corporate globalization. The WTO was particularly special in its power to legally enforce and penalize countries, taking away the policy space of governments, and on several occasions, forcing them to change their national laws in order to implement global free trade rules."

While affirming that "Trade is needed but a different kind of trade, one that is not based on the exploitation of people and nature and whose rules benefit the communities and not the corporations. The kind of trade we need is complementary and equitable trade not corporate free trade", the Declaration concludes by stating that "To really address the climate crisis, a world without the WTO and the FTAs, one that is not dominated by transnational corporations and the global free trade regimes, is necessary!"

The effects of the movements organised by "alter-globalisation" organisations in Seattle (1999), Cancun (2003) or Hong Kong (2005) cannot be denied. They have contributed to bringing a series of challenges for international negotiations to public attention. However, it must be noted that the issue of the rejection of international trade negotiations as they are organised today results in organisations such as WTO being considered a compact unit in a neo-liberal posture, while Member States such as the USA, the EU, China or BRICS (such as India or Brazil) have different interests and positions. Alliances are possible based on shared or convergent interests. More generally, such an approach, that is essentially defensive, leads to the view that the development of trade exchanges at global level systematically consolidates the system.

## 9.3 Promoting the Values and Interests of the EU

In fact, as the Lisbon Treaty outlines ("In its relations with the wider world, *the Union shall uphold and promote its values and interests*"), there is another possible strategy, an offensive one, which consists of supporting the objectives and aims of the European Union and the values they rest on, even in international trade

[8]ATTAC—España, Attac—France, Center for Encounter and active Non-Violence—Austria, Corporate Europe Observatory, Critical Information Collective, East and Southern Africa Small-scale farmer's Forum (ESAFF) Zambia, Ecologistas en Acción, Entrepueblos—España, ETC Group, Fairwatch—Italy, Focus on the Global South, Global Exchange, Global Forest Coalition, Grassroots Global Justice Alliance—US, Grassroots International, Health of Mother Earth Foundation—Nigeria, Indigenous Environmental Network, JA! Justiça Ambiental / FOE Mozambique Kalikasan People's Network for the Environment (Kalikasan PNE)—Philippines, La Via Campesina, Migrants Rights International, No REDD in Africa Network (NRAN), Oilwatch International, Partido Humanista—Vigo, Plataforma Boliviana Frente al Cambio Climático, Polaris Institute, REPEM América Latina y El Caribe, The Democracy Center—Bolivia, Transnational Institute, Unión Universal Desarrollo Solidario.

negotiations, to build alliances, aiming not to exclude a specific area but to enrich the process of globalisation and trade exchanges based on new foundations.

At this point, we return to the possibilities presented by the Lisbon Treaty in order to illustrate this approach.

Article 2 TEU identifies the EU's main values: "The Union is founded on the values of respect for human dignity, freedom, democracy, equality, the rule of law and respect for human rights, including the rights of persons belonging to minorities. These values are common to the Member States in a society in which pluralism, non-discrimination, tolerance, justice, solidarity and equality between women and men prevail." We do not intend to open a debate on the universality of these values,[9] but we see that there may be some scope here to open debates in international negotiations in order to integrate those values that are subject to convergence into the framework of the objectives of trade agreements.

Another area that has been mentioned above concerns services of general interest. Since the Amsterdam Treaty they have been considered "common values of the European Union". The Lisbon Treaty identifies the main elements in Protocol 26 attached to the two treaties (TEU and TFEU) which has the same legal value:

> THE HIGH CONTRACTING PARTIES,
> WISHING to emphasise the importance of services of general interest,
> HAVE AGREED UPON the following interpretative provisions, which shall be annexed to the Treaty on the European Union and to the Treaty on the Functioning of the European Union:
>
> **Article 1**
> The shared values of the Union in respect of services of general economic interest within the meaning of Article 14 of the Treaty on the Functioning of the European Union include in particular:
>
> - the essential role and the wide discretion of national, regional and local authorities in providing, commissioning and organising services of general economic interest as closely as possible to the needs of the users;
> - the diversity between various services of general economic interest and the differences in the needs and preferences of users that may result from different geographical, social or cultural situations;
> - a high level of quality, safety and affordability, equal treatment and the promotion of universal access and of user rights.
>
> **Article 2**
> The provisions of the Treaties do not affect in any way the competence of Member States to provide, commission and organise non-economic services of general interest.

"The promotion of EU values and interests in its relations with the rest of the world", i.e. the further development of bilateral and international trade agreements, can lead to:

- non-economic services of general interest being excluded from the area of negotiations and agreements which should remain within the competence of the states with regard to their definition, organisation and financing;

[9] For us, "universal values" are only those that are recognised as such, and therefore internalised and recognised as being legitimate, by the large majority of States and people.

- not promoting the obligation to uniformly apply the liberalisation principles but instead focusing on the needs and preferences of users, their democratic choice and therefore on the large discretionary power of national, regional and local authorities with regard to services of general economic interest, which involves combining unity and diversity by taking into account different geographical, social or cultural situations;
- the introduction of references to a high level of quality, safety and affordability, equal treatment and the promotion of universal access and of user rights in negotiations.

This strategy suggests reversing the perspective: alignment with the current dominant rules of international trade is either unavoidable or required; it suggests introducing issues surrounding aims and objectives "ensuring that the agreements negotiated are compatible with internal Union policies and rules", and therefore, their primacy.[10] It is not about the EU having an "imperial" attitude or giving lessons to the rest of the world but, following an open and offensive approach, furthering the acquis of a long history aiming to contribute to the creation of an international framework based on responding to the needs of the population.

Naturally, such an approach does not exclude the possibility of standing firm with regards to some areas and in certain moments. Thus, in the field of public procurement, the EU has opened its market to competition from foreign companies for 352 billion of around 500 billion euros per year, compared with 178 billion euros open to foreign companies in the USA and 27 billion euros open to foreign companies in Japan.

[10]Article 207 TFEU.

# Chapter 10
# Public Services Exemptions in EU Free Trade and Investment Agreements

**Markus Krajewski**

**Abstract** This chapter analyses the various approaches used in free trade agreements to safeguard regulatory space for the provision, financing and organisation of public services. It focuses on agreements signed by the EU including texts of recently negotiated agreements and drafts of agreements under negotiation. After a brief overview of the current state-of-affairs of existing free trade agreements of the EU and of current negotiations the chapter explains why the obligations of free trade agreements may potentially conflict with the special function of the provision and organisation of public services. The main part of the chapter is devoted to the development and explanation of an analytical framework concerning the various exemptions and clauses which allows an assessment of the impact of a particular free trade agreement independently of a specific existing model. Based on this analytical framework, the current approach of the EU regarding public service exemptions in free trade agreements is assessed. The chapter concludes with some reform proposals.

## Contents



M. Krajewski (✉)
Public and International Law, University of Erlangen-Nuremberg, Erlangen, Germany
e-mail: markus.krajewski@fau.de



M. Krajewski (ed.), *Services of General Interest Beyond the Single Market*, Legal Issues of Services of General Interest,
DOI 10.1007/978-94-6265-063-3_10

## 10.1 Introduction

Academic analyses and public debates about the impact of trade agreements on the provision and organisation of public services have so far mostly focussed on the General Agreement on Trade in Services (GATS).[1] Bilateral agreements including those signed by the European Union (EU) have largely gone unnoticed in this context. This changed only recently, in particular with the conclusion of the negotiations between the EU and Canada on Comprehensive Trade and Economic Agreement (CETA) and the ongoing negotiations of the EU and the US about a Transatlantic Trade and Investment Partnership (TTIP). While scholarly contributions are still rare, the public debate about public services and these agreements is in full swing.[2]

Observers of the discussions about the impact of GATS on public services may have noticed a few déjà-vus as many aspects which are relevant in the GATS context also play a role concerning bilateral agreements. Analysing and discussing the impact of EU agreements on trade and investment can therefore partly rely and built on existing knowledge concerning the GATS and public services as the impact of the EU's bilateral free trade agreements on public services mirrors the impact of the GATS on public services in a number of aspects. However, there also are new issues which need to be addressed because the GATS framework and bilateral trade also differ. In some cases, bilateral agreements provide greater legal flexibility for the provision of services of general interest while other agreements tend to be stricter. New issues, specifically with regards to the "new generation" free trade agreements (FTAs) of the EU, include the structure of specific commitments in trade agreements ("negative list" or "positive list" approach), the emergence of new rules on sectoral regulations and competition, and the increasing inclusion of chapters on investment—and most recently on investment protection in bilateral trade agreements.[3]

[1]See Chap. 2 in this volume by Arena as well as Krajewski 2003; Leroux 2006; Adlung 2006.

[2]'Protecting public services in TTIP and other EU trade agreements', http://trade.ec.europa.eu/doclib/press/index.cfm?id=1115. Accessed 29 January 2015; 'TTIP—A threat for public services', http://ttip2014.eu/blog-detail/blog/Services%20TTIP%20threat.html. Accessed 29 January 2015.

[3]For a general discussion of investment law and public services see Chap. 4 in this volume by Costamagna.

Most international trade agreements contain some form of exemptions for public services or exclude instruments regulating the organisation and provision of public services from the disciplines of trade agreements. They are based on the traditional understanding that liberalisation obligations should be made at the international level, whereas the regulation of services should remain within the domestic ambit. The respective model hence aims at defending policy space at the national level for the regulation of public services through various "public services exemptions". "Public policy exemptions" are those provisions of trade agreements which exempt public services or aspects of their provision, financing and regulation from all or some disciplines of those agreements.[4] Against this background, this chapter analyses the various approaches used in free trade agreements to safeguard regulatory space for the provision, financing and organisation of public services. The chapter focuses on agreements signed by the EU including texts of recently negotiated agreements and drafts of agreements under negotiation. As a comparison, the chapter also takes other free trade agreements into account where they use interesting other models of managing the interplay between trade liberalisation and public services.

The chapter is structured as follows: Sect. 10.2 contains a brief overview of the current state-of-affairs of existing free trade agreements of the EU and of current negotiations. Section 10.3 explains why the obligations of free trade agreements may potentially conflict with the special function of the provision and organisation of public services. The main part of the chapter, Sect. 10.4, is then devoted to the development and explanation of an analytical framework concerning the various exemptions and clauses which allows an assessment of the impact of a particular free trade agreement independently of a specific existing model. Based on this analytical framework, Sect. 10.5 assesses the current approach of the EU regarding public service exemptions in free trade agreements. The paper concludes with some reform proposals (Sect. 10.6) and a summary of its main findings (Sect. 10.7).

## 10.2 Overview of Agreements and Negotiations

The European Union is party to a number of bilateral free trade agreements and in the process of negotiating further agreements with various partners. The existing bilateral free trade agreements consist of two groups. Traditional free trade agreements are based on the WTO-model. Examples are the EU-Mexico and the EU-Chile agreement. A "new" or "second generation" of free trade agreements was signed after and based on the "Global Europe" trade strategy of the EU in

[4]For a similar definition see Arena 2011, p. 495. This chapter uses the term "public services" as a general proxy for different types of definitions including services supplied in the exercise of governmental authority, public utilities, services of general interest, etc.

2007.[5] The free trade agreements of the second generation contain comprehensive services and investment chapters, but only with regards to investment liberalisation, but not concerning investment protection. The "second generation" agreements often also include sector-specific regulatory frameworks and sometimes also provisions on competition law. The first and archetypical agreement of the second generation is the EU-Korea FTA, which is in force since 2011. Other agreements of the new generation are the EU-Colombia and Peru FTA, signed in 2012 and provisionally applicable since 2013 and the EU-Central America (Honduras, Nicaragua and Panama) FTA, signed in 2012 and provisionally applicable since 2013.

The conclusion of the negotiations with Canada in September 2014[6] and with Singapore in October 2014[7] could mark the rise of a third group of agreements. These agreements do not only address matters of trade law, but also contain chapters on investment protection based on the new EU competence in the field of the common commercial policy for foreign direct investment. In addition they also contain enhanced forms of regulatory cooperation. The ongoing negotiations with the United States on a Transatlantic Trade and Investment Partnership Agreement (TTIP) which commenced in July 2013 have a similar objective. In addition, the EU is currently negotiating FTAs with India (since 2007), Malaysia (since 2010), Mercosur (resumed in 2010), Vietnam (since 2012), Thailand (since 2013) Japan (since 2013) and Morocco (since 2013).[8]

Other relevant agreements in the present context are the Economic Partnership Agreements (EPAs) with African, Caribbean and Pacific Countries (ACP) based on the Cotonou Agreement of 2000. Of these only the EU-CARIFORUM EPA contains a full chapter on services which is comparable to the new generation FTAs. Interim EPAs with some African and Pacific States exclude services, but contain so-called "rendezvous" clauses which mandate negotiations on services in the future. The EU is currently also negotiating further EPAs with some ACP countries and regions. These negotiations also cover trade in services.

Two further negotiations deserve to be mentioned in the present context. The EU is engaged in plurilateral negotiations of some 22 countries on a Trade in Services Agreement (TiSA) since 2012.[9] This agreement is built on the GATS and aims at further liberalisation commitments of the participating WTO Members.

---

[5]European Commission, Global Europe—A stronger Partnership to Deliver Market Access for European Exporters, COM(2007) 183 final, 18 April 2007.

[6]The text of CETA is available at http://trade.ec.europa.eu/doclib/docs/2014/september/tradoc_152806.pdf. Accessed 30 January 2015.

[7]The text of the EU-Singapore FTA is available at http://trade.ec.europa.eu/doclib/press/index.cfm?id=961. Accessed 30 January 2015.

[8]See European Commission, Overview of FTA and other trade negotiations, 27 January 2015, available at http://trade.ec.europa.eu/doclib/docs/2006/december/tradoc_118238.pdf. Accessed 29 January 2015.

[9]On TiSA see Marchetti and Roy 2014.

The agreement is controversial as it is not clear if and how the agreement can be integrated into the WTO framework. In addition, the EU is also engaged in negotiating bilateral agreements covering investment protection only. Since November 2013, the EU is negotiating a comprehensive investment protection agreement with China while trade negotiations remain stalled.[10]

## 10.3 Areas of Potential Conflict Between Trade Agreements and Public Services

The potential conflict between international trade agreements and the provision, financing and organization of public services depends on the specific obligations of a trade agreement. The most important of these are market access, national treatment and potential disciplines for domestic regulation. In addition, provisions on monopolies, subsidies and government procurement are of relevance if they contain binding obligations for the provision and organisation of public services.

### *10.3.1 Market Access*

The market access obligations of GATS and bilateral trade agreements prohibit maintaining of adopting specified quantitative and qualitative restrictions on market access. For example, market access requires the abolition and precludes the establishment of public monopolies or exclusive service suppliers unless specific limitations to the commitment have been scheduled.[11] Monopolies and exclusive service suppliers are, however, regulatory instruments which are often used in the context of public services. Since the GATS and most trade agreements do not contain justification clauses such as Article 106(2) TFEU,[12] any monopoly or exclusive service supply arrangement is a violation of the market access principle unless the schedules contain a limitation or a restriction covering that arrangement. Furthermore, market access requires that the number of services suppliers is not limited unless specifically stated in its schedule.

Another element of the market access obligation is the prohibition of so-called economic needs tests. Economic needs tests are regulatory measures which restrict the number of service suppliers on the basis of economic needs in order to manage

---

[10]See above note 7.

[11]Delimatsis and Molinuevo 2008, pp. 382–384.

[12]But see Article 129(2) of the EU-CARIFORUM EPA or Article 11:4(1) of the EU-Korea Agreement, which however only apply to the competition law chapter of that agreement. See Sect. 10.3.4.

competition.[13] The aim of such measures is to avoid ruinous competition which would affect the quality and security of services. Economic needs tests can be used in the context of regulating the number of taxi service providers or of emergency ambulance services. While the GATS and older trade agreements treat economic needs tests like other market access restrictions, some of the more recent negotiation proposals adopt a general prohibition of them. Typically, restrictions or requirements of specific types of legal entities are also considered to be market access restrictions. With regards to public services this may be relevant if certain activities are restricted to special forms of public law such as the French *établissement public* or *groupement d'intérêt public* or the German *Anstalt des Öffentlichen Rechts*.

By generally prohibiting monopolies, exclusive service supplier arrangements, economic needs tests and restrictions with regards to legal forms, market access obligations target traditional instruments of providing and regulating public services and put pressure on governments which want to maintain or reintroduce such measures.

Recent practice of trade agreements suggests that countries become more aware of the potential risks market access obligations pose on regulatory matters. In this context, it is noteworthy that the draft CETA text on market access contains a number of useful clarifications. In particular the respective provision states that certain measures are not considered to be a market access restriction. These include measures concerning zoning and planning regulations affecting the development or use of land, measures requiring the separation of the ownership of infrastructure from the ownership of the goods or services provided through that infrastructure to ensure fair competition as well as measures restricting the concentration of ownership ("unbundling") and measures seeking to ensure the conservation and protection of natural resources and the environment, including limitations on the availability, number and scope of concessions granted, and the imposition of moratoria or bans. The last clarification seems to be addressed at the concerns that the prohibition of certain environmentally dangerous or controversial activities could be seen as a market access violation. These clarifications are therefore useful instruments to ensure that domestic regulatory space is not limited unduly. However, it should be noted that the clarifications do not apply to public services in general.

### 10.3.2 National Treatment

National treatment requires that foreign services and service suppliers are treated no less favourable than domestic services and service suppliers, if foreign and domestic services or service suppliers are "like". This obligation is therefore generally at odds with any formal discrimination between foreign and domestic services

[13]Delimatsis and Molinuevo 2008, p. 384.

and suppliers. Consequently, subsidies which are only given to domestic service suppliers violate the national treatment obligation unless the subsidies are exempted from this obligation on the basis of the specific commitments and reservations.[14] National treatment obligations could therefore interfere with the provision and regulation of services if the competent authority favours local or regional service suppliers in order to assure that the services are supplied "as closely as possible to the needs of the users" (Article 1 Protocol No. 26 on Services of General Interest).

In addition, the principle of national treatment also covers indirect or disguised discrimination. This exists in cases where a formally neutral measure places a heavier burden on foreign services and service suppliers than on like domestic ones.[15] The determination of the notion of "likeness" is of special importance in the context of public services if public domestic service suppliers (e.g. a municipal hospital or a communal sewage operator) are faced with competition from private (foreign or domestic) service suppliers.[16] While it seems likely that a public entity run by a local government would not be considered "like" a multinational company,[17] it may be argued that the services they provide are "like". This raises the difficult question whether entities providing "like" services are also "like" service suppliers as suggested by the WTO's panel in the *EC—Bananas* case.[18]

These considerations show that while market access and national treatment obligations usually do not prevent the establishment and maintenance of special regimes for the provision of public services as such they influence the adoption and implementation of specific regulatory instruments. Certain forms of supplying and organising these services may be prohibited by the market access and national treatment obligations.

### *10.3.3 Positive and Negative List Approaches*

In most trade agreements market access and national treatment apply subject to specific commitments or reservations laid down in the respective country's schedules of commitments or reservation annexes. Countries can therefore determine whether and to which extend market access and national treatment obligations apply to specific sectors. In order to assess the impact of a trade agreement on public services the approach of the agreement towards scheduling is of significant importance.

---

[14]See Sect. 10.3.3.

[15]Diebold 2010, p. 38.

[16]Lang 2004, pp. 823–826; Connolly 2015.

[17]Lang 2004, p. 824.

[18]*European Communities—Regime for the Importation, Sale and Distribution of Bananas*, Report of the Panel, 22 May 1997, WT/DS/27/R, para 7.311. For a critical assessment of this view see Zdouc 1999, p. 333.

If the agreement adopts a "positive list"-approach (or bottom-up approach[19]), market access and national treatment only apply in sectors with specific commitments and only subject to any limitations and conditions laid down in schedules of specific commitments. If the agreement adopts a "negative list"-approach (or top-down), market access and national treatment apply unless the respective country specifically listed measures it wants to exclude from these obligations in annexes to that agreement. In both cases, the actual scope of these disciplines depends on the level of the commitments.

The differences between the two approaches are significant[20]: A negative list approach means that the core obligations of market access and national treatment apply generally, unless the parties of the agreement explicitly include existing or potential measures which would violate these obligations in the relevant annexes. Under a positive list approach these core obligations only apply to sectors, which are positively included in a list, and only subject to the conditions contained in such a list. NAFTA and other free trade agreements signed by the United States follow a negative list approach, while GATS follows a positive list approach.

Most EU agreements so far also followed a positive list approach, but recent negotiations suggest a shift: The CETA agreed between Canada and the EU adopts a negative list approach. The negotiations of the Trade in Service Agreement seem to be based on a hybrid approach which uses a negative list in the context of national treatment and a positive list for market access.[21] A similar approach seems to be favoured for the Transatlantic Trade and Investment Partnership (TTIP). In this context, it is important to recall that the European Parliament in its Resolution on EU-Canada trade relations of 8 June 2011 considered that the negative list approach in the CETA "should be seen as a mere exception and not serve as a precedent for future negotiations".[22]

A negative list approach usually distinguishes two types of reservations which are often associated with an Annex I and an Annex II to the agreement.[23] Measures listed in Annex I are existing measures which do not conform to the core obligations. Countries can maintain and renew these measures. They may also revise them, but have to ensure that the revision does not decrease the conformity of the measure with the respective obligations of the agreement compared to the level of conformity which existed immediately before the amendment. This requirement leads to a so-called "ratchet effect" which locks-in future liberalisation measures and therefore contains an "autonomous built-in dynamic" towards liberalisation.[24]

---

[19]Adlung and Mamdouh 2014.

[20]Stephenson 2002, p. 193.

[21]See TiSA EU proposal for a core text and scheduling provisions, March 2013, available at http://trade.ec.europa.eu/doclib/html/152687.htm. Accessed 30 January 2015.

[22]European Parliament resolution of 8 June 2011 on EU-Canada trade relations, P7_TA-PROV(2011)0257, 8 June 2011, para 5.

[23]See Chap. 5 in this volume, by VanDuzer.

[24]Stephenson 2002, p. 198.

A country which listed a specific measure in its Annex I reservations and revises this measure in a more liberalising manner cannot re-introduce the original measure because that would be an amendment of the measure which decreases the conformity of the (revised) measure with the agreement.[25] Measures listed in Annex I can therefore only be amended to make them more consistent with the trade agreement. If an exempted measure is amended to be more liberal or eliminated altogether it cannot be restored at its previous level later.

The "ratchet"-mechanism is of specific importance for public services which have been subject to various policy reforms in many EU Member States in the past. While regulatory reform in the 1980s and 1990s referred to liberalisation and abolishing public monopolies, in recent years some countries have opted for re-nationalisation or re-municipalisation: If a country listed a monopoly for a specific service in its Annex I and subsequently abolishes the monopoly autonomously in the context of a general privatisation and liberalisation policy, it may not reintroduce the monopoly at a later stage if liberalisation and privatisation failed.

Annex II enables countries to adopt and maintain measures inconsistent with the core obligations and therefore covers existing and future measures. As a consequence, policy space for future regulations and deviations from the status quo will only be possible if there are appropriate reservations in Annex II. If a country only lists measures in Annex I it is essentially bound to maintain the status quo. According to this mechanism liberalization measures adopted by a country cannot be replaced by new measures which are more restrictive unless there are relevant reservations in Annex II.

While it is possible to maintain certain measures and exclude liberalisation obligations under a "negative list"- and a "positive list"-approach, the negative list approach tends to have a more liberalising effect,[26] because all sectors and measures are subject to the core obligations while a positive list approach requires specific liberalisation commitments. The shift from a positive to a negative list approach requires detailed and careful scheduling disciplines as any "omission" of a measure results in a liberalisation commitment ("list it or lose it"). Furthermore, such a shift complicates the comparison between the different levels of liberalisation commitments.

In conclusion, the distinction between positive and negative list approaches is crucial for the determination of the impact of trade agreements on public services. In particular, while a positive list approach allows countries wishing to maintain a maximum level of regulatory flexibility in a certain sector to refrain from making any commitments in that sector by simply not including it in their schedules, a

[25]See also M. Houde et al. The interaction between investment and services chapters in selected Regional Trade Agreements: Key findings, OECD Trade Policy Working Paper No. 55, 2007, p. 35. OECD Publishing.

[26]For a similar assessment see M. Houde et al. The interaction between investment and services chapters in selected Regional Trade Agreements: Key findings, OECD Trade Policy Working Paper No. 55, 2007, p. 9. OECD Publishing.

negative list approach precludes this technique. Instead, countries must list those sectors specifically in their Annexes and also positively mention those measures they wish to maintain or carefully design a regulatory carve-out for future measures.

### *10.3.4 Disciplines on Domestic Regulation, Procurement, Subsidies and Competition*

Most agreements on trade in services contain rules on disciplines for domestic regulations with a view that such regulations do not provide unnecessary barriers to trade and are no more burdensome than necessary to ensure the quality of the service. GATS and a number of other trade agreements mandate multilateral negotiations on the development of such disciplines while other agreements contain a basic rule which states that domestic regulations may not be more burdensome than necessary. Disciplines on domestic regulation should ensure that domestic regulations including licensing rules, technical standards, and planning restrictions are no more burdensome (no more trade restrictive) than necessary.[27] These disciplines have the potential of greatly reducing governments' regulatory autonomy.[28] Depending on the scope of them and the specific design of a necessity test in such disciplines,[29] domestic regulations such a universal service obligations could be seen as more burdensome than necessary to ensure the quality of the service.[30] As a consequence, governments could find it more difficult to impose such obligations on public service providers.

Unlike in trade in goods there is no specific regime for subsidies in the GATS. In particular, there are no rules on the permissibility of subsidies in services sectors and on possible countervailing measures in the GATS. Some free trade agreements, including most EU agreements, contain provisions on subsidies in the goods context. However, these trade agreements generally contain exemption clauses for subsidies in their chapters on services and establishment. Therefore these chapters do not apply to subsidies relating to services.

However, subsidies are not exempt from the other disciplines of the GATS. Members may therefore not use subsidies in a manner which would be inconsistent with the most-favoured-nation treatment, i.e. a Member may not discriminate between two foreign service suppliers from different countries. In addition, the provision of subsidies must not violate the specific commitments. In particular, if a Member made a full national treatment commitment, it may not discriminate

[27]For a comprehensive discussion see Delimatsis 2008.

[28]Djordjevic 2002, pp. 305–322.

[29]On the problems associated with a necessity test in this context see Neumann and Türk 2003, pp. 223–225.

[30]Arena 2011, p. 511; Adlung 2006, p. 455; Trachtman 2003, p. 68.

between foreign and domestic service supplier regarding subsidisation.[31] Many Members have therefore listed general exemptions for subsidies as limitations in their schedules or have excluded subsidies to public entities from their commitments. For example, the EU stated in its schedule that the subsidisation of a service within the public sector is not in breach of its commitment.[32]

The WTO's regime regarding disciplines for public procurement is split into two regimes.[33] First, a procurement measure affecting trade in services would generally fall within the scope of the GATS. However, Article XIII:1 GATS holds that the obligations of most-favoured-nation treatment, market access and national treatment shall not apply to government procurement. For the time being, government procurement is hence excluded from some of the most important GATS disciplines. Second, government procurement is covered by the plurilateral Agreement on Government Procurement (GPA) revised in 2012. The GPA applies to governmental agencies, public authorities and public undertakings as specified in the Annexes of each party to the GPA. The disciplines of that agreement include general principles such as transparency and non-discrimination as well as detailed tendering requirements for procurement activities which are covered by the agreement. The scope of the GPA as regards to services depends on the services sectors each party to the GPA listed in its Annexes. The EU has submitted transportation services, a number of professional services, some financial and telecommunication services as well as sewage and refuse disposal and sanitation services to the disciplines of the GPA. EU free trade agreements tend to follow the WTO model: They exclude government procurement from the disciplines of the chapter on services and establishment, but contain separate chapters on government procurement which incorporate and amend the principles of the WTO GPA.

The more recent bilateral and regional trade agreements to which the EU is a party include increasingly sector-specific regulatory obligations and elements of competition law. The agreements tend to incorporate the sector-specific regimes on telecommunications[34] and financial services of the GATS, but also contain rules on computer services, postal and courier services, maritime transportation services and sometimes even tourism services. Trade agreements with sector-specific rules on certain services which could be considered as public services such as telecommunications or postal services may have a significant impact of the regulation of these services on the domestic level.

[31]WTO, Guidelines for the Scheduling of Specific Commitments under the General Agreement on Trade in Services (GATS), Adopted by the Council for Trade in Services on 23 March 2001, S/L/92, 28 March 2001, p. 6.

[32]European Communities and their Member States, Schedule of Specific Commitments, GATS/SC/31, 15 April 1994.

[33]See Chap. 3 by Weiß in this volume.

[34]See Chap. 12 by Batura in this volume.

In addition, some free trade agreements also include chapters on basic competition law principles.[35] These provisions may also apply to public services. In this context, it is significant that the agreements contain provisions which are based on Article 106(2) TFEU and excludes the application of the rules on competition for public enterprises and enterprises entrusted with special rights or exclusive rights if the application of the competition law principles obstructs the performance of the particular tasks assigned to them.

## 10.4 Analytical Framework for the Assessment of Public Service Exemptions

The previous brief overview of the potential impact of various obligations of free trade agreements on public services indicates why countries are trying to limit this impact through public service exemption clauses. In order to assess the potential of public service exemption clauses to protect public services, a framework based on two determining factors can be developed. The first determining factor concerns the substantive scope of the respective public services exemption clause[36] and the second factor is the level of protection of the clause.[37] The substantive scope relates to the services covered by the exemption clause. The level or protection concerns the application of the clause to obligations of the trade agreement and whether the clause excludes all obligations or only certain parts and elements of the agreement.

### *10.4.1 Substantive Scope*

The substantive scope of public services exemption clauses can either be determined by functional definitions or by sector-based categorisations. The former rely on an abstract definition of specific activities or functions while the latter list those sectors which are covered by the exemption clause. In recent trade agreement practice, the two approaches have also been combined.

[35] On this see P. Sauvé and N. Ward, The EC-Cariforum Economic Partnership Agreement: Assessing the Outcome on Services and Investment, ECIPE Paper, January 2009.

[36] See also Arena 2011, p. 495, who calls this the "objective scope".

[37] In Arena's terminology, this concerns the "effects" of the exemption clause, Arena 2011, p. 495.

#### 10.4.1.1 Functional Definitions

Traditionally, trade agreements exclude activities which are associated with the exercise of governmental or official authority. The best-known example of such a clause is Article I:3(b) and (c) GATS. It states that the agreement does not apply to "services supplied in the exercise of governmental authority" which are defined as services "supplied neither on a commercial basis, nor in competition with one or more service suppliers." Similar provisions can be found in many free trade agreements concluded by the EU, such as the EU-CARIFORUM Economic Partnership Agreement,[38] the EU-Korea Free Trade Agreement,[39] the EU-Peru/Colombia FTA[40] and the EU-Central America Free Trade Agreement.[41] The CETA and the EU-Singapore Free Trade Agreement also contain GATS-type exception clauses as does the EU proposal for the TiSA core text.

The clauses built on the GATS adopt a functional model of the description of public services. They refer to a specific governmental function (exercising public authority) and do not specify to which sector the exemption clause applies. While it is normally assumed that activities such as public administration, the administration of justice, correctional services, police and military activities are covered by the notion of "exercising governmental authority" it is not clear whether this could also apply to other activities in particular if only the government engages in them by maintaining a public monopoly. For example, until the liberalisation in the late 1990s, postal services were considered part of governmental functions in many EU countries, but this perception changed through the liberalisation of the sector.

The ambiguous concept of "governmental authority" may have been the reason why the GATS negotiators chose to further define the notion of governmental authority with references to "commercial basis" or "in competition". According to Article I:3(c) GATS a service supplied in the exercise of governmental authority "means any service which is supplied neither on a commercial basis, nor in competition with one or more service suppliers", a definition which has also been used

[38]Economic Partnership Agreement between the CARIFORUM States, of the one part, and the European Community and its Member States, of the other part, *OJ* 2008 L 289/3.

[39]Free trade Agreement between the European Union and its Member States, of the one part, and the Republic of Korea, of the other part, *OJ* 2011 L 127/6.

[40]Trade Agreement between the European Union and its Member States, of the one part, and Colombia and Peru, of the other part, *OJ* 2012, L 354/3.

[41]Agreement establishing an Association between the European Union and its Member States, on the one hand, and Central America on the other, *OJ* 2012, L 346/3. However, it should be noted that Article 162 of that agreement which addresses the scope of the chapter on establishment (Mode 3 under the GATS) defines "economic activity" as not to include "activities carried out in the exercise of governmental authority, for example, activities carried out neither on a commercial basis nor in competition with one or more economic operators" (emphasis added). Contrary—and contradictory—the chapter on cross border supply of services (Modes 1 and 2 under the GATS) contains the traditional GATS-type clause without the qualification "for example" in Article 169(2)(b).

in other agreements. Much has been said and written about the scope and value of such an additional definition which does not need to be repeated here.[42] It seems sufficient to recall that the notions "on a commercial basis" or "in competition" mean that even services which are provided in a semi-market environment or on heavily regulated market would not fall under that exception clause.

There seems to be a growing consensus in academic literature and trade practice that the functional approach referring to governmental or public authority—with or without additional definition—only covers those governmental activities which are considered as core sovereign functions (*acta iure imperii, foctions régaliennes*).[43] This means that most public services, including social, health, educational services as well as network-based and universal services are not covered by this exemption clause.[44] In fact, it may very well be argued that the additional definition is probably circular, because activities considered as "governmental authority" are by definition inconsistent with ideas of commerce and competition.[45]

In this context, the deviation from the standard model in the EU-Central America Free Trade Agreement is noteworthy.[46] By adding the words "for example" between the term and the definition, the drafters turned the narrow definition into a broader concept which might include approaches other than the functional definition.

A second—not so common—exemption clause is similar, but does not contain an additional definition. An example can be found in Article 135(2) of the EU–Chile Agreement Association Agreement of 2002[47] which holds that the "provisions of this Title shall not apply to the Parties' respective social security systems or to activities in the territory of each Party which are connected, even occasionally, with the exercise of official authority." The same provision is contained in Article 29(2) of Decision 2/2001 of the EU-Mexico Joint Council on trade in services implementing Article 6 of the 1997 EC-Mexico Partnership and Cooperation

[42]See Chap. 2 in this volume by Arena. See also Leroux 2006; Krajewski 2003.

[43]Arena 2011, p. 505.

[44]This understanding seems to be shared by the European Commission, Reflections Paper on Services of General Interest in Bilateral FTAs (Applicable to both Positive and Negative Lists), TRADE.B.1/SJ D(2011), 28 February 2011, available at http://www.epsu.org/IMG/pdf/Reflections_Paper_on_SGIs_in_Bilateral_FTAs.pdf. Accessed 30 January 2015, pp. 2–3. See also European Commission, Commission Proposal for the Modernization of the Treatment of Public Services in EU Trade Agreements, TRADE.B.1/SC/am D(2011) 1146318, 26 October 2011, available at http://www.epsu.org/IMG/pdf/154b-11_EC_paper_on_public_services_.pdf. Accessed 30 January 2015, p. 2.

[45]Leroux 2006, p. 352.

[46]See note 4.1.

[47]Agreement Establishing an Association between the European Community and its Member States, of the one part, and the Republic of Chile, of the other part of 18 November 2002, *OJ* 2002 L 352/3.

Agreement.[48] Both provisions seem to be built on Article 51 TFEU. The main difference between these provisions and the GATS-type exemption clause is that the former do not have a definition as to what amounts to services supplied in the exercise of governmental authority. It seems that the EU has been using the unqualified clause in the first phase of its bilateral trade agreements while the GATS-type exemption clause has been applied in the FTAs of the "second generation".[49]

#### 10.4.1.2 Sector-Based Categorisations

A second approach for public service exemptions is based on sectoral categorisations. This approach has not yet been used by the EU, but by the Members of NAFTA and Latin American countries. Historically the oldest type of a sectoral public services exemption clause can be found in Article 1201.3 NAFTA[50] which holds: "Nothing in this Chapter shall be construed to: (…) (b) prevent a Party from providing a service or performing a function such as law enforcement, correctional services, income security or insurance, social security or insurance, social welfare, public education, public training, health, and child care, in a manner that is not inconsistent with this Chapter." The Canada-Chile Free Trade Agreement of 1996 contains an identical provision. Similar provisions can be found in the investment chapters of these agreements (e.g. Article 1101:4 NAFTA). A number of Mexican free trade agreements with Central American countries contain similar clauses.

It should be noted, however, that this provision is not an exemption clause in the formal sense, because the services mentioned are still covered by the agreement. In particular, the last part of the provision "in a manner that is not inconsistent with this Chapter" could be interpreted in such a way that the provision of these services on a discriminatory basis or in fragrant violations of the agreement would not be justified. It might even be questioned whether such a provision would be able to justify a deviation from the disciplines of the agreement at all or whether it only contains a symbolic statement.[51]

Unlike the functional approach of Article I:3(b) and (c) GATS and similar agreements, a sector-based public service exemption clause implies greater clarity which activities are covered by the prospective clause. In particular, it is clear that the NAFTA-type exemption clause covers in any case social and welfare services, as well as public education and health services. Hence, it is possible that the NAFTA-clause has a wider scope of application than functional approaches

[48]Decision 2/2001 of the EU-Mexico Joint Council of 27 February 2001, *OJ* 2001 L 70/7.

[49]See Sect. 10.2.

[50]It should be noted that pre-NAFTA agreements on trade in services such as the Protocol on Trade in Services to the Australia New Zealand Closer Economic Relations Trade Agreement and Canadian-United States Free Trade Agreement, which entered into force in 1989, do not contain an exception clause for governmental services.

[51]See Chap. 5 by VanDuzer in this volume.

based on governmental authority. However, the exact contours of these sectors may also be open to debate and discussion. It is therefore not clear whether the scope of a sector-based exemption clause is in fact more precise than the functional approaches mentioned above. Furthermore, sector-based exemption clauses could be static if they are based on an exhaustive list of sectors. In this case, these clauses cannot accommodate changes in the way certain services are provided and do not take into account that the conception and understanding of "public services" varies over time. Sector-specific approaches which are based on non-exhaustive lists provide for greater flexibility and allow for a dynamic understanding of the respective scope.

#### 10.4.1.3 Hybrid Approaches

Functional and sectoral definitions of public services can also be combined. The "public utilities"-clause used by the EU in its free trade agreements and concepts built on EU law terminology such as services of general interest are examples of hybrid approaches.

*The public utilities-clause*

The so-called "public utilities"-clause is one of the most important instruments of the EU in the context of trade agreements and trade negotiations.[52] It reads as follows: "In all EC (or EU) Member States services considered as public utilities at a national or local level may be subject to public monopolies or to exclusive rights granted to private operators." Accordingly, the EU and its Member States maintain the right to establish or maintain monopolies or to grant exclusive rights to service providers in public utilities. The "public utilities"-clause therefore only covers these types of market access restrictions.[53]

The "public utilities"-clause is usually supplemented by an following explanatory footnote stating that

> [p]ublic utilities exist in sectors such as related scientific and technical consulting services, R&D services on social sciences and humanities, technical testing and analysis services, environmental services, health services, transport services and services auxiliary to all modes of transport. Exclusive rights on such services are often granted to private operators, for instance operators with concessions from public authorities, subject to specific service obligations. Given that public utilities often also exist at the sub-central level, detailed and exhaustive sector-specific scheduling is not practical.

This clause was first used in the EC's GATS schedule in 1994 and has also been used in the schedules of the EU-Chile, the EU-CARIFORUM, the EU-Korea and EU-Peru/Colombia agreements. The EU also used the "public utilities"-clause in

[52]See 'Protecting public services in TTIP and other EU trade agreements', available at http://trade.ec.europa.eu/doclib/press/index.cfm?id=1115&title=Protecting-public-services-in-TTIP-and-other-EU-trade-agreements. Accessed 30 January 2015.

[53]See Sect. 10.4.2 under 'Limitations or Reservations of Specific Commitments'.

its Annex II reservations in the CETA with Canada and in the schedules of the EU-Singapore FTA. While in most of these agreements the explanatory footnote is similar,[54] the EU-Singapore FTA follows a slightly different approach. Instead of referring to specific sectors in the explanatory footnote, the footnote states that since "public utilities often also exist at the sub-central level, detailed and exhaustive sector-specific listing is not practical. To facilitate comprehension, specific footnotes in this list of commitments will indicate in an illustrative and non-exhaustive way those sectors where public utilities play a major role." Following this approach, many sectors or subsectors listed in the schedules of specific commitments contain a footnote which states that the horizontal "public utilities"-clause applies. Mostly, the respective services fall into the categories of energy activities and services, transportation, social and health services and cultural services.[55] Interestingly, education services are not marked with a reference to the "public utilities"-clause.

The explanatory lists used in the "public utilities"-clauses are non-exhaustive. They are therefore not limited to the sectors specifically mentioned in that clause, but can apply to sectors with similar characteristics. This would also be the case with regards to the technique employed in the EU-Singapore FTA although it may be difficult to argue that a sector which is not specifically mentioned as one to which the "public utilities"-clause applies to, also contains public utilities.

The term "public utilities" has no specific meaning in international trade or EU law. The ordinary meaning of the term public utilities relates the concept to large network industries, in particular energy and water supply, and transportation.[56] This understanding seems narrower than the understanding of the term according to the footnote(s) in the EU schedules. However, the ordinary meaning of the term utilities emphasises the fact that a utility is needed by everyone or necessary to the community. In fact, the word utility includes a notion of necessity. This "public need" aspect of the term public utility can be used for the interpretation of the EU schedules. Public utilities would therefore be all services, which are considered

[54]In the EU-Korea agreement the footnote is supplemented by the following qualification: "This limitation does not apply to telecommunications services and to computer and related services."

[55]The sectors include mining and quarrying; manufacture of refined petroleum products; transmission and distribution on own account of electricity, gas, steam and hot water; research and development services; technical testing and analysis services, which are compulsory for the granting of marketing authorisations or for utilisation authorisations (e.g. car inspection, food inspection); distribution of chemical products, of pharmaceuticals, of products for medical use such as medical and surgical devices, medical substances and objects for medical use, of military equipment and precious metals (and stones) and, in some Member States of the European Union, also to the distribution of tobacco and tobacco products and of alcoholic beverages; environmental services; health services and social services; libraries, archives, museums and other cultural services; port services and other maritime transport services requiring the use of the public domain; rail transport services requiring the use of the public domain; road transportation; freight transportation; services auxiliary to transport; energy services; spa services and non-therapeutical massages provided in domains of public utility such as certain water sources.

[56]Geddes 2000, p. 1162; Graham 2000, p. 1.

necessary for a community.[57] This interpretation seems to coincide to a large extent with the various notions of public services in the EU Member States and the term 'services of general economic interest' in EU law. This interpretation is supported by the non-binding French and Spanish versions of the 1994 GATS schedule of the EC,[58] which refer to "services considérés comme services publics" and "servicios considerados servicios públicos" respectively. These translations of the term 'public utilities' point to the broad understanding of public services in the French and Spanish legal traditions.[59]

Nevertheless, it should be emphasised that the ordinary meaning of the term is not clear as the interpretation suggested above requires additional means of interpretation. It is therefore understandable that the Commission considered the term "public utilities" as ambiguous in its "Reflections Paper on Services of General Interest in Bilateral FTAs" published in February 2011.[60]

*Services of general (economic) interest*

Another approach which also follows a hybrid understanding is based on the EU law concept of services of general economic interest. In trade agreements clauses using this term have so far only been introduced in chapters relating to competition law. An example of such a clause can be found in Article 11:4 of the EU-Korea agreement. It states that regarding public enterprises and "enterprises entrusted with special rights or exclusive rights" the parties "shall ensure that such enterprises are subject to the competition laws set out in Article 11.2, in so far as the application of these principles and competition laws does not obstruct the performance, in law or in fact, of the particular tasks assigned to them". An explanatory footnote further defines the notion of enterprises entrusted with special rights: "Special rights are granted by a Party when it designates or limits to two or more the number of enterprises authorised to provide goods or services, other than according to objective, proportional and non-discriminatory criteria, or confers on enterprises legal or regulatory advantages which substantially affect the

[57]The Commission seems to have a broader understanding of the term "utilities", because it defines it as service which is "of utility the public" only to conclude that this applies to all services. See European Commission, Commission Proposal for the Modernization of the Treatment of Public Services in EU Trade Agreements, TRADE.B.1/SC/am D(2011) 1146318, 26 October 2011, available at http://www.epsu.org/IMG/pdf/154b-11_EC_paper_on_public_services_.pdf. Accessed 30 January 2015, p. 4.

[58]Only the English version of the EC's GATS Schedule of 1994 is binding.

[59]See also Krajewski 2009, pp. 208–210. This seems to be the perspective of the Commission as well, see European Commission, Commission Proposal for the Modernization of the Treatment of Public Services in EU Trade Agreements, TRADE.B.1/SC/am D(2011) 1146318, 26 October 2011, available at http://www.epsu.org/IMG/pdf/154b-11_EC_paper_on_public_services_.pdf. Accessed 30 January 2015, p. 4.

[60]European Commission, Commission Proposal for the Modernization of the Treatment of Public Services in EU Trade Agreements, TRADE.B.1/SC/am D(2011) 1146318, 26 October 2011, available at http://www.epsu.org/IMG/pdf/154b-11_EC_paper_on_public_services_.pdf. Accessed 30 January 2015, p. 4.

ability of any other enterprise to provide the same goods or services." Article 129 EU-CARIFORUM EPA and Article 280 of the EU-Central America FTA contain a similar clause as does CETA.

These provisions are based on the model of Article 106(2) TFEU which restricts the application of EU competition law to enterprises which have been entrusted with the task to provide service of general economic interests.[61] Based on this concept a distinction between services of general economic interest and non-economic services of general interest was suggested in two trade policy documents of the EU Commission in 2011, the "Reflections Paper on Services of General Interest in Bilateral FTAs" of February 2011[62] and a subsequent paper entitled "Commission Proposal for the Modernisation of the Treatment of Public Services in EU Trade Agreements" of October 2011.[63] In the Reflections Paper the Commission introduced three categories based on concepts which have already been used in the EU internal market[64]: Non-economic services of general interest; services of general economic interest considered to be network industries; and services of general interest other than network industries. While the definition of the term services of general economic interest in the EU context is a functional one, the proposal of the European Commission combined functional and sectoral aspects when defining and describing the different categories. According to the proposal, non-economic services of general interest include "police and judiciary, prisons, statutory social security schemes, border security, air traffic control, etc." This list is non-exhaustive. The proposal also stated that the notion of non-economic services of general interest is "essentially equivalent to the GATS definition of services carried out in the exercise of governmental authority".[65] According to the Commission's proposal network industries are "large network infrastructures—telecoms, energy, transport, postal, environmental". This list is considered to be exhaustive. Lastly, services of general interest other than network industries include "healthcare, social services, education, employment and training services,

[61]See Chap. 6 by Van de Gronden in this volume.

[62]European Commission, Reflections Paper on Services of General Interest in Bilateral FTAs (Applicable to both Positive and Negative Lists), TRADE.B.1/SJ D(2011), 28 February 2011, available at http://www.epsu.org/IMG/pdf/Reflections_Paper_on_SGIs_in_Bilateral_FTAs.pdf. Accessed 30 January 2015.

[63]European Commission, Commission Proposal for the Modernization of the Treatment of Public Services in EU Trade Agreements, TRADE.B.1/SC/am D(2011) 1146318, 26 October 2011, available at http://www.epsu.org/IMG/pdf/154b-11_EC_paper_on_public_services_.pdf. Accessed 30 January 2015.

[64]For an in-depth analysis of the Commission proposals see M. Krajewski, Public Services in Bilateral Free Trade Agreements of the EU, available at SSRN: http://ssrn.com/abstract=1964288. 1 November 2011. Accessed 30 January 2015.

[65]European Commission, Commission Proposal for the Modernization of the Treatment of Public Services in EU Trade Agreements, TRADE.B.1/SC/am D(2011) 1146318, 26 October 2011, available at http://www.epsu.org/IMG/pdf/154b-11_EC_paper_on_public_services_.pdf. Accessed 30 January 2015, p. 2.

certain cultural services, etc." The proposal stated that it may be possible to "narrow down the scope through a description of the characteristics (services of an economic nature subject to specific services obligations by virtue of a general interest criterion)." Apart from one offer in the negotiations with Canada, the approach of the Reflections Paper and the October Proposal have not been used in current negotiations of the EU.

#### 10.4.1.4 Assessment

The major challenge of all definitions of public services in trade agreements concerns the dynamic and flexible nature of the concept of public services. Public services are determined by a particular society in a distinct historical, social and economic context based on the values of that society. As pointed out above, this involves social and policy choices which may be different in different parts of the world and at different moments in time. The variety and flexibility is therefore a key element of the concept of public services.[66] In fact, many services which were traditionally considered public services have been subject to liberalization and privatization processes in recent years which lead to a limited scope of public services.[67] More recently, however, there are trends towards a re-municipalisation in some countries suggesting that the scope of public services may increase again in the near future. Public service exemption clauses in trade agreements therefore need to be sufficiently flexible and open to accommodate the dynamic notion of public services, but also need to be precise in order to ensure that they exclude those sectors and services which are considered as public services from the scope of trade agreements.

Public service exemption clauses which are based on exhaustive lists may be precise and transparent, but they may not provide sufficient flexibility. Functional approaches such as Article I:3(b) and (c) GATS may offer flexibility, but their scope varies depending on the organization of the supply of the service. Provisions in a trade agreement referring to legal concepts which can only be found in specific legal systems, such as the EU's notion of services of general interest may be interpreted and understood differently in an international context.

### *10.4.2 Level of Protection*

Apart from their substantive scope, public service exemption clauses can be distinguished on the basis of which provisions of a trade agreement they apply to.

[66]See also Article 1 Protocol No. 26 on Services of General Interest.

[67]Geddes 2000, pp. 1162–1163.

#### 10.4.2.1 Complete Carve-Out

Public service exemption clauses such as Article I:3(b) and (c) GATS apply to all provisions of an agreement and exclude the activities to which they apply completely from the respective trade agreement. These clauses are typically located in the framework agreement. They have the most far-reaching scope. Their scope is not limited to market access and national treatment, but applies to any other obligation (most favoured nation-treatment, transparency, disciplines on domestic regulation, etc.) as well. Exemption clauses of this type also apply to annexes or later revisions of the agreement. In short: Activities which are covered by these exemption clauses are not subject to the trade agreement at all. The rationale for such general exemptions in the framework agreement is that the activities covered by these clauses are typically not considered to be economic or commercial activities which can or should be subject to liberalisation. A public service exemption clause in the framework agreement also applies to all parties of the agreement in the same manner, because the framework agreement is binding on all Members unlike the specific schedules which only bind the respective Member.

It should be noted, however, that because of their general scope of application, these exception clauses tend to be construed narrowly. In a 1998 meeting of the WTO's Council for Trade in Services it was suggested that "the exceptions provided in Article I:3 of the Agreement needed to be interpreted narrowly."[68] In a similar way, the ECJ held the official authority exemption of Article 51 TFEU must be interpreted in a manner limiting its scope to what is strictly necessary to protect the interests of the Member States.[69] It must also be recalled that the substantive scope of these complete carve-out clauses tends to be limited as it is restricted to core governmental functions. It could be argued that the broad level of protection of these clauses corresponds with their narrow substantive scope.

#### 10.4.2.2 Limitations or Reservations of Specific Commitments

Apart from public services exemption clauses in the framework of trade agreements, exemption clauses can be found as limitations of specific commitments (positive list approach) or as reservations (negative list approach) in the schedule of commitments of each country. As such they only apply to the country which use them and only to those disciplines which are subject to the commitments or reservation. Under a traditional GATS-type positive list approach market access and national treatment are the only disciplines which are subject to specific

[68] WTO, Council for Trade in Services, Report of the Meeting Held on 14 October 1998, Note by the Secretariat, S/C/M/30, 12 November 1998, para 22(b).

[69] CJEU, Case C-147/86 *Commission of the European Communities v. Hellenic Republic* [1988] ECR 1637, para 7 and CJEU, Case C-114/97 *Commission of the European Communities v. Kingdom of Spain* [1998] ECR I–6717, para 34.

commitments. Two approaches of limitations or reservations concerning specific commitments can be distinguished: Horizontal limitations and sector-specific limitations.

*Horizontal limitations*
Public service exemption clauses can be part of the horizontal section of a schedule of specific commitments based on positive list. In this case, the exemption clause applies to all sectors in which commitments were made. Similarly, exemptions can apply to "All sectors" in a negative list-type schedule of reservations.

An example for a horizontal exemption clause is the traditional "public utilities" clause used by the EU in many trade agreements. This clause excludes public utilities from the application of the market access disciplines, but only regarding monopolies and exclusive service suppliers. Furthermore, it only applies to Mode 3 (commercial presence) in GATS and to the commercial presence or establishment sections of the EU's free trade agreements. Hence, the other modes of supply (cross-border supply, consumption abroad or movement of natural persons) are not covered. While the "public utilities"-clause was originally developed in the context of "positive list"-approaches the EU is also using it in "negative list"-agreements. For example, Annex II of the EU's commitments in CETA contains the usual reference to public utilities. However, even though it applies to all sectors it remains limited to monopolies and exclusive service suppliers.

The "public utilities"-clause therefore has a broader scope of application than Article I:3(b) and (c) of the GATS, because the notion of "public services" covers more activities than the concept of "services supplied in the exercise of governmental authority". However, the level of protection of the public utilities clause is lower than that of Article I:3(2) and (3) GATS as it only applies to parts of the market access obligation.

*Sector-specific limitations*
Public service exemptions can also be integrated into sector-specific commitments or limitations. Such an approach excludes or limits the application of the trade agreements and/or their core obligations in the context of sectoral commitments or limitations. Instead of regulating the scope of application at the horizontal level, countries exclude those elements of a service which they consider public services at the sectoral level.

Examples for this type of exemptions are the EU's GATS commitments in education services which are limited to "privately funded education services". A reference to the public or private nature of the funding of the services has also been used in recent trade negotiations including in the context of social and health services. This reference may seem attractive at first sight as it implies that only privately funded services are subject to liberalisation commitments. However, the devil is in the details: First, it needs to be determined whether "publicly-funded" covers only a complete (100 %) public funding or whether the dominant part needs to be publicly financed. Concerning health services it needs to be established if contributions by members of a public sickness fund constitute "public funding", because they are based on a law while insurance fees paid to private insurers constitute "private funding". Second, it is unclear whether the nature of the funding relates to the service or the service supplier. For example, in the case of a graduate programme of a public university which is funded by high student fees and corporate sponsors, would the privately-funded service or the publicly funded service supplier (i.e. the university) determine whether the commitments apply?

Some of these problems can be avoided if the exemption clause refers to services "which receive public funding or State support in any form", because this does would include fully and partially State-funded institutions. This term has been introduced in the CETA agreements. For example, in the EU's Annex II the reservation concerning education services refers to "educational services which receive public funding or State support in any form, and are therefore not considered to be privately funded." The same definition can be found with regards to health services. The broad term public funding or State support in "any form" suggests that even a small contribution to the service by the public purse excludes them from the application of the specific commitments.

Excluding publicly-funded services from specific commitments is hence a public service exception clause of an intermediate level of protection. It applies to national treatment and market access and offers hence a higher level of protection than the "public utilities"-clause which only applies to parts of the market access obligation but offers a lower level of protection than the exception for services in the exercise of governmental authority, because this clause applies to all provisions of an agreement.

#### 10.4.2.3 Exemptions Applicable to Other Obligations

In addition to public service exemptions in the relevant schedules which are only applicable to specific commitments, trade agreements may also include exemptions which apply to other obligations. For example, such clauses can reduce the application of certain general rules of a free trade agreement such as disciplines for subsidies or government procurement. These provisions would therefore not exempt from the entire agreement, but only from certain obligations or parts thereof.

The exemption clauses for public enterprises and enterprises entrusted with special rights applicable to competition law mentioned above[70] are also example of a clause which is only applicable to a specific set of rules of the trade agreement. These exemption clauses have a limited scope of application as they only apply to the respective obligation (or set of obligations). Their potential to reduce the impact of a trade agreement on public services may therefore be small. However, since public services exemptions at the level of specific commitments only apply to those obligations, public services would remain unprotected from the impact of the competition law principles in those agreements without such specific exemption clauses.

[70]See Sect. 10.4.1 under 'Services of General (Economic) Interest'.

#### 10.4.2.4 Assessment

The level at which countries choose to introduce public service exemptions is of particular importance regarding the breadth of application. Exemptions which are located in the core agreement apply to all parts of the agreement and therefore exclude public services to the extent they are covered by the respective provision from the agreement altogether. It follows that an exemption clause at that level offers by far the most comprehensive protection of public services from the impact of the disciplines of trade agreements. Contrary to this, exemptions located at the level of commitments or reservations only apply to specific disciplines, usually national treatment and market access. Other obligations of trade agreements such as disciplines on domestic regulation, subsidies and government procurement would apply nonetheless if they cover trade in services. Furthermore, sector-specific public services exemptions in the schedules of commitments or reservations only apply to the specific sector and have generally no impact on other public services in other sectors. The level of protection of public services exemptions therefore decreases in the following order: Framework agreement, sector-specific annex, horizontal section of the schedule, sectoral section of the schedule, exemption clause only applicable to a specific set of rules.

### *10.4.3 Summary*

The previous discussion reveals an inverse relationship between the substantive scope of public service exemption clauses and their level of protection. While general carve-outs like Article I:3(b) and (c) GATS provide the highest level of protection, they only have a very narrow substantive scope, which has only a very limited impact on public services. Sectoral carve-outs which limit commitments to "privately-financed" services have a larger scope as they aim to protect all activities of the respective sector which would be considered as "publicly financed". They have, however, a more limited level or protection as they only exclude the applicability of key disciplines such as market access and national treatment. Lastly, public service exemption clauses such as the "public utilities" clause or the public services clause have the largest substantive scope. However, so far they only apply to two types of market access limitations and have therefore the most limited scope of application.

## 10.5 The Multi-layer System of Public Services Exemption Clauses in EU Trade Agreements

Since the conclusion of the GATS in 1994 and in all subsequent trade agreements the EU has followed a specific model combining public services exemption clauses at different layers. The first layer is an exemption clause for services supplied in the exercise of governmental or official authority (e.g. Article I:3(b) and (c) GATS) which excludes these activities from the scope of the agreement. These activities are therefore neither subject to specific commitments nor to general obligations. All public services which are not covered by this exemption clause are subject to all obligations of the respective agreement.

The second layer of the traditional EU approach concerns sectoral definitions limiting the scope of the commitment. One possibility is to limit the commitments to privately funded activities. Prominently, the EU used this technique in education and health services.

The third layer is the "public utilities" clause in the horizontal section of the EU's GATS schedule. As mentioned above, this clause only applies to commercial presence and covers certain aspects of market access, in particular monopolies and exclusive service suppliers. However, the public utilities exemption is applicable to all sectors and therefore not limited regarding its sectoral scope. While the exact meaning of term "public utilities" remains unclear it seems safe to assume that it is not restricted to certain network services, but covers all services which are considered as "public services" by the competent national, regional or local authority.

The traditional approach is based on three principles: First, activities which are considered as exercise of governmental functions should not be subject to trade agreements. Second, certain sectors may include elements which are considered public services and elements which are of a commercial nature. One way of distinguishing the two sets of services is through the way they are financed. Third, there are certain aspects of public services which should be protected in all sectors such as the right to establish or maintain monopolies and exclusive service suppliers.

It should be noted that the elements of the traditional approach are not based on a coherent theoretical model. It combines functional, sectoral and hybrid definitions and uses terms which are not necessarily linked with each other. Nevertheless, the underlying concept of the three levels or layers of protection is a useful approach as it allows countries to distinguish between different activities and rationales for protecting them from parts or the whole of the GATS. However, the concrete application of the model and its terminology is problematic: It employs ambiguous concepts (definition of services supplied in the exercise of governmental authority, public utilities, private funding) and it only exempts public utilities from two elements of the market access obligation while all other obligations of the trade agreements apply to public services. This does not provide sufficient regulatory space and flexibility from the domestic regulation perspective.

The CETA agreement, the EU-Singapore Free Trade Agreement and the recent negotiations about the TTIP suggest a refinement of this approach. The EU-Singapore Agreement uses clearer indications concerning the sectors which are covered by the public utilities clause. CETA and possibly TTIP are agreements based on the negative list approach which means that the public utilities clause needs to be incorporated into the Annex II reservations. The CETA agreement also contained a precise definition of publicly funded services which allows for a clearer line between the commitments and the non-committed sectors.

However, the CETA agreement did not adopt an approach based on the notion of services of general interest as suggested in the 2011 Reflections Paper or the Proposal of the EU Commission.[71] While the EU's Draft offer of 29 July 2011 in the CETA negotiations contained an exemption of public services referring to "services of general economic interest which are subject to specific public service obligations imposed by public authorities on the provider of the service in order to meet certain public interest objectives" the final version of the EU's commitments have returned to the "public utilities". It is unclear whether the EU will revisit the idea to align the terminology of trade agreements and of Article 106 para 2 TFEU in future trade negotiations.

## 10.6 Proposals for Reform

The analysis of the existing public service exemptions, in particular their scope and level of protection have highlighted that they all have their limits: On the one hand, they lack legal and conceptual clarity and on the other hand they do not seem to be sufficiently flexible to accommodate changing political and social approaches towards public services. In general, the existing provisions do not offer public services a sufficient level of protection from the impact of the obligations of trade agreements. Any reform proposals will have to strike a balance between an sufficient degree of legal clarity and an appropriate amount of legal flexibility. What follows are two different reform proposals which strike the balance between these two aspects in different ways. The two proposals also differ regarding their compatibility with the current trade regime. While the first follows the dominant logic of trade liberalisation and attempts to create specific carve-outs, the second proposal challenges the locking-in function of trade agreements and is therefore at odds with orthodox trade agreement logic.

### *10.6.1 Increasing Legal Certainty and Providing for Specific Carve-Outs*

As shown above, the GATS-type exemption clause covering "services supplied in the exercise of governmental authority" has an ambiguous content due to its confusing definition of this term which does not increase the scope of the clause or

[71] European Commission, Reflections Paper on Services of General Interest in Bilateral FTAs (Applicable to both Positive and Negative Lists), TRADE.B.1/SJ D(2011), 28 February 2011, available at http://www.epsu.org/IMG/pdf/Reflections_Paper_on_SGIs_in_Bilateral_FTAs.pdf. Accessed 30 January 2015, and European Commission, Commission Proposal for the Modernization of the Treatment of Public Services in EU Trade Agreements, TRADE.B.1/SC/am D(2011) 1146318, 26 October 2011, available at http://www.epsu.org/IMG/pdf/154b-11_EC_paper_on_public_services_.pdf. Accessed 30 January 2015.

its level of protection. It is therefore proposed to abandon the additional definition and simply exclude the application of the trade agreement to "activities considered as exercise of governmental authority in the jurisdiction of the respective Party/ Member". Such a provision would make it clear that core governmental functions as defined by the legal system of each country would be excluded from the scope of the trade agreement.

For the remaining, large area of public services which fall under the scope of the agreement, Members should use the term "public services" and define it as "services which are subject to special regulatory regimes or special obligations imposed on services or service suppliers by the competent national, regional or local authority in the general interest". This definition would reflect a generally shared understanding of public services in most, if not all, countries of the world and would avoid the ambiguity of the term "public utilities".

Based on this definition, Members could then choose which provisions of the trade agreement should be applicable to public services and which should be excluded. This could be achieved either through specific public service clauses in the framework agreement. For example, a provision of subsidies could read: "The provisions of this agreement do not apply to the direct or indirect subsidisation of the provision of public services". In addition, Members could limit the impact of disciplines for domestic regulation on the provision of public services, by either excluding public services from the scope of future disciplines altogether or by specifying that certain public service regulations are not considered more burdensome than necessary. A possible provision could read: "The imposition of a public service obligation (or: universal service obligation) on a service supplier in a transparent and non-discriminatory manner is not considered as more burdensome than necessary".

Furthermore, Members could restrict the application of the specific market access and national treatment obligations and exclude public services from the scope of their commitments. In the context of a positive list approach, this could be achieved through a horizontal restriction. Compared with the current EU public utilities clause, such a broader public service limitation would provide more legal clarity as it would avoid the ambiguous term "public utilities". Furthermore, it should not be restricted to only two aspects of the market access obligation (monopolies and exclusive service suppliers). In the context of a negative-list approach, a public service exemption clause would need to apply to "all sectors" and to reservations for future measures (Annex II). Such a reservation could have the following wording: "With regards to public services, [Party to the agreement] reserves the right to limit the number of services and service suppliers, impose special obligations on service suppliers and regulate the provision of these services in the general interest."

It should be noted that the approach suggested in this section would not exclude public services from the application of general obligations. More importantly, the approach would not increase the flexibility of a country after it made its commitments. In fact, commitments would be binding and countries which adopted a liberal approach towards public services would be bound by their original commitments. Furthermore, the logic of progressive liberalisation which is inherent to all trade agreements would still apply. In sum, the proposal would provide for greater regulatory flexibility and policy space but not fundamentally alter the existing relationship of trade agreements and public services, which is characterised by carve-outs and exemptions. The underlying principle of this regime is that trade liberalisation and market-based operations are the rule whereas market intervention and the provision of public services remain exemptions.

### *10.6.2 Providing More Flexibility: The Case for a Simplified Procedure to Modify Commitments*

The last considerations lead to a more fundamental proposal for reform. A key problem of the impact of trade agreements on public services or domestic regulation in general is that the agreements are too restrictive. A substantial reform should therefore not be based on a refinement of exemption clauses. Instead, it would need to reduce the impact of binding commitments on domestic regulation. This could be done through a simplified mechanism for the modification of commitments. The possibility to modify commitments as contained in Article XXI GATS and similar provisions in free trade agreements is currently a very difficult and burdensome procedure[72] without a predictable outcome. It requires the notification of the intended modification to all WTO Members and negotiations about compensations in the form of additional commitments with all interested other members. Should these negotiations not result in a compensatory agreement an arbitrator will determine the level of compensations. The procedure to modify schedules has so far only been used by the EU in the context of the consolidations of its schedule after two rounds of enlargement,[73] by the United States as a reaction to the Appellate Body ruling in the Gambling case[74] and by Bolivia concerning its commitments in health services.[75]

In order to increase the flexibility of the GATS, a simplified modification procedure could be introduced in trade agreements. This procedure could include a

[72]See WTO, Council for Trade in Services, Procedures for the Certification of Rectifications or Improvements to Schedules of Specific Commitments, Adopted by the Council for Trade in Services on 14 April 2000, S/L/84, 18 April 2000.

[73]See WTO, Council for Trade in Services, Communication from the European Communities and its Member States, Certification, Draft Consolidated GATS Schedule, S/C/W/273, 9 October 2006.

[74]*United States—Measures Affecting the Cross-Border Supply of Gambling and Betting Services*, Report of the Appellate Body, WT/DS285/AB/R. See WTO, Council for Trade in Services, Notification from the United States Pursuant to Article XXI of the General Agreement on Trade in Services (GATS), Restricted Document, 8 May 2007.

[75]WTO, Council for Trade in Services, Notification from Bolivia Pursuant to Article XXI of the General Agreement on Trade in Services (GATS), Restricted Document, 11 November 2008.

requirement to announce the modification of a schedule, a period of comments by other parties of the agreement, a requirement to take those comments into consideration and the obligation to compensate any service supplier who lost significant values of his investment or commercial expectations on the basis of a case-by-case arbitration. In addition, one could impose a grace period of 1 or 2 years after the entry into force of the agreement in order to ensure a certain degree of legal stability.

A simplified modification procedure developed along those line could reduce the "regulatory chill" factor of trade agreements significantly because it would limit the impact of the claim that a particular regulatory measure violates the commitments. It would also provide countries with a real possibility to alter their international obligations in case of fundamental policy shifts regarding public services in that country. This would also create space for countries which review their current liberalisation policies and remove the restrictions created by the current "lock-in" rationale of trade agreements. A more limited version of such a simplified modification procedure could be restricted to public services only, but it might also be worth considering applying such a modification procedure to all sectors.

## 10.7 Conclusion

Trade agreements contain a number of different provisions, techniques and instruments aimed at limiting the impact of the obligations of these agreements on the provision of public services. This paper suggested an analytical framework which can be used to assess the effect of these clauses. Specifically, the paper showed that the ambit of public service exemption clauses depends on their sectoral scope, i.e. which activities and services they cover, and on the level of protection of these clauses, i.e. which provisions of the agreements they exclude or modify. The paper applied this analytical model to the most commonly used public service clauses, in particular the exclusion of services supplied in the exercise of governmental authority, the "public utilities"-clause of the EU and sector-specific restrictions such as those limited to privately-funded health and social services. The discussion of these clauses and provisions showed that they have some potential to protect public services from the application of disciplines of trade agreements which would be problematic for public services. However, it has also been shown that many provisions suffer from ambiguities and could therefore be improved. It has been suggested that such improvements should address two elements: They should increase legal certainty without restricting the policy space for public entities in charge of organising public services and they should provide more flexibility in particular for a modification of commitments.

# References


Adlung R (2006) Public services and the GATS. J Int Econ Law 9(2):455–485

Adlung R, Mamdouh H (2014) How to design trade agreements in services: top down or bottom-up? J World Trade 48(2):191–218

Arena A (2011) The GATS notion of public services as an instance of intergovernmental agnosticism: comparative insights from the EU supranational dialectic. J World Trade 45(3):489–528

Connolly K (2015) Finding space for regulatory autonomy in GATS Article XVII after EC—seals: public services and the 'Likeness' of public and private service providers. Leg Issues Econ Integr 42(1):57–83

Delimatsis P (2008) Determining the necessity of domestic regulations in services—the best is yet to come. Eur J Int Law 19(2):365–408

Delimatsis P, Molinuevo M (2008) Article XVI GATS market access. In: Wolfrum R, Stoll PT, Feinäugle C (eds) WTO—trade in services. Brill, Leiden, pp 367–395

Diebold N (2010) Non-discrimination in international trade in services. CUP, Cambridge

Djordjevic M (2002) Domestic regulation and free trade in services—a balancing act, legal issues of economic integration. Legal Issues Econ Integr 29(3):305–322

Geddes R (2000) Public utilities. In: Bouckaert B, De Geest G (eds) Encyclopedia of law and economics: the regulation of contracts, vol III. Edward Elgar, Cheltenham, pp 1162–1205

Graham C (2000) Regulating public utilities—a constitutional approach. Hart Publishing, Oxford

Krajewski M (2003) Public services and trade liberalization: mapping the legal framework. J Int Econ Law 6(2):341–367

Krajewski M (2009) Protecting a shared value of the union in a globalized world: services of general economic interest and external trade. In: van de Gronden JW (ed) EU and WTO Law on services: limits to the realisation of general interest policies within the services markets? Kluwer Law International, Alphen aan de Rijn, pp 187–213

Lang A (2004) The GATS and regulatory autonomy: a case study of social regulation of the water industry. J Int Econ Law 7(4):801–838

Leroux E (2006) What is a "service supplied in the exercise of governmental authority" under Article I:3(b) and (c) of the general agreement on trade in services? J World Trade 40(3):345–385

Marchetti JA, Roy M (2014) The TISA initiative: an overview of market access issues. J World Trade 48(4):683–728

Neumann J, Türk E (2003) Necessity revisited—proportionality in World Trade Organization Law after Korea—Beef, EC—Asbestos and EC—Sardines. J World Trade 37(1):199–233

Stephenson SM (2002) Regional versus multilateral liberalisation of services. World Trade Rev 1(2):187–209

Trachtman J (2003) Lessons for the GATS from existing WTO rules on domestic regulation. In: Mattoo A, Sauvé P (eds) Domestic regulation and service trade liberalization. World Bank Publications, Washington, pp 57–81

Zdouc W (1999) WTO dispute settlement practice relating to the GATS. J Int Econ Law 2(2):295–346

# Chapter 11
# Services of General Interest in the European Neighbourhood Policy

**Narine Ghazaryan**

**Abstract** The debate about services of general interest can be extended to the European Neighbourhood Policy (ENP), a policy embracing different types of legal or quasi-legal instruments. This chapter analyses the role of the services of general interest within the EU as a subject of normative export that can become part of the transposition of the EU's model of governance. Next, the ENP is discussed to establish the policy-specific avenues for normative export. The role of the SGI is then traced within the policy on the basis of the analysis of general policy documents and bilateral cooperation instruments between the EU and partner states of the Eastern Neighbourhood.

## Contents



N. Ghazaryan (✉)
Lecturer in Law, Brunel University London, Uxbridge, UK
e-mail: narine.ghazaryan@brunel.ac.uk



M. Krajewski (ed.), *Services of General Interest Beyond the Single Market*, Legal Issues of Services of General Interest,
DOI 10.1007/978-94-6265-063-3_11

## 11.1 Introduction

The services of general interest (SGI) within the foreign relations of the European Union (EU) have surfaced previously in debates on EU trade agreements.[1] This debate can be extended beyond one type of international legal instrument of the EU to an entire policy embracing different types of legal or quasi-legal instruments.

The European Neighbourhood Policy (ENP) is a cross-Treaty policy initiated in 2003 to offer certain level of integration to the European and non-European neighbours of the EU without an ultimate promise of membership.[2] Exporting the EU law and values is not a chief objective of the ENP. It is rather a means to an end, which is achieving wider policy objectives of securing a stable and a safe zone around the post-2004 and 2007 enlargement borders of the EU.[3] The presumption is that the more the neighbours replicate the EU values, the safer and secure the EU will be. The ENP applies to the Eastern and Southern neighbours with varying intensity as some countries have seemingly advanced in their cooperation with the EU, while others have not agreed on a basic framework of cooperation. Few years following its inception, the ENP has been divided into regional flanks with the Eastern Partnership (EaP) and the Union for the Mediterranean emerging respectively in the East and South through the course of 2008 and 2009.[4] The EaP promised a more enhanced cooperation with the neighbours in the East,[5] and it constitutes the subject of the discussion that follows for a number of reasons.[6] First, the countries concerned are comparable in terms of their legal background stemming from the common Soviet heritage and their participation in the Commonwealth of Independent States (CIS) which provided models for normative regulation in certain areas.[7] Although in recent years the organisation envisaged an action on consolidating the legal framework for the provision of healthcare

[1]See for instance Krajewski 2011a.

[2]The following countries are addressees of the policy (some do not have immediate borders with the EU at present): Ukraine, Moldova, Belarus, Georgia, Armenia, Azerbaijan, Egypt, Algeria, Tunisia, Morocco, Israel, Occupied Palestinian Territories, Syria, Jordan, Lebanon, Libya.
The 'cross-Treaty' nature of the ENP refers to the legal scope of the policy which includes EU competences provided both in the TEU and the TFEU, see Ghazaryan 2014, pp. 32, 62, 179.

[3]For the centrality of security considerations within the ENP see Smith and Webber 2008, p. 81; Wallace 2003 p. 27; Zaiotti 2007, p. 149; Cremona and Hillion 2006, p. 24.

[4]Council of the European Union, Brussels European Council Conclusions of 19–20 June 2008, p. 19; Council of the European Union, Brussels European Council Conclusions of 13–14 March 2008, p. 19.

[5]The EaP countries include Ukraine, Moldova, Belarus, Armenia, Georgia and Azerbaijan.

[6]Belarus is excluded from the analysis of bilateral relations below due to the absence of bilateral documents between the latter and the EU.

[7]With the exception of Georgia, the EaP states are part of the CIS. Georgia has withdrawn its membership in 2009.

services and social assistance,[8] it has not been translated into a comprehensive normative approach towards public services. Judging by the constitutions of the countries concerned certain regulation of services of public interest can be expected as they all highlight the social underpinnings of the new legal orders.[9] However, there is no uniform approach to the concept of 'public service' in the countries concerned. While in Armenia this term would be comparable to SGI,[10] in other countries it might be used to denote civil services,[11] or administrative services provided by the state. Other notions, such as 'services of vital importance' are also used.[12] On the other hand, social services are a more familiar category where specific legislation exists in some EaP countries.[13]

The presence of SGI related regulations in the legal orders of the countries concerned might question the issue of EU intervention in this area. However, despite the existing regulation there is no adequate standard of SGI provision in many vital areas as can be observed from the annual review by the Commission of the progress of the EaP countries. Besides, even though the countries concerned might have developed certain model of providing SGI, the issue of legal approximation is at the centre of the ENP and more so of the EaP, requiring transposition of the relevant *acquis*.

The export of EU values and *acquis* early on transpired as the means to the 'Europeanisation' of the neighbouring states through the ENP.[14] Ambitious in its scope, the policy aimed to integrate the neighbouring states to the EU in an extensive range of areas without a promise of membership.[15] In view of the ENP's

---

[8]Decision on the Conception of Future Development of CIS and the Plan on Central Measures for its Implementation, Council of Head of States of CIS, 5 October 2007, available at http://www.e-cis.info/page.php?id=3616.

[9]Article 1 of the Constitution of Ukraine, 28 June 1996; Article 47 of the Constitution of the Republic of Moldova 29 July 1994; Articles 1, 30.2 and 38 of the Constitution of the Republic of Armenia, 5 July 1995; Preamble and Article 33 of the Constitution of the Republic of Georgia, 24 August 2005; Preamble of the Constitution of the Republic of Azerbaijan, 12 November 1995.

[10]According to Article 2 of the Law on the Public Services Regulatory Commission public services include water, energy and electronic communication services. See also Article 30.2 of the Constitution of the Republic of Armenia.

[11]See European Commission, *Implementation of the European Neighbourhood Policy in 2009, Progress Report Georgia*, SEC(2010) 518 final, 12 May 2010, pp. 4–5.

[12]Article 33 of the Georgian Constitution mentions 'services of vital importance' in the context of strikes.

[13]Ukrainian Law on Social Services, N 966-IV, 2003; Moldovan Law on Social Service No 123, 2010; Azerbaijan Law on Social Services, 2012. Georgia and Armenia have laws on social assistance from 2006 and 2005 respectively.

[14]The term 'Europeanisation' is used here in its outwards understanding as an export of 'forms of political organisation' of the EU; Olsen 2002, p. 924; European Commission, *Communication on a Wider Europe-Neighbourhood: A New Framework for Relations with our Eastern and Southern Neighbours,* COM (2003) 104 final, 11 April 2003, pp. 4, 10.

[15]European Commission, *Communication on a Wider Europe-Neighbourhood: A New Framework for Relations with our Eastern and Southern Neighbours,* COM (2003) 104 final, 11 April 2003, p. 5.

focus on opening of markets to free trade based on competition, it is apt to ask whether the calls to liberalise the market and trade are accompanied with social underpinnings as it increasingly is the case in the EU.

The debate on the SGI in the EU, in particular the distinct emphasis on the services of general economic interest (SGEI) and service of general non-economic interest, has become prominent within the last two decades. The very terminology used in this area has been one of the sources of complexity,[16] including 'public services', 'social service of general interest', 'universal service' as part of the EU jargon.[17] Although the exclusion of SGI-related services from the scope of the Service Directive 2006 was considered to be an indication of their increasing importance,[18] the Directive was seen to have complicated the terminology further by dividing the into a number of subgroups.[19] Despite referring to these various terms in their particular context in the discussion that follows, they are nevertheless viewed as part of an overarching concept of SGI as an EU-specific term.

Within this context the chapter aims to explore the following issues. In Sect. 11.2, the role of the SGI within EU would be discussed to identify the subject of normative export that can become part of the transposition of the EU's model of governance. Next, in Sect. 11.3 the ENP is discussed to establish the policy-specific avenues for normative export. The role of the SGI is then, in Sect. 11.4, traced within the policy on the basis of the analysis of general policy documents and bilateral cooperation instruments between the EU and EaP partner states. Finally, the chapter concludes with a brief summary of findings in Sect. 11.5.

## 11.2 Services of General Interest: Identifying the EU Model?

The debate on the role of the SGI in the EU currently revolves around the arguably shifting balance between the so called market values and social objectives of the EU. The original EEC was based on market economy with 'a very limited degree of social-policy-related intervention' with non-economic policies remaining with the Member States.[20] The Rome Treaty made a single reference to the SGEI as an

[16]European Parliament, Committee on Employment and Social Affairs, Report on Social Services of General Interest in the European Union, 6 March 2007; European Parliament, Resolution on the Commission's White Paper on Services of General Interest, 27 September 2006, para 10.

[17]The Commission avoids using the term 'public service' outside the context of Article 93 TFEU; European Commission, *Communication on a Quality Framework for Services of General Interest in Europe,* COM(2011) 900 final, 12 December 2011, pp. 3–4.

[18]Sauter makes this observation as regards the SGEI; Sauter 2008, p. 192.

[19]Ross 2007, pp. 1058–1059.

[20]Semmelmann 2010, p. 519.

exception from competition rules in Article 90 EEC.[21] However, even this marginal appearance testified to the special role of these services. Although the SGEI is a supranational concept, the definition of activities that constitute SGEI is left to the Member States,[22] subject to the review for manifest error of assessment.[23] There is therefore no communitarian definition of the SGEI which is inter alia explained by their dynamic nature.[24] Outside the rules on competition a distinction has been made by the Court of Justice between economic and non-economic interests in relation to the provision of services: the latter group emerged as a legitimate justification for non-discriminatory restriction on free movement.[25]

### *11.2.1 SGI as an EU Value?*

The SGI has become much more prominent in the EU through the acknowledgement of the social dimension of the single market.[26] The 1996 Commission Communication was first to use the term of SGI: the latter was presented as an element of the 'European model of society',[27] and it became part of the future vocabulary of this discourse with a distinction being made between the SGEI and non-economic services of general interest.[28] According to Bauby, this development signified a move towards a horizontal approach in departure from previous sector-driven liberalisation.[29]

Although there is no supranational definition of either SGEI or non-economic services of general interest, certain supranational aspects have been added to the SGI via the specification of the content of such services, or specific groups of

---

[21]Article 77 EEC made a reference to 'public service' in transport area; Treaty Establishing the European Economic Community, 1957. Hennig considers that 'public service' in former Article 77 EEC (current Article 93 TFEU) denominates the same idea as SGEI; Hennig 2011, p. 191.

[22]CJEU, Case C-157/94 *Commission v Netherlands* [1997] ECR I-5699, para 40.

[23]CFI, Case T-17/02 *Fred Olsen* [2005] ECR II-2031, para 216; CFI, Case T-289/03 *BUPA and Others v Commission* [2008] ECR II-81, para 165; European Commission, *Communication on Services of General Economic Interest in Europe, OJ* 2001 C 17/ 4, para 22.

[24]Sauter 2008, p. 175.

[25]CJEU, Case C-120/78 *Cassis de Dijon* [1979] ECR 649, para 8.

[26]European Commission, *Communication on a Single Market for 21st Century Europe,* COM(2007) 724 final, 20 November 2007, p. 3.

[27]European Commission, *Communication on Services of General Interest in Europe,* COM(96) 443 final, 11 September 1996, p. 1.

[28]For instance European Commission, *White Paper on Services of General Interest,* COM(2004) 374 final, 12 May 2004; *Communication on Services of General Interest, including Social Services of General Interest: A New European Commitment,* COM(2007) 725 final, 20 November 2007; *Communication on a Quality Framework for Services of General Interest in Europe,* COM(2011) 900 final, 20 December 2011.

[29]Bauby 1999, p. 52.

services within the SGI or the obligations attached to their provision. For instance the 2000 Commission Communication on SGEI mentions high quality at affordable prices as an attribute of such services.[30] The Commission's 2003 Green Paper on SGI emphasised the concept of universal service established in certain network areas.[31] The subsequent White Paper referred to the 'existence of a common concept of services of general interest in the Union' which includes universal service, continuity, quality of service, affordability, as well as user and consumer protection.[32] Soft law has been used also in relation to another group of SGI that is social services of general interest ultimately influencing the modelling and provision of these services in the Member States.[33]

Importantly, former Article 16 EC added by the Amsterdam Treaty acknowledged the increasing importance of the SGEI by placing them among 'shared values' of the EU. Although it did not per se introduce new exemptions to the previously established rules,[34] it divided opinions as to its significance.[35] Ultimately, it was perceived to have added a positive connotation introducing the SGEI as a shared value within the EU in difference to their previous negative perception as an obstacle to free trade and competition.[36] Thus, already prior to the Lisbon Treaty the SGI have been increasingly referred to as one of the pillars of EU citizenship and part of the European social model.[37]

Following the reshuffling of EU objectives in the Lisbon Treaty, social and economic considerations both occupy a prominent role therein.[38] The current wording of Article 3(3) TEU is seen as an indication that the European integration should not be achieved at the expense of eroding the social systems of the Member States.[39] Meanwhile the previous goal of competition has been ousted from the text of the Treaty to Protocol 27 suggesting a shift in the balance of values.[40]

---

[30]European Commission, *Communication on Services of General Economic Interest in Europe*, *OJ* 2001 C 17/ 4, para 8.

[31]European Commission, *Green Paper of Services of General Interest*, COM(2003) 270 final, 21 May 2003, paras 50–51.

[32]European Commission, *White Paper on Services of General Interest,* COM(2004) 374 final, 12 May 2004, para 2.1.

[33]Van de Gronden 2011, p. 150.

[34]Behrens 2001, pp. 470–471.

[35]See on different interpretations of the significance of Article 16 EC Ross 2007, pp. 1072–1073; Szyszczak 2011, p. 5; Schwintowski 2003, p. 372.

[36]Ross 2009, p. 131; Heritier, 2001, p. 829; Ross 2000, pp. 28–35.

[37]European Commission, *Green Paper of Services of General Interest*, COM(2003) 270 final, 21 May 2003, p. 2.

[38]Fiedziuk 2011, p. 233.

[39]Azoulai 2008, p. 1337.

[40]According to Article 51 TEU protocols have the same legal value as the Treaties. Semmelmann doubts that this development signifies major practical changes, as the legislative means to create a social Europe are limited; Semmelmann 2010, pp. 521–522.

Perhaps, further support for the shifting balance of objectives can be found in the legally binding Charter of Fundamental Rights stipulating a number of provisions related to social protection.[41]

Although the term SGI as such does not feature in the main text of the Treaties, the latter features in the title and the text of the Protocol on SGI attached to the Lisbon Treaty under the pressure from the Dutch government.[42] Article 2 of the Protocol for the first time mentions the concept of SGI in a Treaty context elevating it from secondary legislation to primary.[43] The preamble of the Protocol emphasises the 'importance of [SGI]' and as such does not amend the pre-existing status of SGI in EU, in particular as regards the Member States discretion when it comes to the SGEI and non-economic services of general interest. The Member States have absolute discretion as regards non-economic services, while in case of economic services their discretion extends to the definition of the general interest via the imposition of public service obligations on the providers of such services.[44]

Article 1 of the Protocol, together with the case law, has been considered to provide the minimum common supranational criteria or principles for SGEI,[45] including inter alia respecting the diversity of services, high level of quality, safety and affordability, equal treatment and promoting universal access, upholding user rights. Not only it is said that the principles were established with the Commission's policy in mind,[46] but they also make appearance as *values* that are applicable also to the SGI according to the Commission.[47] These values or criteria are therefore common to the SGEI and non-economic services which highlight a unitary basis for the SGI as an overarching concept.

Nevertheless, the delimitation between the two groups of services is far from clear.[48] The importance of the delimitation is linked to the Member States discretion but also the application of rules on free movement.[49] The lack of clarity surrounding the delimitation is all the more visible when one considers the definition

---

[41]Chapter IV, Charter of Fundamental Rights of the European Union, *OJ* 2000 C 364/15.

[42]Bauby 2011, pp. 19–36.

[43]The reference to secondary legislation means Article 2(2)(a) of the Services Directive excluding SGI from the scope of its application; Fiedziuk 2011, p. 233.

[44]Behrens 2001, p. 483.

[45]CFI, Case T-289/03 *BUPA and Others v Commission* [2008] ECR II-81, para 172; Ross 2009, pp. 134–136; Sauter 2008, p. 173.

[46]Van de Gronden 2009, p. 261.

[47]European Commission, *Communication on a Quality Framework for Services of General Interest in Europe,* COM(2011) 900 final, 12 December 2011, p. 2.

[48]Cygan 2008, p. 530.

[49]According to the Court's jurisprudence the non-economic nature of general interest is what makes a difference in terms of derogations form Treaty rules on free movement of trade (economic goals cannot justify restrictions on free movement); Behrens 2001, pp. 480–481.

of social services of general interest used by the Commission.[50] However, establishing a common definition for SGI would be even more problematic than that of the SGEI as it will not be easy to find a common denominator applicable across various sectors, but also applicable in different areas of law, including EU competition law and free movement rules.[51] On the other hand, the lack of definition of non-economic services has been viewed as causing uncertainty as to their performance.[52]

As far as the economic services are concerned, the amended Article 14 TFEU has divided opinions similar to its predecessor Article 16 EC. Some consider that in combination with Article 106(2) and Article 36 of the Charter it shields the SGEI 'from the full force of the economic rules of the TFEU',[53] while others see its significance in the 'value statement fulfilling the concept of European Social Model'[54] and a 'fundamental principle' denoting more than a mere derogation from Treaty rules.[55] On the other hand, the nature and language of Article 14 TFEU does not lead to directly effective rights for EU citizens. Nor does the Charter of Fundamental Human Rights, which in its Article 36 'recognises and respects access to [SGEI]', create any new rights.[56] Article 14 TFEU nevertheless highlights the value dimension to the SGEI specifically.

The various Treaty developments noted above suggest the gradual emergence of the SGI, and specifically SGEI, as an EU value which could be traced in EU foreign policy, including within the ENP, within the value-driven foreign policy framework established by the Lisbon Treaty.

### *11.2.2 Acquis as a Subject of Normative Export*

In addition to the possible projection of the SGI in EU foreign policy as *a value*, their presence in the EU foreign policy can also be considered within the context of promoting EU *acquis*, taking into account the legislative developments of the last two decades regarding the SGEI in network areas.

[50]According to the Commission the social nature of the services does not per se classify the service, which can be both economic and non-economic; European Commission, *Communication on a Quality Framework for Services of General Interest in Europe,* COM(2011) 900 final, 12 December 2011, pp. 3–4.

[51]Fiedziuk 2011, p. 235.

[52]Bauby 2011, p. 34.

[53]Davies and Szyszczak 2011, p. 157.

[54]Bekkedal 2011, pp. 92, 98, 99.

[55]Schweitzer 2011, p. 53.

[56]Fiedziuk 2011, pp. 236–237; Cruz 2005, p. 178.

Despite the adoption by the Commission of certain directives for liberations of former state-owned corporations or monopolies on the basis of Article 106(3),[57] the opposition by the Member States, the Parliament and the Council resulted in a limited number of acts adopted through this legal basis and led to the liberalisation of relevant sectors with the participation of the Parliament and the Council[58] The latter group of measures includes *acquis communautaire* in such areas as communications,[59] energy markets,[60] and postal services.[61] Most importantly, these measures were adopted not only with the view of market liberalisation but also of securing obligations regarding public service. Liberalising measures have been established also in the area of transportation, although they do not necessarily impose public service obligations.[62]

In difference with former Article 16 EC, the amended Article 14 TFEU provides for a new legislative competence for the European Parliament and the Council based on the ordinary legislative procedure. It is nevertheless doubted whether any new framework measure would be adopted soon taking into account the Commission's

[57]For instance Commission Directive 88/301/EEC of 16 May 1988 on competition in the markets in telecommunications terminal equipment, *OJ* 1988 L 131/73; The Commission Decision of 28 November 2005 on the application of Article 86(2) EC (now Article 106(2) TFEU) to state aid in the form of public service compensation granted to certain undertakings entrusted with the operation of SGEIs.
This power of the Commission was confirmed by the Court of Justice in the following cases: CJEU, Joined Cases C-188-190/80 *France, Italy and United Kingdom v Commission* [1982] ECR 2545; CJEU, Case C-2020/88 *France v Commission* [1991] ECR I-1223 para 14.

[58]Schweitzer 2011, p. 42; Heritier 2001, pp. 843–844; Sauter 2008, p. 170.

[59]Directive 2002/21/EC of the European Parliament and of the Council of 7 March 2002 on a common regulatory framework for electronic communication networks and services (Framework Directive) *OJ* 2002 L 108/33; Directive 2002/19/EC of the European Parliament and of the Council of 7 March 2002 on access to, and interconnection of, electronic communications networks and associated facilities (Access Directive), *OJ* 2002 L 108/7; Directive 2002/20/EC of the European Parliament and of the Council of 7 March 2002 on the authorisation of electronic communications networks and services (Authorisation Directive), *OJ* 2002 L 108/21 and Directive 2002/22/EC of the European Parliament and of the Council of 7 March 2002 on universal service and users' rights relating to electronic communications networks and services (Universal Service Directive), *OJ* 2002 L 108/51.

[60]Directive 2003/55/EC of the European Parliament and of the Council of 26 June 2003 concerning common rules for the internal market in natural gas, *OJ* 2003 L176/57; Directive 2003/54/EC of the European Parliament and of the Council of 26 June 2003 concerning common rules for the internal market in electricity, *OJ* 2003 L 176/37.

[61]Directive 97/67/EC of the European Parliament and of the Council of 15 December 1997 on common rules for the development of the internal market of Community postal services and the involvement of quality of service, *OJ* 1998 L 15/14.

[62]For instance in the area of air transport, see Prosser 2005, p. 205.

reluctance and its preference for sector-based approach.[63] However, if any measure is adopted through this new legal basis, it will become a subject of normative export.

Thus, in addition to the SGI as a value of the EU, one can expect the export of the EU rules on the SGEI, particularly the liberalising and harmonising measures in network sectors, as well as rules on state aid and public procurement and any future secondary legislation adopted on the basis of Article 14 TFEU.

## 11.3 The ENP and the Export of SGI

In his analysis of universal service provisions in EU trade agreements, Krajewski considers the shift from derogation to a positive obligation within the value-driven framework of EU foreign policy. Similar value dimension is prevalent within the ENP.

Since the Commission, to a certain extent the mastermind of the ENP,[64] accorded an important role to the SGI within the 'European model of society',[65] devising the ENP in a way to 'share everything, but institutions'[66]—as was planned originally—would have implied a positive projection of existing EU rules within the ENP. Because both the original policy documents and the main bulk of the bilateral documents are soft law in nature, one would expect finding more of a value projection rather than derogation which would be more appropriate in hard legal instruments. The following section explores the conditionality as a central element of the ENP with a view of placing the SGI within the latter.

### *11.3.1 ENP Avenues for Exporting EU Values and Acquis*

As noted above the Lisbon Treaty introduced a number of provisions which have added a value dimension to the pursuit of EU external policy objectives. If one is to consider the ENP within the Treaty framework on the foreign policy, the emphasis on EU values in Articles 3(5) and 21 TEU appears to be demanding in

---

[63]European Commission, *Communication on a Quality Framework for Services of General Interest in Europe,* COM(2011) 900 final, 12 December 2011, p. 5; European Commission, *Communication on Services of General Interest, including Social Services of General Interest: A New European Commitment,* COM(2007) 725 final, 20 November 2007, p. 12; European Commission, *Report to the Laeken European Council: Services of General Interest*, COM (2001) 598, s 5–6; European Commission, *Green Paper of Services of General Interest,* COM(2003) 270 final, 21 May 2003, s 40; European Commission, *White Paper on Services of General Interest,* COM (2004) 374 final, 12 May 2004, s 4.1.; Sauter 2008, pp. 172–173.

[64]For the role of EU institutions within the ENP see Ghazaryan 2012; Ghazaryan 2014, pp. 36–53.

[65]European Commission, *White Paper on Services of General Interest,* COM (2004) 374 final, 12 May 2004, p. 4.

[66]R. Prodi, A wider europe—a proximity policy as the key to stability. http://europa.eu/rapid/press-release_SPEECH-02-619_en.pdf. Accessed 11 November 2014.

terms of entire foreign policy of the EU.[67] Although Article 21(3) TEU applies the common list of objectives to the EU external action covered by Title V of the TEU and by Part Five of the TFEU (which technically leaves Article 8 TEU on the neighbourhood policies outside its scope), the ENP as a cross-Treaty policy comprising elements from various areas of EU foreign action, necessarily has to pursue the objectives in Article 21 TEU.[68] Besides, Article 8 TEU is itself constructed upon the premise of a value-driven policy: 'The Union shall develop a special relationship with neighbouring countries … *founded on the values of the Union …*'.[69] In any case, the value dimension of the ENP was present since its initiation due to conditionality being embraced as one the methods of achieving policy objectives.

Conditionality is described as the linking by an international organisation or a state of perceived benefits to another state to the fulfilment of economic and/or political conditions.[70] Although the ENP was introduced as an alternative to the accession policy, it was elaborated predominantly based on the pre-accession instruments and methodology, including the accession conditionality.[71] Nevertheless, this has been far from a straightforward borrowing not only due to the exclusion of the main carrot, but also due to the manner of setting the conditions for cooperation.

The ENP conditionality can be described as undermined, muted, and non-prioritised. The lack of a membership perspective or other clearly defined incentives is one of the factors which has undermined the policy conditionality for years following its initiation.[72] The conditionality is non-prioritised as the documents setting conditions for cooperation failed to set a clear set of actions to be achieved within a certain time-frame.[73] In this connection the conditionality can also be viewed as muted due to the fact that the accession criteria have been replaced with

[67]See Eeckhout in Chap. 9 in this volume.

[68]Ghazaryan 2014, p. 32.

[69]Emphasis added.

[70]Smith 2005, p. 28.

[71]The relationship between the enlargement policy and the ENP has been extensively explored, see for instance Kelley 2006; A. Magen, The shadow of enlargement: can the European Neighbourhood Policy achieve compliance? Centre on Democracy, Development and the Rule of Law, Stanford Institute for International Studies, Working Papers No 68, 2006; G. Meloni, Is the same toolkit used during enlargement still applicable to the countries of the new neighbourhood? A problem of mismatching between objectives and instruments. In: Cremona M, Meloni G (eds) The European Neighbourhood Policy: A New Framework for Modernisation? EUI Working Papers, LAW 2007/21, pp. 97–111; Balfour and Rotta 2005.

[72]Ghazaryan 2014, pp. 78–81; Hill and Smith 2005, pp. 287–288; Cremona and. Hillion 2006, p. 39; Missiroli 2004, p. 19.

[73]Kochenov 2008, p. 116; Magen, The shadow of enlargement: can the European Neighbourhood Policy achieve compliance? Centre on Democracy, Development and the Rule of Law, Stanford Institute for International Studies, Working Papers No 68, 2006, p. 15; N. Tocci, Can the EU promote democracy and human rights through the ENP? The case for refocusing on the rule of law. In: Cremona M, Meloni G (eds) The European Neighbourhood Policy: A New Framework for Modernisation? EUI Working Papers, LAW 2007/21, pp. 23–35, at p. 31; Emerson 2005, p. 20; Seeberg 2010, p. 676.

the concept of 'shared values'.[74] The prospect of closer economic integration with the EU depends on the progress in demonstrating shared values.[75] Making a distinction between *acquis* and non-*acquis* or value conditionality, Kochenov attaches fewer expectations to the fulfilment of non-*acquis* conditionality.[76] The question is where to place the SGI within this dual conditionality?

It can be argued that the discourse on the SGI can be translated to the ENP via both channels of conditionality. First, narrow and wide approaches to value conditionality can be envisaged. If understood narrowly the value conditionality would be based only on Article 2 TEU which defines the EU values to include respect for human dignity, freedom, democracy, equality, the rule of law and respect for human rights, including minority rights. Such narrow reading would exclude the SGI as an EU value. The article however continues to specify that the values are common to the Member States in a society in which pluralism, non-discrimination, tolerance, justice, solidarity and equality between women and men prevail. If one is willing to read into the idea of 'solidarity' it might be even possible to link the SGI to Article 2 TFEU values, as some do indeed.[77] On the other hand, a wider approach is also conceivable where 'values' can be understood to include ethical considerations other than those mentioned in Article 2 TFEU. Ultimately, Article 8 TEU on the neighbourhood policy mentions the value basis of the relationship with reference to the 'values of the Union' without confining them to Article 2 TEU. Such wide understanding can also include other values of the EU, including at least the SGEI as a 'shared value' of the Union in Article 14 TFEU and Article 1 of the Lisbon Protocol on SGI.

Returning to the distinction between value and *acquis* conditionality, the relationship between the two is somewhat problematic. First of all, there is no hierarchy between the two. At the same time, hierarchy might not be deemed essential because it can be argued that *acquis* is based on the EU values. Here it should be noted that the progress of the ENP partners does not solely depend on the adherence to shared values, but also the 'will and capacity to implement agreed priorities'.[78] On the other hand, it can be argued that both value and *acquis* conditionality have to be translated to the priorities of cooperation to have any effet utile. The value conditionality would become an abstract notion if it was not included within the priorities of cooperation. Some of the established priorities are not necessarily based on the EU *acquis*, as in many areas prioritised in the bilateral cooperation no *acquis communautaire* exists as such.[79] They should therefore be deemed to be based on value

---

[74]Tulmets 2006, p. 30.

[75]European Commission, *Communication on a Wider Europe-Neighbourhood: A New Framework for Relations with our Eastern and Southern Neighbours,* COM (2003) 104 final, 11 April 2003 p. 4; European Commission, *European Neighbourhood Policy Strategy Paper,* COM(2004) 373 final, 12 May 2004 (hereinafter ENP Strategy Paper), p. 8; On 'common values' see further Leino and Petrov 2009.

[76]Kochenov 2008, pp. 108–110.

[77]Ross 2007; Wernicke 2009.

[78]ENP Strategy Paper, p. 8.

[79]For instance, conflict resolution.

projection. Thus, the SGI as a value can be traced within the ENP on a rhetorical level, but also within the priorities of cooperation in addition to the relevant *acquis*.

### *11.3.2 The ENP Policy Documents and the SGI*

It is the ENP strategy-setting documents that have laid the ground for exporting EU values and laws in many areas of EU competence. Thus, before turning to the bilateral instruments spelling out the conditions for cooperation, the former should be considered first to identify whether the SGI-related aspects of 'social Europe' have been projected onto the neighbourhood, and if so whether they take a form of a derogation or of a positive value projection or *acquis* promotion.

The ENP exists through a wide range of instruments predominantly with no traditional legal obligations, which can be brought under the general concept of soft law, suggesting no binding force per se, although with a possibility of inducing certain practical or even legal effects.[80]

The initial Wider Europe Communication (a rather rhetorical document) referred to striving towards social cohesion, reduction of social division and promotion of social inclusion.[81] More substantively the Communication made reference to the EU *acquis* in transport, energy and telecommunications networks as 'a well-established model' which the neighbours should replicate. The subsequent ENP Strategy Paper, which narrowed certain policy ambitions following the Council's intervention,[82] emphasised the eagerness of the Union to establish dialogue and cooperation 'on the social dimension', defined widely to include such issues as poverty reduction, reducing regional disparities, employment, and even reforming national welfare systems.[83] Similar to the previous document the Strategy Paper refers to the ambition of connecting the neighbourhood in transport, energy, and information society sectors. Subsequent ENP policy and revision documents, although consider various aspects of social policy, do not mention SGI or SGEI.[84]

---

[80]The main ideas of the ENP were circulated through the conclusions of the Council and the European Council, Commission communications and other policy documents, including papers and non-papers, joint letters, statements, EP resolutions and recommendations. See the definition of soft law in Senden 2005, p. 112.

[81]European Commission, *Communication on a Wider Europe-Neighbourhood: A New Framework for Relations with our Eastern and Southern Neighbours,* COM (2003) 104 final, 11 April 2003, pp. 3, 8.

[82]Zaiotti 2007, p. 157.

[83]ENP Strategy Paper, p. 14.

[84]For instance the 2006 Communication on Strengthening the ENP mentions the benefits of a multilateral dialogues in network and other areas; European Commission, *Communication on Strengthening the European Neighbourhood Policy,* COM(2006) 726 final, 4 December 2006, p. 8. The Communication on *Implementation of the ENP* in 2008 considers the progress made in 'social reform', COM(2009) 188/3, 23 May 2009. The Communication on *Taking Stock of the ENP Communication* considers various social policy issues as part of the ENP, COM(2010) 207, 12 May 2010, p. 8.

Following the Arab Spring Revolutions, the ENP has been revised to allegedly respond to new challenges. A 'more for more' approach was adopted to reward with more significant benefits those neighbours which distinguish themselves with a fast pace of reform.[85] In this respect, the 'more for more' principle was extended to the areas of energy and transport with a focus on market integration.[86] The social debate is reflected also in the most recent strategy papers of the ENP, highlighting the importance of a more inclusive economic development,[87] and even mentioning social cohesion as one of the values constituting the basis for closer cooperation between the parties.[88] This suggests that the concept of 'values' deployed within the ENP is rather fluid and is not restricted to those defined in Article 2 TEU. Besides, the policy documents reveal that the economic liberalisation appears to be accompanied by social considerations, including an agenda for legislative approximation in the network areas. Similar outlook is present within the EaP.

The EaP Communication was meant to signal a step-change in the relations between the EU and its Eastern neighbours. It appeared to reinforce the prospect of new association agreements leading to the creation of a network of FTAs that can eventually evolve into a neighbourhood economic community.[89] In addition to more intensified cooperation via previously established bilateral track the EaP added new fora for multilateral high-level meetings, going beyond 'classical association'.[90] Four thematic platforms have been established for a multilateral cooperation in a form of exchange of practice operating through meetings held twice a year at the level of senior officials. The platforms are on democracy,

[85]European Commission/High Representative, *Joint Communication on A New Response to a Changing Neighbourhood: A Review of the European Neighbourhood Policy*, COM(2011) 303, 25 May 2011, pp. 2, 8–9, 20–21; European Commission/High Representative, *Joint Communication on Delivering on a New European Neighbourhood Policy,* JOIN (2012) 14 final, 15 May 2012, pp. 2–4.

[86]European Commission/High Representative, *Joint Communication on a New Response to a Changing Neighbourhood: A Review of the European Neighbourhood Policy,* COM(2011) 303, 25 May 2011, p. 10.

[87]European Commission/High Representative, *Joint Communication on Delivering on a New European Neighbourhood Policy,* JOIN (2012) 14 final, 15 May 2012, p. 9.

[88]European Commission/High Representative, *Joint Communication on European Neighbourhood Policy: Working towards a stronger partnership,* JOIN (2013) 4 final 2013, 20 March 2013, p. 2.

[89]European Commission, *Communication on Eastern Partnership,* COM (2008) 823 final, 3 December 2008, p. 10. For a more detailed discussion of the Eastern Partnership see Hillion and Mayhew 2009; Ghazaryan 2014, pp. 84–94.

[90]The structural platform consists of meetings of the heads of the states or governments of Eastern partners held every 2 years and annual spring meetings of Ministers of Foreign Affairs; Hillion and Mayhew 2009, pp. 8–9.

good governance and stability; economic integration and convergence with EU policies; energy security; and contacts between people. Its added value should therefore be sought in its multilateral framework. The objectives for the platform on economic cooperation include taking into account the social aspects of the market, convergence in some network areas, as well as approximation in competition rules.[91]

The EaP policy documents similarly envisage legal approximation in network areas inclusive of also the bilateral track.[92] In a Joint Communication establishing a Roadmap to the EaP summit in 2013, the concept of 'public services' featured for the first time in the ENP common policy documents.[93] The context is one of establishing a dialogue on labour markets and social policies as part of expected achievements by the summit, to promote exchanges inter alia on 'social protection and social inclusion policies, involving public services and social partners as stakeholders'. It is noteworthy that the term 'public service' found its way to the document despite the Commission's reluctance to use it in internal context, and because the term is mostly used to denote other services than SGI in the countries concerned as mentioned earlier. One might argue that 'public service' is used to denote social services as the context above would suggest. On the other hand, the passage enumerates a number of expected achievements without much elaboration, which can suggest that the reference is made without attaching much significance to it.

It can therefore be summarised that despite certain rhetoric being present on social considerations accompanying the market liberalisation, there is no realistic imposition of the SGI or SGEI as a Union value outside the discourse on the liberalisation of network sectors. To which extent this rhetoric is translated into bilateral instrument is considered next.

## 11.4 Bilateral Instruments of Cooperation with the EaP States

A few generations of ENP bilateral documents can be envisaged within the bilateral cooperation. Although the ENP established its own instruments, it also inherited the previously concluded with the Eastern neighbours Partnership and

[91]Core Objectives and Proposed Work Programme 2009–2011, available at http://eeas.europa.eu/eastern/platforms/docs/platform2_151109_en.pdf.

[92]European Commission, *Communication on Eastern Partnership,* COM (2008) 823 final, 3 December 2008, pp. 9–10.

[93]European Commission/High Representative, *Joint Communication on Eastern Partnership: A Roadmap to Autumn 2013 Summit,* JOIN(2012) 13 final, 15 May 2012, p. 13.

Cooperation Agreements (PCAs).[94] Alongside these pre-ENP documents, Action Plans as the first official ENP bilateral instruments were established with each party. Accession Partnership (to date established only with Ukraine) represent the next generation of ENP bilateral instruments, with the possible Association Agreements to become the latest generation.

### *11.4.1 Pre-association Agreement Instruments*

It should be noted that due to the possibility of creating a free trade area the PCAs concluded with Moldova and Ukraine, so called Westerns CIA countries, have been perceived as more advanced in comparison with the PCAs with the South Caucasian countries.[95] Thus, there are certain distinctions, but also commonalities, between on the one hand the Moldovan and Ukrainian and on the other the South Caucasian PCAs.[96] Among common features, the PCAs provide for social cooperation as an objective for bilateral relations.[97] They envisage that the economic reforms should be guided by harmonious social development, while simultaneously providing for cooperation in network sectors, including energy and telecommunications.[98] Although only transport is mentioned from network sectors among the specific areas for legislative approximation, other areas as far as the SGEI are concerned would include the rules on competition.[99] Another notable provision is the common article on postal services and telecommunications, which inter alia mentions enhancing *efficiency and quality of service*.[100] A social cooperation-specific provision, despite its health and employment oriented core, mentions that

---

[94]Partnership and Cooperation Agreement between the European Communities and their Member States, of the one part, and the Republic of Armenia, of the other, *OJ* 1999 L 239/3; Partnership and Cooperation Agreement between the European Communities and their Member States, of the one part, and the Republic of Azerbaijan, of the other, *OJ* 1999 L 246/3; Partnership and Cooperation Agreement between the European Communities and their Member States, of the one part, and the Republic of Georgia, of the other, *OJ* 1999 L 205/3; Partnership and Cooperation Agreement between the European Communities and their Member States, of the one part, and the Republic of Moldova, of the other, *OJ* 1998 L 181; Partnership and Cooperation Agreement between the European Communities and their Member States, of the one part, and Ukraine, of the other, *OJ* 1998 L 049; European Commission, *Communication on a Wider Europe-Neighbourhood: A New Framework for Relations with our Eastern and Southern Neighbours,* COM (2003) 104 final, 11 April 2003, p. 15; Council of the European Union, Thessaloniki European Council Conlusions, 19–20 June 2003.

[95]See for instance Article 4, PCA with Moldova; Maresceau and Montaguti 1995, pp. 1340–1341; Berdiyev 2003, pp. 463–464.

[96]See Ghazaryan 2010, p. 225.

[97]Common Article 1.

[98]Article 51 EU-Moldova PCA; Article 52 EU-Ukraine PCA; Article 44 EU-Armenia PCA.

[99]Article 50(2) EU-Moldova PCA, Article 51(2) EU-Ukraine PCA; Article 43 EU-Armenia PCA.

[100]Article 63 EU-Moldova PCA; Article 66 of EU-Ukraine PCA; Article 57 EU-Armenia PCA.

social reforms should aim at developing methods of protection intrinsic to market economics and shall comprise all directions of social protection.[101] While these provisions suggest certain positive obligation imposed on the parties, an article on cooperation in the area of competition special to Moldovan and Ukrainian PCAs provides for a derogation-like clause similar to Article 106(2) TFEU:

> In the case of public undertakings or undertakings to which [the Parties] grant exclusive rights, the Parties declare their readiness … to ensure that there is neither enacted nor maintained any measure distorting trade between [the Parties] to an extent contrary to [their] respective interests. This provision shall not obstruct the performance, in law or fact, of the particular tasks assigned to such undertakings.[102]

Despite the obvious similarity in the rationale of the Article to that of Article 106(2) TFEU, the terminology of undertakings to which which 'exclusive rights' were granted replaces the 'undertakings entrusted with the operation of services of general economic interest' suggesting flexibility in using relevant terminology. This provision demonstrates that the promise of a closer cooperation in a form of a potential free trade area is accompanied with certain projection of the EU model into the relations with the neighbours concerned.

The key ENP bilateral instruments, the non-binding Action Plans establishing priority areas of cooperation with the majority of the Eastern partners have continued the trend of distinguishing between the Western NCIS and South Caucasian countries.[103] The Ukrainian and Moldovan Action Plans are much more detailed and extensive in setting the priority agenda. Although the discourse on social cohesion and social policy reform is adopted in all Action Plans,[104] a few aspects can be singled out in terms of the SGI. The Moldovan and Ukrainian Action Plans establish priorities for legal convergence not only in network sectors of transport, energy and communications, but also on rules of competition and public procurement.[105] Certain features of the SGI do however make a sporadic appearance in the documents. For instance, the Moldovan Action Plan in the priority on information society requires adoption of a comprehensive regulatory framework including *universal service and users' rights.*[106] Although no reference to EU *acquis* is made in this priority area, it is evident that the debate is informed by the basic concepts of the Universal Service

[101] Article 71 EU-Ukraine PCA; Article 68 EU-Moldova PCA; Article 60 EU-Armenia PCA.

[102] Article 48(2)(5) EU-Moldova PCA; Article 49(2)(5) of EU-Ukraine PCA.

[103] Georgia, Armenia and Azerbaijan have originally been excluded from the ENP and were included in 2004; ENP Strategy Paper, pp. 10–11.

[104] The Introduction to all Action Plans mentions promotion of social cohesion as one of the objectives of the document. See also Priority Area 2.3 of EU-Moldova Action Plan; Priority Area 21 of EU-Ukraine Action Plan; Priority Area 3 of EU-Georgia Action Plan; Priority Area 3 of EU-Armenia Action Plan; Priority Area 6 of EU-Azerbaijan Action Plan.

[105] See Priority 37, 40, 57, 63 and 67 of EU-Moldova Action Plan; Priority Area 39, 42, 51, 52, 58 of EU-Ukraine Action Plan.

[106] Priority Area 67, EU-Moldova Action Plan.

Directive 2002/22 in the area of electronic communications.[107] On the other hand, the Ukrainian Action Plan requires the latter to undertake measures to improve social cohesion, including *social services with access for all.*[108] While no sectoral *acquis* exists in this area, it can be argued that the Commission's soft law has influenced the drafting of this priority area, particularly the 2004 White Paper which prior to the establishment of the Action Plan recognised that social services of general interest, based on the principle of solidarity, are 'an integral part of the European model of society'.[109] In addition, the specific references in the individual Action Plans can be claimed to have been reflective of the lacuna that existed in the national legislation of the countries concerned. For instance, although a Law on Social Services existed in Ukraine since 2003, the access to these services was not available to all groups.[110]

The Action Plans with the South Caucasian countries contain fewer and much more generally phrased priorities.[111] In comparison with the previously considered Action Plans these documents come across as being more rhetorical in nature, and the following references might be argued to be devoid of legal significance. Although the references serve as evidence to the EU internal debate surrounding the SGI being to a certain extent reflected in the ENP, their location within the documents is rather discouraging. They appear within 'general actions' the status of which is far from clear. They are neither priorities nor conditions for cooperation: rather a general call for action.

The Georgian Action Plan within its general actions makes provision for health and other social services 'with access for all' and affordable healthcare for whole population.[112] Similarly the general actions of the Armenian Action Plan provide for the modernisation of public sector to ensure 'better access to basic services for all', and improve social cohesion, 'including social services with access for all'.[113] In relation to health sector reform, the document requires improving 'access and affordability of services'.[114] The concept of 'universal service' also makes appearance in the area of communications in the Armenian and Azerbaijani Action Plans.[115] The latter also

[107]See for instance the preamble and Article 3 of the Universal Service Directive, *OJ* 2002 L 108/51.

[108]Priority Area 22, EU-Ukraine Action Plan.

[109]European Commission, *White Paper on Services of General Interest,* COM(2004) 374 final, 12 May 2004, p. 16.

[110]For instance the access for migrants was noted to be problematic even in 2009, European Commission, *Implementation of the European Neighbourhood Policy in 2009, Progress Report Ukraine,* SEC(2010) 524, 12 May 2010, p. 13.

[111]For the criticism of the Action Plans with South Caucasian countries see Ghazaryan 2014, pp. 125–140.

[112]S 4.4 and 4.7.2 of General Actions, EU-Georgia Action Plan.

[113]S 4.3 of General Actions, EU-Armenia Action Plan.

[114]S 4.7.2 of General Actions, EU-Armenia Action Plan.

[115]S 4.6.3 of General Actions, EU-Armenia Action Plan; S 4.6.4 of General Actions, EU-Azerbaijan Action Plan.

refers to the improved access and affordability of healthcare for entire population.[116] These references are notable for a number of reasons. First, they might be suggestive of the EU's acknowledgment of the lack of regulation in the countries concerned. In line with the Ukrainian and Moldovan Action Plans they also suggest that the Action Plans are necessarily informed by the EU's internal debate on SGI. While in some areas, such as communications, the language used is directly reflective of the EU *acquis*, in others, such as social services and healthcare, the references to access and quality of services echo the elements of the SGI as defined in soft law, projecting the role of the SGI as an emerging EU value.

Within the instrumental progression of the ENP, the Association Agenda with Ukraine, a so called 'second-generation' ENP instrument,[117] should be noticed. It was established with Ukraine in 2009 to replace the EU-Ukraine Action Plan and to prepare the ground for the new association agreement,[118] by arguably 'hardening' the soft law framework of the Action Plan.[119] It has a more focused approach towards legislative approximation inter alia in network areas. For instance the Agenda mentions the necessity of compatibility of Ukrainian law with the Directive 2003/55/EC liberalising and imposing public service obligations in natural gas sector. This confirms the presumption made that the secondary legislation will be the main export subject via the ENP as far as the SGEI is concerned.

### *11.4.2 Association Agreements as the Future Generation of Bilateral Instruments*

In terms of instrumental progression, association agreements have been promised to all EaP states with the exception of Belarus. The association agreement containing a Deep and Comprehensive Free Trade Area (DCFTA) was expected to be signed with Ukraine and those with Moldova, Armenia and Georgia were expected to be initiated at the Vilnius EaP summit in November 2013. Due to political pressure from Russia, Armenia declared in September 2013 that it would join the Eurasian Economic Community,[120] therefore sabotaging the prospect of establishing a DCFTA with the EU. In an even more surprising turn prior to the EaP summit the Ukrainian President declared that the process of concluding the Association Agreement with the EU would be suspended which led to a national uprising.[121] Although the new interim Ukrainian government reversed this decision, the future

[116] S 4.7.2 of General Actions, EU-Azerbaijan Action Plan.

[117] Van Vooren 2011a, pp. 203–210.

[118] EU-Ukraine Association Agenda, p. 2.

[119] Van Vooren 2011b, p. 169.

[120] 'Armenia chooses Russia over EU' *European Voice*, 3 September 2013.

[121] 'EU "disappointed" by Ukraine decision' *European Voice*, 22 November 2013.

of the agreement is not yet certain.[122] Notwithstanding the future events, the leaked draft of EU-Ukraine Association Agreement is indicative of the EU's approach to the SGI in its neighbourhood, as it represents the maximum cooperation offered to any of the neighbours due to Ukraine's previous role as a frontrunner in the region. The agreements with Moldova and Georgia have been negotiated within a rather limited period of time suggesting that the Ukrainian template would have been used for these countries.

The draft agreement has a DCFTA as its component as noted above. A 'comprehensive' FTA refers to liberalisation of trade in both goods and services, while 'deep' FTA entails regulatory approximation and reduction of non-tariff barriers.[123] A DCFTA which constitutes a part of the agreement is rather far reaching as in addition to the market liberalisation in all areas it implies also legislative approximation to EU norms and regulations. The membership of the WTO has been a precondition for entering negotiations on the DCFTA, which would suggest that the latter would be reflective of the GATS regime on the liberalisation of services. A cursory examination of the draft reveals a significant role for the SGEI. A question to be mindful of here is whether the role of SGEI in the agreement is more reflective of the GATS regime or the EU's internal market model.

Although the general objectives and principles of the cooperation established highlight the economic and political core of the agreement without reference to social cohesion as in the case of the PCAs,[124] the SGEI occupy a prominent role within the agreement. Not only they make a frequent appearance within the derogations intended to shield domestic policies in a number of areas, but they also feature prominently through positively promoted SGEI-related concepts and approximation agenda. The most scrupulous legislative approximation agenda annexed to the Treaty already promises much in this respect. These two strands are in accordance with the two approaches towards public services found in trade agreements identified by Krajewski. While the first approach excludes specific services from the full impact of the trade agreement, the second aims to regulate certain aspects related to specific services or their provision.[125]

The presence of specific derogations in an agreement is indicative of a balance the parties intend to strike between market liberalisation and non-market considerations.[126] In many respects the draft Association Agreement is comparable to other free trade agreements concluded but the EU. In line with the EU's previous practice, the agreement provides for general exceptions in Article 141 from the rules on establishment, trade in services and electronic commerce for social security systems or activities connected to the exercise of official authority of each of the parties.

[122]'Ukraine ready to sign association agreement during March EU summit' *Euractiv*, 27 February 2014.

[123]Gstohl 2012, p. 98.

[124]Articles 1 and 3 of the Draft EU-Ukraine Association Agreement.

[125]Krajewski 2011b, p. 6.

[126]Arena 2011, p. 494.

This provision is similar to other FTA provisions concluded by the EU in line with GATS I:3(b) and (C), and has been viewed to refer to 'core governmental functions' as opposed to most services of general economic interest.[127]

In relation to services, the proposed EU-Ukraine agreement follows GATS's approach of a positive list regarding the market access and national treatment rule.[128] In difference with GATS, a general exception is made in regards to audiovisual services, which has been the case also in previous trade agreements explained by EU's or its Member States' sensitivity in this area.[129] Cultural services, other than audiovisual services, have not been excluded from the scope of the agreement. The agreement can be compared to other trade agreements concluded by the EU in respect of a horizontal reservation regarding public utilities which are economic activities which may be subject to public monopolies or to exclusive rights granted to private operators. For instance, while EU-Chile FTA provides for a horizontal reservation for the EU from the market access regime for cross-border supply of services in relation to public utilities, the EU-Ukraine draft agreement makes a horizontal reservation to national treatment rule on establishment related to 'public utilities'. Further, the list of commitments on cross-border services is clarified to be without prejudice to the existence of public monopolies and exclusive rights as described in the list of commitments on establishment, therefore referring to public utilities. This is reflective of the EU's horizontal reservations in GATS Schedule except for express exclusion for telecommunication and computer services.[130]

In terms of sector-specific reservations, the following areas concerning SGI can be noted:

- Publicly funded health, social and education services are excluded from the EU national treatment and MFN commitments.[131] As to privately funded education services, nationality conditions may apply, and specific commitments are specified for the majority of the Member States as regards primary, secondary, higher education and other education services.[132] Similarly, Member-State specific reservations are made for privately funded health and social services.[133]
- No reservations are made for postal and telecommunication services with the exception that 'service providers in this sector may be subject to obligations to safeguard general interest objectives related to the conveyance of content through their network in line with the EU regulatory framework for electronic communications'.[134]

---

[127]Krajewski 2009, p. 206; Krajewski 2003, p. 73.

[128]See Articles 93–94 of EU-Ukraine draft Association Agreement; Krajewski 2009, p. 208.

[129]Krajewski 2011c, p. 182.

[130]Such conclusion was drawn by Krajewski as regards EU-Chile agreement, Krajewski 2009, p. 209.

[131]See ANNEX XVI-A.

[132]See ANNEX XVI-B, s 5 of the list of sub-sectoral commitments.

[133]See ANNEX XVI-B, s 8 of the list of sub-sectoral commitments.

[134]See ANNEX XVI-B, s 2 of the list of sub-sectoral commitments.

- The commitments in environmental services are without reservations with an exception of consulting services for cross border trade.[135]

So far, this is reflective of the EU's common commercial policy and is comparable to FTAs concluded by the EU.

It has been noted that the scope of GATS exemptions are limited in comparison to the EU regime, particularly with reference to Article 106(2) TFEU.[136] It is important therefore to look into this issue to identify whether the regime proposed in the Treaty is also reflective of the EU's internal market. First all, it should be mentioned Article 257 is reminiscent of the Article 49 of the Ukrainian PCA noted above. Although it does not refer to the SGEI, it however considers the activity of 'public enterprises' or 'enterprises entrusted with special or exclusive rights' within the Article 106(2)-like language of 'performance obstruction'. Most important however for the rationale of the EU internal market, is the fact that approximation of laws including on Article 106 and its implementing legislation is an obligation under the agreement.[137] Although the specific measures and their timetable mentioned in Article 256 do not include those related to Article 106(2), the provision includes also approximation as regards 106(2) since the 'competition laws' referred to in the Article are defined to include also Article 106 TFEU.[138]

That the internal market rationale has been projected into the agreement is evident also from further derogation, this time specifically for 'SGEI'. Article 262(4) on state aid provides that undertakings entrusted with the operation of SGEI shall be subject to the general rules, in so far as they do not obstruct the performance, in law or in fact, of the particular tasks assigned to them.

The projection of the internal market rationale is also evident as regard the postal and communication services regarding universal service obligations which the parties are free to define and which will not be considered to be anticompetitive per se.[139] It should be noted that the concept of a universal service, defined on the basis of EU secondary legislation, constitutes the foundation of the Ukrainian commitments in certain sectors. For instance draft Article 109 defines universal service in postal areas on the basis of the definition in Article 3(1) of the Directive 97/67 on postal services.[140] Meanwhile the provisions on energy cooperation of the draft agreement adopt the relevant language of the EU secondary regulation, exemplified by 'public service obligations' in Article 337. Besides, the general

---

[135]Reservation is related to Mode 1, See ANNEX XVI-B, s 6 of the list of sub-sectoral commitments.

[136]Steinicke 2012, p. 340.

[137]Article 256 of Draft EU-Ukraine Association Agreement.

[138]Article 253(2), ibid.

[139]See Articles 111 and 120 of Draft EU-Ukraine Association Agreement.

[140]Directive 97/67/EC of the European Parliament and of the Council of 15 December 1997 on common rules for the development of the internal market of community postal service and the improvement of quality of service, *OJ* 1998 L 15/14; Article 115(g) does the same for communications sector.

principles of the relevant secondary legislation are specified in the provision referring to 'access to affordable energy for consumers, including vulnerable groups'.[141] The reliance on the terminology of 'public service' here demonstrates the positive correlation to the internal regulation of particular services. Article 389 on information society also reflects the elements of SGEI, which is better quality of services and affordable prices. Most importantly, the draft agreement details the plan of legislative approximation which involves the network areas liberalised in the EU, which impose public service obligations on the Member States.[142] This can be argued to be an evidence that the trade component of the proposed association agreement stretches beyond the common commercial policy and indeed reflects an extension of the internal market rationale with its rules as far as the SGEI are concerned.

## 11.5 Conclusion

The discussion above reveals that there is certain social accompaniment to the trade liberalisation core of the cooperation offered through the ENP reflective of the value-driven policy framework. Public interest has featured early on in relations with the Eastern neighbours through the provisions of the PCAs, although more intensely with those of the Western CIS countries. While embracing the PCAs, the ENP policy documents also indicate towards the presence of certain social agenda within the policy. Thus, the policy documents, even if only rhetorically, introduce social elements aimed at social cohesion, and poverty reduction in addition to the call for economic liberalisation. While the latter reveals a legislative approximation agenda in network areas, the rhetoric more generally can be argued to be informed by the role of the SGI as an EU value, since in many areas concerned no *acquis* exists as such. This trend has found continuity within the ENP, and has been translated into the instruments of bilateral cooperation.

The Action Plans preserve the rhetoric on social cohesion, but they also invite neighbours attention to the purpose of legislative approximation in network areas (Ukraine and Moldova), as well as to the importance of providing SGI in some areas although without mentioning the term, but referring to such elements of the

---

[141]See for instance Article 3(2) and (5) of Directive 2003/54/EC of the European Parliament and of the Council of 26 June 2003, *OJ* 2003 L 176/37; Article 3(2) and (3) of Directive 2003/55/EC of the European Parliament and of the Council of 26 June 2003, *OJ* 2003 L 176/57.

[142]Specifically Universal Service Directive, *OJ* 2002 L 108/51; Directive 2003/55/EC of the European Parliament and of the Council of 26 June 2003 concerning common rules for the internal market and natural gas, *OJ* 2003 L 176/57; Directive 2003/54/EC of the European Parliament and of the Council of 26 June 2003 concerning common rules for the internal market in electricity, *OJ* 2003 L 176/37; Directive 97/67/EC of the European Parliament and of the Council of 15 December 1997 on common rules for the development of the internal market of Community postal services and the improvement of quality of service, *OJ* 1998 L 15/14.

latter as universality, affordability and quality (Armenia, Azerbaijan, Georgia). Although, such references can be viewed as devoid of practical significance, as the Action Plans with the three South Caucasian countries are rather rhetorical in nature, the rhetoric similar to the general policy documents is informed by the values of the EU. In this respect it should be noted that a more noticeable focus on SGI is present once the cooperation advances into a traditional hard-law based stage. The draft Association Agreement with Ukraine serves as a testimony to this, demonstrating that the internal debate on the SGI and specifically the SGEI has been embraced by the ENP both in a form of a derogation and positive policy promotion. Most importantly, it also demonstrated that draft agreement stretches beyond the GATS regime and projects the EU's own model as far as the SGEI are concerned. Ultimately, the ENP is certainly reflective of the internal developments around the notion of SGI.

## References


Arena A (2011) The GATS notion of public services as an instance of intergovernmental agnosticism: comparative insights from the EU supranational dialectic. J World Trade 45(3):489–528

Azoulai L (2008) The Court of Justice and the social market economy: the emergence of an ideal and the conditions for its realisation. Common Mark Law Rev 45(5):1335–1355

Balfour R, Rotta A (2005) Beyond enlargement: the European Neighbourhood Policy and its tools. Int Spect 40(1):7–57

Bauby P (1999) Public service: forging a European conception. In: Haibach G (ed) Services of general interest in the EU: reconciling competition and social responsibility. European Institute of Public Administration, Maastricht, pp 49–62

Bauby P (2011) From Rome to Lisbon: services of general interest in primary law. In: Szyszczak E, Davies J, Andenæs M, Bekkedal T (eds) Developments in services of general interest. T.M.C. Asser Press, The Hague, pp 19–36

Behrens P (2001) Public services and the internal market: an analysis of the Commission's communication on services of general interest in Europe. Eur Bus Organ Law Rev 2:469–492

Bekkedal T (2011) Article 106 TFEU is dead. Long live Article 106 TFEU! In: Szyszczak E, Davies J, Andenæs M, Bekkedal T (eds) Developments in services of general interest. T.M.C. Asser Press, The Hague, pp 61–102

Berdiyev B (2003) The EU and former Soviet Central Asia: an analysis of the partnership and cooperation agreements. Yearb Eur Law 22:463–481

Cremona M, Hillion C (2006) L'Union fait la force? Potential and limitations of the ENP as an integrated EU foreign and security policy. In: Copsey N, Mayhew A (eds) European Neighbourhood Policy: the case of Europe. Sussex European Institute, SEI seminar papers series, pp 20–44

Cruz JB (2005) Beyond competition: services of general interest and European community law. In: de Burca G (ed) EU law and the welfare state in search of solidarity. OUP, Oxford, pp 167–212

Cygan A (2008) Public healthcare in the European Union: still a service of a general interest? Int Comp Law Q 57:529–560

Davies J, Szyszczak E (2011) Universal service obligations: fulfilling new generations of services of general economic interest. In: Szyszczak E, Davies J, Andenæs M, Bekkedal T (eds) Developments in services of general interest. T.M.C. Asser Press, The Hague, pp 155–177

Emerson M (2005) Is there to be a real European Neighbourhood Policy? In: Youngs R (ed) Global Europe: new terms of engagement. Foreign Policy Centre, London, pp 15–22
Fiedziuk N (2011) Services of general economic interest and the Treaty of Lisbon: opening doors to a whole new approach or maintaining the 'status quo'. Eur Law Rev 36:226–242
Ghazaryan N (2010) The ENP and the Southern Caucasus: meeting the expectations. Whitman R, Wolff S (eds) The European Neighbourhood Policy in perspective: context, implementation and impact. Palgrave, Basingstoke, pp 223–246
Ghazaryan N (2012) Pre and post-Lisbon institutional trends in the EU's neighbourhood. In: Cardwell PJ (ed) EU external relations law and policy in the post-Lisbon era. T.M.C. Asser Press, The Hague, pp 199–216
Ghazaryan N (2014) The European Neighbourhood Policy and democratic values of the EU: a legal analysis. Hart Publishing, Oxford
Gstohl S (2012) What is at stake in the internal market? Towards a neighbourhood economic community. In: Lannon E (ed) The European Neighbourhood Policy's challenges. College of Europe Studies, P.I.E. Peter Lang, Brussels, pp 85–108
Hennig M (2011) Public service obligations: protection of public service values in a national and European context. In: Szyszczak E, Davies J, Andenæs M, Bekkedal T (eds) Developments in services of general interest. T.M.C. Asser Press, The Hague, pp 179–193
Heritier A (2001) Market integration and social cohesion: the politics of public services in European regulation. J Eur Public Policy 8:825–852
Hill C, Smith M (2005) International relations and the European Union. OUP, Oxford
Hillion C, Mayhew A (2009) The Eastern partnership: something new or window-dressing. SEI working paper no 109
Kelley J (2006) New wine in old wineskins: policy learning and adaptation in the new European Neighbourhood Policy. J Common Mark Stud 44:29–55
Kochenov D (2008) The ENP conditionality: pre-accession mistakes repeated. In: Delcour L, Tulmets E (eds) Pioneer Europe? Testing EU foreign policy in the neighbourhood. Nomos, Baden Baden, pp 105–120
Krajewski M (2003) National regulation and trade liberalisation in services: the legal impact of the General Agreement on Trade in Services (GATS) on national regulatory autonomy. Kluwer Law International, The Hague
Krajewski M (2009) Protecting a shared value of the Union in a globalised world: services of general economic interest and external trade. In: van de Gronden J (ed) The EU and WTO law on services: limits to the realisation of general interest policies within the services market. Kluwer Law International, The Hague, pp 188–213
Krajewski M (2011a) Universal service provisions in international agreements of the EU: from derogation to obligation? In: Szyszczak E, Davies J, Andenæs M, Bekkedal T (eds) Developments in services of general interest. T.M.C. Asser Press, The Hague, pp 231–252
Krajewski M (2011b) Public services in bilateral free trade agreements of the EU. http://www.epsu.org/IMG/pdf/PublicServicesFTAs_FinalVersion.pdf. Accessed 11 Nov 2014
Krajewski M (2011c) Of modes and sectors: external relations, internal debates and the special case of (trade in) services. In: Cremona M (ed) Developments in EU external relations law. OUP, Oxford, pp 172–215
Leino P, Petrov R (2009) Between 'common values' and competing universals: the promotion of the EU's common values through the European Neighbourhood Policy. Eur Law J 15:654–671
Maresceau M, Montaguti E (1995) The relations between the European Union and Central and Eastern Europe: a legal appraisal. Common Mark Law Rev 32(6):1327–1367
Missiroli A (2004) The EU and its changing neighbourhood. In: Dannreuther R (ed) European Union foreign and security policy: towards a neighbourhood strategy. Routledge, London, pp 12–26
Prosser T (2005) The limits of competition law: markets and public services. OUP, Oxford

Ross M (2000) Article 16 EC and services of general interest: from derogation to obligation? Eur Law Rev 25:22–38
Ross M (2007) Promoting solidarity: public services to a European model of competition. Common Mark Law Rev 44:1057–1080
Ross M (2009) A healthy approach to services of general economic interest? The BUPA judgement of the Court of First Instance. Eur Law Rev 34:127–140
Sauter W (2008) Services of general economic interest and universal service in EU law. Eur Law Rev 33:167–193
Schweitzer H (2011) Services of general economic interest: European law's impact on the role of markets and of Member States. In: Cremona M (ed) Market integration and public services in the European Union. OUP, Oxford, pp 11–62
Schwintowski HP (2003) The common good, public subsistence and the functions of public undertakings in the European internal market. Eur Bus Organ Law Rev 4:353–382
Seeberg P (2010) The European Neighbourhood Policy, post-normativity and pragmatism. Eur Foreign Affairs Rev 15:663–680
Semmelmann C (2010) The European Union's economic constitution under the Lisbon Treaty: soul-searching shifts the focus to procedure. Eur Law Rev 35(4):516–542
Senden L (2005) Soft law in European community law. Hart Publishing, Oxford
Smith KE (2005) Engagement and conditionality: incompatible or mutually reinforcing? In: Youngs R (ed) Global Europe: new terms of engagement. The Foreign Policy Centre, London
Smith ME, Webber M (2008) Political dialogue and security in the European Neighbourhood Policy: the virtues and limits of 'new partnership perspective'. Eur Foreign Aff Rev 13(1):73–95
Steinicke M (2012) Trade in services. In: Olsen BE, Steinicke M, Engsig Sorensen K (eds) WTO law: from a European perspective. Kluwer Law International, The Hague, pp 321–352
Szyszczak E (2011) Introduction: why do public services challenge the European Union? In: Szyszczak E, Davies J, Andenæs M, Bekkedal T (eds) Developments in services of general interest. T.M.C. Asser Press, The Hague, pp 1–16
Tulmets E (2006) Adapting the experience of enlargement to the neighbourhood policy: the ENP as a substitute to enlargement? In: Kratochvil P (ed) The European Union and its neighbourhood: policies, problems and priorities. Institute of International Relations, Prague, pp 29–57
Van de Gronden JW (2009) The EU and WTO law on free trade in services and the public interest: towards a framework directive on services of general economic interest? In: van de Gronden JW (ed) The EU and WTO law on services: limits to the realisation of general interest policies within the services market. Kluwer Law International, The Hague, pp 249–279
Van de Gronden JW (2011) Social services of general interest and EU law. In: Szyszczak E, Davies J, Andenæs M, Bekkedal T (eds) Developments in services of general interest. T.M.C. Asser Press, The Hague, pp 123–153
Van Vooren B (2011a) External relations law of the EU and the European Neighbourhood Policy: a paradigm for coherence. Routledge, London
Van Vooren B (2011b) The European Union as an international actor and progressive experimentation in its neighbourhood. In: Koutrakos P (ed) European foreign policy: legal and political perspectives. Edward Elgar Publishing, Cheltenham, pp 147–171
Wallace W (2003) Looking after the neighbourhood: responsibilities for the EU-25. Notre Europe, Policy Papers no 4
Wernicke S (2009) Services of general economic interest in European law: solidarity embedded in the economic constitution. In: van de Gronden JW (ed) The EU and WTO law on services: limits to the realisation of general interest policies within the services market. Kluwer Law International, The Hague, pp 121–137
Zaiotti R (2007) Of friends and fences: Europe's Neighbourhood Policy and the 'gated' Community syndrome. Eur Integr 29(2):143–162

# Part III
# Specific Services Sectors

# Chapter 12
# Towards an International Regime of Regulating Electronic Communications

**Olga Batura**

**Abstract** This chapter compares the regulatory framework of telecommunications at the EU and the international level. It claims that the comparative superiority of the EU framework rests on technological cognisance and strong consideration of social needs. The chapter begins with a brief characterisation of the EU legal and regulatory framework for electronic communications. Against this background and in relation to it, the chapter provides an overview of the existing international legal and regulatory arrangements. In order to demonstrate the differences and similarities of the regimes more clearly, their correspondence to technological developments and on specifics of regulation of electronic communications as a public service is examined. The concluding section summarises the findings and discusses the lessons learnt from the EU experience and the EU's role in shaping an international regime for electronic communications.

## Contents



---

Lecturer in European Law.

---

O. Batura (✉)
European Humanities University and University of Bremen, Bremen, Germany
e-mail: batura@uni-bremen.de



M. Krajewski (ed.), *Services of General Interest Beyond the Single Market*, Legal Issues of Services of General Interest,
DOI 10.1007/978-94-6265-063-3_12

## 12.1 Introduction

The notion of electronic communications is quite a recent phenomenon, known only to a handful of legal orders. Among transnational regimes, so far only the European Union's (EU) legislation contains a precise notion of what electronic communications networks and services are. There, an electronic communications network refers to a transmission system which permits the conveyance of signals by wire, radio, optical or other electromagnetic means (Article 2(a) Framework Directive[1]). The generic definition is intended to cover all kinds of networks capable of and used for carriage of electromagnetic signals: satellite networks, circuit-switched and packet-switched fixed telecommunications networks, Internet, mobile terrestrial networks, electricity cable systems, networks for radio and television broadcasting and cable television networks.

An electronic communications service is a service which consists wholly or mainly in the conveyance of signals on electronic communications networks (Article 2(c) Framework Directive). This definition allows transport services, which transmit an electromagnetic signal, to be distinguished from content-related services, which provide or exercise editorial control over the transmitted information. It further delimits them from information society services (Recital 10 Framework Directive in conjunction with Article 1 Directive 98/34/EC[2]), which cover a wide range of online activities from e-commerce to professional services to online entertainment.[3]

The above concepts have developed only recently: throughout the 20th century electronic communications was synonymous with computer (or data) communications. When, due to technological advances, digitalisation of audio and video

[1]Directive 2002/21/EC of the European Parliament and of the Council of 7 March 2002 on a common regulatory framework for EC networks and services, amended by Regulation (EC) No 717/2007 of the European Parliament and of the Council of 27 June 2007 on roaming on public mobile telephone networks within the Community, OJ 2002 L 108.

[2]Directive 98/34/EC of the European Parliament and of the Council of 22 June 1998 laying down a procedure for the provision of information in the field of technical standards and regulations and of rules on Information Society services, OJ 1998 L 204/37.

[3]See Recital 18 Directive 2000/31/EC of the European Parliament and of the Council of 8 June 2000 on certain legal aspects of information society services, in particular electronic commerce, in the Internal Market, OJ 2000 L 178/1. This latter distinction is, however, not entirely clear due to deficiencies of the definition of information society services, which leaves open the question of whether at least some of them are simultaneously EC services. Also noted by Kariyawasam 2007, pp. 90–91.

analogue signals became possible, both telecommunications and broadcasting went (completely or partially) digital. Digitalisation has brought about a slow demise of dedicated communications networks which were built in order to optimally fulfil the specific requirements of particular kinds of analogue signals. Digital signal has the same binary form regardless of what it is carrying—audio, video, image or data—and can be sent over any network. The wider implications of this technological development have become known as convergence and are being felt far beyond communication technologies: on top of the amalgamation of broadcasting, IT and telecommunications, boundaries between relevant industries and markets are also blurring. It is only logical, therefore, that the EU has come to amend its legal framework in order to account for these changes in the communication environment (Recital 5 Framework Directive).

Thus, when talking about an international regime for electronic communications, one seems to adopt an EU perspective because such a notion does not exist at the international level yet. Yet, the adopted perspective is regime-specific only at first glance: electronic communications emerges due to technological convergence and the EU is simply one of the first regimes to recognise that and to reflect it in the legislation. Thus, it can be argued that the EU perspective is to a certain extent a technological and, therefore, universal one.

An examination of the international regime through the prism of electronic communications shall allow a better comparison between the EU and international levels and it shall shed more light on the deficits and fragmentation of international regulation. Ultimately, an analysis of the rules covering individual elements of electronic communications networks and services is aimed at uncovering comparative advantages of the EU experience and at a discussion of their transferability to the international level.

This chapter argues that the comparative superiority of the EU framework rests on two objective qualities that are conditioned by specifics of the sector: technological cognisance and strong consideration of social needs. Technological cognisance, understood as consideration of technological reality and technological possibilities in the regulation, is an indispensable feature of regulation of a famously technology-intensive sector. Consideration of social needs in electronic communications regulation reflects the enormous (and growing) importance of the EC sector for all aspects of our life and shall prevent technological determinism. Technology is shaped by society and legislation and regulation are the designer tools that project social expectations about the role of the respective technologies.

This chapter leaves assessment of the respective rules as an economic regulation largely untouched, firstly, in order not to go beyond the limited scope of the contribution and, secondly, because a comprehensive comparison between the international and EU levels in this regard is very complicated due to the very different nature and objectives of the regimes.

The discussion will consist of the following aspects. Section 12.2 intends a brief but, as much as possible, comprehensive characterisation of the EU legal and regulatory framework for electronic communications. Against this background and in relation to it, Sect. 12.3 provides an overview of the existing international legal and regulatory arrangements. In order to demonstrate the differences and similarities of the regimes more clearly, both Sections examine their correspondence to technological developments and on specifics of regulation of electronic communications as a public service. The concluding Sect. 12.4 summarises the findings and discusses the lessons learnt from the EU experience and the EU's role in shaping an international regime for electronic communications.

## 12.2 EU Regulatory Framework as a Prototype of International Regime for Electronic Communications

### *12.2.1 Technological Cognisance of the EU Regulatory Framework*

Having embraced technological convergence, the EU legal framework has largely abandoned the sectoral approach to regulation of communications and adopted a functional one instead. The sectoral approach, dominant in the 20th century, treated communications networks—broadcasting, telecommunications and IT—and communications services differently depending on over what network they were transported. By contrast, a functional approach reaches deeper, taking into account what the network or service is used for. Thus, it regards all the networks used for transmission of electromagnetic signals as a single infrastructure and all the services consisting wholly or mainly of conveyance of electromagnetic signals over those networks as transport services. Accordingly, a holistic regulation of these types of activity is adopted.

The most important expression of the functional approach—and one of the major regulatory novelties of the EU framework—is the idea of technological neutrality of regulation. It means that regulations shall not artificially promote certain technological choices above the others or discriminate in favour of use of a particular kind of technology (Recital 18 Framework Directive, Recital 25 Universal Service Directive[4]). Essentially, all electronic communications networks and services shall be treated the same disregarding the underlying transmission technology.

The departure from the sectoral approach has resulted in a tentative, most likely unintentional adoption of the so-called layered regulatory model.[5] Regulatory frameworks relevant for information and communications sectors are structured

[4]Directive 2002/22/EC of the European Parliament and of the Council of 7 March 2002 on universal service and users' rights relating to electronic communications networks and services, OJ 2002 L 108/51.

[5]Mindel and Sicker 2006, pp. 136–148; Frieden 2003, p. 248.

not vertically, along the lines of the industries of telecommunications, broadcasting and IT, but horizontally according to the layers, originally known from IP network architecture. In the EU level regulation, an explicit dividing line runs between the content layer, comprising the conveyed information, and the conduit/carrier layer, used for transporting the information. Some scholars, however, advocate a more subtle distinction with content, applications, transport and access layers being the bare necessity for regulatory purposes.[6]

The layered model combined with a functional approach allows for a more effective and precise regulation of market entry and market conditions[7]—central aspects of the sector-specific *ex ante* regulation that was introduced in the EU in order to ensure a transition from national telecommunications monopolies to the competitive internal market. The liberalised market for electronic communications already mainly relies on regulation through general competition law. However, occasional *ex ante* interventions are justified, for example, to create a level playing field for network operators and service providers and to promote effective competition in a technologically neutral manner and, eventually, at the infrastructural level.

While general competition law, naturally, covers all the market behaviour of providers of electronic communications networks and/or services, the mentioned sector-specific *ex ante* regulation addresses only the most critical issues. An in-depth study of the EU's sector-specific regulatory framework would go far beyond the scope of this contribution and, in fact, has been done elsewhere.[8] Therefore, this chapter confines itself to indicating some of the issues most relevant from the perspective of this contribution.

Internal market and effective competition mean equal conditions of competition for and in the market, not only for domestic and foreign providers but also—from the perspective of technological convergence—for legacy telecommunications providers and alternative providers, including operators of other networks originally used for different purposes and subject to different regulation. Regulation has to account for technologically and economically reasonable separation between networks, services and content, and address the specific problems of each subject-matter. For electronic communications networks operation and services provision, the convergence-related aspects are access to essential facilities and coordination of the performance of different networks—or, in other words, interconnection[9] and interoperability.[10] Because technological convergence drives the development in the direction of new generation networks (NGN)—an overarching network

[6]For a brief, but quite comprehensive overview of various layered models see Kariyawasam 2012, pp. 225–231.

[7]ACMA—Australian Communications and Media Authority, Converged legislative frameworks—International approaches. Occasional paper. http://www.acma.gov.au/~/media/Regulatory%20Frameworks/pdf/converged_legislative_frameworks_paper%20pdf. p. 2. Accessed 28 February 2014.

[8]To name just a few major studies, Nihoul and Rodford 2004; Koenig et al. 2009.

[9]See, for instance, K. Werbach, Only Connect. http://ssrn.com/abstract=964991. 20 February 2007. Accessed 28 February 2014.

[10]See Gasser and Palfrey 2007.

environment consisting of heterogeneous parts, the ability to interconnect and interoperability are central for the functioning of the diverse parts of NGN. Services carried, devices attached and applications used need to interoperate to cope with the infrastructure variety. Regulation that considers these aspects is not only technology-responsive, but also technology-fostering.

Measures of the Access Directive[11] cover a great many issues for a satisfactory provision of interconnection and interoperability. They address the possible technical barriers (technical specifications, network characteristics), economic complexities (accounting information, prices) and legal hurdles of public and private law nature (terms and conditions for use and supply, conditions limiting access to and/or use of services and applications). Measures directed at unbundling the local loop[12] require that physical access to it shall be granted at any feasible network point, even if facility sharing is necessary, and in a non-discriminatory technologically neutral manner. Restrictions, necessary to protect network integrity, shall also be technologically neutral and based on objective criteria defined in advance.

Harmonised numbering rules, especially promotion of the European Telephone Numbering Space, uniform policy on European access codes, emergency and social services, may facilitate convergence on the market. However, limited numbering portability, namely excluding porting of numbers between fixed and mobile networks, and the existence of geographic numbers somewhat hamper convergence from the user perspective.[13]

Indispensable for the provision of interconnection and for ensuring interoperability is the existence of common standards—or at least a common frame of reference. The Framework Directive (Article 17) prescribes the Commission to draw up and publish a list of non-compulsory standards and/or technical specifications and, where necessary, to request that standards be drawn up by the European standards organisations. Where interoperability has not been granted due to inadequate implementation of standards, the Commission may make certain standards compulsory (Article 17 paras 3–4 Framework Directive). A special case of standardisation is quality of service, regulated only tentatively in Article 22 Universal Service Directive[14] that intends to harmonise requirements with quality of electronic com-

[11]Directive 2002/19/EC of the European Parliament and of the Council of 7 March 2002 on access to, and interconnection of, EC networks and associated facilities, OJ 2002 L 108/7.

[12]Regulation (EC) No 2887/2000 of the European Parliament and of the Council of 18 December 2000 on unbundled access to the local loop, OJ 2000 L 36/4; Commission Recommendation 2000/417/EC of 25 May 2000 on unbundled access to the local loop: enabling the competitive provision of a full range of EC services including broadband multimedia and high-speed Internet, OJ 2000 L 156/44.

[13]For the relevant rules and restrictions, see Article 30 in conjunction with Annex I Part C of the Directive 2002/22/EC of the European Parliament and of the Council of 7 March 2002 on universal service and users' rights relating to EC networks and services, OJ 2002 L 108/51.

[14]Directive 2002/22/EC of the European Parliament and of the Council of 7 March 2002 on universal service and users' rights relating to EC networks and services, OJ 2002 L 108/51.

munications services, provided on a universal service basis within the EU internal market, as regards, for example, non-network and network performance.

The harmonious and comprehensive approach and regulatory system at the EU level crumbles slightly when an external dimension is considered in addition to the above described internal one. In its free trade agreements (FTAs), the EU has to seek a compromise between the innovative concepts and approach of its internal framework, demands of its counterparts and requirements of international trade law. A comprehensive analysis of the EU's FTAs will go beyond the scope of this contribution, therefore only several typical examples of deviation from the EU's domestic practices shall be named.

Most notable is the absence of the notion of electronic communications in the FTAs. Instead, the terms "telecommunications services" and "telecommunications networks" are used,[15] following the custom of international trade agreements (discussed further in Sect. 12.3). The content of this term slightly differs from FTA to FTA. While its definition is a broad one (Article 109(a) EU-Chile Agreement, Article 94 para 1(a) EU-CARIFORUM Agreement, Article 7.27 para 2(a) EU-Korea Agreement), the content is defined rather restrictively and includes either only basic telecommunications services in the sense of the GATS's "Services Sectoral classification list" (EU-Korea Agreement) or basic and some value-added telecommunications services (EU-Chile Agreement, EU-CARIFORUM Agreement). The approach is restrictive and technologically non-neutral, as will be explained further in Sect. 12.3 of this contribution, and it contradicts the EU's efforts at the international level, aimed at promotion of a functional approach and a greater alignment of the international framework with its internal framework through a reform of services classification in the telecommunications sector.[16]

Naturally, this has further implications for other relevant provisions of FTAs, which in general lag behind the technological developments in the sector. By contrast to the EU's internal framework, FTAs' rules can be said to follow the lines dividing the ICT sector according to technologies of signal transmission to a greater extent. One of the indicators for this is a rather detailed regulation of issues of interconnection between telecommunications networks, essential for international provision of telecommunications services (although in some FTAs it

[15]See, for instance, Section 3 of Agreement establishing an association between the European Community and its Member States, of the one part, and the Republic of Chile, of the other part, OJ 2002 L 352/3 (hereinafter—EU-Chile Agreement); Section 4 of Economic Partnership Agreement between the CARIFORUM States, of the one part, and the European Community and its Member States, of the other part, OJ 2008 L 289/I/3 (hereinafter—EU-CARIFORUM Agreement); Chapter Seven Section E Sub-Section D of Free Trade Agreement between the European Union and its Member States, of the one part, and the Republic of Korea, of the other part, OJ 2011 L 127/6 (hereinafter—EU-Korea Agreement).

[16]See WTO Council for Trade in Services Special Session Committee on Specific Commitments, Communication from the European Communities, Classification in the Telecom Sector under the WTO-GATS Framework, TN/S/W/27, S/CSC/W/44, 10 February 2005.

is limited only to major suppliers (EU-Chile Agreement) or to suppliers of public telecommunications networks and services (EU-Korea Agreement), but lack of provisions guaranteeing interoperability between various types of networks.

### *12.2.2 Consideration of Social Needs in the EU Regulatory Framework*

Technological sensitivity of regulation seems to be a sensible approach for both the economy and society as it does not promote unrealistic expectations and does not pose impossible requirements, and it can be more effective in terms of advancement of societal goals.

Speaking of social regulation of electronic services provision, one has to point out the great variety of social concerns addressed at the EU level. Security of usage of electronic communications networks and services is addressed by a great number of legislative measures. For instance, security of provision of connection and services is partially ensured by the Universal Service Directive, but also by several measures adopted within police and justice cooperation in criminal matters.[17] Data protection and privacy in the electronic communications sector are covered by harmonised rules, currently under reform.[18] Consumer rights issues regarding electronic communications are dealt with in the Universal Service Directive, while consumer protection regarding e-commerce is regulated by the e-Commerce Directive. Use of electronic communications for security purposes has its regulatory content in the Data Retention Directive[19] and in provisions on emergency services in the Universal Service Directive.

Implications of technological convergence for information pluralism—another social interest—are covered by two EU directives focusing on audiovisual

[17]For example, Council Framework Decision 2005/222/JHA of 24 February 2005 on attacks against information systems, OJ 2005 L 69/67.

[18]Directive 2002/58/EC of the European Parliament and of the Council of 12 July 2002 concerning the processing of personal data and the protection of privacy in the EC sector, OJ 2002 L 201/37. Directive 95/46/EC of the European Parliament and of the Council of 24 October 1995 on the protection of individuals with regard to the processing of personal data and on the free movement of such data, OJ 1995 L 281/31 will be soon superseded by a General Data Protection Regulation, see European Commission, Proposal for a Regulation of the European Parliament and of the Council on the protection of individuals with regard to the processing of personal data and on the free movement of such data (General Data Protection Regulation), COM(2012) 11 final, 25 January 2012.

[19]Directive 2006/24/EC of the European Parliament and of the Council of 15 March 2006 on the retention of data generated or processed in connection with the provision of publicly available EC services or of public communications networks and amending Directive 2002/58/EC, OJ 2006 L 105/54.

services.[20] At the same time, regulatory activities in the field of electronic communications shall account for the links between the carrier and content levels in order to guarantee media pluralism and cultural diversity (Recital 5 Framework Directive).

The immense significance of access to information and the role of communication of any kind (political, economic, cultural, personal) in the emerging "digital age" substantiates the primary societal interest in having quality network access everywhere and at affordable cost. Over this access one should be able to use electronic communications services necessary to fulfil individual communication needs. The EU Universal Service Directive, drafted in a technologically neutral manner, ensures that in case of a market failure to provide an established minimum of electronic communications services of a particular quality and at an affordable price, a special mechanism of designation of a universal service provider, which can use any technology to accomplish its mission, can be employed.[21]

Regulation of universal service provision at the EU level is a substantive one; both the concept and the instrument of its realisation are drafted in great detail resulting in full harmonisation of most of its aspects. The Universal Service Directive determines an EU-wide minimum set of services to be available on the universal service basis (Articles 4–7 USD); it specifies their quality (Article 11 USD) and provides for guarantees for price and affordability (Articles 3 and 9 USD). It further establishes the primacy of the market as a means of universal service provision and regulates the conditions and form of state intervention in this context (Recitals 3–5 and Article 1 para 1 and Article 3 USD). For this purpose, in place of the former national tools of *Daseinsvorsorge* and *service public* it introduces a universal service instrument, which takes the form of universal service obligations imposed on designated providers, selected in a special procedure (Article 8 USD). The Universal Service Directive also foresees that a non-market provision of universal service may require special financing arrangements: according to Articles 12–13 USD where universal service obligation results in an unfair financial burden for a designated provider, the excessive cost can be compensated either through a special fund or by cost sharing with other electronic communications providers.

Implementation falls on Member States (Article 3 para 1 USD) who have relatively little discretion in selection of the means to secure the EU-defined goals: they are to establish an affordable price in the light of the national conditions

[20]Council Directive 89/552/EEC of 3 October 1989 on the coordination of certain provisions laid down by Law, Regulation or Administrative Action in Member States concerning the pursuit of television broadcasting activities, OJ 1989 L 298/23; Directive 2010/13/EU of the European Parliament and of the Council of 10 March 2010 on the coordination of certain provisions laid down by law, regulation or administrative action in Member States concerning the provision of audiovisual media services (Audiovisual Media Services Directive), OJ 2010 L 095/1. For critical assessment of both documents from the convergence perspective see Geach 2008.

[21]For shortcomings in terms of technological neutrality of universal service regulation see, for example, Bohlin and Teppayayon 2009, p. 283.

(Article 9 para 2 USD); they can determine the number of designated universal service providers and the procedure of their designation (Article 8 USD) and choose one of the methods of financing suggested by the Universal Service Directive (Article 13 para 1 USD).

Questions of social regulation relevant for bilateral trade in telecommunications services are addressed in a strikingly different way in the EU's FTAs. The EU-Chile and EU-Korea Agreements contain a provision on universal service declaring a sovereign right of each Party to define the kind of universal service obligations for itself and requiring guarantees for non-discrimination and competitive neutrality for their administration to be set (Article 115 and Article 7.34 respectively). By comparison, Article 94 para 1(f) and Article 100 EU-CARIFORUM Agreement sound like a summary of the Universal Service Directive and contain all the main elements of the EU's universal service concept: a particular set of services, a specified quality, an affordable price, possibility of designation of an operator to fulfil universal service obligation.[22] These rules constitute a more sensible limitation on the legislative sovereignty of the Parties, but bind all of them to the benchmark set by the EU. To this end, one can speak of export of the EU universal service model and regulation.[23] Arguably, such export is made possible by the relatively less developed telecommunications law and policy of the CARIFORUM states and their weaker negotiation position, on the one hand, as well as by their aim to establish a CARICOM Single Market and Economy[24] and therefore their inclination to adopt the European experience, on the other hand.

### *12.2.3 European Framework for Electronic Communications—A Holistic Regime?*

At the EU level there is a unique case of a holistic regulation of electronic communications networks and services for the internal market. The extensive framework seems to cover most of the issues significant for market provision of the subject matter, yet it goes much further than simple economic regulation considering most seriously such factors as technological development and social interests. Remarkably, the EU framework is mainly aimed at creation of an internal market in electronic communications (the EU does not have other competences in regulation of electronic communications), yet it seems to respond well to wider societal concerns and contains rules of social regulation, most prominently universal service, for the whole internal market. The level of detail and the depth of

[22]For a more detailed examination see Krajewski 2011, pp. 231–252.

[23]Krajewski 2011, p. 247, comes to the same conclusion.

[24]Revised Treaty of Chaguaramas Establishing the Caribbean Community Including the CARICOM Single Market and Economy Community of 2001. http://www.caricom.org/jsp/community/revised_treaty-text.pdf. Accessed 28 February 2014.

responsiveness of the EU regulation, which are almost national-law-like, can be taken as a benchmark of what is possible at a transnational level (as well as evidence of a high degree of integration).

However, externally the EU bears away from its internal approach, at times considerably. Only the EU-CARIFORUM Agreement stands out as an example of the transfer of the internal model to external rules. In agreements with other more technologically savvy and economically and politically weighty counterparts the EU follows the approach developed in the GATS.

## 12.3 Overview of International Rules for Electronic Communications

### *12.3.1 An Incomplete "Who Is Who" of International Regulations on Electronic Communications*

At the global level, several organisations possess competences in regulating different aspects of electronic communications. Arguably, the most comprehensive mandate belongs to the oldest international organisation—the International Telecommunications Union (ITU). Its overall objective can be summarised as the "establishment and maintenance of international telecommunications on a general basis".[25] In detail its objectives are listed in Article 1 ITU Constitution[26] and include maintaining and extending international cooperation, promoting and offering technical assistance to developing countries, promoting the development of technical facilities and their efficient operation, extending the benefits of new technologies, promoting the use of telecommunications for peaceful relations, and harmonising the actions of ITU members to achieve these and other objectives.

The ITU is an intergovernmental organisation with the Plenipotentiary Conference of the State Members being its supreme organ that determines general policies and decides on other important questions of the ITU's existence and functioning (Articles 8–9 ITU Constitution). The Council, elected by the Plenipotentiary Conferences from the State Members, carries out every-day administrative functions (Article 10 ITU Constitution) and other international conferences adopt decisions on specific questions. However, the main substantive work is done in the Sectors, which are organised thematically as the Radiocommunication Sector (ITU-R), the Telecommunication Standardisation Sector (ITU-T) and the newest one, created as a result of the institutional reform in the 1990s, the Telecommunication Development Sector (ITU-D) (Articles 12–24 ITU Constitution).

---

[25] Lyall 2011, p. 131.

[26] Constitution and Convention of the International Telecommunication Union: Final Acts of the Additional Plenipotentiary Conference, Geneva, 22 December 1992, Geneva: ITU, 2011. http://www.itu.int/pub/S-CONF-PLEN-2011/en. Accessed 28 February 2014.

Being an international organisation, the ITU can set legally binding rules only in the forms accepted by international public law.[27] According to Article 4.1 ITU Constitution, only the Constitution itself, the ITU Convention and the administrative regulations bind the Member States in their own operations. A vast majority of the documents produced by the Sectors are substantive recommendations which have a non-binding character. However, they are generally observed by the States, other types of Members[28] and non-state actors due to requirements regarding international provision of telecommunications and restrictions of the laws of physics[29] and can be therefore described as "authoritative law".[30]

The transmission of information over the "network of networks" uses telecommunications channels and therefore should be subject to the ITU regulation.[31] However, due to the history of Internet development, central questions of Internet regulation, namely routing protocols, administration of top-level domains and allocation of Internet numbering resources, have happened to slip the ITU's reach. The functions which have been named are carried out by the Internet Corporation for Assigned Names and Numbers (ICANN) which is a unique global governance body: it is a non-profit private law entity, incorporated in California, which performs its tasks under a contract with the US government.[32] The ITU only participates as an observer in the Governmental Advisory Committee (GAC) and has not managed so far to get a foot in the door of the regulation of vital Internet infrastructure issues due to strong opposition from the United States and bitter disappointment on the part of developing countries.[33] Nevertheless, the ITU and the ICANN have been cooperating on some issues as there are a number of fields of

[27]On the ITU law-making from the public international law perspective see an insightful analysis by Hinricher 2004.

[28]The ITU has categories of Sector and Associate membership for non-state actors, such as network operators, equipment manufacturers, service providers, NGOs, academia and other. Their rights are limited in comparison to State Members, most notably in respect of voting at Plenipotentiary Conferences. At the same time, they are numerous (currently over 700) and exercise a serious influence on the agenda of the ITU and on the content of the documents adopted by the Sectors. See alternative approval procedure for standards in Recommendation ITU-T A.8 (10/2008) "Alternative approval process for new and revised ITU-T Recommendations" and MacLean 2007, p. 34.

[29]Lyall 2011, p. 164.

[30]D. Westphal, International Telecommunication Union (ITU). Max Planck Encyclopedia of Public International Law. http://opil.ouplaw.com/view/10.1093/law:epil/9780199231690/law-9780199231690-e514?rskey=1mYV3z&result=3&prd=EPIL, para 24. Accessed 28 February 2014.

[31]Lyall 2011, pp. 188–189.

[32]See http://www.icann.org/en/about/welcome.

[33]For a detailed account of the battle over the domain governance see Mueller 2002; Kleinwächter 2009; S. Simpson, The Evolution of International Policy Agendas in the Regulation of Electronic Communications: the Internet and Telecommunications. http://usir.salford.ac.uk/18397/3/IPSAECPR%252817.1.11%2529.pdf. 2011. Accessed 28 February 2014.

common interest for the two organisations,[34] and the ITU continues to work on many Internet-related issues, like cybersecurity, combatting spam and the digital divide. Although the decisions, adopted by the ICANN, are not legally binding, they are "more widely and more strictly accepted and respected than binding decisions of most international organisations", according to some observers,[35] due to the obvious reason that they are indispensable for the operation of the Internet.[36]

In the mid-1990s the regulatory centre of telecommunications shifted to the newly established World Trade Organisation (WTO) that played a prominent role in the liberalisation of trade in services and promotion of foreign direct investment. With the adoption of the General Agreement on Trade in Services (GATS), trade aspects of various communications services fell under the scope of this international organisation's competence.

According to Article I GATS, no services sector, traded in one of the four modes, is apriori excluded from the general obligations of most favoured nation treatment (MFN) and transparency (Articles II and III GATS respectively). Thus, the GATS covers telecommunications services, computer and data processing services, and audiovisual services (broadcasting and information services)—all listed in the "Services Sectoral classification list" (W/120).[37] Besides, according to the Annex on Telecommunications, services suppliers, depending on their activity on public telecommunications networks, and services shall have access to them under non-discriminatory conditions (Article 1 Annex). Just like MFN and transparency, the Annex on Telecommunications represents a horizontal obligation and applies to all GATS signatories.

Besides general obligations, GATS Members may enter into specific commitments only regarding particular services, outlined in detail in schedules of commitments. Specific commitments include market access (Article XVI GATS), national treatment (Article XVII GATS) and additional commitments (Article XVIII GATS), the latter—only for basic telecommunications—contained in the Reference Paper on regulatory principles.

Thus, the WTO legal framework for electronic communications consists of mainly liberalising rules with a few regulatory provisions, that cover only few electronic communications services and were adopted to account for various domestic concerns in order to promote free international trade. Regulation of telecommunications services provision is, however, of great importance in this context because the network character of the industry in question requires coordination and cooperation in order to provide for interconnection and interoperability

[34]See H. Zhao, ITU-T and ICANN reform. http://www.itu.int/ITU-T/tsb-director/itut-icann/ICANN%20Reform.pdf. 17 April 2002. Accessed 28 February 2014; L-R. Chetty, A new season of cooperation between ICANN and ITU. http://itu4u.wordpress.com/2012/12/05/a-new-season-of-cooperation-between-icann-and-itu/. 5 December 2012. Accessed 28 February 2014.

[35]Hartwig 2010, p. 576.

[36]Wessel 2011, p. 85.

[37]WTO, Services Sectoral classification list, Note by the Secretariat, MTN.GNS/W/120, 10 July 1991.

between separately developed national systems. Thus, activities of the ICANN, the ITU and other standardisation organisations are taken into consideration by the GATS (Article XXVI GATS, para 6 Annex on Telecommunications).

### *12.3.2 International Rules and the Pace of Technological Change in Electronic Communications*

General observations on the technological up-to-dateness of regulation at the international level are difficult due to the specifics of each international organisation in question. As a reminder, electronic communications networks encompass all types of networks capable of and used for transmission of electromagnetic signals, namely broadcasting, telecommunications and data networks, wired and wireless. Such a notion is absent at the international level, which obscures the regulatory landscape. The ITU deals with telecommunications in the broadest sense, covering all communications networks and services that involve transmission of an electromagnetic signal. Their definition is strikingly similar to 'electronic communications' in the EU legal framework: Telecommunications are any transmission, emission or reception of signs, signals, writing, images and sounds or intelligence of any nature by wire, radio, optical or other electromagnetic systems (Article 2.1 International Telecommunication Regulations[38]). Hence, the ITU definition distinguishes transport level from the content and is comparable with the EU's notion of electronic communications.

The terminology used by the other organisations complicates the matter. As indicated above, the ICANN focuses solely on communications over IP networks, which also fall under the definition of the ITU's subject-matter. Under the GATS, due to the positive list approach to scheduling, different types of communications services are treated differently: all of them are subject to most favoured nation and transparency principles, but all other commitments differ considerably across sectors and countries and, actually, only the limited category of basic telecommunications services is regulated relatively comprehensively.[39] Thus, while the ITU and the ICANN keep pace with technological development,[40] the GATS is lagging seriously behind both due to the use of the outdated classification list W/120[41] and the distinction between basic and value-added services, not justifiable from

[38]International Telecommunication Regulations: Final Acts of the World Conference on International Telecommunications, Dubai 2012.

[39]Difference in treatment of communications service is concisely, but accurately outlined by Luff 2012, pp. 81–84.

[40]This statement needs to be somewhat qualified in relation to the ITU: one of the central issues of telecommunications services provision—tariff and accounting principles—seems to be quite outdated and cries for reform. Yet, due to political reasons, this step has been taken only half-heartedly. See, for example, Cowhey 2004, pp. 34–50; Guermazi 2004, pp. 83–129.

[41]Zhao 2003/2004, pp. 8–9; Weber and Burri 2012.

technological and regulatory points of view.[42] Principally, the GATS continues to follow the sectoral approach that was dominant at the time of the GATS's conception and is therefore not technologically neutral.[43]

Putting aside this serious shortcoming, the content of the international rules of all organisations, similarly to the EU rules, focuses on interconnection and interoperability. Another significant issue in international cooperation refers to common efficient use of scarce resources, such as numbering, radio frequencies and geostationary orbit slots. The reasons for these priorities are, however, different from the motives of the European legislators. Due to the historically conditioned differences in national communications networks, equipment and standards,[44] common arrangements on interconnection and interoperability are absolutely indispensable for a cross-border provision of communications services. The necessity of orchestrating the allocation of scarce resources is based mainly on the conflicting claims and interests of nation states rather than the creation of a level playing field for different technologies.

To this end, the regulations of the three organisations can be said to complement each other. Thus, for interconnection and interoperability, the GATS sets up a regulatory framework of a principled nature, however, only for telecommunications. Broadcasting and IT services, among which are both content and transport services, are subject mainly to horizontal obligations of most favoured nation treatment and transparency. The GATS reaches beyond the purely technical framework for the operation of the telecommunications industry and addresses the economic and legal factors, hinting at a particular form of provision, namely through the market. The GATS Annex on Telecommunications prescribes provision of access to public telecommunications transport networks and services for all—also broadcasting, information and data—services providers, using them, on reasonable and non-discriminatory terms and conditions. The GATS Reference Paper on regulatory principles applies to basic telecommunications and lays out conditions for effective competition in provision of such services internationally: public availability of licensing criteria in order to enter the market (Section 4 PR), guarantee of interconnection under non-discriminatory, transparent and reasonable conditions (Section 2 RP), and access to essential facilities and commercially relevant information necessary to provide services (Section 1 RP). The ITU and ICANN rules and standards complete the regulatory framework with detailed provisions necessary for operation in the communications industry within their mandates. The ITU addresses transmission issues concerning all kinds of communications, while the ICANN deals with IP networks. Standards and recommendations adopted cover a wide range of transmission related issues from procedures and practices to compatibility between equipment to operating protocols for all kinds of networks to security of networks.

[42]For example, Bronckers and Larouche 2008, p. 325; Burkart 2007.

[43]Luff 2012, pp. 84–85.

[44]Tegge 1994, pp. 28–30, 37–38.

The interplay of the WTO, the ITU and ICANN rules in the similar format as indicated above continues in the field of scarce resources, especially frequencies, numbering and rights of way (Section 6 RP). The GATS Reference Paper on regulatory principles—in relation to basic telecommunications—requires their allocation in an objective, timely, transparent and non-discriminatory manner. Technically minded, the ITU administers international numbering resources for different types of communications, while the ICANN deals with Internet numbering resources. Furthermore, due to specifics of the mandate, the use of the radio frequency spectrum both for terrestrial and space communications and the use of the geostationary satellite orbit are managed by the ITU. For this, the ITU administers the Master International Frequency Register, undertakes studies into the technical issues and resolves disputes. In the ITU's activity technical and physical laws play the central role: economic factors may be taken into account only when comparing technical or operational alternatives.[45]

All in all, jointly the ITU, the GATS and the ICANN cover major issues from the perspective of technological developments in electronic communications. Interconnection, interoperability and joint management of scarce resources are as necessary for the international provision of communications as they are indispensable for the convergence of communications technologies. At least the general principles of the GATS—objectivity, transparency, non-discrimination—will remain relevant for the environment where providers using different communications technologies compete against each other, as the EU's experience shows.

Unfortunately, technical, financial and procedural aspects reach only as far as the competences of the organisation adopting the rules allow. Technological aptness of the regulation is to this end relative and limited, which may potentially deter technological development and the spread of its benefits across the globe. Besides, the use of divergent services classifications and definitions causes overlaps and legal uncertainty for providers. This may have adverse implications for international trade and competition as well as the development of (new) markets and communication products.

### *12.3.3 Elements of Social Regulation at the International Level*

Social problématique of electronic communications networks and services provision is to some extent addressed by the intergovernmental organisations the ITU and the WTO, while, by contrast, social concerns are largely neglected by the ICANN.[46] The ICANN does not "promote the global public interest", but instead

[45] Lyall 2011, p. 160.

[46] See the comparative legitimacy study by Take 2012, esp. at pp. 14–15.

concerns only the "operational stability" of the IP communications networks and the means for achievement of this goal are limited and relate to particular issues of operability (safety, interconnectivity).[47]

The coverage by the ITU, especially regarding the public service nature of telecommunications services, is most extensive. The ITU's International Telecommunication Regulations[48] contain some provisions of socio-political nature, related to the concept of universal service. Accordingly, the signatory State Members have to ensure a sufficient supply of international telecommunications facilities and services to meet the demand. Besides, they are to improve their availability to the public. By national laws and to the greatest extent practicable, Member States shall endeavour to ensure satisfactory quality of service of at least a form of telecommunication service which is reasonably accessible to the public. Within its standardisation activities, the ITU-T has extensively addressed questions of the quality of service regarding both different kinds of communications services and networks.[49]

Related to universal service, the problem of digital divide has been one of the primary focuses of the ITU's attention for decades. The ITU is to promote the extension of the benefits of the new information and communication technologies to all the world's inhabitants and it is to do so by fostering and offering technical assistance to developing countries, mobilising human capital, material and financial resources. The special ITU-D Sector attends to these tasks diligently.

Other socially important aspects of communications—personal data protection, privacy protection, consumer rights—are being studied by special groups of the ITU,[50] but no regulatory measures of any kind have been produced so far. Emergency use of electronic communications is dealt with by both the Radiocommunication and Standardisation Sectors.

Despite the ITU's active efforts in the field mentioned, their results are quite modest. It can be argued that one of the main reasons for this is that social policy is a sensitive matter for State Members and heavy-duty legal instruments are not usually used to address them at the international level directly. Another important factor is the fact that cooperation on socially important matters is not essential for cross-border communication or, rather, is necessary only to a certain, quite limited extent. Each nation state takes care of the social needs of its citizens according to

---

[47]See para 3 of Articles of incorporation of Internet Corporation for Assigned Names and Numbers.

[48]See Articles 3–4 International Telecommunication Regulations: Final Acts of the World Conference on International Telecommunications, Dubai 2012.

[49]See http://www.itu.int/en/ITU-T/studygroups/2013-2016/12/Pages/default.aspx. Accessed 28 February 2014.

[50]See, for instance ITU, Privacy in cloud computing. ITU-T Technology Watch Report. http://www.itu.int/dms_pub/itu-t/oth/23/01/T23010000160001PDFE.pdf. March 2012. Accessed 28 February 2014; ITU, Regulation and consumer protection in a converged environment. http://www.itu.int/en/ITU-D/Regulatory-Market/Documents/Regulation%20and%20consumer%20protection.pdf. March 2013. Accessed 28 February 2014.

the political and legal requirements of the day and economic possibilities. At the international level, the efforts often aim at securing the national provision and not interfering with more important common international interests.

A vivid example of the latter logic is the requirements for domestic provision of universal service in basic telecommunications by the Member States in the GATS. Due to its potential to obstruct an effective liberalisation of trade in telecommunications services[51] (but also in other services), this was a pivotal issue which is explicitly dealt with in Section 3 of the GATS Reference Paper on regulatory principles. The right of each Member to define a national universal service is recognised; the sole limitation is the scope of commitments and application of the Reference Paper, which applies only to basic telecommunications services. What can, however, create trade barriers is not so much universal service scope, but the mode of its realisation. Therefore, the principles for the design of domestic regulation of universal service provision have a procedural character. They require the respective universal service obligations to be administered in a transparent, non-discriminatory and competitively neutral manner and to be no more burdensome than necessary for the kind of universal service the Members wish to maintain.

Digital divide is not directly a trade issue and is therefore not addressed by the GATS. The GATS Annex on Telecommunications only contains a developing countries clause (Sections 5(g) and 6).

All in all, socially important issues related to electronic communications are insufficiently addressed at the international level. As regards the range of socially-relevant topics picked out, researched and/or brought to global attention, the ITU definitely stands out. But the ITU lacks teeth, and its modest efforts are overshadowed by the trade-enhancing rules of the GATS.[52] Among the reasons for this state of affairs is the lack of strong competences in this field, as indicated above, conditioned by the lack of interest and feeling of common concern. Partially overlapping competences and absence of a consistent approach to electronic communications among the three organisations exacerbate the situation not only due to an inadequate level of services liberalisation, but also because of inconsistent social regulation.

### *12.3.4 Fragmented Regulation at the International Level?*

A "one-shop" regulation of the kind found at the EU level does not exist at the international level. Instead, several international organisations are responsible for different aspects of electronic communications. This situation is conditioned by the history of communications technologies. Different communications technologies

---

[51] Batura 2011, p. 270.

[52] See *Mexico—Measures Affecting Telecommunications Services*, Report of the Panel, WT/DS204/R; Batura 2011, p. 271.

developed at different times and separately from each other, focusing on transmission of particular content and services. In addition to this, there is the strong governmental interest in communications that resulted in the technical and economic specifics of communications networks deployment and maintenance, and in different equipment and standards developed according to local requirements, meaning communication could not freely flow across national borders.[53] The fragmented character of international cooperation as well as the body of correspondent international law reflects the needs to address issues of common concern (e.g. emergency communications), issues essential for the effective functioning of cross-border communications (e.g. standardisation and interconnection at national borders) and issues necessary to secure communications within national borders (e.g. avoidance of harmful interference of wireless communications). With the growing importance of international trade in services, cooperation on economic aspects of communications is added to this list.

At first glance, international regulation looks heterogeneous and fragmentary: at least three international organisations have their say in the regulation of electronic communications with none of them clearly having the upper hand. Even though at the moment it looks as though the GATS is becoming the most influential,[54] this does not turn the WTO into the defining regulatory hub. The overall confusion is enhanced by overlaps in competences, differences in regulatory approaches (functional versus sectoral), a varying level of binding force and a different degree of clarity of the provisions. In this situation, in the absence of a clear hierarchy of norms or other conflict law rules, potential conflicts are to be solved through less satisfactory "consideration rules" and cooperation mechanisms between the organisations mentioned above (cooperation agreements, observer statuses, common working groups).

Yet, impressively, the remit of issues covered at the international level is on a par with the coverage by the EU framework, so that fragmentation in this regard is less noticeable. Technologically important questions and social needs recur at both levels and in all organisations which can be explained first and foremost by the network character of the industry (economics and externalities are the same) and global nature of technological advance (also conditioned by the network character of the industry). The central social aspects and implications of electronic communications—especially the necessity of universal service provision and challenges of digital divide—are taken into consideration to a degree. Regrettably, the arrangements on socially important issues lose out by comparison to the regulation of other issues: the approaches of the ITU, the WTO and the ICANN range from complete neglect (ICANN) to an inferiority of social issues in relation to trade issues (WTO) to special high-level attention, yet without serious means of influence (ITU).

[53]Tegge 1994, p. 30.

[54]*Mexico—Measures Affecting Telecommunications Services*, Report of the Panel, WT/DS204/R, paras 7.168–7.184.

## 12.4 Towards an International Regime for Electronic Communications

Considering the above conclusions about the international regime of regulating electronic communications and keeping in mind the achievements at the EU level, one cannot but wonder what direction the international-level regulation may take and, of course, what developments are desirable.

The EU framework as a prototype demonstrates what regulation is possible beyond a nation state. Yet the EU experience is likely to remain mainly just that. Due to the specifics of the EU legal order and very particular objectives of European integration, the EU experience can only be transferred to the international level in few instances (at least at the moment). The most plausible candidates for this are the general regulatory approach (functional instead of sectoral), the regulatory principle of technological neutrality and possibly even the notion of electronic communications or at least a revision of the notion of telecommunications. Especially in the field of telecommunications, the WTO/GATS framework was greatly inspired by the respective EU regulatory framework. Besides, the EU remains one of the biggest markets in the respective field and boasts a modern innovative regulation for it. Yet, most importantly, with the adoption of the functional regulatory approach, the principle of technological neutrality and a new notion for communications, the EU has kept pace with technological and market developments. These changes are objective and universal and cannot be reversed or ignored at the international level much longer. It seems that a proper, coordinated regulatory reaction to them is just a matter of time, especially considering the fact that the ICANN is basically a product of technological developments and the ITU is taking tentative, largely non-binding steps in the same direction.[55] The EU is working on transferring its experience to the GATS framework: its negotiations proposal for the telecommunications sector reflects the internal approach and, where possible, it exports its regulatory model through FTAs.

Can dynamism and depth of regulation, similar to the EU regime, be expected at the international level? The first answer to come to mind is negative: due to the great number of actors involved and the diversity of their agendas, decision-making in even the most narrowly specialised organisations takes years and contains only the most general aspects. However, even a quick glance at work and developments in the ITU and the ICANN prove this answer wrong. Both organisations—to a different extent—make use of new forms of governance and

[55]Such simple, yet fundamental changes at the international level are necessary and overdue which is also understood by some actors of the international community. See, for example, WTO Council for Trade in Services, Telecommunication Services, Background Note by the Secretariat, S/C/W/299, 10 June 2009; WTO Council for Trade in Services Special Session, Communication from Australia, Negotiating Proposal for Telecommunications Services, S/CSS/W/17, 5 December 2000; WTO Council for Trade in Services Special Session, Communication from Switzerland, GATS 2000: Telecommunications, S/CSS/W/72, 4 May 2001.

decision-making[56] which results in relatively prompt adoption of comprehensive detailed normative documents mainly in the form of standards. The specifics of the sector—its network and its large technological component—require intense expert knowledge and more detailed regulation internationally than some other services sectors.

As regards social concerns, a proper detailed, legally binding regulation at the international level is, however, less likely in the near future. As mentioned above, none of the venues has the necessary competences and/or teeth to exercise them. The states are not necessarily willing to radically reform this situation: to take just one example, the interest in bridging the digital divide and providing everyone with a proper electronic communications set-up is shared by the international community only superficially. The actual understanding of the problem and the proposed solutions vary greatly between countries. Besides, first and foremost, countries attend to their own domestic digital divide before turning to search for effective solutions for the international one.

The situation at the international level seems to suggest possibilities of institutional clashes and turf wars[57] due to the proliferation of international organisations with competences on the subject matter which does not disintegrate, but—on the contrary—emerges as one entity as a result of the amalgamation of different subjects. This will further fragment electronic communications regulation. Against this background, is an EU-style venue for general regulation of electronic communications possible at the international level?

At the moment, it seems as though all three organisations are precluded from assuming this role due to the constraints of their competences: specialisation and focus on very particular objectives means that each organisation covers only some aspects of electronic communications. Competition law that could catch some of the issues through *ex post* intervention does not exist at the international level: the GATS framework contains only a few competitive safeguards in order to ensure an effective opening-up of the previously monopolistic national markets.[58] However, the organisation coming closest to a general regulator—the ITU—may have potential. Its own history shows that bringing together separate but related regulatory bodies under one roof and under one general framework is reasonable and beneficial: The modern ITU is a result of the fusion of the International Telegraph Union and the International Radio Union in 1932, which until then mainly functioned completely independently of one another.[59]

---

[56]On this subject for the ICANN see Mueller 2010; for the ITU see Noll 2001; MacLean 2003; S. Simpson, The Evolution of International Policy Agendas in the Regulation of Electronic Communications: the Internet and Telecommunications. http://usir.salford.ac.uk/18397/3/IPSAE CPR%252817.1.11%2529.pdf. 2011. Accessed 28 February 2014.

[57]The ongoing battle over Internet regulation between the ITU and ICANN mentioned previously (see n 33) and an earlier battle over telecommunications regulation between the WTO and ITU, see Frühbrodt 2002; Tegge 1994.

[58]See especially Preamble and Section 1 GATS Reference Paper on regulatory principles.

[59]Lyall 2011, pp. 17–73.

Yet the probability and desirability of a holistic regulation by one organisation—for the time being—are questionable. Although it makes sense in terms of bringing all the relevant issues to one forum and efficiency savings due to the absence of need for coordination, such a solution may strain its decision-making capacity, as the stalled WTO Doha Round negotiations demonstrate. Multiple specialised forums allow for small successes and partial advances, which may develop spill-over effects and be transferred to other forums due to shared membership.

## References


Batura O (2011) Embedded transnational markets for telecommunications services. In: Joerges C, Falke J (eds) Karl Polanyi, globalisation and the potential of law in transnational markets. Hart Publishing, Oxford, pp 255–275

Bohlin E, Teppayayon O (2009) Broadband universal service: a future path for Europe? Int J Manag Netw Econ 1:275–298

Bronckers M, Larouche P (2008) A review of the WTO regime for telecommunications services. In: Alexander K, Andenæs M (eds) The World Trade Organization and trade in services. Martinus Nijhoff Publishers, Leiden, pp 319–379

Burkart P (2007) Moving targets: introducing mobility into universal service obligations. Telecommun Policy 31:164–178

Cowhey P (2004) Accounting rates, cross-border services and the next WTO round on basic telecommunications services. In: Geradin D, Luff D (eds) The WTO and global convergence in telecommunications and audio-visual services. CUP, Cambridge, pp 34–50

Frieden R (2003) Adjusting the horizontal and vertical in telecommunications regulation: a comparison of the traditional and a new layered approach. Fed Commun Law J 55:207–250

Frühbrodt L (2002) Die Liberalisierung der Telekommunikationsdienste. Vom nationalen Monopol zum globalen Wettbewerb. Deutscher Universitäts-Verlag, Wiesbaden

Gasser U, Palfrey J (2007) Fostering innovation and trade in the global information society: the different facets and roles of interoperability. In: Burri M, Cottier T (eds) Trade governance in the digital age. CUP, Cambridge, pp 123–153

Geach N (2008) Converging regulation for convergent media: an overview of the Audiovisual Media Services Directive. J Inf Law Technol 8(1). http://go.warwick.ac.uk/jilt/2008_1/geach

Guermazi B (2004) Reforming international accounting rates: a developing country perspective. In: Geradin D, Luff D (eds) The WTO and global convergence in telecommunications and audio-visual services. CUP, Cambridge, pp 83–129

Hartwig M (2010) ICANN—Governance by technical necessity. In: Von Bogdandy A, Wolfrum R, Von Bernstorff J, Dann P, Goldmann M (eds) The exercise of public authority by international institutions: advancing international institutional law. Springer, Heidelberg, pp 575–605

Hinricher J (2004) The law-making of the International Telecommunication Union (ITU)—providing a new source of international law? Zeitschrift für ausländisches öffentliches Recht und Völkerrecht 64:489–501

Kariyawasam R (2007) International economic law and the digital divide: a new silk road? Edward Elgar, Cheltenham

Kariyawasam R (2012) Better regulation of digital markets: a new look at the reference paper. In: Burri M, Cottier T (eds) Trade governance in the digital age. CUP, Cambridge, pp 225–231

Kleinwächter W (2009) Multistakeholderism and the IGF: laboratory, clearinghouse, watchdog. In: Drake W (ed) Internet governance: creating opportunities for all. UN Department of Economic and Social Affairs, New York, pp 76–90

Koenig C, Bartosch A, Braun J-D (eds) (2009) EC competition and telecommunications law. Kluwer Law International, The Hague

Krajewski M (2011) Universal service provisions in international agreements of the EU: from derogation to obligation? In: Szyszczak E, Davies J, Andenæs M, Bekkedal T (eds) Developments in services of general interest. T.M.C. Asser Press, The Hague, pp 231–252

Luff D (2012) Convergence: a buzzword to remain? In: Burri M, Cottier T (eds) Trade governance in the digital age. CUP, Cambridge

Lyall F (2011) The international telecommunications union and the universal postal union. Ashgate, Farnham

MacLean D (2003) The quest for inclusive governance of global ICTs: lessons from the ITU in the limits of national sovereignty. Inf Technol Int Dev 1:1–18

MacLean D (2007) International Telecommunication Union (ITU). Global information society watch, pp 29–38

Mindel J, Sicker D (2006) Leveraging the EU regulatory framework to improve a layered policy model for US telecommunications market. Telecommun Policy 30:136–148

Mueller M (2002) Ruling the root: internet governance and the taming of cyberspace. MIT Press, Cambridge

Mueller M (2010) Networks and states: the global politics of internet governance. MIT Press, Cambridge

Nihoul P, Rodford P (2004) EU electronic communications law: competition and regulation in the European telecommunications market. OUP, Oxford

Noll A (2001) The ITU in the 21st century. Singapore J Int Comp Law 5:63–70

Take I (2012) Regulating the internet infrastructure: a comparative appraisal of the legitimacy of ICANN, ITU, and the WSIS. Regul and Governance 6:499–523

Tegge A (1994) Die Internationale Telekommunikations-Union: Organisation und Funktion einer Weltorganisation im Wandel. Nomos, Baden-Baden

Weber R, Burri M (2012) Classification of services in the digital economy. Schulthess, Zürich

Wessel R (2011) Regulating technological innovation through informal international law: the exercise of international public authority by transnational actors. In: Heldeweg M, Kica E (eds) Regulating technological innovation: a multidisciplinary approach. Palgrave, Basingstoke, pp 77–94

Zhao Y (2003/2004) Further liberalization of telecommunications services in the framework of the WTO in the 21st century. Int J Commun Law Policy 8:1–30

# Chapter 13
# Services of General Interest and the External Dimension of the EU Energy Policy

**Panagiotis Delimatsis**

**Abstract** Services of general interest (SGI) are a key component of the EU economy, accounting for 26 % of GDP and 30 % of employment within the EU. They cover economic and non-economic activities alike. They are to be distinguished from services of general economic interest (SGEI), which are economic activities which deliver outcomes in the overall public good and which would be supplied under conditions less favourable to the consumers in terms of quality, safety, affordability, equal treatment or universal access if the State did not intervene. As the SGEI is a particularly developed concept within the EU, the relevant discussions inevitably focus on their function and organization at the EU level. Less is said about the external aspects of such services. One of the most promising areas for such discussions is the energy sector, whereby the EU is called upon to show leadership not only due to global concerns relating to sustainable development, but also due to the EU's dependence on external energy sources. Against this backdrop, this chapter discusses the external dimension of the EU energy policy in the area of SGI. After a review of the role of SGI in the energy sector, the chapter focuses on the external aspects of the EU energy policy, tentatively discussing ends and means. In the next section an analysis of the SGI within the broader scope of the EU external action is offered. In this regard, the concept of public services in the context of energy is examined through a discussion of the relevant rules in the WTO General Agreement on Trade in Services (GATS), the role of energy services in the GATS and some relevant provisions in a number of free trade agreements (FTAs) that the EU concluded jointly with its Member States.

Professor of European and International Trade Law and Director.

P. Delimatsis (✉)
Tilburg Law and Economics Center (TILEC), Tilburg University, Tilburg, The Netherlands
e-mail: p.delimatsis@uvt.nl



M. Krajewski (ed.), *Services of General Interest Beyond the Single Market*, Legal Issues of Services of General Interest,
DOI 10.1007/978-94-6265-063-3_13

## Contents



## 13.1 Introductory Remarks

SGI are a key component of the EU economy, accounting for 26 % of GDP and 30 % of employment within the EU.[1] SGI are to be distinguished from services of general economic interest (SGEI).[2] Having said this, SGEI is a subset of SGI, without however any definition given by any EU institution as to the actual coverage of SGI.[3] The Court of Justice of the European Union (CJEU) has accepted various services as SGEI, including water, gas and electricity, distribution, countrywide collection and delivery of mail, the operation of unprofitable airlines, ambulance transport or the pharmaceuticals wholesale business.[4]

The new Article 14 of the Treaty on the Functioning of the European Union (TFEU) culminated a decade-long debate on the manner that SGI should be treated at the EU level.[5] SGI came to the forefront in public policy discourse in

---

[1]SGI are 'services that public authorities of the Member States classify as being of general interest and, therefore, subject to specific public service obligations (PSOs).' PSOs, in turn, constitute obligations which a given undertaking would not assume—or would not assume to the same extent or under the same conditions—if it were to consider its own commercial interests. See Note of DG Energy & Transport on Directives 2003/54/EC and 2003/55/EC on the internal market in electricity and natural gas, 'Public Service Obligations', 16 January 2004, quoting the definition used in Article 2 of the Regulation 1191/69 concerning PSOs in inland transport.

[2]European Commission, *Communication on a Quality Framework for Services of General Interest in Europe,* COM(2011) 900 final, 20 December 2011, p. 3.

[3]For simplicity reason, we will treat the two concepts interchangeably, taking into account that SGI also include SGEIs. When necessary, we will refer to non-economic services which are not to be regarded as SGEIs.

[4]See Conclusions of AG Colomer of 20 October 2009 in CJEU, Case C-265/08 *Federutility and Others* [2010] ECR I-3377.

[5]Starting with the European Commission's first Communication, *Services of General Interest in Europe*, *OJ* 1996 C 281, and later on with the Commission's *Green Paper on Services of General Interest*, COM(2003) 270 final, 21 May 2003. See also Article 36 of the EU Charter of Fundamental Rights, which after the entry of the Treaty of Lisbon is upgraded into EU primary law.

the 90s once it was realized that liberalization and privatization of various services was here to stay and that the market alone would not be able to meet certain public interest requirements. It was only at that moment that accessibility and affordability of certain essential services entered the (de-)regulatory discussion in the EU. Article 14 TFEU confirms that SGI are no longer to be regarded as an exception confined within the competition law discourse but rather a concept that forms part of the shared values of the EU and play an important role for the promotion of territorial and social cohesion nowadays.[6] Article 14 refers to the joint responsibility of the EU and the Member States to ensure high-quality supply of services of general interest and constitutes a legal basis for the EU to act, without prejudice to the competences of the Member States.[7] It is actually for the latter to define, organize, finance and monitor SGI.[8] Typically, the state imposes certain obligations on undertakings[9] in liberalized sectors in order to safeguard public interests which the market forces alone would not protect. In return, these undertakings may receive direct financial support through the public purse; special or exclusive rights; contributions by market participants; tariff averaging or solidarity-based financing, to name but a few.

Additionally, Protocol 26 highlights the importance of certain characteristics that EU Member States believe they should be safeguarded when organizing SGI such as high quality, safety and affordability, non-discrimination, universal access as well as user and consumer protection. These principles governing the supply of SGI appear for the first time in the form of EU primary law. Another novelty enshrined in the Protocol is the reference to non-economic services of general interest in primary law for the first time, confirming that their supply, commissioning and organization is a prerogative of the Member States.[10]

However, the role that SGI play in the EU external action has been largely neglected in the literature. This is quite astonishing particularly in areas such as energy, given the high degree of EU's dependence on external energy sources. Against this backdrop, this chapter discusses the external dimension of the EU energy policy in the area of SGI to see the potential impact of EU external action and international economic law on the regulation of SGI within the EU. After a review of the role of SGI in the energy sector, the chapter focuses on the external aspects of the EU energy policy, tentatively discussing ends and means. In Sect. 13.4 an analysis of the SGI within the broader scope of the EU external action is offered. In this regard, the concept of public services in the context of

[6]Cf. Ross 2000, p. 31.

[7]See European Commission, *Communication on Services of General Interest, Including Social Services of General Interest: A New European Commitment*, COM(2007) 725 final, 20 November 2007.

[8]See also Protocol No 26 annexed to the TFEU.

[9]Undertakings are broadly defined within EU law: See CJEU, Joined Cases C-180/98 to C-184/98 *Pavlov and Others* [2000] ECR I-6451.

[10]See also Fiedziuk 2011.

energy is examined through a discussion of the relevant rules in the WTO General Agreement on Trade in Services (GATS), the role of energy services in the GATS and some relevant provisions in a number of free trade agreements (FTAs) that the EU concluded jointly with its Member States.

## 13.2 SGI and the Energy Sector

In an ever-changing regulatory environment and with various alternative forms of regulation emerging, the State sometimes has to re-invent itself and re-define its role in regulating economic and non-economic activities. Indeed, while the State has become a rule-taker in various economic sectors as the result of private ordering, there are services sectors where the welfare State can improve resource allocation as a last resort in cases where market is incapable of doing it alone. This is particularly the case with vulnerable groups or outermost regions which ensures availability of a given service to those who could not otherwise buy essential services for themselves. In this regard, universal service emerged as a key EU concept to ensure effective access of vulnerable consumers to essential services. The concept of universal service entails a right for consumers to access certain services but also an obligation to service suppliers to offer such services according to pre-specified conditions, including complete ('universal') territorial coverage and at an affordable price. Universal service obligations (USOs) may be imposed on one, more or all undertakings that are active in a given sector.[11]

At the EU level, both Member States and the Commission initially considered a sector-specific approach as the more apposite one for the regulation of SGEIs.[12] However, this changed with the two so-called 'Altmark packages' in 2005 and 2012, in an attempt by the EU legislature to bring more coherence to the legal framework on SGEIs. In the area of energy, an important network industry, in particular, the EU regulatory approach is encapsulated in the gradual completion of the internal market for electricity and gas through three subsequent packages,[13] moving from a highly monopolistic, vertically integrated, state-controlled industry into a competitive services sector, albeit with various complicated outstanding matters and with meaningful competition being unevenly applied in the various Member States.[14] Effective unbundling of natural monopolies (transmission system operators—TSOs) and the separation of the function of transmission has been

[11]See also European Commission, DG Competition, *Services of general economic interest and state aid: Non-paper*, 12 November 2002, para 9.

[12]European Commission, *White Paper on services of general interest,* COM(2004) 374 final, 12 May 2004, p. 11.

[13]See Hancher and Larouche 2011.

[14]Cf. European Commission, *Communication on prospects for the internal gas and electricity market*, COM(2006) 841 final, 10 January 2007.

a key element of the liberalization efforts[15]: no genuine internal market could be created without the possibility for new players to access national networks and markets. At the political level, the European Council pledged to complete the internal market for electricity and gas by 2014, noticing that no Member State should remain isolated from the European gas and electricity networks after 2015.[16]

With respect to PSOs,[17] which would cover energy security and continuity of supply as well as affordability of electricity and gas for all domestic users, the first Directives would call for a balance between security and predictability, on one side, with open markets and consumer choice on the other.[18] In the second energy package of 2003, additional protection would be provided to vulnerable consumers through suppliers of last resort and USOs (the latter, only in the case of electricity), whereas independent regulatory authorities (NRAs) at the national level would ensure the smooth function of the domestic energy markets and non-discriminatory access to transmission systems. USOs in particular have been a safety valve against the deleterious effects of liberalization to the weaker groups of society, ensuring the continuity and affordability of a given service without compromising its quality. Competition law matters would be dealt with by the relevant national competition authorities or the DG Competition.

In the meantime, the CJEU decided in *Almelo*[19] that an undertaking which 'must ensure that throughout the territory in respect of which the concession is granted, all consumers, whether local distributors or end-users, receive uninterrupted supply of electricity in sufficient quantities to meet demand at any given time, at uniform tariff rates and on terms which do not vary save in accordance with objective criteria applicable to all customers' provides a SGEI. Thus, in cases like *Almelo*, the CJEU identified the main elements that constitute a SGEI such as continuity (uninterrupted supply of the service); universality (benefitting the consumers throughout a given territory); and equality (supply with uniform tariffs and of similar intensity regardless of specific situations or profitability). Nowadays, this triptych is complement by the equally important principles of transparency and affordability.[20] Furthermore, in *Altmark*, The CJEU found that under certain

[15]See, for instance, Recital 6 of Directive 2009/73/EC of the European Parliament and the Council of 13 July 2009 concerning common rules for the internal market in natural gas and repealing Directive 2003/55/EC (the 'Gas Directive'), *OJ* 2009 L 211/94.

[16]European Council Conclusions of 4 February 2011.

[17]PSOs are imposed on undertakings by way of entrustment and on the basis of a general interest criterion which makes sure that the service is provided under conditions allowing them to fulfill their mission. See also European Commission, *Communication on the application of the European Union State aid rules to compensation granted for the provision of services of general economic interest, OJ* 2012 C 8/4, at p. 12.

[18]See Cross et al. 2007.

[19]CJEU, Case C-393/92 *Municipality of Almelo and Others* [1994] ECR I-1477, para 48.

[20]See for instance, recitals 42, 45, 50, 51 and Article 3 of the Directive 2009/72/EC of the European Parliament and the Council of 13 July 2009 concerning common rules for the internal market in electricity (the 'Electricity Directive'), *OJ* 2009 L 211/55.

conditions, state funding of a SGEI will constitute compensation for the extra costs incurred by an undertaking discharging its PSOs, and will thus not fall under the EU State aid rules.[21]

With respect to reference price fixing, whereas the second energy package was supposed to liberalize prices, the CJEU found that Member States still had substantial leeway to ensure that the price of natural gas in the downstream markets would be reasonable irrespective of market forces. However, it was for the national courts to assess whether such measures were proportionate, taking into account the objective of liberalization and the imperatives of an operational internal market for gas. More specifically, such measures must be transitional, i.e. limited in duration; strictly necessary to achieve consumer protection; and comply with the principles of transparency and non-discrimination.[22] Between the second and third energy package, Member States ensured that the controversial—and potentially far-reaching—Services Directive would not apply to the electricity and the gas sectors.[23]

In the third energy package of 2009 that entered into force in March 2011, extensive (including ownership) unbundling is required, calling for structural unbundling of TSOs regarding production and supply functions. The new Directives entail rules for PSOs for electricity and gas and ensure universal service for all household customers in the case of electricity,[24] and call upon Member States to adopt national rules to protect vulnerable consumers against energy poverty, such as those relating to the adoption of national energy action plans; the granting of benefits in social security systems to ensure the necessary electricity supply to vulnerable consumers, or support energy efficiency projects.[25] To avoid unnecessary litigation as to the target group, the Directives urge Member States to clearly delineate the concept of vulnerable consumers.[26] Furthermore, they reiterate the principles of transparency, continuity, non-discrimination, verifiability and equality. In addition, environmental sustainability and energy efficiency as well as the use of renewables are parameters that shall play an important role in organizing and defining PSOs taking into

---

[21]CJEU, Case C-280/00 *Altmark Trans GmbH and Regierungspräsidium Magdeburg* [2003] ECR I-7747, para 95.

[22]See also CJEU, Case C-265/08 *Federutility and Others* [2010] ECR I-3377; also CJEU, Case C-242/10 *Enel Produzione*, [2011] ECR I-13665.

[23]See Article 17 of Directive 2006/123/EC of the European Parliament and the Council of 12 December 2006 on services in the internal market, *OJ* 2006 L 376/36.

[24]According to the Electricity Directive, universal service is the right to be supplied (if needed, through a supplier of last resort) with electricity of a specified quality within their territory at reasonable, easily and clearly comparable, transparent and non-discriminatory prices. See Article 3:3 of the Electricity Directive above n 20. The unbundling requirements—and the third energy package, more generally—have been at the heart of a WTO complaint launched by Russia in May 2014. See Russia's request for consultations addressed to the European Union, WT/DS476/1.

[25]Article 3 of the Electricity Directive above n 20 and Article 3 of the Gas Directive above n 15.

[26]See also European Commission, *Commission Staff Working Paper, An Energy Policy for Consumers*, SEC(2010) 1407 final, 11 November 2010, p. 4.

account the Europe 2020 policy.[27] To date, implementation of the third energy package has been disappointing, whereas infringements proceedings against Member States under the second energy package are still pending.[28]

As harmonization in the energy sector grows bigger and liberalization intensifies, the scope of the Member States to attribute special or exclusive rights in return for the imposition of PSOs shrinks. Settled case-law developed by the CJEU suggest that PSOs cannot be attached to services that are already provided under conditions such as price, objective quality characteristics, continuity and access to the service, consistent with the public interest, as defined by the State, by undertakings operating under normal market conditions. Member States have a wide margin of discretion is assessing whether this is the case, the control of the Commission being limited as to whether a manifest error on the side of the Member State exist as to the application of the EU State aid rules.[29] This would mean, for instance, that certain services that are fully liberalized or regulated at the EU level such as oil transmission, or electricity and gas transmission and distribution by TSOs would no longer be regarded as SGEI to which exclusive or special rights can be awarded. Similar considerations would probably lead electricity and gas storage activities to be outside the scope of SGEI.[30]

Further integrationist endeavours at the political level should once again limit the scope for attaching PSOs to energy service providers within the EU. In attempting to give a new boost to the integration of an important enabler of growth amidst the sovereign debt crisis, in October 2012, the European Commission included the development of fully integrated energy networks within the EU among the top priorities of the Single Market Act II initiative.[31] The Commission recalled the major benefits for consumers that full integration could entail, but also was reminiscent of the important investments that are necessary to modernize EU's energy infrastructure, decarbonize systems and make them energy efficient, including through the use of smart grids.[32] Along with the recent finalization of

[27]A resource-efficient EU is one of the Europe 2020 flagship initiatives: see European Commission, *Communication on Energy 2020: A Strategy for Competitive, Sustainable and Secure Energy*, COM(2010) 639 final, 10 November 2010; and *A Resource-Efficient Europe—Flagship Initiative Under the Europe 2020 Strategy*, COM(2011) 21, 26 January 2011.

[28]See European Commission, *Commission Staff Working Paper, 2009–2010 Report on progress in creating the internal gas and electricity market*, 9 June 2011.

[29]See European Commission, above n 17, at p. 11; also CJEU, Case C-320/05P *Olsen v Commission* [2007] ECR I-131(confirming the General Court's view in T-17/02, para 216).

[30]Cf. European Commission, *Paper of the Services of DG Competition containing draft Guidelines on environmental and energy aid for 2014–2020*, 2013 (on file with the author). The final Guidelines entered into force in July 2014. See European Commission, *Communication on Guidelines on State aid for environmental protection and energy* 2014–2020 [2014] OJ C 200/1.

[31]European Commission, *Communication on Single Market Act II—Together for new growth*, COM(2012) 573 final, 3 October 2012.

[32]See also European Commission, *Communication on Making the internal energy market work*, COM(2012) 663 final, 15 November 2012, to which the Commission annexed an action plan leading to the completion of the internal energy market.

the reform of government procurement rules in the sector,[33] major changes in the sector should be expected in the medium run. In June 2013, the Council reiterated the importance of the implementation of the third energy package for a fully functioning, interconnected and integrated internal energy market. Interestingly, the Council made reference to end-user price regulation measures at the domestic level, inviting Member States, while taking into account USOs, to review measure which do not focus on well-defined groups of vulnerable consumers; are not of limited duration; and are not justified by wholesale markets that are uncompetitive due to their geographical isolation or their temporary lack of interconnections or diversity of supply.[34]

In parallel, the climate and energy package was adopted in the same year, highlighting the close interconnection between energy and climate action for the EU.[35] According to this package on the 20-20-20 policy, the EU has committed to three headline targets relating to reductions of GHG emissions, renewable energy and energy savings.[36] In this respect, an important ('flagship') initiative relates to the realization of a resource-efficient EU, which included the preparation of roadmaps for a low-carbon economy by 2050 and a resource-efficient EU as well as the revision of common policies such as those relating to agriculture and fisheries.[37]

The EU's energy strategy focuses on (i) achieving energy efficiency (20 % savings by 2020 and even more by 2050); (ii) building an integrated EU energy market (eliminating anticompetitive practices and fragmentation); (iii) providing secure, safe and affordable energy for consumers and businesses; (iv) promoting energy technology and innovation (also spelled out in the Energy Roadmap 2050); and (v) strengthen the external dimension of the EU energy market.[38] This latter objective would include the identification of new energy supply sources and routes by 2020, and the integration of the EU energy market and regulatory framework with the EU neighbours. Quite ironically, the above-mentioned major internal reforms coincided with the major interruption of gas flows from Russia to Europe in early 2009, alluding to the EU vulnerability to unexpected disruptions of external energy sources of which it has no, or perhaps limited, control.[39] At the same

[33]See Directive 2014/25 of the European Parliament and of the Council of 26 February 2014 on procurement by entities operating in the water, energy, transport and postal services sectors, *OJ* 2014 L 94/243.

[34]See Council of the European Union, Council Conclusions on the Commission Communication 'Making the internal energy market work', 6–7/10 June 2013.

[35]See also European Commission, *Green Paper—A 2030 framework for climate and energy policies*, COM(2013) 169 final, 27 March 2013. Such a close interconnection is also obvious in primary law: see, for instance, Article 194:2 TFEU in conjuction with 192:2(c) TFEU.

[36]European Commission, *Communication on Europe 2020—A strategy for smart, sustainable and inclusive growth*, COM(2010) 2020 final, 3 March 2010.

[37]Above n 27.

[38]Above n 27.

[39]See also European Commission, *Staff Working Document, The January 2009 Gas Supply Disruption to the EU: An Assessment,* SEC(2009) 977 final, 16 July 2009.

time, such disruptions show the urgency of an alternative energy policy for the EU based on solidarity, efficient energy use and storage, and the development, as a matter of priority, of renewable energy sources. In times of austerity, important public spending obligations are derived from these objectives and the legislative acts that include them.

## 13.3 The External Dimension of the EU Energy Policy

The EU and its Member States share competences in the area of energy.[40] Article 2:2 TFEU provides that when the Treaties provide for a shared competence in a given area, the EU and the Member States may legislate and agree on legally binding acts in that area. When the competence is shared, Member States can exercise their competence to the extent that the EU has not exercised its competence (that is, it has not occupied the field), or to the extent that the EU has decided to cease exercising its competences. Article 194 TFEU confirms this sectoral competence, introducing a legal basis for action in the area of energy.[41]

Thus, international energy agreements would be mixed agreements, which are negotiated, concluded and managed jointly by the EU and its Member States. As the EU has occupied the field in the areas of electricity and gas to a large extent internally, it is reasonable to assume that in the case of an international agreement in these areas, the EU would have exclusive competence,[42] particularly if one of the conditions of Article 3:2 TFEU is met, that is, if the international agreement is necessary to enable the Union to exercise its internal competence or insofar as its conclusion affects common rules or alters their scope. This is so, even if, contrary to Article 191:1 TFEU relating to the EU environmental policy, Article 194:1 TFEU does not explicitly refer to measures taken at the international level.

However, it is clear that issues such as energy security or interconnection of networks cannot be seen nor tackled in isolation; the external dimension is an essential element for efficiently tackling such challenges, notably in view of the fact that the EU is a net importer of energy. In addition, in areas of shared competence, the duty of loyalty or genuine cooperation set out in Article 4:3 TFEU plays a crucial role in ensuring coherence in the external action and the unity in the international representation of the EU, and eliminating any incompatibility between EU law and bilateral agreements concluded unilaterally by Member States before of after their accession to the EU.[43]

---

[40]Article 4:2(i) TFEU.

[41]See also CJEU, C-490/10 *Parliament v Council* [decided on 6 September 2012 nyr], para 66.

[42]See, by analogy, CJEU, Opinion 2/91 (*ILO Convention*) [1993] ECR I-1061; For some further guidance on these terms (e.g. what 'to a large extent' or 'affecting common rules' means), see CJEU, Opinion 1/03 (*Lugano Convention*), [2006] ECR I-1145.

[43]Cf. CJEU, Case C-246/07 *Commission v Sweden (PFOS)* [2010] ECR I-3317. See also Neframi 2010, p. 323. Also Eeckhout 2011, p. 249 ff.

Whereas no meaningful external/exclusive competence is claimed by the EU at the external level, the least that one would expect nowadays, particularly in view of the completion of the internal market for electricity and gas, is coordination between Member States and the Commission as to possible international agreements that the former may plan to conclude. However, more than simple cooperation would be necessary to ensure uninterrupted energy supply to a geographical area that imports over 60 % of its gas and over 80 % of its oil.

To date, various Member States have concluded bilateral agreements with third countries in the area of energy, but it seems that unified action by the EU is not among the immediate plans of the EU political institutions nor its Member States.[44] Rather, soft involvement of the EU institutions is called for, whereby EU documents refer to shared *responsibilities* among Member States, the Commission, national regulatory authorities as well as undertakings.[45] Another reason that coherence in energy external action in the field of energy may not be achieved anytime soon is the fact that energy supply is very much in the hands of private companies with only indirect involvement of the respective Member States. At the same time, internally the EU has evolved into such a sophisticated regulatory area with rules touching upon every possible aspect of private economic activity that this argument may be losing any credibility.

In 2012, Decision 994/2012/EU of the European Parliament and the Council established an information exchange mechanism that would bring more transparency as to existing and future agreements that Member States concluded with third countries in the area of energy.[46] However, as energy security becomes a recurring theme in all major fora, more coordination among the EU and its Member States is warranted. In this regard, joint action should be streamlined in international organizations such as the International Energy Agency (IEA), the International Energy Forum (IEF), the International Partnership for Energy Efficiency Cooperation (IPEEC) and the International Renewable Energy Agency (IRENA). The same goes for G-8 or G-20, when issues such as price volatility in energy markets or fossil fuel subsidies arise. A better-coordinated approach would also most likely have a higher impact on increasing awareness as to the collective character of energy security, thereby stimulating global cooperation on energy matters.[47]

As energy security grows in prominence, one should expect that the supranational angle, as expressed by the involvement of the Commission, will increase, particularly when it comes to large-scale infrastructure projects linking the EU energy network to third countries. For instance, as a reaction to the call by the

[44]See also De Jong and Schunz 2012, p. 165.

[45]Cf. European Commission, *White Paper on services of general interest,* COM(2004) 374 final, 12 May 2004, p. 4.

[46]Decision No 994/2012/EU of the European Parliament and of the Council of 25 October 2012 establishing an information exchange mechanism with regard to intergovernmental agreements between Member States and third countries in the field of energy, *OJ* 2012 L 299/13.

[47]See also Baumann 2010, p. 77.

European Council on 4 February 2011 for the development of strategic corridors for the transport of large volumes of gas to the European market, the Council gave a mandate to the European Commission to negotiate a treaty with Azerbaijan and Turkmenistan allowing for the creation of a Trans-Caspian Gas Pipeline. Even if the result of the negotiations remains uncertain,[48] the willingness expressed by MS to task the Commission with such negotiations is quite telling for the conduct of the EU external energy policy of the future.

The EU energy policy is very much focused on combating climate change. However, at the external level, it aims at limiting the EU's external vulnerability to and dependence on imported hydrocarbons through energy partnerships but also by raising pressure for more market transparency, better control of market volatility and less supply shocks and disruptions. Thus, security of supply (including through diversification), along with sustainability, become central objectives of the EU policy on energy, particularly when one takes into account that the EU is the world's largest energy importer (the EU imports some 60 % of its gas and over 80 % of its oil, with an upward trend), but also the importance of sustainable energy sources for the competitiveness of EU industries.

Being an energy importer itself, the EU is highly dependent on free and transparent energy markets globally to decrease the leverage of the energy-exporting countries. This is coupled with the intensified effort domestically for unprecedented energy savings, decarbonization and extensive development of renewable energy sources. However, stable and secure international partnerships (including through the European Economic Area and particularly Norway, whose exports of natural gas to the EU matched Russia's in 2012; its Neighboring Policy-ENP; or the expansion of the Energy Community Treaty-ECT) with important upstream (producer) countries are essential. This also includes transit and consumer countries on the East side of Europe but also on the South.[49] Partnerships of any form with these countries cover a wide array of issues, ranging from energy security to the investment environment (particularly for large-scale infrastructure projects) to sustainability.[50] Such partnerships are important in view of the forthcoming construction of the Southern Gas Corridor, bringing natural gas from the Caspian region to the EU.

[48]See European Commission, *Report on the Implementation of the Communication on Security of Energy Supply and International Cooperation and of the Energy Council Conclusions of November 2011*, COM(2013) 638 final, 13 September 2013.

[49]See European Commission, *Communication on Energy Roadmap 2050*, COM(2011) 885 final, 15 December 2011. See also the Roadmap on EU-Russia Energy Cooperation until 2050 of March 2013, providing for the creation of a common energy space, including harmonized minimum rules on third party access and competition, thereby leveling the playing field. The Roadmap is available at http://ec.europa.eu/energy/international/russia/doc/2013_03_eu_russia_roadmap_2050_signed.pdf (Accessed 13 September 2013). For a list of international instruments and initiatives that the EU employs in its energy diplomacy, see European Commission, *Commission Staff Working Paper, Key facts and figures on the external dimension of the EU energy policy*, SEC(2011) 1022 final, 7 September 2011, p. 13 ff.

[50]See also infra the discussion about the ECT and the Energy Charter Treaty.

Two significant existing legal instruments can be (or are already being) used to provide a framework for such regional cooperation: the Energy Community Treaty[51]; and the Energy Charter Treaty.[52] With the deadline for the completion of the internal market for gas and electricity approaching quickly, the EU has to move full speed towards the implementation of a coherent external energy policy to complement the internal dimension of this policy, which would entail, inter alia, the negotiation of EU-level agreements, whereby a negotiating mandate would give the authorization to the Commission to start negotiations on behalf of the EU.[53]

In addition, energy and climate action is closely associated with the EU development policy and the achievement of the Millennium Development Goals (MDGs) is equally dependent on effective action within these areas.[54] Even if energy is not among the sectoral priorities of the EU policy coherence for development (trade and finance; climate change; food security; migration; security), it is directly or indirectly relevant for the achievement of these priorities.[55] Issues such as technology transfer and energy security, price volatility or access (through interconnection of energy infrastructures and networks) to secure, affordable, clean and sustainable energy services are of outmost importance to the developing world.[56] Such objectives, for instance, have become part and parcel of the EU discussions with Southern Mediterranean countries. In addition, the EU participates in the Sustainable Energy for All Initiative, aiming to provide energy access to 500 million people by 2030, with a particular focus on Africa. In addition, the EU policy on renewables and biofuels, if not monitored and adequately designed, may have deleterious impact on developing countries by decreasing their competitiveness, increasing food prices and causing shortages on certain products or bringing about carbon leakage.[57]

Whereas it is clear that a well-functioning internal energy market is a prerequisite for delivering to all EU consumers energy products and services of high quality, but still affordable for them, the EU external energy policy is equally important to achieve these objectives in a region that is highly dependent on external energy

[51]See European Commission, *Report from the Commission to the European Parliament and the Council under Article 7 of Decision 2006/500/EC (Energy Community Treaty)*, COM(2011) 105 final, 10 March 2011.

[52]See Bamberger and Wälde 2007, p. 145.

[53]Cf. European Commission, *Communication on security of energy supply and international cooperation—"The EU Energy Policy: Engaging with Partners beyond Our Borders"*, COM(2011) 539 final, 7 September 2011.

[54]See European Commission, *Green Paper—EU development policy in support of inclusive growth and sustainable development, Increasing the impact of EU development policy*, COM(2010) 629 final, 10 November 2010.

[55]Note that policy coherence forms part of the EU primary law: See Article 208 TFEU.

[56]See European Commission, *Communication on Increasing the impact of EU Development Policy: An Agenda for Change*, COM(2011) 637 final, 13 October 2011, p. 9.

[57]European Commission, *Commission Staff Working Document, Policy Coherence for Development Work Programme 2010–2013*, SEC(2010) 421 final, 21 April 2010.

sources and uninterrupted energy supply. In addition, one should not lose sight of the semantics. The energy policy of the EU is based on the principle of solidarity, alluding to social cohesion and the specific preferences of the European society relating to universal access to certain essential services, including energy.

These preferences or values are also reflected in the EU external action. Article 21 TEU provides that the EU external action shall be guided by the principles that have also shaped the evolution of the EU internally, including the principles of equality and solidarity. Any external policies, including in energy matters, shall safeguard such values. Finally, the principle of consistency among the EU external policies but also between them and internal policies also leads to the conclusion that when acting at the international level, the principles of equality, continuity, universality, affordability, transparency, and solidarity indeed inform any measures adopted or commitments undertaken at the international level. Thus, considerations relating to public service obligations only play an indirect role in the EU external energy policy: in order to be able to serve properly the EU populace with uninterrupted energy sources, the EU would need to ensure diversification of energy sources and have stable partnerships with predictable interlocutors (be they energy producer, transit countries or private companies), which remain unaffected by exogenous factors.[58]

## *13.3.1 The Energy Community Treaty (ECT)*

The ECT was established in 2006[59] between the EU and a number of Southeastern European countries, some of which may become EU Members in the future.[60] Initially concluded for a period of 10 years,[61] the ECT extends the EU *acquis* relating to energy, environment (including energy efficiency and renewable energy) and competition to third countries.[62] The adoption of the EU relevant legislation is continuous: in this respect, the EU third energy package is also implemented within the Energy Community. However, the adaptation to the EU acquis is not automatic.[63] Rather unanimous decisions by the ECT Ministerial Council endorsing adaptation are warranted. Interestingly, the ECT adopts a quite flexible

---

[58]Cf. European Commission, *Communication on Second Strategic Energy Review: an energy security and solidarity action plan*, COM(2008) 781 final, 13 November 2008, under 2.2.

[59]See Council Decision 2006/500/EC of 29 May 2006 on the conclusion by the European Community of the Energy Community Treaty, *OJ* 2006 L 198/16ff.

[60]For instance, Serbia has a formal EU candidate status.

[61]For the EU, deepening and extending the validity of the ECT beyond 2016 is a strategic priority. See European Commission's Communication, above n 53, p. 8.

[62]This type of extension of the EU acquis to third countries in a particular economic sector was termed 'sectoral multilateralism'. See Lazowski 2008, p. 1436.

[63]See also Blockmans and Van Vooren 2012, p. 590.

governance model, whereby stakeholder involvement, including industry, regulators, industry representative groups and consumers, is critical.

The ECT is a political project of sectoral integration in South East Europe, but it is no less economic: It is focused towards economic development and social stability, security of energy supply and infrastructural investment. It is an important means for the EU to achieve an integrated energy network through key interconnections with key (notably energy transit) countries. In this respect, ECT contributes to the materialization of the EU external action objectives in the area of energy.

With regard to SGI, the ECT refers explicitly to the importance of PSOs for economic prosperity, thereby extending an EU concept to the territories of the third countries participating in the ECT. According to Article 32 ECT, the concept of PSOs is to be interpreted pursuant to the EU acquis on energy. However, much of the acquis remains to be fully implemented, whereas enforcement of the rules adopted still is in its infancy.[64] In addition, the ECT suffers from the lack of private investment. As rules are increasingly implemented and enforced, the ensuing legal security and regulatory convergence should create more optimal conditions for such investment.[65]

### 13.3.2 The Energy Charter Treaty

The Energy Charter Treaty entered into force in April 1998. It is the most important energy-specific international legally binding agreement with significant rules on the protection and promotion of energy-specific investment and detailed obligations on energy transit. The Treaty also adopts a WTO 'by reference' approach, which leads to the application of WTO rules to parties to the Treaty which are not WTO Members.[66]

Interestingly, the Energy Charter Treaty, counting 54 contracting parties (EU and Euratom being separate contracting parties), includes energy producer, consumer and transit countries, of varying degrees of development and involving the European and Asian continents. Initially intended to foster dialogue between the developed economies of Western Europe and Japan and the former Soviet Union countries, the Energy Charter Treaty acquired global status when countries like Japan and Australia or Central Asian States joined. To increase its global coverage, later on the US, Canada, China, Venezuela and various Middle East energy producing countries became observers. However, ratification is pending in various

---

[64] See also Petrov 2012, p. 331.

[65] See also European Commission, *Report from the Commission to the European Parliament and the Council under Article 7 of Decision 2006/500/EC (Energy Community Treaty)*, COM(2011) 105 final, 10 March 2011.

[66] See Selivanova 2012, p. 311.

energy producing signatories, such as Russia, Norway or Australia, although Russia has accepted to provisionally apply the Treaty. This reluctance shows that energy producing countries may soon opt for a new framework for cooperation on energy outside the Energy Charter Treaty.

The Energy Charter Treaty combines binding rights and obligations notably relating to the post-investment phase, which are enforceable through a compulsory arbitration system or through GATT-type dispute resolution (thus, both investor-State and State-to-State dispute resolution; the latter is not limited to investment matters),[67] with soft law provisions on issues such as competition, energy efficiency and the environment, or technology transfer and access to capital. Thus, the ECT includes various investment-related provisions such as fair and equitable treatment standard or the principle of full compensation following expropriation that are found in bilateral investment treaties (BITs). Quite interestingly, the Treaty can be regarded as a intra-EU BIT, whereby investment claims by EU investors against EU MS are adjudicated through recourse to the Treaty proceedings rather than the ECJ.[68] The Treaty provisions on investment apply to any investment associated with an economic activity in the energy sector, from exploration, extraction, refining, production or storage, to land transport, transmission, distribution, trade, or marketing and sale. The Treaty includes a pervasive non-discrimination provision, protecting the investors of the parties against State arbitrariness. Again, due to the breadth of material scope, the Treaty is more than a typical investment treaty. However, for the EU, the Treaty should focus on the core areas of trade, transit and investment protection, while extending its geographical reach to North Africa and Far East, thereby showcasing a potential for becoming a far-reaching multilateral instrument.[69]

## 13.4 Energy, the GATS and the EU Free Trade Agreements

### *13.4.1 Energy Services in the GATS*

The GATS is the first multilateral agreement setting rules on trade in services. Its scope is potentially unlimited in that it covers any possible measure, taken by governments, public authorities at all levels of government or by non-governmental

[67]For an overview of the arbitration mechanism, see Hober 2010, p. 153.

[68]See, for instance, the recent dispute that Vattenfall, a Swedish energy company which runs two nuclear power plants in Germany, has brought against Germany before ICSID based on the Energy Charter Treaty, after Germany's decision to phase out nuclear power. See http://www.encharter.org/index.php?id=213&L=0#Vattenfall2. See also, more generally, Kleinheisterkamp 2012, p. 85.

[69]See also European Commission Communication, above n 53, at p. 13.

bodies with delegated regulatory powers, which may affect trade in services.[70] The GATS legal framework is vested with considerable flexibility. This is made possible also due to the four modes of supplying services through which trade in services is defined: cross-border supply (Mode 1, where only the service moves); consumption abroad (Mode 2, where only the service recipient moves); commercial presence and temporary movement of natural persons (Modes 3 and 4, where only the service supplier moves—in the second case only temporarily). Mode 3 is the most important mode of supply, as over 50 % of services trade is conducted through Mode 3.[71]

In the years during which the WTO treaty was negotiated (the Uruguay Round of trade negotiations), electricity and gas were supplied predominantly by state-run vertically integrated monopolies which were in charge of exploration and production to marketing and sale to the downstream markets.[72] Essentially, trade in energy was regarded as trade in goods, with services being an ancillary element to enable such trade. The everything but straightforward distinction between goods and services would only add to the confusion.[73] While oil or solid fuels would clearly be goods, the answer was not that clear for electricity or gas, which are by nature intangible. Again, gas can be transformed in liquefied natural gas (LNG) to be transported, so it can eventually be regarded as having tangible characteristics. Electricity, on the other side, seems to be generally regarded as a commodity despite being generally non-storable.[74] Be this as it may, the heavy state involvement and the monopoly/vertical integration ownership resulted in a general view that there was no room for trade in energy services.[75]

Thus, at the end of the Uruguay Round, when the schedules of specific commitments of each WTO Member were finalized, energy-related services were not a priority for—nor were they used as a negotiating chip by—the negotiators. Rather, they preferred focusing on sectors where trade was already significant.[76] The little focus on energy services is also reflected in the GATS classification list: Energy or energy-related services is not a separate comprehensive category in the MTN.GNS/W/120,

[70]Article I GATS. According to the Appellate Body, the word 'affect' implies a broad scope of application: *European Communities—Regime for the Importation, Sale and Distribution of Bananas (EC—Bananas III)*, Report of the Appellate Body, WT/DS27/AB/R, 9 September 1997, para 220.

[71]J. Magdeleine and A. Maurer, Measuring GATS Mode 4 Trade Flows, WTO Staff Working Paper ERSD-2008-05. http://www.wto.org/english/res_e/reser_e/ersd200805_e.pdf. Accessed 18 November 2014.

[72]See WTO, Council for Trade in Services, Energy Services, Background Note by the Secretariat, S/C/W/311, 12 January 2010, p. 2.

[73]See also Cossy 2008, p. 411.

[74]Cf. CJEU, Case C-158/94 *Commission v. Italy* [1997] ECR I-5789, para 17.

[75]See also Cottier et al. 2011, p. 213 ff.

[76]See WTO, Council for Trade in Services (Special Session), Communication from the United States, Energy Services, S/CSS/W/24, 18 December 2000, para 4.

the Services Sectoral Classification List.[77] The same observation applies to the United Nations Central Product Classification (CPC) on which the W/120 is based.[78] Instead, energy-related services, e.g. transport, distribution, construction, engineering, energy-related financial services, consultancy or research and development are scattered across several existing sectoral classifications within the W/120.[79]

Only three subsectors explicitly mentioned in the W/120 are energy-specific. Two of them are classified under 'business services': *services incidental to energy distribution* (which the CPC 887 defines as transmission and distribution services on a fee or contract basis of electricity, gaseous fuels and steam and hot water to household, industrial, commercial and other users e.g. power management and monitoring services) and *services incidental to mining* (which, according to the CPC 883 and 5115, include site preparation work for mining or services rendered on a fee or contract basis at oil and gas fields such as drilling or repair services). Thus, both downstream and upstream energy-related activities are thereby covered. The third relevant subsector is *pipeline transportation of fuels*, classified under 'transport services' (CPC 7131), which includes all services related to the actual operation of a pipeline.[80]

However, activities relating to the planning, construction and management of a pipeline would come under various categories of the W/120 such as engineering, construction or other business services. For instance, construction work for long distance pipelines and power lines is classified under CPC 5134, which comes under the W/120 category of 'general work for civil engineering'. Finally, several energy-related services are classified within various CPC sub-categories. For instance, wholesale trade services of solid, liquid and gaseous fuels and related products is classified under CPC 62271, which is a category of distribution services under the W/120. Of course, Members could deviate from the W/120 nomenclature and undertake commitments on a cluster of energy-related services. The 1993 Scheduling Guidelines allows for this possibility as long as the scope of the commitment and the classification used is sufficiently clear.[81] This latter option, however, was not used in the early years of the GATS.

Overall, Members' commitments in energy-related services were limited at the closure of the Uruguay Round negotiations in 1994.[82] Indeed, some of the major developed and developing economies listed commitments on energy-related

[77]See WTO, Services Sectoral Classification List, Note by the Secretariat, MTN.GNS/W/120 (the 'W/120'), 10 July 1991.

[78]See *United States—Measures affecting the cross-border supply of gambling and betting services (US—Gambling)*, Report of the Appellate Body, WT/DS285/AB/R, DSR 2005:XII, 5663 (Corr.1, DSR 2006:XII, 5475), para 172.

[79]See also the US Communication, above n 76, Annex A.

[80]See above n 72, p. 11.

[81]Also *United States—Measures affecting the cross-border supply of gambling and betting services (US—Gambling)*, Report of the Appellate Body, WT/DS285/AB/R, DSR 2005:XII, 5663 (Corr.1, DSR 2006:XII, 5475), paras 202–203.

[82]Evans 2003, p. 174.

services almost twenty years ago. Thus, these commitments no longer reflect the contemporary landscape relating to energy. In contrast, the countries that became Members of the WTO after 1995 were much more willing—and sometimes obliged, owing to the asymmetrical WTO accession process—to undertake commitments on energy-related services.

As a result of intensive liberalization attempts, core energy services relating to transport, transmission, and distribution were unbundled and are nowadays provided by private entities (sometimes former public monopolies which have been privatized) under conditions of competition in many countries. This came only to confirm that the private sector can very well serve the public and provide goods with public good features.[83] With respect to energy, the trend towards privatization and liberalization resulted in a great deal of confusion as to whether specific economic activities related to energy raise questions that should be dealt with under the GATT, the GATS, or both.[84] It has also revealed possible imbalances that may appear due to this 'sorting out' of previously bundled activities. Because the final consumption of energy is the outcome of a series of associated activities, market access may be a prerequisite in a considerable number of services sectors for energy service suppliers to provide their services adequately. In the current energy-related business landscape, the GATS schedules of commitments are outdated, do not encapsulate contemporary market realities and are in sharp contrast with the rise in prominence of energy security, sustainability and climate change adaptation. Therefore, the creation of a new entry in the Services Classification List is warranted that would allow WTO Members to undertake specific commitments on energy. This approach would allow WTO Members to clarify their level of openness in energy services and undertake energy-specific commitments. The recent WTO accession of various energy producer or transit countries such as Russia, Saudi Arabia or Ukraine, created a new momentum for progress in energy liberalization at the current round of trade negotiations (the Doha Round).

The most important development relating to energy services during the Doha Round was the collective request submitted by ten WTO Members to twenty-three requested Members in March 2006 in accordance with the Hong Kong Ministerial Declaration allowing for plurilateral negotiations to complement the traditional bilateral request-offer type of negotiations at the WTO.[85] After reiterating Members' right to regulate to achieve non-economic policy objectives and recognizing the full sovereignty of each Member over its energy resources, the requesting

[83]See also Coase 1974, p. 357.

[84]Consistent WTO case-law confirms that the two Agreements are not mutually exclusive. *United States—Measures affecting the cross-border supply of gambling and betting services (US—Gambling)*, Report of the Appellate Body, WT/DS27/AB/R, DSR 1997:II, 591, para 221; also *Canada—Certain measures affecting the automotive industry (Canada–Autos)*, Report of the Appellate Body, WT/DS139/AB/R, WT/DS142/AB/R, paras 159–166.

[85]The requesting Members were Australia, Canada, the EU, Japan, Norway, Saudi Arabia, Korea, Chinese Taipei (Taiwan), Singapore, and the United States.

Members identify 11 sub-sectors (both onshore and offshore) which currently belong to three main services sectors: business services (e.g. Engineering; management consulting; technical testing); construction services (e.g. long distance and local pipelines; construction for mining) and distribution (e.g. Wholesale trade services for fuels excluding electricity and gas; retailing services). It is worth noting that the request, while thorough, does not make reference to other key energy services such as services incidental to energy distribution or the pipeline transportation of fuels. The most significant requests for commitments relate to Mode 3 (commercial presence), whereby removal or substantial reduction is requested of foreign equity limitations; requirements for joint ventures or joint operations; economic needs tests; and discriminatory licensing procedures. Further requests related to the facilitation of temporary movement for intra-corporate transferees and contract service suppliers.

Another proposal that did not in the end gain considerable support was the adoption of a reference paper for energy services, modeled on the reference paper relating to Basic Telecommunications. The similarities between the two sectors are substantial, although energy services need a more careful approach due to matters relating to energy security and environmental protection. The reference paper would call for more transparency in the sector and non-discriminatory third-party access to and interconnection with energy networks and grids in reasonable terms and cost-oriented rates that are transparent. It would further include provisions on anticompetitive practices. In addition, like the reference paper on basic telecommunications, it could reiterate Members' right to define USOs. The telecoms reference paper considers such obligations as not being anti-competitive 'provided that they are administered in a transparent, non-discriminatory and competitively neutral manner and are not more burdensome than necessary for the kind of universal service defined by the Member.'[86]

### *13.4.2 Public Services, Energy and the GATS*

Aware of the importance of a particular set of services which are supplied in the public interest, the GATS drafters exempted from the scope of the GATS any services supplied in the exercise of governmental authority.[87] Pursuant to Article I:3(c) GATS, services fall within this category provided that they are not supplied on a commercial basis nor in competition with one or more service suppliers. The two conditions are cumulative in that failure to meet one would lead to the full application of the GATS.[88] For instance, supply by a State monopoly of electricity

[86]See also Krajewski 2011, p. 239.

[87]Article I:3(b) GATS.

[88]See Leroux 2006, p. 345.

in low-density and thus non-profitable geographic areas to meet USOs would fall under the exception. On the other hand, preferential access to the grid in profitable regions is less likely to escape the GATS scrutiny.[89] Thus, as one can infer, many public services as provided today would not come under the current, rather narrow definition of governmental authority.[90]

Article VIII relating to monopolies and exclusive service suppliers is also relevant for energy services. By virtue of this provision, monopoly suppliers are not allowed to act in a manner inconsistent with the WTO Member's obligations under the MFN and its specific commitments. It further prohibits abuse of monopoly (not dominant) position outside the scope of the monopoly rights but which is subject to specific commitments. This obligation applies to both public and private monopolies.[91]

Article VI GATS is also important when we consider the social character of energy services. Non-discriminatory measures imposing particular licensing requirements to energy service providers (for instance, USOs or other PSOs) would not need to be scheduled, but abide by the requirements of Article VI. The same goes for certain technical standards or specificities that energy service providers would need to abide by (for instance, various standards allowing for interoperability of networks).

When it comes to SGEI, the EU Schedule provide that 'services considered public utilities at a national or local level may be subject to public monopolies or to exclusive rights granted to private operators', thus leaving the door open for the identification of public service markets even at a later stage.[92] Such open-ended and thus ambiguous limitation may leave important leeway to the domestic regulator, but it creates uncertainty as to scope of the EU commitments, which the EU Member States seem to have a *carte blanche* to modify. Providing new exclusive rights in the energy sector may under certain conditions, as noted above, be justified under EU law,[93] but compensation would need to be granted to the EU's trading partners according to GATS rules. The same would go for investors who are protected by an investment agreement in case of indirect expropriation.

The explanatory note in the EU schedule provides that public utilities exist in various 'sensitive' sectors, including social services, environmental and health services, or transport services. It also informs that, within the EU, exclusive rights on such sectors are often granted to private operators subject to specific (public service) obligations. This is a non-discriminatory market access limitation, as it

[89]However, one would also need to see whether this specific WTO Member also undertook commitments in the relevant sector relating to energy distribution.

[90]Cf. Krajewski 2003, p. 341; also Adlung 2006, p. 464.

[91]Article XXVIII(h) GATS.

[92]See Arena 2011, p. 499.

[93]Again, rolling back liberalization may violate EU rules. See European Commission, above n 17, para 48.

restricts the number of possible service suppliers.[94] Energy services are not mentioned in the list, but the list is illustrative and, in any case, the concept of public utilities generally includes the energy sector. The note suggests that an exhaustive sector-specific scheduling would be impracticable, thereby allowing for flexibility to the national and local level with EU Member States to organize SGEI. Then, although the EU has included in its Schedule commitments in energy-related services, the wide discretion of EU Member States to define, organize and manage SGEI in the area of energy remains unaffected. However, in a global trade context, such a broad exception may trigger the other party's unwillingness to liberalize. This can be an unwelcome development for the EU export-oriented companies which are active in energy-related business activities.

### *13.4.3 The EU Free Trade Agreements (FTAs)*

The EU FTAs follow the GATS approach when it comes to SGEI (alias, public services), including for the energy sector.[95] In addition, the EU typically excludes from the scope of its FTAs all subsidies for public services. Furthermore, the EU FTAs, contrary to NAFTA, do not contain substantive disciplines specifically directed at the energy sector, but rather refer to the general concept of 'public utilities', which has been used in various EU FTAs, including the ones concluded with Chile, CARIFORUM, and Korea. In certain cases such as the EU-Chile FTA, the parties will include a best-efforts provision calling for cooperation or consolidation of economic relations in key areas such as the energy sector.[96]

More generally, the public utilities concept is central in the discussion relating to the external dimension of EU public services, although both EU law and WTO law are agnostic to the concept.[97] The European Parliament's resolution relating to the negotiation of a plurilateral Trade in Services Agreement (TiSA)[98] also makes reference to the high quality of EU's public utilities and connects the concept with Protocol No 26, thereby insinuating that, for the EU political institutions the concepts of "public utilities" and SGI are to be used interchangeably, but also reminding the negotiators of the status of SGI as "shared values of the Union". However, a different explanation would suggest that the Parliament, taking into account that the plurilateral agreement is to be negotiated within the WTO, decided to use the

[94] See European Commission, DG Trade, *Commission Proposal for the Modernisation of the Treatment of Public Services in EU Trade Agreements*, 26 October 2011, p. 2.

[95] Ibid.

[96] See WTO, above n 72, p. 21.

[97] See Krajewski's contribution in this volume.

[98] As of September 2013, participants in the TISA include Australia, Canada, Chile, Chinese Taipei (Taiwan), Colombia, Costa Rica, European Union, Hong Kong, Iceland, Israel, Japan, Liechtenstein, Mexico, New Zealand, Norway, Pakistan, Panama, Paraguay, Peru, Republic of Korea, Switzerland, Turkey, and the United States.

term that the EU had previously used in its Schedule. Be this as it may, public utilities are regarded as at least encompassing large network industries and therefore energy can come under this concept.

DG Trade has suggested that such an open-ended concept used in the GATS and other trade agreements is untenable and thus proposed the introduction of separate individual, transparent limitations which would define more precisely the situation for those national/regional level public services, while maintaining some leverage solely to measures of this type taken at the local level. In a positive list approach, this change would be of a horizontal nature, i.e. applying to all sectors. In a negative list, the reservation would be inserted in the relevant sector hindering market access (for instance, inscription of a monopoly for the provision of electricity to a given region, with no phase out in sight). The reservation under a negative list could also reserve the right to maintain or adopt a measure that would confer exclusive rights to certain energy services. Such a limitation would be inconsistent with both market access and national treatment.

For instance, the EU-Korea FTA,[99] which used a positive list in scheduling, entails a GATS-like exception relating to 'public utilities' under the horizontal limitations relating to establishment. At the same time, it excludes from its scope telecommunications and to computer and related services. Whereas the former is indeed an important network industry, the latter could be hardly considered as a public service. One would assume that Korea asked for some clarity (and, to be sure, legal certainty) as to the exact scope of the public utilities exception, whereas the EU export-oriented companies would like to ensure that no protection would be unduly granted to the Korean computer-related industries. With respect to energy, the agreement includes a best-effort provision inviting the EU and Korea to facilitate and promote trade and investment in renewables and energy efficiency. However, the EU has hardly made any meaningful energy-related commitments. The production, distribution and transmission of electricity and gas remained unbound, that is, no liberalization commitments were undertaken and this is the case for most energy services. However, commercial presence for services incidental to mining is fully liberalized under the agreement. Furthermore, commercial presence for services incidental to the distribution of gas is also liberalized. Again, the schedule makes reference to the application of the horizontal limitation relating to public utilities. Under the part of the EU schedule relating to energy services, the EU has no limitations for Modes 1 and 2 under services relating to mining. However, it made no liberalization commitments under pipeline transportation of fuels, energy-related wholesale trade services, retailing services of motor fuel or services incidental to energy distribution. In the latter case, only supply of consultancy services under Modes 1 and 3 is liberalized. On the other side, Korea liberalized commercial presence for most of the energy-related services. A possible interpretation of this discrepancy as to openness on energy-related services is

[99]Free Trade Agreement between the European Union and its Member States, of the one part, and the Republic of Korea, of the other part of 15 October 2009, *OJ* 2011 L 127/6.

that Korea decided to focus its efforts of opening the EU market on services sectors which are of export interest to Korean high-tech companies.

In the EU-CARIFORUM economic partnership agreement (EPA),[100] similar observations apply. Under commercial presence, the EPA entails a horizontal limitation as to the existence of monopolies or exclusive rights granted to private operators at the national or local level. Under commercial presence, the EPA, just like the EU-Korea FTA, provides that investors from energy producer countries may be prohibited from obtaining control in services sectors relating to production, transmission and distribution of electricity, gas, steam and hot water. Regarding energy services, the EPA has no limitations on cross-border supply and commercial presence regarding services incidental to mining and consultancy services in energy distribution with the caveat regarding public utilities still being applicable. Other than that, commercial presence in energy services within the EU is foreclosed. CARIFORUM States, on the other hand, are equally reluctant to pursue liberalization under energy-related services. Thus, there is no commitment under the heading relating to production, transmission and distribution of electricity, gas, steam and hot water.

In the EU-Central America FTA, under cross-border supply, Costa Rica, Nicaragua, Guatemala and Honduras included a horizontal limitation similar to the EU GATS public utilities exemption. The particularity of the Schedules of Costa Rica and Nicaragua is that they include a footnote listing various public services in an illustrative manner. Importantly, energy-related services such as electric energy supply, including generation, transmission, distribution and commercialisation are mentioned. El Salvador also included a similar exception suggesting that no provisions of the FTA can be interpreted as requiring a party to privatize the supply of public services in the exercise of governmental authority. The EU, on its side, inscribed full liberalization for cross-border supply and commercial presence of services incidental to mining and consultancy services incidental to energy distribution. Interestingly, the EU has not included any horizontal public utilities exception under cross-border supply, but only with respect to commercial presence.

Overall, the Central American countries inscribed more liberalization commitments on energy services than the EU for both cross-border supply and commercial presence. El Salvador and Guatemala liberalized fully the cross-border supply of energy services relating to the pipeline transportation of fuels. Guatemala went a step further and liberalized cross-border supply in all energy services except for retailing services of electricity, gas, steam and hot water. Panama also inscribed far-reaching commitments under cross-border supply of energy services. Honduras was also bold in its commitments, but still reserved sales of petroleum products and retailing services relating to electricity, gas, steam and hot water. Nicaragua also liberalized cross-border wholesale trade services in energy and

[100]Economic Partnership Agreement between the CARIFORUM States, on the one part, and the European Community and its Member States, of the other part of 15 October 2008, *OJ* 2008 L 289/I/3.

retailing services. Costa Rica, on the other hand, made virtually no reservation in commercial presence with respect to energy services. This divergence among the Central American countries is indicative of the varying level of integration and approach to sector-specific liberalization already within the CAFTA partners. Certain partners wished to maintain a more reluctant view than others towards liberalization in this sensitive sector, also reflecting differences in domestic regulatory approaches. This resulted in significant variance as to the openness of the bloc vis-à-vis the EU. It also weakened the concessions that the group could get on the side of the EU.

Overall, the EU approach with respect to energy-specific trade liberalization has been reluctant to date, but is expected to become more sophisticated in the near future, as the EU adopts a more aggressive outward-looking strategy towards energy security and sustainability. This will include traditional Eastern European partners but also other countries beyond this area such as Mexico or the ASEAN countries.[101]

## 13.5 Conclusion

Whereas the literature about SGI within the EU abounds, this is not the case with regard to the EU external action and the role of SGI. This chapter attempted to fill this gap, by focusing on the energy sector. Due to the typically dialectical relationship between the EU internal regulatory convergence and the EU external action, one would expect a much more coherent stance on the side of the EU, notably in an area of such strategic importance as the energy sector. It was argued that this fragmentation is in part due to the EU internal constitutional structure and the division of competences between MS and the EU. It may also be attributed to specific traits of the energy sector. As the EU has undertaken limited liberalization commitments to date both in the WTO and in free trade agreements, it would be safe to say that the impact of EU external action to the regulation of SGI within the EU has been limited. Within the WTO and the GATS, there has not been yet significant impetus for substantial liberalization in the energy sector similar to the forces that brought about liberalization in telecommunications and financial services within the WTO during the late-90s. In addition, and contrary to the EU, the GATS still lacks a comprehensive set of rules relating to subsidies and government procurement, thereby leaving outside its scope some of the most restrictive trade practices that States use to assign exclusive rights towards particular service suppliers. Discussions about such rules are ongoing, but chances for a deal in this negotiating round are low. Currently, there is a patchwork of exceptions and country-specific reservations exempting public services from the scope of trade regulation at the multilateral or preferential level.

[101]Cf. European Commission's Report, above n 48.

However, as the EU may become more outward-looking due to the increasing export orientation of its energy-related companies, it will seek liberalization of energy-related services by its trading partners, either at the bilateral level or through the WTO. When this happens, the EU will most likely need to show more flexibility with respect to the openness of its own market for energy-related services. While it is true that activities in the energy sector have public good characteristics (for, instance, providers of SGI serve the public interest, but they also are there to *safeguard* it; take the case of TSOs in their role as gatekeepers), regulatory intervention and trade restrictions would need to be better justified than by simply adding a broad carve-out in a trade agreement.

## References

Adlung R (2006) Public services and the GATS. J Int Econ Law 9(2):455–485

Arena A (2011) The GATS notion of public services as an instance of intergovernmental agnosticism: comparative insights from EU supranational dialectic. J World Trade 45(3):489–528

Bamberger C, Wälde T (2007) The Energy Charter Treaty. In: Roggenkamp M, Regwell C, Del Guayo I, Ronne A (eds) Energy law in Europe. OUP, Oxford, pp 145–194

Baumann F (2010) Europe's way to energy security—the outer dimension of energy security: from power politics to energy governance. Eur Foreign Aff Rev 15:77–95

Blockmans S, Van Vooren B (2012) Revitalizing the European "Neighbourhood Economic Community": the case for legally binding sectoral multilateralism. Eur Foreign Aff Rev 17(4):577–604

Coase R (1974) The lighthouse in economics. J Law Econ 17(2):357–376

Cossy M (2008) The liberalization of energy services: are PTAs more energetic than the GATS? In: Marchetti J, Roy M (eds) Opening markets for trade in services—countries and sectors in bilateral and WTO negotiations. CUP, Cambridge, pp 405–434

Cottier T, Malumfashi G, Matteotti-Berkutova S, Nartova O, de Sepibus J, Bigdeli S (2011) Energy in WTO law and policy. In: Cottier T, Delimatsis P (eds) The prospects of international trade regulation—from fragmentation to coherence. CUP, Cambridge, pp 211–244

Cross E, Delvaux B, Hancher L, Slot PJ, Van Calster G, Vandenberghe W (2007) EU energy law. In: Roggenkamp M, Redgwell C, Rønne A, Del Guayo I (eds) Energy law in Europe—national, EU and international regulation, 2nd edn. OUP, Oxford, pp 225–392

De Jong S, Schunz S (2012) Coherence in European Union External Policy before and after the Lisbon Treaty: the cases of energy security and climate change. Eur Foreign Aff Rev 17(2):165–187

Eeckhout P (2011) EU external relations law, 2nd edn. OUP, Oxford

Evans P (2003) Strengthening WTO member commitments in energy services: problems and prospects. In: Mattoo A, Sauvé P (eds) Domestic regulation and services trade liberalization. OUP, Oxford, pp 167–189

Fiedziuk N (2011) Services of general economic interest and the Treaty of Lisbon: opening doors to a whole new approach or maintaining the "Status Quo". Eur Law Rev 36(2):226–242

Hancher L, Larouche P (2011) The coming of age of EU regulation of network industries and services of general economic interest. In: Craig P, De Burca G (eds) The evolution of EU law, 2nd edn. OUP, Oxford, pp 743–781

Hober K (2010) Investment arbitration and the Energy Charter Treaty. J Int Dispute Settl 1(1):153–190

Kleinheisterkamp J (2012) Investment protection and EU law: the intra- and extra-EU dimension of the Energy Charter Treaty. J Int Econ Law 15(1):85–109

Krajewski M (2003) Public services and trade liberalization: mapping the legal framework. J Int Econ Law 6(2):341–367

Krajewski M (2011) Universal service provisions in international agreements of the EU: from derogation to obligation? In: Szyszczak E, Davies J, Andenæs M, Bekkedal T (eds) Developments in services of general interest. TMC Asser Press, The Hague, pp 231–252

Lazowski A (2008) Enhanced multilateralism and enhanced bilateralism: integration without membership in the European Union. CML Rev 45(5):1433–1458

Leroux E (2006) What is a "service supplied in the exercise of governmental authority" under Article I:3(b) and (c) of the General Agreement on Trade in Services? J World Trade 40(3):345–385

Neframi E (2010) The duty of loyalty: rethinking its scope through its application in the field of EU external relations. Common Market Law Rev 47:323–359

Petrov R (2012) Energy community as a promoter of the European Union's "Energy Acquis" to its neighbourhood. Legal Issues Econ Integr 39(3):331–355

Ross M (2000) Article 16 E.C. and services of general interest: from derogation to obligation? Eur Law Rev 25:22–38

Selivanova Y (2012) The Energy Charter and the international energy governance. Eur Yearb Int Econ Law 3:307–342

# Chapter 14
# The Impact of Free Trade Agreements on Local Self-government—The Provision of Drinking Water by Local Utilities in Germany as a Case Study

**Britta Kynast**

**Abstract** This chapter addresses the potential impact of free trade agreements on services of general interest which are provided in the context of local self-government and discusses how these agreements could interfere with Article 4(2) TEU. The chapter uses the provision of drinking water by local utilities in Germany as an example case study. The chapter begins with a brief overview of the current regime for the supply of drinking water, particularly with regard to the involvement of structures of self-government. Next, the chapter examines whether the provision of drinking water and the involvement of local self-government therein are likely to be influenced by free trade agreement regulation and, if so, to what extent. Finally, the results of the former analysis will be presented in relation to the EU primary law provision of Article 4(2) TEU.

## Contents



B. Kynast (✉)
University of Erlangen-Nuremberg, Erlangen, Germany
e-mail: britta.kynast@gmail.com



M. Krajewski (ed.), *Services of General Interest Beyond the Single Market*, Legal Issues of Services of General Interest,
DOI 10.1007/978-94-6265-063-3_14

## 14.1 Introduction

A large number of services of general interest are organised by public authorities which are subject to self-government. Therefore, when considering whether or not free trade agreements have an impact on services of general interest, it is also interesting to look at those services which are embedded in structures of self-government. The supply of drinking water by local utilities in Germany represents such a service and shall therefore serve as a case study.

With the entry into force of the Treaty of Lisbon, the proponents of self-government claimed a success, as local (and regional) self-government was mentioned in prominent sections of the revised European primary law.[1] Probably the most important[2] new provision is Article 4(2) of the Treaty on the European Union (TEU) which states: "The Union shall respect the equality of Member States before the Treaties as well as their national identities, inherent in their fundamental structures, political and constitutional, inclusive of regional and *local self-government*".[3]

This chapter will focus on the potential impact of free trade agreements on services of general interest which are provided in the context of local self-government and how these agreements could interfere with Article 4(2) TEU.

The chapter uses the provision of drinking water by local utilities in Germany as an example case study.

To begin with, the current regime for the supply of drinking water will be studied, particularly with regard to the involvement of structures of self-government. Secondly, this chapter will examine whether the provision of drinking water and the involvement of local self-government therein are likely to be influenced by free trade agreement regulation and, if so, to what extent. Finally, the results of the

---

[1]For example press release of the Association of German Cities (Deutscher Städtetag), 18 September 2009, available at: http://www.staedtetag.de/presse/mitteilungen/058308/index.html; press release of the German County Association (Deutscher Landkreistag), 4 November 2009, available at: http://www.kreise.de/__cms1/presseforum/pressemitteilungen/39-pres. This assessment is confirmed in the European Parliament resolution of 18 May 2010 on new developments in public procurement (2009/2175(INI)), para 9: "Points out that the Lisbon Treaty, which came into force on 1 December 2009, incorporates an acknowledgement of the right to regional and local self-government into European Union primary law for the first time (Article 4(2) of the Treaty on European Union); (...)".

[2]Supporters of subsidiarity might argue otherwise, however, the principle of subsidiarity is not a new one and the involvement of *local* authorities remained—even when taking into account the new Protocol No. 27—limited.

[3]Emphasis added by the author.

former analysis will be presented in relation to the EU primary law provision of Article 4(2), first sentence, TEU.

## 14.2 Legal and Political Background

### *14.2.1 Services of General Interest Before and After the Treaty of Lisbon*

Prior to the Treaty of Lisbon, the debate about services of general interest focused on services of general *economic* interest, as the regimes of these services matched clear competences of the European Union (EU) regarding internal market and competition rules.

Arguably the Treaty of Lisbon represented a fundamental turning point with regard to the acknowledgement of the important role of services of general interest in the EU. Evident in several changes made to primary law, services of general interest are deemed to have been accorded higher value.[4] In terms of a more general observation, it seems that the goal of establishing an internal market might no longer be an unconditional overall policy objective of the Union.[5] These assessments seem to be correct when looking at the wide range of changes to European primary law.

Article 14 of the Treaty on the Functioning of the European Union (TFEU) states a new competence for legislation related to services of general economic interest. Even though, for example, the European Parliament would have welcomed if this new article was chosen as a legal basis in the "State Aid Modernisation" process in the last years,[6] it has not yet been used in practice. Consequently, the impact of Article 14 TFEU remains unclear. Whilst some claim that it did not include any requirement for action from European legislators, nor would it set any particular directions,[7] others argue that Article 14 TFEU could regulate and secure the principles applicable to services of general interest.[8] Hence, whether or not Article 14 TFEU will be used in the coming years, and in which way, will surely be of particular interest to both jurists and political actors. The creation of a new competence already shows the increased importance of services of general (economic) interest for the European Commission's policies.

The new Protocol No. 26 on Services of General Interest[9] also attracted academic attention; however, its legal relevance, for example, in case law, has not yet been proven. After the negative referenda of France and the Netherlands on the

---

[4]Critical analysis e.g. Fiedziuk 2011.

[5]Fiedziuk 2011, p. 236.

[6]Szyszczak 2013, p. 5.

[7]Fiedziuk 2011, p. 242.

[8]Buendía Sierra and Munoz de Juan 2012, p. 64; Righini 2012, p. 5.

[9]Protocol on services of general interest, *OJ* 2007 C 306, p. 158 f., hereinafter: Protocol No. 26.

Treaty establishing a Constitution for Europe, the European Commission first proposed an interpretative declaration on services of general interest; however, this did not satisfy the needs of the Dutch government, which desired a tool in European law. As a consequence, Protocol No. 26 was developed[10] which has, according to Article 51 TEU, the same legal status as the Treaties. The protocol makes explicit reference to Article 14 TFEU, in addition to linking services of general *economic* interest with local authorities, thus possibly with local self-government: "(…) The shared values of the Union in respect of services of general economic interest within the meaning of Article 14 of the Treaty on the Functioning of the European Union include in particular:—*the essential role and the wide discretion of* national, regional and *local authorities in providing, commissioning and organising services of general economic interest as closely as possible to the needs of the users*; (…)".[11] The relevance of Protocol No. 26 is highly disputed. Some argue that the protocol adds little in substance[12] and, foremost, does not include any regulation for the European Commission, its policies and decision making on services of general interest.[13] These opinions neglect the fact that the protocol has the same legal status as the European Treaties, and hence forms part of European primary law. Others argue that the protocol shall serve as a concretisation of the provision of Article 14 TFEU and will also influence the application of Article 106(2) TFEU.[14] Even the creation of an independent legal remedy through the protocol is discussed.[15] As the relevance of Protocol No. 26 has yet to be thoroughly examined academic discussions are still in the early stages and its interpretation by the European courts is difficult to predict; at this stage even far-reaching claims as to its meaning cannot be excluded definitively. The newly established link between the provision of services of general *economic* interest and the local level ("local authorities") in European primary law may gain momentum in future conflicts about the provision of such services through local municipalities.

### 14.2.2 Local Self-government Before and After the Treaty of Lisbon

It was not a European institution but the Council of Europe which first addressed local self-government on a European level in its European Charter of Local Self-Government.[16] This Charter dates back to the year 1985. In its preamble, local

[10]Bauby and Similie 2012, p. 11.

[11]Emphasis added by the author.

[12]Sauter 2008, p. 173.

[13]Fiedziuk 2011, p. 233.

[14]Hatje 2012b, para 15.

[15]Bauby and Similie 2012, p. 47.

[16]European Charter of Local Self-Government of 15 October 1985, entry into force: 1 September 1988, CETS No.: 122, available at: http://conventions.coe.int/Treaty/en/Treaties/html/122.htm.

authorities are described as one of the main foundations of any democratic regime. As the ratifying states can choose 20 paras from the Charter,[17] it is referred to as an "à la carte menu". The Charter is a multilateral international agreement which was not signed by the EU itself; however, it was ratified by all 28 member states.[18] The Charter outlines, inter alia, the concept of local self-government and its scope with regard to tasks fulfilled at the local level. Article 3(1) of the Charter describes this concept as follows: "Local self-government denotes the right and the ability of local authorities, within the limits of the law, to regulate and manage a substantial share of public affairs under their own responsibility and in the interests of the local population". Article 4 deals with the scope of local self-government and states in para 2: "Local authorities shall, within the limits of the law, have full discretion to exercise their initiative with regard to any matter which is not excluded from their competence nor assigned to any other authority." Article 4(4) makes further reference to powers given to local authorities which "shall normally be full and exclusive. They may not be undermined or limited by another, central or regional, authority except as provided for by the law". These three quoted paragraphs are applicable to all EU member states as none have made a declaration which states otherwise.[19]

The paragraphs underline the commitment of the member states towards local self-government, as well as the independence of the local level in fulfilling its own duties and tasks.

The Committee of the Regions, the most important institution for local and regional interests at the EU level, was created under the Treaty of Maastricht in 1992, and had its first meeting in 1994.[20] The Committee is currently comprised of 353 representatives from the local and regional level. In the case of Germany, the majority of members (21 out of 23) represent the regional governments.

According to a number of studies, approximately 70 % of all EU legislation is implemented on the regional or local level.[21] The Committee of the Regions shall advocate the interests of the territorial areas, regions, cities and local municipalities in Europe.[22] Such advocacy is, inter alia, needed for matters which concern services of general interest: since the beginning of the 1990s, municipalities have faced problems with European law and politics when providing services of general interest as

[17]Article 12 of the European Charter of Local Self-Government.

[18]See the Chart of signatures and ratifications, available at: http://conventions.coe.int/Treaty/Commun/ChercheSig.asp?NT=122&CM=1&DF=&CL=ENG.

[19]See the list of declarations, reservations and other communications, available at: http://conventions.coe.int/Treaty/Commun/ListeDeclarations.asp?NT=122&CM=1&DF=&CL=ENG&VL=1; Hungary is not included in this list, however, according to the Treaty Office, it made no declaration under Article 12 of the Charter and is considered bound by the Charter in its entirety without exception.

[20]See e.g. Article 4 para 2 of the Maastricht Treaty.

[21]See Committee of the Regions, Key facts, available at: http://cor.europa.eu/en/about/Pages/key-facts.aspx.

[22]Mission Statement of the Committee of the Regions of 21 April 2009.

part of their own economic activities. In particular, the objective of the establishment of an internal market led, and still leads, to conflicts between the interests and needs of local self-government and EU policies.[23] At present, state aid rules and areas of public procurement (including concessions) seem to be the most sensitive topics for the local level. Regulations in these areas have the potential to threaten the organising and financing of tasks which are administered at the local level, especially with regard to the cooperation of municipalities, which is very common in Germany.

With the entry into force of the Treaty of Lisbon in 2009, the "blindness" of European law towards the concerns of the local level in the EU member states is deemed to have ceased once and for all.[24] With respect to local self-government, the most important new stand-alone legal provision should be the above-quoted Article 4(2), first sentence, TFEU. This provision is often deemed to mark a turning point in the acknowledgement of structures of local self-government in European law. It is therefore important to discuss whether and to what extent local self-government can be actively protected through this article.

In contemporary political debate, the principle of subsidiarity is often discussed as another possible tool for the protection of the regional and local level against excessive European law-making. The new Article 5(3), first sentence, TEU makes reference to the local level in the context of the principle of subsidiarity by stating: "Under the principle of subsidiarity, in areas which do not fall within its exclusive competence, the Union shall act only if and in so far as the objectives of the proposed action *cannot be sufficiently achieved by the Member States*, either at central level or at regional and *local level*, but can rather, by reason of the scale or effects of the proposed action, be better achieved at Union level".[25] Despite this new provision, the progress with regard to local self-government should not be overstated: the principle of subsidiarity is not new, and the involvement of *local* authorities remains limited, even when taking into account the new Protocol No. 27.

However, in general, both post-Lisbon Articles 4 and 5 TEU strengthened and continue to strengthen the role of local self-government in European politics by making explicit references to the local level and to self-government on this level.

### *14.2.3 Services of General Interest and Self-government Since the Beginning of the Euro Crisis*

In times of austerity, citizens have to rely more than usual on services provided by modern social welfare states which include, to a great extent (if not exclusively), services of general interest.

As a consequence of the crisis, the local level faces great challenges. Local budgets are heavily dependent on stable revenues as they are burdened with a high

---

[23]Ruge 2008, p. 263.

[24]Ruge 2008, p. 264.

[25]Emphasis added by the author.

amount of regular costs; however, these revenues decrease whilst, at the same time, the public's need for services of general interest increases. When trying to reduce the burdens on providers of such services, the local level often finds itself in conflict with EU competition policies, such as state aid regulations.

The European Commission is under considerable strain as well. In light of the rising scepticism towards "Europe", or even "Europe bashing", the Commission's policies and actions have to be justified more than usual. In this context, it is interesting to note that, for example, with regard to state aid for important utility services, stricter rules were introduced whilst a "softer" system was maintained for social services and the health sector.[26]

However, services of general interest did not remain untouched; on the contrary, some were subject to extensive reforms during the crisis. In Greece and Portugal, the privatisation of public utilities, including water supply, took place on initiative of "the Troika", consisting of the European Commission, the International Monetary Fund, and the European Central Bank, which caused uproar among civil society organisations.[27]

But not only initiatives which targeted services of general interest in crisis states received public attention. The discussions surrounding the Concessions Directive depicted European citizens as increasingly sensitive to policies concerning services of general interest. The proposal for a new directive on the award of concession contracts[28] included service concessions to "ensure a real opening up of the market and a fair balance in the application of concession award rules in the water, energy, transport and postal services sector".[29] This proposal was perceived as an attempt to privatise water by the back door through its rules on concessions.[30] The vivid public protests (including the first successful European citizens' initiative) caused an exclusion of the water sector from the directive.[31]

This new sensitivity in society is also apparent in current negotiations of free trade agreements, where reservations are expressed particularly with regard to a possible liberalisation of the water sector.[32]

---

[26]Sauter 2012, p. 313.

[27]See for example the exchange of letters between, inter alia, EPSU and Commissioner Rehn, available at: http://www.epsu.org/a/9019.

[28]European Commission, *Proposal for a Directive of the European Parliament and of the Council on the award of concession contracts,* COM(2011) 897 final, 20 December 2011.

[29]European Commission, *Proposal for a Directive of the European Parliament and of the Council on the award of concession contracts,* COM(2011) 897 final, 20 December 2011, recital 11.

[30]See "Water services: Directive on concessions will not lead to forced privatisation", http://ec.europa.eu/archives/commission_2010-2014/barnier/headlines/news/2013/01/20130124_en.html. Last accessed 5 March 2015.

[31]See n. 30.

[32]The Commission reacted to this during the TTIP negotiations by publishing a paper which shall prove that the water sector forms no part of the negotiations. (http://trade.ec.europa.eu/doclib/docs/2013/december/tradoc_152029.pdf; paper available in German only.).

## 14.3 Impact of Free Trade Agreements on Services of General Interest and Local Self-government—Case Study: Drinking Water Utilities in Germany

With regards to an analysis of the interdependence of free trade agreements, services of general interest and local self-government, it is important to recall that free trade agreements do not use the expression "services of general interest", as this is a term which derives from EU law and which has in itself no legal meaning in, for example, WTO law.[33] Furthermore, free trade agreements include provisions regarding cross-border trade in services. However, they usually do not regulate the structure and organisation of public administration.

### *14.3.1 The Provision of Drinking Water to Citizens—A Service of General Interest*

The notion of services of general interest emerges from European law[34]; however, it is not defined in European primary law,[35] and neither the jurisprudence nor the European Commission has developed a uniform definition. Nevertheless, the provision of drinking water is broadly acknowledged as a service of general economic interest (as is the treatment of waste water).[36] Hence, the provision of drinking water by local utilities in Germany constitutes a good example for a case study of a service of general interest, more specifically a service of general *economic* interest, the provision of which could be influenced by a free trade agreement.

### *14.3.2 The Provision of Drinking Water by Local Utilities in Germany*

The provision of drinking water to consumers has a one-hundred-year history in Germany.[37] Municipal regulations[38] and sometimes the constitutions of the

[33]See Chap. 3 by Weiß in this volume.

[34]See Article 14 TFEU, Article 106 para 2 TFEU, Protocol No. 26 on services of general interest, Article 36 of the Charter of Fundamental Rights.

[35]Kamaris 2012, p. 55.

[36]European Commission, *Communication accompanying the Communication on "A single market for 21st century Europe", Services of general interest, including social services of general interest: A new European commitment*, COM(2007) 725 final, 20 November 2007, "Other services of general economic interest, such as those in the area of waste management, water supply or waste water treatment, are not subject to a self-standing regulatory regime at EU level.", p. 4.

[37]German Federal Environmental Agency (Umweltbundesamt), Rund um das Trinkwasser. http://www.umweltbundesamt.de/sites/default/files/medien/378/publikationen/rund_um_das_trinkwasser.pdf, p. 14. Accessed 28 November 2014.

[38]E.g. Article 57 para 3, first sentence Bavarian Municipal Code.

German Länder[39] stipulate that the supply of drinking water constitutes an obligation of the municipalities as a general rule. Exceptions to this are, for example, domestic wells in sparsely populated areas where a central supply of drinking water simply does not represent the best solution with regards to technical, hygienic and financial aspects. Municipalities can decide how they wish to organise their local provision of drinking water. For this purpose, they may choose from different forms of business organisations which are regulated by the individual laws of the Länder: public and private enterprises as well as cooperation with other municipalities.[40] When local authorities choose to organise the provision of drinking water through a legal body which belongs to them, for example as majority shareholders, the supply is arranged through a concession contract.

In the view of the German Constitutional Court, the provision of drinking water is a traditional task of local municipalities[41] and therefore forms part of the right to self-government.[42]

### *14.3.3 The Provision of Drinking Water and the "Public Utilities Clause"*

In current EU free trade agreements, a clause is usually included which is based on the public utilities clause of the GATS: "In all EC Member States services considered as public utilities at a national or local level may be subject to public monopolies or to exclusive rights granted to private operators".[43] In the context of this clause, the meaning of the term "public utilities" is strongly debated.[44] However, even when accepting the narrowest possible interpretation, the supply of drinking water as an infrastructure-related service consumed by the public, respectively a service "of utility to the public" represents a public utility in the sense of the public utilities clause used by the EU.[45]

---

[39]E.g. Article 83 para 1 Bavarian Constitution.

[40]ATT et al. 2011, p. 19, 20. Municipalities can be members of self-governing corporations under public law as well. These corporations were usually founded for historical reasons.

[41]German Constitutional Court, Decision of 16 May 1989, 1 BvR 705/88.

[42]German Federal Administrative Court, Judgements of 20 January 2005, 3C 31.03, p. 9; Judgements of 16 March 2006, 4A 1075.04, para 480; German Constitutional Court, Judgement of 10 December, BVerfGE 38, 258(270); Judgement of 7 June 1977, BVerfGE 45, 63(78); Judgement of 23 June 1981, BVerfGE 58, 45(62).

[43]Usually there is a footnote added which reads as follows (or similarly): "Public utilities exist in sectors such as related scientific and technical consulting services, R&D services on social sciences and humanities, technical testing and analysis services, environmental services, health services, transport services and services auxiliary to all modes of transport. Exclusive rights on such services are often granted to private operators, for instance operators with concessions from public authorities, subject to specific service obligations. Given that public utilities often also exist at the sub-central level, detailed and exhaustive sector-specific scheduling is not practical.".

[44]On this see Chap. 10 by Krajewski in this volume.

[45]October Proposal, p. 4, point 3.1.

In 2011, the European Commission worked on proposals for reform with regard to the negotiations of new free trade agreements and prepared the confidential Reflections Paper on Services of General Interest in Bilateral FTAs which was leaked.[46] This Reflections Paper dealt with the common public utilities clause (and possibilities to replace it) as well as strategies for a negative list approach. In the Reflections Paper the public utilities clause was re-designed as a "services of general economic interest clause"; however, network industries would have been excluded from the newly designed reservation: "Network industries of telecommunications, energy, transport, environmental, and postal services are excluded from the scope of this reservation."[47] The category "environmental" was listed without further explanation under the scope of network industries. "Environmental" usually refers to CPC category 940 "Sewage removal, treatment and disposal services"; nevertheless, as reference was made to "large network infrastructures" in the explanatory part of the Reflections Paper,[48] listing the category "environmental" was interpreted as a possible effort to liberalise the water sector as a whole, thus concerning both the provision of drinking water and sewage water treatment.[49]

The leaked Reflections Paper was met with strong public criticism.[50] As a consequence, the European Commission published the Commission Proposal for the Modernisation of the Treatment of Public Services in EU Trade Agreements in October 2011[51] in which the "fundamental role" of public services was underlined.[52] The Commission upheld the proposed new design of the public utilities clause, with reference to services of general economic interest as a sector, but added "in all sectors" to this reference ("Sector: Services of general economic interest in all sectors"). As regards "water production, distribution and waste handling", the proposal went even further, putting forth a reservation from market access and national treatment applicable to all levels of government: "Country X reserves the right to maintain or adopt any measure with respect to the collection, purification and distribution of water, including drinking water, to water

[46]Hereinafter referred to as "Reflections Paper".

[47]Reflections Paper, p. 5. The analysis in this chapter will focus on a negative list approach as this will probably be applied in currently negotiated trade agreements.

[48]Reflections Paper, p. 2.

[49]The Reflections Paper included a reservation for the sector "water for human use and wastewater management". However, this reservation was limited and read as follows for mode 3: "EU: None, except that waste management at local level may be subject to monopoly or exclusive rights granted to private operators." For mode 4 it was indicated "Unbound; except as indicated in the horizontal section." Therefore, unlike the title suggests, there was no exemption for water supply.

[50]See for example Arbeiterkammer [(Austrian) Federal Chamber of Labour], Services of General Interest in Bilateral Free Trade Agreements—Reflection Paper of the European Commission, 2011.

[51]Hereinafter referred to as "October Proposal".

[52]October Proposal, p. 1.

management, and to waste water management. This includes the right to limit the number of suppliers of privately funded water production, distribution and waste handling services by establishing or maintaining monopolies, or granting a concession or exclusive rights on a non-discriminatory basis to a service provider or service providers". Clearly the Commission was impressed by the publicly expressed criticism of several stakeholders.

### *14.3.4 Current Negotiations of Free Trade Agreements*

Currently, free trade agreements with Canada (CETA, Comprehensive Economic Trade Agreement) and the USA (TTIP, Transatlantic Trade and Investment Partnership) are being negotiated. Within both free trade agreements—unlike in previous ones—a negative list approach ("list it or lose it") shall be introduced.

In the mandate for the negotiations of the TTIP,[53] reference is made to services of general interest in para 19 which states: "The high quality of the EU's public utilities should be preserved in accordance with the TFEU and in particular Protocol No. 26 on Services of General Interest, and taking into account the EU's commitment in this area, including GATS". Allegedly, such a paragraph shall also exist in the CETA mandate.

Especially with regard to its reference to Protocol No. 26, the content of which is highly disputed (see above), the meaning of this passage is anything but clear. Apart from its disputed legal meaning, this clause shows that the importance of services of general interest has been acknowledged by the political actors as they saw the need to add a separate paragraph to the mandate.

### *14.3.5 Possible Impact of Currently Negotiated Free Trade Agreements on the Provision of Drinking Water by Local Utilities in Germany*

For the purposes of this case study on the possible impact that free trade agreements currently being negotiated could have on the provision of drinking water by local utilities in Germany it is presumed that the "classic" public utilities clause of the GATS will be used.

In the given scenario, the German model of provision of drinking water by local utilities could be contested foremost because of rules on market access and national treatment as well as the effects of a separate chapter on public procurement.

[53]According to Article 207(3) TFEU the European Commission negotiates international agreements for the member states. The Council has a mandate for these negotiations. The mandate was made public and can be found at http://data.consilium.europa.eu/doc/document/ST-11103-2013-DCL-1/en/pdf. Last accessed 5 March 2015.

#### 14.3.5.1 Market Access and National Treatment

As shown above, there are several models of public utilities clauses[54] which could be used for a new generation of free trade agreements. Based on the Reflections Paper, as well as on the October Proposal,[55] a reservation for services of general economic interest would be limited to market access and would only refer to monopolies and exclusive service suppliers, not to economic needs tests. This can be taken as an indication that the European Commission would limit a "classical" public utilities clause to this scope as well.

While this reservation would still allow the granting of exclusive rights to an operator, for example concessions to a public utility, it would not cover national treatment, thus a more favourable treatment of local suppliers would not be possible.

It is not clear whether local utilities might generally be deemed to enjoy a more favourable treatment compared to foreign providers. For instance, it could be questioned whether it constitutes an infringement of the national treatment obligation that municipalities may found companies which are subject to public law, such as a *Zweckverband* (cooperation association between local authorities), whereas foreign companies cannot form such a cooperation.

Article 1 of Protocol No. 26 on services of general interest underlines "the wide discretion of (…) local authorities in providing, commissioning and organising services of general interest *as closely as possible to the needs of the users*.[56] It makes sense to engage with a local public utility, especially with regard to water supply, to ensure sustainable water management throughout the whole life cycle of drinking water. For example, it is much easier to reach an agreement with farmers to use less fertilizer if the negative effects directly concern the ground water (from which drinking water is produced) of their own community. It is also questionable whether such considerations could be taken into account when granting a concession to a local utility or if this would interfere with national treatment obligations.

Moreover, even if such narrow interpretations of the national treatment obligations could not be confirmed in the end, a conceivable discrimination already causes legal uncertainty and thus might put pressure on both the market and regulatory policies.

#### 14.3.5.2 Public Procurement

Most importantly, it is unclear how a horizontal reservation for public utilities would affect and be affected by a procurement chapter which might comprise

[54]On this subject, see Chap. 10 by Krajewski in this volume.

[55]See above n. 46 and n. 51.

[56]Emphasis added by the author.

detailed regulations on tendering for public utilities. In other words, if the tendering of a concession contract for drinking water supply was necessary under a public procurement chapter, it is unclear whether the public utilities clause would prevent this obligation from being enforced as this clause does not mention the procedure through which the exclusive right is granted to an operator.

For the TTIP agreement, a newly designed template for the procurement chapter was announced which will not be based on the GPA. As regards para 24 of the TTIP Mandate, the negotiated agreement "shall aim for the maximum ambition" and "will aim at enhanced mutual access to public procurement markets at all levels (national, regional, local) and in the fields of public utilities".[57] Before the fourth round of the TTIP negotiations in March 2014, the European Commission addressed regulations on concessions in the TTIP in a communication to the member states.[58] As to the published *state of play* of the sixth round of negotiations, the negotiating partners discussed questions on their regimes on concessions and Public private partnerships.[59]

As water supply was exempted from the scope of the European concessions directive,[60] its incorporation in a procurement chapter of a free trade agreement could undermine the regulatory flexibility which currently exists in this sector, and which enables publicly owned local utilities to provide water services.

Moreover, rules on PPP, which were also addressed by the European Commission, are not covered by the current GPA. Rules on PPP may have a huge impact on local water supply providers as some of them often—for historical reasons—have private minority shareholders.

Both rules on concessions in general and rules on PPP could result in new obligations to tender with regard to companies from free trade partners.

In summary, a new procurement template with the above described features could force local municipalities to tender water supply, even though they are exempted from the obligation to tender under current EU legislation. As concessions for the supply with drinking water are long-term contracts, lost tenders would imply the closure of public utilities, respectively the water branches in public utilities active in several sectors.

#### 14.3.5.3 Conclusions

The limitation of the public utilities clause to market access and, especially, the creation of a new public procurement chapter could lead to pressure which would work towards an opening of the drinking water services market and, ultimately, to liberalisation.

---

[57]See TTIP Mandate, see no. 53.

[58]Arbeiterkammer [(Austrian) Federal Chamber of Labour], Positionspapier Behandlung von Öffentlich-Privaten Partnerschaften (ÖPP) und Konzessionen in der TTIP, 2014.

[59]European Commission, State of Play of TTIP negotiations after the 6th round, 29 July 2014.

[60]See above under Sect. 14.3.3.

As a consequence, the provision of drinking water would no longer be in the hands of local municipalities and therefore would no longer represent a task which they execute under their right to self-government.

Although, at present, there may not be offensive interests from companies in the territory of potential trading partners[61] to enter the drinking water market, a free trade agreement would most probably be valid for an indefinite period of time,[62] thus an attempt to crack open the market of German drinking water utilities cannot be excluded.

#### 14.3.5.4 Remark with Regard to Environmental Issues

It should be noted that these findings concentrate exclusively on the potential structural effects of free trade agreements on the supply of drinking water by local utilities.

Another result of the conclusion of these kinds of agreements could be their direct and indirect effect on environmental issues.

Free trade agreement regulation could lead to a mutual recognition of environmental standards. Fertilizers, for example, usually end up in the ground water from which drinking water is produced at some point in their life cycles, and have to be dealt with by local utilities.

Another highly discussed issue is the impact of ISDS mechanisms on national, regional and local policy making. In Germany, the protection of drinking water reservoirs against possible environmental threats caused by the use of fracking technology is subject to public debate. Shale gas companies have already reserved claims for the exploitation of (possible) gas fields. These claims might be a protected right under the investment protection chapter of a free trade agreement. Although only compensation can be sought, it can very well be argued that a high compensation sum might de facto influence policy decisions or motivate parties to agree on a settlement which could involve an allowance for a project.

### *14.3.6 Infringement of Article 4(2) TEU by Future Free Trade Agreement Regulation?*

Article 4(2), first sentence, TEU, as introduced by the Lisbon Treaty, clarifies that local self-government forms part of the national identities of the member states.[63]

---

[61]At least no stakeholder association or individual companies expressly articulate such interests for the moment.

[62]See, for example, the EU-Korea agreement which states in Article 15.1 para 1 that the agreement shall be valid indefinitely.

[63]Hatje 2012a, para 14; Geiger 2010, para 3, Streinz 2012, para 16, contra: Puttler 2011, paras 18, 19.

Although the content of Article 4(2), first sentence, TEU should be interpreted autonomously by EU law, the member states and, in particular, their constitutional courts decide on the features of "their national identities, inherent in their fundamental structures, political and constitutional, inclusive of regional and local self-government".[64]

In order to determine whether the provision of drinking water by local utilities forms part of the "national identity" of Germany protected under Article 4(2) TEU, it has to be analysed whether this provision of services is "inherent" in the fundamental constitutional structures of Germany.

#### 14.3.6.1 German Constitutional Law as a Starting Point

Article 28(2) of the German Basic Law states: "Municipalities must be guaranteed the right to regulate all local affairs on their own responsibility, within the limits prescribed by the laws. Within the limits of their functions designated by a law, associations of municipalities shall also have the right of self-government according to the laws". In the view of the German Constitutional Court, the constitutional right to local self-government does not guarantee municipalities a right to exercise a specific task. However, Article 28(2) Basic Law ensures that the municipalities are responsible for all matters of a local nature as part of their right to self-government.[65] The very fact that a task could be provided in a cheaper or more efficient way beyond the local level does not justify an exception to this rule. Only an otherwise disproportionate increase in costs could legitimate an exemption.[66]

Water supply in Germany is traditionally locally organised through networks, supply and the production of water. The demand for water is also of a local nature. Water supply therefore constitutes a typical matter of a local nature in the sense of Article 28(2) Basic Law, which is also acknowledged by the German Constitutional Court.[67] Hence, water supply forms part of the constitutional right to self-government in Germany. It is therefore covered by Article 4(2), first sentence, TEU.

This assessment is not changed by the fact that drinking water supply is not organised by local utilities and is not a task of local self-government in all member states. The explicit goal of Article 4(2), first sentence, is to protect the individual

---

[64]Bogdandy and Schill 2013, para 22.

[65]German Constitutional Court, Judgement of 23 November 1988, BVerfGE 79, 127 II, 150.

[66]German Constitutional Court, Judgement of 23 November 1988, BVerfGE 79, 127 II, 153.

[67]German Constitutional Court, Decision of 16 May 1989, 1 BvR 705/88, German Constitutional Court, Judgement of 10 December 1974, BVerfGE 38, 258(270); Judgement of 7 June 1977, BVerfGE 45, 63(78); Judgement of 23 June 1981, BVerfGE 58, 45(62).

characteristics of the member states, thus these features do not need to have an equivalent in other member states.[68]

#### 14.3.6.2 The European Union Law Perspective

Under Article 4(2), first sentence, TEU, the EU "shall respect" the national identities of the member states. The term "shall respect" usually means a prohibition of disproportionate measures in EU law, for example, in the context of the Charter on Fundamental Rights.[69] As regards Article 4(2), first sentence, TEU, there is also a practical reason for assuming an inherent criterion of disproportionality: a general prohibition of any measure which would have an impact on local self-government would not be feasible in times in which 70 % of EU law is implemented on the regional or local level.[70] Such a strict approach would hinder European integration and would indeed not be necessary.

Some argue that a measure which is in conflict with the *core* of the identity of a member state should be forbidden in any case (without assessing its proportionality).[71] Examples for the core of the national identity of a member state include the fundamental decision to be a democratic state, the formation as a federal state and the language used in a state's territory.[72] Compared to these examples, the provision of drinking water by local utilities does not have the same outstanding position with regard to the identity of the German state, meaning that the dispute about the legal implications of conflicts with the *core* of the national identities of states can remain open.

It is also argued that a case based on a violation of Article 4(2), first sentence, TEU should be well-reasoned and an obligation should be included that a complaint was already filed by the respective member state during the legislative procedure in question.[73] It is true that in German law the interests of the local level shall generally be represented by the Bundesrat, the assembly of the

---

[68]Compare CJEU, Case C-244/06, *Dynamic Medien Vertriebs GmbH* [2008] ECR I-505, para 44, where the Court decided on the discretion of member states with regards to different concepts of child protection which justify an exemption from Article 28 EC. The measures of the member states did not have to be aligned as the European law intended to respect the individual standards in the member states. This is also true for Article 4(2), first sentence, TEU, as otherwise the protection of "national" identities would be led ad absurdum.

[69]Bogdandy and Schill 2013, para 25.

[70]See no. 23.

[71]Hatje 2012a, at para 18 with reference to Bogdandy and Schill, who do not share this view in the current edition of Das Recht der Europäischen Union: EUV/AEUV.

[72]Bogdandy and Schill 2013, at paras 19–26.

[73]Hatje 2012a, at para 20. The nature of this complaint is not defined any further.

German Länder.[74] However, this is a national attempt to protect and engage the local level in European law and policy making processes, and does not render obsolete judicial protection on the EU level. An obligation to notify an infringement during a legislative procedure would mean an additional criterion with regard to Article 4(2), first sentence, and go far beyond what is stipulated in the Treaty. Creating further prerequisite conditions for the use of Article 4(2), first sentence, TEU would contradict the special acknowledgement of local self-government after the Treaty of Lisbon. Such an added obligation must therefore be rejected.

The same argumentation is valid for the presumption that Article 4(2), first sentence, TEU shall only be used in "extreme situations".[75]

In sum, a measure which affects the provision of drinking water by local utilities has to be proven to be disproportionate to constitute an infringement of Article 4(2), first sentence, TEU.

It is disputed whether a proportionality test under EU law is based on two ("appropriateness", "necessity") or three ("appropriateness", "necessity", "reasonableness") criteria. In some judgements, the European Court of Justice only refers to the appropriateness and the necessity of a measure.[76] However, ideas of reasonableness are sometimes merged into the evaluation of necessity and, in some judgements, are even directly addressed when the structure of the case demands it. Therefore, it seems that all three criteria belong to a proportionality test. The criterion of reasonableness, however, is only addressed when it appears to be decisive from the point of view of the court.[77]

As the facts on the free trade agreements currently being negotiated are still very limited, the proportionality test can only be based on the scenarios presented in the previous sections.

The free trade agreements currently being negotiated aim to remove tariff and non-tariff barriers to trade in order to achieve positive effects for the economies of the states involved. This is a legitimate goal, also with regard to Article 3(3) TEU.

It is not certain whether this economic objective can be realised; while some studies indicate advantages, others see very few positive effects.[78] In general, there does not seem to be substantial interest regarding an opening of the market in the drinking water sector. However, as positive effects of the trade agreements cannot be rebutted with certainty, the planned trade agreement can be deemed to be appropriate.

[74]See for example Section 12 EuZBLG (Gesetz über die Zusammenarbeit von Bund und Ländern in Angelegenheiten der Europäischen Union), IntVG (Gesetz über die Wahrnehmung der Integrationsverantwortung des Bundestages und des Bundesrates in Angelegenheiten der Europäischen Union).

[75]Hatje 2012a, at para 19.

[76]Trstenjak and Beysen 2012, p. 270.

[77]Trstenjak and Beysen 2012, p. 270 with detailed references.

[78]E.g. Bertelsmann Stiftung and Global Economic Dynamics, Die Transatlantische Handels- und Investitionspartnerschaft (THIP) Wem nutzt ein transatlantisches Freihandelsabkommen? http://www.bertelsmann-stiftung.de/cps/rde/xbcr/bst/xcms_bst_dms_38052_38053_2.pdf. Accessed 28 November 2014; ÖFSE and Austrian Foundation for Development Research 2014.

The second criterion of the proportionality test is "necessity". A measure is necessary when there is no less intrusive and equally effective alternative.

Without free trade agreements, the costs of entering foreign markets for interested market participants are usually high which is a deterring factor for business. Changing the relevant rules on a state-by-state basis to encourage foreign market participants would still challenge the German model of providing drinking water through local utilities. Hence, the free trade agreement regulation in question can be deemed to be necessary as there is no less intrusive alternative.

Finally, the reasonableness of the planned free trade agreement regulation has to be assessed, weighing up the positive outcomes of the envisaged measures and the negative effects on the protected rights.

On the one hand, especially in the context of the euro crisis, promoting economic growth is an important objective. Moreover, the market forces in an open market could theoretically lead to lower and thus more affordable prices. In a global economy with emerging markets and other attempts to create free trade zones, such as in the Pacific area, the EU has to safeguard its competitiveness.

On the other hand, the local level could face a potentially irreversible liberalisation of the drinking water market. Thereby, local authorities would be denied the right to self-organise this task, even though the independent performance of duties and responsibilities is one of the major features of local self-government and, as such, is protected under German constitutional law (see above). Moreover, water supply is not just any task for local municipalities in Germany, but has an extensive history of being organised by local utilities.

In European primary law, Protocol No. 26 underlines "the essential role and the wide discretion" of, inter alia, local authorities "in providing, commissioning and organising services of general economic interest as closely as possible to the needs of the users." As described in the previous sections, this wide discretion of local authorities would be severely limited if it came to a liberalisation of the drinking water sector.[79] At present, no agreement exists in principle, whether in German or in European policies, on a desire to liberalise the water sector, therefore the possible effects of free trade agreement regulation described cannot be deemed to be part of an ongoing political process or consensus.

It is true that drinking water infrastructures in Germany may require large investments in the future[80] (as may, for example, infrastructures in the USA,

[79]A possible justification because of problems with other features of Protocol No. 26, such as "a high level of quality, safety and affordability, equal treatment and the promotion of universal access and of user rights" which would ask for a European intervention is not evident with regards to water supply by local utilities in Germany.

[80]Partially because prices were kept low for the citizens, partly because climate and demographic changes will necessitate technical adjustments. See e.g. for figures on the estimated need of investment: KfW Bankengruppe, KfW Kommunalpanel 2014. https://www.kfw.de/PDF/Download-Center/Konzernthemen/Research/PDF-Dokumente-KfW-Kommunalpanel/Kommunalpanel-2014.pdf. May 2014, pp. 14–15. Accessed 28 November 2014.

a potential future trading partner[81]); however, investments could be achieved through other measures than free trade agreements, such as, for example, appropriate price increase, state funding or minority investments from private shareholders.

In sum, the negative effects of the free trade regulation in question are far-reaching and therefore outweigh the probably not exorbitant positive effects that could be expected. Consequently, the envisaged measures cannot be deemed to be reasonable and are, thus, disproportionate.

A liberalisation of water supply services in Germany caused by free trade agreement regulation would, therefore, be in conflict with Article 4(2), first sentence, TEU.

This result takes into account the *current* situation in Germany. Should this situation change, for instance, with regard to the applicable rules on concessions for water services, the results of the case study would have to be re-assessed. Moreover, it is important to stress that clauses, which mirror the state of play in European law nowadays, could be incorporated into free trade agreement regulation, for example in a public procurement chapter (e.g. through dynamic references to existing exceptions from the duty to tender in EU law), in order to avoid conflicts with Article 4(2) TEU.

## 14.4 Concluding Remarks

The case study conducted shows that free trade agreement regulation can have severe effects on the provision of a service of general interest and thereby on the underlying structure of its organisation. With respect to the supply of drinking water by local utilities in Germany, the rules of a possible procurement chapter would affect tasks which are exercised under the regime of local self-government.

Free trade agreement regulation, as described in the scenario of the case study, would constitute an infringement of Article 4(2), first sentence, TEU. In order to avoid such a conflict with European primary law, an adequate reservation from the obligation of the procurement chapter for Germany (at least) would have to be inserted. For instance, it could be stipulated that no further requirements than those already existing under the current regime could be imposed on local utilities which provide water supply. A public utilities clause which incorporates a reservation from national treatment would prevent legal uncertainty with regard to legal bodies under public law.

However, it should be clarified that operating local utilities which are founded under public law, such as *Zweckverbände,* means no infringement of national treatment obligations. Moreover, free trade regulation should not be able to deprive the local level of its duties, respectively its rights, with regard to Protocol No. 26 on Services of General Interest.

---

[81]See Studie: Infrastruktur, Unterfinanzierung und Nachhaltigkeit im Fokus der US-Versorger *EUWID*, 30 June 2014.

In sum, the case study shows that, although the importance of services of general interest seems to be more acknowledged in European policies and European law at present, this does not mean that the European institutions and, especially, the European Commission can initiate *any* changes and reforms in that sector.

As shown above, Article 4(2), first sentence, TEU has practical effects on the work of European law and policy makers. With regard to services of general interest, this may implicate that there could be interesting future developments as many of these services are provided by local authorities which are subject to self-government.

## References

Association of Drinking Water from Reservoirs (ATT) et al (2011) Profile of the German water sector. wvgw Wirtschafts- und Verlagsgesellschaft Gas und Wasser mbH, Bonn

Bauby P, Similie MM (2012) Providing high-quality public services in Europe based on the values of Protocol No. 26 of the Lisbon Treaty on Services of General Interest study. CESI Académie Europe. Brussels

Von Bogdandy A, Schill S (2013) Artikel 4 EUV. In: Grabitz E, Hilf M, Nettesheim M (eds) Das Recht der Europäischen Union: EUV/AEUV, 51st supplement. C.H. Beck, München

Buendía Sierra JL, De Munoz Juan M (2012) Some legal reflections on the Almunia package. Eur State Aid Law Q Suppl 2:63–81

Fiedziuk N (2011) Services of general economic interest and the Treaty of Lisbon: opening doors to a whole new approach or maintaining status quo. Eur Law Rev 36:226–242

Geiger R (2010) Artikel 4 EUV. In: Geiger R, Khan D, Kotzur M (eds) EUV/AEUV, 5th edn. C. H. Beck, München

Hatje A (2012a) Artikel 4 EUV. In: Schwarze J, Becker U, Hatje A, Schoo J (eds) EU-Kommentar, 3rd edn. Nomos, Baden-Baden

Hatje A (2012b) Artikel 14 AEUV. In: Schwarze J, Becker U, Hatje A, Schoo J (eds) EU-Kommentar, 3rd edn. Nomos, Baden-Baden

Kamaris G (2012) The reform of EU state aid rules for services of general economic interest in times of austerity. Eur Compet Law Rev 2:55–60

ÖFSE, Austrian Foundation for Development Research (2014) ASSESS_TTIP: assessing the claimed benefits of the Transatlantic Trade and Investment Partnership (TTIP), Vienna

Puttler A (2011) Artikel 4 EUV. In: Calliess C, Ruffert M (eds) EUV/AEUV, 4th edn. C.H. Beck, München

Righini E (2012) The reform of the state aid rules on financing of public services. Eur State Aid Law Q Suppl 2:3–16

Ruge K (2008) Kommentar zu den Auswirkungen des Protokolls über Dienste von allgemeinem Interesse auf Daseinsvorsorge und Vergaberecht. Wirtschaft und Verwaltung 4:263–272

Sauter W (2008) Services of general economic interest and universal service in EU law. Eur Law Rev 33:167–193

Sauter W (2012) The Altmark Package Mark II: new rules for state aid and the compensation of services of general economic interest. Eur Compet Law Rev 7:307–313

Streinz R (2012), Artikel 4 EUV. In: Streinz R (ed) EUV/AEUV, 2nd edn. C.H. Beck, München

Szyszczak EM (2013) Introduction. In: Szyszczak EM, van de Gronden JW (eds) Financing services of general economic interest: reform and modernization. T.M.C. Asser Press, The Hague, pp 1–32

Trstenjak V, Beysen E (2012) Das Prinzip der Verhältnismäßigkeit in der Unionsrechtsordnung. Zeitschrift Europarecht 3:265–284

# Chapter 15
# Health Systems and Policy Space for Health in the Context of European Union Trade Policies

**Meri Koivusalo**

**Abstract** European Union trade policies have been evolving towards more emphasis on bilateral agreements and addressing non-tariff barriers to trade with an increasing number of trade negotiations with focus on services, government procurement and investment. Maintaining national policy space is a challenge for governments due to negotiation focus, practices and priorities. This is further affected by the changing relationship between national health systems and European Union law. While national health systems have become commercialised, this has not been recognised as part of trade negotiations. The variety of health systems within the European Union also creates challenges for Member States wishing to maintain full policy space for cost-containment and regulation, and return to public provision of services. This paper explores emerging concerns regarding maintaining policy space from a Member State perspective in the context of evolving European Union law, and priorities and practice in trade negotiations.

## Contents



M. Koivusalo (✉)
National Institute for Health and Welfare, Helsinki, Finland
e-mail: meri.koivusalo@thl.fi



M. Krajewski (ed.), *Services of General Interest Beyond the Single Market*, Legal Issues of Services of General Interest,
DOI 10.1007/978-94-6265-063-3_15

## 15.1 Introduction

The relationship between health and trade arises from a contested ground and is likely to remain so in the foreseeable future. This is due to three concerns and conflicts of interest with respect to health and trade policies: (1) epidemics and the spreading of infectious diseases; (2) contrasting policy priorities between health and commercial industries (e.g. tobacco), and (3) governance and management of national health systems to achieve universal coverage and solidarity, and ensure the sustainability of financing for health systems.

This chapter focuses on the third concern and argues why health services need to be considered a "sensitive" sector, where protection of essential policy space in publicly funded services is necessary but not sufficient for national health care systems. It then discusses how this aim relates to European Union trade policies, politics and practice of multilevel governance.

## 15.2 Health Systems and European Union Policies

The perceived and actual relevance of European Union policies to national health care systems was still negligible into the 1990s. While the first internal market-related cases at the European Court of Justice date back to the 1980s and health was present as part of the Maastricht Treaty (1992), the idea that European Union policies would be of major relevance to national health systems was neither discussed nor recognised broadly until key European Court of Justice cases emerged in the late 1990s. Indeed, when new member states Finland, Sweden and Austria joined the European Union in the mid-1990s, the Finnish government and policymakers were of the opinion that this would not have an impact on the national health care system, its organisation and financing.

The relevance of health was a public health issue for the European Union, in particular, due to the potential threats of epidemics and negative impacts of public health crises to the functioning of internal markets. This overall concern over public health was at the core of the public health Article 152 in the Amsterdam Treaty (1997) and the Nice Treaty (2001). Article 152 reiterated the requirement to ensure a high level of health protection in all policies, but kept any European Union competence complementary and strictly limited to public health.[1]

The Treaty of Amsterdam was important in making public health-related responsibilities part of broader European Union competence; however, the focus

[1]Article 152:5 of the Treaty establishing the European Community (Nice consolidated version) states that "Community action in the field of public health shall fully respect the responsibilities of the Member States for the organisation and delivery of health services and medical care. In particular, measures referred to in para 4(a) shall not affect national provisions on the donation or medical use of organs and blood."

on health services became more prominent as a result of key decisions by the European Court of Justice. The role of ECJ decisions was crucial for further engagement of the European Commission with health services. Hatzopoulos has described this as judicial activism in the creation of a European Union institutional role and presence in an area which, on the basis of Treaty, should have been preserved for Member States.[2] The first cases, known as the Kohll[3] and Decker[4] cases, were related to Luxembourg, Belgium and Germany, and it was initially considered that the problems were not applicable to national health services—NHS-type health systems (UK, Sweden, Finland). However, the subsequent Watt[5] case made it clear that this was not the case.[6] In addition to further court cases,[7] the changing context between national health systems and European Union policies was reflected on several fronts over the following 10 years:

(1) General economic and financial policies and concern over health and long-term care as a driver for high public spending as health and long-term care cover a substantial part of public spending[8]

[2]Hatzopoulos 2013, p. 125.

[3]CJEU, Case C-158/96 *Raymond Kohll v. Union des caisses de maladie* [1998] ECR I-1931.

[4]CJEU, Case C-120/95 *Nicolas Decker v. Caisse de maladie des employés privés* [1998] ECR I-1831.

[5]CJEU, Case C-372/04 *Yvonne Watts v. Bedford Primary Care Trust and Secretary of State for Health* [2006] ECR I-4325. In these healthcare systems access to services is defined on the basis of residence and free (or mostly free) at the point of use.

[6]Nedwick 2006, pp. 1645–1668 has brought up a number of difficulties with the ECJ approach to healthcare, whereas Hatzopoulos 2002, pp. 683–729 has emphasised how the ECJ had prioritised individual rights over governance of health care in the decisions and created a market in health care. See also, Brooks 2012, pp. 33–37.

[7]See e.g. CJEU, Case C-368/98 *Abdon Vanbraekel a.o. v. Alliance nationale des mutualités chrétiennes* [2001] ECR I-5363; CJEU, Case C-157/99 *B.S.M. Geraets-Smits v. Stichting Ziekenfonds VGZ and H.T.M. Peerbooms v. Stichting CZ Groep Zorgverzekeringen* [2001] ECR I-5473; CJEU, Case C-385/99 *V.G. Müller-Fauré v. Onderlinge Waarborgmaatschappij OZ Zorgverzekeringen UA and E.E.M. van Riet v. Onderlinge Waarborgmaatschappij ZAO Zorgverzekeringen* [2003] ECR I-4509; CJEU, Case C-444/05 *Aikaterini Stamatelaki v. NPDD Organismos Asfaliseos Eleftheron Epangelmation* [2007] ECR I-3185.

[8]The control of costs of health and pension systems has been part of economic policy focus for a longer time. See, for example Council of the European Union, The 2004 Update of the Broad Guidelines of the Economic Policies of the Member States and the Community (for the 2003–2005 period), 10676/04, 21 June 2004. However, after economic crisis health is increasingly an important part of European Semester process with European Commission providing guidance as part of Health 2020 and European Semester for Member States due to importance of health and long-term costs for public spending, see e.g. European Commission, Thematic summary on health and health systems, available from: http://ec.europa.eu/europe2020/making-it-happen/key-areas/index_en.htm. Accessed 27 November 2014 ; Council of the European Union, Conclusions on the sustainability of public finances in the light of aging populations, Press Release, 15 May 2012, para 3.

(2) Open coordination process with emphasis on health care and long-term care[9] and high level process of reflection on patient mobility[10]
(3) Services of general interest[11]
(4) Constitutional treaty negotiations and changes to the Treaty of Lisbon (2007)
(5) Services directive[12] and Directive on patient rights and mobility in cross-border care
(6) Changes in the focus of the European Union Health Programme with explicit engagement with health services and pharmaceutical policies as part of the European Union Health Programme[13]

The economic case with respect to the public funding of health care can be seen as providing legitimacy and relevance for the introduction of an open method of coordination, in particular, for long-term care. The high-level reflection process on patient mobility can be seen as paving way to the inclusion of health under the services directive and the later development of the directive on patient rights and mobility in cross-border care. The Open Method of Coordination on long-term care can also be seen as a means of legitimating the European Union's role in health services as this was later reflected in the Lisbon Treaty through Article 168 of the Treaty on the Functioning of the European Union (TFEU), opening up scope for European Union engagement with health services. The incremental and increasing engagement with health services building first on European Court of Justice decisions, but later on commission initiatives, was not left unobserved by the Member States. Perhaps the clearest and strongest statement was made in 2006

[9]European Commission, Modernising social protection for the development of high-quality, accessible and sustainable health care and long-term care: support for national strategies using the 'open method of coordination', COM(2004) 304 final, 20 April 2004, p. 11 makes an interesting interpretation on how responsibilities for the organisation and funding of the health care and elderly care sector rests primarily with the Member States, which are bound, *when exercising this responsibility, to respect the freedoms defined and rules laid down in the Treaty.*

[10]European Commission, High level process of reflection on patient mobility and health care developments in the European Union, HLPR/2003/16, 9 December 2003.

[11]See e.g. European Commission, Green paper on Services of General Interest, COM(2003) 270 final, 21 May 2003; European Commission, White paper on Services of General Interest, COM(2004) 374 final, 12 May 2004.

[12]Directive 2006/123/EC of the European Parliament and of the Council of 12 December 2006 on services in the internal market, *OJ* 2006 L 376/36; Directive 2011/24/EU of the European Parliament and of the Council of 9 March 2011 on the application of patients' rights in cross-border health care, *OJ* 2011 L 88/45.

[13]See European Commission, Proposal for a Regulation of the European Parliament and of the Council on establishing a Health for Growth Programme, the third multi-annual programme of EU action in the field of health for the period 2014–2020, COM(2011) 709 final, 9 November 2011. Pharmaceutical policies were moved from DG enterprise to Health and Consumer affairs in 2009, see European Commission, President Barroso unveils his new team, Press Release, IP/09/1837, 27 November 2009.

in the Council conclusions and Statement on Common Values and Principles, which made it clear that[14]:

> This is a statement by the 25 Health Ministries of the European Union, about the common values and principles that underpin Europe's health systems. We believe such a statement is important in providing clarity for our citizens, and timely, because of the recent vote of the Parliament and the revised proposal of the Commission to remove health care from the proposed Directive on Services in the Internal Market. We strongly believe that developments in this area should result from political consensus, and not solely from case law.
>
> We also believe that it will be important to safeguard the common values and principles outlined below as regards the application of competition rules on the systems that implement them.
>
> This statement sets out the common values and principles that are shared across the European Union about how health systems respond to the needs of the populations and patients that they serve. It also explains that the practical ways in which these values and principles become a reality in the health systems of the EU vary significantly between Member States, and will continue to do so. In particular, decisions about the basket of health care to which citizens are entitled and mechanisms used to finance and deliver that health care, such as the extent to which it is appropriate to rely on market mechanisms and competitive pressures to manage health systems must be taken in the national context.

The fact that health services were carved out from the services directive has had implications for European Union commercial policies in relation to what is taken for granted for the negotiation of bilateral trade agreements, as internal markets and the services directive are often used to imply reference to European internal powers that entitle the Commission to act on behalf of Member States. This remains a broader concern in the context of the European Commission's increasing involvement in health, although the specific carve out of health services by the European Parliament made it more explicit that health is not just "any service" governed by the service directive as part of internal markets.[15]

The Lisbon Treaty, however, has enabled the definition of health services as an area of complementary action in Article 168 TFEU, building on engagement with the open method of coordination in para 2, and also removed explicit references to Community action on public health in para 7:

> 2. The Union shall encourage cooperation between the Member States in the areas referred to in this Article and, if necessary, lend support to their action. It shall in particular encourage cooperation between the Member States to improve the complementarity of their health services in cross-border areas.

---

[14]Council conclusions on common values and principles in European Union Health Systems, *OJ* 2006 C 146/1, Statement paras 1–3.

[15]This is to some extent compromised by the fact that in spite of initial concerns the new proposal was not based only or, in particular, on the TFEU public health Article 168, but essentially on TFEU Article 114 (95 TEC) on functioning of internal markets, which was claimed as the "appropriate" article based on the claim that "functioning of internal markets on the basis of Article 114(3) requires that, in achieving harmonisation, a high level of protection of human health is to be guaranteed taking account in particular of any new development based on scientific facts.", Directive 2011/24/EU of the European Parliament and of the Council of 9 March 2011 on the application of patients' rights in cross-border healthcare, *OJ* 2011 L 88/45.

> Member States shall, in liaison with the Commission, coordinate among themselves their policies and programmes in the areas referred to in para 1. The Commission may, in close contact with the Member States, take any useful initiative to promote such coordination, in particular initiatives aiming at the establishment of guidelines and indicators, the organisation of exchange of best practice, and the preparation of the necessary elements for periodic monitoring and evaluation. The European Parliament shall be kept fully informed.
>
> 7. Union action shall respect the responsibilities of the Member States for the definition of their health policy and for the organisation and delivery of health services and medical care. The responsibilities of the Member States shall include the management of health services and medical care and the allocation of the resources assigned to them. The measures referred to in para 4(a) shall not affect national provisions on the donation or medical use of organs and blood.

The implications from changes to Article 168 TFEU can be interpreted in different ways. On the one hand, it can be argued that the role of the EU has become now legitimately mentioned as this relates to health services, and that restriction of community action on public health has been changed, opening scope for increasing EU involvement in health services.[16] On the other hand, it can be emphasised that it includes a stronger reference to Member States' responsibility for definition of their health policies and management of health services.[17] What has taken place since would support the former interpretation of the shift of competence to the European Commission more strongly, as since the Lisbon Treaty negotiations the European Commission has engaged increasingly with health services on the grounds of expressed necessities with respect to patient mobility and cross-border care. While the White Paper on the strategic approach for the European Union discussed public health further, its title now focused on health rather than public health.[18] However, in spite of the strategic focus on public health, major efforts were geared towards health services as part of separate consultation.[19] Indeed, the new health programme for the years 2014–2020 has a substantial focus on health services.[20] The result of these changes is that while Member States still have responsibilities for the financing of health care, the role of the European Commission in the regulatory context of health systems governance has been

[16]Article 152.5 ECT (Nice version) had a clear and explicit focus on public health: "Community action in the field of public health shall fully respect the responsibilities of the Member States for the organisation and delivery of health services and medical care. In particular, measures referred to in para 4(a) shall not affect national provisions on the donation or medical use of organs and blood."

[17]Foreign and Commonwealth Office 2008, p. 14.

[18]European Commission, White paper, Together for Health: A Strategic Approach for the EU 2008–2013, COM(2007) 630 final, 23 October 2007.

[19]European Commission, Consultation regarding Community action on health services, SEC(2006) 1195/4, 26 September 2006.

[20]European Commission, Proposal for a Regulation of the European Parliament and of the Council on establishing a Health for Growth Programme, the third multi-annual programme of EU action in the field of health for the period 2014–2020, COM(2011) 709 final, 9 November 2011.

increasing in the field, both in the context of DG5 responsible for Health and Consumer Affairs and in the requirement that Member States follow Treaty obligations, requirements for economic and financial policies, and the broader regulatory framework established as part of internal markets and commercial policy.[21]

The carve out of health from the service directive resulted in consequent communication and a proposal for a directive on patient rights and cross-border care.[22] This was, however, approved only in late 2011 after substantial amendments in Parliament and substantial delays. The views of several Member States have been described by the term animosity,[23] but the proposed directive was (finally) approved by a vote, with Austria, Poland, Portugal, and Romania voting against approval and Slovakia abstaining, in 2011.[24] In Austria national legislation was in compliance with the directive, but the background was the federal organisation and financing of hospitals.[25] In this context, the active engagement of the European Commission in bringing health systems under internal markets was reflected in a Court of Justice case on free movement against the requirements of prior authorisation for reimbursement of costs in a case against France.[26] The ability to require prior authorisation for mobility of patients was a major sticking point between Member States and the European Commission, as Member States argued this would make planning and allocation of resources within health systems impossible, in particular, for major health care costs, even if these were applied to services outside national hospitals as was the case with France.

Thus, while European Court of Justice decisions were initially the "cause" for Commission engagement with health, decisions by the European Court of Justice have now come full circle in support of Member States policy space to ensure the financial sustainability of health systems against the Commission.

The financial sustainability of health systems is of interest, in particular, due to the use of intra-European Union investment agreements to challenge governments, such as Poland and Slovakia, which backed away from health care privatisation programmes.[27] Poland refused to privatise the majority of its health insurance system and backed off from further privatisation after the government changed.[28]

---

[21]See e.g. Van de Gronden et al. 2011; Mossialos et al. 2010; Tritter et al. 2009, pp. 76–94; European Commission, A Quality Framework for Services of General Economic Interest in Europe, COM(2011) 900 final, 20 December 2011.

[22]European Commission, Proposal for a Directive of the European Parliament and of the Council on the application of patients' rights in cross-border healthcare, COM(2008) 414 final, 2 July 2008; Koivusalo 2010, pp. 263–280.

[23]Hatzopoulos 2013, p. 126.

[24]Council of the European Union, Directive on cross-border care adopted, Press Release, 7056/11, 28 February 2011.

[25]Kostera 2013, pp. 149–156.

[26]CJEU, Case C-512/08 *European Commission v. French Republic* [2010] ECR I-8833.

[27]See Hall 2010.

[28]See e.g. FACTBOX-Poland, Eureko meet to settle PZU dispute, Reuters, 17 January 2008, available at: http://www.reuters.com/article/2008/01/17/pzu-idUSL17499172008O117.

In Slovakia a similar story of overambitious liberalisation of the public health insurance system was followed by more restrictive action by the next government.[29] A key aspect was limiting mobility of capital through the requirement of non-profit status. Slovakia refused to pay and in May 2013 its assets were frozen at the value of 29.5 million euros on the basis of information provided by the Dutch insurance company Achmea, involved as a claimant in the case.[30]

There is a broader question of the applicability of intra-European Union investment agreements, where the case has been a landmark case confirming the scope for application of intra-EU BITs.[31] The reality is that arbitration cases within Europe have created scope for investment arbitration in the field of health care and health insurance services, including against such measures that governments use to constrain costs. It is not surprising that the focus has been on new Member States as these have undertaken more market-oriented health care reforms and there has been international interest in prospective health care markets in CEE markets as the result of changes in legislation.[32] On the other hand, as the case has not so far been judged by the European Court of Justice, we do not have evidence as to whether consideration of the financial sustainability of health systems would have in practice weighed more than Treaty obligations regarding free mobility of capital.

Emphasis in European Court of Justice cases that health services are services in the context of internal markets has meant that they have often been more part of the problem than the solution in efforts to ensure the financial sustainability of health systems. Furthermore, the particular trail of European Court of Justice decisions on health services has been complemented by judgements on freedom to provide services, government procurement and state aid in the area of social security and, in particular, services of general interest.[33] For example, European Court of Justice decisions on the AOK and Oymanns cases have been seen as controversial in terms of their further influence on the German health system as this relates to competition and government procurement law.[34] However, while it is and would

---

[29]See case *Eureko B.V. v. the Slovak Republic*, PCA Case No. 2008-13, Award on Jurisdiction, Arbitrability and Suspension, 26 October 2010. While this case applies to the intra-EU issue it has some discussion with respect to the case itself.

[30]See Achmea, Dutch insurer Achmea seizes Slovak assets. http://news.achmea.nl/dutch-insurer-achmea-seizes-slovak-assets. 22 May 2013. Accessed 24 February 2014.

[31]*Eureko B.V. v. the Slovak Republic*, PCA Case No. 2008-13, Award on Jurisdiction, Arbitrability and Suspension, 26 October 2010.

[32]See e.g. Koivusalo 2013, pp. 93–117.

[33]See e.g. Deutsche Sozialversicherung, Social Security as 'social service provision' in the Internal Market: not an appropriate concept for Europe, Joint Position Paper of the Umbrella Organisations representing the German Social Security System. http://www.deutsche-sozialversicherung.de/en/europe/documents/verweis_healthcare/Konzept_fuer__Europa_englisch.pdf. April 2005, p. 1. Accessed 24 February 2014.

[34]Welti 2011, p. 320; CJEU, Case C-264/01 *AOK Bundesverband a.o. v. Ichthyol-Gesellschaft Cordes, Hermani & Co.* [2004] ECR I-2493; CJEU, Case C-300/07 *Hans & Christophorus Oymanns GbR, Orthopädie Schuhtechnik v. AOK Rheinland/Hamburg* [2009] ECR I-4799.

be a matter of European policies to address a lack of balance within European Union social and economic treaty obligations, changes are more difficult to make if the current state is bound further on the basis of trade and investment agreements.

Trade and services negotiations also broadly affect national health systems through what is negotiated in the context of professional services and mode 4 negotiations. These areas are also reflected in the European legal framework as it concerns the mobility of people. In the European Union, free mobility of workers is laid down in Article 39 TFEU and has been further developed in regulation 1612/68. Mutual recognition of qualifications was initially provided for in Directive 2005/36/EC. A further revision of the regulation on mutual recognition of qualifications was approved in 2013, allowing more policy space to tackle language requirements as well as to address concerns over rogue professionals moving from one country to another.[35] The Green Paper on the European workforce for health further established the role and presence of the European Union in the field.[36]

### 15.2.1 Services of General Interest and Health Systems

Services of general interest have been important in the definition of limits of internal markets and part of European discourse since the Treaty of Rome.[37] Broader debate on services of general interest was initiated on the basis of green and white papers with respect to the role, nature and scope of services of general interest.[38] Health and social services have also become explicitly defined as part of services of general interest.[39] A further process of clarification and guidance has taken

[35]Directive 2013/55/EU of the European Parliament and of the Council of 20 November 2013 amending Directive 2005/36/EC on the recognition of professional qualifications and Regulation (EU) No. 1024/2012 on administrative cooperation through the Internal Market Information System, *OJ* 2013 L 354/132.

[36]European Commission, Green paper on the European Workforce for Health, COM(2008) 725 final, 10 December 2008.

[37]See the original Rome Treaty of 1957, Article 90 EEC.

[38]See e.g. European Commission, Green paper on Services of General Interest, COM(2003) 270 final, 21 May 2003; European Commission, White paper on Services of General Interest, COM(2004) 374 final, 12 May 2004; European Commission, Services of general interest, including social services of general interest: a new European commitment, COM(2007) 725 final, 20 November 2007; European Commission, Staff Working Document, Progress since the 2004 White Paper on services of general interest, SEC(2007) 1515, 20 November 2007; European Commission, Staff Working Document, Biennial Report on social services of general interest, SEC(2008) 2179, 2 July 2008.

[39]See e.g. European Commission, Services of general interest, including social services of general interest: a new European commitment, COM(2007) 725 final, 20 November 2007; European Commission, Staff Working Document, Progress since the 2004 White Paper on services of general interest, SEC(2007) 1515, 20 November 2007.

place and is continuing, in particular for social services.[40] However, while there have been substantial discussions concerning the definition of services of general interest, the key problem for health systems is how a distinction between services of general interest and services of general economic interest is made. The most recent report on services of general interest clarifies the relationship with state aid, emphasising that state aid rules apply to the financing of social services of an economic nature, even if the body providing the service has non-profit status.[41]

As long as services of general interest (SGI) remains a more residual category in the context of internal markets in practice,[42] a substantial part of health services will become defined as services of general economic interest and subject to internal market regulations and competition law. This implies that SGI is not a sufficient basis for exclusion from trade and investment negotiations. Furthermore, Article 2 of the Lisbon Treaty Protocol on services of general interest (Protocol No. 26) makes it explicit that: "The provisions of the Treaties do not affect in any way the competence of Member States to provide, commission and organise *non-economic services* of general interest."

On the other hand, debates and discourse on services of general interest have been a channel for major discontent regarding the implications of single markets, in particular with provision of social services.[43] In European policies the role of SGI has been followed and promoted by nongovernmental organisations with substantial public scrutiny. The danger is that while rhetorics would emphasise the values and the role of SGI and the contribution of Social Europe to the trading partners of the rest of the world, this is not associated with adequate consideration of how this can be achieved, with the consequence of SGI becoming merely a replacement for GATS Article I:3 (see below).

---

[40]European Commission, Staff Working Document, Guide to the application of the European Union rules on state aid, public procurement and the internal market to services of general economic interest, and in particular to social services of general interest, SEC(2010) 1545 final, 7 December 2010; European Commission, Staff Working Document, Second Biennial Report on social services of general interest, SEC(2010) 1284 final, 22 October 2010; European Commission, A Quality Framework for Services of General Economic Interest in Europe, COM(2011) 900 final, 20 December 2011; European Commission, Staff Working Document, Investing in Health, SWD(2013) 43 final, 20 February 2013; European Commission, Staff Working Document, Guide to the application of the European Union rules on state aid, public procurement and the internal market to services of general economic interest, and in particular to social services of general interest, SWD(2013) 53 final/2, 29 April 2013.

[41]European Commission, Staff Working Document, Guide to the application of the European Union rules on state aid, public procurement and the internal market to services of general economic interest, and in particular to social services of general interest, SWD(2013) 53 final/2, 29 April 2013, p. 9.

[42]This is reflected, for example, in CJEU, Case C-309/99 *Wouters a.o. v.* Algemene Raad van de Nederlandse Orde van Advocaten [2002] ECR I-1577.

[43]This is also reflected in formal reports on the Single Market, such as in M. Monti, A new strategy for the single market. At the service of Europe's economy and society. Report to the President of the European Commission Jose Manuel Barroso, 9 May 2010. http://ec.europa.eu/bepa/pdf/monti_report_final_10_05_2010_en.pdf, p. 73. Accessed 1 March 2014, where, according to Monti: 'Since the nineties, the place of public services within the single market has been a persistent irritant in the European public debate.'

### *15.2.2 Commercial Policy and Health Systems*

European Union competence on health remained complementary and restricted to public health during the intergovernmental conference and negotiations of the Treaty of Nice. This provides the background as well as context for the way in which this relationship was reflected as part of European Union commercial policy in the Treaty of Nice, where a specific carve out was left for particular services: cultural and audiovisual, educational, social and human health services were carved out from shared majority voting to unanimous decision-making and shared competence in these fields:

Article 133. 6 ECT stated:

> An agreement may not be concluded by the Council if it includes provisions which would go beyond the Community's internal powers, in particular by leading to harmonisation of the laws or regulations of the Member States in an area for which this Treaty rules out such harmonisation.
>
> In this regard, by way of derogation from the first subparagraph of para 5, agreements relating to trade in cultural and audiovisual services, educational services, and social and human health services, shall fall within the shared competence of the Community and its Member States.
>
> Consequently, in addition to a Community decision taken in accordance with the relevant provisions of Article 300, the negotiation of such agreements shall require the common accord of the Member States. Agreements thus negotiated shall be concluded jointly by the Community and the Member States.

In health services the articulation of the problem during Treaty of Nice negotiations was relatively straightforward. As Member States had competence for organisation and financing of health care, they should have been able to maintain policy space within the sector in relation to commercial policy negotiations. Cultural, audiovisual, educational, social and health services became known as "sensitive services" in the context of European Union commercial policy. However, while international trade negotiations on services were stalled, the situation with respect to health services started to change more prominently in relation to European Union internal policies, services and health.

The Lisbon Treaty version of the Article on common commercial policy (Article 207 TFEU) has further limited the scope for carve out on services, but is still relevant to current trade negotiations as it gives support to arguments concerning "sensitive services" as well as, ultimately, a right to veto if there is a concern over the financial sustainability of health services in a member state as expressed in Article 207(4):

> 4. For the negotiation and conclusion of the agreements referred to in para 3, the Council shall act by a qualified majority.

> For the negotiation and conclusion of agreements in the fields of trade in services and the commercial aspects of intellectual property, as well as foreign direct investment, the Council shall act unanimously where such agreements include provisions for which unanimity is required for the adoption of internal rules.
>
> The Council shall also act unanimously for the negotiation and conclusion of agreements:
>
> (a) in the field of trade in cultural and audiovisual services, where these agreements risk prejudicing the Union's cultural and linguistic diversity;
>
> (b) in the field of trade in social, education and health services, where these agreements risk seriously disturbing the national organisation of such services and prejudicing the responsibility of Member States to deliver them.

The carve out represents in many ways the concern of Member States of maintaining policy space in a context where European Union engagement in the sector is increasing. A reservation for unanimity only for those areas where unanimity is required for internal rules was thus not sufficient to ensure policy space for these services, which required a specific carve out. On the other hand, it applies not only to services, but also to negotiations on foreign direct investment and commercial aspects of intellectual property rights. In light of the existing arbitration cases, as well as pressures from trade, this is of importance to national pricing policies and cost-containment in the field of medicines.[44] The scope for Article 207(4) TFEU carve out is thus broader than was initially assumed necessary to ensure policy space arises in a greater proportion from the existing, more contested relationship between national health systems and internal markets.

An interesting element in this is that Article 207 TFEU uses almost the same language as the initial Court of Justice case C-120/95, Decker, in para 39, which states:

> It must be recalled that aims of a purely economic nature cannot justify a barrier to the fundamental principle of the free movement of goods. However, it cannot be excluded that the risk of seriously undermining the financial balance of the social security system may constitute an overriding reason in the general interest capable of justifying a barrier of that kind.

This "emergency brake" provision has potential to both a help and a hindrance in taking health services better into account as part of trade negotiations (see Sect. 15.2.5). There is also a risk that some of these services are considered "more sensitive" than others. While audiovisual services were excluded from services and establishment chapter in the directives for EU-USA negotiations, there was only a minor reference to recognising the "sensitive nature" of certain sectors[45]:

---

[44]For example, Finland is already on the United States 301 pressure list due to reference to pricing and promotion of generic medicines; see United State Trade Representative, 2013 Special 301 Report. United States, Washington D.C. http://www.ustr.gov/sites/default/files/05012013%202013%20Special%20301%20Report.pdf. May 2013, p. 48. Accessed 1 March 2014.

[45]Council of the European Union, Directives for the negotiation on the Transatlantic Trade and Investment Partnership between the European Union and the United States of America, 17 June 2013, para 15.

> The aim of negotiations on trade in services will be to bind the existing autonomous level of liberalisation of both Parties at the highest level of liberalisation captured in existing FTAs, in line with Article V of GATS, covering substantially all sectors and all modes of supply, while achieving new market access by tackling remaining long-standing market access barriers, recognising the sensitive nature of certain sectors. Furthermore, the US and the EU will include binding commitments to provide transparency, impartiality and due process with regard to licensing and qualification requirements and procedures, as well as to enhance the regulatory disciplines included in current US and EU FTAs.

The narrow application of GATS I:3 as discussed elsewhere in this volume[46] implies that, in principle, where governments have outsourced services with a liberal legislation allowing market access to foreign providers, this will not provide sufficient protection for policy space. Furthermore, the language regarding sensitivities is reduced to recognising sensitivities while "tackling remaining long-standing market access barriers".

From the perspective of a European Union Member State seeking to maintain necessary policy space for health, further Commission engagement on negotiation of bilateral treaties has not been straightforward, and in health services has led to the incremental inclusion of new areas for all Member States. For example, the European Union did make commitments with respect to privately funded mobility of patients in the CARIFORUM (2012) agreement,[47] which has formed the basis and precedent for new negotiations on health services in bilateral agreements including mode 2 in health services to BITs since the CARIFORUM agreement. The precedence factor is important as it is increasingly difficult for a Member State to back down from compromises made in one BIT in negotiations of another, unless further arguments on the matter can be made with respect to the particular country.

As the Lisbon Treaty increased the rights of the European Parliament with respect to the conclusion of trade agreements, this was accompanied by diminishing powers of national parliaments in relation to trade agreements.[48] Health and social policies are at the core of this problem as national parliaments remain responsible for the financing of health within countries, whereas financing of health care or the sustainability of financing of health care is not at the core of European Parliament concerns.

### 15.2.3 Policy Space for Health

The understanding of national health systems is often based either on an assumption that trade and investment issues do not matter at all, or that there are no issues that would imply that the health sector is different from any other sector. In practice both

[46]See Chap. 2 by Arena in this volume.

[47]CARIFORUM-EC Economic Partnership Agreement 2012, available at: http://ctrc.sice.oas.org/Trade/CARIFORUM-ECEPA/CARIFORUM-ECEPA_e.asp, accessed 5 January 2012.

[48]See e.g. Krajewski 2012, p. 311.

of these assumptions are wrong. In reality national health systems are based on and engage with commercial sector operators more than is usually assumed, but health services cannot be seen as equal to consumer or more "market" driven services due to substantial market failures in health services markets.

The term policy space for health is functional and can be defined as "the freedom, scope, and mechanisms that governments have to choose, design, and implement public policies to fulfil their aims".[49] It draws on an understanding of and discussions on economic policy space, which has been taken up in the context of UNCTAD and the Accra declaration.[50] However, it is particularly feasible for addressing trade negotiations on non-tariff barriers to trade, domestic regulation, government procurement, regulatory cooperation and investment liberalisation and protection, which are more likely than tariffs to have an influence on **how** governments regulate both public and private services in particular sectors. The issue is thus not only about the right of governments to set standards at a level they desire, but also the ways in which trade agreements change the process of how and on what basis governments can regulate.

Policy space for health is useful in this context as it extends from public health-related measures, health-related standards and standard setting to the scope and measures that governments can use to contain costs within health systems, to ensure universal provision of services, equity and affordable access to services. In many ways this would imply, in particular, government interventions of the type that are required for the purpose of services of general interest. In health care these types of activities include cross-subsidisation across services provided for the rich and healthy and those provided for the sick and poor. Statutory social security systems do this through insurance funds, whereas in NHS-type services this is done through pooling of funding and provision of services.

A particular trend in current health policy developments in a number of European Union Member States has been to introduce more contractual and competitive arrangements to health care provision. In some countries, such as Germany, hospitals have been privatised.[51] In others, such as the Netherlands, active measures have been implemented to achieve regulated competition within health care, but so far this has not reduced overall costs.[52] In Finland municipalities have contracted out primary health care services to private sector companies.[53] In Sweden consum-

---

[49]Koivusalo et al. 2009, p. 105.

[50]The Accra Declaration states in para 16 that: " While development is the primary responsibility of each country, domestic efforts should be facilitated and complemented by an enabling international environment based on multilaterally agreed and applied rules. It is for each Government to evaluate the trade-off between the benefit of accepting international rules and commitments, and the constraints posed by the loss of policy space…/…". http://unctad.org/en/Docs/iaos20082_en.pdf. Accessed 27 February 2014.

[51]Mosebach 2009, pp. 65–98.

[52]E. Schut, S. Sorbe and J. Hoj, Health care reform and long-term care in the Netherlands. OECD Economics Department Working Papers, No. 1010, 2013. OECD Publishing.

[53]Tritter et al. 2009, pp. 132–151; Eronen et al. 2013.

ers are allowed to choose between private and public providers.[54] The United Kingdom government has introduced competition to the NHS as part of the new health and social care bill with substantial criticism over the process and likelihood of compounding economic pressures.[55]

While commercialisation and reliance on choice and markets have been sought as a means for cost-containment, this does not imply that government intervention is not required in order to achieve benefits and ensure equity and quality of services. Furthermore, there remain concerns that expectations from more "consumer driven care" have been too high.[56] It has long been known that, depending on incentive mechanisms, service providers in competitive markets tend to cream, dump and skimp when it comes to patients.[57] In Finland a substantial number of local governments moved back to provision of their own health care as result of cost increase.[58] It is not surprising that Poland and Slovakia have engaged with more market restrictive initiatives, as before accession the major players in the CEE/CIS countries were the World Bank and the USAID with a predominant American influence via World Bank and US government-funded programmes in the region.[59] Backing off from health care markets, for example, in the United Kingdom could result in investment arbitration.[60] As a result health care systems have been more commercialised with a more substantial role for private insurance companies and private hospitals than in other European Union health care systems.

The problem with respect to health care systems, commercialisation and choice as a means to lower costs is that on the basis of OECD comparison (Fig. 15.1),[61] more commercialised and private insurance-based health care systems tend to have higher costs. Furthermore, there are not, as one may expect, more medical doctors per head of population in the United States, where there are relatively few medical doctors per head of population in spite of the high costs, in comparison to many European Union Member States.[62] The interface between internal market regulations and broader public interests within national health systems is likely to face increasing tensions in the future as a result of patient mobility. The economic crisis and subsequent concern over public spending is likely to impose further financial and reform pressures on the health care sector. While moves towards further

[54]See e.g. Blomqvist 2004, pp. 139–155; Dahlgren 2008, pp. 697–715; Tritter et al. 2009.

[55]Reynolds et al. 2012, pp. 213–217; N. Timmins, Never again? The story of the health and social care act 2012. Kings Fund and Institute of Government, London. http://www.kingsfund.org.uk/sites/files/kf/field/field_publication_file/never-again-story-health-social-care-nicholas-timmins-jul12.pdf. Accessed 2 March 2014; Klein 2013, p. 237.

[56]Okma and Crivelli 2013, pp. 105–112.

[57]See Ellis 1998.

[58]Eronen et al. 2013.

[59]See e.g. Shakarashvili and Davey 2005, p. 15.

[60]Koivusalo and Tritter 2014, pp. 93–111.

[61]OECD 2013.

[62]OECD 2013.

commercialisation of health services provision do not usually create problems with respect to commercial policies, investment and markets, it is likely that further restrictions or shifts towards public or non-profit provision of health care would do so. It is this policy space for cost-containment measures that is particularly at stake as part of trade negotiations as it would constrict and affect services trade and the expectations of investors from European health care markets.[63]

Measures for ensuring the financial sustainability of health systems is an area where the context of European internal markets differs from the context of international trade agreements due to the fact that the European Court of Justice has clearly judged that the financial sustainability of national health care systems is a valid reason for government intervention. Furthermore, the Article 207 TFEU carve out for health and social services is based on the same concern.

The paradox of the health care sector and commercial policy is that for regulatory purposes there is no need to articulate policy space if health services and their operation are strictly under direct public "command and control". The more commercialised the provision of health services becomes, the more important it is to ensure sufficient policy space for regulation and cost-containment. It is also about priorities for government action. It is necessary for governments to decide whether their priorities with respect to the health care system are those related to commercial opportunities, foreign investors and export prospects for services or for access and quality of services that citizens receive within the country, as these are unlikely to coincide. There remains a major discrepancy between requirements for a well-functioning publicly funded service and a highly profitable commercial industry both in terms of the aims and focus of these services.

### *15.2.4 Policy Space for Health in the Context of Trade and Investment Agreements*

In terms of policy space the largest scope can be achieved through broad exemption for health systems in a way that would be extensive enough to also apply to

[63]This is often impeded by restrictions and limits on the use of competition to lower costs of medicines as a result of trade-related measures in the field of intellectual property rights. Particular attention needs to be paid in this regard to the negotiations of the Transatlantic Trade and Investment Partnership (TTIP), where European technology assessment measures, reference pricing and price controls in the field of pharmaceutical policies have already been raised as a potential concern for the United States. As national health systems—and those who are ill—will, to a large extent, pay for pharmaceuticals (OECD 2008), it is not entirely clear how much of the share of the estimated gains for pharmaceutical markets as result of addressing non-tariff measures in the field of pharmaceuticals would actually be spent on jobs in the EU and what it would imply for prices of medicines paid for by national health systems and consumers in European Union and United States (Ecorys Nederland BV, Non-Tariff measures in EU-US Trade and Investment—An Economic Analysis. http://trade.ec.europa.eu/doclib/docs/2009/december/tradoc_145613.pdf, pp. 99–106. Accessed 2 March 2015.

social care and care for the elderly as these cannot necessarily be separated.[64] A generic exemption covering all aspects of trade and investment agreements would be simplest from the perspective of national health policies. Furthermore, from the perspective of policy space, it should cover not only services with **any public funding**, but also privately funded services. Publicly and privately funded services also rely on the same pool of expertise and professional work-force.

It is not always feasible to make a strict separation between publicly and privately funded services. Government obligations include regulation of privately funded health services and the quality of care that is provided. Lack of oversight or regulation of private practice can also become a burden for the publicly funded services. Failures of private sector providers to follow guidelines or provide adequate quality of care can result in serious consequences, which then need to be treated under publicly funded care.

For example, European Commission negotiators' assumptions of the non-problematic nature of liberalising health tourism in the form of the privately funded mode 2 in trade in health services can be easily challenged by cases where patients have contracted a multi-resistant hospital bacteria in a privately financed operation in another country and brought it to—publicly funded—hospitals in the home country.[65] Promotion of trade in privately funded services is often considered as irrelevant if not beneficial to publicly funded services. However, if this trade brings in an epidemic of multi-resistant hospital bacteria or results in the need for correctional operations, the costs of it can easily far outweigh the benefits.

Health policies will require the right to exclude and ban provision, establishment or advertising of particular services, even if these could be claimed to put foreign providers at a disadvantage or disproportionately affect foreign providers. The GATS dispute settlement case on gambling is a case in point in this respect. Government action to ban—without discrimination—the provision of online gambling services was considered a matter of restriction of market access and setting a quota of zero for services.[66]

One crucial question with respect to trade agreements is whether governments would have the right to regulate for cost-containment through, for example, restriction of patient choice to a limited number of providers. According to Luff,[67] cost-containment mechanisms have an unclear status in the GATS and, in principle, full commitments in the health sector could render the granting of special or exclusive rights to hospitals untenable in health care systems.

---

[64]See Chap. 10 by Krajewski in this volume.

[65]See e.g. Kumarasamy et al. 2010, pp. 597–602, Another ethical dilemma relates to trade and trafficking of organs.

[66]*United States—Measures affecting the Cross-Border Supply of Gambling and Betting Services*, Report of the Appellate Body, WT/DS285/AB/R, para 5.67.

[67]Luff 2003, p. 213.

Issues with respect to the impact of domestic regulation on health systems have been raised and discussed in WTO consultations on domestic regulation.[68] Licensing procedures, technical standards and recognition of qualifications remain important means of regulation in practice. Member States have already responded to emerging problems with mobility of health professionals within the European Union; for example, the UK NHS Federation has been engaged in lobbying to correct problems with language skills, training requirements and clinical competence.[69]

The scope to tighten qualifications or introduce new qualifications is also a matter of health and safety when these measures focus on private providers. For example, a UK Department of Health report on cosmetic interventions emphasised the need to tighten regulation, including with respect to qualifications required for those using dermal fillers in accordance with several other governments considering or already engaged in tightening regulations.[70]

Government procurement requirements have allowed some flexibility and limitation in implementation within the European Union. However, it is not certain that flexibilities gained as part of European Union internal policies will remain as these elements become subject to international trade disputes. The change from GATS provisions on services to separate chapters on investment liberalisation and protection are perhaps the most problematic for policy space and regulation of health systems. The case with respect to Slovakia implies that there is a real risk of a "one way street" when further liberalisation is introduced to a health system. Concerns with respect to investment arbitration apply also to health promotion and public health-related services and measures, as has been the case with respect to the known investment arbitration case on plain packaging legislation between Philip Morris and Australia.[71]

### *15.2.5 Governance Challenges to Health Systems and Trade in the European Union*

The governance challenge with respect to national health systems and health priorities in the context of European commercial policies includes both intended and unintended consequences of the increasing number of negotiated agreements and

---

[68]See e.g. WTO Working Party on Domestic Regulation, Regulatory Issues in Sectors and Modes of Supply, Note by the Secretariat, S/WPDR/W/48/Add.1, 30 April 2013.

[69]See e.g. NHS European Office, New EU law on mobility of health professionals across Europe, briefing October 2013, Issue 15. http://www.nhsconfed.org/Publications/briefings/Pages/New-EU-law-health-professionals-move.aspx. Accessed 24 February 2014.

[70]See Department of Health, Review of the Regulation of Cosmetic Interventions. https://www.gov.uk/government/uploads/system/uploads/attachment_data/file/192028/Review_of_the_Regulation_of_Cosmetic_Interventions.pdf. April 2013. Accessed 24 February 2014.

[71]*Philip Morris v. Australia*, Notice of Arbitration, 21 November 2011, available at: http://www.ag.gov.au/internationalrelations/internationallaw/pages/tobaccoplainpackaging.aspx. Accessed 24 February 2014.

their expanding and more complex nature, as well as changes and combinations of negotiation tactics geared towards more extensive inclusion of services and sectors. The large number of bilateral negotiations results more easily in mistakes and omissions in country schedules and often leads to incremental liberalisation in practice. The increasing depth and simultaneous expansion to investment and government procurement negotiations also creates a lack of focus and understanding of details on which commitments have been made and where. Investment agreements and, to some extent, bilateral agreements have been and, to some extent, remain negotiated under different governance practices with less public consultation than in multilateral negotiations on the General Agreement on Trade in Services.[72] As commitments made in one bilateral agreement are then used as precedence for the negotiation of the next one, it is difficult for Member States to back down from commitments made.

As commercial policy negotiators engage, in particular, with "barriers" to trade, it is likely that they are more informed about "protectionist" practices and problems that multinational industries face in different countries. This "bias" becomes more prominent in European Union level negotiations as these concern trade and health. Multinational industries within the health sector have an incentive to negotiate at European level for access to 27 different markets. On the other hand, due to assumptions of the "complementary" role of European Union and limited interest in trade, governments may not realise where and how health-related priorities should be defended as part of negotiations.

National governments may or may not consult with health ministries regarding their policies, and health ministries may or may not have sufficient understanding of the potential implications of negotiations. European negotiators are likely to be more informed of the need to exclude audiovisual services than health services. The lack of adequate consultation on negotiation mandate is reflected also in the European Parliament in the resolution on the opening of negotiations on a plurilateral agreement on services where para 5 makes it known that it "regrets the fact that the Council granted a mandate without having taken Parliament's view into consideration".[73] This contrasts with the claimed powers that the European Parliament were given as part of Lisbon Treaty negotiations and also potentially undermines the scope of the European Parliament to block processes, as was the case with ACTA negotiations. Indeed, the rejection of ACTA was the first time the European Parliament used powers from Article 207 TFEU.[74]

[72]R. Adlung, Trade in health care and health insurance services: the GATS as a supporting actor(?), WTO Staff Working Paper ERSD-2009-15.

[73]European Parliament, Opening of negotiations on plurilateral agreement on services, 4 July 2013, http://www.europarl.europa.eu/sides/getDoc.do?type=TA&language=EN&reference=P7-TA-2013-325. Accessed 1 March 2014, para 5.

[74]See e.g. European Parliament, European Parliament rejects ACTA, Press Release, 4 July 2012, available at: http://www.europarl.europa.eu/news/en/news-room/content/20120703IPR48247/html/European-Parliament-rejects-ACTA. Accessed 24 February 2014.

The lack of consideration of health applies also to consultations and other practices, such as sustainability impact assessments, where health system or health policy considerations are not a main concern and broader public policy interests, such as maintaining regulatory policy space, are not necessarily brought up by those participating in consultations on impact assessments.[75] This would of course imply that impact assessments had relevance for decisions made. The European Parliament resolution on the opening of negotiations on a plurilateral agreement on services notes that[76]:

> The EU's negotiating mandate was proposed by the Commission and adopted by the Council *without any impact assessment*; insists that the Commission follow up on its intention to prepare a sustainability impact assessment and that it must do so in consultation with the relevant stakeholders as regards social, environmental and other concerns; demands that the Commission publish the sustainability impact assessment with a view to taking its conclusions into account in the negotiations.

The reality of European trade negotiations is that audiovisual services are better protected than social security, health and social services—or services of general interest. The potential for the use of Article 207(4) powers through a veto if the negotiated agreement does not fulfil the requirements of adequate consideration of these services can, nevertheless, be useful in ensuring that policy space for regulation is prioritised. Whether a government will want to use the "emergency brake" clause to turn down the whole agreement when substantial political capital has been invested in the process is another issue. However, it is important to recognise that there is always scope for using this as leverage in order to secure adequate consideration for "sensitive" services.

### *15.2.6 Policy Space and Negotiation Processes*

A key challenge to ensure that a service sector is kept outside a trade agreement is the "normalisation" of liberalisation in the context of trade negotiations. The assumption that market access or a lack of non-conforming legislation implies that

---

[75]Representation of health interests in the context of trade in the European Union has been traditionally based more on trade unions and development-oriented nongovernmental organisations, although nongovernmental organisations working on public health have now followed TTIP and TiSA more. Participation in sustainability impact assessment consultations has been limited, where inclusion of health considerations has been weak or lacking. In the European Union–Canada (CETA) agreement sustainability impact assessment health was taken up, in particular in the Canadian context, but gained little focus due to expectations that services negotiations would not cover health. See e.g. Kirkpatrick C et al., A trade SIA related to the negotiation of a Comprehensive Economic and Trade Agreement (CETA) between the EU and Canada. Trade 10/B3/B06. http://trade.ec.europa.eu/doclib/docs/2011/september/tradoc_148201.pdf. June 2011, p. 125. Accessed 1 March 2014.

[76]European Parliament, Opening of negotiations on plurilateral agreement on services, 4 July 2013, http://www.europarl.europa.eu/sides/getDoc.do?type=TA&language=EN&reference=P7-TA-2013-325. Accessed 1 March 2014, para 19 (emphasis by author).

a service or a sector can be included as part of a trade and investment agreement is particularly problematic. This may be a result of recent liberalisation and "under-regulation" or merely a reflection of the major role of public sector operators and professional associations within the sector. This is why policy space to undertake regulatory measures and tighten oversight can be the particular reason why governments have not included health services as part of trade agreements in the first place. For example, in Finland legislation on health is liberal and foreign investors are allowed into the sector, which lead to the initial inclusion of health services as part of the EU-Mexico FTA in 2001. However, the government had not intended to include health services as part of the agreement.

Another challenge is anticipating and understanding where commitments have been made. While the General Agreement on Trade in Services (GATS) offered governments and their ministries scope to assess where to make commitments and how, the focus on negotiations on the basis of "negative" listing changes this context profoundly. In contrast to knowing what they want to liberalise, governments now need to know what not to liberalise. Furthermore, when inclusion of services is done on the basis of existing legislation on market access it can suddenly imply inclusion of services and sectors which governments did not intend to include as part of a trade agreement. There are negative listing elements in the GATS in relation to broader sectoral coverage of different types of services; for example, the dispute settlement case on gambling made it clear how online gambling was included in GATS commitments as part of much broader group of "other recreational services" at a time when online gambling was not yet as prominent as it currently is.[77] The problem is a lack of flexibility to react to "market failures" in the most efficient way as part of national policies or to limit the scope of markets where unanticipated problems or practices emerge.

The focus on negative listing forces governments to anticipate their future regulatory needs, which is usually impossible, in particular, for such sectors which have been recently liberalised. This also makes the ratchet effect a problem as newly liberalised sectors are automatically included as part of agreements. If a government makes a mistake in liberalising a service with adverse consequences, the flexibility to move back is very difficult or in practice no longer a possible option. The focus on standstill assumes that there is no need to tighten regulation or introduce new non-conforming measures. This is particularly challenging to the newly liberalised sectors, more likely to be under-regulated or be prone to problematic trading practices or a lack of competition, which may have influenced government engagement in the field in the first place. Allowing for policy space does not imply that a government should introduce non-conforming measures, but provides scope for doing so, in particular, to achieve cost-containment, universal service provision and equity in access to services, the key values emphasised as part of Lisbon Treaty protocol on services of general interest.

---

[77]See *United States—Measures affecting the Cross-Border Supply of Gambling and Betting Services*, Report of the Appellate Body, WT/DS285/AB/R, para 5.67.

While it would be meaningful to seek broad and extensive European Union level exclusion for both publicly and privately funded health and social services and health and social insurance services, it is more likely, on the basis of prior European Union level measures, that a European level of exclusion would cover only public utilities or publicly funded services. In this context, as discussed elsewhere in this book, the most extensive form of exclusion would be any publicly funded services. Furthermore, in order to maintain policy space it should be part of negotiations for cross-border trade in services and investment liberalisation, and also apply to public procurement. Exclusions should also cover professional services and negotiations concerning mutual recognition of qualifications, even if these were to be negotiated separately from other services. Any carve out of health and social services would need to apply also to horizontal provisions affecting policy space, such as provisions on domestic regulation, regulatory cooperation, performance requirements and subsidies. Removal of investment protection provisions from negotiations would provide the most policy space. If this is not possible, it is necessary to ensure that exemptions made apply both to investment liberalisation and investment protection provisions and that adequate scope for health promotion and protection is ensured. This is a challenge if investment protection is negotiated separately from investment liberalisation, leading easily to a situation where governments may assume false security of policy space on the basis of excluding services from investment liberalisation when these could still be subject to investment protection provisions.

Governments have choice and flexibility in what is included under government procurement obligations of services within Europe. However, this may be lost or not appropriately secured in the context of trade agreements. For example, the TTIP negotiation directives are ambitious, seeking to cover all sectors, thresholds and services contracts and markets at all administrative levels with rules and disciplines to address local content or local production requirements for contracts.[78] Government procurement obligations can affect both health insurance and NHS-type health systems and are likely to have implications for any publicly funded services and their outsourcing in health and long-term care, as well as measures to cross-subsidise provision of services across regions.

While those inclined towards preference of free markets might assume that there is no need to return to public provision once services are outsourced, this is, of course, not always the case in practice. Indeed, a neutral position would support flexibility. For example, a recent survey found that in Finland around a third of local governments have returned from outsourced health services to public provision due to lower costs and administrative simplicity.[79] The problem of commitments made with respect to investment agreements is that if a government moves out of contractual markets or more liberalised insurance markets, multinational investors may call for compensation as a result of loss of potential income from outsourced services.

---

[78]Council of the European Union, Directives for the negotiation on the Transatlantic Trade and Investment Partnership between the European Union and the United States of America, 17 June 2013, para 24.

[79]Eronen et al. 2013.

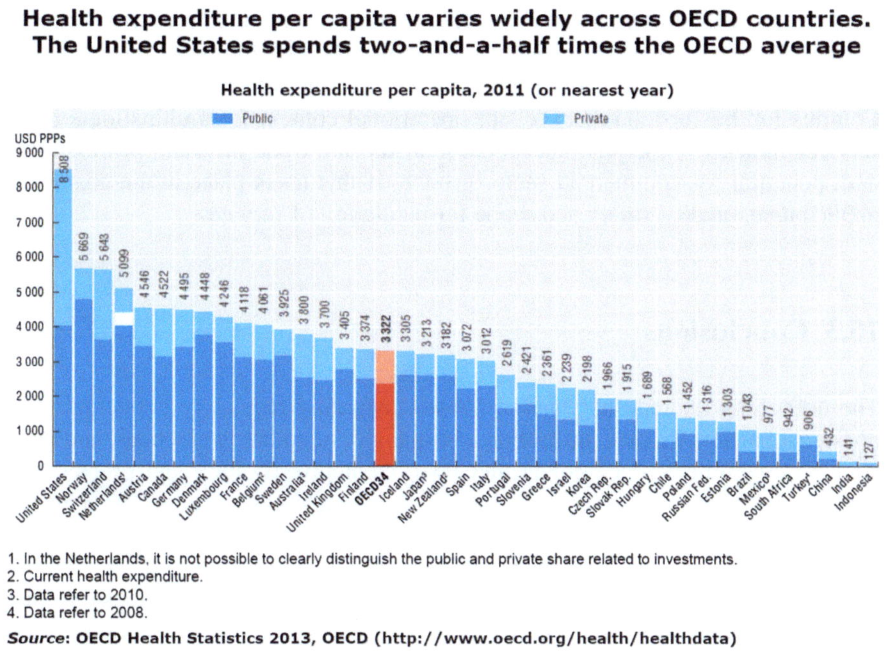


**Fig. 15.1** Health expenditure per capita

The paradox of national health systems is that the more commercialised and liberalised governments wish their health systems to be in terms of service provision, the more important is to maintain regulatory policy space for cost-containment, equity and quality of services. Experiences of commercialisation in the field of health care provision in Finland would suggest that liberalisation and concentration takes place quite quickly in health and social services, with the danger of moving from public to private sector monopolies and market dominance.[80] Indeed, the question of the dominant position in health insurance markets can be seen as one of the issues in the Polish arbitration case.

From the perspective of policy space for health and safeguarding future regulatory policy space on the basis of health policy needs and priorities, the issue is not whether existing standards or legislation can be maintained, but whether legislation can be made more market restrictive and how the sustainability of financing of national health systems can be maintained. The comparison of "like services" can also be deceptive as there is, for example, a major difference in spending on health between European Member States and the United States[81] (see Fig. 15.1).

[80] In Finland markets for private contractors of publicly funded services have developed in the last 5 years with increasing involvement of large actors in service provision, as well as elements of concentration in the field of provision. See e.g. Eronen et al. 2013; Tritter et al. 2009.

[81] See OECD 2013.

Furthermore, while investment protection might not make the return from markets impossible, it can make it very expensive and represents unwise use of public funds. European Member States may not be delighted to find that the European Commission has negotiated excellent operational context for multinational health services industries, the pharmaceutical industry and trade in health professionals, with potential for commercial sector growth, if this takes place at the cost of the public purse, quality, safety and scope for regulation of services.

## 15.3 Conclusions

The deepening of trade negotiation agenda regarding regulatory cooperation and non-tariff barriers to trade, utilisation of expansive negotiation practices, and inclusion of government procurement and investment liberalisation and protection in negotiations all add to the complexity of current trade negotiations. The new generation trade agreements require a broader assessment and analysis, in particular with respect to services, investment, government procurement and horizontal rules negotiations so as to understand their implications upon health and social security systems financing, organisation and functioning. Trade in health services is also likely to bring new and mostly unexpected challenges and demands for a review in relation to mobility of health professionals and mobility of patients, which have not been adequately discussed or addressed as part of trade negotiations. The changing scope and complexity of trade negotiations puts particular pressure on European Union multilevel governance and the division of obligations and competences within the European Union.

Maintaining national policy space for health has been important for public health and health promotion measures, but also needs to be recognised in the context of services and investment negotiations and in relation to health systems. This is not only a matter of the number of personnel, quality, public health and safety within services, but applies, in particular, to cost-containment, cross-subsidisation and wise use of public funds.

The commercialisation of national health systems in European Union Member States has brought up a new regulatory context, where old assumptions of what public services entail are no longer adequate in ensuring sufficient policy space for European Member states to govern their health systems adequately.

Furthermore, the current context of trade negotiations with an emerging number of bilateral agreements, changing context and basis of negotiations, and increasing tendency for more ambitious and comprehensive trade agreements with focus on investment, services and government procurement poses a challenge for cost-containment, equity and quality of care within health systems. Furthermore, they have a risk of leading to commitments which are made without adequate consideration or full understanding of their future implications.

The division of competences and responsibilities between the European Union and Member States creates a void of accountability, as multinational health care-related industries have an interest in ensuring their priorities become reflected in trade agreements, while there is limited understanding and focus in ensuring that Member States, responsible for the financing of health systems, will have sufficient means for ensuring cost-containment, equity and quality within health systems.

The new negotiations with high-income countries with focus on regulatory cooperation, domestic regulation and investment liberalisation and protection have particular relevance for maintaining policy space for health and capacities of governments to tackle issues emerging from recently commercialised services, unethical practices, novel trends in health care provision or challenges by multinational health care industries and investors.

Trade and investment agreements are negotiated on the basis of expected benefits rather than products of natural laws. It is important that all implications, including those for public policies, are adequately assessed. There are grounds for requiring policy space for health systems if governments seek to provide and finance theses services in the long-term. Securing policy space for health, social and education services—or audiovisual services—is a matter of governments' values and political priorities.

## References


Blomqvist P (2004) The choice revolution: privatisation of Swedish welfare services in the 1990s. Soc Policy Admin 38(2):139–155

Brooks E (2012) Crossing borders: a critical review of the role of the European Court of Justice in EU health policy. Health Policy 105:33–37

Dahlgren G (2008) Neoliberal reforms in Swedish primary health care: for whom and for what purpose? Int J Health Serv 38(4):697–715

Ellis RP (1998) Creaming, skimping and dumping: provider competition on the intensive and extensive margins. J Health Econ 17(5):537–555

Eronen A et al (2013) Sosiaalibarometri. SOSTE, Helsinki

Foreign and Commonwealth Office (2008) A comparative table of the current EC and EU Treaties as amended by the Treaty of Lisbon. HMSO, Norwich

Hall D (2010) Challenges to Slovakia and Poland health policy decisions: use of investment treaties to claim compensation for reversal of privatisation/liberalisation policies. PSIRU, Greenwich

Hatzopoulos V (2002) Killing national health and insurance systems but healing patients? The European market for health care services after the judgments of ECJ in Vanbraekel and Perbooms. Common Mark Law Rev 39(4):683–729

Hatzopoulos V (2013) Actively talking to each other: the Court and the political institutions. In: Dawson M, De Witte B, Muir E (eds) Judicial activism at the European Court of Justice. Edward Elgar, Northampton, pp 102–141

Klein R (2013) Sleepwalking into a political fiasco. Health Econ Policy Law 8:237–242

Koivusalo M (2010) Constitutional issues in European health policies. In: Tuori K, Sankari S (eds) The many constitutions in Europe. Ashgate Publishing, Surrey, pp 263–281

Koivusalo M (2013) We are all in this together—European policies and health systems change. In: Watson P (ed) Health care reform and globalisation. The US, China and Europe in comparative perspective. Routledge Advances in Health and Social Policies. Routledge, Abingdon, pp 93–118

Koivusalo M, Tritter J (2014) Trade creep and the implications of the EU-USA TTIP Agreement on the NHS in the United Kingdom. Int J Health Serv 44(1):93–111

Koivusalo M, Labonté R, Schrecker T (2009) Globalization and policy space for health and social determinants of health. In: Labonté R et al (eds) Globalization and health: pathways, evidence and policy. Routledge, New York, pp 105–130

Kostera T (2013) Subnational responsibilities for healthcare and Austria's rejection of the EU's patients' rights Directive. Health Policy 111(2):149–156

Krajewski M (2012) The reform of the Common Commercial Policy. In: Biondi A, Eeckhout P, Ripley S (eds) EU law after Lisbon. OUP, Oxford, pp 292–311

Kumarasamy K et al (2010) Emergence of a new antibiotic resistance mechanism in India, Pakistan, and the UK: a molecular, biological and epidemiological study. Lancet Infect Dis 10(9):597–602

Luff D (2003) Regulation of health services and international trade law. In: Mattoo A, Sauve P (eds) Domestic regulation and services trade liberalisation. World Bank and OUP, New York, pp 191–220

Mosebach K (2009) Commercializing German hospital care? Effects of new public management and managed care under neoliberal conditions. Ger Policy Stud 5(1):66–98

Mossialos E et al (2010) Health systems governance in Europe: the role of European Union law and policy. CUP, Cambridge

Nedwick C (2006) Citizenship, free movement and health care: cementing individual rights by corroding social solidarity. Common Mark Law Rev 43(6):1645–1668

OECD (2008) Pharmaceutical pricing policies in a global market. OECD, Paris

OECD (2013) Health at a glance. OECD, Paris

Okma KGH, Crivelli L (2013) Swiss and dutch "consumer-driven health care": ideal model or reality? Health Policy 109(2):105–112

Reynolds L et al (2012) Competition-based reform of the National Health Service in England: a one-way street? Int J Health Serv 42(2):213–217

Shakarashvili G, Davey K (2005) Trends in reforming the provision and financing of health care services in CEE/CIS regions during the 1990s. In: Shakarashvili G, Davey K (eds) Decentralisation in health care. Open Society Institute, Budapest, pp 3–43

Tritter J et al (2009) Globalisation, markets and healthcare policy: redrawing patient as consumer. Routledge, London

Van de Gronden JW et al (2011) Health care and EU law. T.M.C. Asser Press, The Hague

Welti F (2011) EU law and the organization of health care: experiences from Germany. In: van de Gronden JW et al (eds) Health care and the EU law. T.M.C. Asser Press, The Hague. pp 319–336

# Index




M. Krajewski (ed.), *Services of General Interest Beyond the Single Market*, Legal Issues of Services of General Interest,
DOI 10.1007/978-94-6265-063-3

MIX
Papier aus verantwortungsvollen Quellen
Paper from responsible sources
FSC® C105338

If you have any concerns about our products,
you can contact us on
**ProductSafety@springernature.com**

In case Publisher is established outside the EU,
the EU authorized representative is:
**Springer Nature Customer Service Center GmbH**
**Europaplatz 3, 69115 Heidelberg, Germany**

Printed by Libri Plureos GmbH
in Hamburg, Germany